I0827870

Also By The Terminal Press:

The J.G. Ballard Book
Deep Ends: The J.G. Ballard Anthology 2014
Deep Ends: The J.G. Ballard Anthology 2015
Deep Ends: The J.G. Ballard Anthology 2016
Deep Ends: A Ballardian Anthology 2018
Deep Ends: A Ballardian Anthology 2019
Deep Ends: A Ballardian Anthology 2020

Dominika Oramus - Grave New World: The Decline of the West in the Fiction of JG Ballard

Lawrence Russell - Radio Brazil
Lawrence Russell - Outlaw Academic

Rick McGrath - Straight Man: Rock Star Interviews, Reviews & Photos From The 1970s Underground Press
Rick McGrath - The Disenchanted Forest

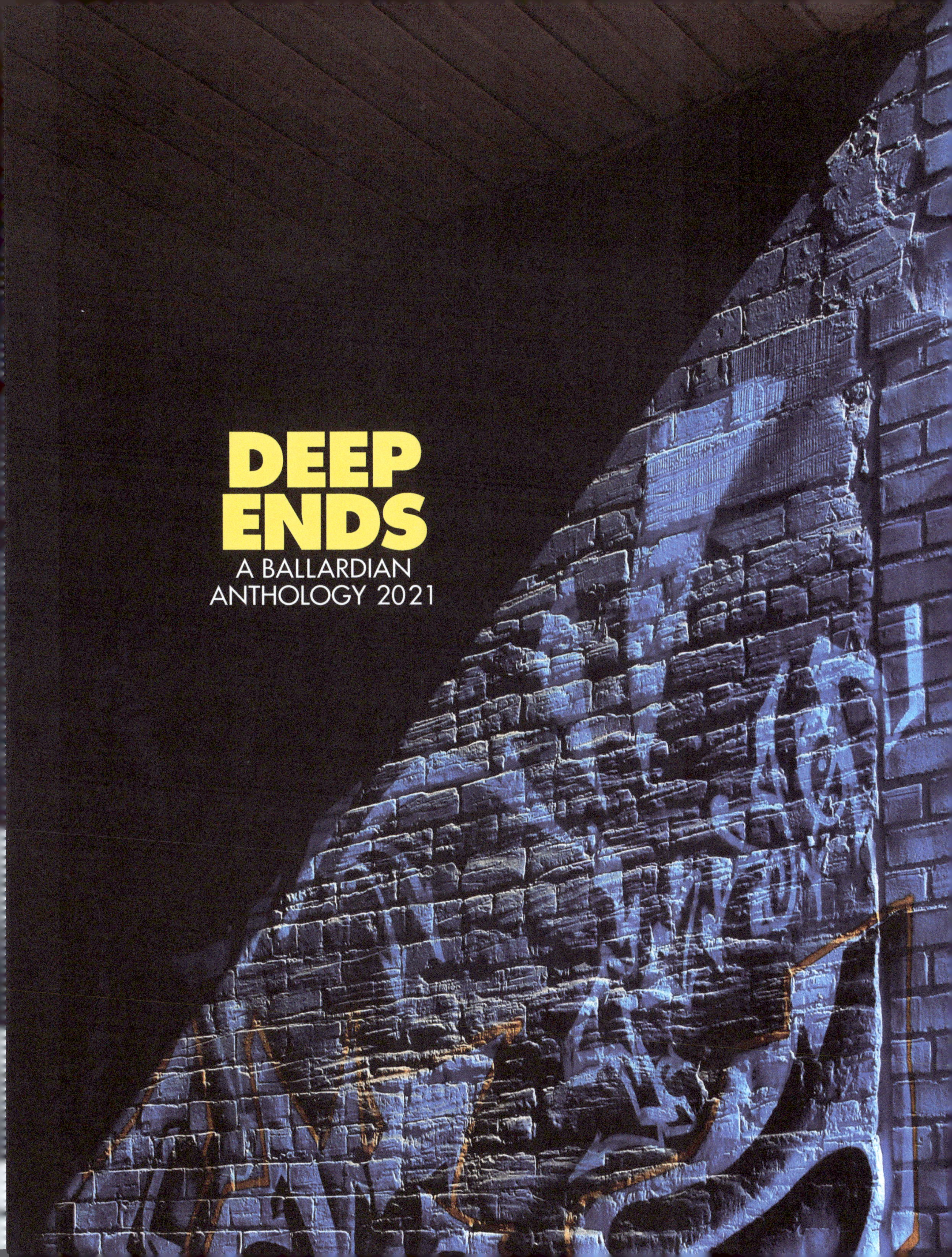
DEEP ENDS
A BALLARDIAN ANTHOLOGY 2021

First Edition

Published By
The Terminal Press
Powell River, BC, Canada
October 2021

Editor & Designer: Rick McGrath

ISBN: 978-1-7753679-8-7

Visit us: www.facebook.com/theterminalpress

Acknowledgements

The publisher gratefully acknowledges that the manuscript pages of *The Drowned World, Crash* and *High-Rise* are Copyright © J.G. Ballard, are used by the kind permission of The J.G. Ballard Estate and the Wylie Agency (UK) Limited. The publisher also gratefully acknowledges that the illustrations by Robert Smithson are used by the kind permission of the Holt/Smithson Foundation, through the Artists Rights Society.

Contents:

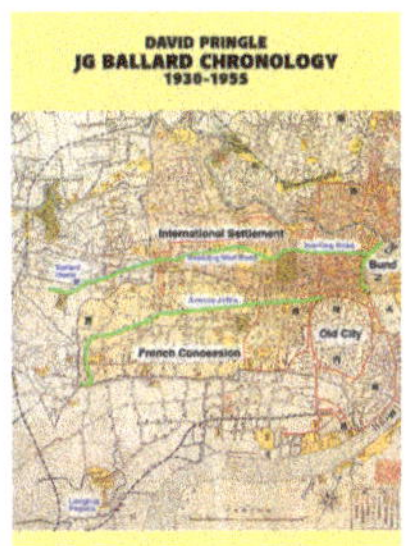

David Pringle
JG Ballard Chronology, 1930-1955
Page 8

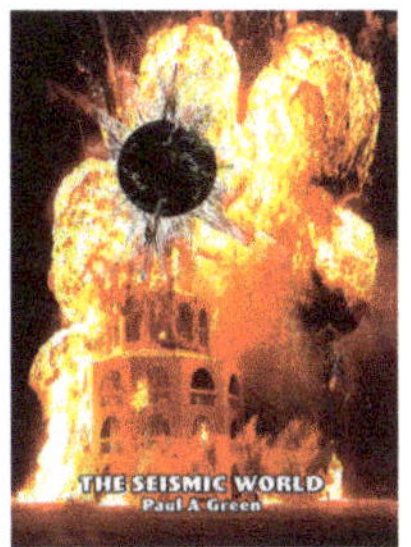

Paul A. Green
The Seismic World
Page 84

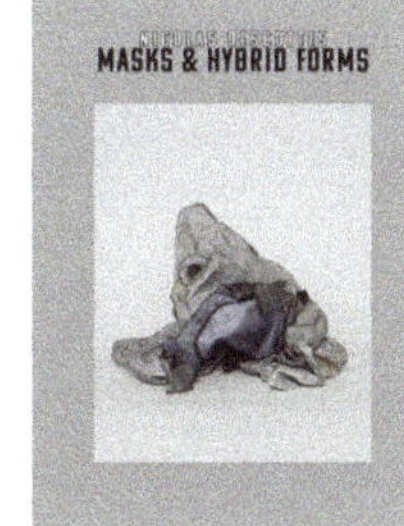

Nicolas Descottes
Masks and Hybrid Forms
Page 94

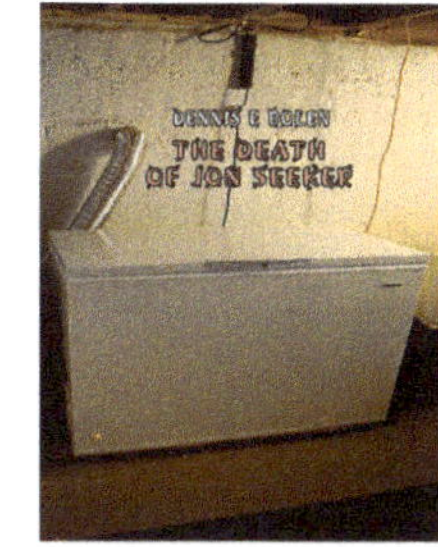

Dennis E. Bolen
The Death of Jon Seeker
Page 102

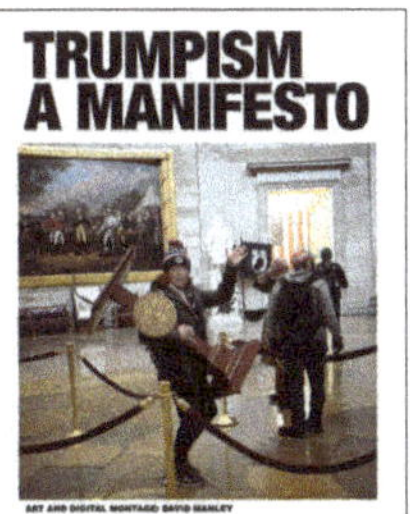

David Manley
Trumpism
A Manifesto
Page 116

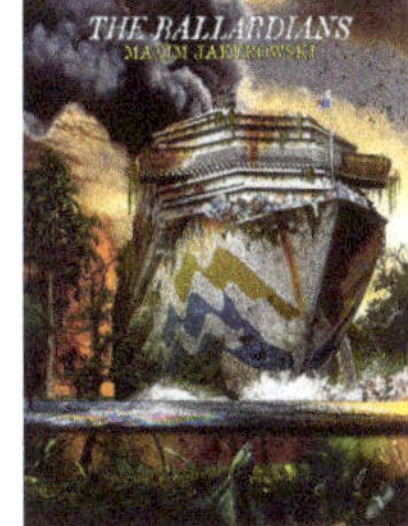

Maxim Jakubowski
The Ballardians
Page 130

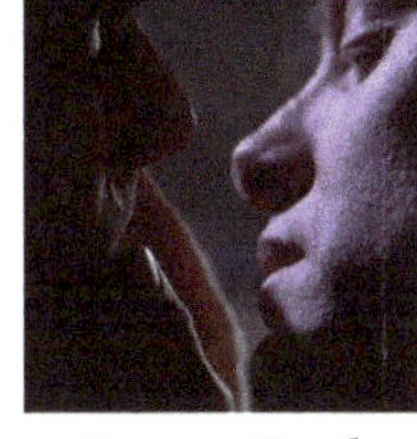

Jeremy Reed
The Homoerotics of Ballard's *Crash*
Page 136

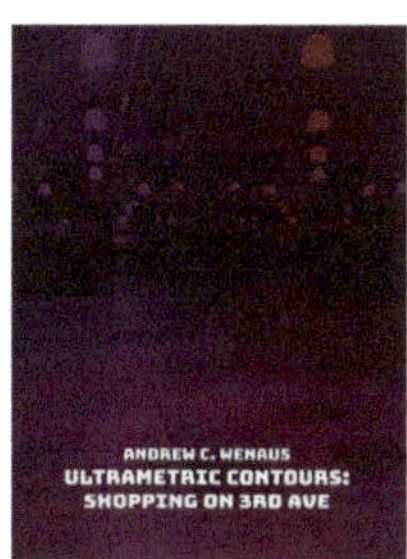

Andrew C. Wenaus
Ultrametric Contours: Shopping on 3rd Ave
Page 142

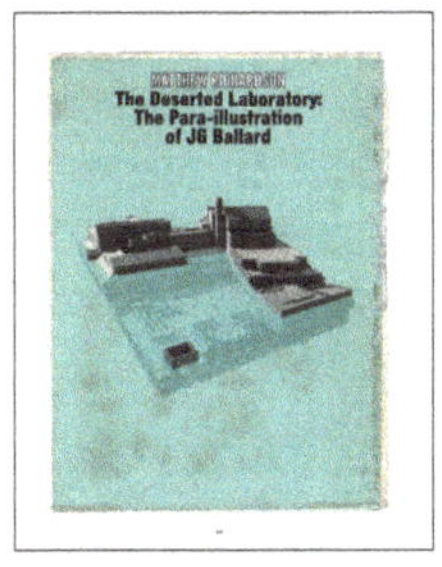

Matthew Richardson
The Deserted Laboratory: The Para-Illustration of JG Ballard
Page 150

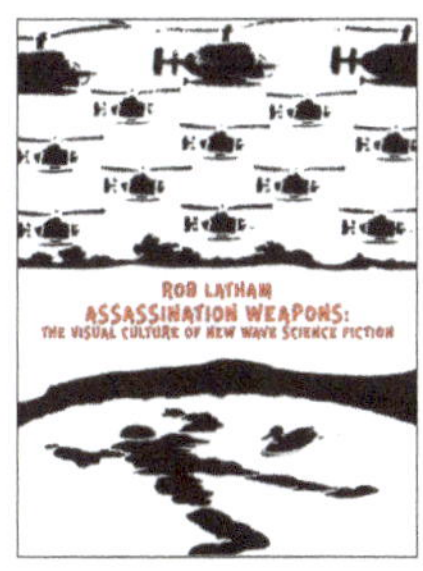

Rob Latham
Assassination Weapons: The Visual Culture of New Wave Science Fiction
Page 170

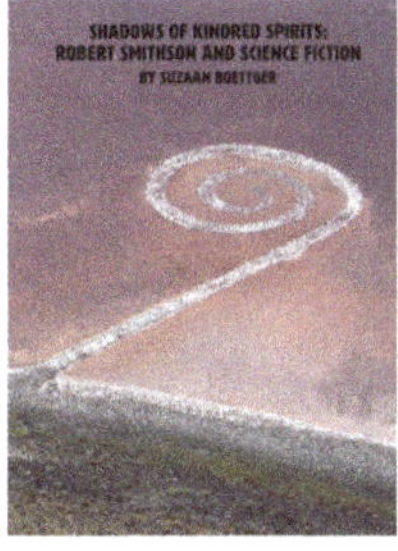

Suzaan Boettger
Shadows of Kindred Spirits: Robert Smithson and Science Fiction
Page 176

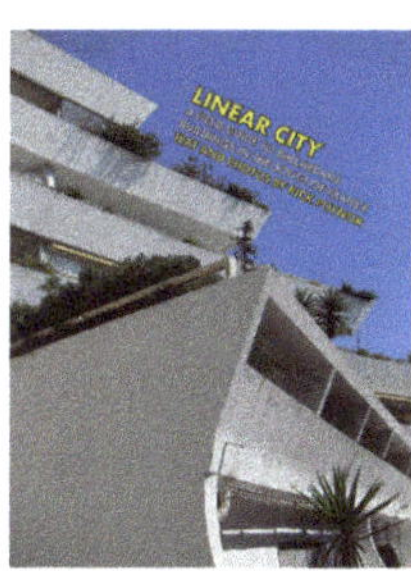

Rick Poynor
Linear City: A Field Guide to Ballardian Buildings in the South of France
Page 184

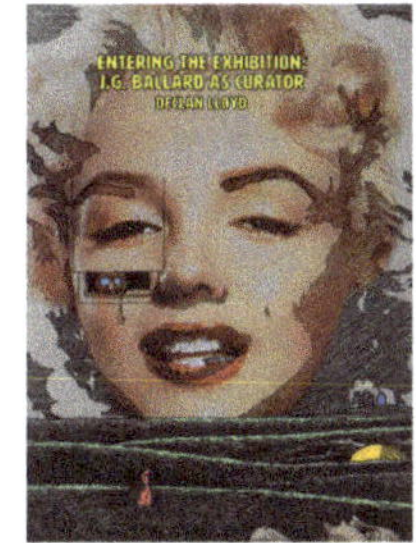

Declan Lloyd
Entering The Exhibition: JG Ballard as Curator
Page 198

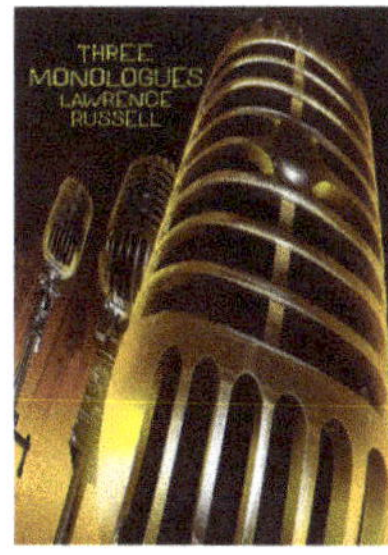

Lawrence Russell
Three Monologues
Page 206

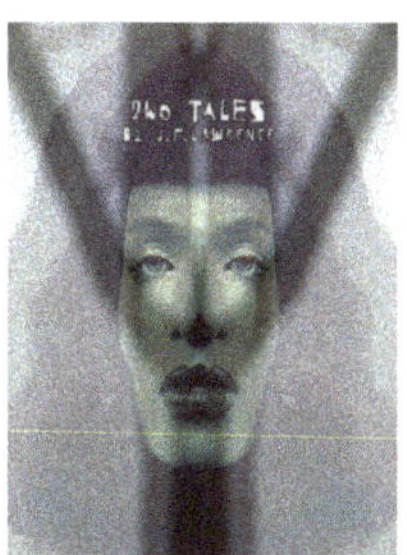

J.F. Lawrence
2wo Tales
Page 212

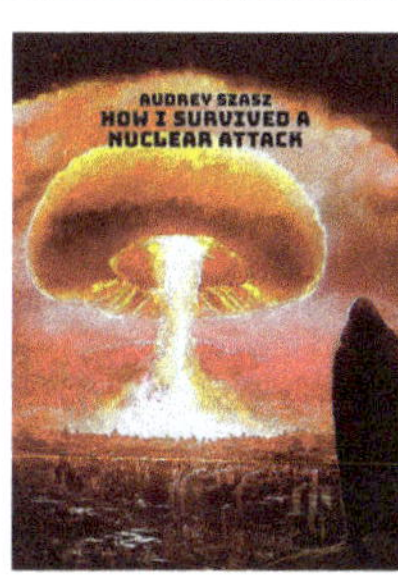

Audrey Szasz
How I Survived A Nuclear Attack
Page 216

Cover Photos: Rick McGrath

Our Contributors:

Dennis E. Bolen. Dennis has published five novels — *Stupid Crimes, Stand in Hell, Krekshuns, Toy Gun, Kaspoit!*; two books of short fiction—*Gas Tank and Other Stories, Anticipated Results*; and a poetry collection—"*Black Liquor*". He holds an MFA in creative writing from the University of British Columbia and was fiction editor at *sub-TERRAIN* magazine for ten years; has been a part-time editorial writer and reviewer for *The Vancouver Sun*; literary reviewer for *The Georgia Straight*; freelance critic for numerous publications.

Suzaan Boettger. Suzaan is an art historian, critic and lecturer based in New York City and Professor Emerita at Bergen Community College. She has published features and reviews in major art magazines and is the author of *Earthworks: Art and the Landscape of the Sixties* (University of California, 2003), acclaimed by the *New York Times Book Review* as the "definitive history." The Boston Psychoanalytic Society and Institute awarded her the 2020 Silberger Prize for psychoanalytic criticism for an essay derived from research for her book, *The Passions of Robert Smithson, Art and Biography*, forthcoming fall 2022 from the University of Minnesota Press. https://SuzaanBoettger.academia.edu Instagram: @NatrCultr #UnknownSmithson

Nicolas Descottes. Nicolas is a french artist based in Paris and in Antwerp. He has published a few books about the disappearance and the metamorphosis of territories: the Aral Sea disaster in Kazaksthan and the frozen forest in Ukraine. His work is frequently exhibited, and in 2021 he participed in the collective project named *Dust: The Plates In The Present* at The Centre Pompidou, then in Istanbul for a project entitled *The Year Of The Thirteen Moons*. Conducting a study on the Paris "yellow vest" riot on December 8 2018, Nicolas was injured in the face by a flash ball shot, deliberately targeted by a policeman. Miraculously, he escaped with some minor after-effects!

Paul A. Green. More from "Brother" Paul Green, whose stories and articles have appeared in every edition of *Deep Ends*. His books include *The Gestaltbunker—Selected Poems* (Shearsman Books 2012), and *Shadow Times* (QBS Productions 2019). His audio work can be found on the CD *Sounds and Symbols* (Phantom Airship 2017) and at www.culturecourt.com. His novels consist of *The Qliphoth* (Libros Libertad 2007) and *Beneath the Pleasure Zones I & II* (Mandrake of Oxford 2014/2016). A selection of his plays for radio and stage has been published in *Babalon* (Scarlet Imprint 2015) His website is paulgreenwriter.co.uk. His latest book is *Dream Clips of the Archons*.

Maxim Jakubowski. Another writer first featured in *Deep Ends 2018*, Maxim met JG Ballard in the 1960s and they remained friends until Jim's passing, travelling together to events in France and Italy on various occasions. A British author and publisher active in crime, fantasy & SF, and erotica, Maxim won a handful of awards across these genres for his writing and editing. A winner of the Anthony award for non fiction, and the author of 20 novels, he lives in London where he is, amongst other things, currently the Vice Chair of the Crime Writers' Association and chairs its Dagger awards. He has been the crime reviewer for *The Guardian* for 12 years, and prior to that at *Time Out London*, and Joint Director of *Crime Scene*, London's International Crime & Mystery Film and Literary Festival. His latest novel is *The Louisiana Republic*, 2018.

Rob Latham. Rob is a life-long Ballardophile and a recovering academic. A co-editor of the journal *Science Fiction Studies* for almost two decades, he is the author of *Consuming Youth: Vampires, Cyborgs, and the Cultural of Consumption* (2002), editor of *The Oxford Handbook of Science Fiction* (2014) and *Science Fiction Criticism: An Anthology of Essential Writings* (2017), and co-editor of *The Wesleyan Anthology of Science Fiction* (2010). He lives in the California high desert, a very Ballardian landscape.

J.F. Lawrence is a writer, poet (as Jim Lawrence), translator and semi-retired psychedelic blues guitar wrangler who likes Jack Daniels, chess and Elizabeth Taylor. He is a contributor to *Red Phone Box*, a multi-author urban fantasy novel from Ghostwood Books, and has been published in various poetry zines. He is based in Southampton, UK, where he follows his obsessions.

Declan Lloyd. Declan is a postdoctoral researcher and associate lecturer within the literature and art departments at Lancaster University. His work primarily looks to the intersections of literature and art in the Modernist period and beyond. His research on Ballard has appeared in *The Guardian* and *Foundation* and his PhD thesis examined Ballard's influence and philosophical affinities with Salvador Dali. He is currently in the final stages of editing his first academic monograph entitled *Painterly Poetics: Four Authors and Art Movements of the Twentieth Century.*

David Manley. David is a Sydney based artist. He holds a 1st-class Honours degree and Masters degree in Fine Arts (photo-media) and is currently a PhD candidate at the University of New South Wales Art and Design, Sydney. He is a lecturer in lens-based art at the National Art School Australia.

Rick Poynor. Rick is Professor of Design and Visual Culture at the University of Reading in the UK. His latest book is *David King: Designer, Activist, Visual Historian* (Yale University Press, 2020). His other books include three collections of his essays: *Design Without Boundaries* (1998), *Obey the Giant: Life in the Image World* (2001) and *Designing Pornotopia* (2006). He has written about visual interpretations of J.G. Ballard's writing for *Eye magazine*, the *Design Observer* website, and *The J.G. Ballard Book*.

David Pringle. David has been in every *Deep Ends*, most recently with his chronology of JGB which started in *Deep Ends 2015* and continues in this edition. David was the editor of *Foundation*, an academic journal, from 1980 through 1986, during which time he became one of the prime movers of the collective which founded *Interzone* in 1982. By 1988 he was publisher and editor of *Interzone*, a position he retained until 2004. For two-and-a-half years, in 1991–1993, he also edited and published *Million: The Magazine About Popular Fiction*. *Interzone* was nominated several times for the Hugo award for best semiprozine, winning the award in 1995. In 2005, the Worldcon committee gave David a Special Award for his work on *Interzone*. He wrote the first short monograph on Ballard, *Earth is the Alien Planet: J.G. Ballard's Four-Dimensional Nightmare* (Borgo Press, 1979) and compiled *J.G. Ballard: A Primary and Secondary Bibliography* (G.K. Hall, 1984). He has also written *Science Fiction: The 100 Best Novels* (1985) and *Modern Fantasy: The 100 Best Novels* (1988).

Jeremy Reed. Jeremy is one of Britain's most outstandingly original and controversial poets. His recent collections include *Piccadilly Bongo, Sooner Or Later Frank, Voodoo Excess, Candy4Cannibals* and *Psychedelic Meadow*. JG Ballard contributed a preface to his collection *West End Survival Kit* claiming his 'talent is almost extraterrestrial in its brilliance.' His recent non-fiction books include *Waiting For The Man Lou Reed, The Dilly: A Secret History of Piccadilly Rent Boys* and the recently published London memoir *Bandit Poet*. He lives in London and performs with the Ginger Light.

Matthew Richardson. Matthew is a UK artist and illustrator working across physical and digital media, producing collages, assemblages, books and films. He has worked on projects with the V&A, the British Library, Folio and the Poetry Society and shown work at Tactile Bosch, g39, Transition and Outpost. He has taught at a number of UK art colleges including UCA Maidstone, Norwich University of the Arts and the RCA. His work is about exploring the way meanings, messages and the stories we tell change and mutate over time, using a process of sifting, gathering together and building with the leftovers and residue of material culture. The work in *Deep Ends* is part of a practice-based PHD based at Kingston School of Art and funded by the AHRC through the London Doctoral Design Centre. More work and information on this and other projects can be found at: matthew-richardson.co.uk

Lawrence Russell. Born in Northern Ireland, educated in the U.K, Canada, and California. Playwright, fiction writer, critic, musician and multi-media artist. Formerly Professor of Writing & Film, University of Victoria. Twice winner of the Canadian Broadcasting Corporation's Literary Competition. His stage plays have been produced in all the major Canadian venues, including the National Arts Theatre (Ottawa) and the Stratford (Ontario) Festival's 3rd Stage. His drama and electronic sound-text compositions have been broadcast on the C.B.C., A.B.C., Radio Canada International, N.P.R. (National Public Radio, US), the Pacifica Radio Network and other broadcast networks. Books include *Penetration* (5 plays), *Repeat This & You're Dead* (stories), *Radio Brazil* (novel) and the recent non-fiction work *Outlaw Academic* (criticism/metafiction/autobiography). LR's website is: culturecourt.com

Audrey Szasz. Audrey (aka Zutka) is a London-based writer, performer and sound designer with roots in Central Europe. She has been described alternately as 'the postmodern heir to the disarranged novels of Anna Kavan and more closely, Ann Quin,' and 'a deviant genius of surreal and perverse image-play.' Audrey's debut in print, *Plan for the Abduction of J.G. Ballard* (a collaboration with author and poet Jeremy Reed) was published in 2019 via Infinity Land Press. In 2020, Amphetamine Sulphate issued her first solo novella, *Invisibility: A Manifesto*, and her debut full-length novel, *Tears of a Komsomol Girl*, was released several months later. In June 2021, Audrey's hour-long sound and spoken-word performance *Deposition: Agent Erdély* was published on the Nearest Truth podcast, whilst her latest novella, *A-Z of Robomasochism,* is included in the Amphetamine Sulphate sci-fi anthology *AS/SF Vol.1 Human Rights*, set to be released in 2021.

Andrew C. Wenaus. Andrew is an assistant professor at the University of Western Ontario's Department of English and Writings Studies and a member of Western's Complex Adaptive Systems Lab. He is also a composer and, with Christina Willatt, has recorded, arranged, and performed electro-acoustic scores for theatre, dance, film, and contemporary classical ensemble. He is the author of *The Literature of Exclusion: Dada, Data, and the Threshold of Electronic Literature* (Lexington Books, 2021) and has a book, *Jeff Noon's Vurt*, forthcoming from Palgrave Macmillan in 2022.

DAVID PRINGLE

JG BALLARD CHRONOLOGY
1930–1955

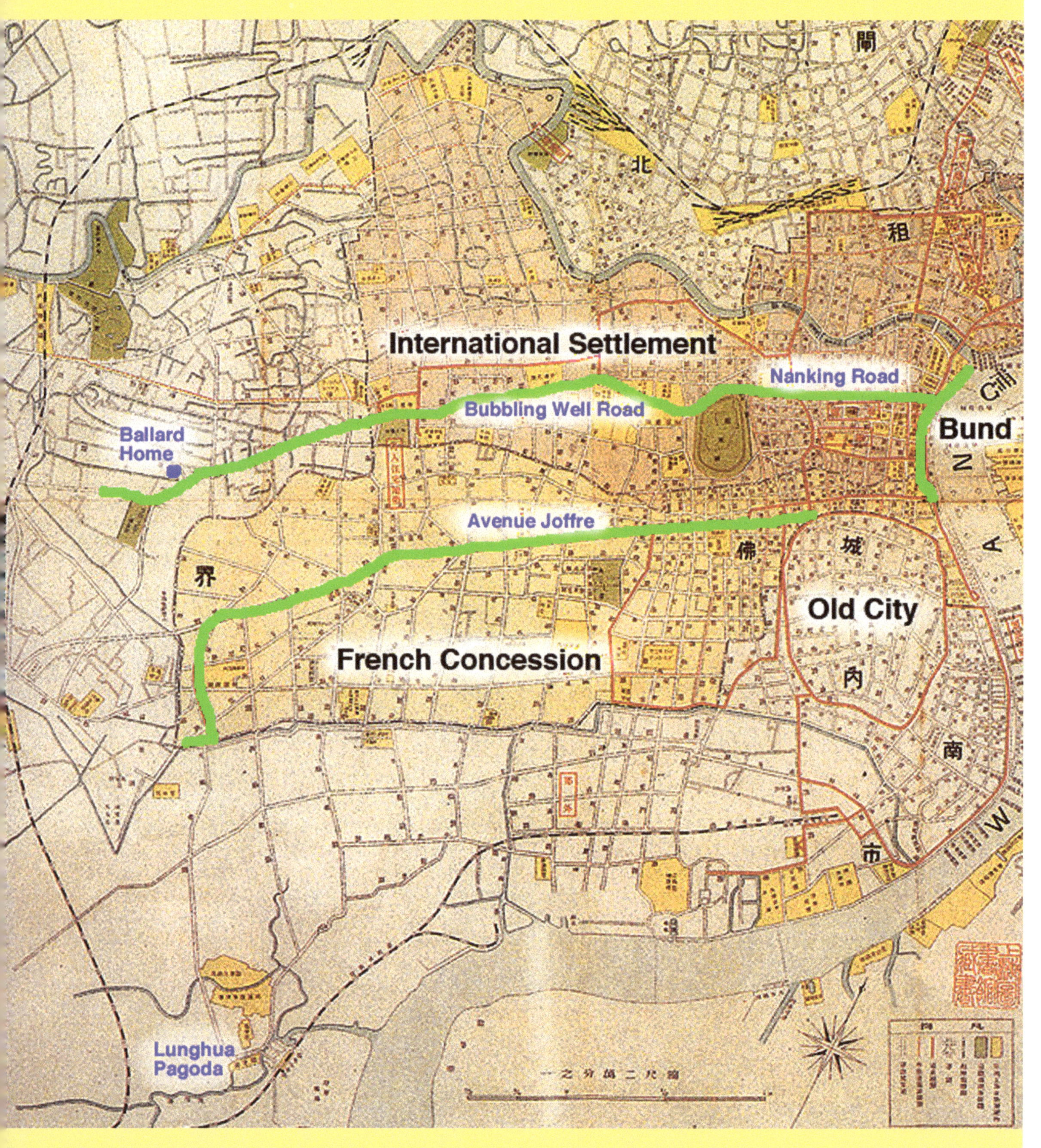

1930

1930 — February (mid-month) — The child who would be named James Graham Ballard was conceived in "a suburb of Manchester" on or about St Valentine's Day. As one of the few ancient saints' days still remembered by most Westerners—the day before the even more ancient Roman Feast of Lupercalia, dedicated to Faunus, god of fertility—it is quite likely that this particular 14th of February, which fell on a Friday, was celebrated by some of the residents of Manchester's suburbs with parties or dances. Did one particular young couple, James Ballard (b. 1901) and Edna (Johnstone) Ballard (b. 1905)—whose address at the time of their marriage in 1929 was 36 Church Lane, Romiley, Stockport, near Manchester—attend some Valentine's Day event? Possibly. At any rate, we can be reasonably sure that sometime around that weekend, that Lupercalia, they seeded a baby. "If my parents had decided not to go out to China in 1929 [sic] and I'd been born in a suburb of Manchester, I might never have become a writer at all." (Ballard, interviewed by Jeremy Isaacs, BBC 2, 7 November 1989.) Although in later years JGB would refer to his parents going to China in 1929, the shipping records tell us otherwise: it was in April 1930 that the Ballards left England.

1930 — February (mid-month) — "The past is enshrined in us, of course, and our minds contain the materials of huge mythic quests formed probably long before we were even born, probably at the moment of conception. ... I accept the collective unconscious—I don't think it's a mystic entity, I think it's simply that whenever an individual is conceived, a whole set of operating instructions, a set of guidebooks, are meshed together like cards being shuffled. A whole set of unconscious mythologies are nestled and locked into one another to produce this individual, who will then spend the whole of his life evolving and fulfilling that private mythology for himself, and setting it, testing it against the universe around him. We all enshrine within ourselves vast Homeric journeys; we're all clusters of mythological systems that begin to unwind the moment we're born." (Ballard, interviewed by Graeme Revell, 1983, in *Re/Search 8/9*, 1984.)

1930 — February 25 (Tuesday) — Mr James Ballard's new passport was issued to him from London on this date. He had no doubt owned an earlier one, which he must have used to take his bride Edna to Paris on honeymoon in 1929, but British passports required renewal every few years. "My mother was a 25-year-old newly married woman who had never been out of England, except for a honeymoon trip to Paris." (Ballard, *Miracles of Life*, p51.) They had first met at a holiday hotel in the English Lake District, "one of the hydros which were very popular with young people in the 1920s," and had married at Stockport Register Office, Cheshire, on 9 August 1929, so it is likely that their Parisian honeymoon had been in the latter part of that month. They had renewed their vows in a Church of England ceremony on 23 December 1929, held in West Bromwich, Staffordshire, and presumably undertaken to satisfy Edna's parents, who lived in that Midlands town.

1930 — March 2 (Sunday) — Death of D. H. Lawrence (b. 1885), British novelist, poet and essayist, author of *Sons and Lovers* (1913), *Women in Love* (1920), etc, in Vence, France, of tuberculosis at age 44.

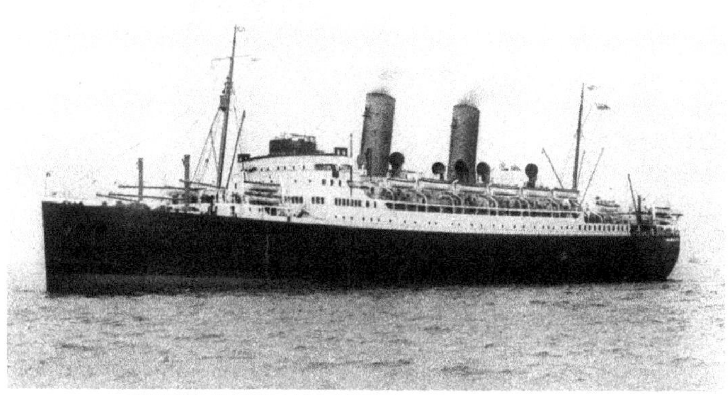

CANADIAN PACIFIC LINER "DUCHESS OF YORK." 20,000 TONS

1930 — April 4 (Friday) — Mr James Ballard and Mrs Edna Ballard departed England from the port of Liverpool, aboard the SS *Duchess of York*, a new liner of the Canadian Pacific Steamship Company. Along with their unborn first child, they were travelling to China via Canada.

1930 — April 11 (Friday) — Mr and Mrs Ballard arrived in Saint John, New Brunswick, Canada. According to their disembarkation details, James Ballard, 28, born in Blackburn and described as a "manager," and Edna Ballard, 24, born in West Bromwich and described as a "housewife," were "in transit to China" and their destination while still in Canada (which they would reach via the Canadian Pacific Railway) was "Hotel Vancouver, Vancouver, B.C." James Ballard's father's name and address were also given—"Mr E. Ballard, 158 Redlands, Blackburn" ("Redlands" seems to have been an error for Redlam)—as well as the number, date and place of issue of James's passport. So Canada was the first place outside England that the unborn child travelled to: unknowingly in transit across half the world, foetal JGB floated comfortably in his mother's womb.

1930 — April (mid) — Leaving Saint John, New Brunswick, on its way west, the Canadian Pacific train bearing the Ballards travelled through part of the US state of Maine, which sticks up into Canada like a fat thumb. So the second country the unborn boy entered, after Canada, was the United States. Later, en route across Canada to the west coast, the train must also have passed through Moose Jaw, Saskatchewan—where, almost 25 years later, JGB would find himself stationed as a trainee pilot in the RAF. After their long train journey, under the big skies and over the Canadian Rockies, Mr and Mrs Ballard stayed at the Hotel Vancouver before taking ship again to cross the Pacific to China. "Many famous people stayed at this hotel, including Winston Churchill, Sarah Bernhardt, Babe Ruth, Ethel Barrymore, and Anna Pavlova. It was also much loved by the people of Vancouver, who made its rooftop dining room and dance floor, the Panorama Roof, a favourite place for a night out." (Wikipedia.)

1930 — May (early) — It was around this time that James and Edna Ballard arrived in Shanghai aboard their Canadian Pacific steamer, he to take up a management post in the China

Printing and Finishing Company (a subsidiary the Manchester Calico Printers' Association), and she to become a housewife and mother—she was about two-and-a-half months pregnant. It is likely that their first permanent address in the city was an apartment at 39 Great Western Road, in the International Settlement, Shanghai. (Homeric journeys. Did the Ballards, including foetal JGB, stop at Hawaii, on their way across the Pacific from Vancouver to China? It is not known, but it is certainly possible, as they would stop over there on later trips.)

1930 — August 18 (Monday) — Noel Coward's play "Private Lives" premiered at the King's Theatre in Edinburgh. He had written it in only four days while staying at the newly-opened Cathay Hotel in Shanghai. Sir Victor Sassoon (of the wealthy Sassoon family, erstwhile opium traders) had built the hotel: situated at No. 20, The Bund, Shanghai, the office portion of the structure was called Sassoon House. The remainder was the Cathay Hotel, which had a nightclub under the roof. Sassoon, who was a bachelor, lived in the penthouse. Built in 1929, the whole hotel and office complex was pyramid-topped, and in the Moderne (later known as Art Deco) style.

1930 — October 23 (Thursday) — W. Olaf Stapledon's *Last and First Men: A Story of the Near and Far Future* was first published by Methuen of London, in an edition of 2,036 copies priced at 7/6. "In this brilliant romance, a man living on Neptune 2,000,000,000 years hence tells the story of humanity from our day to his," said the publisher's dust-jacket blurb. Meanwhile, in Shanghai, the gestating baby Ballard continued his nine-month journey towards birth. "The fact that I am who I am is a gigantic accident. This is a paradox we all have to live with: each of us has a unique character and identity which is an enormous accident, a complete billion-to-one chance against, while at the same time it's totally real. For each of us, existence is like being the winner of some enormous lottery prize!" (Ballard, interviewed by Graeme Revell, 1983.)

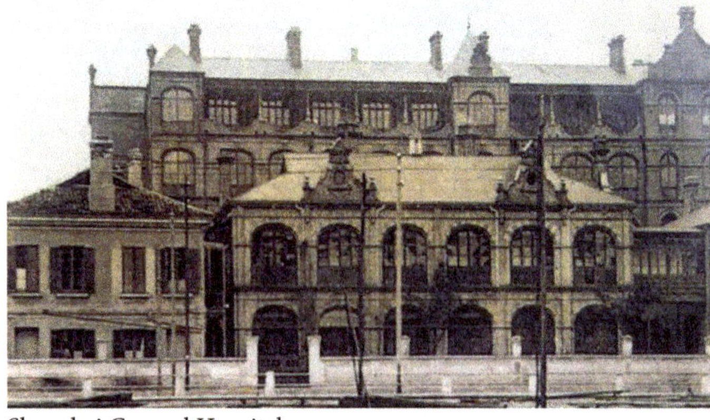

Shanghai General Hospital

1930 — November 15 (Saturday) — After his long amniotic dream, James Graham Ballard was born in China, to parents James and Edna Ballard. "I was born in Shanghai General Hospital on 15 November 1930, after a difficult delivery that my mother, who was slightly built and slim-hipped, liked to describe to me in later years, as if this revealed something about the larger thoughtlessness of the world. Over dinner she would often tell me that my head was badly deformed during birth, and I feel that for her this partly explained my wayward character as a teenager and young man (doctor friends say that there is nothing remarkable about such a birth)." (Ballard, *Miracles of Life*, 2008, p3.) It sounds as though it was probably a forceps delivery, a common procedure in the past which often left infants' soft skulls temporarily misshapen.

1930 — November 16 (Sunday) — In Shanghai, a tiny boy puzzled over his earliest impressions, after being pulled from his mother's womb. "I think there are landscapes of the mind that tap something deep in your central nervous system. We obviously inherit through our genes a whole visual apparatus —grids and patterns are laid down in the brain. A human baby takes a long time to cope with its world, though recent research seems to suggest that babies of even a few hours are beginning to activate these pattern-recognition systems in their brains which are triggered off by everything—the mother's presence, a smell, a smile. They are beginning to assemble all the basic building-blocks of perception. ... I'm a firm believer in the enduring quality of these pre-childhood experiences... It's not just the visual world, but the emotional world and our perception of our relationship with our mothers. These structures endure into adult life and are fed into our imaginations." (Ballard, interviewed by Lynne Fox, 20 January 1991.)

1930 — Sigmund Freud published his short book *Des Unbehagen in der Kultur*, which was swiftly translated into English as *Civilization and Its Discontents*. Here he stated that men are "creatures among whose instinctual endowments is to be reckoned a powerful share of aggressiveness. As a result, their neighbour is for them not only a potential helper or sexual object, but also someone who tempts them to satisfy their aggressiveness on him, to exploit his capacity for work without compensation, to use him sexually without his consent, to seize his possessions, to humiliate him, to cause him pain, to torture and to kill him. *Homo homini lupus* [Man is wolf to man]. Who, in the face of all his experience of life and of history, will have the courage to dispute this assertion?"

1931

1931 — January 17 (Saturday) — Mr James and Mrs Edna Ballard registered the birth of their son, James Graham Ballard, with the British Consulate—some two months after he was born. The address they gave as their residence was 39 Great Western Road, Shanghai. The baby boy now existed officially, and was a British citizen.

1931 — February 15 (Sunday) — James Graham Ballard, aged three months, was baptised at the Holy Trinity Church (familiarly known as the Anglican Cathedral), Shanghai. According to the certificate of baptism, the address his parents gave as their home was still 39 Great Western Road. Why did they give him the middle name Graham? Possibly it was in honour of his father's maternal grandmother Ellen Ward, née Ellen Graham (b. 1837).

1931 — May 1 (Friday) — The 102 storey Empire State Building was officially opened in New York City. A 3,000-man construction crew had completed the building in one year and 45 days.

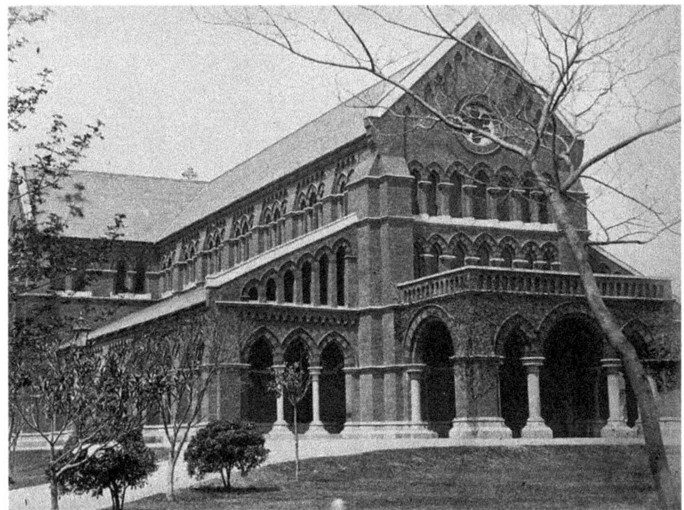
Holy Trinity Church

1931 — May 27 (Wednesday) — Professor Auguste Piccard of Switzerland, together with and physicist Paul Kipfer, made the first-ever flight into the stratosphere, in an airtight ball attached to a hydrogen balloon, reaching an altitude of 15,606 metres (51,200 feet). They landed in the Austrian Alps after more than 18 hours in the air. "The moral authority of science was colossal in the 1930s. I can remember myself that children's encyclopaedias were loaded with scientific marvels the greatest bridge in the world, the longest tunnel, the biggest ship, Professor Piccard in his stratosphere balloon." (Ballard, interviewed by Lynn Barber, August 1970.)

1931 — June 10 (Wednesday) — A British joint passport was issued on this date in Shanghai, China, to Mrs Edna Ballard and her seven-month-old son James Graham Ballard. Why should this have been necessary? Was she planning a journey somewhere with her baby but without her husband? The likelihood is that she was intending to take a ship from Shanghai to the coastal resort of Tsingtao in northern China. Many European Shanghai residents (known as "Shanghailanders") were in the habit of taking their summer holidays there during the hot months, if they could afford to do so, and passports would facilitate their travel there, from one westernized enclave of China to another. (It was a former German colony.)

1931 — June 19 (Friday) — Death of Silas Aaron Hardoon (b. 1851), Shanghai millionaire and philanthropist, at about 80. Born in Baghdad, educated in Bombay, he joined the firm of David Sassoon & Co., Ltd., moved to E. D. Sassoon & Co., and in 1911 launched into Shanghai property dealing. He died worth $150,000,000. "Among those who had made immense fortunes by bringing in opium was the 'Baghdad Jew', Hardoon. Starting life as a watchman, he had risen like a phoenix from the ashes of the millions of pipefuls of the drug he had provided for the emaciated sots who were in its deadly grip. But, as if to atone for the misery his trading success had caused, he adopted a family of about nine orphaned children of many races who lived with him in a palatial mansion on Bubbling Well Road." (Ralph Shaw, *Sin City*, 1973.) "[My father showed me] the vast Hardoon estate in the centre of the International Settlement, created by an Iraqi property tycoon who was told by a fortune-teller that if he ever stopped building he would die, and who then went on constructing elaborate pavilions all over Shanghai, many of them structures with no doors or interiors." (Ballard, *Miracles of Life*, p9.)

1931 — Summer — It was probably in July or August of this year that young Jamie Ballard had his first experience of the seaside at the coastal resort of Tsingtao—and it was very nearly his last: "My mother often told me that when I was a baby ... the amah [nanny] pushing my pram missed her footing on the grassy slope above the cliffs and lost control of the pram. It sped downhill towards the cliff's edge, where a chance British visitor ran forward and caught the pram before it went over..." The "amah," he explained, was "a middle-aged Chinese woman, hobbling on her bound feet... Parents in the 1930s took what now seems a remarkably detached view of their children, whose welfare if they could afford it was assigned to servants, whatever the hazards." (Ballard, *Miracles of Life*, p43-44.)

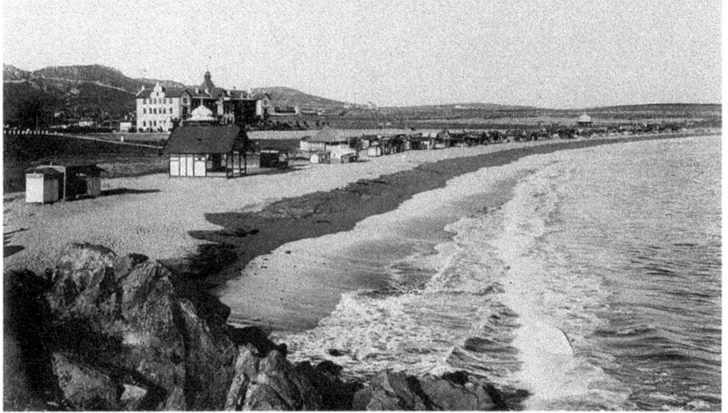
Tsingtao beach with the Strand Hotel

1931 — August 3 (Monday) — The Huang He River in the Yangtse-Kiang area of China flooded more than 40,000 square miles and killed a great many people.

1931 — August 18 (Tuesday) — The floods in China reached their worst point when the Yangtse peaked. The consequent widespread famine would lead to the deaths of an estimated 225,000 people, making this flood season one of the worst natural disasters in history.

1931 — Late Summer — As Mrs Edna Ballard and her nine-month-old son, Jamie, returned to Shanghai by ship from their holiday in Tsingtao, the vast country on the edge of which they made their home endured the aftermath of a huge disaster. "China's angry dragon, the Yangtse River, was dropping a few inches a day last week. The flood peak had definitely passed. But there was no respite from death and destruction. Hankow, 'Chicago of China,' was still awash with germ-laden, stinking waters. Gendarmerie headquarters estimated 250,000 dead in the vicinity. It was the typhoon season. After furious storms, the Grand Canal (running north and south between Hangchow and Tientsin) gave way in 15 places and washed out the thriving city of Yangchow; 200,000 were reported killed, 6,000,000 more made homeless. A missionary reached Shanghai last week from the flooded region and reported the creation of a great shallow inland sea, 200 miles long, yellow and endless to the horizon." (*Time*, 7 September 1931.)

1931 — September 18 (Friday) — The "Mukden Incident"

was initiated by the Japanese Kwangtung Army in Mukden, Manchuria. It involved an explosion that occurred on the Japanese-controlled South Manchurian Railway. Next day, the Japan's invasion of Manchuria would begin, and within three months Japanese troops would spread throughout the country.

1931 — October 2 (Friday) — Charles Lindbergh, world-famous American aviator, and his wife Anne Morrow had a mishap in China. "In a thousand newspaper offices the hearts of a thousand editors gave an extra-hard thump one day last week when the wire service tickers gave them the words: 'Lindberghs ... crash.' In a moment it was clear that both Colonel & Mrs. Lindbergh were safe. They had been fished out of the filthy Yangtze River at Hankow by a lifeboat crew from the British aircraft carrier Hermes. Still, a crash was a crash and many a page-wide headline shrieked the news that afternoon. Next day it was being called a 'ducking'... Flyers and plane were hauled back aboard the Hermes which steamed for Shanghai, where the plane was to be repaired." (*Time*, 12 October 1931.)

1931 — November 15 (Sunday) — J.G. Ballard's 1st birthday. He was still an infant, probably unable to walk as yet, but: "One year. Stands holding furniture. Stands alone for a second or two, then collapses with a bump. Babbles two or three words repeatedly. Drops toys, and watches where they go. Cooperates with dressing, waves goodbye, understands simple commands." (Child Development Stages, Wikipedia.)

1932

1932 — January 28 (Thursday) — Following anti-Japanese boycott activities and racial disorders in the Hongkew district of Shanghai, and the failure of Chinese military forces to withdraw from near the Settlement boundaries, Japanese naval forces made a direct attack on the Chinese army in the Chapei district. Troops landed from ships, and planes bombed the district, killing thousands in the first-ever terror-bombing of civilians. Astonishingly, all this was going on just a few miles north of where the Ballards and many other Westerners lived, but they were unharmed by it.

1932 — January 30 (Saturday) — *Brave New World*, a satirical, futuristic novel by Aldous Huxley, was first published (London: Chatto & Windus). It envisioned a world of conditioned uniformity and constant mindless entertainment enhanced by mood-altering drugs.

1932 — February 1 (Monday) — In Shanghai, the majority of the International Settlement and the French Concession remained untouched by the bloody Sino-Japanese conflict in Chapei, and it was often the case that the more foolhardy western civilians would treat the battle as a spectacle, watching the war from the banks of Soochow Creek.

1932 — February 12 (Friday) — Marlene Dietrich, German actress and singer, starred in the Hollywood film *Shanghai Express* (dir. Josef von Sternberg), first released on this date. Also starring Clive Brook, Anna May Wong and Warner Oland, it would become the highest-grossing US movie of 1932, perhaps boosted by the fact that Shanghai was in the news.

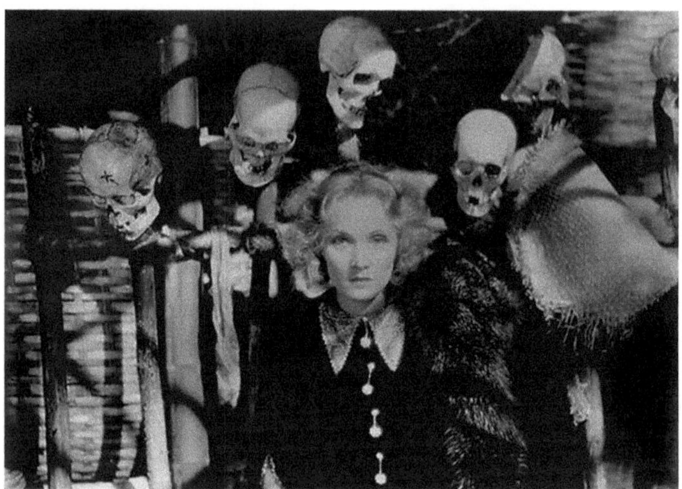

Marlene Deitrich in *Shanghai Express*

1932 — May 5 (Thursday) — A Sino-Japanese armistice was signed, terminating the "undeclared war" which would be known as the Shanghai Incident.

1932 — November 15 (Tuesday) — J.G. Ballard's 2nd birthday. "Two years. Able to run. Walks up and down stairs two feet per step. Builds tower of six cubes. Joins two–three words in sentences." (Child Development Stages.)

1932 — December 25 (Sunday) — King George V became the first monarch to deliver a Christmas Day message by radio, on the newly-launched BBC Empire Service. His speech to the Empire was written by Rudyard Kipling, and recorded on the Blattnerphone.

1932 — The song "The Teddy Bears' Picnic" became a hit in Britain. It had begun life as a 1907 musical piece written by the American Tin Pan Alley composer John Walter Bratton, but gained new prominence in 1932 when the Northern Irish lyricist Jimmy Kennedy added words and it was recorded by the popular Henry Hall and his BBC Dance Orchestra, featuring Val Rosing as lead vocalist—a version which sold a million copies. "When I was a small boy, I was given one of those windup gramophones [and] 'Teddy Bear's Picnic,' which I played hundreds of times in my bedroom. By the time I grew up, I couldn't bear the sound of that song—everything about it drove me mad. And then I discovered, in my 60s, that actually I rather liked the song again. Perhaps I felt that my childhood was slipping away from me for the last time. Now, I could listen to it happily forever." (Ballard, interviewed by Mike Doherty, CBC.ca, 2 October 2006.)

1933

1933 — January 30 (Monday) — Adolf Hitler was appointed chancellor of Germany, and the Nazis celebrated with a torchlight parade in Berlin. Hitler's aide Rudolf Hess would praise his leader in a speech: "Do not seek Adolf Hitler with your mind. You will find him through the strength of your hearts! Adolf Hitler is Germany and Germany is Adolf Hitler. He who takes an oath to Hitler takes an oath to Germany!"

1933 — February 27 (Monday) — The Reichstag, Germany's

parliament building, was set on fire in an act of arson, and heavily damaged. The police quickly found one Marinus van der Lubbe, shirtless, inside the building: he was a Dutch unemployed bricklayer, recently arrived in Germany. The Nazis, blaming the Communists, would use the fire as a pretext for suspending civil liberties and increasing their power.

1933 — February 28 (Tuesday) — Billy Wilder, Austrian-born screenwriter and film director-to-be, boarded a train from Berlin to Paris with $1,000 secreted about his person. Abandoning Germany on the day following the Reichstag fire, he would soon make his way via France and Mexico to America, to Hollywood, where in due course he would direct such movies as *Double Indemnity, The Lost Weekend* and *Sunset Boulevard.*

1933 — March 4 (Saturday) — Franklin D. Roosevelt was inaugurated as the 32nd President of the USA in Washington, DC, in succession to Herbert Hoover.

1933 — April 3 (Monday) — Douglas Douglas-Hamilton, Marquess of Clydesdale, and David McIntyre, a Royal Air Force lieutenant, flying two open-cockpit Westland aircraft, completed the first over-flight and aerial photographic survey of Mount Everest. The British team battled extreme cold and high winds as they photographed the previously unknown crest of the 29,028-foot peak. The flight was funded by Lucy, Lady Houston.

1933 — July 14 (Friday) — Death of Raymond Roussel (b. 1877), French "poet, novelist, playwright, musician, chess enthusiast, neurasthenic, drug addict, and likely suicide," of a barbiturate overdose at 56. He wrote *Impressions d'Afrique* ("Impressions of Africa," 1910) and *Locus Solus* (1914).

1933 — November 15 (Wednesday) — J.G. Ballard's 3rd birthday. "Three years. Goes up stairs one foot per step and downstairs two feet per step. Builds tower of nine cubes. Constantly asks questions. Speaks in sentences. Cooperative play. Imaginary companions." (Child Development Stages.)

1933 — December — Raymond Chandler (b. 1888) first contributed to *Black Mask*, with "Blackmailers Don't Shoot" (December 1933 issue). American-born, but educated in England, Chandler had worked for a decade in the Los Angeles oil industry before losing his job as a result of his drinking. "Wandering up and down the Pacific Coast in an automobile I began to read pulp magazines, because they were cheap enough to throw away... This was in the great days of the *Black Mask* (if I may call them great days) and it struck me that some of the writing was pretty forceful and honest, even though it had its crude aspect. I decided that this might be a good way to try to learn to write fiction and get paid a small amount of money at the same time. I spent five months over an 18,000-word novelette and sold it for $180. After that I never looked back, although I had a good many uneasy periods looking forward." (Chandler, letter to Hamish Hamilton, 1950.)

1934

1934 — January 7 (Sunday) — The first episode of Alex Raymond's "Flash Gordon" comic strip, a creation of the King Features Syndicate, was published in US newspapers. It was inspired by, and created to compete with, the already established "Buck Rogers" science-fiction strip.

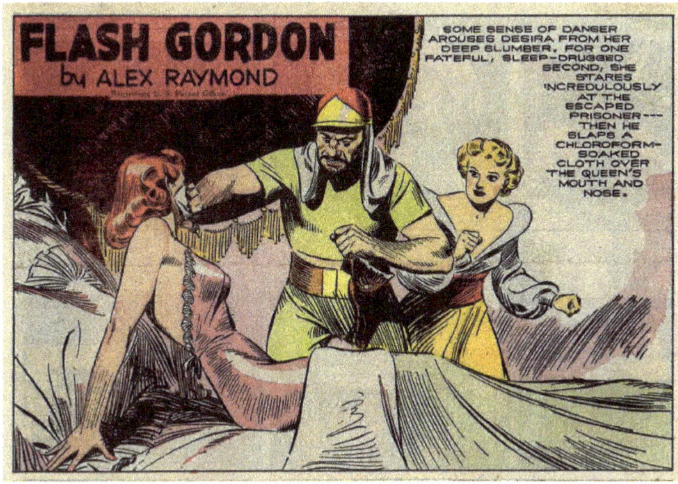

1934 — April 16 (Monday) — Kingsley Amis's 12th birthday (he was born in London on 16 April 1922). "I have been a devotee of science fiction ever since investigating, at the age of twelve or so, a bin in the neighbourhood Woolworth's with the label YANK MAGAZINES: Interesting Reading. Those stories of twenty-five years ago, of course, with their exploitation of violence and horror, were as far below the level of contemporary science fiction as the music of the B.B.C. Dance Orchestra was below that of Louis Armstrong's Hot Five; but the first coverful of many-eyed and -tentacled monsters was enough assurance for me, as it must have been for thousands of others, that this was the right kind of stuff." (Amis, *New Maps of Hell*, London: Gollancz, 1961.)

1934 — May 15 (Tuesday) — J.G. Ballard's three-and-a-halfth birthday, and possibly the time from which his earliest memories dated. "I have a vague recollection of being introduced to Madame Sun Yat-Sen." (Ballard, quoted in *World Authors*, 1975.) "Jim ... remembered a garden party at the British Embassy. 'Once I was introduced to Madame Sun Yat-Sen... I was only three and a half.'" (Ballard, *Empire of the Sun*, Ch. 11.) The lady in question was Soong Ching-ling (1893–1981), also known as Rosamond Soong Ching-ling, who had married Sun Yat-sen, 26 years her senior, on 25 October 1915 and become his widow when he died on 12 March 1925. Fluent in English, she lived in a house in the French Concession of Shanghai until 1937.

1934 — May 16 (Wednesday) — It must have been around this date that the Ballard family departed Shanghai once more by ship, bound for Canada and England. After four years in the great Chinese city, Mr Ballard was no doubt due to take his first long leave from his managerial work at the China Printing and Finishing Company—a break long enough to allow him to take his small family on a home visit to Britain to see older relatives.

1934 — May 23 (Wednesday) — The *Empress of Canada*, a

passenger liner of the Canadian Pacific Steamship Company which had begun its voyage at Manila (but must have called at Shanghai en route), docked at Victoria, British Columbia, Canada. From it disembarked James Graham Ballard, aged three, with his father James and his mother Edna. Their status in Canada was that of "tourists," their country of residence was listed as China, and their ultimate destination address was given as c/o A. Johnstone, 11 Lodge Road, West Bromwich, England. Young Ballard was travelling on a passport shared with his mother, issued in Shanghai on 10 June 1931.

1934 — May 28 (Monday) — The Dionne quintuplets were born to Olivia and Elzire Dionne near Callander, Ontario, Canada, becoming the first quintuplets to survive infancy. The babies Emilie, Yvonne, Cecile, Marie and Annette averaged two pounds 11 ounces each, and attracted worldwide attention. No doubt the Ballard family, crossing Canada at the time, heard the news.

1934 — June 4 (Monday) — The *Montcalm*, a passenger steamer of the Canadian Pacific Line, docked at Southampton, England. From it disembarked James Graham Ballard, aged three, with his father James and his mother Edna. Their country of "last permanent residence" was listed as China, and their "proposed address in the United Kingdom" was stated as 11 Lodge Road, West Bromwich, Staffordshire. That address was the house of young Jamie Ballard's maternal grandparents, Archibald and Sarah Annie Johnstone, music teachers long resident in the Midlands town of West Bromwich, near Birmingham.

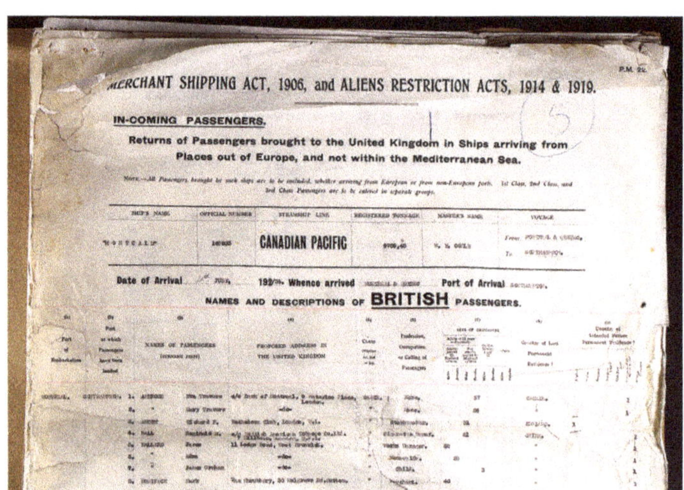
P.M. 22.

MERCHANT SHIPPING ACT, 1906, and ALIENS RESTRICTION ACTS, 1914 & 1919.

IN-COMING PASSENGERS.

Returns of Passengers brought to the United Kingdom in Ships arriving from Places out of Europe, and not within the Mediterranean Sea.

CANADIAN PACIFIC

Date of Arrival ... 193 ... Whence arrived ... Port of Arrival ...

NAMES AND DESCRIPTIONS OF BRITISH PASSENGERS.

1934 — June-July? — Young Jamie Ballard met the Johnstones, his maternal grandparents, for the first time in this period, staying with them in the Black Country town which had been his mother's birthplace. Apparently, he would remember nothing of this visit, but would later write: "My mother rarely talked about her life in West Bromwich... The only thing she ever told me about her schooldays was that the future film actress Madeleine Carroll was in the same class at the West Bromwich Grammar School for Girls. For a brief period she worked as a teacher in a junior school in West Bromwich, and was appalled by the dreadful poverty of many of the children." (Ballard, *Miracles of Life*, p50-51.) Whether or not young Jamie noticed any dire poverty in the town (probably not), the actress Madeleine Carroll would undoubtedly have been a subject of conversation at the time of the Ballards' visit, as in 1934 she had just made her first film in Hollywood (*The World Moves On*, directed by John Ford) and, back in Britain, was about to star in Alfred Hitchcock's forthcoming *The 39 Steps* (1935) — not many English actresses of the 1930s achieved greater fame and success.

1934 — August-September? — During his long stay in England, young Jamie also met his other grandparents, Ernest Ballard (b. 1871), Master Tailor, and Emma Ballard (née Ward; b. 1872), who had married on 20 December 1900 in the Lancashire town of Blackburn, and still resided there. Unfortunately, though, he would not remember them, and in later years would simply say: "I never met my father's parents: they lived in Blackburn in my father's youth." (Ballard, interviewed by David Pringle, 24 July 1981.) In fact, part of the purpose of this lengthy stay in Britain had been to enable the little boy to meet his grandparents, both sets; and sadly, there would never be another opportunity to do so in the case of the elder Ballards, as both Ernest and Emma would die before the family's next return home from China. Someone else Jamie is likely to have met on this trip was his father's younger brother, Edward Ballard (b. 1904), also a resident of Blackburn and also in the tailoring business (it is not known whether JGB would have any contact with his Uncle Edward in later years).

1934 — October 12 (Friday) — The *Ranpura*, a passenger steamer of the P&O line, departed from the port of London. Aboard were James Graham Ballard, aged three, with his father James and his mother Edna. Their destination was Shanghai, China, and their "last address in the United Kingdom" was given as 158 Redlam, Blackburn, Lancashire. They had been in England since 4 June 1934, a period of just over four months.

1934 — November 15 (Thursday) — J.G. Ballard's 4th birthday. Newly returned from their long stay in England, it may have been around this time that Mr James Ballard and his family set up home at 31A Amherst Avenue, Shanghai, a newly-built spacious house situated in the suburbs, or "New Roads" area, outside the western boundary of the International Settlement (that is, outside the part of Shanghai which, in the mid-19th century, had been conceded to Britain and the USA as a trading zone). "My childhood home in Amherst Avenue... had been built in the early 1930s in the classic stockbroker-Tudor style of the Home Counties, though the interior was that of an American house with five bathrooms, air conditioning and a squash-court-sized kitchen." (Ballard, "Unlocking the Past," *Telegraph*, 21 September 1991.)

1934 — The Park Hotel in Shanghai (initially the Shanghai Joint Savings Society Building), designed by László Hudec, was a prime example of *Art Moderne* architecture, facing the race track on Bubbling Well Road. Upon its completion in December 1934, it was Asia's tallest building, at 275 feet, with a retractable roof over its 22nd-floor nightclub.

1934 — J.B. Priestley published his book *English Journey*, in which he described his travels round the country in the autumn of 1933, during which he had discerned "three Englands": (1) "The 'Old England' of the cathedrals, the Cotswolds and the colleges of the ancient universities." (2) "The 19th-century England, the industrial England of coal, iron, steel, cotton,

The Ballard Home at 31A Amherst Avenue.

Below: A floorplan of the house, drawn by JG Ballard in 2007.
Bottom: Main door to the house.
Top right: Southeast view of the exterior.
Middle right: South view of the exterior.
Bottom right: East view of the exterior.

Photos taken by Peter Brigg in 1984.

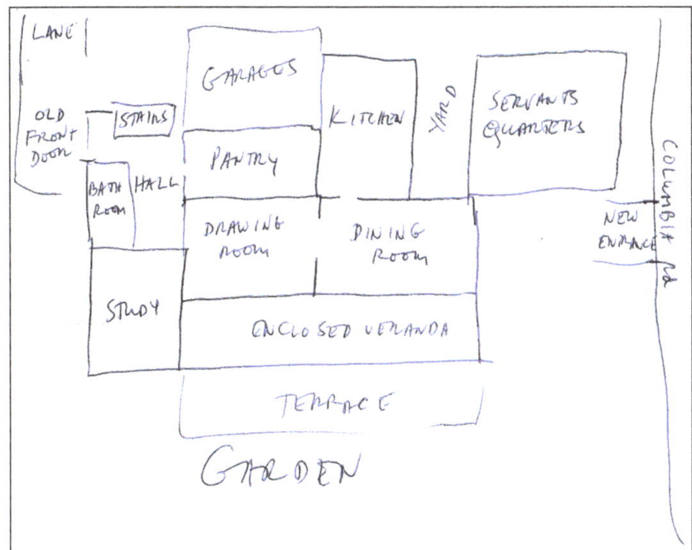

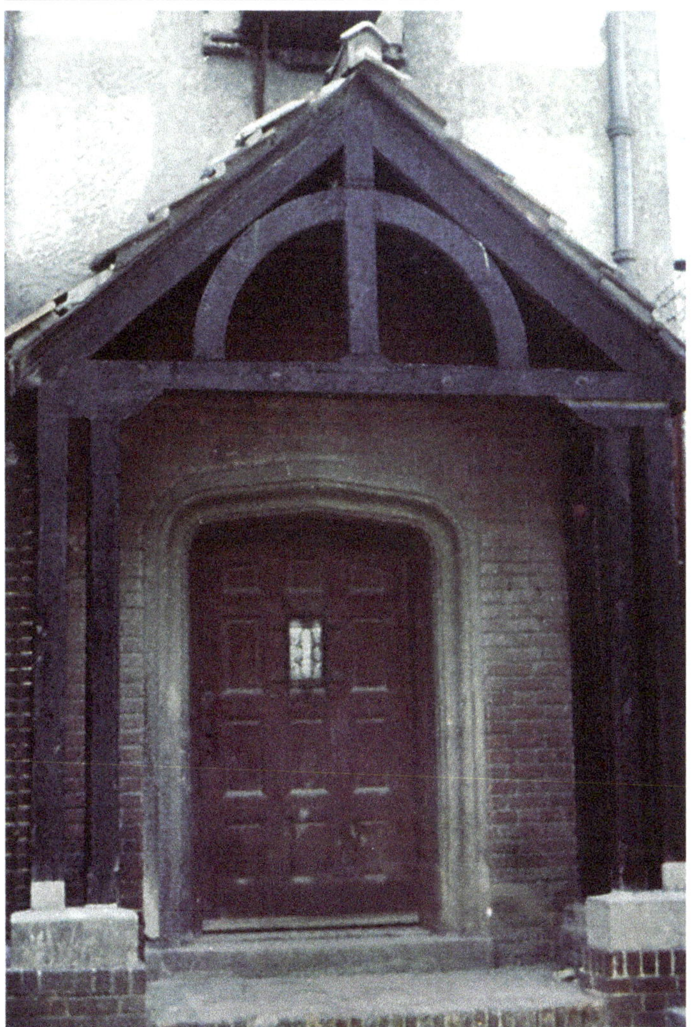

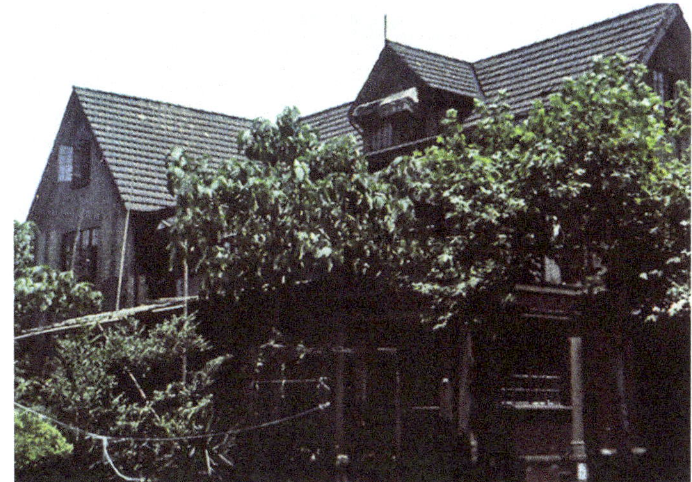

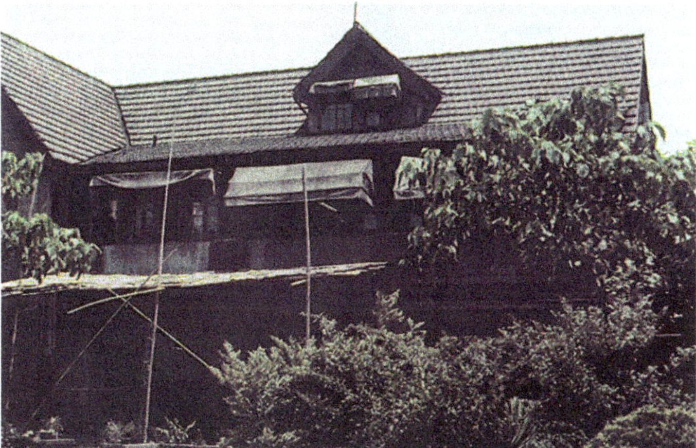

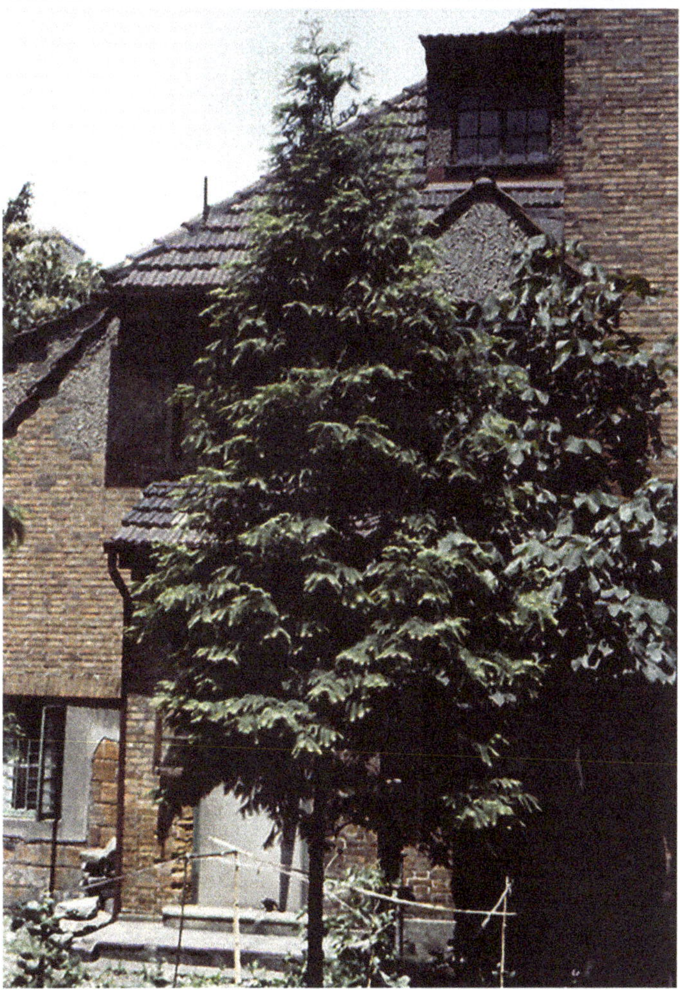

wool, railways... mills, foundries, warehouses." (3) "The third England, I concluded, was the new post-War England... America, I suppose, was its real birthplace. This is the England of arterial and by-pass roads, of filling stations and factories that look like exhibition buildings, of giant cinemas and dance-halls and cafés, bungalows with tiny garages, cocktail bars, Woolworths, motor-coaches, wireless, hiking, factory girls looking like actresses, greyhound racing and dirt tracks, [and] swimming pools..."

1935

1935 — January 6 (Sunday) — In his comic strip "Terry and the Pirates," Milton Caniff introduced the character called the Dragon Lady on this date. The phrase would become a part of the language, applied to any powerful Chinese or East-Asian woman and to characters of that type played in Hollywood films by the actress Anna May Wong and others. Young JGB would come to regard this as his favourite strip, though probably not until a couple of years later: "By the thirties, perhaps in response to the Depression, crime and detective strips were well established, led by Chester Gould's *Dick Tracy*... [A]s a boy in Shanghai I had my own problems trying to find the exotic world of *Terry and the Pirates*, an Oriental farrago of inscrutable mandarins, dragon ladies and sinister pagodas, among the department stores and art deco cinemas of the real city in which the strip was set." (Ballard, "How to Tear a Strip Off a Culture," *Guardian*, 21 March 1991.)

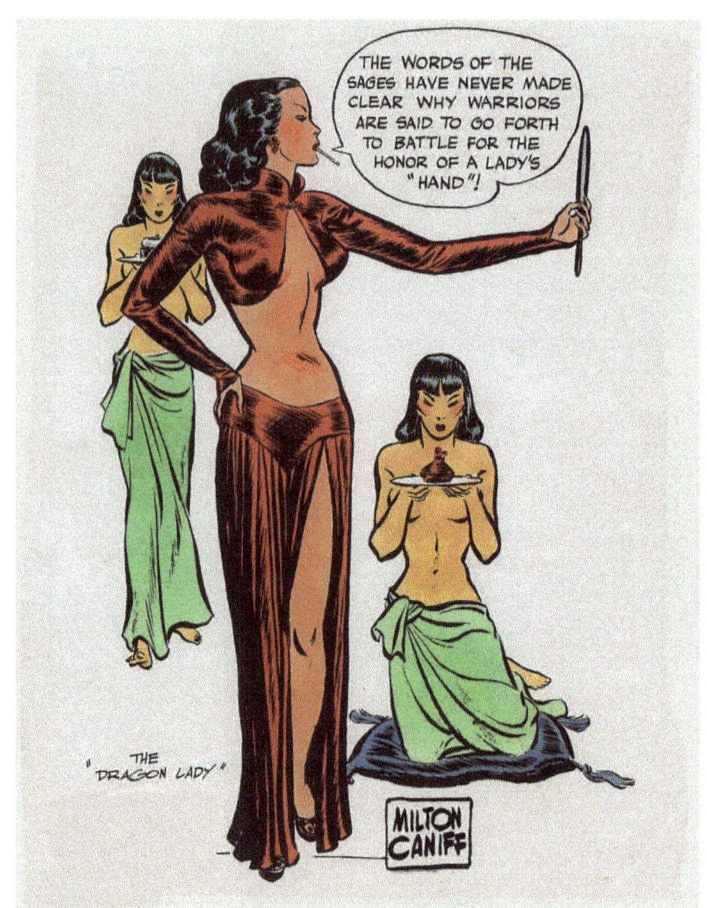

1935 — February 28 (Thursday) — Ballard's paternal grandmother, Emma Ballard (b. 1872) of 158 Redlam, Blackburn, died (aged about 63), leaving effects worth £148 14s. 2d. to her husband, Ernest Ballard, tailor, of the same address. (Probate records, 1935.) She had lived long enough to meet her first grandchild when he had been brought to England a few months earlier, but she would not be remembered by him in after-years.

1935 — Spring — A new cotton spinning and weaving mill at Pootung (Pudong Point), opposite the Bund at Shanghai, was opened by the China Printing and Finishing Company. In due course, Ballard's father would rise to become chairman and managing director of the company. Meanwhile, his young son was often in the care of a Russian nanny: "I climbed to the top floor and stood in my childhood bedroom, which still had its original blue paint and the bookshelves where I had methodically arranged my *Chums* annuals and American comics... In the bathroom there was even the original lavatory seat on which, as a small boy, I had been ordered by the punitive White Russian nanny to sit uselessly for hours—the 1930s baby-minding equivalent of television, and probably far more educational." (Ballard, "Unlocking the Past," *Telegraph*, 21 September 1991.) "My parents were busy with their expat social life and I was brought up by Chinese servants who never looked at me and never spoke to me." (Ballard, "Look Back at Empire," *Guardian*, 4 March 2006.) "I can remember the bad-tempered amahs of my childhood, ruthless and hard-fisted little women darting about on their bound feet. At the other end of the social scale were the dragon ladies—tycoon's wives or successful businesswomen—in their long fur coats and immaculate make-up, who could petrify a small boy at 50 paces with their baleful stares." (Ballard, "Survival Instincts," *Sunday Times*, 1 March 1992.)

1935 — May 15 (Wednesday) — J.G. Ballard's four-and-a-halfth birthday. "What may be one of my earliest memories is of the floods that came to Shanghai every spring. Every street, every drive and garden was almost a foot deep in brown flood-water as the Yangtse overflowed its banks. I must have been about five when I put on a pair of my father's Wellington boots and shuffled slowly through the water to the end of the drive, amazed that there was all this water around me but my lower legs were still dry. Then a passing car churned past and threw a wave over the boots, filling them with water. I still remember my surprise." (Ballard, notes for *Miracles of Life*, circa 2007, British Library archive, p6.) "Shanghai was founded [in] an area of swamp, virtually, with a water table that was literally about two feet below the ground. One of my childhood pastimes was digging wells—which sounds extremely laborious, but in fact there's nothing easier on earth: you just put a spade in and within three minutes you had a fully-functioning well. I think it was quite a problem to my parents' gardener, constantly seeing these wells appearing everywhere!" (Ballard, "Grand Tour," BBC Radio 4, 17 November 1990.)

1935 — June 6 (Thursday) — Alfred Hitchcock's film *The 39 Steps*, based on the novel by John Buchan and starring Robert Donat, Madeleine Carroll and Godfrey Tearle, premiered at the New Gallery Theatre in London.

1935 — June 7 (Friday) — Stanley Baldwin (b. 1867),

Conservative Party leader, became Prime Minister in Britain's National Government, replacing the former Labour Party leader Ramsay MacDonald.

1935 — July 30 (Tuesday) — Penguin Books introduced modern mass-market paperbacks in Britain, priced at sixpence each. The first ten Penguins, paper-covered reprints of titles previously published in hardback, were all issued on the same day by publisher Allen Lane.

1935 — August — The new Shanghai Stadium was opened in this month. Built by the Chinese Nationalist government, with *Art Moderne* finishes, it was the largest sports stadium in the Far East at the time of its completion, and its complex included a gymnasium, a swimming pool, a baseball field and tennis courts.

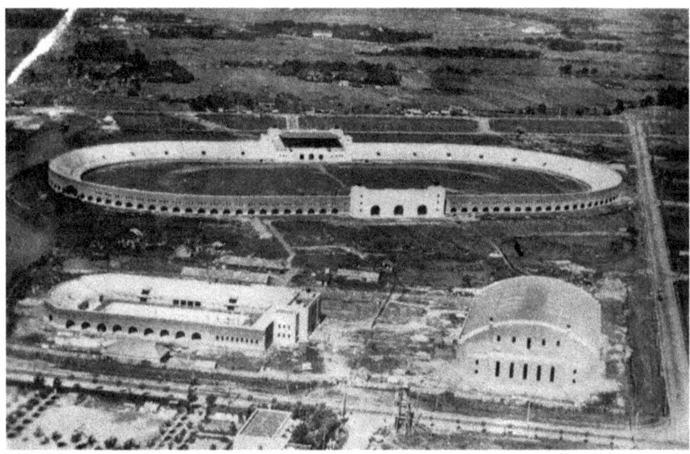

1935 — November 15 (Friday) — J.G. Ballard's 5th birthday. "Mah-jong was reinvented in the 1930s by an American, living in Shanghai, and I think the very first sounds I ever heard were the sounds of Mah-jong tiles, these tiles, clacking away. In the mid '30s my mother and all the other ex-pat European, American ladies in Shanghai, played Mah-jong constantly. ... [T]here might be two tables, eight ladies or nine in fact, one would circulate the canapés and listen in on the latest gossip on the telephone. So the noise of these ivory tiles clacking away was ferocious. And as a five-year-old I used to listen to this sort of gnashing of tiles, and it probably was the first sound I ever heard." (Ballard, Joan Bakewell interview, Channel 4, 29 April 1993.) "The cook's son was a boy of my age... I tried desperately to make friends with him, but never succeeded. He was not allowed into the main garden, and refused to follow me when I invited him to climb the trees with me. He spent his time in the alley between the main house and the servants' quarters and his only toy was an empty Klim tin that had once held powdered milk. There were three holes in its lid, through which he would drop small stones, then remove the lid and peer inside. He would do this for hours, mystifying me completely... Aware that I had a bedroom filled with expensive British and German toys (ordered every September from Hamleys in London), I made a selection of cars, aeroplanes, lead soldiers and model battleships and carried them down to him. He seemed bemused by these strange objects, so I left him to explore them. Two hours later I crept back and found him surrounded by the untouched toys, dropping stones into his tin. ... The toys had been a genuine gift, but when I went to bed that night I found that they had all been returned." (Ballard, *Miracles of Life*, p13.)

1935 — December — Young Jamie Ballard had probably learned to read by the end of this year. "I can no longer remember my nursery reading, though my mother, once a school-teacher, fortunately had taught me to read before I entered school at the age of five." (Ballard, *The Pleasure of Reading*, edited by Antonia Fraser, 1992.) "I remember very little before the age of 5 or 6, when I joined the junior form of the Cathedral School for boys. The school was run on English lines with a syllabus aimed at the School Certificate examinations or their pre-war equivalent, heavily dominated by Latin and scripture classes. The masters were English, and we were made to work surprisingly hard... There were two hours of Latin every other day and a great deal of homework. The headmaster was a Church of England clergyman called the Reverend Matthews, a sadist who was free not only with his cane but with his fists, brutally slapping quite small boys. ... Miraculously I escaped his wrath..." (Ballard, *Miracles of Life*, p17-18.)

1936

1936 — January 18 (Saturday) — Death of Rudyard Kipling (b. 1865), British novelist (*Kim*), short-story writer (*The Jungle Book*) and poet (*Barrack-Room Ballads*), Nobel Prize laureate, of a perforated duodenal ulcer at 70.

1936 — January 20 (Monday) — Death of King George V (b. 1865), at Sandringham House, Norfolk, after a four-day bronchial illness. Like Kipling, he was 70. His eldest son, the Prince of Wales, succeeded him as King Edward VIII.

1936 — February 21 (Friday) — The science-fiction film *Things to Come*, produced by Alexander Korda, directed by William Cameron Menzies, written by H. G. Wells, and starring Raymond Massey, premiered in London.

1936 — April 6 (Monday) — The first "chapter" of *Flash Gordon*, a 13-part science-fiction film serial, was released by Universal Pictures in the US. Directed by Frederick Stephani, it starred former swimming champion Larry "Buster" Crabbe as the eponymous hero, Jean Rogers as his girlfriend Dale Arden, Charles Middleton as the Emperor Ming the Merciless, and Priscilla Lawson as Princess Aura of the planet Mongo.

1936 — July 1 (Wednesday) — Salvador Dali gave a speech at the International Surrealist Exhibition in London. "Dali's lecture was delivered whilst wearing a deep-sea diving suit. Nearly suffocating during the presentation, Dali had to be rescued by the young poet David Gascoyne, who arrived with a spanner to release him from the diving helmet." (Source: *International Surrealist Bulletin*, Number 4, September 1936.)

1936 — Summer — In Shanghai, it may have been around this time that young Ballard learned to swim: "During school holidays we would drive every morning to the Country Club, where I spent hours in the swimming pool with my friends. I was a strong swimmer, and won a small silver spoon for coming first in a diving competition..." (Ballard, *Miracles of*

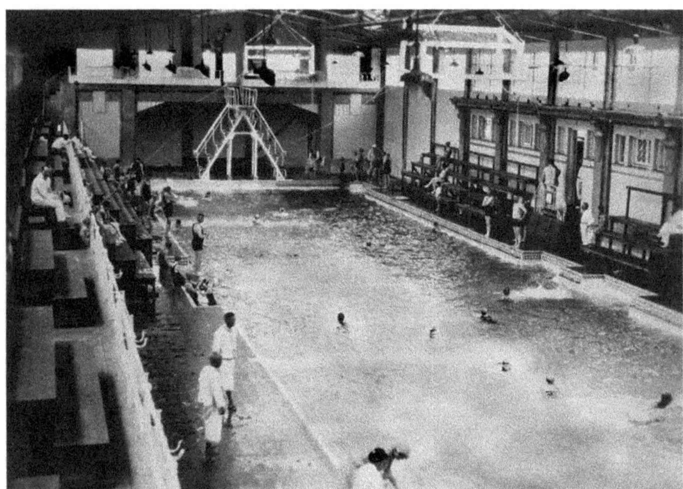

The French Club swimming pool.

Life, p19, 5.) It is likely that his swimming instructor was the ex-bantamweight boxer Billy Tingle, a popular figure among western parents and schoolchildren in the Chinese city. About this time a friend of Jamie Ballard's, almost six months his senior, was Ursula Keir Simpson, the daughter of a Shell oil company employee: many years afterwards, perhaps in the late 1990s, she would write a story mentioning Billy Tingle's name, about a little girl and a little boy swimming in the sea while on a family holiday at Tsingtao. "[S]he was a very strong swimmer and keen diver, so she must have learnt her skills from him! I'm guessing my mother wrote this story ... possibly inspired by a trip back to Shanghai to visit her childhood home. ... I have found a handwritten draft which suggests she was planning to write an extended novella surrounding this story which would have covered 1936-37 Shanghai, featuring her illness and recovery from TB and 'playing with "Hamish" at his house on Saturdays'." (Keiran Ure [daughter of Ursula Simpson Ure], e-mail to DP, 10 June 2019.)

1936 — Summer — Ursula Simpson's daughter would also write: "My mother was born in the Country Hospital Shanghai on 25th May 1930. Her family lived in a mock Tudor house in Ave Joffre in the French Concession nicknamed Gasoline Alley as the houses were owned by Asiatic Petroleum Company/Shell for whom my grandfather Stanley Pare Simpson worked. ... She attended the Cathedral School and I'm not sure if it's then she met Jamie, as she knew him, or whether they already knew each other. My mother was an only child with a huge imagination and I believe was quite lonely as her parents were very tied up with work and social engagements. My mother contracted TB and therefore was off school a lot, [and she] and Jamie spent many happy hours playing together in their respective gardens, coming up with all sorts of stories and adventures. Their families also spent the summer[s] in Tsingtao together... They used to enjoy playing with the trainee Buddhist monks who were a similar age to them, and were both particularly impressed by the incense marks on their shaved heads where the incense had burned down. The large spiders that did battle with the servants' brooms and the land crabs that might eat you when you slept [as mentioned in the story Ursula wrote] were also a huge source of fascination and horror." (Keiran Ure [daughter of Ursula Simpson Ure], e-mail to DP, 11 June 2019.)

1936 — November 2 (Monday) — The official opening took place of the world's first regular high-definition television service, operating from the BBC studios at Alexandra Palace in north London.

1936 — November 15 (Sunday) — J.G. Ballard's 6th birthday. The young Ballard attended the Cathedral School in Shanghai. "There were no cheerful posters or visual aids in those days, apart from a few threatening maps, in which the world was drenched red by the British Empire. The headmaster was a ferocious English clergyman whose preferred bible was Kennedy's *Latin Primer*. From the age of six we were terrorized through two hours of Latin a day..." (Ballard, *The Pleasure of Reading*, 1992.) "His disillusion with God began when he was a child in pre-war Shanghai. He was alarmed by the religious ravings of his Russian governess and depressed by a superfluity of worship at the Cathedral School. 'The governess used to say she heard God speak, but I soon realized it was just the thunder,' he chuckles throatily. 'At school the Church of England iconography—prayers, sermons, organ voluntaries—hung over our lives like a headache. Years later, when I went to King's College, Cambridge, as a student, I couldn't bring myself to set foot in the chapel. The headmaster of the school was a C of E clergyman. He was a sadist and would, without doubt, be behind bars today. He's dead now, thank God,' Ballard smiles. 'I hope he's suffering the same torments of Hell he put the small boys through.' His parents were non-practising Anglicans. He believes his father to have been an atheist. At the age of five Ballard himself embraced atheism. 'Going to school I would see small coffins decorated with paper flowers by the wayside. If there was a God he wasn't presiding over the streets of Shanghai.'" (Ballard, interviewed by Frances Welch, *Sunday Telegraph*, 20 March 1994.)

1936 — December 10 (Thursday) — Britain's King Edward VIII agreed to abdicate the throne in order to marry American divorcee Wallis Simpson. The next day, Parliament would pass His Majesty's Declaration of Abdication Act, and the King would perform his last act as sovereign by giving royal assent to it. His brother Prince Albert, Duke of York, would accede to the throne as King George VI. This was the major domestic news story of the decade for British citizens, including no doubt the Ballard family in Shanghai.

1937

1937 — January 11 (Monday) — The first issue of *Look* magazine went on sale in the United States. Large-format and copiously illustrated, it would be one of the glossy American magazines to which the Ballard family in Shanghai evidently subscribed. "These names were taken from the editorial mastheads of *Look*, *Life* and *Time*... [of which] I have been a keen reader since the late 1930s." (Ballard, annotations to *The Atrocity Exhibition*, 1990, p101.)

1937 (early?) — "When I was six, before the Japanese invasion in 1937, an old beggar sat down with his back to the wall at the foot of our drive, at the point where our car paused before turning into Amherst Avenue. I looked at him from the rear seat of our Buick, a thin, ancient man dressed in rags, undernourished all his life and now taking his last breaths. He rattled a Craven A tin at passers-by, but no one gave him anything. After a few days he was visibly weaker and I asked my mother if No. 2 Coolie would take the old man a little food. Tired of my pestering, she eventually gave in, and said that Coolie would take the old man a bowl of soup. The next day it snowed, and the old man was covered with a white quilt. I remember telling myself he would feel warmer under this soft eiderdown. He stayed there, under his quilt, for several days, and then he was gone." (Ballard, *Miracles of Life*, p15-16.)

1937 — May 6 (Thursday) — The Hindenburg, the hydrogen-filled German dirigible, burned and crashed in Lakehurst, New Jersey, killing 36 of the 97 people on board. A newsreel film of the disaster was made, and the explosion of the airship was reported 'live' on the radio.

1937 — May 12 (Wednesday) — King George VI and Queen Elizabeth were crowned at Westminster Abbey in London. BBC Television transmitted the Coronation procession, the first official outside broadcast, seen by 50,000 viewers.

1937 — May 28 (Friday) — Neville Chamberlain (b. 1869) became Prime Minister of the United Kingdom, following Stanley Baldwin's retirement.

1937 — May 29 (Saturday) — "Shanghai, Saturday. An accident marred the debut of the 'Hell Drivers' at the Better Homes Exhibition on the racecourse here when one of the cars, driven by Dick Acton, vaulted off an incline at 40 miles an hour, swerved to the side of the course and crashed into a stand injuring seven foreigners." (*Straits Times*, 30 May 1937, p1.) Jamie Ballard would become a fan of the Hell Drivers, although at six-and-a-half he was still a bit too young to have been present for this incident.

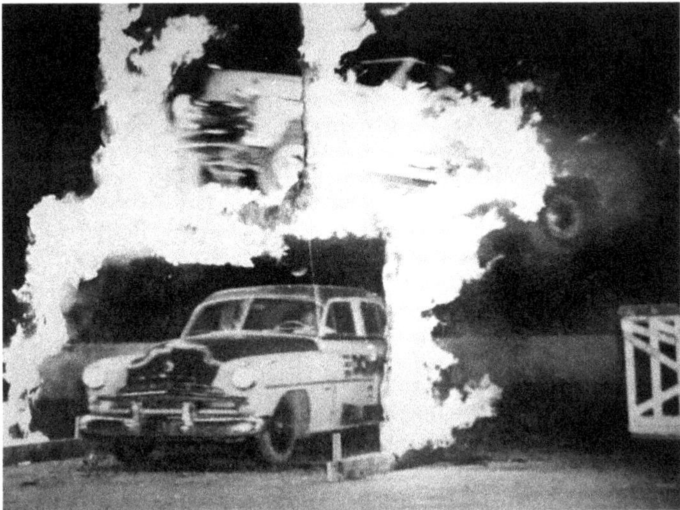

The Hell Drivers in action.

1937 — Summer — "Tsingtao, on the north China coast near Peking, was a German naval base during World War I, and later became a popular beach resort where I spent the summers in the 1930s. As a seven-year-old I was deeply impressed by the huge blockhouses and the maze of concrete tunnels where the tourist guides pointed to the bloody handprints of (they claimed) wounded German gunners driven mad by the British naval bombardment. For some reason these were far more moving than the dead Chinese soldiers in the battlegrounds around Shanghai which I visited with my parents, though they were sad enough." (Ballard, annotations to *The Atrocity Exhibition*, Re/Search, 1990.)

1937 — August 14 — "Bloody Saturday": war had broken out again in the Shanghai area. The Japanese launched bombing raids on Nationalist Chinese positions, and the Chinese air force responded: Northrop bombers attacked Japanese supply ships and the warship Idzumo, moored on Shanghai's Whangpoo River, which served as the Japanese military headquarters. Unfortunately, they missed their intended targets. One of the 550-pound bombs fell at the crowded intersection of Nanking Road and the Bund, while two more fell on the busy Avenue Edward VII. The bombs hit crowds of mainly Chinese civilians, and the loss of life was horrific—1,740 people killed and 1,873 injured, according to one account. Jamie Ballard was probably on his seaside holiday in Tsingtao at the time this happened, but he would use a fictional version of the incident in the opening chapter of his novel *The Kindness of Women*, imagining his younger self caught up in the carnage.

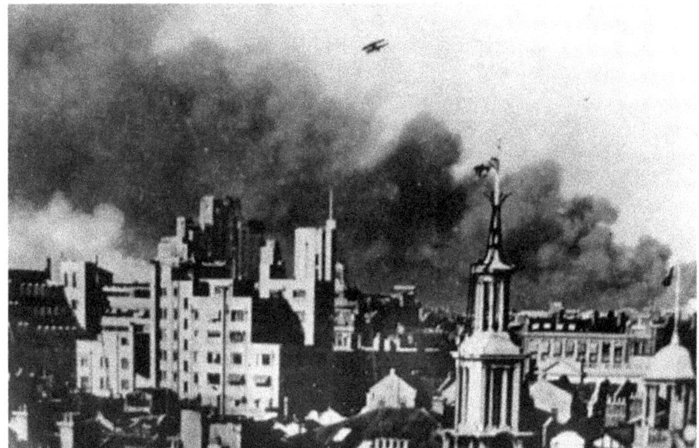

The Chinese air force mistakenly bombs Shanghai.

1937 — August 26 (Thursday) — As the Japanese were bombing targets around Shanghai, they attacked a car carrying Britain's ambassador, Sir Hughe Knatchbull-Hugessen, who was badly injured. He would be hospitalized in Shanghai and then invalided home to Britain.

1937 — September — "War in all its forms was institutionalized in Shanghai, after the Sino-Japanese War began in 1937. I remember having to leave our house on the outskirts of the city and move into a rented house in the centre of Shanghai, because the Chinese and Japanese forces were firing shells whose trajectories went right overhead." (Ballard, interviewed by David Pringle, 24 July 1981.) "For three months fierce fighting raged around Shanghai, and my own family, who lived outside the British-run International Settlement, left for the French Concession, a safe haven from the fighting, when shells from rival Chinese and Japanese artillery guns began to fly over our roof." (Ballard, "Licence to Kill," *Sunday Times*, 21 February 1999.) "[W]e moved to a rented house in the comparative safety of the French Concession. Neglected by its owner, the swimming pool had begun to drain. Looking down at its sinking surface, I felt that more than water was ebbing away." (Ballard, "The End of My War," *Sunday Times*, 20 August 1995.)

1937 — September 11 (Saturday) — Jamie's sister, Margaret Ann Ballard, was born in Shanghai. "My sister Margaret ... was delivered by Caesarean... The seven-year gap between us meant that she never became a childhood friend. When I was 10 she was still a toddler." (Ballard, *Miracles of Life*, p3, p32.) The following is from a fictional context, but may reflect some of young boy's feelings: "His infantile anger as he shouted aloud for Catherine reminded him of how, as a child, he had once bellowed unwearyingly for his mother while she nursed his younger sister in the next room. For some reason, which he had always resented, she had never come to pacify him, but had let him climb from the empty bath himself, hoarse with anger and surprise." (Ballard, *Concrete Island*, p51.)

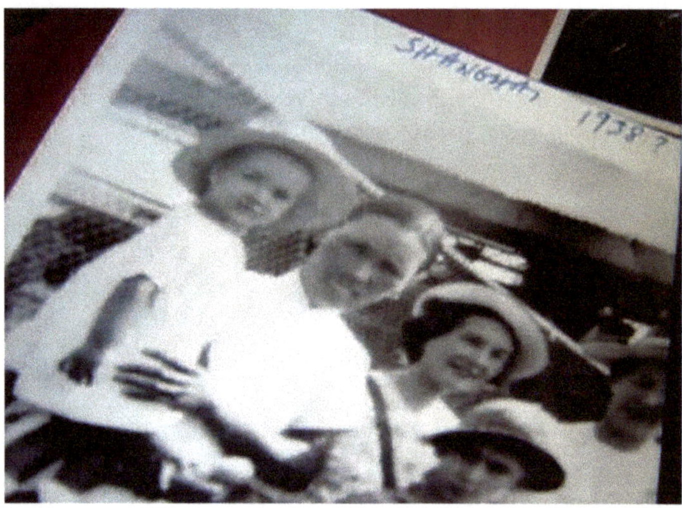

One-year-old Margaret Ballard is being held by her amah. Edna Ballard is beside her, and the eight-year-old Jamie is below his mother.

1937 — September 15 (Wednesday) — In the US, "News of the Day," the newsreel company formerly known as "Hearst Metrotone News" (until 1936), advertised its most recent episode: "LATEST FILMS OF WAR TERROR IN SHANGHAI! *News of the Day* brings another installment of remarkable pictures of the conflict in China made by staff cameramen at risk of life. The bombing of the great South Station, the attempted 'Hobson' blockade of the Whangpoo, the destruction of the Nantao drydock, the sinking of gunboats, new air raids and other spectacular scenes."

1937 — Autumn? — The family of Jamie Ballard's childhood friend Ursula Simpson moved away from Shanghai, never to return, as her daughter would explain: "My mother remembered the dogfights that took place over their house in Shanghai when she would be dragged in to safety, and I still have the bullets she collected from the garden. She remembered counting bodies in the river when travelling by boat and seeing a family running through a field until she realised they weren't moving because they had been burnt to death. Refugees had started pouring into the city and one family took shelter in their garden much to the horror of the servants, as they worried the house would be overrun and my grandmother had to insist the family receive shelter and food. Sometime around 1937-38 Shell was anticipating investing in building roads into the interior of China and my grandfather was given the opportunity to travel to Canada or New Zealand to study similar projects. As a native of New Zealand he naturally chose to return there so that his family could discover the country and Mum could spend time with her grandmother. Nine months later the study was complete and they prepared to return to the family home in Shanghai when my grandfather was told by Shell that the project was being pulled and it was considered just too dangerous for them to return. This came as a terrible shock to both my grandmother and mother as they never had the opportunity to say goodbye. I don't think my mother ever recovered from the shock of losing her beloved Amah who had been a much loved surrogate grandmother to her. They were posted to Cairo where they lived all through the war." (Keiran Ure [daughter of Ursula Simpson Ure], e-mail to DP, 11 June 2019.)

1937 — November 9 (Tuesday) — Japanese troops, consolidating their hold on Shanghai, set up a puppet regime in the Greater Shanghai Municipality—i.e. those areas outside the International Settlement and the French Concession, the neutrality of which was, for the time, respected. "As soon as the fighting ended, the Cathedral Boys' School moved from the cloisters of Shanghai Cathedral, not far from the Great World Amusement Park, and took over part of the Cathedral Girls' School on the western edge of the International Settlement. I could now cycle to school, and no longer needed to be chauffeured in the family car, with the nanny keeping an interfering watch over me." (Ballard, *Miracles of Life*, p28.)

1937 — November 15 (Monday) — J.G. Ballard's 7th birthday. "Shanghai was an American zone of influence... We had Coca-Cola and American-style commercial radio stations. We used to listen to the radio a lot. Shanghai itself had about ten English-language radio stations, and they were blaring out American programmes and radio serials. ... I spent a great deal of time reading as a child all the childhood classics, like *Alice in Wonderland, Robinson Crusoe* and *Gulliver's Travels*, as well as American comics and the American mass magazines of the day, *Collier's, Life* and so on. I don't think I read any Jules Verne, though I certainly read H. G. Wells. There were popularized versions of Wells's novels in the American comic books..." (Ballard, interviewed by David Pringle, 24 July 1981.) "Not only can I remember, half a century later, my first readings of *Treasure Island* and *Robinson Crusoe*, but I can sense quite clearly my feelings at the time—all the wide-eyed excitement of a seven-year-old, and that curious vulnerability, the fear that my imagination might be overwhelmed by the richness of these invented worlds. Even now, simply thinking about Long John Silver or the waves on Crusoe's island stirs me far more than reading the original text. I suspect that these childhood tales have long since left their pages and taken on a second life inside my head. ... Left to myself for long periods, I read everything I could find—not only American comics, but *Time, Life, Saturday Evening Post* and the *New Yorker*. At the same time, I read the childhood classics—*Peter Pan*, the Pooh books and the genuinely strange William series, with their Ionesco-like picture of an oddly empty middle-class England. Without being able to identify exactly what, I knew that something was missing, and in due course received a large shock when, in 1946, I discovered the invisible class who constituted three-quarters of the population but never appeared in the *Chums* and *Boy's Own Paper* annuals." (Ballard, *The Pleasure of Reading*, 1992.)

1937 — November (late?) — "I remember seeing a lot of troops, and going out frequently to the battlefields around Shanghai where I saw dead soldiers lying around, dead horses in the canals and all that sort of thing. The Japanese were sitting around the city, and in fact occupied all but the International Settlement." (Ballard, interviewed by David Pringle, 24 July 1981.) "Tens of thousands of Chinese civilians were killed in the fighting, as we saw when we later drove out to the silent battlefields. I remember the procession of chauffeur-driven Packards and Buicks that stopped near a devastated village, and the hundreds of dead Chinese lying by the roadside and in the abandoned paddy fields. Wearing their silk dresses, my mother and the other wives stepped with their husbands among the bright cartridge cases, a sight that even at the age of seven struck me as bizarre." (Ballard, "Licence to Kill," *Sunday Times,* 21 February 1999.) "A week after the ceasefire my parents and their friends set out on a tour of the silent battlefields to the south of Shanghai. A motorcade of chauffeur-driven Packards and Buicks, filled with children, smartly dressed mothers and their straw-hatted husbands, moved past the shattered trenches and earth bunkers, like the landscapes of the Somme I had seen in the sepia photographs of the *Illustrated London News*. Skirts in their hands, my mother and her fellow wives stepped through the hundreds of cartridge cases. The skeleton of a horse lay on the bank of a creek, and the canals were filled with dead Chinese soldiers, arms and legs stirred by the water. Belts of machine-gun bullets snaked through the grass, and live ammunition was scattered among the discarded webbing. A boy at the Cathedral School who picked up a grenade during another outing lost his hand when it exploded. Later, to his credit, he became a champion swimmer." (Ballard, "The End of My War," *Sunday Times*, 20 August 1995.) Another British boy, Desmond Power (b. 1923), recalled this last incident from his schooldays in Tientsin: "The Headmaster announces... 'I have to bring to your attention some harrowing news... You will all remember Wesley Morris, the bright young lad from Form Four Lower School [Tientsin Grammar School]. Tragically, the day before yesterday, while exploring a battlefield on the outskirts of Shanghai, he got hold of a grenade. It blew off his hand. He is in critical condition. But the doctors think he has a chance...'" (Power, *Little Foreign Devil*, 1996, p104.) Wesley Morris would live a full life, dying in Canada in 2012 at the age of 86.

1937 — December 13 (Monday) — The Japanese army occupied Nanking, China, as the Chinese army retreated in disorder. In what would be known as the "Rape of Nanking," the Japanese sacked and pillaged the city and its suburbs. "When the city fell on December 13, the triumphant Japanese soldiers unleashed an orgy of murder, rape and torture that lasted for six weeks and killed more than 300,000 Chinese civilians, shocking even the German Nazi party members who were resident in the city. The 90,000 Chinese soldiers who surrendered were quickly rounded up, roped together and moved to improvised killing grounds outside the city, where they were shot, beheaded, used for human bayonet practice or soaked with petrol and burnt alive. Mounds of Chinese corpses formed huge dykes along the Yangtze. All this was photographed by Japanese reporters, and one newspaper ran an illustrated article about the friendly rivalry between two officers under the heading 'Contest to kill first 100 Chinese by beheading'. Once all military opposition was out of the way, the Japanese soldiers turned on the city's civilians. For the next six weeks they moved from house to house, bayoneting the men and raping the women, from girls as young as eight to grandmothers in their seventies. After they were raped most were killed... Sadistic torments were devised, involving live burials, castrations, disembowellings, and the forcing of Chinese parents to have sex with their children before they were killed. Mutilated corpses rotted in the streets. Amazingly, much of this was documented in photographs..." (Ballard, "Licence to Kill," *Sunday Times*, 21 February 1999.) Although he would later write about it in reviewing Iris Chang's book on the subject, the seven-year-old Ballard, 170 miles away in Shanghai, did not witness any of these events.

1938

1938 — January 10 (Monday) — Japanese forces in China followed up their successes of 1937 by capturing the port and beach resort of Tsingtao.

1938 — February 4 (Friday) — *Snow White and the Seven Dwarfs*, Walt Disney's first feature-length animated film, which had been premiered in Los Angeles just before Christmas of 1937, went on general release in the United States. It would be released in Shanghai, China, at a somewhat later date. "Now and then I would go with my mother or the nanny to the cinema, one of the vast art deco theatres that loomed over Shanghai. The first film I saw was *Snow White*, which frightened the wits out of me. The wicked queen, the purest essence of evil radiating across the auditorium..." (Ballard, *Miracles of Life*, 2008, p19.) "That vicious queen, with her 'mirror, mirror on the wall,' took up residence inside my six-year-old brain for months afterwards." (Ballard, "Movie Memories," *Sight and Sound*, May 1996; in fact, he must have been seven when he saw it.)

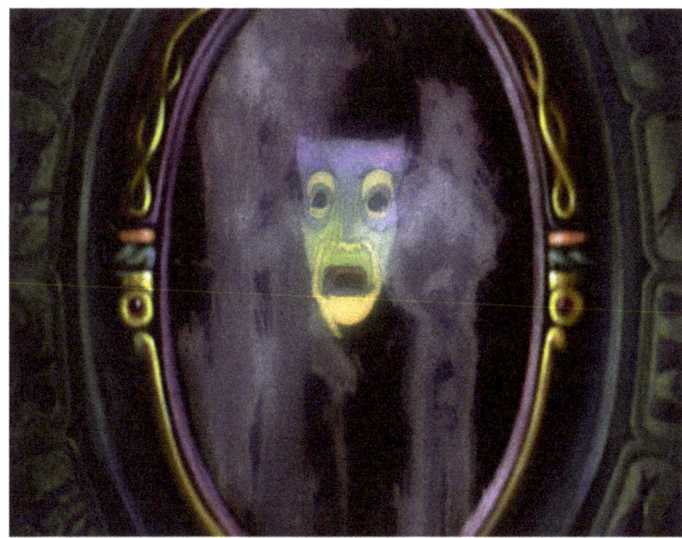

1938 — April 18 (Monday) — "Superman," the creation of cartoonists Jerry Siegel and Joseph Shuster, made his first appearance in Action Comics issue #1 (dated June 1938), from National Allied Publications in the US.

1938 — June 2 (Thursday) — The children's section at London Zoo was opened by Robert and Ted Kennedy, two of the young sons of Joseph P. Kennedy, United States ambassador to Britain. Jamie Ballard would see its equivalent: "Even now I can vividly remember the enormous ancient alligator housed in a narrow concrete pit half-filled with cigarette packets and ice-cream cartons in the reptile house at the Shanghai zoo, who seemed to have been jerked forward reluctantly so many tens of millions of years into the 20th century." (Ballard, "Time, Memory and Inner Space," *Woman Journalist*, Spring 1963.)

1938 — July 3 (Sunday) — The locomotive "Mallard" set the world speed record for steam by reaching 126 mph. "I remember vividly as a child in the 1930s the intense curiosity and excitement about the future you found in popular encyclopaedias, popular magazines, magazines like *Popular Mechanics*. All the American and British magazines I saw as a boy in Shanghai were filled with accounts of another land speed record broken, the fastest train, a plane that can fly at 200 miles an hour, next year they will be 300 miles an hour, within five years we may fly around the world in a day. This excitement really extended into almost every aspect of life." (Ballard, interviewed by Jonathan Weiss, 2005.)

1938 — August 15 (Monday) — Ballard's paternal grandfather, Ernest Ballard (b. 1871) of 158 Redlam, Blackburn, died (aged about 67), leaving effects worth £468 2s. to Edward Ballard, shop manager, and Thomas Marsden, retired insurance inspector. (Probate records, 1938.)

1938 — October 21 (Friday) — After months of bombing, the city of Canton, in southern China, fell to the Japanese.

1938 — November 9 (Wednesday) — "Kristallnacht," or the night of broken glass, took place in Germany. Nazi activists looted and burned synagogues as well as Jewish-owned shops and houses, and scores of Jews were killed.

1938 — November 15 (Tuesday) — J.G. Ballard's 8th birthday. "I remember reading children's editions of *Alice in Wonderland, Robinson Crusoe* and Swift's *Gulliver's Travels* at the same time as American comics and magazines. Alice, the Red Queen and Man Friday crowded a mental landscape also occupied by Superman, Buck Rogers and Flash Gordon. ... Later, when I was seven or eight, came *The Arabian Nights*, Hans Andersen and the Grimm brothers, anthologies of Victorian ghost stories and tales of terror, illustrated with threatening, Beardsley-like drawings that projected an inner world as weird as the surrealists'. Looking back on my childhood reading, I'm struck by how frightening most of it was, and I'm glad that my own children were never exposed to those gruesome tales and eerie coloured plates with their Pre-Raphaelite gloom, unearthly complexions and haunted infants with almost autistic stares. The overbearing moralistic tone was explicit in Charles Kingsley's *The Water Babies*, a masterpiece in its bizarre way, but one of the most unpleasant works of fiction I have ever read... The greatest exception was *Treasure Island*, frightening but in an exhilarating and positive way—I hope that I have been influenced by Stevenson as much as by Conrad and Graham Greene, but I suspect that *The Water Babies* and all those sinister fairy tales played a far more important part in shaping my imagination. Even at the age of ten or eleven I recognized that something strangely morbid hovered over their pages..." (Ballard, *The Pleasure of Reading*, 1992.)

1938 — Some 20,000 Jewish refugees arrived in Shanghai from Europe. "It was an extraordinary place, in that every day there was some new surprise, some new marvel. And there was a huge amount of crime—great gangster syndicates were operating there; kidnapping and Chicago-style machine-gunnings were commonplace. I remember seeing a man called Two-Gun Cohen, known because he always carried two guns, stepping out of a big black limousine. He was the bodyguard of some very famous Chinese warlord. It was a city unlike any other, I imagine, before or since." (Ballard, "Grand Tour," BBC Radio 4, 17 November 1990.) "Once, when my father took me to his office in the Szechuan Road, near the Bund, a Chinese family had spent the night huddling against the steel grille at the top of the entrance steps. They had been driven away by the security guards, leaving a dead baby against the grille, its life ended by disease or the fierce cold." (Ballard, *Miracles of Life*, p14-15.)

1938 — Rachel Field's novel *All This, and Heaven Too*, based on the true story of her great-aunt, a 19th-century French children's governess, was published in the US, and became very popular. It is likely that among its readers was Jamie Ballard's mother, many of whose choices of books would also be read by her young son over the next few years: "I read American bestsellers, such as *All This and Heaven Too, Babbitt, Anthony Adverse* and *Gone With the Wind*." (Ballard, *Miracles of Life*, p20.)

1939

1939 — January 28 (Saturday) — Death of W. B. Yeats (b. 1865), Anglo-Irish poet and playwright, Nobel Prize laureate, in Menton, France, at 73.

1939 — February 6 (Monday) — Raymond Chandler published *The Big Sleep*, his first novel, introducing the Los Angeles private eye Philip Marlowe.

1939 — February 24 (Friday) — Eight-year-old Jamie Ballard, together with his mother and infant sister, is likely to have left Shanghai around this time aboard the liner Ranchi, bound for England.

1939 — March 24 (Friday) — A P&O ship named the SS *Ranchi*, sailing from Yokohama, Japan (via Shanghai), docked at London, and from it disembarked James Graham Ballard, aged eight, his mother Edna and his baby sister Margaret Ann. Their country of "last permanent residence" was listed as China, and their destination address in Britain was stated as

11 Lodge Road, West Bromwich, Staffordshire. No doubt Mrs Ballard was keen to introduce her new daughter to her parents, Archibald and Sarah Johnstone.

1939 — April 5 (Wednesday) — The Ballard family, newly back in the UK and staying near Birmingham, had arrived in the midst of an Irish Republican bombing campaign, which may have reminded them of Shanghai, although luckily it was all on a smaller scale. "Fresh bomb outrages have been perpetrated at Liverpool, Coventry and Birmingham. ... Three bomb explosions in the centre of Birmingham early this morning extensively shattered windows, but no one was injured." (*Sydney Morning Herald*, 6 April 1939.)

1939 — April 10 (Monday) — Despite IRA bombs, it was pleasant in England. "LONDON. England had the sunniest Easter for twelve years. The maximum temperature in London yesterday was 63 degrees, and there were eleven hours' sunshine. The Prime Minister, Mr Chamberlain, and his wife spent two hours in Kew Gardens in the afternoon admiring the magnolias and daffodils until the crowds recognised them, when they fled." (*Sydney Morning Herald*, 11 April 1939.)

1939 — April 15 (Saturday) — Following the Easter holidays, which presumably she had spent with her parents in West Bromwich, near Birmingham, Mrs Edna Ballard rented a house in or near Worthing, in Sussex. There she would enrol her son James, probably for a full term, at Sompting Abbotts preparatory school, where the headmaster was a Mr A. C. Rutherford. The school's later publicity would say: "Set in a magnificent site on the edge of the South Downs, Sompting Abbotts overlooks the English Channel with views towards Beachy Head and the Isle of Wight. The imposing Victorian house has some 30 acres of sports fields, woodlands, gardens and activity areas."

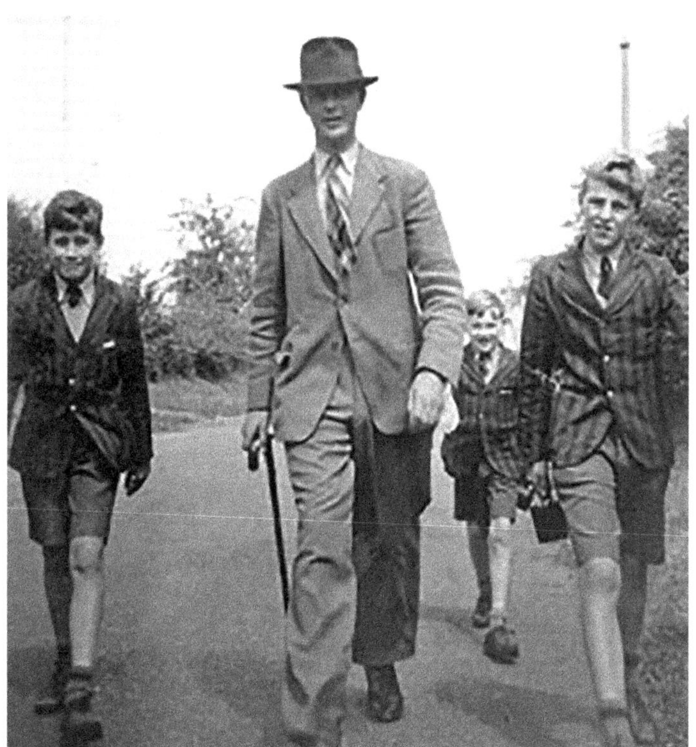

Headmaster A.C. Rutherford of Sompting Abbotts prep school.

1939 — April 17 (Monday) — Mr James Ballard (whose wife and children were currently in England) departed from Shanghai aboard the liner *Empress of Canada*, bound for Honolulu, Hawaii. Meanwhile, his eight-year-old son would be starting school at Sompting Abbotts in the following days.

1939 — May 4 (Thursday) — *Finnegans Wake*, James Joyce's long-awaited work-in-progress, parts of which had appeared in magazines or as separate booklets, was published in complete form by Faber & Faber, London. "In *Finnegans Wake*, a gigantic glutinous pun, Joyce in effect brought the novel up to date, circa 1940, with his vast cyclical dream-rebus of a Dublin publican who is simultaneously Adam, Napoleon and the heroes of a thousand mythologies." (Ballard, "Myth Maker of the 20th Century," *New Worlds*, May/June 1964.)

1939 — May 5 (Friday) — Mr James Ballard arrived in San Francisco aboard a ship named the SS *Matsonia*, from Honolulu, Hawaii. Presumably enjoying his first long leave since 1934, he would continue across the United States to New York City. How was his young son coping with an unfamiliar school in Sussex? We do not know, as in later years JGB would never mention his time at an English prep school; indeed, he would never mention this months-long stay in the home country, and would like to give the impression that he had spent his entire childhood, up to the age of 15, in Shanghai.

1939 — May 23 (Tuesday) — Mr James Ballard arrived at Southampton, on the liner *Aquitania* from New York. He had crossed the Atlantic to rejoin his wife and children in England. His journey from Shanghai, with various stops along the way, appears to have been quite a leisurely one.

1939 — June 7 (Wednesday) — While Mr Ballard was absent on his long leave, there was trouble at the mill of which he was a manager. "SHANGHAI. Mr. R.M. Tinkler, an employee of a British finishing mill at Pootung, who was critically wounded during an encounter with Japanese, has died as a result of his wounds. The British Consulate denies that the affray in which Mr. Tinkler was wounded, resulted from a clash with strikers at the mill. It declares that there was no strike, but says that Mr. Tinkler became involved when paid agitators armed with clubs attacked a Chinese foreman, who was going to the mill. Japanese marines were summoned to 'restore order,' and Mr. Tinkler was bayoneted. ... It is stated here that the Japanese often employ agitators to provoke factory disorders after which they insist on placing a military guard over the factory. The Japanese naval spokesman at Shanghai alleges that Mr. Tinkler was involved in disorders. He says that he was disarmed by a Japanese marine and then surrounded by Japanese with fixed bayonets, during which process he might have come in contact with a bayonet. The spokesman denied, however, that Mr. Tinkler had been wilfully stabbed. Mr. Tinkler, whom the Japanese had arrested, was taken to hospital at Hongkew. He had three bayonet wounds in the abdomen, a head wound from a blow with a rifle butt, and an injured foot." (*Sydney Morning Herald*, 8 June 1939.)

1939 — June 19 (Monday) — Pocket Books, Inc., brought the mass-market paperback book to America. The new company founded by Robert de Graff in partnership with Simon &

Schuster put out its first ten titles, priced at 25¢ each: James Hilton's *Lost Horizon*, William Shakespeare's *Five Great Tragedies*, Agatha Christie's *The Murder of Roger Ackroyd*, Samuel Butler's *The Way of All Flesh*, Emily Brontë's *Wuthering Heights*, Thorne Smith's *Topper*, Thornton Wilder's *The Bridge of San Luis Rey*, Dorothea Brande's self-help *Wake Up and Live*, Dorothy Parker's collection of light verse *Enough Rope*, and Felix Salten's juvenile *Bambi*.

1939 — June 25 (Sunday) — "LONDON. After a period of quiescence London's week-end quiet was broken last night by further bomb explosions attributed to the Irish Republican Army. Bombs that burst at the corner of Piccadilly Circus, Shaftesbury Avenue, and elsewhere constituted the most daring outrages yet perpetrated in London. Nineteen people were treated at Charing Cross Hospital for injuries. ... An incendiary bomb burst in a pillar-box outside Madame Tussaud's Exhibition of Waxworks in the Marylebone Road." (*Sydney Morning Herald*, 26 June 1939.)

1939 — July 2-4 (Sunday-Tuesday) — The First World Science Fiction Convention ("Worldcon") was held in the Caravan Hall, New York City, in conjunction with the New York World's Fair (themed as "The World of Tomorrow"). Guest of Honour was the science-fiction illustrator Frank R. Paul, and the event was chaired by Sam Moskowitz. Other notable attendees included editor John W. Campbell, author L. Sprague de Camp, and the very young writers Isaac Asimov and Ray Bradbury. "Sold at U.S. newsstands are about a dozen pulp magazines with such titles as *Amazing Stories, Astounding Stories, Startling Stories, Strange Stories, Fantastic Adventures, Thrilling Wonder Stories, Unknown, Marvel Science Stories, Weird Tales*. In the pulp trade they are known as 'pseudo-scientifics' or 'scientifiction.' This week in Manhattan this amazing group of publications produced an amazing show: a convention of their fans. *Scientifiction*, which deals almost exclusively with the world of tomorrow and life on other planets, was inspired by Jules Verne's and H. G. Wells's fantasies." (*Time*, 10 July 1939.)

1939 — July (mid) — By this time Jamie Ballard's three months as a prep-school boy in England was nearing its end. How had he fared? He left no account, so we do not know. His silence on the matter may mean that he was unhappy there, but there is no evidence for that and perhaps he simply forgot all about this period in his life. On a trivial level, eight-year-old Jamie may have encountered British comics for the first time during this stay. He would make a curious aside in a review he wrote many years later: "In Britain, which lacked the necessary social and geographical mobility, the comic strip was virtually monopolised by children's humour, of a peculiarly warped and introverted kind, from which I'm glad to have been saved." (Ballard, "How to Tear a Strip Off a Culture," *Guardian*, 21 March 1991.) Which comics may have given him this impression? Given that they were enjoying their first flush of popularity at this time, it is all too likely that he was thinking of *The Dandy*, launched in 1937, and *The Beano*, launched in 1938, both issued by D. C. Thomson & Co. of Dundee, Scotland, but successful throughout the UK. Was it the likes of Keyhole Kate, or Lord Snooty and His Pals, who failed to impress the boy?

1939 — July 22 (Saturday) — The summer term must have been over at Sompting Abbotts preparatory school, Sussex. It was probably around this time that the Ballard family left England once more, to return, via Canada, to China.

1939 — August 5 (Saturday) — By this time the Ballard family, recently in England, may have been staying in the vicinity of Vancouver, Canada. "[W]hile waiting with my parents for a boat back across the Pacific to Shanghai, I lived in a rented flat ... near Vancouver... We spent a couple of months [there]..." (Ballard, interviewed by Thomas Frick, 1983.)

1939 — August 25 (Friday) — With war looming, shipping lines, airlines and even telephone services were over-booked. "LONDON. Shipping and aerial services to America and Australia cannot cope with the demand for passages. Widespread anxiety about the plans of relatives and friends is causing acute telephone congestion in England, and between England and America. The public has been requested to use telephones only when urgently necessary." (*Sydney Morning Herald*, 26 August 1939.)

1939 — September 1 (Friday) — 4:45 am — World War II began when the Germans attacked Poland with their strategy of Blitzkrieg, or lightning war.

1939 — September 3 (Sunday) — Britain and France declared war on Germany, two days after the Nazi invasion of Poland and after Germany had ignored Britain's ultimatum to stop the invasion.

1939 — September (early) — Around this time: "I was in Vancouver, with my parents, soon after the outbreak of World War II in 1939. I remember buying the first Batman comic. I mean really the first, the first one! I think it was September 1939." (Ballard, interviewed by Catherine Bresson, 1982.) Note: the first comic book wholly devoted to Batman was dated Spring 1940, and appeared no earlier than April of that year. If young Ballard did buy a comic featuring Batman in 1939, it must have been an issue of *Detective Comics*, where the character had made his debut in May 1939. He would also say, of this time: "I went to the same school [after the war] as Malcolm Lowry, the Leys in Cambridge, and curiously enough, in September 1939, while waiting with my parents for a boat back across the

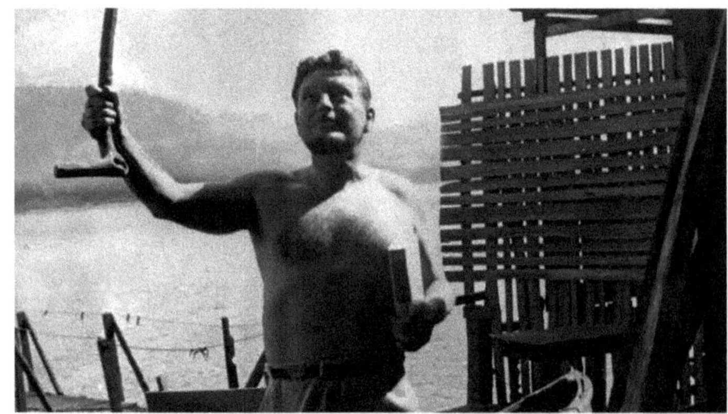

Malcolm Lowry on the deck outside his oceanside squatter's shack in Dollarton, on the north shore of the Vancouver harbour. He lived there until 1954, when he returned to the UK and died in 1957.

Pacific to Shanghai, I lived in a rented flat on the same shoreline near Vancouver and Victoria Island where he had his shack... we spent a couple of months at a time when he was there. His father came from the same Manchester cotton industry background as mine." (Ballard, interviewed by Thomas Frick, 1983.)

1939 — September 12 (Tuesday) — "OTTOWA. The Prime Minister, Mr. Mackenzie King, said in the [Canadian] House of Commons yesterday that German submarines were operating not only in the Atlantic, but also in the Pacific." (*Sydney Morning Herald*, 13 September 1939.) However, this warning did not deter the Ballards, temporarily stranded in Vancouver, from taking ship to China when they could.

1939 — September 19 (Tuesday) — "OTTAWA. 'I consider this moment as grave as any in the history of the Empire,' said the Governor-General, Lord Tweedsmuir (formerly John Buchan, the novelist), in addressing the Canadian Legion. 'It is a grave moment,' he added, 'because the war the Empire has entered has a serious purpose—a more momentous purpose than any of the older wars in which we fought for security, defence of territory, balance of power, or similar reasons. We have entered this war for the preservation of those spiritual values which alone make life worth living. However long and however desperate this struggle may be, we are not going to flinch, and we are going to win.'" (*Sydney Morning Herald*, 20 September 1939.)

1939 — September 23 (Saturday) — Death of Sigmund Freud (b. 1856), Austrian founder of psychoanalysis, in Hampstead, London, of a morphine overdose after suffering for some time with inoperable cancer of the jaw at 83.

1939 — September (late) — By this time, the Ballard family, on their way home to Shanghai from Vancouver, Canada, may well have been in Hawaii. During their stopover in the islands, they stayed at the Royal Hawaiian Hotel on Waikiki Beach in Honolulu: "I was there in 1939, staying at the Royal Hawaiian Hotel with my parents." (Ballard, letter to Vale, 6 November 2005.) It is possible that while they were there young Ballard was jokingly nicknamed "Kimo"—which is the Hawaiian form of Jim.

1939 — October (early-mid?) — The Ballards arrived back at their home in the western suburbs of Shanghai, having been away for about six months.

1939 — November 15 (Wednesday) — J.G. Ballard's 9th birthday. "My closest friends were an English family called the Kendall-Wards, who lived at the far end of Amherst Avenue... During the holidays I would cycle over and spend most of the day with them. There were three brothers, whom I remember well, but it was the parents who made a powerful and lasting impact on me... The Kendall-Ward home was the complete opposite of 31 Amherst Avenue, and an influence that has lasted all my life." (Ballard, *Miracles of Life*, p21-22.)

1939 — December 13 (Wednesday) — The Battle of the River Plate took place in the South Atlantic, off the coast of Uruguay, between three Royal Navy cruisers and the German pocket battleship, *Admiral Graf Spee*. In a day-long running battle, HMS *Exeter* sustained heavy damage from the 11-inch guns of the *Graf Spee*, which could fire 670 pound shells for 17 miles. HMS *Ajax* and HMS *Achilles* attacked the *Graf Spee* from two sides, making it impossible for her to fight them both off, and drove the German vessel to seek refuge in Montevideo harbour.

1939 — December 15 (Friday) — "Yesterday [came] news of the greatest naval action since Jutland. The British cruisers *Exeter, Ajax*, and *Achilles* encountered an enemy battleship—since shown to have been the *Admiral Graf Spee*—off the coast of Uruguay, brilliantly engaged and damaged her in a running action, and drove her into the harbour of Montevideo. There she lies, with the watchful eyes of the cruisers upon her, awaiting internment or the time when she must put to sea to almost certain destruction. This, it is clear, was an action in the finest traditions of the British Navy, fought with skill and daring, and triumphantly successful in that the *Admiral Graf Spee*'s career of mischief has evidently been ended." (*Sydney Morning Herald*, 15 December 1939.) Chapter 3 of Ballard's memoir begins thus: "In September 1939 the European war began, and quickly reached across the world to Shanghai. ... My father spent a great deal of time listening to the short-wave radio broadcasts from England which brought news of the sinking of HMS *Hood* and the hunt for the *Bismarck*, then later of Dunkirk and the Battle of Britain." (Ballard, *Miracles of Life*, p37.) JGB's chronology is badly awry, and in mentioning the sinking of the *Hood* and the hunt for the *Bismarck*, which took place in 1941, a year after the retreat from Dunkirk and the Battle of Britain, he was probably confusing those events with the Battle of the River Plate and the defeat of the *Graf Spee*— a naval victory that delighted the British and Commonwealth public at the time and would be the subject of books and films in years to come.

1939 — December 17 (Sunday) — Following the Battle of the River Plate near Montevideo, the British navy had trapped the pocket battleship *Admiral Graf Spee*. German Captain Hans Langsdorff, believing false radio reports that a superior British force was about to arrive, sailed to a point just outside Uruguay's waters, transferred his crew to other vessels, and then, at sunset, scuttled his ship with explosives, thinking that resistance was hopeless. (A few days later, he committed suicide in Buenos Aires, Argentina: he lay on his ship's battle ensign and shot himself.)

1939 — December 29 (Friday) — The film *The Hunchback of Notre Dame* (dir. William Dieterle), the latest adaptation of Victor Hugo's 1831 novel, starring Charles Laughton as the deformed Quasimodo and Maureen O'Hara as the beautiful Esmeralda, was first released in the US. Some time later, it would also open in Shanghai: "Bizarre advertising displays—the honour guard of fifty Chinese hunchbacks outside the film premiere of *The Hunchback of Notre Dame* sticks in my mind—were part of the everyday reality of the city..." (Ballard, *Miracles of Life*, p4.)

1940

1940 — February 7 (Wednesday) — The premiere of *Pinocchio*, Walt Disney's second animated feature film, was held in New York City. Based on Carlo Collodi's children's novel, it featured the voices of Dickie Jones as the wooden puppet-boy and Cliff Edwards as Jiminy Cricket. (It would go on general release two weeks later.) "The first film I saw was *Snow White*, which frightened the wits out of me [as did *Pinocchio* a little later]." (Ballard, *Miracles of Life*, p56; phrase in square brackets from the notes for the same, circa 2007, British Library archive, p10.)

1940 — March 11 (Monday) — George Orwell's first collection of his shorter writings, *Inside the Whale and Other Essays*, was published in London by Victor Gollancz. Among the striking passages was this: "To say 'I accept' in an age like our own is to say that you accept concentration camps, rubber truncheons, Hitler, Stalin, bombs, aeroplanes, tinned food, machine-guns, putsches, purges, slogans, Bedaux belts, gas-masks, submarines, spies, provocateurs, press-censorship, secret prisons, aspirins, Hollywood films and political murders."

1940 — May 10 (Friday) — Neville Chamberlain, British Prime Minister, resigned following a debate in the House of Commons in which many Conservative MPs had failed to support him. King George VI asked Winston Churchill to form a new government, and he accepted: he would serve as Prime Minister and Conservative head of a coalition with the Labour and Liberal Parties.

1940 — May 13 (Monday) — The Nazis had launched their blitzkrieg conquest of France, and the period known as the Phoney War was over. In his first speech as Prime Minister of the UK, Winston Churchill told the House of Commons, "I have nothing to offer you but blood, toil, tears and sweat."

1940 — June 4 (Tuesday) — The massive evacuation of British and French troops from — Dunkirk in northern France came to an end. Ships and small boats had ferried the men across the Channel to England, and Churchill made a famously defiant speech in the Commons: "We shall fight on the beaches, we shall fight on the landing grounds, we shall fight in the fields and in the streets, we shall fight in the hills; we shall never surrender."

1940 — June 18 (Tuesday) — Churchill spoke to the House of Commons: "[T]he 'Battle of France' is over. I expect that the Battle of Britain is about to begin. ... Let us therefore brace ourselves to our duties, and so bear ourselves, that if the British Empire and its Commonwealth last for a thousand years, men will still say, 'This was their finest hour.'"

1940 — August 12 (Monday) — Carl Gustav Jung wrote in a letter to a friend: "This year reminds me of the enormous earthquake in 26 B.C. that shook down the great temple of Karnak. It was the prelude to the destruction of all temples, because a new time had begun. 1940 is the year when we approach the meridian of the first star in Aquarius. It is the premonitory earthquake of the New Age..." (*Letters of C. G. Jung: Volume I*, 19061950, p285.)

1940 — August 20 (Tuesday) — As the Battle of Britain reached its peak, Winston Churchill paid tribute to the Royal Air Force, saying, "Never in the field of human conflict was so much owed by so many to so few." In Shanghai, a boy would follow the news: "School was often interrupted so that we could visit one of the cinemas for screenings of British newsreels, thrilling spectacles that showed battleships in line ahead, and Spitfires downing Heinkels over London. Fund-raising drives were held at the Country Club, and I remember the proud announcement that the British residents in Shanghai had financed their first Spitfire." (Ballard, *Miracles of Life*, p37.)

1940 — September 11 (Wednesday) — It was Margaret Ballard's third birthday, in Shanghai. In the following months, young Jim would find her presence an annoyance: "My sister, aged three, irritated me immensely, and I tried to devise entire days when I never set eyes on her. Breakfast was always a problem, with school deciding when I sat down to my mango and scrambled egg, and having to endure my sister's babbling across the table. With a small boy's logic, I took advantage of Mr Kendall-Ward's carpentry room to construct a large plywood screen which I placed in the centre of the dining table. I equipped it with a spyhole through which I could ferociously keep watch on my astonished sister, and a miniature hatch cover that I would flick into place when she noticed my staring eye. Amazingly, my parents took all this with good humour..." (Ballard, *Miracles of Life*, p41.)

1940 — November 15 (Friday) — J.G. Ballard's 10th birthday. "I think our characters, our personalities, are set at an early age. Probably by the time we're 10, our world views are virtually hard-wired into our brains." (Ballard, interviewed by John Walsh, 14 September 2003.) "I was sent to the Cathedral School in Shanghai... A very authoritarian English clergyman was the headmaster there, and he used to set lines. It's the most time-wasting enterprise one could imagine, but he would say '500 lines, Carruthers! 600 lines, Ballard!' for some small infringement. Five hundred lines was about 30 pages of a school exercise book. You were supposed to copy out school texts, and I remember starting to copy from a novel about the Spanish Armada. It was something like G. A. Henty, or it might have been Kingsley's *Westward Ho!* (I remember that. It has a marvellous last paragraph which has stayed with me all my life; the last paragraph of that novel is a fine piece of prose, and you ought to find echoes all over my fiction.) Anyway, I started copying out this high adventure narrative. I suddenly realized—I was only about nine or ten—that it was easier, and it would save a lot of effort, if I just made it up. Which I did. So from then on I would make up my own narratives. I think the authoritarian clergyman must have scanned my lines because he reprimanded me by saying: 'Ballard, next time you pick a book to copy your lines from don't pick some trashy novel like this!' He didn't realize I'd written it myself." (Ballard, interviewed by David Pringle, 24 July 1981.)

1940 — December 21 (Saturday) — Death of F. Scott Fitzgerald (b. 1896), American novelist and screenwriter, in Hollywood of a heart attack at 44.

1940 — December 29 (Sunday) — Germany began dropping incendiary bombs on London. Many famous buildings, including the Guildhall and Trinity House, were damaged or destroyed. Among the sectors of British life badly affected was the book-publishing industry. "On just one night (29 December) fire bombs dropped by wave after wave of German

Heinkels and Dorniers had fallen on the London premises of Longman, Collins, Eyre and Spottiswoode, Hutchinson and many smaller firms, destroying some 5 million books. The vast majority were, of course, the publishers' back-stocks... [but] paper rationing meant that it was impossible to reprint even new titles." (Hugh David, *The Fitzrovians*, 1988, p211.)

1941

1941 — January 5 (Sunday) — Amy Johnson (b. 1903), British aviator, the first woman to fly from England to Australia (in 1930), disappeared in a flight over the Thames estuary and was assumed drowned at 37. "Aviation was then so new that there were few social or career restraints, and a large number of women pilots carried out record-breaking flights and became even greater stars than most of their male rivals—the American Amelia Earhart, who vanished in the Pacific; the English woman Amy Johnson, who plunged into the Thames estuary during the war; the wonderfully promiscuous Beryl Markham, who gave her own private spin to the notion of the erotic cathexis of flight. There were a host of others, usually photographed in white overalls leaning against their flying machines. Flight and beauty fused, and it's hard to believe that any of these remarkable women would die." (Ballard, "Up with the Celestial Helmsmen," *Guardian*, 7 May 2005.)

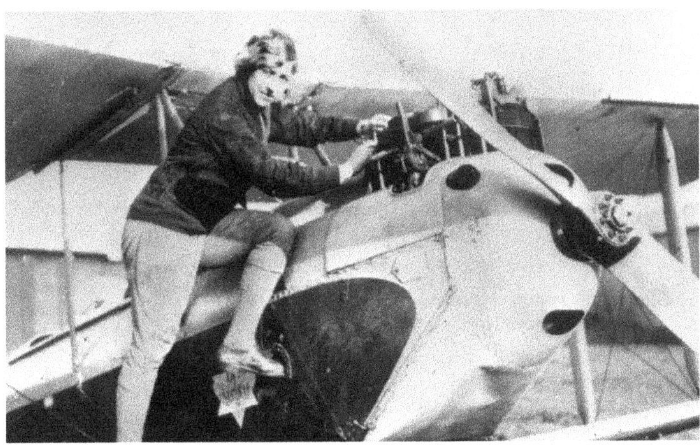

Amy Johnson in her white overalls.

1941 — January 13 (Monday) — Death of James Joyce (b. 1882), Irish novelist, short-story writer and poet, in Zurich, Switzerland, following surgery for a perforated duodenal ulcer at age 58.

1941 — January 23 (Thursday) — In Shanghai, Mr W. J. "Tony" Keswick, chairman of the Shanghai Municipal Council, was shot and wounded by an enraged Japanese ratepayer during an Annual General Meeting of ratepayers held at the city's race course.

1941 — February 10 (Monday) — Patrick Geoffrey Mulvaney, aged ten, travelling with his mother, Annie Elizabeth Mulvaney, aged 38, left Shanghai aboard the SS *President Cleveland,* bound for San Francisco. "Extraordinary inversions [were] taking place all the time... I mean, I remember this little boy, his name was Patrick Mulvaney, he was my best friend, he lived in an apartment block in the French Concession, and I remember going there and suddenly finding that the building was totally empty, and wandering around all those empty flats with the furniture still in place, total silence, just the odd window swinging in the wind... it's difficult to identify exactly the impact of that kind of thing. I mean, all those drained swimming pools that I write about in my fiction were there, I remember going around looking at drained swimming pools by the dozen." (Ballard, interviewed by Charles Platt, 1980.)

1941 — March 28 (Friday) — Death of Virginia Woolf (b. Virginia Stephen, 1882), British novelist and essayist, in Rodmell, near Lewes, Sussex, a suicide at 59. She feared a mental breakdown, wrote a note to her husband, filled her coat pockets with stones and drowned herself in the River Ouse near her home. (Her body would not be found until 18 April.)

1941 — May 1 (Thursday) — *Citizen Kane*, a film directed by, co-written by and starring Orson Welles, aged 25, premiered in New York City. The co-writer was Herman J. Mankiewicz, and the cast also included Joseph Cotten and Dorothy Comingore. Later frequently voted the best film ever made, it did not receive a widespread release and, despite seven Oscar nominations, it would win nothing. Because the central character, Charles Foster Kane, was transparently based on press magnate William Randolph Hearst, the latter's newspapers refused to carry advertising for the film.

1941 — May 17 (Saturday) — A sports day was held at the Cathedral School, Shanghai (headmaster P.C. Matthews, MA). The ten-year-old James Graham Ballard was among the participants. No doubt he took part in many sports days during his school years, but this is one for which documentary evidence exists in the British Library's Ballard archive: unfortunately, it gives no further details as to which events he participated in.

1941 — May 24 (Saturday) — The German battleship *Bismarck* and the heavy cruiser *Prinz Eugen*, were sighted in the strait between Greenland and Iceland. The British battle-cruiser HMS *Hood* and the battleship HMS *Prince of Wales* engaged the German vessels, but the *Hood* was soon hit, suffered a huge magazine explosion, and sank in the cold North Atlantic. There were only three survivors, and 1,415 men died. The *Prince of Wales* withdrew, damaged, but had hit the *Bismarck* three times, partially crippling her.

1941 — May 27 (Tuesday) — In the North Atlantic, Fairey Swordfish aircraft from the carrier HMS *Ark Royal* had inflicted more damage on the German battleship *Bismarck* in a torpedo attack. Further battered by two British battleships, HMS *King George V* and HMS *Rodney*, and two cruisers, the *Bismarck*, Germany's most famous battleship, sank with the loss of about 2,100 lives. In Shanghai, Jamie Ballard, listening to the radio with his father, would remember this major naval event in later years, even if he would become confused as to the sequence of things.

1941 — June 22 (Sunday) — Nazi Germany suddenly invaded the Soviet Union, in the largest invasion of another country ever. German and Axis troops took Russia by surprise, violating the 1939 Russo-German nonaggression pact.

1941 — October 3 (Friday) — *The Maltese Falcon* (dir. John Huston), based on Dashiell Hammett's novel, starring Humphrey Bogart and Mary Astor, premiered in New York City. It would come to be seen as beginning a new style of Hollywood crime film that, some years later, would be called "film noir."

1941 — November 15 (Saturday) — J.G. Ballard's 11th birthday. "I remember the very first little book I produced. Of course it was never printed, but it was my first effort at a book. It was about how to play Contract Bridge. I learned to play the game at an early age, because Bridge-playing was all the rage. I must have been only about 11... My mother used to hold Bridge parties, almost every afternoon it seemed. To a child the bids conjure up a whole world of mystery because they don't seem to be related to anything. 'One heart, two hearts, three diamonds, three no trumps, double, redouble' what the hell does all this mean? I used to pace around upstairs listening to these bids, trying to extract some sort of logical meaning. I finally persuaded my mother to explain how Contract Bridge was played. I was so impressed by the discovery of what bidding meant deciphering these cryptic and mysterious calls, particularly when I discovered that they relate to the whole world of conventions so that they are a code within a code that I wrote a book. I think I filled a school exercise book on the basic rules of Contract Bridge and what the conventions were. I even had a section on 'psychic bidding,' which was pretty good for an 11 year old! It was quite an effort of exposition." (Ballard, interviewed by David Pringle, 24 July 1981.)

1941 — December 7 (Sunday) — At 7:55 am (Hawaiian time) Japan launched a surprise aerial attack on the United States naval base at Pearl Harbor, home of the US Pacific fleet. Some 363 Japanese fighters, dive-bombers and torpedo planes sank or damaged eight battleships and three light cruisers, destroyed 188 planes and killed 2,418 Americans in just over two hours.

1941 — December 8 (Monday) — In the early hours, Japanese forces sank a British naval ship, the *Peterel*, commanded by Lieutenant Polkinghorn, off the Bund in Shanghai. "HMS *Peterel*, a small river gunboat, and the USS *Wake*, a ship of approximately the same size, were the sole remaining representatives of allied naval might in Shanghai by December 1941. They had been left moored in the Whangpoo River off the Shanghai Bund principally to enable the embassies to maintain direct radio communication with their capitals." (Hugh Collar, *Captive in Shanghai*, 1990, p14.)

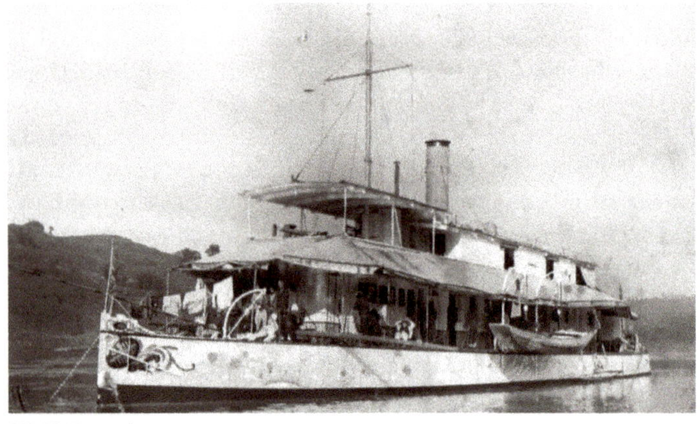

HMS *Peterel.*

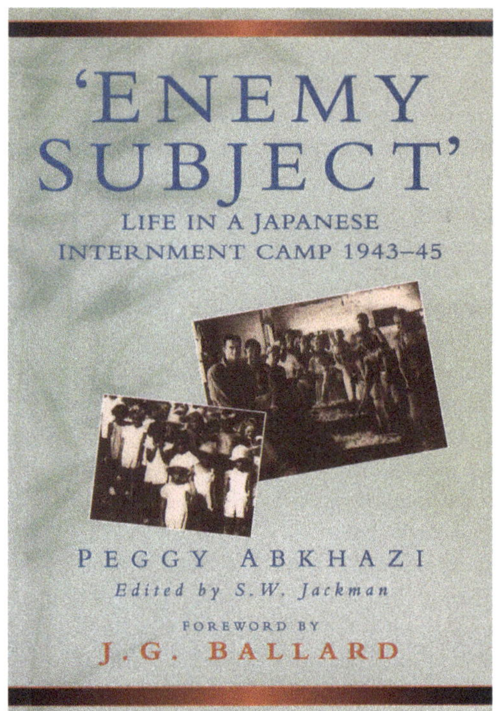

1941 — December 8 (Monday) — A British resident in Shanghai, Peggy Pemberton-Carter, wrote: "The war started for me when I heard the furious sound of planes rushing over the house at 6:50 a.m. I thought sleepily 'how angry they sound' and then a few minutes later Manfred Voigt rang up to tell me that Japan was at war with America and Great Britain. They had seen and heard the heavy firing on the river at 4 a.m., the sinking of the *Peterel* and the peaceful surrender of the *Wake* as we learned later..." (Peggy Abkhazi, '*Enemy Subject*,' p21.)

1941 — December 8 (Monday) — Japanese tanks rolled into the International Settlement at Shanghai. "I was going to do the scripture exam at the end-of-term examinations at the school I went to. Pearl Harbor had just taken place, the previous night I suppose, and I heard tanks coming down the street. I looked out the window and there were Japanese tanks trundling around." (Ballard, interviewed by J. Goddard & D. Pringle, 4 January 1975.)

1941 — December 8 (Monday) — An American ship, the SS *President Harrison*, was deliberately grounded by its captain, Orel Pierson, on a small island in the mouth of the Yangtse, in an attempt to evade capture by the Japanese. (The senior officers would spend the war in prison camps in Japan, but the ordinary crew of about 150—sailors, deck stewards, room stewards, mess-men, cooks, waiters, laundry-men, etc— would eventually be released into the population of Shanghai, and then interned in civilian prison camps in 1943. All but a handful would survive the war.)

1941 — December 10 (Wednesday) — Two great capital ships, HMS *Prince of Wales* and HMS *Repulse*, sailing from Singapore with four destroyers to prevent Japanese landings on the Malayan coast, were both sunk by Japanese bombers in the China Sea. The destroyers HMS *Electra* and HMS *Vampire* rescued survivors of the *Repulse*, while HMS *Express* rescued those from the *Prince of Wales*. Over a thousand were saved but 840 sailors were lost.

In Shanghai, there would be dismay when the news broke: "[T]he sinking of the British battleships *Repulse* and *Prince of Wales* devastated us all." (Ballard, *Miracles of Life*, p56.)

1941 — December 12 (Friday) — Peggy Pemberton-Carter wrote: "Queued again at the bank for the second withdrawal of $500. Alec Forbes a few ahead of me, and afterwards we walked home together. ... To what has the war reduced him! Aside from losing his job, the same handkerchief for two days, and shirt for four. He looks badly, taking it very hard. ... We all tried to convince ourselves that the report of the sinking of the *Prince of Wales* and *Repulse* wasn't true—but I'm afraid it is." (Abkhazi, '*Enemy Subject*,' p23.)

1941 — December (mid) — "The Japanese seized the International Settlement, and everything changed. Now, that was quite a surprise to an 11-year-old—the Japanese Gendarmerie, their equivalent to the Gestapo, visiting our house, and I could see that my mother was keeping her poise but in great danger from these men, and I suddenly realized too that British power had ended, and that in a sense the whole great Western party, which had been running in Shanghai since the 1890s, really, was over." (Ballard, "Grand Tour," BBC Radio 4, 17 November 1990.)

1941 — December 29 (Monday) — Peggy Pemberton-Carter wrote: "All private cars have been off the roads for just a week, and it has taken just that time for the Chinese population to forget anything they ever knew about traffic regulations. They amble down the middle of the roads, rickshaws go four abreast and little boys spin their tops in the middle of Avenue Foch and it is all rather enchanting; very like a holiday place. The tempo of life has slowed down to a delightful leisureliness... The new era includes no more barber or manicures, no sweets, cigarettes, drinks, coffee or movies. And this plain living and high thinking seems to conduce to the healthiest possible appearance in almost everyone. Though the older men are looking a great deal older." (Abkhazi, '*Enemy Subject*,' p28-29.)

1942

1942 — January 20 (Tuesday) — In Shanghai, Peggy Pemberton-Carter wrote: "Richard Lang went out with the pig food, and found the barricades shut; Inspector Sharrock had been assassinated.* However, by the afternoon they were opened again, and normal traffic resumed. ... Bicycle convoys have been instituted, to combat the epidemic of being hit on the head and your bike removed from between your legs, which has broken out along Hungjao road. Most men ride along armed with knuckle dusters and lead coshs..." (Abkhazi, '*Enemy Subject*,' p31.) *Her editor adds a note: "Inspector Sharrock's death was the first real sign of overt disorder and a sign of things to come."

1942 — February 15 (Sunday) — British forces in Singapore surrendered to General Tomoyuki Yamashita. The Japanese prevailed when Lieutenant General Sir Arthur Percival and 130,000 Empire troops gave up the fight. "My parents spent hours listening to the shortwave radio broadcasts from Britain and America. ... The surrender of Singapore, the capture of the Philippines and the threat to India and Australia sounded the death knell of Western power in the Far East and the end of a way of life. ... Despite my admiration for the Japanese soldiers and pilots, I was intensely patriotic, but I could see that the British Empire had failed." (Ballard, *Miracles of Life*, p56.)

1942 — February 17 (Tuesday) — In Shanghai, Peggy Pemberton-Carter wrote: "Singapore has gone; hard to accept that fact... We are all just steeped in gloom over the news. ... The Japanese are understandably tremendously elated at their victory, and huge victory parades here and all over Japan are planned..." (Abkhazi, '*Enemy Subject*,' p32-33.)

1942 — Spring — "The Japanese took over the place, and they segmented Shanghai into various districts with barbed wire, so you couldn't move from Zone A to Zone B except at certain times. They'd block off everything for security reasons, and on certain days the only way of going to school was to go to the house of some friends of my parents who lived on one of these border-zones, between I think the French Concession and the International Settlement. There was an abandoned night club, a gambling casino called the Del Monte—a huge building in big grounds. We'd climb over the fence and go through, and go up the main driveway on the other side of the border-zone, and go to school. This abandoned casino, a multi-storied building, was decorated in full-blown Casino Versailles style, with figures holding up great prosceniums over bars and huge roulette tables. Everything was junked. I remember a roulette table on its side and the whole roulette wheel section had come out, exposing the machinery inside." (Ballard, interviewed by J. Goddard and D. Pringle, 4 January 1975.)

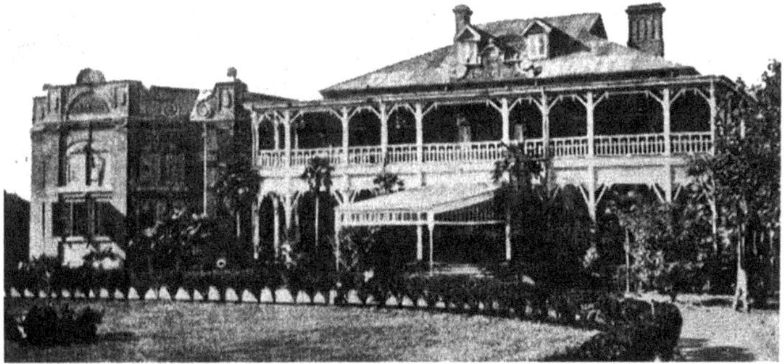

"The Del Monte was old school Shanghai class, Jewish and mostly about the gambling. Run for years by Californian Al Israel, the Del Monte was considered way out of town—almost in Siccawei (Xujiahui) when it opened before the Great War. Al ran the joint with his wife Bertha and 200-pound Great War vet brother-in-law 'Demon' Hyde. Shanghai said Al was crazy to open out in the western suburbs, but he laid out a car park, hired a turbaned Sikh watchman, strung colored lights up to the entrance and decorated the whole place just like the Palace of Versailles (but with roulette tables). Shanghai duly fell in love with the automobile, and The Del Monte was packed. The Badlands grew up around Al, and he didn't get on so well with the gangster element that moved in. He was murdered in the long hot summer of 1938 and Demon took the place over. It eventually fell to wrack and ruin and a young English boy living in the area, called James Graham (J.G.) Ballard, used to play in the ruins among the Versailles statuary." Paul French, *City of Devils* (2018).

Where Blockade Was Enforced

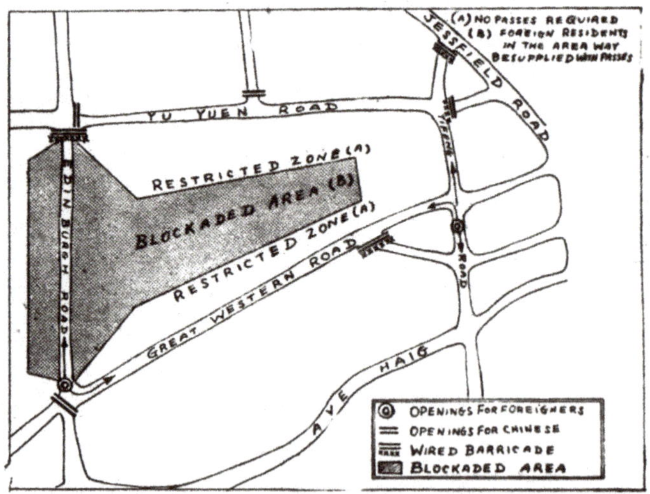

This map of the blockaded western area shows the various zones. The latter, it will be seen, were divided by wired barricades. The Japanese authorities, who issued this map, stated that should any person encounter difficulties not foreseen by this map he or she should apply to the Gendarmerie station at 94 Jessfield Road.

1942 — June 4 (Thursday) — The Battle of Midway took place. Aircraft from three US Pacific fleet carriers ambushed a huge Japanese fleet bound for Midway Island. With four of their aircraft carriers lost, it was Japan's first major defeat in World War II.

1942 — Summer — In Shanghai: "Money was increasingly scarce, and accommodation was becoming crowded. The currency was depreciating and prices rising to what even then seemed to be fantastic levels. Gone altogether was the luxurious living of the past. ... One great hope buoyed us up, one word —repatriation. It was the cheering song in everyone's heart. Our government would send big ships to take us all away... I, of course, being in constant contact with the Swiss Consulate, knew that negotiations for repatriation were going on and that snags were being slowly ironed out. Numbers were fixed and a tentative date mentioned. There would be so many places for British, so many for Dutch, so many for other nationals." (Hugh Collar, *Captive in Shanghai*, 1990, p49-50.)

1942 — August 12 (Wednesday) — The lights went out in Shanghai. "War had made Shanghai dull, although the cabarets did not close, and the gambling continued merrily. But inflation soared, housing became a real problem, and corruption slowly became ingrained. On 12 August 1942 the neon lights of the electric city were turned off for the duration. In the new Shanghai dark, the SMC [Shanghai Municipal Council] decided in October 1942 to legalize brothels... That same month, 'enemy nationals'—Britons, Americans and other Allied civilians—were barred from cinemas, nightclubs, theatres, the racecourse, the Hai Alai stadium and the Canidrome." (Robert Bickers, *Empire Made Me*, p317.)

1942 — October 3 (Saturday) — Wernher von Braun and his team conducted the first successful launch of an A-4 rocket from Peenemünde, Germany. (This was the prototype of the V-2 missile.) It reached a height of 84.5 kilometres, and was considered the first manmade object to reach space. "This third day of October, 1942, is the first of a new era in transportation, that of space travel." (Speech at Peenemünde on the day, by Major Walter R. Dornberger.)

1942 — November 5 (Thursday) — In Shanghai, Hugh Collar, Chairman of the British Residents' Association, was finally arrested by the Japanese Gendarmerie and sent into detention in the Haiphong Road camp in the Western District of the city. "It was the last many of us were to see of the outside world for two and a half years... When the round-up was completed, we had about 360 men in all in the Haiphong Road Camp. They consisted of approximately 270 British, 60 Americans, 20 Dutch, 14 Greeks, one Norwegian and one Belgian. They proved to be as complete a cross section of humanity as one could hope to see. Every kind from Taipans to beachcombers, they ranged in age from 20 to 72. We never did find out how the selection had been made. Were we political prisoners? Were we selected as hostages? Had we been picked at random out of the telephone book? None of these explanations quite fitted the bill." (Collar, *Captive in Shanghai*, 1990, p64, 73.) Among the detainees was one Robert Patterson, from Northern Ireland, father of an "orphaned" boy that Jamie Ballard would come to know in the following year.

1942 — November 10 (Tuesday) — Winston Churchill gave a speech at the Lord Mayor's Luncheon, in the Mansion House, London, announcing the news of a great Allied victory against German forces at El Alamein in Egypt. "Now this is not the end," he said. "It is not even the beginning of the end. But it is, perhaps, the end of the beginning."

1942 — November 15 (Sunday) — J.G. Ballard's 12th birthday. "For a year the Ballards continued to live in Amherst Avenue: 'Our cars were surrendered and we moved around on bicycles. Adults had to wear red armbands with numbers on them. There were no visits to the cinema, no gymkhanas, no military tattoos, no hell drivers—they were Americans who used to crash cars spectacularly on the racecourse. We had to stop at a checkpoint on the way to school. But on the whole, it was still a very comfortable life.'" (Ballard, interviewed by Elizabeth Dunn, *Telegraph*, 9 November 1991.)

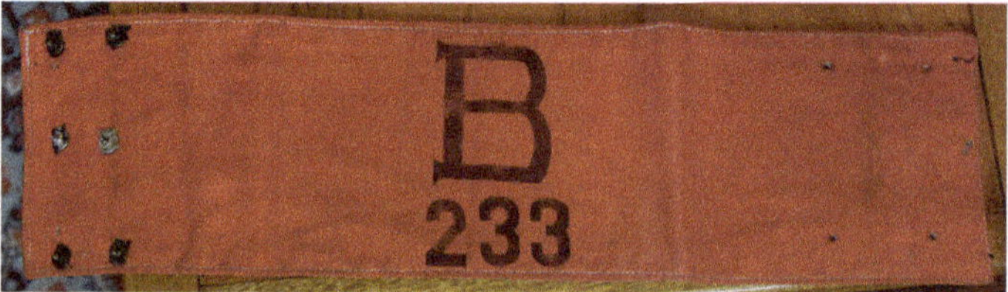

"B" for British armband.

1942 — November 26 (Thursday) — The movie *Casablanca* (dir. Michael Curtiz), produced by Hal B. Wallis, scripted by Julius and Philip Epstein with Howard Koch, and starring Ingrid Bergman, Humphrey Bogart, Paul Henreid and Claude Rains, had its world premiere at the Hollywood Theatre, New York. "Most critics consider *Citizen Kane* the best film ever made, but the best-liked must be *Casablanca*. Yet no one involved in making the film ever imagined that it would achieve its legendary status. ... *Casablanca* is rich in supporting roles that give the film a telling authenticity the cast-list is packed with Jewish refugees, some of them playing refugees, and the others playing the Nazis." (Ballard, *Daily Telegraph*, 20 February 1993.)

1942 — December 28 (Monday) — "The dapper Spanish painter Salvador ('soft watches') Dali has published his autobiography, *The Secret Life of Salvador Dali* (Dial, $6). It is a wild jungle of fantasy, posturing, belly laughs, narcissist and sadist confessions. It is stuffed with Dali's paranoiac paintings, sketches and constructions, is one of the most irresistible books of the year. ... Dali is a superb draftsman, whose painting technique reveals the sheen of an old master. In both his painting and writing he is sensationally packaging fantasies of his own, plus ideas inspired by Freud." (*Time*, 28 December 1942.) A British edition of this same translation of the book—i.e. translated from the French *La Vie Secrete de Salvador Dali* by Haakon M. Chevalier—would appear in 1948 from Vision Press, London, and would be relished by the student Ballard.

1943

1943 — January 11 (Monday) — Britain and the United States signed treaties relinquishing their "extra-territorial" rights in China. Their rights in parts of Shanghai and other ports were given up to the Chinese Nationalist government now based in Chungking (although the Japanese were actually in control of most of the ports at the time). Thus Shanghai's International Settlement formally ceased to exist. (A few months later, in July 1943, the Vichy government of France would also renounce the Concession that it had held to Chinese territory in Shanghai since 1849.)

1943 — January 31 (Sunday) — In Japanese-occupied Shanghai, a general internment of "enemy" civilians began, "and by the end of the year about 7,500 British, American and other allied civilians in the city—barring the elderly and the infirm—were moved into a converted school, empty godowns and other installations making up [the] 'Ash Camp,' 'Pootung,' 'Lunghwa' addresses, for the duration, of the Shanghailander... [A]nd it was boring. The treatment the great majority of those interned received was bearable, but wearyingly dull as three summers and two winters of captivity passed. A third winter's internment would have seen a higher death rate due to malnutrition, but the horrors of camps in south-east Asia were not visited on the Shanghailander." (Bickers, *Empire Made Me*, p318-319.)

1943 — March 17 (Wednesday) — To the south of Shanghai, a large batch of western "enemy" civilians was interned by the Japanese at Lunghua Civil Assembly Centre (i.e. prison camp), at the site of the former Kiansu Middle School, Minghong Road. They were probably the first to enter the camp.

1943 — April 5 (Monday) — Another batch of British and other western civilians was interned by the Japanese at Lunghua camp. Peggy Pemberton-Carter wrote, a couple of days later: "We arrived at the Lunghua Middle School about 15 miles outside Shanghai, right out in the country near the historic old Pagoda, in half an hour... Visions of leisured hours under trees evaporated at once. The nearest approach to shady trees for purposes of solitary meditation being provided by two piles of devastated buildings and an acre of bricks. The actual school buildings are fairly impressive at first sight, and the men have been marvellous beyond all words, accomplishing miracles of repair, cleaning, building and organizing, and hauling our beds and heavy baggage. The fortnight-old inhabitants were up on the roofs and at all the windows, waving us in. One wit had produced a banner inscribed: WELCOME HOME." (Abkhazi, *'Enemy Subject,'* p51.)

1943 — April 7 (Wednesday) — In Lunghua, Peggy Pemberton-Carter wrote: "We have electric light, which I hadn't expected. The lamp and switch are over my bed, for which I yield thanks... The rations are quite good as regards quality and being served hot, but the quantity would leave a void in one's interior if it weren't for being able to supplement with one's private store, either of tinned food or the fresh food we brought in with us." (Abkhazi, *'Enemy Subject,'* p52.) Two days later she would add: "Really life isn't too bad, there's not

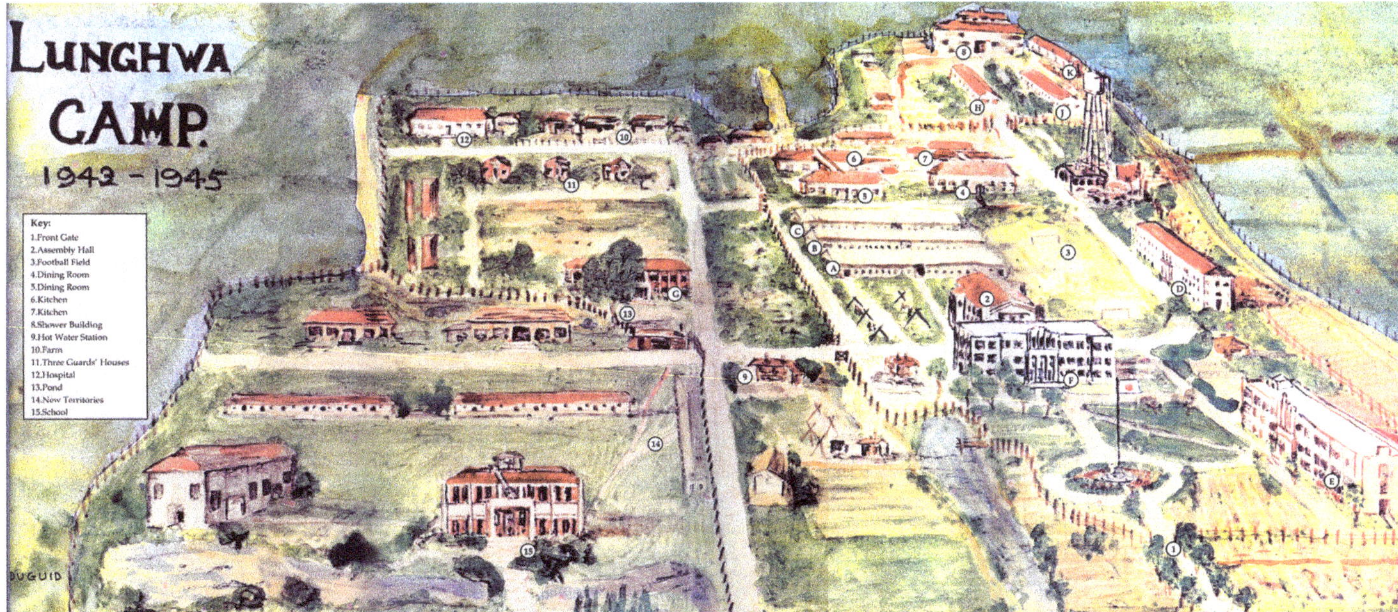

Map of the Lunghua Camp drawn by internee Irene Duguid Kilpatrick.

an anxiety, our duties are all prescribed, the food at present is adequate. And most important of all, one meets kindness and generosity on all sides. I wonder if these qualities will dwindle once deadly monotony gets us in its grip." (Abkhazi, *'Enemy Subject,'* p55.)

1943 — April 19 (Monday) — Well over a year after the Japanese occupation of central Shanghai, Jamie Ballard was interned with his parents and five-year-old sister in the civilian prisoner-of-war camp. "[I remember] the day we were bussed into Lunghua from our assembly point at the American Club near the Great Western Road. I can still see the huge crowd of Brits, many of the women in fur coats, sitting with their suitcases around the swimming pool, as if waiting for the water to part and lead them to safety." (Ballard, "Look Back at Empire," *Guardian*, 4 March 2006.) "Together we waited around the swimming pool, sitting at the tables where the American members of the club had once sipped their bourbons and mint juleps. Then the Japanese guards arrived with a small fleet of buses, and we were on our way across the open countryside, among the last group of Allied nationals to be interned." (Ballard, *Miracles of Life*, p63.) "There were about 2,000 prisoners, mostly from the British settlement in Shanghai—businessmen like his father, missionaries, professional people—with a sprinkling of Belgians and Dutch and American sailors... Few of the internees had arrived in the camp expecting the war to last long some came with nothing but their clothes—but Ballard's parents were among those with foresight... Forced to abandon their splendid Shanghai mansion to invading Japanese officers, they carefully packed text-books for their children: Latin, science, history, Shakespeare, an anthology of English poetry compiled by Robert Lynd..." (Ballard profile by Claire Tomalin, *Sunday Times*, 9 September 1984.) Peggy Pemberton-Carter wrote later: "On the 19th a huge batch of newcomers arrived —some say the last lot we'll have, as our numbers are now up to 2,000. Our [single women's] hut is full to bursting, with 53 inhabitants of all ages, classes, habits and nationalities and religions. A liberal education in the humanities! Apart from superficial irritations, I think it is wonderful how well we have all shaken down together. It would appear that the difficult minority are nearly always becoming assimilated by the more normal majority. So here we are, Belgians, Dutch, Russians, British, Dutch-Japanese, South African, genuine Portuguese and half castes, French and American, of all ages between 13 and 60." (Abkhazi, *'Enemy Subject,'* p59.)

1943 — April 25 (Easter Sunday) — Easter occurred on the latest possible date in the year. In Lunghua, Peggy wrote: "Two days of heavy rain have provided the nearest approach we shall probably ever know to rest and relaxation, with time for comparatively uninterrupted reading, writing and mending. The rain has also given us a holiday from gardening, not unwelcome to aching hands and blistered backs. ... We have already prepared and sown acres of beans, cabbage, tomatoes, corn, cucumbers and pumpkins. ... One may call the place a Civil Assembly Centre, but it is really nothing but a labour camp, granted that the labour is for ourselves. The men are really beyond all praise. Office workers are transformed into road builders, garbage collectors, stokers, stove builders, hot water firemen, cooks, butchers, and kitchen toilers." (Abkhazi, *'Enemy Subject,'* p62.)

1943 — May — Ray Bradbury (b. 1920) published one of his first notable stories, "The Crowd," in *Weird Tales* (issue dated May 1943), a fantasy about the ghoulish crowds that gather round car crashes.

1943 — May — The first anthology of "science fiction" (eo nomine) was published by the mass-market paperback house of Pocket Books, New York. Edited by Donald A. Wollheim, *The Pocket Book of Science-Fiction* contained reprinted magazine stories by Stephen Vincent Benet, Ambrose Bierce, John Collier, H. G. Wells, T. S. Stribling, Wallace West, Stanley G. Weinbaum, "Don A. Stuart" (John W. Campbell), Theodore Sturgeon and Robert Heinlein.

1943 — May 12 (Wednesday) — In Lunghua, Peggy Pemberton-Carter wrote: "Summer has arrived, [with] the grilling heat of the past two days. ... One of the ten little Abrahams, number seven, I think, was getting her water and Irene Rayden said to her: 'I didn't know you were British.' 'We weren't until there was a B.R.A.' (British Residents Association, which helped out greatly, financially and otherwise before we were interned, and during the calling-up period.) A vivid memory of this same Abraham family. As there were the two parents and the ten children, they were assigned a room to

Dew Drop Inn from 'F' roof.

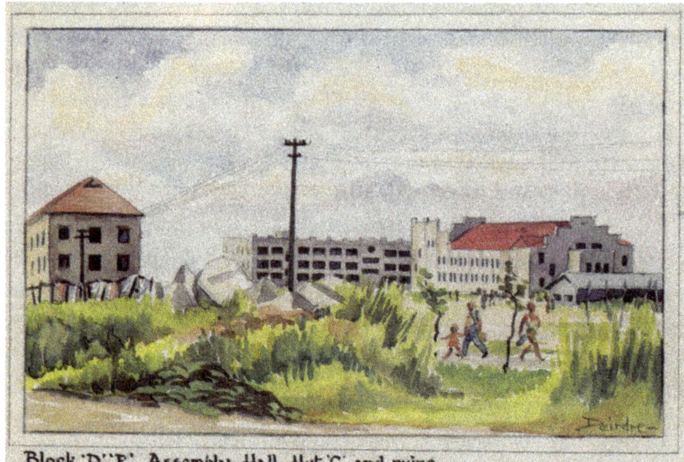

Illustrations of the Lunghua Camp drawn by internee Deirdre Fee.

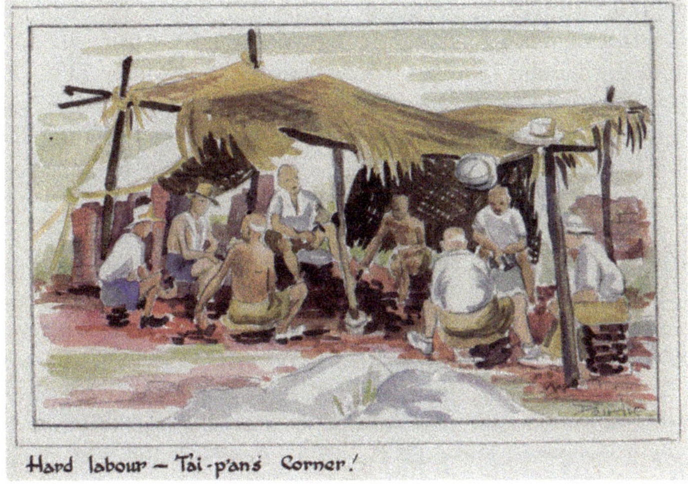

Hard labour – Tai-pan's Corner!

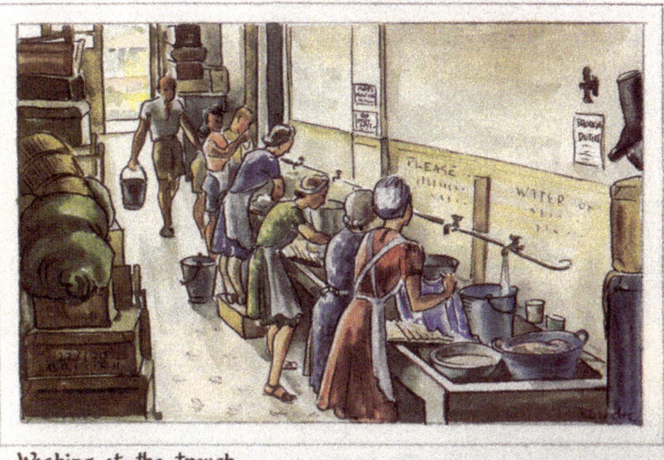

Washing at the trough.

themselves. It was an inspiration, a vision of peace and faith to pass by their open door on a Sabbath evening and see the whole family keeping that holy hour—a white cloth on the table, and the seven-branched candlestick; ten as-clean-as-possible children with their mother, and their father intoning the age-old prayers. One was reminded of other days, other worlds, and that this messy phase of life was only an interlude." (Abkhazi, *'Enemy Subject,'* p69-70.)

1943 — May 12 (Wednesday) — One of the "little Abrahams" mentioned by Peggy would later give his own account: "Isaac Abraham spent his childhood years just outside Shanghai in the same Japanese internment camp as the author J.G. Ballard... Mr Abraham's parents and his nine siblings were rounded up along with their compatriots... Mr Abraham, 69, said: 'The Japanese interned us from April 1943 until the end of the war...' Some of Mr Abraham's strongest memories of the time are of Ballard's father, a larger-than-life character who acted as a leader in the camp. 'They modelled the camp along the lines of an English village and we had a council and had elections and the ones we elected were the ones who negotiated between the inmates and our wardens and tried to ameliorate situations. So J.G. Ballard's father was one of those and there were songs made up about him. We had troupes of players called the *Nungwha Sophomores* among the inmates who put on Gilbert and Sullivan productions, like the 'Pirates of Penzance' and 'Trial by Jury.' And in one of those, they referred to the fact that we always had rumours going around camp. There was a song which referred to him and the three places we got our water from in the camp, which were called Waterloo, Bubbling Well and Lucky Dip. The song went: *They are serving beer at Waterloo, that's the rumour today, Ballard and Bradewood [sic*] are first in the queue, that's the rumour today.* It had such a big impact on me, these were the only sort of entertainment we had and I have remembered them ever since.' Of the 1,700 people in the camp, Mr Abraham said the majority were British, while others were from countries allied with the British. But all the children went to *Nungwha Academy*, the British-style school for primary and secondary students, which even held exams recognised by the University of London. All internees were put to work, using their skills from the outside world. Only bankers and shopkeepers had less use, and were put to stoking the fire in the kitchens. 'But it wasn't a summer camp by any means,' said Mr Abraham. 'It could have been a lot worse, but food was scarce, and clothes wore out and there was no way of replenishing anything. Also, we had no liberty. We were punished if people tried to escape, and had a curfew, or roll calls, to show we were all there. The worst thing was that we did not know when it would end. We were in prison and there was no way out.'" (Sophie Kummer, *Hendon Times*, 9 September 2004.) *"Bradewood" is a reference to Mr W.G. Braidwood.

1943 — May? — "The novelist J.G. Ballard recalls performances of 'Pirates of Penzance' and 'Trial by Jury' in the camp in Lunghua where he was interned as a child: 'The music was probably played on a piano I can't remember any kind of orchestra. There was a stage at the end of the dining hall where productions were held. Everything was in full costume. Prisoners of war and civilian internees had vast amounts of idle time and a great deal of ingenuity so it would not have been difficult to assemble scenery and costumes. Gilbert and Sullivan was very popular I have never seen a G & S production since leaving the camp but can still recite large sections of the libretti partly or largely because they are so English. My impression is that they were quite elaborate productions. They certainly held me mesmerised.'" (Ballard, quoted in Ian Bradley, *Oh Joy, Oh Rapture!: The Enduring Phenomenon of Gilbert and Sullivan*, OUP, 2005, pviii.)

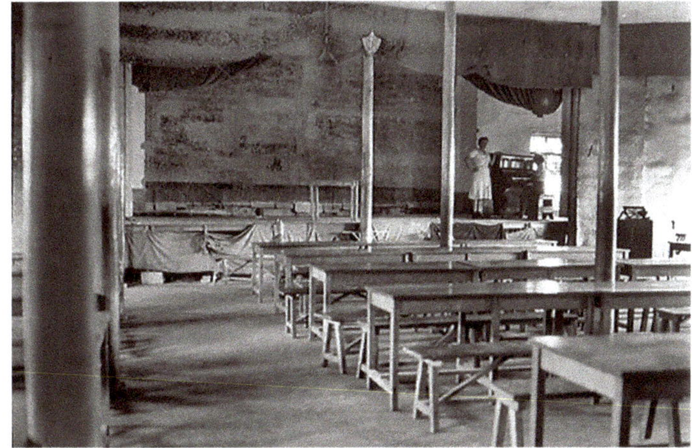

The Lunghua Camp mess hall and stage.

1943 — May-June — "Most of the British nationals there were people from the professions, senior management personnel, and most had university training of various kinds. A school was started in the camp, and the headmaster was a missionary called the Reverend George Osborn. (Oddly enough, I discovered years later that he was the father of Martin Bax's wife Judy—Martin Bax is the editor of *Ambit.*) There were a lot of missionaries like him who had been teaching all their professional lives. So a school was started and ran most of the time though towards the end when the Japanese wanted to penalize the adults in the camp the first thing they did was to close the school and impose a curfew. All the parents were stuck in their tiny little rooms, trapped with their noisy offspring! But I think that people like Osborn did a very good job, because I didn't feel when I got to England, despite very nearly three years in the camp, that I was much behind. I think in many areas I was absolutely up to scratch, for all the interruptions." (Ballard, interviewed by David Pringle, 24 July 1981.)

1943 — June 1 (Tuesday) — Peggy Pemberton-Carter wrote: "As from June 1st, we were ordered to sleep under mosquito nets, certainly for our own good, but to hear the grumbles from some of the free-born Britons and others, you would have thought it was a special punishment devised for their greater torment. But in that delightful Proclamation I quoted to you, they [the Japanese] forgot to mention in their lyrical enthusiasm over all the Civil Assembly Centres, that Lunghua in particular is a malaria infested swamp." (Abkhazi, *'Enemy Subject,'* p76.)

1943 — July 7 (Wednesday) — In Lunghua, Peggy P-C wrote: "Yesterday ... as well as letters, the Red Cross brought in our monthly parcels from our contacts in Shanghai. Parcel day is always a great excitement, something like prize giving at school. The children are always the first to see or hear the lorries lumbering along the main road, before they turn into our private lane. And from them the cry goes up, to be caught and carried along by all and sundry 'Parcels...parcels' and then they are unloaded by our camp Service Men, and carried into the dining rooms, there to be searched by the gendarmes, and a few hours later, we are allowed to collect them. That same evening, all over camp and in every corner, parties are in progress." (Abkhazi, *'Enemy Subject,'* p80-81.)

1943 — July 10 (Saturday) — Peggy Pemberton-Carter, who was one of the volunteer teachers at 'Lunghua Academy,' wrote: "An overheard conversation between two boys: 'What was your report like?' 'Awful, and yours?' 'Rotten.' 'And Jack's?' 'Rotten.' 'I know what it is, the masters here aren't paid, so they tell the truth.'" (Abkhazi, *'Enemy Subject,'* p85.) Could the boy who made that last remark have been the 12-year-old Ballard? It is just possible, and it sounds rather like him.

1943 — July 20 (Tuesday) — In the camp, Peggy P-C wrote: "The great heat is upon us. If only one could be really clean, and have no physical chores, the least of which is completely exhausting — in other words, if one wasn't in camp, a summer at Lunghua would be very agreeable, at least 10 degrees cooler than the city. But being as we are, it needs every ounce of self control not to blaze up in irritation at the flies, the noise, the smells, the crowds, the scarcity of water, the perspiration, and the unappetizing stews during the day, and at night, the rats and mosquitoes. And at all hours overwhelming tiredness." (Abkhazi, *'Enemy Subject,'* p86.)

1943 — July 28 (Wednesday) — President Roosevelt spoke on US radio about the fall from power of Benito Mussolini. He said that the dictator "and his Fascist gang will be brought to book, and punished for their crimes against humanity. No criminal will be allowed to escape by the expedient of 'resignation.' So our terms to Italy are still the same as our terms to Germany and Japan --'unconditional surrender.'"

1943 — August 11 (Wednesday) — The inmates of Lunghua camp experienced a "wind from nowhere." Peggy Pemberton-Carter wrote: "A typhoon has been raging since 5 a.m. We hope it reached its peak half an hour ago—4 p.m. ... All afternoon we heard the howling wind and the rain thundering on the roof, sheets of iron and pieces of wood banging and blowing on the wind like bits of paper, bamboo matting and straw floating around on the small sea which is all that is visible of our gardens. And then the cries: 'C West has gone, A East has gone, B East has gone,' it seemed impossible that our roof could hold out. But it did, except for some leaks that could be dealt with by means of basins and buckets." (Abkhazi, *'Enemy Subject,'* p87-88.)

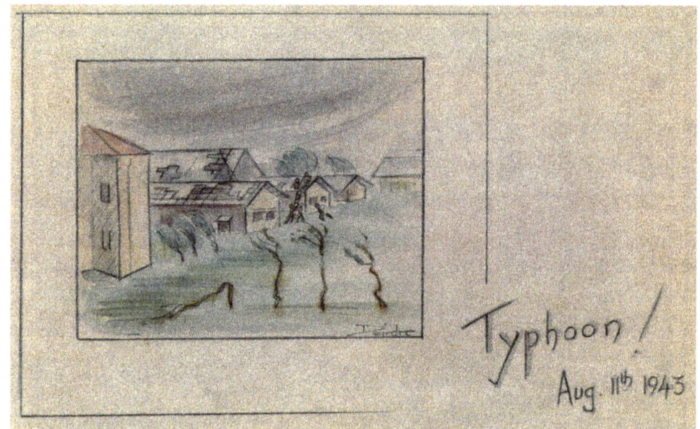

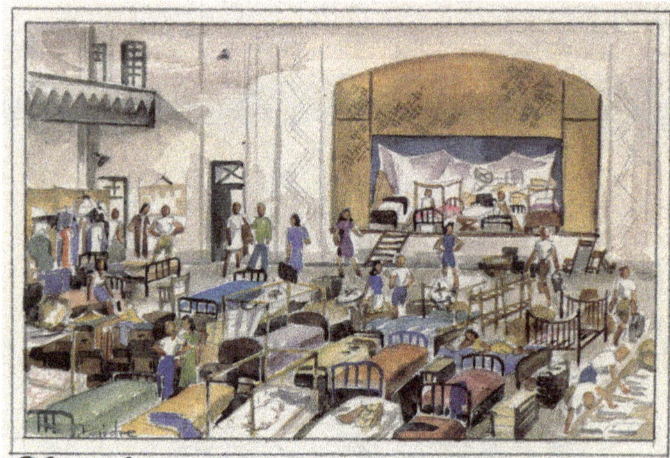

Refuge in Assembly Hall - morning after Typhoon.

1943 — August 12 (Thursday) — The next day, Peggy added: "The typhoon blew for twenty-six hours. It is now just an ordinary gale. Last night was an unforgettable experience. From 1 o'clock to 4 the wind and rain were terrific, and we gave up hope that the roof could hold any longer. But excepting that the leaks grew bigger, and one sheet of iron got partly loosened and clanged monotonously above the noise of the storm, it remained intact. ... We were a pale and exhausted-looking crew this morning, but we all revived when the men, bless them! arrived with buckets of hot water for us to wash in, and later they returned with our breakfast rations, tea and cracked wheat. The poor souls from the wrecked huts had spent a miserable night in the Assembly Hall, cold, wet and mosquito bitten. The Commandant, Mr Hiyashi, was very concerned and did his best to console them by serving out a tot of saki to each one." (Abkhazi, *'Enemy Subject,'* p89.)

1943 — September 9 (Thursday) — "A visible sign of the Italian collapse was the decision by the sailors on the *Conte Verde* to prevent their ship being sequestered by the Japanese navy. The Lloyd Trestino liner had been lying idle in Shanghai harbour since the outbreak of the Pacific War... At 7.00 a.m. on 9 September 1943, the crew scuttled the ship within sight of Americans held in the Pootung internment camp. The 615 ton Italian river gunboat *Lepanto* was also sunk. For months the two hulks lay overturned side by side in shallow water opposite the Bund. The crews of both ships as well as of another Italian gunboat, *Carlotta*, were all interned." (Bernard Wasserstein, *Secret War in Shanghai*, 1999, p244-245.)

1943 — September 17 (Friday) — Peggy Pemberton-Carter wrote: "The news of Italy's capitulation gave me a joyful idee fixe during the alternate burnings and freezings of Lunghua malaria. So much better than the hobgoblins that sometimes haunt one in high fevers. According to schedule, I was up and around, though very tottery, after three days... The compound, formerly occupied by the military who just folded up their tents and stole silently away one early morning, has been turned over to our use. This should relieve some of the chaos and congestion produced by the typhoon. There is talk that the school can be removed there bodily from its present odd holes and corners." (Abkhazi, *'Enemy Subject,'* p90-92.)

1943 — September 20 (Monday) — In Lunghua camp: "Pathetic sight: truck containing body of Mrs Ackerman who died of heart failure in the morning, followed to the gate by her friends. The wicker basket in back of truck with other things. First death in camp, though two in Shanghai." (Ruth Hill Barr, *Ruth's Record*, p173.)

1943 — September 27 (Monday) — Peggy Pemberton-Carter wrote: "I have changed my occupation... I am now a fully fledged French schoolmarm, with nineteen classes weekly, all ages, from 7 to 70. The elder ones come to the Polytechnic classes, and the others I teach in the school. Great changes have occurred there, it has been moved en bloc to the 'New Territory,' to the buildings recently vacated by the military. And with all the deficiencies and drawbacks, it is a great improvement on trying to give classes in the dining rooms and in odd corners of the Assembly Hall or out in the grounds." (Abkhazi, *'Enemy Subject,'* p93-94.)

1943 — September 27 (Monday) — Peggy P-C added: "This afternoon a large batch of men arrived here from Pootung, ostensibly to help with the heavy work of this camp... As I say, the ostensible reason is to help with the heavy work, but we do hear rumours that Pootung won't be sorry to see the last of some of the lads. And I must add that amongst these arrivals are several answers to Lunghua maidens' prayers." (Abkhazi, *'Enemy Subject,'* p94.) The new arrivals, about 70 in all, included the 20-year-old Desmond Power and a number of Americans from the SS Harrison. "So long Pootung! ... I had the feeling somehow this was going to be a beautiful day, a day of wonderful surprises. I wasn't wrong. Soon as the river tender skirted *Conte Verde*'s rusting bilge, we could see, parked on the Bund, two buses waiting to pick us up. So, no twelve-mile route march... By golly, we were off on a charabanc outing via Shanghai's western suburbs to the fresh green countryside. And what a rousing welcome from the swelling concourse of internees at Lunghua's main gate! And what wolf whistles they got from us! How could there be so much pulchritude concentrated in one place? And how rich the variety—slim, buxom, tall, petite, fair, dark!" (Desmond Power, *Little Foreign Devil*, 1996, p183.)

1943 — September 27 (Monday) — Jamie Ballard was excited by the newcomers. "There was a group of thirty American merchant seamen, captured on board an American freighter. As civilians, they were not sent to a POW camp, and must have realised their good luck. They passed their time loafing on their beds in E Block, though now and then they would rouse themselves and amble out to the assembly ground for a game of softball. I liked them immensely, for their good humour, verbal inventiveness and enormously laid-back style. Life in their company was always interesting, and they remained cheerful to the end, unlike many of the British internees. They always seemed glad to see me, throwing back the curtains of

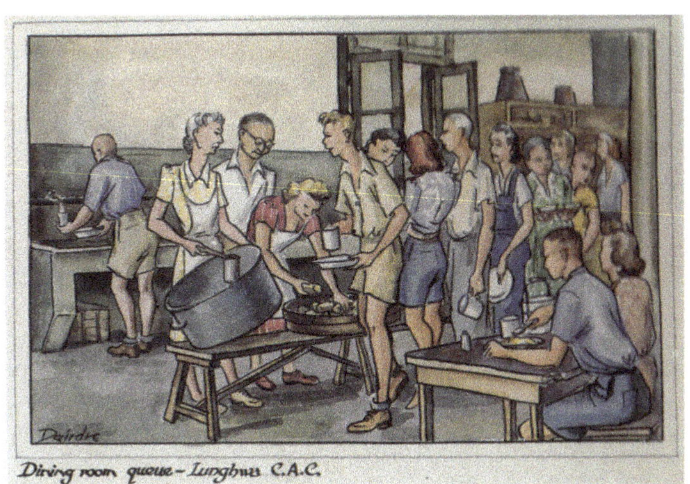

Dining room queue - Lunghua C.A.C.

French Water Truck at the old "Lucky Dip"
Lunghwa C.A.C.

their miniature cubicles, and would go to elaborate lengths to make me the butt of friendly practical jokes, which I took in good part. Among their other virtues, the Americans had a substantial stock of magazines—*Life, Time, Popular Mechanics, Collier's*—which I devoured, desperate for the kind of hard information on which my imagination fed." (Ballard, *Miracles of Life*, p72-73.) "[M]en from Pootung arrived... Some negroes included among Harrison crew, split up so as not to cause so much trouble in one camp." (Ruth Hill Barr, *Ruth's Record,* p175.) The interesting fact that some of his merchant-seamen friends were black would not be mentioned by JGB in after-years.

1943 — Autumn — "I'd never really been allowed to meet any working-class people in pre-war Shanghai, and then I met them and found they have a colossal vitality because they're not repressed like the British middle class. And you see, in a place like an internment camp, parents have none of the levers with which they can control their children, particularly teenage boys. My mother once described me years later as a free spirit —and I think I was." (Ballard, interviewed by Lynn Barber, 27 December 1991.) "My real existence took place in the camp, wheedling dog-eared copies of *Popular Mechanics* and *Reader's Digest* from the American merchant seamen in the men's dormitory, hunting down every rumour in the air... My mind was expanding to fill the possibilities of the war, something I needed to do on my own. ... Lunghua was a grimy bidonville, a slum township where, as in all slums, the teenage boys ran wild. There were unwatched screwdrivers or penknives to be snaffled, heroic arguments with a bored clergyman about the existence of God, buckets of night soil to be hoisted from the G-block septic tank and poured into the tomato and cucumber beds that were supposed to keep us alive when the Japanese could no longer feed us. In a bombed-out building I found a broken Chinese bayonet, sharpened the stump of blade and used it to prise away the bricks of the kitchen coal store, filling a sack with precious coke that would briefly break the chill of our unheated concrete building. My father said nothing, feeding the coke into a miniature brazier as he rehearsed his lecture on science and the idea of God. I ran off, and nagged the off-duty Japanese guards in their bungalows until they let me wear their kendo armour, laughing as they thumped me around the head with their wooden swords." (Ballard, "Look Back at Empire," *Guardian*, 4 March 2006.)

1943 — November 9 (Tuesday) — In Lunghua: "Took Dick [a 13-year-old son] to [Doctor] Ranson who ordered him to bed to rest his tummy." (Ruth Hill Barr, *Ruth's Record*, p181.) The Ranson referred to was Paddy Ranson, a "red-haired Irish doctor" (Ballard's words in a letter to DP) whose name would be half-borrowed by JGB for the character of Dr Ransome in *Empire of the Sun*.

1943 — November 15 (Monday) — J.G. Ballard's 13th birthday. "I came to puberty in the camp, so I avoided the strangled attitudes to sex you get in most English public schools. Girls were everywhere, and there was far less privacy than there is in ordinary life. Actually, I think it was the best possible upbringing in that respect." (Ballard, interviewed by Lynn Barber, 27 December 1981.) "What was your most embarrassing moment of the war? 'Missing roll-call by a few minutes in the camp and having to run down the corridor past all the English families standing to attention outside their rooms while the Japanese guards blew on their fingernails. I've been punctual ever since.' What is your greatest treasure? 'The chess set I carried with me into Lunghua camp and which is the only possession I have from my childhood.'" (Ballard, *Sunday Express*, 20 August 1995.) "Within a few weeks, as I roamed around the camp, chess set under my arm, I was soon on good terms with dozens of men. Architects, lawyers, engineers and plant managers, they were bored enough to play a game of chess and dispense a little cynical wisdom to an impressionable young ear." (Ballard, "The End of My War," *Sunday Times*, 20 August 1995.)

1943 — December 23 (Thursday) — In Lunghua, Peggy Pemberton-Carter wrote: "The first real cold came without any warning on December 1st, and caught us unprepared (as well it might, seeing that one is accustomed in Shanghai to having reasonably warm sunny weather until after Christmas) in even those things that we could do something about. Camp conditions in general had prepared us for the fact that though the stoves might be erected, we should rarely, if ever, have enough coal this year to light them as we did when we first came into camp. The draughts whistled through the floors, through the cracks in the wooden walls, only one plank thick, anyhow, and through the warped window frames." (Abkhazi, *'Enemy Subject,'* p96.) Young Jamie and his parents and sister were living in a small room, number 117, in Lunghua's G Block: "This was the room in which he would watch his father melt down candles, soak cloth in the wax, to refashion as window panes for the camp. 'Broken panes were OK in summer but in winter it was just so cold.' By the way, 'I certainly didn't hero worship him,' Ballard says. 'What he did was unheroic and that's the important thing... This was a stoical, thoughtful, considerate response to the endemic crisis that existed.'" (Ballard, interviewed by Susie Mackenzie, *Guardian*, 6 September 2003.)

1943 — December 25 (Saturday) — In Lunghua: "To Church in Dining Room D after a breakfast of bacon & eggs. Guests to tea: Bernard Read, Geo. Osborn... Block Xmas tree with lights." (Ruth Hill Barr, *Ruth's Record*, p184.)

1943 — "In G Block a boy named Bobby Henderson was so resented by the couple on whom he was billeted that he constructed a cubicle like a beggar's hovel around his narrow bed. This was his private world that he defended fiercely. He was dressed in cast-offs, and saved his shoes for the winter months. In the summers he wore a pair of wooden clogs with the heels completely worn away leaving two slivers of wood that ended in his insteps. Bobby was a close friend, though I never really liked him, and found something threatening about his tough and self-reliant mind. I sensed that circumstances had forced him to fight too hard to survive, and that this had made him ruthless not only with others, but with himself. He allowed me to tag along with him, but regarded my endless curiosity and roaming around the camp as a waste of time and energy, and my interest in chess, bridge and kite building, and in the complex skipping games that some of the girls brought into camp with them, as frivolous and distracting. His parents were interned in Peking, but he never spoke about them, which baffled me at the time, and I suspect that he had forgotten what they were like." (Ballard, *Miracles of Life*, p69-70.)

1943 — Who was "Bobby Henderson"? It is highly likely that he was actually a boy called Bobby Patterson, who I was able to pick out from a short list of possible candidates that Greg Leck, an expert on the subject of the internment camps, kindly sent to me. Whether JGB simply misremembered the surname, or altered it deliberately to disguise the youth's identity, I do not know, but I suspect the former. Henderson and Patterson are names with a similar ring to them, and perhaps easy to confuse in the memory (DP). "Robert Thomas Harold Patterson (born 1929), father interned in Haiphong Road (a camp for internees the Japanese had identified as having the potential to cause problems), mother not interned and whereabouts unknown. ... [He] was in camp until liberation, and then would have remained for a month or more. His father had been transferred to Fengtai [a camp near Peking] in June 1945 and would not return to Shanghai until October 10, 1945." (Greg Leck, compiler of the 738-page book *Captives of Empire: The Japanese Internment of Allied Civilians in China, 1941-1945* (2007), e-mails to David Pringle, 23 November 2011.)

1944

1944 — January 2 (Sunday) — Peggy Pemberton-Carter wrote: "The whole camp had been allowed [a] three hour extension because of it being New Year's Eve, so a fancy dress dance was the highlight of entertainment for the young. We enjoyed our party, little dreaming of the drama that was about to be unfolded. The drama concerned the one, whom for want of a better name, we have always referred to as 'our problem child.' ... She is one of the most beautiful young women I have ever met. ... And then she opens her mouth, and you hear the most appalling accent, with, as often as not, a flow of profanity to match. ... But by 9 a.m. it was proved that she and a couple of her young boy friends had escaped. ... All this morning has been spent with questioning by Authority... Since Authority has departed from the hut, looking very wise, we have been waiting around, uneasily, wondering what further restrictions we shall inherit in the way of punishment. ... I was just putting this away, when Muriel, our monitor, came in with the notice from the Commandant regarding our punishment ... Excepting for one item, not nearly so severe as we had expected. ... The bad item is that the whole New Territory is put out of bounds, including the school buildings, which is really catastrophic for the 300 children, who were just getting used to a more orderly school routine, and feeling the benefit (though they wouldn't know it!) of improved discipline. Now when the new term opens, we shall have to go back to our odd holes and corners, and things will slip back into the bad old ways." (Abkhazi, *'Enemy Subject,'* p99-101.)

1944 — January 16 (Sunday) — In Lunghua, Peggy P-C wrote: "Cold! Cold! Cold! that is the monotonous tune that accompanies every action of stupid, numbed limbs. And as for thought, one's brain feels like a frozen sponge. Consequently, tempers are short, and there are daily rows over lights, space, curtains, open windows, the time, loaned articles, jerries, and what have you... ... Today we have been officially informed that the three escapers have been recaptured at a brothel in Yalu Road. Their story was that the girl and one of the lads left to get married, and the third lad tagged along to be the witness. This has provoked much laughter in our low neighbourhood." (Abkhazi, *'Enemy Subject,'* p101.)

1944 — January 31 (Monday) — Desmond Power was transferred from Lunghua camp to Weihsien camp in northern China, to be with his family. "In Pootung I got to know several from the crew of the SS *Harrison*. When the Japanese transferred internees from Pootung to Lunghua I was with the twenty or so of the crew who were included in the move. Lunghua's Assembly Hall was converted into a dormitory to receive the Pootung arrivals. Members of the *Harrison* crew were assigned spaces in the auditorium while I had my bunk on the stage. Visitors from other Blocks were frowned upon, too many personal items pilfered, so Ballard must have sweet-talked his way into

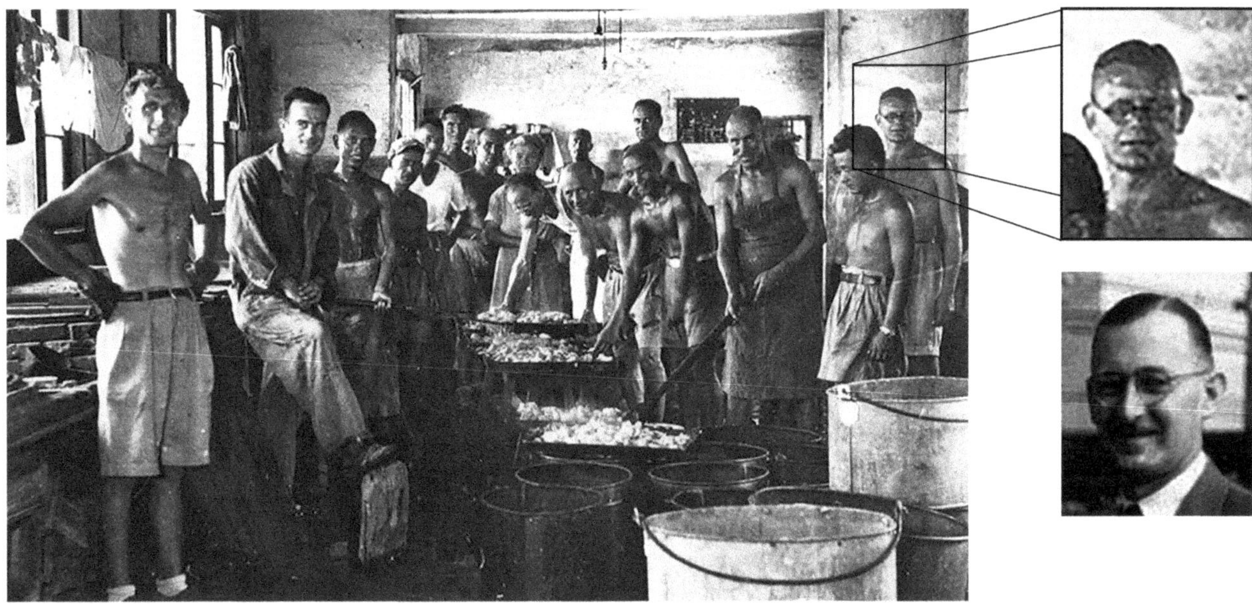

Photograph of the Lunghua Camp cooking area. Question: is the man in the photo James Ballard, JG Ballard's father?

the auditorium to get to know his 'sailor' friends. When I was transferred to Weihsien in 1944 fourteen of the crew signed their names on a farewell sheet in my autograph album. I can tell you that three of the fourteen were negroes, one was from the Islands, and the rest whites, which gives you an idea of the mix of races." (Power, e-mail to DP, 22 November 2011.) The 14 men who signed Desmond's autograph album (circa 30 January 1944) were: Blacky Kelleher, Chief Oke Doke, Ed Doner, W. White, Mike Barrasa, John Kulesha, Chester Piekos, A. Mortensen, John Bondaruk, Charles H. Edwards, Gilbert Monreal, Cecil Richards, Hank Behrens, and Bob Wakeland. Which of these men may have served as the original of "Basie" in *Empire of the Sun*? The character was probably drawn from several of them.

1944 — February 17 (Thursday) — United States' forces landed on Eniwetok Atoll in the Pacific. The battle against the Japanese occupiers there would end in an American victory on 22 February.

1944 — April 5 (Wednesday) — In Lunghua, Peggy P-C wrote: "I haven't written for over two months. The bitter coldness, making it difficult to hold a pencil even in mittened hands, has been largely responsible, and the endless monotony holds one in its grip for weeks on end. But today is an anniversary of sorts! [She first entered the camp on 5 April 1943.] The most exciting thing that has happened to us during this past year was the arrival, at the end of last month, of our first Red Cross parcels from America. If I could only tell you or the Red Cross how wonderful those parcels are..." (Abkhazi, *'Enemy Subject,'* p103.)

1944 — May 23 (Tuesday) — Five more men escaped from Lunghua Civil Assembly Centre. They were Reggie Euluch, Tommy Huxley, Mike Levy, Roy Scott and, "the escape leader," Lewis Murray-Kidd. (Power, *Little Foreign Devil*, p209.) "Discovered in early am that 5 men had escaped. New territory closed. No school for children." (Ruth Hill Barr, *Ruth's Record*, p208.)

1944 — May 27 (Saturday) — Jean-Paul Sartre's play "Huis Clos" (*No Exit*) was first produced at the Théâtre du Vieux-Colombier in Paris. It depicted the dawning realization by three people that they are in hell and are each other's punishment: "L'enfer, c'est les autres" (Hell is other people).

1944 — May 30 (Tuesday) — In Lunghua, Peggy P-C wrote: "A week of excitement. Two attempted suicides, one of them in our hut, Russian, plus insomnia, plus love. ... And last Tuesday morning it was discovered that five men had escaped. Judging by official reticence on the subject we judge that they have reached safety by now—we hope so, as we shall be punished either way. ... As the New Territory is closed to us, school has once more come to an abrupt end, and all teachers are enjoying an indefinite holiday. If it goes on too long, even my sluggish conscience will creak a bit. Meanwhile the comparative leisure has been a boon..." (Abkhazi, *'Enemy Subject,'* p107.)

1944 — June 6 (Tuesday) — D-Day: tens of thousands of Allied troops — American, British, Canadian and others—landed on the beaches of Normandy.

1944 — June 9 (Friday) — In Lunghua, Peggy Pemberton-Carter wrote: "The news of the invasion came officially in yesterday's newspapers, though we had already had flurries of rumours on the subject, via our bamboo wireless. We are all sick with excitement and anxiety. It is the first break in our stupid, doldrummy existence." (Abkhazi, *'Enemy Subject,'* p108-109.)

1944 — June 12 (Monday) — Peggy P-C added: "A delightful, if apocryphal, story has just drifted in, to the effect that Hiyashi has just received a post card from Chungking from one member of the last escaping gang, Murray Kidd, which reads: 'Arrived safely. Wish you were here.' Well, the shower bath enthusiasts have had their last warm showers, because the boilers are to be removed by the Japanese military to help boost Japan's war effort scrap metal collection." (Abkhazi, *'Enemy Subject,'* p109-110.)

1944 — June 13 (Tuesday) — One week after the Normandy invasion, the first German V-1 flying bombs—which would be variously nicknamed by the British as "robots," "buzz-bombs" or "doodlebugs"—were launched at London.

1944 — July 25 (Tuesday) — Bing Crosby and the Andrews Sisters recorded Cole Porter's "Don't Fence Me In" in Los Angeles for Decca Records. Many years later it would become one of Ballard's Desert Island Discs.

1944 — July 31 (Monday) — Death of Antoine de Saint-Exupery (b. 1900), French aviator and writer, at 44. "Saint-Exupery was a complex but attractive figure. The great poet of the sky, the author of *Night Flight* and the children's classic *The Little Prince*, Saint-Ex wrote mystically about the solitude of the cockpit, the wonder of clouds and airborne time, the terror of storms and the pilot's inevitable desire for death. A tall, shambling figure, he was unhappily married and the most romantic hero that aviation has yet produced, dying at the controls of his Lightning fighter when he was shot down into the sea near Toulon in 1944." (Ballard, "Up with the Celestial Helmsmen," *Guardian*, 7 May 2005.)

1944 — August 18 (Friday) — In Lunghua, Peggy Pemberton-Carter wrote: "It has been a long and trying summer. It began at the end of June and has continued unbroken until the end of last week. Day after day of grilling sunshine, never a drop of rain, and nights of suffocation under the nets, with compulsory lights out at 9:30 p.m. ... This last week there has been a brisk northeast breeze, no typhoon so far, 'from which may the Lord deliver us,' which has cooled things down." (Abkhazi, *'Enemy Subject,'* p110.)

1944 — August 21 (Monday) — There was an incident in Lunghua camp: "After the mid-day meal, a crowd of children were turned out to play on the football field. I, as usual, was lying on my bed, when suddenly I heard screams, roars, and the sounds of beating, hissing and booing. All the awful sounds of the mob, which make one realize how thin is the veneer of good manners and orderliness. I thought 'they' had turned upon the children. But it was S. (the friend and next door neighbour of one of the escapers) who had been questioned for the past five hours by the gendarmes, who had broken away from his questioners, and was running across the field. Seeing two guards closing in, he hit them, then a third gendarme joined in the chase and caught him, whilst the other two held him down. No. 3 beat him until he streamed with blood from scalp wounds. The windows of all the buildings had been filled with horrified onlookers, who then poured out on to the field, the men at a strange, almost primeval crouching run, they all closed round the guards, who were pressed back to back, looking green with fear. If they had touched their revolvers they would certainly have been torn limb from limb. The crowd then rescued S. and took him back to the doctors for attention. The guards were carried along to F Block by the furious crowd, where they were met by the Commandant, who was seized by his lapels by an angry woman, who shook him like a rat, and called him a B..., a brute and a swine." (Abkhazi, *'Enemy Subject,'* p111-112.)

1944 — August 24 (Thursday) — Peggy P-C wrote: "Everyone is chafing under the enforced confinement, though mercifully the book punishment has been waived [the Japanese had announced that no reading matter would be allowed, but then evidently thought better of it]. Confined to billets means what it says so literally, that we are not even allowed to go to the washing lines... The last two nights have been difficult. At evening Roll Call, slaps and hits galore... During the night we were twice awakened with the whistle and order for Roll Call." (Abkhazi, *'Enemy Subject,'* p114.)

1944 — September 8 (Friday) — Germany's V-2 rocket offensive against England began. Without warning, a missile hit Chiswick in south-west London: three people died and 17 were seriously injured.

1944 — September 30 (Saturday) — At Lunghua camp, a typed document was drawn up listing the internees and giving their ages (last birthday) as at this date. The Ballard family were listed as follows: James Ballard, age 42 (M); Edna Ballard, age 29 (F); James G. Ballard, age 13 (M); and Margaret Ann Ballard, age 7 (F). There was an evident typing error: Edna's age was given as "29" when it should have been 39.

1944 — October 25 (Wednesday) — The USS *St Lo* was sunk by a Japanese kamikaze plane, with the loss of 140 men. "The first official suicide pilot was Lieutenant Yukio Seki, who crashed his Zero fighter into the US carrier *St Lo* at the Battle of Leyte Gulf. The *St Lo* sank within hours, blown apart by its own exploding torpedoes. During the next three months, more than a thousand suicide pilots lost their lives attacking the American fleet near the Philippines. A further 2,000 kamikaze pilots died in the bitter struggle for Okinawa in the spring of 1945, most of them shot down into the sea by resolute gunners. More than 30 US warships were sunk or damaged..." (Ballard, "The Ultimate Sacrifice," *New Statesman*, 9 September 2002.)

1944 — November 8 (Wednesday) — In Lunghua, Peggy Pemberton-Carter wrote: "It is a long time since I have written anything... Our Commandant, Hiyashi, was demoted as a result of the August escapes (coming on top of the others) ... and about two weeks ago his successor, Yamashita, arrived. He appears to be a much more dignified, reserved man, and with his arrival we were declared as completely forgiven; and the last privileges (excepting the roofs for sitting and concerts) newspaper and entertainments were restored to us. But the threat was added that another escape would entail temporary punishments being made permanent, plus the stopping of our Red Cross parcels, and either confiscating or puncturing all our private stocks of tinned food." (Abkhazi, *'Enemy Subject,'* p117-118.)

1944 — November 12 (Sunday) — Peggy P-C wrote: "Yesterday morning we had our first thrilling moment since coming into camp... At exactly 9 a.m. as the guard entered our hut for morning Roll Call, there was a run of terrific explosions, and we knew at once that it must be an Allied air raid, so long waited for, and so greatly longed for. We all played our parts well in the comedy, the guard walking past us, with impassive face, and ourselves mechanically calling out our numbers. But the suppressed excitement, after all these years of dull monotony, was almost more than one could bear. After the guard left the hut, our excitement broke loose, and we all shouted and cheered, and hung out of the windows, trying in vain to catch a glimpse of the planes." (Abkhazi, *'Enemy Subject,'* p119.)

1944 — November 15 (Wednesday) — J.G. Ballard's 14th birthday. "I have—I won't say happy, but not unpleasant memories of the camp. I was young, and if you put four or five hundred children together they have a good time whatever the circumstances. I can remember the acute shortage of food in the last year, and a general breakdown of facilities. Drinking water was no longer brought in by road tanker to the camp for the last year or more, once the tide turned against the Japanese. I remember a lot of the casual brutality and beatings-up that went on—but at the same time we children were playing a-hundred-and-one games all the time! There was a great deal of illness, and about three-quarters of the people in the camp caught malaria—though not my family, thank God. My sister, who is seven years younger than me, nearly died of some kind of dysentery. I know my parents always had very much harsher memories of the camp than I did, because of course they knew the reality of the circumstances. ... I saw it all from a child's eye, and didn't notice the danger. Right next to the camp was a large Japanese military airfield. This was under constant attack in the last year or so from American bombers and low-flying fighters. Although we had a curfew imposed by the Japanese during the air attacks, they became so frequent—almost continuous towards the closing stages that we were often out in the open with anti-aircraft shells bursting over our heads. I daresay my parents were driven frantic by all this, but children don't remember." (Ballard, interviewed by David Pringle, 24 July 1981.)

1944 — November 25 (Saturday) — A German V-2 rocket hit a crowded Woolworth's store in New Cross Road, Deptford, south-east London, killing 168 people, the highest death toll caused by a single V-2 in Britain.

1944 — December 25 (Monday) — In Lunghua, Peggy Pemberton-Carter wrote: "At Christmas the Swiss Consulate and our private contacts were unbelievably generous in sending in parcels of fresh foodstuffs, and bulk supplies of meat, cereals and vegetables, so for that week we lived really well. ... After this burst of high living, we returned to our life of steadily diminishing everything." (Abkhazi, *'Enemy Subject,'* p121.)

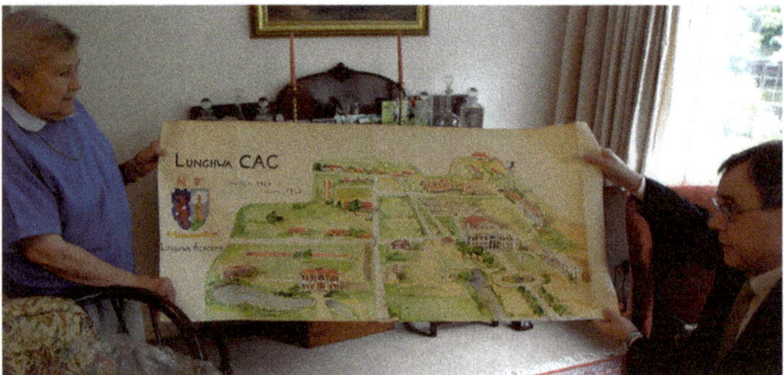

Internee Irene Duguid shows David Pringle one of the two maps she drew of the Lunghua complex.

1944 — "Ballard's description of how the internees behaved in camp [in the fictional context of *Empire of the Sun*] was outrageously inaccurate. The internees were depicted as useless, depraved and incompetent... Lunghua Camp was one of the most efficient, hygienic and best run of all the camps even though it was the largest... It was extremely well organized by a number of elected committee members who very efficiently and fairly organized the billets, distribution of food, schooling, games and entertaining... Jimmy Ballard was a young boy in Lunghua camp and his best friend Bill Weight was the brother of my friend Jean so I saw quite a lot of him... He lived in G Block with his parents and sister. He did seem to live in a dream world making up tales about talking to the Jap pilots of the planes in the nearby aerodrome which was impossible." (Mrs Irene Duguid Kilpatrick, letter to Rick McGrath, 29 April 2007.)

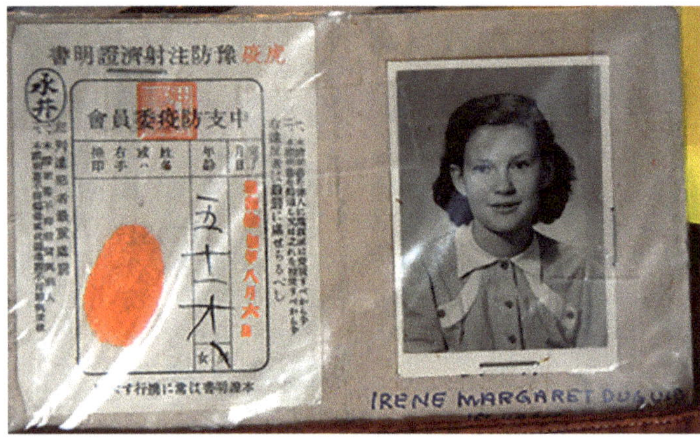

Irene Duguid in 1943 with her Japanese identification card.

1944 — Among Ballard's fellow internees in Lunghua was an older youth who would later become famous in Britain as an actor. "Peter Wyngarde was in the camp, under his real name of Cyril Goldbert. We came to England on the *Arrawa* [sic], and I bumped into him once or twice in the 1950s. The last time, when he had begun to be successful, he cut me dead in St James's Park. In interviews he claims that his father was a French diplomat and is vague about his age, sometimes claiming to be younger than me. In fact, he is at least four years older than me, and played adult roles in the camp Shakespeare productions." (Ballard, letter to DP, 2 December 1994.)

1945

1945 — January 18 (Thursday) — Nazi personnel began to empty the Auschwitz concentration camp system. As Soviet forces approached the camp complex from the east, the SS evacuated prisoners to the west. Nearly 60,000 people, mostly Jews, were forced on a series of cold-weather death marches. Tens of thousands marched to the cities of Loslau and Gleiwitz in Upper Silesia. Those too weak or sick to walk were left behind. During the marches, SS guards shot anyone who could not continue, and as many as 15,000 died. (In Loslau and Gleiwitz, the surviving prisoners would be put on unheated freight trains and sent to camps in Germany.) Among the marchers from one of the Auschwitz-Birkenau sub-camps was a Jewish boy named Reinhard Frank. Miraculously, he and a small group of other youths were able to break away from their death march and head south to Czechoslovakia. After weeks of wandering, Reinhard would survive to become a refugee in postwar England, where he would be a schoolmate of J.G. Ballard's in Cambridge. "I had a few close friends... There was also a boy called Frank who was an Auschwitz survivor and had his number prominently tattooed on his arm. He was adopted after the war by an émigré Cambridge physicist and his wife, and attended The Leys as a day boy. To begin with, he spoke no English, but he was well-liked." (Ballard, *Miracles of Life*, p135.)

1945 — February 13-14 (Tuesday-Wednesday) — British aircraft fire-bombed the city of Dresden in eastern Germany, attacking at night with Lancaster heavy bombers. They were followed by American B-17 heavy bombers, flying daylight raids over Dresden just hours after the British assault. About 25,000 people died in the two bombings and in the resulting firestorm.

1945 — March 9-10 (Friday-Saturday) — American B-29 bombers launched incendiary bomb attacks against the city of Tokyo, Japan, causing widespread devastation and killing up to 100,000 people.

1945 — March 21 (Wednesday) — Peggy Pemberton-Carter wrote: "The grim and so much dreaded prospect of our second winter here more than fulfilled itself. My mind is just a blur as to what really happened from the end of November until now; a frozen, stupefying blanket numbed all my faculties—and everybody else's too. I thought our first winter here was about all anyone could bear, but this one places that one under the heading of temperate weather. According to official figures, it is the longest and coldest ever recorded in the Shanghai area, with 79 days of unbroken freezing and below freezing temperatures. ... Chilblains, frostbite septic hands and feet and sores and cuts that couldn't heal because of the cold were all accepted as inevitable." (Abkhazi, *'Enemy Subject,'* p120.) "During the years of internment I saw a great many adults weakened by hunger and malaria, gradually losing hope that the war would ever end. Parents in the camp were unable to feed their children, protect them or even keep them warm. Lunghua was in effect an enormous slum, and as in any slum the teenage boys ran wild. Though I was not aware of it, all this probably led to the estrangement between my parents and myself that lasted all my life." (Ballard, "Secrets of the Emperor's Bunker," *Guardian*, 13 September 2005.)

1945 — March 27 (Tuesday) — One of the final V2 rockets to fall on London hit Hughes Mansions, a block of flats in Stepney, killing 134 people.

1945 — April 1 (Easter Sunday) — In Lunghua, Peggy Pemberton-Carter wrote: "Today is Easter Sunday, glorious weather, sunny and warm, and the birds are singing, and at last things are growing after the terrible winter. I am writing to you out of doors... We are also well fed again. A couple of weeks ago we each received four Red Cross parcels... And even more thrilling than the parcels, we have, from time to time, actually seen the Allied planes flying over—we have heard bombings somewhere in the direction of Woosung quite often, but to actually see the planes makes all the difference." (Abkhazi, *'Enemy Subject,'* p122.)

1945 — April 3 (Tuesday) — Peggy P-C added: "Yesterday we had our first real air raid over the Lunghua area. American planes swooping so low that we could see every marking, and even the crews, shrapnel flying around and falling on our roof, bombs dropping and huge fires started at Lunghua aerodrome, the cement works and Hungjao aerodrome. Can you imagine our excitement to see something really happening at last." (Abkhazi, *'Enemy Subject,'* p123.)

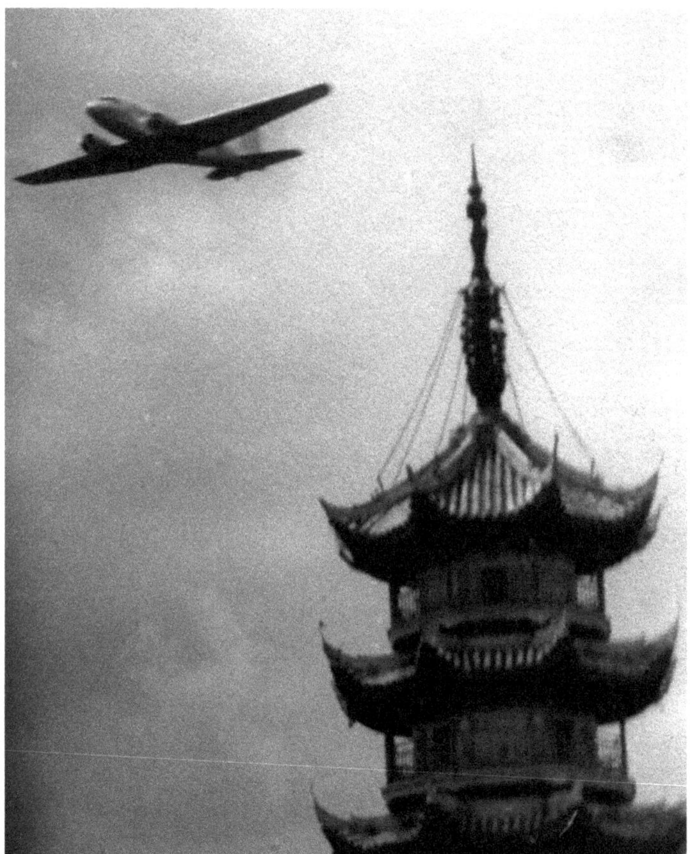

American bomber flies over the Lunghua Pagoda.

1945 — April 12 (Thursday) — Death of Franklin D. Roosevelt (b. 1882), 32nd President of the United States, of a cerebral haemorrhage at 63. He was succeeded by his Vice-President, Harry S. Truman.

1945 — April 15 (Sunday) — British and Canadian troops liberated the Nazi concentration camp of Bergen-Belsen, and found some 10,000 corpses, dead of starvation and disease.

1945 — April 30 (Monday) — Death of Adolf Hitler (b. 1889), Nazi dictator of Germany, a suicide at age 56 along with his wife of one day, Eva Braun (b. 1912), 33. He shot himself and she took a cyanide pill.

1945 — May 7 (Monday) — In Lunghua, Peggy Pemberton-Carter wrote: "No newspapers for the last two days. But the food cart, and other sources, have brought us the news that Germany has at last capitulated; the news of the past week has pointed to this being on the point of happening, and now we really can allow ourselves to believe in the indescribable lightening of one's heart. ... Well, the two most malign influences have gone—Hitler and Mussolini ... and one of the benign influences. Roosevelt's death was announced to us by an official bulletin. What tragic irony that he couldn't live to see the completion of his work. We were allowed to hold a memorial service for him... The two minutes silence was the most complete silence imaginable, all the more moving because one of the characteristics of camp life is incessant noise during all the waking hours. ... Rumours are very persistent that we are to be moved inland somewhere, and are only to be allowed to take hand baggage which we can ourselves carry... An alternative, and more unpleasing rumour, is that we shall all be shot the moment the Allies land." (Abkhazi, *'Enemy Subject,'* p125-126.)

1945 — May 8 (Tuesday) — V-E Day (Victory in Europe Day). Winston Churchill announced Germany's unconditional surrender in a radio broadcast. "Our gratitude to our splendid Allies goes forth from all our hearts in this Island and throughout the British Empire," he said. "We may allow ourselves a brief period of rejoicing; but let us not forget for a moment the toil and efforts that lie ahead. Japan, with all her treachery and greed, remains unsubdued. The injury she has inflicted on Great Britain, the United States, and other countries, and her detestable cruelties, call for justice and retribution. We must now devote all our strength and resources to the completion of our task, both at home and abroad."

1945 — May 31 (Thursday) — Peggy P-C wrote: "[T]hese weeks since Germany's collapse are the hardest (psychologically speaking) that we have had to live through. So much movement and changes for the better in Europe, and our life here is as usual, with still further decreases in rations, which have now reached their lowest level—so far! No breakfast on four days a week, except for a ladle of green tea, and on the other three days 1 oz of congee. Today's mid-day meal consisted of 1 ladle of watery cabbage soup with a few strings of tripe in it, 1 oz of potatoes and 2 ozs of beetroot. And we do not have an evening meal. The bread ration has been increased from 12 ozs to 1 lb daily, but since the increase it has become quite uneatable, heavy and sour and mouldy. ... It was very opportune that the Swiss Consul, Emil Fontanelle, visited us today, and was genuinely horrified when he was shown the bulletin posted up, which gave our daily official ration and the number of calories, 300! He left with promises to do everything possible to have bulk supplies sent into us." (Abkhazi, *'Enemy Subject,'* p126.)

1945 — June 17 (Sunday) — Peggy P-C wrote: "The Swiss Consul was as good as his word, and through him the International Red Cross are doing valiantly in sending in supplies, against heavy odds of Japanese officialdom and a currency gone to glory. ... The most disquieting rumour that we have had lately is that the men in Haiphong Road are to be moved up north very soon. A horrible thought, for heaven only knows what will happen to them once they are so far away from all communications. ... Rumours of our own removal are once more very persistent; so can only hope that something drastic will happen before they have time to get us started on our journey." (Abkhazi, '*Enemy Subject,*' p127.) One of the men due to be moved "up north" from the Haiphong Road camp was Mr Robert Patterson, father of the youth Bobby Patterson who was a friend of Jimmy Ballard's.

1945 — June 29 (Friday) — The school term ended at "Lunghwa Academy," and reports were drawn up for the pupils, including J.G. Ballard, whose age was given as 14 years and seven months. The boy's report showed that he did well in history and geography, but rather less well in English literature, composition and grammar ("term work disappointing, but 4th in tests") and in French ("careless at times"). His results in mathematics and the sciences were spotty ("fairly good, but must work more carefully"), although he received an 85% mark in trigonometry ("very good"). His lowest mark was in the Latin exam ("gross inattention in class accounts for poor results"). The report was signed by Enid B. Phillips, B.Sc. Hons. Lond., form mistress, and by George R. Osborn, M.A. Cantab, headmaster.

LungHwa Academy

Report of James Ballard *For Term Ending* 29th June 1945

Form V b Age 14 - 7 Average age 16 - 5 No in Form. 25

Tudor House.

	1st. Period Ending	2nd. Period Ending	3rd. Period Ending	EXAMINATION	
Marks %					**FINAL FOR TERM** Marks %
Position in Form					Position
Times late					Times late
Times absent					Times absent 3
Order Marks					Order Marks 11 GOOD 5 BAD
	Term %				
Scripture	63			?. 50 A. 47	Fairly good work done. W.L.P.
English: Literature				61.	
Composition	58.			68.	Term work disappointing, but 4th in tests. M.D.
Grammar					
Recitation					
Reading					
Writing					
Dictation					
Geography	76			75	Has done good work. ?.
History				85	Very good, marked improvement. E.B.P.
Arithmetic			With Trig. Credit standard reached	57	Fairly good, but must work
Geometry				54	more carefully. E.B.P.
Algebra				39	Algebra Exam disappointing
~~Nature~~ Physics				40.	Did very badly in term exam. Obviously no preparation. ?.
~~Botany~~ CHEMISTRY				51	Fair D.7
~~Hygiene~~ Trigonometry				85	Very good E.B.P.
Latin	55			32	gross inattention in class accounts for poor results
French	58			53.	Very Fair Careless at times ?.
Drawing					
Needlework					
Handwork					
Drill					Fairly good, shows little interest. W.L.P.
General Neatness					

Conduct

General Remark

GENERAL REMARKS FOR TERM.
A general improvement but steady application to work will be necessary to reach School Certificate standard by December.
Form next term: Lower V a

Signature of ~~Parent~~ HOUSE MASTER John Barry M.A. B.Sc. Glasgow

Enid B. Phillips B.Sc. Hons. Lond. *Form Mistress*

George R. Osborn M.A. Cantab. *Head* Master ~~*Mistress*~~

Next Terms begins on Tues. Sep. 11th *at* 9.30 *A.M.*

P.T.O.

1945 — July 1 (Sunday) — In G Block, Lunghua camp: "Dick [Barr] had 7 guests to tea [it was his 15th birthday]: Roger Phillips, Gordon Biggs, Ian Tulloch, Frank Uhlick, Jamie Ballard, Bill & Buddy Perry. Scorching hot day." (Ruth Hill Barr, *Ruth's Record*, p264.)

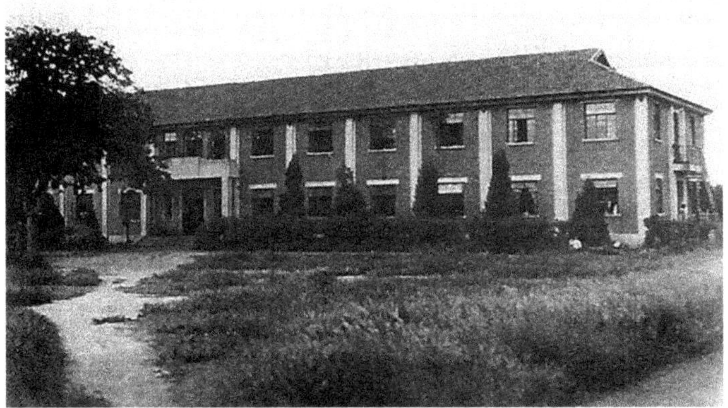

G Block at Lunghua

1945 — July 16 (Monday) — The first US test explosion of an atom bomb was made at Alamogordo Air Base, south of Albuquerque, New Mexico.

1945 — July 26 (Thursday) — General Election results were announced in Britain. Winston Churchill resigned as Prime Minister when his Conservatives were soundly defeated by the Labour Party. Clement Attlee became the new Prime Minister, as his party gained a 146 seat majority.

1945 — August 6 (Monday) — 8.15 am — Hiroshima, Japan, was struck by a uranium bomb, nicknamed "Little Boy," dropped from a B-29 airplane.

1945 — August 9 (Thursday) — 11.02 am — Nagasaki, Japan, was hit by a plutonium bomb, code-named "Fat Man," dropped from another B-29 plane.

1945 — August 11 (Saturday) — In Lunghua, Peggy Pemberton-Carter wrote: "We are seething with excitement... Of all the different ways I had pictured hearing the news of the end of the war, I never dreamed of the actual one! Some of the young girls of the hut rushed in shouting and laughing—'The war is over! The war is over!' And then miraculously one heard the same cry echoing from the whole camp. And yet if you asked how they knew, or who had told them, nobody could say. They just heard someone calling the news, so they took up the cry. My first reaction: 'I don't believe it.' And yet— it could be true." (Abkhazi, *'Enemy Subject,'* p127-128.)

1945 — August 13 (Monday) — Peggy P-C wrote: "What a day of anticlimax! Confused and contradictory rumours pour in all the time. One moment the war is definitely over, the next it is irrefutably proved that fighting is still going on. So I just give up. ... The very latest news—hot off the grill, is that Japan has been given 24 hours to say yes or no with 'atomic' bombings going on in the meantime. Poor devils! I can't help it. It is quite easy to be magnanimous when one has won." (Abkhazi, *'Enemy Subject,'* p130.)

1945 — August 14 (Tuesday) — Japan gave up the fight, accepting a cease-fire. "In the camp, we weren't certain that the war had ended. We heard on a secret radio that a few people had access to: rumours spread through the camp all the time. Also, the Japanese weren't certain whether the war had ended. I think they left a day or two after the dropping of the atom bombs—the guards left. We thought the war had ended, when in fact it hadn't at that point. Some people tried to walk to Shanghai, got picked up, beaten by the Japanese, and returned. Then a new group of Japanese came and took over the camp. They, in turn, suddenly left, leaving us on our own. Even after Hirohito called on the Japanese people to surrender there were vast armies on mainland China that had been falling back to the coastal areas like Shanghai—millions of men who had been there since 1937 and had no intention of surrendering. They were well armed and well equipped, and they planned to make a last stand there. So it was a very confused period. Unpopular though it is to say so, there's no doubt that the dropping of the two atom bombs saved us. I'm sure of that, because the Japanese had well-known plans to march the inmates of the camps around Shanghai into the interior and probably get rid of them there (as they'd done elsewhere in the Far East). I think the sudden nature of the Japanese surrender, tripped off by the atom bombs, probably saved us." (Ballard, interviewed by Colin Greenland, 1 August 1984.)

1945 — August 15 (Wednesday) — V-J Day. American airman Warren "Jeff" Arnett was the pilot of one of three planes that flew low over Shanghai dropping leaflets before landing at the Lunghua airstrip. The aircrews spent the night at the Swiss Consul's residence. Next morning, on returning to their aircraft, the crews were met by teenagers from Lunghua camp who asked them to fly low over the camp as a sign that the war was really over. As the planes flew over, it seemed to Arnett that the entire camp was on the rooftops waving madly. "Returning to our plane we found five or six teenagers from Lunghwa camp waiting for us. They, with permission, had been sent to the field in the first charcoal-burning truck I had ever seen to confirm that Americans were actually on the ground in Shanghai. They were SO excited, jumping up and down. One yelled out 'they'll never believe that we talked to American pilots.' I was excited as well for I was just 20 years old myself and shared their enthusiasm. As we took off for Kunming we flew straight toward where the youngsters said was the location of Lunghwa Camp. It wasn't far and we could see a flat roof jam-packed with people waiting for our appearance, waving any cloth they could get hold of. I get goosebumps now just writing about it for the obvious emotions below stirred us deeply. We flew quite low over the camp and my tough-minded commanding officer was moved enough to tell me to make another pass over the buildings despite our very low gas reserves. This time I stuck my hand out (not easy to do in a C-46) and waved to the crowd." (Jeff Arnett, e-mail to David Pringle, 1 Aug 2006.) "Your lead to J.G. Ballard bore fruit—he just answered my letter with a very nice note. Sixty-one years is a lot to ask of one's memory but Ballard did write, 'I'll never forget the huge impact those US planes had on me and everyone else.' And, 'I spent a lot of time hitching rides to and from the airfield... I might well have been one of those 14-year-old British lads.'" (Arnett, e-mail to DP, 27 August 2006.)

1945 — August 16 (Thursday) — Peggy Pemberton-Carter wrote: "It was officially announced yesterday at 11.00 a.m. by Block Monitors: 'Ladies and Gentlemen, the war is over.' We had had unofficial messages and assurances some hours earlier, but we were a little cautious about accepting them after our disappointment of Monday. By noon, the Japanese had handed over the control of the camp to the Swiss Consulate. Union Jacks blossomed suddenly from the most surprising places, including the top of the water tower. ... Beginning today, we are to be allowed to go for walks in the surrounding countryside. ... The water cart went in to town for the usual water rations, but also laden with the first contingent of men going in to town, to the Consulate, or to see if their offices are still standing, or their homes. They will be back tonight." (Abkhazi, *'Enemy Subject,'* p130-131.)

1945 — August 23 (Thursday) — Peggy P-C wrote: "Yesterday the advance party of doctors and businessmen left camp for good. They are hoping to be able, by occupation, to save their offices and homes from being looted, during this interregnum period between Japanese giving up control and Allied authorities taking over. The weather is glorious, and one feels rather the same as one used to at the end of a rather uncomfortable summer holiday... I am all packed up, except for bedding. ... Now I am only waiting for official permission to leave camp..." (Abkhazi, *'Enemy Subject,'* p133.)

1945 — August 28 (Tuesday) — Peggy P-C added: "One of the most interesting events, because it gave us a vivid idea of how modern armies are supplied by air, was the dropping by parachutes of American food parcels. ... It was a beautiful sight to watch the great B29s roaring over the camp, low enough for us to see the hatch being opened, and the parcels being thrown, and the red, yellow and green parachutes opening like some fabulous flowers—as pretty as a giant's firework display. An ironic commentary has to be added to the above. At one of the other camps a Chinese woman was killed by being hit with one of the containers, their library building was wrecked, and here, considerable damage was done to crops with villagers and camp inmates alike churning over the fields in an effort to get to the parcels first. In short a good deal of harm resulted from a very kindly gesture." (Abkhazi, *'Enemy Subject,'* p133-134.)

1945 — August (late) — "In August, when the war ended, the withdrawal of Japanese authority meant that the whole of the vast metropolis and the surrounding countryside became very dangerous again... [B]andit gangs made up of ex-British and American and Australian POWs were ranging around the countryside in commandeered trucks and old Buicks. I used to go out with these gangs, whom I certainly didn't think of as bandits at the time—we were looking for these air-dropped supplies that the B-29s were now dropping, canisters loaded with Spam and Chesterfield cigarettes and copies of the *Reader's Digest*. I wanted the *Reader's Digests* most of all. Of course, huge Japanese armies were also still sitting around, camping in the fields and by the docks and by the big airfield next to the camp, waiting for the end. It was a hazardous period." (Ballard, interviewed by Colin Greenland, 1 August 1984.)

1945 — August (late) or September (early) — At some point in this period, the Ballards returned to their house at 31 Amherst Avenue. "After the Japanese capitulation we were released and returned to Shanghai. During this unusual period, an interregnum of two months or so, I made a number of visits to our camp, walking across this empty landscape where units of Japanese, American and both Kuomintang and Communist Chinese forces were busy rounding each other up. During this return to peace Shanghai was one of the most exhilarating places in the world." (Ballard, quoted in John Wakeman, ed., *World Authors 1950-1970*.)

1945 — September (early) — "Three weeks after the war ended I walked back to the camp along the Shanghai-Nanking railway line. At the small wayside station an abandoned platoon of Japanese soldiers were squatting on the platform, watching one of their number string up a Chinese youth with telephone wire. Four hundred yards away, on a tank-trap embankment, a group of Kuomintang (Allied) Chinese troops were feeding themselves on the Spam and Nescafé mis-dropped by the B-29's three miles from the camp. Neither of these groups did more than look at me as I walked past. When I reached the camp I found the gates guarded by an American merchant sailor with a Mauser on his hip. Although he had lived in the camp with me for three years he apparently failed to recognize me, and for half an hour I was unable even to convince him that I was English, let alone get in." (Ballard, "Comment on 'End-Game'," *Backdrop of Stars*, 1968). He would give a rather different account of the incident of the Chinese youth and the telephone wire in a later piece—was he walking to the camp or from it? "[A] few days after the war had officially ended, I was walking from the camp and came across a unit of Japanese soldiers at a wayside railway station. One of them, who was slowly strangling a Chinese youth with telephone wire, shouted at me. He had noticed my transparent celluloid belt, which I had wheedled from an American sailor. A long haggle went on, which ended with me unbuckling my precious belt. I remember the soldier's intense pleasure in his new possession as he went back to killing the Chinese, and my own deep sense of loss." (Ballard, "Licence to Kill," *Sunday Times*, 21 February 1999.)

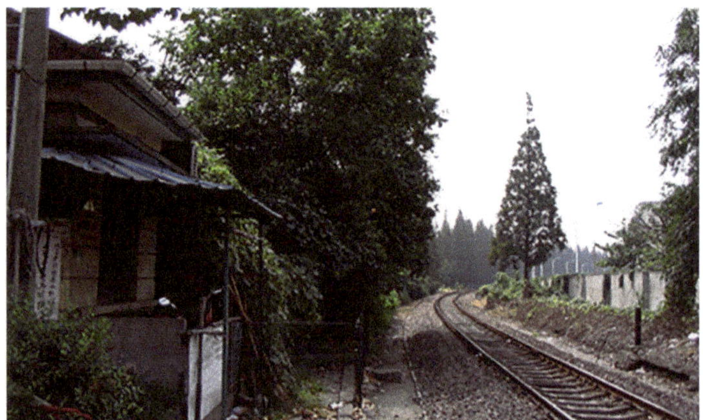

Abandoned World War II wayside station near the Lunghua Pagoda beside the Shanghai-Nanking railway line in 2007. The station has since been demolished.

1945 — September 10 (Monday) — Peggy Pemberton-Carter finally left Lunghua camp, to reside temporarily in a Shanghai private hospital. "[H]ere I am, in this small but pleasant room, by myself. Oh! the indescribable peace and relief to be able to shut the door and be quite alone. A gloriously comfortable bed—and someone to make it for me. ... And how shall I describe the heavenly sensations of silk pyjamas and dressing gown, fresh brewed coffee and milk... And freedom to go out and come in at will — even a tram ride is delightful." (Abkhazi, *'Enemy Subject,'* p136.) She would marry a disinherited prince from Abkhazia in the Caucasus, and they would settle in Victoria, British Columbia, Canada, where they would live for the rest of their lives. Sadly, Ballard would not remember her from the camp, but he would read her diary in the 1990s and write a short appreciation of it for its British publisher: "All the sights and smells of Lunghua camp rush through the pages of Peggy Abkhazi's remarkable diary, as if a window had suddenly opened in the small room that I shared with my father, mother and sister in G Block fifty years ago. ... Everything is here: the stench, the boredom, the fierce winter cold and stifling summers, the moody Japanese guards and equally unpredictable fellow internees. Peggy Pemberton-Carter, as she was in Lunghua, taught me French in the camp school, and I wish I could remember her in person. Her diary suggests a woman of determined character, as critical of herself as she is of the other prisoners who share her dormitory hut." (Ballard, Foreword, *"Enemy Subject": Life in a Japanese Internment Camp 1943-45*, by Peggy Abkhazi, Alan Sutton Publishing, August 1995.)

1945 — September 10 (Monday) — The Reverend George R. Osborn, headmaster of Lunghua Academy, Shanghai, wrote to Dr W.G. Humphrey, headmaster of The Leys school in Cambridge. "Osborn had been a pupil at The Leys himself (from 1918 to 1924) and was now acting as an intermediary for the Ballard family: Mr James Ballard was keen to get a place for his son in a good English school. Osborn described Lunghua Academy, where the young James had been educated for the previous two-and-a-half years, as 'a funny school with lots of shortcomings—not many books, little apparatus, but any number of good teachers.' He expressed the view that the children had not done too badly but nevertheless had of course all had serious interruptions to their education." (Raymond Tait, Cambridge, e-mail to DP, 2007.)

1945 — September (mid?) — "When we returned to our house in Amherst Avenue, we found that the house next door, owned by a German family, had been taken over by two American officers—and they put on little film shows for my sister and I; and the first film they showed us was a film of the Andrews Sisters and Bing Crosby singing 'Don't Fence Me In,' which I thought, really, was tremendously ironic." (Ballard, interviewed by Sue Lawley, "Desert Island Discs," BBC Radio 4, 2 February 1992.) Also in this month Ballard was given an Ernest Hemingway book: *The Viking Portable Hemingway* (Viking Press, New York, 1944). This was the first adult book ever given to me, in 1945, soon after leaving my Japanese internment camp near Shanghai. Superb introduction by Malcolm Cowley, which touches me as deeply now as it did my teenage self." (Ballard, quoted in John Baxter, *A Pound of Paper*, 2002, p313.) Could it have been one of the American officers, mentioned above, who gave him this book?

1945 — September 24 (Monday) — *Life* magazine for this week featured on its cover Colonel Jimmy Stewart (the actor, then serving in the US air force). Among other things, the contents included: a feature on "New Mexico's Atomic Bomb Crater," an article on "The Bombing of Nagasaki" by William L. Laurence, an item entitled "Americans Retake Wake Island," a piece on Pearl Harbor by John Chamberlain (spread over eight pages), an item headed "Peace Comes to Shanghai" by Theodore H. White, and: "Close-Up: Salvador Dali" by Winthrop Sergeant (four-and-a-half pages). Could that last illustrated article have been the young Ballard's first-ever encounter with the work of the surrealist master?

1945 — October 10 (Wednesday) — "The newspapers were worried that day about the lack of an airport for London. Three American airlines had announced that they would soon be reopening their services to Europe, but 'Heath Row, the proposed terminal on the Bath Road, near Hounslow, will not be ready for 18 months or two years.' There were plenty of airfields around London, but the RAF was anxious to hold on to all of them... The dock strike in the north of England had spread to London... On this day the Cabinet agreed to use troops to unload essential food supplies... The Cabinet also decided to let the BBC start up its television service again in the spring of 1946. 'The transmitting apparatus at Alexandra Palace is undamaged,' said The Times, 'but it has been used for war purposes and a certain amount of reconversion is necessary. There has been no radiation for the public since September 1939.' After Hiroshima, the word 'radiation' was already taking on an altogether different connotation, and soon 'broadcasting' would be applied to television as well as radio programmes." (John Simpson, *Days from a Different World*, 2005, p124-125.)

1945 — November 1 (Thursday) — Jimmy Ballard began a six-week voyage of repatriation to Britain with his mother and sister (his father was not with them). They sailed from Shanghai on the SS *Arawa*, a New Zealand freighter which had served as a troop ship. "The *Arrawa* [sic] was a former refrigerated cargo vessel used as a troopship during the war, and the decks and holds were lined with miles of refrigeration piping. ... [T] here was a huge send-off at the pier in Hongkew. Friends and relatives who were staying behind lined the pier and waved as the ship moved out into the Whangpoo, surrounded by scores of American landing craft sounding their sirens. My mother and sister were at the rail, somewhere amidships, but I moved to the stern to be on my own. At the last minute my father turned from my mother and waved to me, and for some reason I have never understood I decided not to wave back. I assume he thought I had lost sight of him, but I have always regretted not waving to him." (Ballard, *Miracles of Life*, p116-117.)

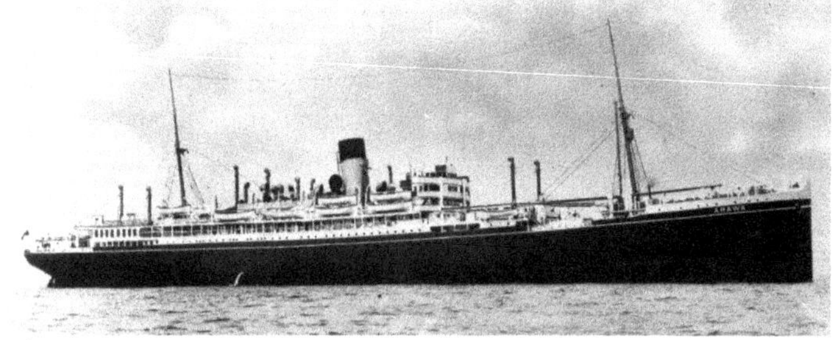

The SS *Arawa*

1945 — November 15 (Thursday) — J.G. Ballard's 15th birthday. He celebrated it on board the *Arawa*, which had sailed from Shanghai via Hong Kong and was probably now at or near Singapore. "I don't think it's possible to escape from one's past. The brain and the imagination are imprinted forever with the images of one's first years. I think puberty is an important turning point, as it is in the case of language acquisition. I lived in Shanghai until I was 15, went through the war and acquired a special 'language', a set of images and rhythms, dreams and expectations that are probably the basic operating formulae that govern my life to this day." (Ballard, interviewed by Hans Ulrich Obrist, January 2003.)

1945 — November 22 (circa) — The *Arawa* continued its voyage. "The troopship carrying former Shanghai internees to England docked briefly at Rangoon [in fact, it was probably at Colombo, Ceylon]. A group of 30 British commandos came aboard, tough-faced young men unlike anything Guy Crouchback encountered during his *Sword of Honour* wanderings. The ship's officers warned the passengers, mostly unaccompanied wives, to take care of themselves and their daughters. As it happened, my mother and sister had nothing to fear. The commandos made straight for the saloon bar on the upper deck. Each morning they bought dozens of bottles of beer, which they stacked on the tables in the saloon, and spent the rest of the day in the leather armchairs, quietly drinking. Eager for tales of derring-do, I and one or two other 15-year-olds tried to draw them out. We had seen the Japanese in victory, never in defeat. But the commandos were reluctant to talk. I noticed that the only heroic deeds they described were those involving former comrades who had died beside them during the suicidal attacks launched by starving Japanese soldiers in the last months of the war. Ever on the look-out for new heroes, I was deeply impressed. Still, I wanted to know, what were the Japanese soldiers like? Cracked, the commandos told me curtly: staring mad, off their rockers. But, I pressed, were they brave? Alas, the word meant nothing to these young warriors. They had seen death coming towards them, armed with sword, grenade and bayonet, and had fought him to a standstill." (Ballard, "Hungry Young Men," *Telegraph*, 10 February 2001.) According to Irene Duguid Kilpatrick, 18 at the time, the ship docked at Colombo and took on board some wounded British personnel; it may be they were soldiers from Burma who had been ferried to Ceylon to join the *Arawa*.

1945 — November 30 (Friday) — About this time, en route to England via the Suez Canal, the *Arawa* docked at Aqaba, "a big British base" situated on a gulf off the Red Sea, part of the Palestine Mandate (soon to become part of the Kingdom of Jordan), and on the way there JGB first saw desert landscapes with dunes. (Ballard, interviewed by Catherine Bresson, 1982.)

1945 — December 14 (Friday) — The *Arawa* arrived in England. According to the official passenger list, among the many on board were Irene Duguid and her mother; Cyril Goldbert (alone); and the Kendal-Ward and Weight families. The latter were: W. A. Weight, male, 51; M. K. Weight, female, 46; J. M. Weight, female, 19 (Irene's friend, Jean Weight); and W. R. Weight, male, 16 (Jimmy Ballard's friend, Bill Weight); and their destination address was: c/o Mr D. Weight, Greycot, The Roman Way, Glastonbury, Somerset. (Ballard would visit and stay with the Weights in the next two years, though whether that was when they were in Glastonbury, or at some other address, is not known.) "I remember when I landed at Southampton ... looking round at the little roads and mean houses by the docks. It was a sad place. The British working class, I suddenly realized, existed. They were nine-tenths of the population and they were appallingly treated. The little side-streets away from the docks were lined with what seemed to be black perambulators with doors—too large for perambulators! —which I assumed were some sort of mobile coal-scuttle used for bunkering ships. Because cars then were all black, you see. English cars were black, whereas American cars were every colour under the sun, in the '30s." (Ballard, interviewed by J. Goddard and D. Pringle, 4 January 1975.)

1945 — December 15 (Saturday) — "We took the train from Southampton to London, and I remember travelling across London and seeing this total devastation—I mean hundreds of acres of the city had been levelled to the ground, the whole place had a shattered look. And everyone looked small and tired and white-faced and badly nourished, they looked like people who had suffered a particularly ugly enemy occupation. The British I met talked as if they had won the war but acted as if they had lost it." (Ballard, interviewed by Danny Danziger, 16 December 1991.)

1945 — December 16 (Sunday) — "We then travelled to Birmingham where my mother's parents lived [at 11 Lodge Road, West Bromwich, Staffordshire], and one never saw the sun, and every chimney-pot belched out clouds of coal smoke. People were obsessed with their tiny butter ration and the tiny portion of stewing steak they were allowed each week. I had spent three years in a Japanese camp, so I could cope with the physical deprivation, but the psychological deprivation from which the English suffered unsettled me far more." (Ballard, interviewed by Danny Danziger, 16 December 1991.) "My mother's maiden name was Edna Johnstone. Her parents lived in West Bromwich, near Birmingham. They were teachers of music. I remember my grandfather as a very straitlaced puritanical Edwardian gentleman. My grandparents were in their 70s, I think, after the war, and were rabidly right-wing Conservatives. They were faced with the apocalypse of the post-war Labour Government, which shattered everything in their world. But in fact, according to my mother, my grandfather was a bit of a maverick. He shocked his very bourgeois family, around the turn of the century, by forming his own band!" (Ballard, interviewed by David Pringle, 24 July 1981.) "My mother's parents were lifelong teachers of music. Both of them taught music at home—usually the piano, and all day long there were two pianos going with various pupils practising their scales or whatever they do. I think this completely turned my mother off to music. Consequently, I don't remember my parents ever playing music of any kind!" (Ballard, interviewed by Vale, 7 February 2003.) "When my grandmother, a small and ungenerous woman, first showed me the single bathroom in this large, gloomy house I blotted my copybook for ever by asking: 'Is this my bathroom?'" (Ballard, *Miracles of Life*, p50.)

1945 — December 23 (Sunday) — Mrs Edna Ballard, newly

arrived in England with her two children, wrote to Dr W. G. Humphrey, headmaster of The Leys school, Cambridge, requesting a place for her son, James, to start in January 1946, and enclosing a letter of introduction written in September by Rev. George Osborn. "My son is just fifteen. I am very anxious to get him back into normal school life after he has missed so much & has had the misfortune to be interned. I wonder if by any chance you have a vacancy & could take him after the Xmas holidays or even later? I realise that he is at least a year older than you would like him to be & that he would be breaking into the school year, also that I am giving you very short notice. If you could overlook this & give his case special consideration I should be most grateful. As regards his standard of work, I do not think you would find him too backward as we were fortunate in having a highly qualified staff in the camp which carried on nobly under Mr. Osborn's direction in very difficult and trying circumstances. I am so sorry to bother you in the middle of your holidays—I realise we have arrived in England at rather an awkward time. Would you be kind enough to let me have an early reply, which I do hope will be favourable."

1946

1946 — January 6 (Sunday) — Mrs Edna Ballard, who must have received a positive reply from Dr Humphrey, filled in an application form for the registration of her son James as a pupil at The Leys school, Cambridge. In the section listing his previous schools and the names of his headmasters, she wrote: "1939. Sompting Abbotts, Worthing. Mr Rutherford. Later Cathedral School, Shanghai. Rev. P. C. Matthews. Latterly Internment Camp School. Rev. George Osborn." (Raymond Tait, "J.G. Ballard at The Leys School," *Deep Ends 2014*, p49.) This document was the clue which, combined with the shipping records, told us that JGB had spent a term as a pupil at Sompting Abbotts school in Sussex, a fact he never mentioned in later years.

THE LEYS SCHOOL

Application for Registration

Sir,

I request that* BALLARD, JAMES GRAHAM.
may be registered for entrance to The Leys School as a pupil, and I enclose a cheque for one guinea in payment of the Registration Fee.

I should like him to enter at the† January term, 1946

If he is accepted, I hereby undertake to pay the School accounts when due, based on the rate of fees in force on the date of entry, and to comply with the Rules and Regulations of the School as set out in the Prospectus in so far as they affect me.

*Names in full in block capitals, surname first

†January May or September

Yours faithfully,

Jan. 6th. 1946 (Date)

E. Ballard. (Signature of Parent or Guardian)

Date of Boy's Birth (date, month, year) 15 November 1930.

Full Name of Parent or Guardian Edna Ballard.

Residence 11, Lodge Rd, West Bromwich. Staffordshire

Profession or Occupation —

Relationship to the pupil Mother.

House preferred B. North House.

Present School or Tutor (if boy is over 10 years old) —

Name of Headmaster of Preparatory School 1939. Sompting Abbotts Worthing. Mr Rutherford. Later Cathedral School Shanghai. Rev. P. C. Matthews. Latterly. Internment Camp School. Rev. George Osborn

NOTES. (1) Any change of Preparatory School should be notified to the Headmaster. (2) If the preference for House cannot be stated at the time of registration, it may be sent to the Headmaster later, provided that this is done before the boy sits for the Common Entrance or Scholarship Examination.

Edna Ballard's application to have JGB admitted to the Leys school.

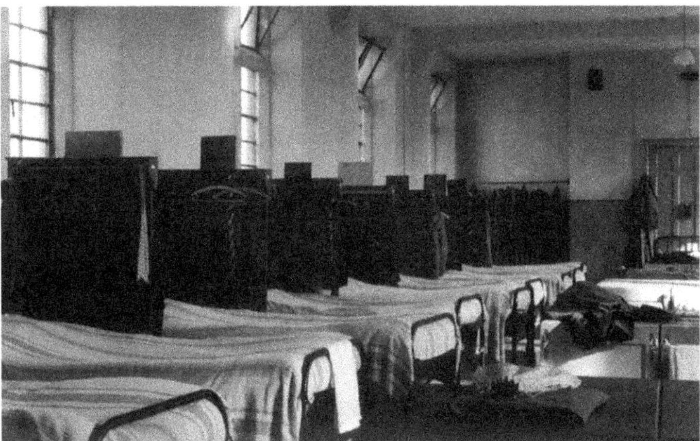

North B House dormitory at the Leys school.

1946 — January (mid) — Jimmy Ballard became a boarder at The Leys school, Cambridge, which he entered half-way through the Fourth Form year. The school had been evacuated to Scotland for several years during the war, and in this month was just resuming its existence in Cambridge. As in many English schools, the boys were divided into "houses," and Ballard was assigned to North B House. A fellow pupil called Barrie Page would write: "When I arrived back at the school in January 1946 I was one of the first to make my way into the daunting grandeur of the junior dormitory of North B, where a line of steel frame beds stretched seemingly forever from the doorway into the far distance. Having spent my first term at The Leys in a small three-boy bedroom in the Atholl Palace Hotel, Pitlochry, the shock was considerable, and it was not a cosy introduction to boarding school life in Cambridge. Apart from the twin rows of beds, ten each side, the huge room was empty, save for one earlier arrival, a boy who seemed to be much larger than me (most boys were at that stage of my life). This boy turned out to be Ballard, no first name use in those days, and so I was probably the first Leys chap to greet him. It would be good to be able to claim that this first contact with a fellow young Leysian marked the beginning of a fabulous friendship for the young Ballard, newly arrived from the rigours of internment in Shanghai. Sadly it was not to be, since I could not have been more of a conforming pupil, keen on sport and on team work generally. James Ballard could not exactly be described as a conformist. I think that he might have been persuaded to play a bit of rough rugby, but he was not by nature a joiner of anything organised. So he did not join the Corps, and certainly not the Scouts, which I suspect he would have regarded with considerable disdain. But even he had to do something on Wednesday afternoons, so he became a leading member of the Non-Cadets, teaming up with another North B rebel, B.V.E. Helliwell. I fancy that I can still see these two, among the fifteen or so other conscientious objectors, wandering around the Quad with shovels over their shoulders, carrying out badly organised maintenance tasks with barely concealed languor. They would then have plenty of time to slope off to distant parts of the grounds for a cigarette or three before returning to base just as the Scouts and the CCF folk came shambling back to North B." (Barrie Page, *Old Leysian Newsletter*, circa 2010.)

1946 — January (mid-to-late) — "The young James did form at least one relationship during 1946, as Barrie Page recalls: 'His main friend seemed to me to be another non-conformer, B.V.E. Helliwell, who was a splendid swimmer but in most other respects did not seem much interested in school activities.' (BP 15.2.94) This was independently echoed by David Spark: 'He did have one close friend called Helliwell, the school bad boy, who was regularly on the "blacklist" for misdemeanours of one kind and another. From Jim Ballard's point of view, befriending Helliwell was probably something of a statement, distancing him from the school establishment without open Helliwell-style rebellion.' (DS 16.2.94) [It was rumoured at the school that] Helliwell had been evacuated to the USA during the war where he had acquired a liking for jazz and a twang to his speech. According to Keith Wollaston the 'E' in his name stood for Ellington and had been, as he put it, 'self-awarded some time after his baptism.' (KW 26.9.94) Barrie Page remembers being 'the butt of some of their teasing—nothing in the way of bullying but strong verbal teasing which to a rather undergrown 14-year-old seemed very unfair at the time.' (BP 15.2.94) A somewhat darker memory of Helliwell is provided by Tony Thornton: 'It would be difficult for me to forget Brian Helliwell. He was a delinquent and caused Mr Morris, our house-master, a lot of heartache. He was a nasty bully and, as a new boy, I suffered at his hands. Several boys seemed to come under his influence. Although James was friendly with him, he was certainly not a bully. In fact he was never anything less than kind and helpful to me.' (TT 13.9.94) This bullying aspect of Helliwell's character was also recalled by Anthony Proudman: 'I do remember Helliwell as a tough chap with longish black hair and inclined to be aggressive to us, his juniors.' (AP 26.9.94) It is not hard to see that James might have been attracted to a boy like Helliwell—he was another outsider... [but] his influence was certainly short-lived as he left the school before the end of 1946." (Notes by Raymond Tait, 2007, based on his research at The Leys in the 1990s.) In fact, Brian Victor Ellington Helliwell was a Yorkshireman from Leeds who had never been to the United States, something verified by David Pringle in a telephone conversation with his widow, Hazel Poulter, on 28 February 2014. It is interesting, though, that his Leys contemporaries mistook him for an evacuee who had spent time in the USA, suggesting that he affected an American accent, perhaps influenced by the jazzmen, such as Duke Ellington and Count Basie, for whose music he had developed a great enthusiasm.

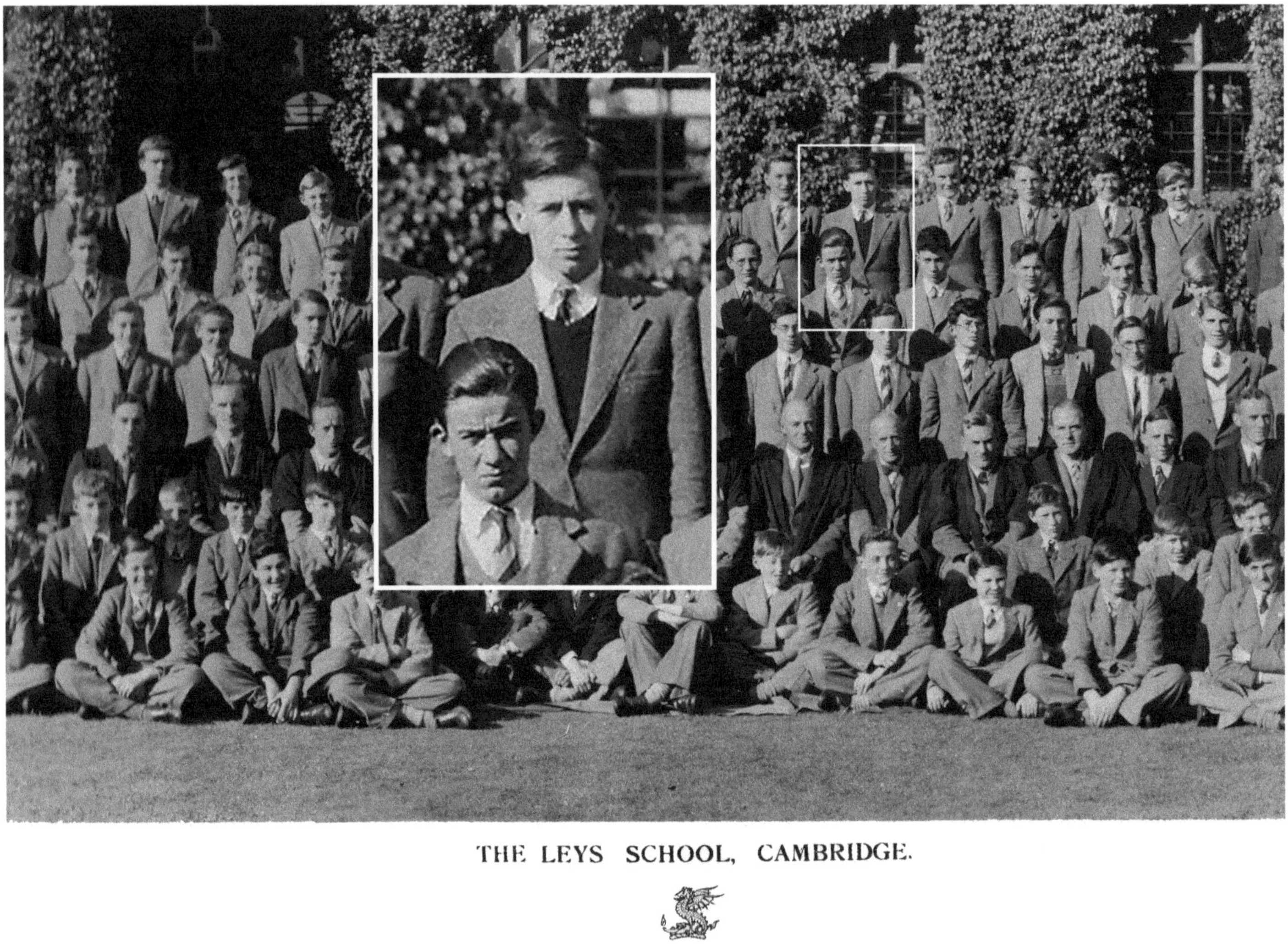

THE LEYS SCHOOL, CAMBRIDGE.

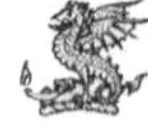

JG Ballard and his "bad boy" friend, Brian Victor Ellington Helliwell, at the Leys school.

1946 — January (mid-to-late) — Ballard would never mention his friendship with Helliwell in later years, and his comments on the school would be general. "I went to The Leys school in Cambridge for a couple of years [sic] in the late 1940s. I disliked it intensely, but I'd been through so many strange experiences before and during the war that it was just another strange experience that I coped with. I wasn't unhappy there, actually. I had a great deal more experience of life in general than almost all the boys that I met there. Although they'd lived in Britain during the war, they'd had very sheltered lives (the school had been evacuated to Scotland). I didn't have anything very much in common." (Ballard, interviewed by David Pringle, 24 July 1981.) Among the boys who had attended The Leys before Ballard's time were the novelists James Hilton, author of the bestseller *Goodbye, Mr Chips* (1934), and Malcolm Lowry, author of *Under the Volcano* (1947), and the actor Michael Rennie, star of the film *The Day the Earth Stood Still* (1951). "The 'Goodbye, Mr Chips' thing was interesting to me. The aged [William] Balgarnie was often seen around the Leys, on speech days, etc., and was well known as Hilton's model. Of course the film then was very much more famous than it is now. I never remember anyone referring to Malcolm Lowry, or for that matter to Michael Rennie, though his film career hadn't taken off then. Infinitely more famous in the film world was the Old Leysian and great benefactor of the school, the flour-milling tycoon J. Arthur Rank. The curious thing is that the Leys, founded by rich Methodists from the north of England as a place where they could educate their sons without any taint of Anglicanism, was very different from the typical ivy-clad public school envisaged by Hilton. A strong emphasis on science, with a lavishly equipped science block, a huge indoor heated [swimming] pool that was the only indoor pool in Cambridge when I was there." (Ballard, letter to D. Pringle, 2 December 1994.)

1946 — February 4 (Monday) — Mr James Ballard, still residing at 31 Amherst Avenue, Shanghai, wrote a letter to the headmaster of The Leys school, Cambridge, about his son: "I was delighted to learn from my wife that you had accepted my son, James, for your school. ... It was my very good fortune to become friendly with George Osborn during our enforced enjoyment of the hospitality of the Japanese at the Lunghwa Internment Camp, and it was his description of Leys School that inspired me with the hope that one day my son would be able to go there. I feel sure you will not regret your kindness in admitting him to your school. I trust you will not think that I am behaving as a doting father when I say that he is a somewhat unusual boy. He has lived for the greater part of his life in the international community of Shanghai and tends to be intolerant of national customs and traditions. He behaved splendidly in camp under somewhat trying conditions but appears to have grown up too quickly and to have lost some of his enthusiasm for normal boyish pastimes. It is my hope that in the atmosphere of your school he will regain a healthy boyish outlook and forget his past experience. J. Ballard 4.2.1946."

1946 — March 1 (Friday) — Mr J. Stirland of The Leys school, Cambridge, wrote to Mrs Edna Ballard about her son James's progress: "In the half-term order of the Lower Fifth Modern he is second out of seventeen boys. ... It is not as easy for a boy of fifteen to settle down in a new school as it is for a youngster of thirteen. It is rather more difficult to make friends and a longer time is required to do so. James understands this; his personality is such that I feel sure that before long he will have found congenial friends who can share his interests." (Raymond Tait, "J.G. Ballard at The Leys School," *Deep Ends 2014*, p50-51.)

1946 — March 5 (Tuesday) — Winston Churchill appeared as President Truman's guest at Westminster College in Fulton, Missouri, and delivered as notable speech: "From Stettin in the Baltic to Trieste in the Adriatic, an iron curtain has descended across the Continent. Behind that line lie all the capitals of the ancient states of Central and Eastern Europe. Warsaw, Berlin, Prague, Vienna, Budapest and Sofia, all these famous cities and the populations around them lie in ... the Soviet sphere."

1946 — April 19 (Good Friday) — During school vacations, Ballard stayed at a house his mother had rented—Little Woodlands, Newton Ferrers, Devon. "We had friends who lived down in the West Country, near Plymouth, and my mother rented a house there for a couple of years. We lived in a sort of Daphne du Maurier-land in fact, there was a little creek which was reputed to have been the source of inspiration for her novel *Frenchman's Creek*, only a few hundred yards away. There was indeed the remains of a great old wooden ship lying there in the mud: it's quite possible that it gave her the idea. It's full of little smuggler's coves and caves, that part of the world." (Ballard, interviewed by David Pringle, 24 July 1981.)

1946 — June — In his editorial in this month's *Horizon*, Cyril Connolly gave a hedonistic wish-list for the new, post-war age. "This list of ten aims, described by Connolly as 'the major indications of a civilized society,' was as follows: (1) abolition of the death penalty; (2) penal reform, model prisons and rehabilitation of prisoners; (3) slum clearance and 'new towns'; (4) light and heating subsidized and 'supplied free like air'; (5) free medicine, food and clothes subsidies; (6) abolition of censorship, so that everyone can write, say and perform what they wish, abolition of travel restrictions and exchange control, the end of phone-tapping or the compiling of dossiers on people known for their heterodox opinions; (7) reform of the laws against homosexuals and abortion, and the divorce laws; (8) limitations on property ownership, rights for children; (9) the preservation of architectural and natural beauty and subsidies for the arts; (10) laws against racial and religious discrimination. This programme was, in fact, the formula for what was to become the permissive society. Indeed, if we leave out some of Connolly's more impractical economic ideas, virtually everything he called for was to be enacted into law in the 1960s." (Paul Johnson, *Intellectuals*, p316-317.)

1946 — June 7 (Friday) — 15:00 — The BBC Television service resumed, for the first time since September 1939, from studios at Alexandra Palace in north London. Jasmine Bligh was the first presenter to appear, greeting watchers with the words: "Good afternoon everybody. How are you? Do you remember me, Jasmine Bligh?" Few people had receivers as yet, and the viewers, all in the London and Home Counties area, numbered about 15,000.

1946 — Summer — "The most representative figure in post-war Britain, after the Ministry snooper, was the spiv. Spivs sprang up in London from nowhere during the summer of 1946, like the weeds on bombed sites, their shallow roots spreading in the general chaos and destruction. No one could even agree where the name had come from... You knew exactly who they were, though: you could tell them from the unfeasibly wide lapels of their double-breasted suits, their narrow waists, their thick-soled suede shoes, their pencil-thin moustaches, the remaining stubs of cigarettes attached to their lower lips, their hats crushed down on their duck's-arse haircuts. And, usually, the wad of notes in their hand." (John Simpson, *Days from a Different World*, p154.)

1946 — July 1 (Monday) — At 8:59 and 45 seconds am local time, the United States exploded a 20-kiloton atom bomb near Bikini Atoll in the Marshall Islands in the Pacific Ocean. This was the fourth atomic explosion, and the first to occur in peacetime. "Husband gets the idea the atom bomb has been a disappointment. I hope it has. I went to bed last night when he turned on for the relay. The awful atmosphere sounded to me too much like the wailings of the poor animals we beastly humans have put on the ships for test." (Edie Rutherford, diary, *Our Hidden Lives*, p241.)

1946 — July 21 (Sunday) — Bread rationing began in Britain, for the first time in history of the UK, by order of the Ministry of Food.

1946 — August 13 (Tuesday) — Death of H.G. Wells (b. 1866), British novelist, scientific romancer (*The War of the Worlds*, etc), social prophet and popular historian, a month before his 80th birthday.

1946 — August 28 (Wednesday) — The French critic Nino Frank first applied the term "film noir" (black, or dark, film) to a group of Hollywood movies recently shown in France: John Huston's *The Maltese Falcon*, Otto Preminger's *Laura*, Edward Dmytryk's *Murder, My Sweet*, Billy Wilder's *Double Indemnity*, and Fritz Lang's *The Woman in the Window*. This summer had been the first opportunity for French audiences to see many of these American crime dramas. Frank's article, "Un Nouveau Genre 'Policier': L'Aventure Criminelle," was published in the weekly magazine *L'Ecran Français*.

1946 — September — Ballard entered the Fifth Form at The Leys school, Cambridge. "Despite my efforts to fit in, I think I was a bit of a misfit at school, an over-aggressive tennis player who would throw a game so that I could slip away to see the latest French film at the Arts Cinema. I was introverted but physically strong, and knew from my wartime experience that most people will back away if faced with a determined threat. One of my classmates called me an 'intellectual thug', not entirely a compliment, and my years in Lunghua had probably given me a tendency to watch other boys' plates in the dining hall. I was also prone to backing up an argument about existentialism with a raised fist. I had a few close friends, an Anglo-Indian boy who went up to Trinity a year ahead of me to study medicine, and an American exchange student. There was also a boy called [Reinhard] Frank who was an Auschwitz survivor and had his number prominently tattooed on his arm... I was drawn to all of them because they were foreigners." (Ballard, *Miracles of Life*, p135.) "At the Leys school, a liberal establishment in Cambridge where he boarded, he kept quiet about his wartime experiences. 'There was one boy in my house who was an Auschwitz survivor. I never mentioned that I had been an internee under the Japanese because it seemed so trivial by comparison.' ... 'I don't think I was unpopular. I think I was regarded as a bit of an odd fish,' he concedes." (Ballard, interviewed by Stuart Wavell, *Sunday Times*, 20 January 2008.) The "Anglo-Indian boy" was Dhun Robin Chand, born in Nottingham of an English mother and an Indian doctor father, so not actually a foreigner. The identity of the "American exchange student" is not known—unless this is a confused reference to the jazz-loving Brian Helliwell, not actually an American but born in Leeds, who was believed by some of the boys to have been a wartime evacuee in the USA and who may have spoken with a faux-American accent.

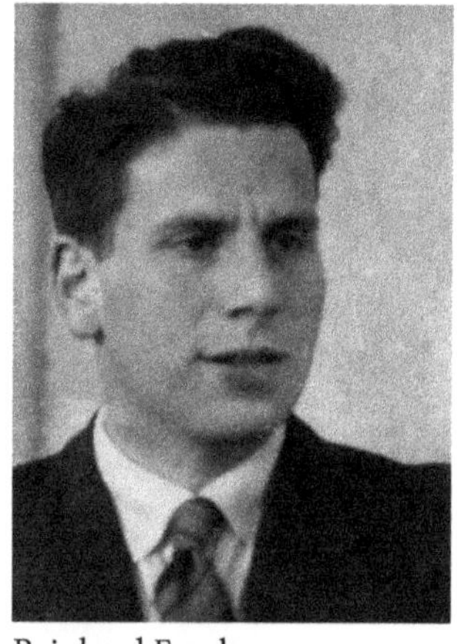
Reinhard Frank

1946 — September 29 (Sunday) — 18:00 — The BBC launched the Third Programme, a cultural radio service. The first unashamedly intellectual radio channel, it would last for 21 years before being absorbed into the new (more music-oriented) Radio 3. Ballard would listen to it, at least on occasions, and in later years he would appear on it.

1946 — November 6 (Wednesday) — The National Health Service Act was passed by Parliament in the UK. (It would take effect in 1948.) "All these middle-class people, my parents' friends and relations and the like, were seething with a sort of repressed rage at the world around them. And what they were raging against was the post-war Labour government. It was impossible to have any kind of dialogue about the rights and wrongs of the National Health Service, which was about to come in, they talked as if this Labour government was an occupying power, that the Bolsheviks had arrived and were to strip them of everything they owned." (Ballard, interviewed by Danny Danziger, *Independent*, 16 December 1991.)

1946 — November 15 (Friday) — J.G. Ballard's 16th birthday. "I once climbed through the fence around a British airfield and crept into one of the parking bays protected by an earth embankment. Security was lax, and none of the service crews was around. There was a four-engined bomber with a tricycle landing gear—probably a Liberator—and I swung myself through the open ventral hatchway, and sat surrounded by the clutter of equipment inside the cockpit. Today I would have been arrested, held in a child remand centre... In fact, I had touched nothing and damaged nothing, and merely gazed through a small window into a dream." (Ballard, *Miracles of Life*, p138.) It is likely the airfield he referred to was RAF Oakington, situated in meadowland five miles northwest of the centre of Cambridge. "Airports and airfields have always held a special magic, gateways to the infinite possibilities that only the sky can offer. In 1946, when I first came to England, a dark and derelict shell of a country, I used to dream of the runways of Wake Island and Midway, stepping stones that would carry me back across the Pacific to the China of my childhood. At school in Cambridge, and later as a medical student at King's College, I would flee all that fossilised Gothic self-immersion and ride a borrowed motorcycle to the American airbases at Mildenhall and Lakenheath, happy to stare through the wire at the lines of silver bombers and transport planes." (Ballard, "Airports," *Blueprint no. 142*, September 1997.)

1946 — November 21 (Thursday) — The film *The Best Years of Our Lives*, directed by William Wyler, starring Dana Andrews, Myrna Loy, Fredric March and a large cast, had its premiere in New York City. (Its London premiere would be on 5 March 1947.) "DP: There's a scene where Dana Andrews is sitting in among the junked American bombers. Do you remember that scene? JGB: Yes, of course I do. That was a great movie too. DP: When I saw that I thought, 'How Ballardian this scene is!' A whole field full of wrecked World War II bombers, and the hero has a kind of fugue and flashback as he sits in the bomb-aimer's cockpit... JGB: Of course, I'd also sat inside wrecked planes in Shanghai, both before the war and after; and there were plenty of airfields in Cambridge, where I was at school in the late 40s. One had semi-derelict planes just stacked around the dispersal areas: we used to climb through the wire and get into these planes. So, all that sort of stuff came from first-hand experience. But I liked the scene, yes: that great field of bombers being dismantled for cheap housing, or whatever it was." (Ballard, interviewed by David Pringle, 30 October 1995.)

1946 — December? — Brian Helliwell, the school "bad boy" and Jimmy Ballard's friend, seems to have left The Leys before the year's end. It is not known if they ever met again—perhaps not. Helliwell would join the Navy, where he would serve as a medical orderly, and he would make an early marriage to a girl called Hazel in Leeds in 1951, fathering two children by her. Tragically, he would die in a van crash in 1959, slamming into a wall late at night, probably while drunk, and breaking his neck. Is it too much to make the claim that traces of Helliwell are to be found all over Ballard's fiction, in the teenage tearaway protagonists of stories like "Chronopolis," "The Ultimate City" (where the youth is called Halloway) and the novel *Rushing to Paradise*, in the character of Vaughan in *Crash*, and even in the character of Basie in *Empire of the Sun* (named after a jazzman)?

1946 — Another, younger, schoolboy in Cambridge had experiences of the place which must have been very similar to Ballard's: "By this time I was at school in Cambridge... I had been disappointed at being sent to the Perse, instead of going back to London, and there were many things I disliked about the place once I got there. Some were endemic to boarding-school life: the lack of privacy, the petty regulations. Others were a consequence of spartan post-war conditions. The food was often vile, none of it viler than the dehydrated egg—'yellow peril'—with which we were frequently compelled to start the day. The harsh winter of 1946-7 and the accompanying fuel crisis left me with my hands covered with chilblains. Still, it could all have been far worse. Discipline was relatively mild, bullying was no more than a minor hazard. And there were compensations, or at any rate consolations—new scenes and new interests... My addiction to the movies grew steadily stronger... I explored the resources of Cambridge, whenever I could, from the big picture houses in the centre of town to an out-of-bounds fleapit in Mill Road where most of the films they showed were leftovers from the thirties... I was learning about better films, too. Roger Manvell's book *Film* (a bible for my generation) steered me towards the big highbrow names. I saw my first French films at the Arts Cinema in Cambridge..." (John Gross, *A Double Thread*, 2001, p107-109.)

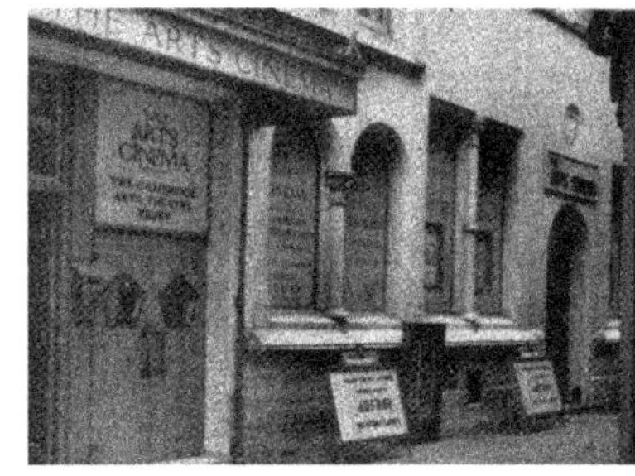
The Arts Cinema

1947

1947 — January 28 (Tuesday) — "LONDON, Jan. 28. Snowdrifts piled up by the blizzard which swept southern England last night threaten to isolate many villages. Up to six inches of snow fell in an hour in some parts. Two deaths due to the cold have been reported. Nearly 2,000,000 London homes had their gas pressure severely curtailed and electricity cuts were widespread." (*Sydney Morning Herald*, 29 January 1947.)

1947 — January? — Edward Glover, Freudian psychoanalyst, published a much expanded edition of his book *War, Sadism and Pacifism* (London: Allen & Unwin, dated 1946 but seemingly delayed until 1947), enlarged by some ten chapters from the original 1933 edition. It was subtitled "Further Essays on Group Psychology and War." In the new final chapter he wrote: "[T]he actual and potential destructiveness of the atomic bomb plays straight into the hands of the Unconscious. The most cursory study of dream-life and of the phantasies of the insane shows that ideas of world-destruction (more accurately destruction of what the world symbolizes) are latent in the unconscious mind. And since the atomic bomb is less a weapon of war than a weapon of extermination it is well adapted to the more bloodthirsty phantasies with which man is secretly preoccupied during phases of acute frustration. Nagasaki destroyed by the magic of science is the nearest man has yet approached to the realization of dreams that even during the safe immobility of sleep are accustomed to develop into nightmares of anxiety." (Glover, p274.) The young Ballard would be impressed by this passage, and would quote phrases from it several times over the years.

1947 — February 12 (Wednesday) — Mrs Edna Ballard wrote to Dr Humphrey, headmaster of The Leys school, Cambridge, saying: "I am shortly leaving England to join my husband in Shanghai. ... I have left Devon & until I sail, probably on February 22 I shall be staying in West Bromwich." She added that her son, James, would be in the care of his grandfather while she stayed in China. (She would take her daughter with her.)

1947 — February 18 (Tuesday) — In Britain, this was "the seventeenth successive day without sunshine anywhere in the country, the longest sunless period since 1880." (Simpson, *Days from a Different World*, p207.)

1947 — March 3 (Monday) — "LONDON, March 3. After the worst February since 1895, England has basked in brilliant sunshine for the first three days of March. ... Temperatures are still low, and many villages are still isolated by snow. Some of them have been cut off for more than six weeks." (*Sydney Morning Herald*, 4 March 1947.)

1947 — March 4 (Tuesday) — The *Strathmore*, a passenger steamer of the P&O line, departed from Southampton. Aboard were Mrs Edna Ballard, aged 41, and her daughter Margaret Ann Ballard, aged nine. Their destination was Shanghai, China, and their "last address in the United Kingdom" was given as 11 Lodge Road, West Bromwich. They had been in England since December 1945, a period of about a year and three months.

1947 — March 15 (Saturday) — The Thames flooded and there was other widespread flooding in England as the exceptionally harsh winter ended in a thaw. "After three months of ice, the thaw came suddenly, with floods of a size never seen before. Forty miles of the River Severn overflowed, the Thames near Windsor was suddenly three miles wide, crops were ruined, livestock was drowned... The following spring and summer were glorious." (Alan Jenkins, *The Forties*, 1977, p68.)

1947 — April 30 (Wednesday) — The Summer term was due to begin at The Leys school, Cambridge, on this day, according to a school report issued at the end of the previous, Spring, term. The report showed that J.G. Ballard was ranked fourth in a form of 22 boys, "V1 Mod." By this time, his closest friend at The Leys may have been Robin Chand, the son of a doctor from Nottingham (his Indian-sounding forename, Dhun, seems not to have been much used), who also had a younger brother at the school, Paul Chand. Both the Chand boys had an interest in the arts, Robin an aspiring painter and Paul perhaps more inclined towards the theatre; however both, no doubt urged by their father, were intending to pursue medical careers.

1947 — Spring? — "Academically Jim seems to have got on very well at The Leys. There were some gaps in his education but he made up the ground..." (Raymond Tait, "J.G. Ballard at The Leys School," *Deep Ends 2014*, p56.) "At school— The Leys —we even attempted Latin conversation. We all agreed that we would far rather take a Latin oral than the French oral, which we detested." (Ballard, interviewed by Thomas Frick, 1983.) "Latin? My first love (at school in England—in the late 40's we even attempted Latin conversation—heroically pointless)." (Ballard, postcard to Angharad Ryder, circa September 1987.) "Sitting the School Certificate in England after the war, I and a group of boys tried to substitute a Latin oral for the French, which we all detested." (Ballard, in Antonia Fraser, ed., *The Pleasure of Reading*, 1992.)

1947 — June 24 (Tuesday) — "A pilot named Kenneth Arnold took off from Chehalis, Washington, in a high-altitude plane to look for a lost C.46 transport that had crashed in the Cascade

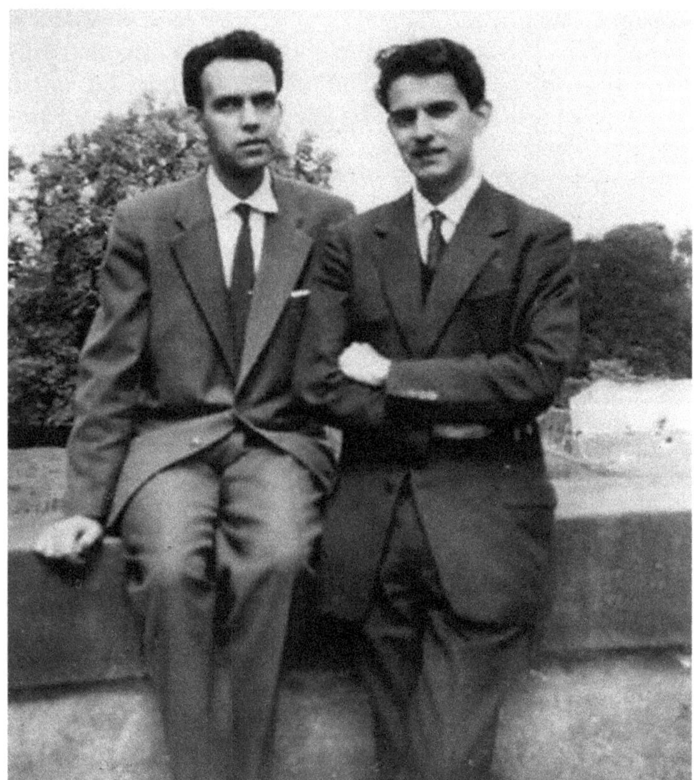
L-R: Brothers Dhun Robin and Paul Chand

Mountains. He reported 'two bright flashes and nine gleaming objects' flying at a vast speed towards Mount Rainier: they resembled 'saucers skimming over water'." (Alan Jenkins, *The Forties*, 1977, p181.) Thus was born the legend of the UFOs (unidentifed flying objects) commonly known as "flying saucers."

1947 — July 3 (Thursday) — "Husband much keyed up about the flying saucers over the American skies. One of his pet subjects. Papers can't report enough about them to satisfy him. Just like a small boy about it." (Edie Rutherford, diary, *Our Hidden Lives*, p416.)

1947 — July 27 (Sunday) — Mr James Ballard wrote from Shanghai to Dr Humphrey, headmaster of The Leys school, Cambridge, saying that he did not want his son, James, to serve in the army after the completion of his Sixth Form years and requesting the school's help to find him a place at a University of Cambridge college. "I am not in favour of him going into the Army if it can be avoided. He has already lost 2½ years of normal education whilst in a Japanese internment camp, and I am informed that this is sufficient to exempt him from any further interruption to his scholastic career. I would very much like to know whether or not exemption on these grounds can be obtained. I understand from his letters that he is keenly interested in biology, and if he should continue to show a liking for this subject, I can think of few careers that I should prefer for him."

1947 — Summer — During vacations, Ballard stayed in the home of his maternal grandfather, Archibald Johnstone, Teacher of Music, 11 Lodge Road, West Bromwich, Staffordshire. "My mother and sister went back to China, and when I wasn't at school in Cambridge I stayed with my grandparents near

Birmingham..." (Ballard, interviewed by David Pringle, 24 July 1981.) "[F]or the next year or so I spent the holidays with my grandparents in West Bromwich, the lowest point in my life that I had by then explored, several miles at least below the sea level of mental health." (Ballard, *Miracles of Life*, p121.) "Life was intensely narrow for them, living in a large, three-storey house where the rooms were always dark, filled with heavy, uncomfortable furniture and interior doors with stained-glass panels. Food rationing was in force, but everything seemed to be rationed, the air we breathed, hope of a better world, and the brief glimpses of the sun..." (Ballard, *Miracles*, p49.) "Forty years ago, according to [Ballard], the typical public sound in Britain, in bus shelters and shops and railway stations was 'of children crying' through misery or rejection or neglect by parents who were too tired and poor to help them." (Ballard, interviewed by Lindsay Mackie, *Scotsman*, 14 March 1988.)

1947 — Summer — Clearly 16-year-old Ballard was very unhappy. His brief comments on "the lowest point in my life" and "below the sea level of mental health" may tie in with a hint from elsewhere that there was a serious falling-out with his grandparents which led to Ballard being banished from their home for a short time and staying with the family of his Shanghai friend, Bill Weight. This information was supplied by Desmond Power, who knew Bill Weight in later years when he had moved to Canada: "I learned from Bill that his family and the Ballards had been close friends in Shanghai and remained so in Lunghua. Of course, Bill and Jim Ballard were pals in camp. In England after the war Jim was expelled from his home by his parents [sic] for gross misbehaviour. The Weights took him in, but he continued on with his bad ways to which Bill was witness. I did not press Bill for the details." Although Desmond said "parents," it must surely have been his grandparents that young Ballard offended, as his father remained in China for several years after the war and his mother had gone to rejoin her husband there in March 1947. What on earth had JGB done, or said, that caused the trouble? Perhaps it was his grandmother, whom he would describe as "a small and ungenerous woman," who took the main offence, but the nature of JGB's transgression remains unknown. "[T]he reason Bill gave for Ballard moving into the Weights' residence was his own family's refusal to accept him for his 'unspeakable' behaviour. ... As for being unable to remember Ballard's misdeeds, it's not a question of my not remembering what Bill Weight told me. He was clearly upset by them, and I didn't press Bill for details." (Power, e-mails to D. Pringle, November 2011.) Unfortunately, Bill Weight, the nearest "witness" to whatever had happened, died in Vancouver, Canada, on 29 December 2002.

1947 — Summer — It is tempting to speculate as to what Ballard's teenage "misdeeds" were, but we lack any real evidence. There is no record of any trouble he might have been in at The Leys: the problem seems to have been domestic. He would describe his grandfather as "very straitlaced [and] puritanical," and quite probably his "ungenerous" grandmother fitted that description to an even greater degree. Perhaps it was some kind of sexual misdemeanour on James's part that offended them. It may have been serious bad behaviour; we do not know, but it is possible that it was something quite trivial, such as a liking for nude sunbathing. It was a warm summer in 1947, and in later years, particularly in the long hot summer of 1976, JGB would be known to surprise his neighbours by sunbathing *au naturel* in his back garden. ("I remember Daddy thinking it would be nice to sunbathe naked in the garden and the neighbours being really shocked" — Fay Ballard, quoted in the *Telegraph Magazine*, 14 September 1996.)

1947 — August 15 (Friday) — India gained independence after some 200 years of mainly British rule. Jawaharlal Nehru became the first Prime Minister.

1947 — August 25 (Monday) — "Alexander Neill's father was a strict Scottish schoolmaster, who used to spank his children rather repetitiously. Young Neill developed a fear of his father that haunted him until early manhood. Years later, when he began studying child psychology, he decided to found a school of his own, to produce children who would go through life free from fear and who would never need to be psychoanalyzed. ... Summerhill is Britain's most progressive school. At his school ('That dreadful school,' he likes to call it), there is no discipline, except for such rules as the children lay down in their weekly meetings. The children are permitted to swear, steal, smash things up, masturbate, lie, play hookey or do anything else that, in schoolmaster Neill's judgment, will rid them of inhibitions... Sex arouses the most curiosity about Summerhill. It is discussed freely and unemotionally. There is no specific sex instruction, but a child is given simple, straightforward answers to anything he asks about. Headmaster Neill is convinced that guilt connected with masturbation is at the root of most 'antisocial' children's disturbances. Says Neill: 'Freedom in masturbation means glad, happy, eager children who are not much interested in masturbation.'" (*Time*, 25 August 1947.)

1947 — August — Nigel Balchin's novel-in-play-form, *Lord, I Was Afraid*, was first published by Collins, London. JGB would read it at some point in the late 1940s. "I loved [Aldous Huxley's] *Ape and Essence* with its story within a film-script, and Nigel Balchin's experimental novel *Lord, I Was Afraid,* now totally forgotten, like the Auden/Isherwood plays, *Ascent of F6* and so on." (Ballard, letter to DP, 20 December 1993.)

1947 — September 1 (Monday) — "LONDON, Sept. 1. The meteorological office to-day reported that 261 hours of sunshine had been recorded in August at Kew. This is the highest figure since August, 1899, when 262 hours were recorded. In addition last month was the driest August since the records began 85 years ago. Some places in England have had no rain since July 28." (*Sydney Morning Herald*, 2 September 1947.)

1947 — September (mid) — Ballard entered the Sixth Form at The Leys school, Cambridge, about this time. Although he concentrated on scientific subjects as a Sixth-Former, he won an essay prize, but did not contribute to the school magazine. "As I entered the Science VIth at 16 I was spending more and more of my time in the school library." (Ballard, *Miracles of Life*, p130.) "I was very interested in psychiatry when I was at school, although I was interested in biology at the same time. In the Sixth Form I took physics, chemistry and biology. When I decided to go to university psychiatry, particularly psychoanalysis, had become my chief interest. You needed a medical degree in order to become a psychiatrist, and as I was interested in biology it seemed natural to study medicine." (Ballard, interviewed by David Pringle, 23 September 1984.)

1947 — November 15 (Saturday) — J.G. Ballard's 17th birthday. "England seemed a very strange country. Both the physical landscape and the social and psychological landscapes seemed fit subjects for analysis extremely constrained and rigid and repressed compared with the sort of background I had. To come from Shanghai, and from the war itself where everything had been shaken to its foundations, to come to England and find this narrow-minded and puritanical world—this was the most repressed society I'd ever known! I became intensely interested in psychoanalysis and began to devour every library I could lay my hands on when I was 16 or 17. I read a good number of Freud's major works then, plus a lot of other works on psychoanalysis and psychiatry. Jung of course, who is really a great imaginative novelist (in a sense, Freud is too). But while I was still at school I was reading not just psychoanalytical texts but all the leading writers of the day—Kafka of course, and Hemingway—the strange sort of goulash of writers and poets that you read when you're that age." (Ballard, interviewed by David Pringle, 24 July 1981.) "I spent far too much time reading in my teens... I try now to remember the novels of Tolstoy, Dostoevsky and Thomas Mann, but really I've forgotten them. At school, as a bet, I read the entire works of Shakespeare in a month—the plays blurred together into one huge historico-comical tragedy and it took me ages to disentangle Caliban from Sir Toby Belch, Malvolio from Macduff." (Ballard, "True Confessions," *Daily Telegraph*, 7th May 1994.)

1947 — November 27 (Thursday) — Ballard was interviewed by L.P. Wilkinson, the Senior Tutor at King's College, Cambridge. "Wilkinson liked what he saw of Jim but was reluctant to make any promises given that he already had fifty per cent more applications for October than he had places. ... In March [1948], however, Wilkinson wrote a fairly positive letter to Dr. Humphrey regarding the likelihood of Jim being offered a place for October 1949, subject of course to his being properly qualified by examination. The intended course of study was to be the Natural Sciences Tripos, Part 1 (Chemistry, Botany and Zoology)." (Raymond Tait, "J.G. Ballard at The Leys School," *Deep Ends 2014*, p56-57.)

1947 — December 16 (Tuesday) — "LONDON, Dec. 16. 'One can almost hear the clanging as thicker plates are riveted to the iron curtain,' is a current comment on the complete failure of the Big Four Conference. On the formal motion of General Marshall, the conference early last evening adjourned indefinitely. The fate of post-war Germany and Austria, two and a half years after the end of the war in Europe, remains undecided. General Marshall took the formal responsibility for moving the adjournment, but only the Communist Press fails to recognise that this step was only a natural consequence of the bitter accusations against the Western Powers by Mr Molotov (Russia) on Friday which produced an insoluble crisis." (*Sydney Morning Herald*, 17 December 1947.)

1947 — Philip K. Dick (b. 16 December 1928) and Ursula Kroeber (b. 21 October 1929; later known as Ursula K. Le Guin), science-fiction writers to be, both graduated from Berkeley High School in Berkeley, California. They were members of the same graduating class (1947) but apparently did not know each other at the time—it was a large school.

1948

1948 — January 5 (Monday) — Dr Alfred Kinsey and his colleagues at Indiana University published *Sexual Behavior in the Human Male*, soon to become famous as "the Kinsey Report." Based on many interviews, it was the first major study of sexual habits, and would sell more than 200,000 copies.

1948 — January 29 (Thursday) — "LONDON, Jan. 29. Britain's official executioner, Albert Pierrepoint, commenced the hangings in Hamelin Prison of 21 German war criminals to-day. The Germans include 14 Gestapo men convicted of the Stalagluft III murders in March, 1944, in which four Australian, two New Zealand, and 44 Allied air force officers were killed after an escape bid. It is the biggest collective execution yet held in the British zone." (*Sydney Morning Herald*, 30 January 1948.)

1948 — January 30 (Friday) — Death of Mohandas Gandhi (b. 1869), Indian nationalist and spiritual leader, murdered by a fellow Hindu at age 78. "I have felt very upset today as Mahatma Gandhi has been assassinated. The story is on the front page of the *Birmingham Mail* and it made me cry. There is a big photo of him which I am cutting out to stick in my big Boots Scribbling Diary which I had for Christmas. The paper says that Gandhi was shot dead with four revolver bullets fired from close range by a young Hindu." (Brian Williams, aged 12, Birmingham, diary.)

1948 — March 16 (Tuesday) — "LONDON, March 16. The ban on pleasure trips abroad would be eased from May 1, the Chancellor of the Exchequer, Sir Stafford Cripps, announced in the House of Commons this afternoon. He said tourists would be allowed to visit Austria, Denmark, France, Italy, the Netherlands, Norway, Portugal, Switzerland, and possibly a few other countries. Expenses, apart from the fare paid in Britain, would not be allowed to exceed £35 for adults and £25 for children annually." (*Sydney Morning Herald*, 17 March 1948.) This would affect the Ballard family.

1948 — April 6 (Tuesday) — Mr James Ballard (46), his wife Edna (42) and daughter Margaret (10), of 31 Amherst Avenue, Shanghai, flew on this day from Honolulu to San Francisco with 145 pounds of luggage in six bags. They had presumably left Shanghai a week or so earlier—and Mrs Ballard and her daughter would never return there. "I was born in Shanghai and brought up there as a child. I well remember the city in the late forties, driving from our house in the western suburbs along Bubbling Well Road, passing all the grand houses on the way and deciding which one I liked best—Spanish with green tiles, or neo-Tudor to remind one of 'home'—past the Majestic Cinema (very modern movement), playing *National Velvet*, past the Park Hotel (so tall) and on to the Nanjing Road to visit Wing On's, the department store." (Margaret [Ballard] Richardson, bdonline.co.uk, 2 June 2006.)

1948 — April 14 (Wednesday) — The United States carried out a nuclear bomb test at Eniwetok Atoll, in the Marshall Islands, for the first time. (Two further explosions would follow there, on 30 April and 14 May 1948, all as part of Operation Sandstone.)

1948 — May — There arrived in food-rationed Britain the first large supply of tins of "snoek," a cheap South African fish. "The Ministry of Food celebrated by putting up snoek posters and publicising eight snoek recipes, including a concoction to go with salad immortally called snoek piquante." (David Kynaston, *A World to Build*, p247.) The public was unenthusiastic.

1948 — May 14 (Friday) — Israel was proclaimed as an independent state, in Tel Aviv, as British rule in the Mandate of Palestine came to an end.

1948 — June 1 (Tuesday) — "LONDON, June 1. With the lifting of the Government's ban on pleasure motoring to-day, Britain's roads will be free again to the country's two million car owners and half a million motor cyclists." (*Sydney Morning Herald*, 2 June 1948.)

1948 — June 3 (Thursday) — James and Edna Ballard arrived back in Britain aboard the liner *Queen Elizabeth*, from New York. Their destination address was 11 Lodge Road, West Bromwich, Staffs. "[W]hen my parents returned from Shanghai on a visit, my mother stepping from their new Buick, dressed in the latest New York fashions, I thought rather critically of how un-English they seemed. I knew, as I thought this, that it marked how English I was becoming, despite all my efforts." (Ballard, *Miracles of Life*, p135-136.)

1948 — June 25 (Friday) — "SINGAPORE, June 25. Shanghai went on a wild buying spree to-day as the China dollar made a sensational plunge in the black market to an exchange rate of four million to one United States dollar—a drop of more than 30 per cent in 24 hours. Unfavourable reports from the civil war front, especially the fall of the Honan capital of Kaifeng, coupled with official statements that the Communists now outnumber Government troops, are believed to have been responsible for the panic." (*Sydney Morning Herald*, 26 June 1948.)

1948 — Summer — "My father remained in Shanghai, returning for a brief visit to England in 1947 [sic], when we toured Europe in his large American car." (Ballard, *Miracles*, p84.) "My father ... took us on a motoring holiday through France and Italy in the spring [sic] of '47 [sic]. I remember being amazed by the abundance that one found in France—there was no rationing and people looked more confident, lives were brighter and more cheerful." (Ballard, interviewed by Danny Danziger, 16 December 1991.) On the subject of middle-class holidays abroad at this time: "If you had enough petrol to get to a port, or an airport which carried cars, you could make a £25—or even a £35—holiday allowance go a long way, for once abroad you could buy foreign petrol. The claustrophobic British drove through the almost empty roads of France, staying at one-star hotels, eating and drinking themselves sick, scoffing a whole week's ration of eggs in one *hors d'oeuvres*, and acquiring new tastes for scampi, bouillabaisse, sea urchins and blackbird paté." (Alan Jenkins, *The Forties*, 1977, p140.)

1948 — September 1 (Wednesday) — Robert Mitchum, Hollywood actor, was arrested for marijuana possession. (He would be convicted, and would serve a short term in prison.) "Marijuana, a drug made from Indian hemp, is sometimes grown furtively on vacant city lots. Medical research has been unable to find positive evidence that it is habit-forming, but it has its constant users. It is said to produce a state of exhilaration in which time seems to move slowly." ("Crisis in Hollywood," *Time*, 13 September 1948.)

1948 — September 16 (Thursday) — Mr James Ballard, who was still in England (but probably about to leave, to return to Shanghai) wrote to Mr J. Stirland, one of his son James's masters at The Leys school, Cambridge. His letter was headed: "Spangate, Bay Estate, Aldwick, Bognor Regis. 16 Sept. 1948." It said: "Dear Mr Stirland, I understand that my son is anxious to concentrate his efforts during the coming term on the subjects which he will be taking in the Higher School Certificate, namely, Chemistry, Biology, & English, and that he would prefer to discontinue his study of Physics as a subject. I am writing to inform you that this meets with my approval. Yours sincerely, J. Ballard." (Raymond Tait, "J.G. Ballard at The Leys School," *Deep Ends 2014*, p57.)

1948 — September 19 (Sunday) — Battle of Britain Day. "LONDON, Sept. 19. A twin-engined Mosquito yesterday crashed into a line of cars and cyclists on their way to an air display at Manston, near Margate. It killed the pilot, the navigator, and ten civilians. Altogether five aircraft crashed at displays throughout Britain yesterday in the 'Battle of Britain' celebrations." (*Sydney Morning Herald*, 20 September 1948.)

1948 — September 22 (Wednesday) — Mrs Edna Ballard wrote to Mr R. Morris, her son James's housemaster at The Leys school, Cambridge. Her letter was headed: "Spangate, The Fairway, Aldwick Bay, Sussex. Tel. Pagham 75. Sept. 22nd, 1948." It said: "Dear Mr Morris, I am sorry I am rather late in notifying you of our change of address to the above. I expect to be in England for at least another year, thus relieving my parents of the responsibility of acting as guardians to James. Would you be kind enough to notify the school office of the change in address? With many thanks, Yours sincerely, Edna Ballard." (Raymond Tait, "J.G. Ballard at The Leys School," *Deep Ends 2014*, p58.) JGB would later say: "My mother returned to England with my sister in 1949 [sic], and rented a house in the Aldwick Bay estate, to the west of Bognor." (Ballard, *Miracles of Life*, 2008, p122.)

1948 — November 9 (Tuesday) — "SHANGHAI, Nov. 9. Three powerful Communist columns to-day converged on the Government's main Central China stronghold of Suchow after cracking the Government's defence system farther north. Foreign and Chinese observers predict that the Communists will overrun virtually the whole of China north of the Yangtze, and take Nanking before the end of the year." (*Sydney Morning Herald*, 10 November 1948.) Mr James Ballard, once more in Shanghai, no doubt followed the news.

1948 — November 15 (Monday) — J.G. Ballard's 18th birthday. "'It is difficult to remember just how formal middleclass life was in the 1930s and 40s,' he says... 'I wore a suit and tie at home from the age of 18. One dressed for breakfast. One lived in a very formal way and emotions were not paraded. And my childhood was not unusual.'" (Ballard, interviewed by Andrew Billen, *Observer*, 7 August 1994.) "I took up painting in my youth and found I hadn't any talent for it, but I always really regretted that I didn't, because I think I would've been far happier as a painter... I would love to have been a painter in the tradition of the surrealist painters who I admire so much. Sometimes I think all my writing is really the substitute work of an unfulfilled painter." (Ballard, interviewed by Richard Kadrey & Suzanne Stefanac, *salonmagazine.com*, 2 September 1997.) "I was very keen on art—I was always sketching and copying... In the late 1940s in England a certain controversy still lingered over Picasso, Braque, Matisse, while the surrealists were utterly beyond the critical pale. The surrealists were a revelation, though reproductions of Chirico, Dali, Ernst were hard to come by and tended to be found in psychiatric textbooks. I devoured them." (Ballard, interviewed by Jeannette Baxter, January 2004.)

1948 — December 6 (Monday) — James Norman Hall, American writer, reported from Tahiti: "An immense buried treasure is being recovered from the lagoon of the island of Bora Bora where the U.S. had a base during World War II. The treasure consists of empty Coca-Cola bottles dumped by Army and Navy personnel during the years 1942-45. The natives have dived up more than 30,000 to date, which they sell to soft-drink emporiums in Papeete at 3 francs per bottle." (*Time*, 6 December 1948.)

1948 — December 7 (Tuesday) — "The 'New York Times' Shanghai correspondent says Britons in Shanghai are planning to remain, 'come what may' in the Chinese civil war. The correspondent says British men and women, organised on a war footing, are setting up a siege camp for 4,000 Britishers still in the city. Cots, food, and medicines have been moved into large warehouses on the waterfront so the Royal Navy can evacuate them as a last resort. The correspondent says: 'Local English businessmen would only leave in the face of full-scale warfare in the city or its burning. The British stake here and in China is too great to be relinquished lightly. British businessmen believe the Communists will have to trade with somebody who can ship goods into China's Pacific ports.'" (*Sydney Morning Herald*, 8 December 1948.) Mr James Ballard was one of those determined to stay.

1948 — "*Ulysses* overwhelmed me when I read it in the sixth form, and from then on there seemed to be no point in writing anything that didn't follow doggedly on the heels of Joyce's masterpiece." (Ballard, in Antonia Fraser, ed., *The Pleasure of Reading*, 1992.) "James Joyce's *Ulysses* opened my eyes to an infinitely richer and more challenging world. Here, I knew, was the authentic voice of heroic modernism that rang through the European and American writers I had devoured at school —Dostoevsky, Rimbaud, Kafka, Camus and Hemingway... It might be set in a single day in a provincial European city, but in Joyce's eye Dublin was the whole world, and that single day lasted longer than a century. Joyce's text seemed to exhaust every conceivable possibility of narrative technique—in fact, technique became the real subject of the novel (a dead end, as the post-modernist writers demonstrate). *Ulysses* convinced me to give up medicine and become a writer, but it was the wrong example for me, an old-fashioned story-teller at heart, and it wasn't until I discovered the surrealists that I found the right model." (Ballard, "James the Great," *Guardian*, 11 October 1990.)

1948 — Raymond Chandler's *The Big Sleep* (1939) first appeared as a Penguin Book in the UK. (It was followed by *Farewell My Lovely* in 1949; *Trouble is My Business* in 1950; *The High Window* in 1951; *The Lady in the Lake* in 1952; and others in later years.) "There was so little competition in those days that I think almost every paperback I read was a Penguin. Raymond Chandler was among the first authors I bought—that was when I was about 17, and I still think he is absolutely brilliant. I remember the green jackets they had on their crime titles, and I must have a couple of those Chandlers around even after all this time." (Ballard, "My First Penguin Paperback," *The Times*, 23 February 1995.)

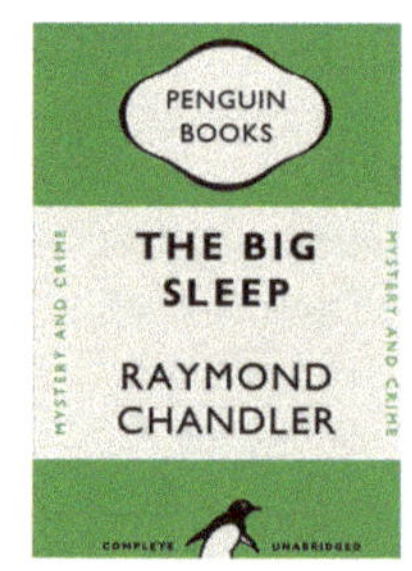

1949

1949 — January 2 (Sunday) — "LONDON, Jan. 2. A heavy storm last night threw the *Queen Mary* on to a sandbar outside Cherbourg, France. The liner remained aground for 12 hours. This was the climax to a day of gales and blizzards, which ushered in the New Year in Western Europe. ... Winds blowing at 80 miles an hour hit parts of Britain's south coast after the wildest New Year's Eve in living memory. At Shoreham-by-sea, Sussex, last night, a tremendous gust blew a double-decker bus off a bridge into the river Adur 20ft below." (*Sydney Morning Herald*, 3 January 1949.)

1949 — January 19 (Wednesday) — Chiang Kai-shek's beleaguered Nationalist Government moved the capital of China from Nanking to Canton.

1949 — March 9 (Wednesday) — Henri-Georges Clouzot's film *Manon* was first released in France. The childlike actress Cécile Aubry (b. 1928), making her debut, played the title part. "I remember Carné's *Les Enfants du Paradis*, a wonderful romp of wartime collaborators led by Arletty; Clouzot's *Le Corbeau* and *Manon* (with the divine child-woman Cécile Aubry, apparently no older than I was and impossible to get out of my 17-year-old [sic] head)..." (Ballard, *Miracles of Life*, p128.)

1949 — March 23-25 (Wednesday-Friday) — At the Cultural and Scientific Conference for World Peace, held at the Waldorf-Astoria Hotel in New York, American Communists and sympathizers, including the composer Aaron Copland, welcomed a delegation of top Soviets. Among those present was the British writer Olaf Stapledon, the only delegate from the UK able to attend.

1949 — April 18 (Monday) — The Republic of Ireland was officially proclaimed in Dublin on the 33rd anniversary of the 1916 Easter Rising. So Eire, formerly known as the Irish Free State, became a republic, and withdrew from the British Commonwealth.

1949 — April 20 (Wednesday) — Royal Navy frigate HMS *Amethyst* sailed up the Yangtse River towards Nanking to evacuate British Commonwealth refugees escaping the advance of the Mao Tse-tung's Communist forces. Under sudden heavy fire from Communist Chinese artillery on the north shore of the Yangtse, she ran aground off Rose Island. A shell mortally wounded her captain; her first lieutenant took over, but was injured too. The *Amethyst* lost 22 men killed and 31 wounded in the ordeal. Rescue attempts by the Royal Navy in the following days would result in another 23 British sailors killed. An assistant naval attaché from the British Embassy at Nanking, Lieutenant John Kerans, would arrive and take command.

1949 — April 24 (Sunday) — "SHANGHAI, April 24. Spearheads of the Chinese Communist armies are now racing south and east beyond conquered Nanking. They threaten to cut off Shanghai, fourth largest city in the world, which is expected to fall in a matter of days. The Communists entered Nanking in force at dawn to-day taking over from the Communist underground fifth column after two days of looting and panic. The whole Nationalist Yangtse defence line has now collapsed." (*Sydney Morning Herald*, 25 April 1949.)

1949 — April 26 (Tuesday) — After an aborted rescue attempt, HMS *Amethyst* was able to refloat, and to anchor ten miles upstream in the Yangtse. Negotiations between Lieutenant Kerans and the Communist forces, to let the ship leave, would drag on for weeks: there was a tense, 103-day stand-off until the frigate would make a daring escape on 30 July.

1949 — May 15 (Sunday) — "HONG KONG, May 15. Shanghai's defenders have withdrawn to a new line averaging no more than five miles from the southern and western borders of the city. ... British Overseas Airways flying-boats stood by in Hong Kong to-day to begin the evacuation of the remaining Britons who wish to leave Shanghai." (*Sydney Morning Herald,* 16 May 1949.)

1949 — May 24 (Tuesday) — A middle-aged English couple, Billy and Gladys Hawkings, refused to leave their large suburban house at Hungjao on the western outskirts of Shanghai. "The attack on the city was in fact launched from the Hawkingses' grounds at Hungjao, which had been under fire for three nights before the final Communist assault. The phone, electricity and water had all been cut off. From time to time heavy firing started up in the daytime, obviously from Communist positions near the airfield or golf course; when this happened Billy and Gladys retired to their bullet-proof redoubt and read by candlelight. Whenever it was time for the BBC world news, 'we went upstairs, sat on the floor in a corner of the drawing room waiting for the magic words, "This is London Calling".' Then they would crawl back to the pantry. The Communists had discovered that some Nationalists were hiding in the grounds ... and without warning there was a lot of banging on the front door and shouts of 'Open up!' [Their servant] Lau Wu went to see what was happening, and came back looking terrified. 'The Communists gave me this, missee,' he said. It was a letter on rough paper headed 'The Advance Unit of the People's Liberation Army,' warning the Hawkingses to move from the house, as the area would be shelled that night. The shelling lasted for three hours. At times Hawkings could hear men moving about outside, but could see nothing. The Communists were, as he discovered later, digging trenches and gun emplacements within a hundred yards of the main house. Finally the Nationalists must have surrendered, for Hawkings could hear shouting and what seemed like the sound of men being marched away." (Noel Barber, *The Fall of Shanghai*, p144-145.)

1949 — May 25 (Wednesday) — "With firing liable to start at any moment, the Hawkingses were virtually trapped in their hide-out for three days and nights. They had a small paraffin stove to heat tins of soup and cups of tea to supplement the iron rations of corned beef and other tinned food. When the firing finally stopped—it had been quiet for three or four hours in the early hours of Wednesday the 25th—Hawkings went to the drawing room to look outside. At the last minute Gladys accompanied him. Just as well, for outside the window was a face silently staring in. Gladys almost shrieked, but in the dim light the Chinese smiled... Billy unbolted the heavy front door and opened it. Then he called out, and three Chinese in green uniforms came running round and bowed politely. When Gladys spoke to them in Chinese they beamed and smiled and insisted on shaking hands. No, they wanted nothing, they were just making sure no enemy troops were hiding... After that Billy and Gladys were able to go upstairs, even sit on the veranda and watch the Red Army troops move on to take Shanghai, thousands of them, often with mules or horses." (Noel Barber, *The Fall of Shanghai*, p145.)

1949 — May (late) — Shanghai fell to the Communist Red Army. There was sporadic fighting, but for the most part the Kuomintang troops just melted away. "My parents, like all the people of their generation, like all the old Far East hands, were absolutely convinced that the zealous Maoist phase would last all of the time it took the commissars to put away their guns, climb down from their tanks and walk into the bars and brothels of downtown Shanghai. It was a big shock when that didn't happen. The thing about the Chinese—for whom I have an enormous respect, as I do the Japanese—is that they're tremendously industrious people. If people are naturally industrious, if their work tempo is three times ours, they're going to find sooner or later some means of expressing this. Maybe the Hong Kong style of capitalism actually serves the Chinese temperament better than the more puritanical and restricted economic life that communism offers." (Ballard, interviewed by David Pringle, 1979.) Mr James Ballard remained in the city at the time of the takeover by Mao Tse-tung's forces: "[H]e spent about a year under the new communist rulers—he had quite a struggle, but he was eventually able to get out, via Canton, and returned to England." (Ballard, "Grand Tour," *BBC Radio 4*, 17 November 1990.)

1949 — June 8 (Wednesday) — *Nineteen Eighty-Four*, George Orwell's last novel, first appeared in London. "In its first year over 400,000 copies were sold in Britain and America." (Michael Shelden, *Friends of Promise*, 1989, p216.) "The phrases and concepts that Orwell minted have become essential fixtures of political language, still potent after decades of use and misuse: newspeak, Big Brother, the thought police, Room 101, the two minutes' hate, doublethink, unperson, memory hole, telescreen, 2+2=5 and the ministry of truth." (Dorian Lynskey, *Observer*, 19 May 2019.)

1949 — June 17 (Friday) — Ballard sat an exam for entry into King's College, University of Cambridge. "Jim duly took the Kings College Entry Examination in Elementary Chemistry and Elementary Biology plus the General Paper on Friday 17 June 1949 and passed." (Raymond Tait, "J.G. Ballard at The Leys School," *Deep Ends 2014*, p57.) "I was impatient with England's mental aspect, the slow and provincial and unimaginative way that people's minds worked, the obsession with petty class distinctions, the lack of interest in 20th-century ideas. At Cambridge, I remember mentioning to one of the senior dons that I was interested in psychoanalysis and this was greeted with gales of laughter. In 1949 Sigmund Freud was still regarded as hilarious." (Ballard, interviewed by Lynn Barber, 27 December 1981.)

1949 — July 14 (Thursday) — Dr Stockdale, the Admissions Tutor at King's College, Cambridge, wrote to Dr Humphrey at The Leys about Ballard, saying "he had talked to various people and that he had now concluded that it was right to allow Jim to divert to medicine although the outcome was still not certain: 'This is a matter for the Council, but the boy starts off with two votes. The Tutor is taking up the matter of the quota with the Registrary [sic]. Wilkinson's view is that Ballard will have to wait for a casual vacancy, that he will get one all right, but that we shall not know definitely until October.'" (Raymond Tait, "J.G. Ballard at The Leys School," *Deep Ends 2014*, p57.)

1949 — July (late) — Ballard must have left his school around this time. "The big saving for me was that The Leys school was in Cambridge itself. I'd sneak off to the Arts Cinema to see all the French films of the 40s. I'd go to the Cambridge Film Society and soak myself in *The Cabinet of Dr Caligari* and all those experimental films of the 20s. And there were always art exhibitions of various kinds on in Cambridge. Also I had two or three friends among the boys in the class above mine who went up to Cambridge University to read medicine, and through them I had an early entry into Cambridge undergraduate life. [The principal friend alluded to was Robin Chand.] I used to visit the colleges. If I'd gone to a school out in a remote corner of Dorset or somewhere it would have been a bit of a strain, but being in Cambridge it was like being a member of a junior college there which was a big help to me." (Ballard, interviewed by David Pringle, 24 July 1981.) "In the three or four years of my late teens I devoured an entire library of classic and modern fiction, from Cervantes to Kafka, Jane Austen to Camus, often at the rate of a novel a day. Trying to find my way through the grey light of postwar, austerity Britain, it was a relief to step into the rich and larger-spirited world of the great novelists. I'm sure that the ground-plan of my imagination was drawn long before I went up to Cambridge in 1949... In fact I now regret that so much of my reading took place during my late adolescence, long before I had any adult experience of the world, long before I had fallen in love, learned to understand my parents, earned my own living and had time to reflect on the world's ways." (Ballard, in Antonia Fraser, ed., *The Pleasure of Reading*, 1992.)

1949 — July 31 (Sunday) — Lieutenant Kerans of HMS *Amethyst*, trapped for weeks in China, had decided to make a break for freedom after nightfall on Saturday. With his vessel under heavy fire from Communist forces on both sides of the Yangtse, he successfully dashed down the river and was able to rejoin the British fleet near Woosung the next morning. Kerans radioed a message to his commander-in-chief: "Have rejoined the fleet. Am south of Woosung. No damage or casualties. God save the King." (He would be regarded as a hero in Britain, and a film would be based on the exploit, *Yangtse Incident* [1957], starring Richard Todd as Kerans.)

1949 — August 4 (Thursday) — "HONG KONG, August 4. The situation in Shanghai is increasingly tense for foreigners, especially since the escape of the British sloop *Amethyst* from the Yangtse. Reports reaching Hong Kong from Shanghai say that the Chinese Communist administration grants exit permits freely, except to heads of firms. In their case, their employees must give consent to the permits. Foreign firms, if they close down, must pay one year's salary to all employees. The administration is making heavy land tax demands on foreigners." (*Sydney Morning Herald*, 5 August 1949.)

1949 — August — Ballard visited France, and in particular Paris, probably in this month, during his long vacation between leaving school and going up to King's College, Cambridge. "I remember the Louvre in 1949 when it was completely deserted, whereas today it is a theme-park where you can enjoy 'the Mona Lisa experience.'" (Ballard, interviewed by Hans Ulrich Obrist, January 2003.) On discovering the books of Henry Miller: "I can still remember reading *Tropic of Cancer* in its Olympia Press edition [sic] when I first went to Paris after the war, and being stunned by the no-nonsense frankness of Miller's language and by the novel's sheer zest and attack. The ozone of sex rushed through Miller's pages, and his prose had a life-hungry energy that made Molly Bloom's soliloquy at the close of Ulysses seem contrived and mannered... Miller, it seems to me, was the first proletarian writer to create a pornographic literature based on the language and sexual behaviour of the working class, and this was the source of his appeal to the American servicemen whose elbows jostled mine in the Paris bookshops of the Forties." (Ballard, "Erotica's First and Finest Working-Class Hero," *Independent on Sunday*, 10 March 1991.) Note: Olympia Press was not founded until 1953, so if he read *Tropic of Cancer* in this year, it would have been in an older Obelisk Press edition. Who accompanied him, if anyone? We do not know, but the Chand brothers, Robin and Paul, with their keen interest in the arts, are likely candidates.

1949 — August 29 (Monday) — The Soviet Union tested its first atomic bomb, in Kazakhstan. The news would not be made public until 23 September.

1949 — September 3 (Saturday) — Carol Reed's film *The Third Man*, with a script by Graham Greene, first went on release in the UK. Ballard saw it probably a month or so later. "A few days ago I saw *The Third Man*, the great Carol Reed film starring Orson Welles, Joseph Cotten and Alida Valli, and it was an extraordinarily moving experience. I first saw the film when it came out in 1949, when I was a medical student at Cambridge, dissecting cadavers in the afternoon before going to the cinema to relax in the evening... It was just four years after the end of the Second World War, and its picture of a shattered and compromised Europe struck me with breathtaking force. Although set in a Vienna still under Four-Power control, it might have been England. There were the same ruins, the same black marketeers and the same corruption and despair. Much as I admired Welles's acting, I was more impressed by the beauty and melancholy passion of Valli... When it was first shown everyone saw it as a newsreel, so close was it to the reality of the bomb-damaged and rationed world in which we lived. The smallest details took me back to the late 1940s—the cut of men's sports jackets, the over-wary gestures of the supporting players and, above all, the moral ambiguities that the naive American, Holly Martins, finds baffling..." (Ballard, *The Times*, 3 October 2002.)

1949 — Autumn — Since the journal in question was due to close down at year's end, it must have been no later than this period when Ballard submitted stories to Connolly's *Horizon*: "I'd tried originally to write stories for English literary magazines like *Horizon*... Just general fiction of an experimental character." (Ballard interviewed by Jannick Storm, 5 July 1968.) "I remember submitting one or two of my early short stories to *Horizon*. There weren't many places to be published then. There were very few magazines at all, and the experimental, impressionistic prose poetry I was writing—free-form was the sort of thing that was just turned down without a second thought by people in charge." (Ballard, interviewed by David Pringle, 24 July 1981.) The editor who read and rejected the young Ballard's submissions may well have been Sonia Brownell (soon to become Sonia Orwell), who had been closely associated with *Horizon* for the past several years: "Cyril Connolly brought her into *Horizon*, where she learned fast and eventually, to the chagrin of some who were not used to receiving editorial decisions from 25-year-old women, more or less ran it." (Jenny Diski, reviewing *The Girl from the Fiction Department: A Portrait of Sonia Orwell* by Hilary Spurling, *London Review of Books*, 25 April 2002.)

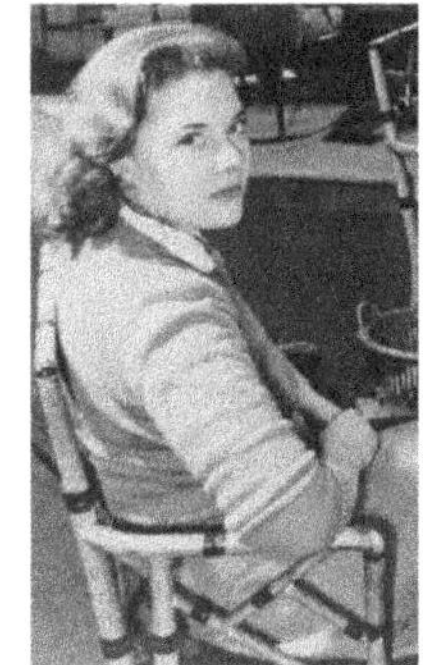

Sonia Brownell

1949 — October 1 (Saturday) — The Communist People's Republic of China was proclaimed under Chairman Mao Tse-tung, with Chou En-lai as premier, in a ceremony in Peking. "In 1949 my father was trapped in Shanghai after the communist take-over and, like all old China hands, confidently expected the ideological purity of the invading armies to last as long as it took them to climb down from their tanks and stroll into the bars and brothels of downtown Shanghai. In fact, their puritan zeal only intensified, and my father found himself on trial, accused of various anti-Communist misdeeds. Fortunately he was able to quote enough Marx and Engels to convince the magistrates that he had seen the error of his ways. He was acquitted and a year later escaped to Hong Kong, aware that the old China of 'squeeze' and corruption had gone for good..." (Ballard, "Let the Women Have Lipstick and High Heels," *Daily Telegraph*, 30 October 1993.)

1949 — October 1 (Saturday) — It was the official beginning of Michaelmas Term at Cambridge University (although, since it fell on a Saturday in this year, the "full" term, or teaching term, would begin a few days later, probably on the following Tuesday). Ballard went "up" to King's, which in fact was situated just a short distance along the road from The Leys. "I became very interested in psychoanalysis while still at school, and read almost all the Freud I could lay my hands on. In fact my chief reason for reading medicine when I went up to King's College was that I wanted to become a psychiatrist a sort of adolescent dream, but I was quite serious about it. ... I [also] became interested in the surrealists at school... I read medicine, and my interest in psychoanalysis abutted surrealism at all sorts of points... I wasn't acquainted with literary surrealism. The French texts probably weren't translated. I remember reading Edmund Wilson's *The Wound and the Bow* as a student, his accounts of writers like Joyce and Hemingway. His chief interests were Eliot, Pound and so on. The Paris in which those writers for the most part lived was also inhabited by the surrealists, but they figured in the margins of the text, in the margins of the biographies of those writers. It was primarily the artists who were referred to. I've never really been interested in literary surrealism." (Ballard, interviewed by David Pringle, 24 July 1981.)

1949 — October 4 (Tuesday) — Michaelmas Term. Ballard became a first-year undergraduate, and he would briefly describe his first day in a novel (a fictional context, but probably an accurate account): "I remember the October morning in the Anatomy Department... With the hundred freshmen joining the medical school, I took my seat in the amphitheatre for the welcoming address by Professor Harris, the head of anatomy. I sat alone in the topmost row, marking my distance from the other undergraduates... Professor Harris entered the theatre and stood at the podium. A small, puckish Welshman, he gazed at the tiers of beefy young men like an auctioneer at a cattle market. He spotted me sitting alone under the roof, asked for my name and told me to put out my cigarette. 'Come and join us—there's no need to be standoffish. You'll find we need each other.' He waited as I crept red-faced to the seats below." (Ballard, *The Kindness of Women*, p77-78.) Henry Harris was in fact the Professor's name, and JGB would mention him again: "Before our first visit to the DR [dissecting room] we were welcomed by Professor Harris, the head of the anatomy school. He was an inspirational lecturer, the child of a modest Welsh family too poor to send their children to university. Harris and his brother were both determined to become doctors, so the younger brother worked for six years to support the older and pay his medical school fees until he qualified. He in turn supported his younger brother for a further six years until both had gained their degrees. In his wide-ranging lectures Harris made clear his belief in the noble calling of medicine, with anatomy at its heart, and I never for a moment doubted him." (Ballard, *Miracles of Life*, p141.)

1949 — October — "When I went into the dissecting room ... as a young man of 18, I had seen a lot of corpses, unlike most of my fellow students. I remember the professor of anatomy giving the welcoming lecture and warning that a few of us would be so unsettled by the experience of dissection that we might not be able to face it. If that were so, we should go and see him quietly, and that would be that. I can understand that some people were shocked, and I was quite. You walked into this huge room, which was a cross between a butcher's shop and a nightclub, with rather eerie overhead lighting, and there were 20 tables, each with a cadaver lying on it. At first it took one's breath away; it was quite unsettling. For dissection purposes a body is divided into five parts: leg, arm, abdomen, thorax, and head and neck. The whole dissection of each part takes a full term, the head and neck take two terms. Once you had separated your part, you took it to a free table where you had more elbow room. And when you'd finished the afternoon's work, each part would be tagged with your name and the identification number of the cadaver. You took the body parts down to huge lockers at the end of the room—and you'd open a locker and find it full of human legs or arms or heads. That was unsettling too. At the end of term, when all the body parts had been dissected, the bones would be gathered together for burial or cremation in the workrooms adjoining the dissecting room, where the laboratory assistants did their stuff. There were wooden tables and a lot of metal dishes, each with a pile of bones and a name tag. It all looked like the remains of some huge cannibal feast." (Ballard, "Raising the Dead," *Sunday Times Magazine*, 7 March 1999; evidently an oral piece, but no interviewer was named.)

1949 — October-November? — It was in this term that Ballard first met the 24-year-old William Spencer, who was a mature undergraduate reading English at St Catharine's College, Cambridge, from 1947 to 1950. "I think I met Jim Ballard (he was always known as 'Jimmy' then) in my second year [sic; it was in fact his third year] at Cambridge—it may have been his first year. It was either at the Cambridge film society or some literary function. I don't know what drew us together, but we did find a good deal to talk about and we met regularly after that." (William Spencer, interviewed by David Pringle, *Interzone* no. 79, January 1994.) On reconsideration, in a later interview, Bill stated that he believed their meeting was at the film society, and that the film they were watching was perhaps *The White Hell of Pitz Palu* (1929), or something equally old. Apparently, Ballard asked him, at the end of the film showing, "What did you think of that?" and then introduced himself with a handshake and "I'm Jimmy Ballard." (Spencer, unrecorded conversation with DP, 23 September 2009.)

1949 — November 15 (Tuesday) — J.G. Ballard's 19th birthday—in the middle of his first term at Cambridge University. "I was impatient with England's mental aspect, the slow and provincial and unimaginative way that people's minds worked, the obsession with petty class distinctions, the lack of interest in 20th-century ideas. At Cambridge, I remember mentioning to one of the senior dons that I was interested in

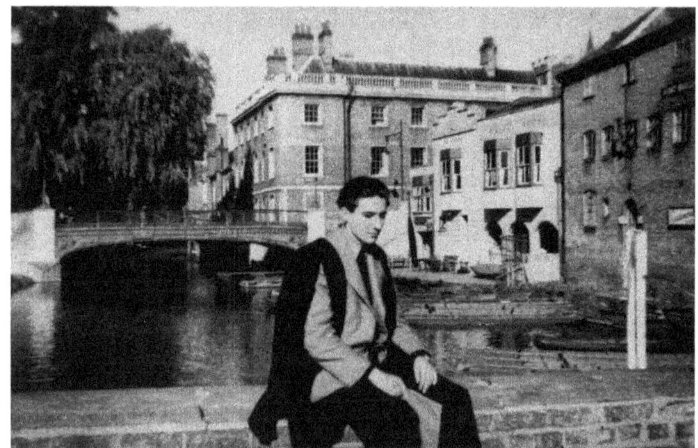
William (Bill) Spencer

psychoanalysis and this was greeted with gales of laughter. In 1949 Sigmund Freud was still regarded as hilarious." (Ballard, interviewed by Lynn Barber, 27 December 1981.) "College life seemed like a quaint and overly folkloric pageant. Where the Cambridge science faculties (Rutherford and the Cavendish, Crick/Watson and DNA, Sanger and so on) were powerfully oriented towards the future, the Cambridge colleges looked back to the past. King's was dominated by its chapel and the musical events that surrounded it. The provost was a classicist, a pantomime parody of the eccentric don. In the dining hall we listened to a long Latin grace that I still know by heart, and sat on benches to eat execrable meals, wearing gowns after dusk and being overseen in the streets of Cambridge by a proctor and his bulldogs (his bowler-hatted aides). We had to be back in college by ten, or perhaps earlier." (Ballard, *Miracles of Life*, p146.) The Provost of King's College, Cambridge, at this time was Sir John Tresidder "Jack" Sheppard (18811968), classicist.

1949 — December — The last issue of *Horizon* appeared, a double issue dated December 1949/January 1950, in which Cyril Connolly wrote: "It is closing time in the gardens of the West and from now on an artist will be judged only by the resonance of his solitude or the quality of his despair."

1949 — December 14 (Wednesday) — Ballard wrote to the secretary at The Leys school: "King's, Cambridge. 14/12/49. Dear Miss de Vincy, I'm sorry to be so dilatory in acknowledging the receipt of my Higher Certificate. Thanks very much for sending it to me; a token of my four years' labour at the Leys. When I last saw you we speculated for some time as to whether any invitation was required to the King's Concerts. I'm pretty sure, though not absolutely certain, that anyone can just stroll in at any time. If however you find that an invitation is required please let me know and I'll get you a box seat. Hoping that everything at the Leys is absolutely bubbling with enthusiasm and excitement, Yours Sincerely, J. G. Ballard." (Raymond Tait, "J.G. Ballard at The Leys School," *Deep Ends 2014*, p59.) This is the earliest JGB letter known to be extant. What happened to any other correspondence of his childhood and student years? Did his mother not keep some? If so, all is now missing, and probably destroyed.

1949 — December 23 (Friday) — "LONDON, Dec. 23. Dr Russell Brain, physician to the London Hospital [author of

Brain's Diseases of the Nervous System], in an address said that a great many writers were insane. Some of them, if not certifiable, were cyclothymes, schizophrenics, obsessional psychopaths, alcoholics, or drug addicts. He named Boswell, Bunyan, Burns, Byron, Dickens, Johnson, Lamb, Ruskin, Shelley, and Tennyson. ... Of Dickens, Dr Brain said his moods and depression, characteristic of his temperament as a 'cyclothyme,' enhanced his sensibility and made him respond with far more feeling than the average man, both to his own experiences and to the sufferings of others. This blended with his sado-masochism." (*Sydney Morning Herald*, 24 December 1949.)

1949 — "I stopped reading only to go to the cinema. The Hollywood films that kept hope alive—*Citizen Kane, Sunset Boulevard, The Big Sleep* and *White Heat*—seemed to form a continuum with the novels of Hemingway and Nathanael West, Kafka and Camus." (Ballard, in Antonia Fraser, ed., *The Pleasure of Reading*, 1992.) "I remember watching *Build My Gallows High* in a Cambridge cinema in 1949 and being gripped by the stylised and affectless violence, where psychopathy was the key to character. Here was a clear look at the dark side of the American dream, and a better guide to the world we were living in than the lectures of Dr Leavis (in fact, I was supposed to be reading medicine)." (Ballard, "A Staircase of Corpses," *New Statesman*, 26 March 2001.) "I first became a moviegoer in 1946 when I came to England, a little lost among its grey, distracted people. Since there was nothing else to do, a large part of the population went to the cinema three times a week. In gigantic art deco Odeons, like smoke-filled cathedrals, I saw the postwar films of Alfred Hitchcock, Howard Hawks, John Ford and Roberto Rossellini when they first came out. Even more exhilarating, I saw Robert Mitchum, Marlon Brando and James Dean before they became stars. On dull afternoons, when I should have been dissecting cadavers, I watched *Sunset Boulevard, Orphée* and *Open City*. A completely new culture and social climate were being created, international in spirit and more urgent than almost any novel." (Ballard, "The Prophet," *Guardian*, 23 July 2005.)

1950

1950 — January — Bill Spencer would say: "There was a great deal of rather orthodox thinking going on at Cambridge in those years immediately following the Second World War. A lot of people saw the university as a place where you went to learn some specific body of knowledge, almost by rote, and you got a qualification and you ended up with a job. But Jim [Ballard] and I tended more towards the unorthodox in our thinking, we were slightly out of alignment with the general current of thought... A place like Cambridge is so steeped in history, you're moving among medieval buildings. In the case of Jim's college, you would come out into the quadrangle and there was this enormous and very magnificent building, King's College Chapel. It dominates the whole of that bit of Cambridge, which is probably the most typical bit. So, while one appreciated all the music and the other cultural offerings that were going on in Cambridge, there was this constant ringing of bells summoning people to worship, which was distinctly jarring. There was also a hidebound quality in a lot of the mundane details of life, you

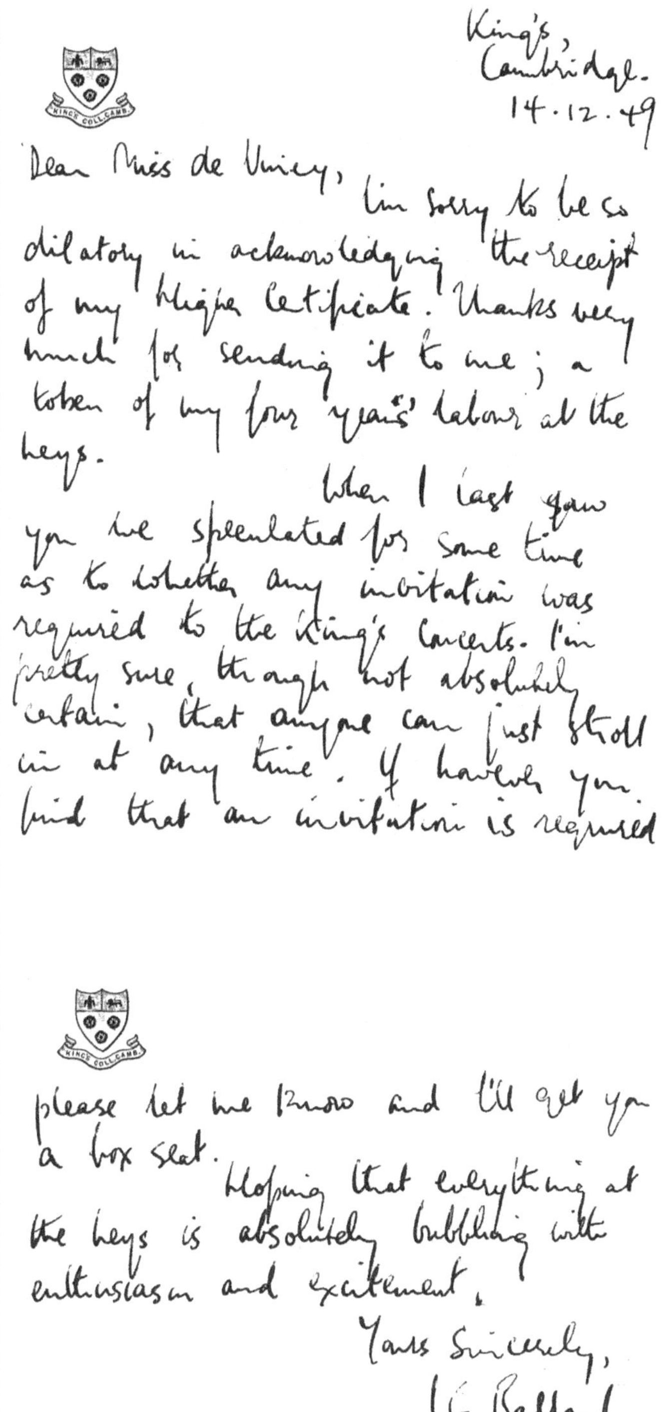

King's,
Cambridge.
14.12.49

Dear Miss de Vincy,

I'm sorry to be so dilatory in acknowledging the receipt of my Higher Certificate. Thanks very much for sending it to me; a token of my four years' labour at the Leys.

When I last saw you we speculated for some time as to whether any invitation was required to the King's Concerts. I'm pretty sure, though not absolutely certain, that anyone can just stroll in at any time. If however you find that an invitation is required please let me know and I'll get you a box seat.

Hoping that everything at the Leys is absolutely bubbling with enthusiasm and excitement,

Yours Sincerely,
J. G. Ballard.

The last of The Leys: Ballard's letter to a Miss de Vincy concerning the receipt of his Higher Certificate. Written 14 December 1949, this is one of the earliest examples of the then 19-year-old Jim Ballard's handwriting.

had to be in your rooms by a certain hour and all that kind of thing. I don't want to suggest that we went round waving banners or tying tin cans to things, or whatever else one does to protest: there was no outward expression of this disquiet other than in discussion, but I think we just felt that much of the mainstream of Cambridge life was happening in some other universe." (William Spencer, interviewed by David Pringle, *Interzone* no. 79, January 1994.)

1950 — January 21 (Saturday) — Death of George Orwell (real name Eric Blair, b. 1903), British novelist and essayist, in London of tuberculosis at 46, just over three months after his sickbed wedding to Sonia Brownell.

1950 — January 31 (Tuesday) — "LONDON, Jan. 31. 'Britain is a country of crushing monotony and infinite boredom,' according to the London correspondent of a Paris newspaper. He says: 'Just one hour from Paris by air, and you are in an entirely different world. Here, the State controls everything and everything depends on the State. The stranger is immediately struck by the drab uniformity of the clothes as much as by the monotony of the menus. England is undergoing a revolution by boredom. There is just one subject of conversation in England to-day: food. I thought at first that the election was a second topic, but it turned out that what the English really want to know is: "How well shall we be eating after the election?"'" (*Sydney Morning Herald*, 1 February 1950.)

1950 — February 23 (Thursday) — This was General Election day in the United Kingdom. Ballard was not yet old enough to vote, but no doubt he took an interest: "... like most students, I was left-wing. I could see that Clement Attlee's post-war government was bringing about some much-needed changes to this country." (Ballard, interviewed by John Walsh, *Independent on Sunday*, 14 September 2003.)

1950 — February 24 (Friday) — The results of the UK General Election, the first since 1945, were announced. The Labour Party was returned to office with a much-reduced majority of just five seats.

1950 — Spring Term? — "I went to one of [F. R.] Leavis's lectures and thought how limited his world was, and remember saying to the English literature student who had taken me: 'It's more important to go to *T-Men* (a classic noir film) than to Leavis's lectures.'" (Ballard, *Miracles of Life*, p148.) "William Spencer was the Eng Lit student mentioned here, and incidentally he shared Ballard's dislike of the Leavis approach to literature. ... The senior tutor of my college Tom Henn (an impressive Anglo-Irishman) was a devotee of Yeats. He held candlelit 'Monday nights' in his rooms (modelled on the soirées of Yeats) at which members of the college were invited to read pieces they had written to the assembled gathering. Discussion then followed. This meant that we were always scratching away at some kind of writing. Attendance was restricted to members of St Catharine's, so when I later met Jim he never took part. But I remember holding at least one joint 'writing session' with him in his room in King's. Curiously enough some of the stuff I was writing then was science fiction, whereas Jim was working on straight fiction." (Spencer, from notes he helpfully wrote on an early version of this timeline, 2010.)

1950 — March 1 (Wednesday) — Klaus Fuchs, German-born nuclear physicist who had been granted British citizenship in 1942, was convicted in London of spying for the Soviet Union by giving them secret atomic bomb data. He was sentenced to 14 years in prison. (Later this day, in Selkirk, Scotland, the compiler of the present chronology, David Pringle, was born.)

1950 — March 22 (Wednesday) — "LONDON, March 22. While Press and Public were clamouring for action against Britain's rising crime wave, the House of Lords yesterday began a two-day debate on flogging. At the end of the day, speakers were fairly evenly divided whether flogging deters crime. The Lord Chancellor, Viscount Jowitt, showed that the Government had not changed its mind since it abolished corporal punishment last year. He said: 'We have no intention of reintroducing it—none whatever.'" (*Sydney Morning Herald*, 23 March 1950.)

1950 — Spring — Bill Spencer would say: "My college was St Catharine's and Jim Ballard's was King's which was next door, so it would happen that I'd walk over to see him or he'd walk over to see me, or we'd occupy a good many mis-spent hours in the Copper Kettle drinking coffee. There was a Cypriot restaurant which we favoured for meals (at the end of the meal we'd often finish with a mysterious dish called yoghurt which was a near-eastern delicacy we'd never heard of). And on sunny days we'd go walking by the river, or take a punt upstream in the direction of Grantchester. I had a girl friend at the time who was a nurse, and because Jim was a medical student they would get involved in these highly anatomical discussions that would leave me feeling distinctly ill. I think Jim, probably like most medical students, often discovered in himself the symptoms of the latest dread disease he'd been studying, so there would be discussions with my nurse friend about this." (William Spencer, interviewed by David Pringle, *Interzone* no. 79, January 1994.) In a later interview, Bill confided that his lady friend was named Maisie, that she was Scottish, an experienced nurse, and that she was somewhat older than him—therefore several years older than Ballard. (Spencer, conversation with DP, 23 September 2009.) "I clearly remember at least one occasion when she and I visited JGB in his room in King's, and there were other occasions when we were together as a threesome. As I mentioned in the *Interzone* interview, Maisie and JGB got on well together, partly as a result of their shared medical background. At that time he was aged about 19, and he adopted the position that he was too young as yet to have a serious girlfriend. I think he was still feeling his way in English society, which in many ways was quite alien to him." (Spencer, e-mail to DP, 3 October 2009.)

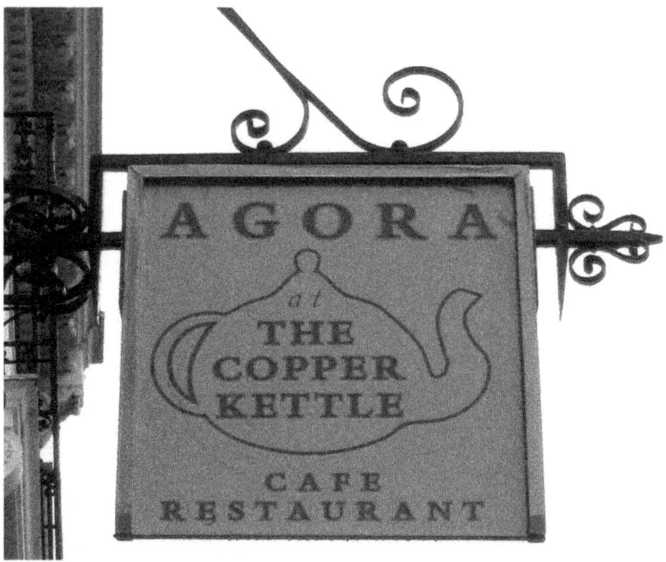

1950 — Spring — Bill Spencer would add: "Try as I may I can't remember Maisie's surname. But I'm fairly certain she was not Mac-anything, and that she came from a smallish community somewhere-in-Scotland, not one of the bigger towns. She was certainly older than me, probably in the range 2 to 4 years. Maisie was just about my first real girlfriend. I'd spent years away in India with the RAF, sweating it out in the depths of the Bengal jungle, or on some remote airfield... In Cambridge, university women were in desperately short supply. You practically had to have an 'honourable' in front of your name, plus an estate in the Home Counties and a private income, to stand any chance. I, with my lack of social skills, and my Nottingham accent revealing that I hadn't attended even the most minor of minor public schools, stood no chance... As well as University women, there were some 'town' rather than 'gown' girls going the rounds, but they tended to be rather coarse and obvious in their approach. (I had a brief tangle with one of these.) Maisie was not like them. She was a nice, serious, sensible girl of equable temperament, who had become wiser than her years through seeing the raw side of life, and death, in her chosen profession. She was quite proud of having risen above the lowest rank in nursing, I think to state registered nurse, SRN. She had earlier worked at Addenbrooke's Hospital in Cambridge, but when I knew her she was employed in a small private nursing home which seems to have specialised in terminally-ill patients. She referred to some of them, in kindly tones, as 'aged prossies' (i.e. sufferers from prostate cancer). They would sometimes leave her small sums in their wills, so she was clearly popular with her charges." (William Spencer, e-mail to DP, 3 October 2009.)

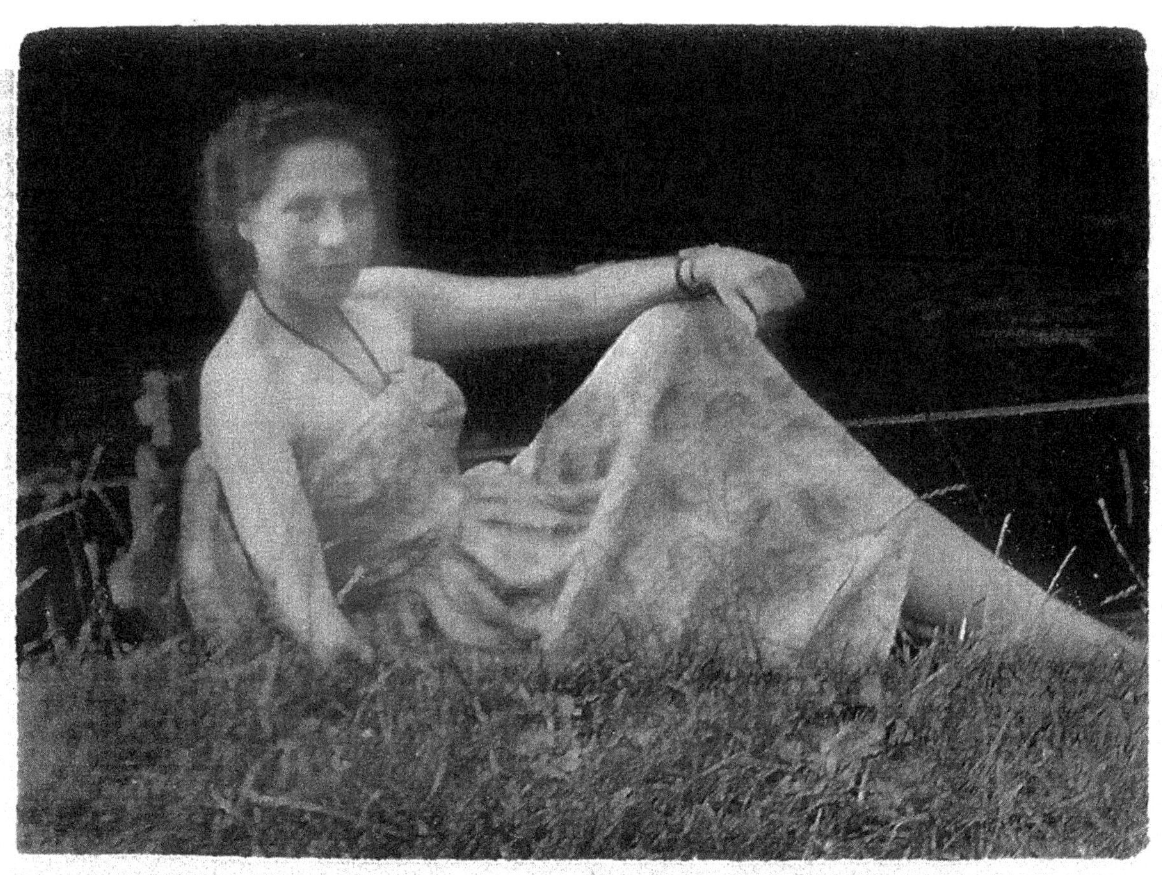

from William Spencer. Photos 1950-62

This one:

"Maisie - My Scottish nurse girlfriend in a punt at the edge of the River Cam. On a summer's day in June 1950, punting towards Grantchester, with Jim & some friends of mine from St. Catharine's.

After I left Cambridge, Maisie remained friendly with Jim."

1950 — Spring — "I was a medical student and medical students tend to have a more relaxed attitude. More importantly, medical students get to know nurses, and nurses—I don't know whether this is still true though no doubt I'll find out in a few years when I'm led off to the terminal ward—nurses in those days were wonderful, life-enhancing, uninhibited things. At 18, thank God, I knew all the nurses at Addenbrooke's and they were much more fun to be in a punt with than girls who were reading English at Newnham. In my forties I started meeting all the women, now prominent in the London literary scene, who were at Newnham when I was there, but somehow I didn't meet them then and I'm rather glad." (Ballard, interviewed by Lynn Barber, 27 December 1981.) Alumnae of Newnham College, Cambridge, included Pat Arrowsmith (b. 1930), Joan Bakewell (b. 1933), Eleanor Bron (b. 1938), A. S. Byatt (b. 1936), Margaret Drabble (b. 1939), Elaine Feinstein (b. 1930), Jane Goodall (b. 1934), Penelope Leach (b. 1937), Jessica Mann (b. 1937), Iris Murdoch (b. 1919), Sylvia Plath (b. 1932), Isabel Quigly (b. 1926), Claire Tomalin (b. 1933) and Katharine Whitehorn (b. 1928)—many of whom were too young to have been JGB's contemporaries, although at least two of those named here, Bakewell (née Rowlands) and Tomalin (née Delavenay), would become acquaintances of his in later years.

1950 — April 24 (Monday) — "For three months the U.S. State Department had tried vainly to evacuate some 1,600 foreigners (including 300 U.S. nationals) from Communist-held Shanghai. Last month the Reds had given a green light for the evacuation, then arbitrarily switched signals at the last minute, leaving the evacuees and their baggage waiting at the Shanghai docks. Last week in Washington, U.S. Secretary of State Dean Acheson decided to call it quits: all plans for a sea rescue from Shanghai were off. He would, he said, ask the Communists to let the Americans travel overland to Tientsin or Hong Kong and try to get private shipping facilities from there. That same day, in Hong Kong, 83 Shanghailanders (including four U.S. citizens) walked down the gangplank of a Danish freighter and onto British soil. The travelers had gone by rail from Shanghai 700 miles north to Tientsin and thence 900 miles south to Hong Kong by ship. Their report on Communist Shanghai described a slowly dying city. Said a Briton: 'A gradual paralysis is setting in, a paralysis of commerce and spirit.' There are few automobiles on the streets. Shanghai's factories are limping along at less than half their capacity production... Nevertheless, some of the travelers who stepped ashore in Hong Kong last week were optimistic, after a fashion, of Communism's future in China. One Briton put it this way: 'As soon as the Communists get over their current troubles, you will see material progress, more than China has ever made before.'" (*Time*, 24 April 1950.)

1950 — May 29 (Whit Monday) — Bank Holiday in the United Kingdom. "LONDON, May 29. More than 1,500,000 cars took to the road yesterday in the biggest Whitsunday rush to the coast and country since 1939. There was plenty of derationed petrol for all. Tankers rumbled out of their depots with nearly a million gallons in preparation for the rush. Country roadhouses, tea-rooms, and refreshment kiosks, some barely able to stay in business during the years of petrol rationing, had the busiest weekend since before the war." (*Sydney Morning Herald*, 30 May 1950.)

1950 — June — Bill Spencer would write: "Exams being over, Maisie and I went with Jimmy [Ballard] and four Cat's men (plus a visiting girlfriend of one of the Cat's men) on a punting picnic up the River Cam in the direction of Grantchester. We sat out on the river bank and sank a beer or two. Jimmy was in high spirits and thoroughly enjoyed himself. In his first year at King's I don't recollect him mentioning any other friends at King's or elsewhere, or any friendship with Addenbrooke's nurses. Was he being overly discreet, or was he in fact a bit of a loner at this time?" (William Spencer, notes on this timeline, 2010.)

1950 — June 5 (Monday) — "By recognizing Communist China last Jan. 6, Britain hoped to protect her huge commercial stake there. Some British optimists also hoped to gain a political advantage; they thought that Mao Tse-tung might become another Tito. In the House of Commons last week, ailing Ernie Bevin sadly dismissed the second hope: 'I think Mao Tse-tung has been receiving advice from Moscow—this is the same kind of attitude as Moscow's.' Although Peking has kept its Communist snoot in the air and has left Britain dangling unrecognized for five months, Bevin still stubbornly defended the first hope: 'We had large interests in China... The advice I gave to the cabinet was right...'" ... A doleful expression of Britain's growing disenchantment came last week from William J. ["Tony"] Keswick, chairman of London's China Association: 'The British stake in Shanghai is withering.' Unless Communist China changes its tactics, said Keswick, 'then clearly, whether we like it or not, the only policy open to us is to close down and shut up shop.'" (*Time*, 5 June 1950.) Mr James Ballard, who had been trying to maintain the China Printing and Finishing Company as a British concern, probably made his escape from Shanghai around this time, returning to the UK via Canton and Hong Kong. "My father was held in Shanghai for about a year after the communists arrived, but eventually he was released and was able to make his way to England. That was in 1950, and they bought a house in the Manchester area [actually in a rural suburb: 'Brynfield,' Townscliffe Lane, Mellor, Cheshire]. By then I was at university. When he arrived here my father became a consultant in the pharmaceutical field. He became director of European operations for an American pharmaceutical company, a big Boston firm which he remained until his retirement." (Ballard, interviewed by David Pringle, 24 July 1981.)

1950 — June 25 (Sunday) — The Korean War began as forces from the communist North unexpectedly attacked the South.

1950 — Summer — "He [Ballard] must have had some literary inclination in his first year at university, and I think that was partly what made the friendship work. I imagine after a morning spent in the dissecting laboratories, it would have been a relief to come and talk about books and art. Also, we were quite big on Freudian and Jungian psychology. (This was one of my approaches to literature, because certainly Marxism didn't appeal to me as a way of profiling literature.) His approach to lots of things was via physiology, and this again was a thing in which we were rather complementary, because I tended to shy away from the physical aspects of existence, I suppose, and go off into some rarefied upper atmosphere of aesthetic discussion. Jim would have much more the physiological understanding of the human brain: the body as a physical reality with lots of tubes and organs running through it and blood pumping around it... And of course Jim was already showing some mastery in writing—he won the *Varsity* story competition the following year." (William Spencer, interviewed by David Pringle, *Interzone* no. 79, January 1994.)

1950 — July — Bill Spencer completed his time at St Catharine's College, Cambridge. "With 'war service allowance' I actually graduated in the English Tripos at the end of two years, but opted to stay on for a third year to complete the full 'peacetime' degree course. (I was then offered a junior research fellowship, but perhaps unwisely turned it down. By then, at 25, I couldn't stand the thought of another two years in Cambridge, which I felt was an artificial, inward-turned environment. I was hungry to see more of the 'real' world.) My final year of study was therefore October 1949 to June 1950. I then remained in Cambridge for a further eight weeks or so working as assistant to Walter Murgatroyd, who was doing postgraduate research in the Cambridge Engineering Laboratory on a magnetic pump for liquid metals. This slightly bizarre arrangement arose because Walter, also a Cats man, knew of my interest in technology and science, and had witnessed some modest skill with my hands on a hobby project. Then, in September or October 1950 I took up a post which the University Appointments Board had found for me as a copywriter for the London advertising agents S. H. Benson." (William Spencer, e-mail to DP, 3 October 2009.)

1950 — August 7 (Monday) — Bank Holiday in the United Kingdom. It was probably some time in this month that Bill Spencer "visited Ballard at the Middleton-on-Sea [Bognor Regis] residence fronting the seashore (in Ballard's summer vacation) and found his mother an impressive lady (she called him 'Jamie'), but did not meet his sister (or of course his father)." (William Spencer, notes on this timeline, 2010.) Apparently Mrs Ballard and daughter had by this time moved from rented accommodation at Aldwick Bay, west of Bognor, to Middleton-on-Sea, east of Bognor.

1950 — August 10 (Thursday) — The film *Sunset Boulevard* (dir. Billy Wilder) had its premiere in New York City. It starred William Holden as Hollywood screenwriter Joe Gillis, with Gloria Swanson as an ageing movie star and Erich von Stroheim as her director. (The London premiere would take place a week later, on 17 August.) "I saw the film when it first came out in 1950. It had a tremendous impact on me, from which I think I've never properly recovered. I was 20 years old and I was a medical student, but I—knew that I was going to become a writer, and the sort of writer I wanted to be was Joe Gillis. The idea of dying face-down in the pool of a great mansion in Beverly Hills struck me as something worthy of Puccini. ... For years after seeing *Sunset Boulevard*, whenever I found myself in a pool I dipped my hat to Joe Gillis by lying face down for a few seconds, imagining myself in a pool in Beverly Hills." (Ballard, interviewed in "Close-Up," BBC 2, 3 April 1995.)

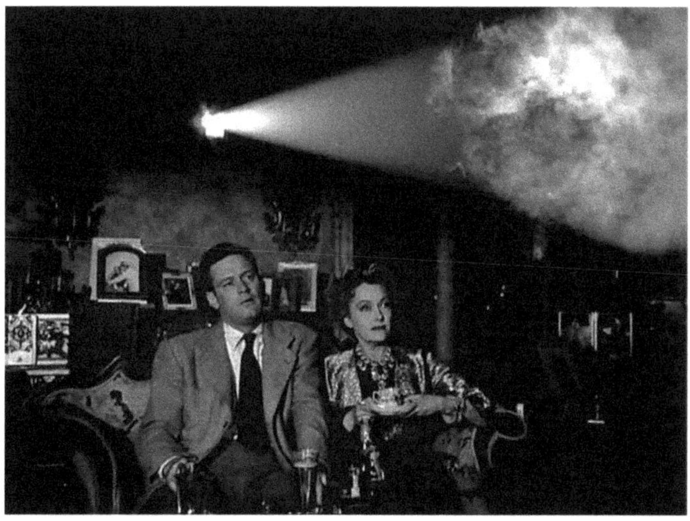
William Holden and Gloria Swanson in *Sunset Boulevard*.

1950 — September 6 (Wednesday) — Death of W. Olaf Stapledon (b. 1886), British philosopher and author of scientific romances, of a heart attack at 64. "The time charts in [Stapledon's] *Last and First Men*—they haven't dated at all, they are still mind-blowing. I've stared at those over the years, thinking, 'Well, I've got a strong imagination, maybe I can do better'—but for once I can't see how you can do that better." (Ballard, interviewed by Jon Savage, *Search & Destroy*, [circa August] 1978.)

1950 — September 29 (Friday) — A film released on this date in France was *Orphée* (dir. Jean Cocteau), which Ballard would come to appreciate. It starred Jean Marais as the Poet, and Maria Casares as Death. "I think Cocteau's *Orphée* was another big influence on the *Vermilion Sands* stories. That has this strange enchantress with her Rolls-Royce and her motorcycle outriders, and mysterious messages that come over a car's radio. The notion is that the woman is the image of death, or rather is Death—not death in general, as she's careful to point out—and that she moves in and out of mirrors. It's a hot mix. I loved that film when I saw it. In fact I have a tape of it, and if I'm bored or I just don't feel like reading I often watch it, because it's enormously sophisticated and it's genuinely a great work of art." (Ballard, interviewed by David Pringle, 30 October 1995.)

1950 — October — Bill Spencer, down from Cambridge, went to work for an advertising agency in London. "When I first joined this particular firm the department I was in had been known as the Literary Department until a few years previously. Dorothy L. Sayers had been a copywriter there. It was S.H. Benson, which no longer exists as a separate firm, but it had a great history: it had been founded in 1893, and it had some very major accounts like Guinness—we had been responsible for producing all those posters: 'My Goodness, My Guinness' and so on. While I was there a man called Julian Yeatman joined, who was the co-author of *1066 and All That*, and another man who was there was Gavin Ewart, who has become quite distinguished as a poet. In the old days the copywriters would come in in the mornings in a rather leisurely mode, and settle down to finish the *Times* crossword-puzzle over a cup of coffee before attempting any serious work. Things had become a little bit crisper and more utilitarian by the time I joined, but it was still a business of sitting in a room with a pencil and pad of paper and maybe hacking out a hundred words in a day: you would write and rewrite those hundred words in every conceivable fashion. So it was a great place to polish one's craftsmanship as a writer." (William Spencer, interviewed by David Pringle, *Interzone* no. 79, January 1994.)

1950 — October 3 (Tuesday) — Michaelmas Term. Ballard began his second year as an undergraduate at King's College, Cambridge. His pal Bill Spencer was no longer around, but he would continue to see Bill's erstwhile girlfriend, Maisie, and he would have other male friends such as his former schoolmates Robin and Paul Chand. It may have been around this time that he produced a double-exposed photographic print of himself, posing moodily with a cigarette holder, somewhat in the style of Cecil Beaton's portrait photographs of the period. A postcard-sized reproduction of a painting visible on his wall was of "The Girl with a Tattered Glove" (1909) by William Nicholson, which he may have first seen in the Fitzwilliam Museum, Cambridge. Many years later the photo would be published in *Re/Search 8/9*, 1984, page 116, with the caption: "Ballard with himself in Cambridge, 1950, aged 19." When asked about it years later still, JGB would say: "The double exposure was a small entertainment—an experiment that seemed to work within the limits of a v. cheesy 1940s (30s) camera—no significance." (Ballard, postcard to Rick McGrath, November 2008.)

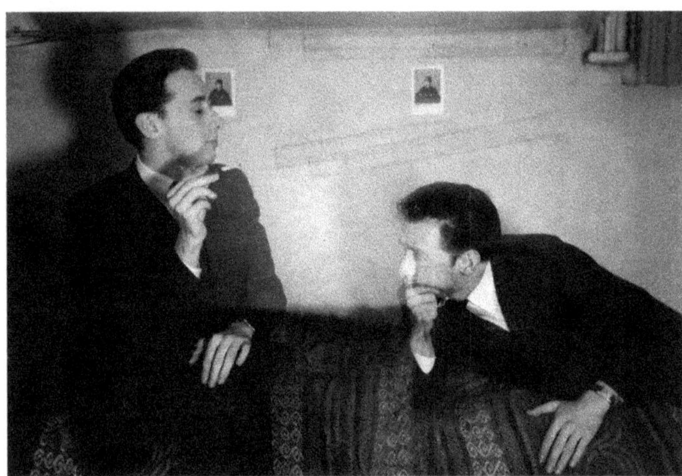

A double exposed J.G. Ballard self portrait at Cambridge.

1950 — November 2 (Thursday) — Death of George Bernard Shaw (b. 1856), British (Anglo-Irish) playwright, novelist, theatre and music critic, social critic and wit, Nobel Prize laureate (1925), at 94.

1950 — November 15 (Wednesday) — J.G. Ballard's 20th birthday. "When I was 20 (in the late 1940s [sic]), there were much greater restraints—going to bed with a girl was a pretty rare occurrence. But because the experience was rarer, it certainly had a powerful charge added to it that casual sex can't have." (Ballard, interviewed by Vale, 29 October 1982.) In fact, he was only 19 "in the late 1940s," or, precisely, for the last six weeks of the 1940s; but could this be a hint as to when he lost his virginity, whether at 19 or at 20? In a later fictional context, he would have his alter ego say of his student period that one of the few women "I had made love to ... [was] a Cambridge prostitute who thought I was an American serviceman posing as an undergraduate" (Ballard, *The Kindness of Women*, 1991, p92)—which could be a reference to an actual incident, but we cannot know for sure.

1950 — November (circa) — "There were no more than nine or ten medical students at King's across all three years, and I was forced to find friends who were reading other subjects. One Kingsman I knew was Simon Raven, whom I would meet in the Copper Kettle after dinner. He told me many years later that he thoroughly enjoyed his time at King's. But he was actively homosexual, and King's was an openly homosexual college, famously home to Maynard Keynes and E.M. Forster, with close connections to the painter Duncan Grant and the Bloomsbury Group... The ethos of the college was homosexual, and a heterosexual like myself who brought in his girlfriends (mostly Addenbrooke's Hospital nurses and free-livers all) was viewed as letting the side down, as well as having made a curious choice in the first place. This was an era when most public schoolboys met no women for the first twenty years of their lives other than the school matron and their mothers, with the result that women in general remained forever in a dead perceptual zone..." (Ballard, *Miracles of Life*, p146-147.) The writer-to-be Simon Raven, aged 22 and still an undergraduate, actually completed his first novel, *An Inch of Fortune*, around this time in 1950. A potentially libellous social comedy, it would remain unpublished for 30 years. It is unlikely that Ballard was given an opportunity to read it in manuscript.

1950 — November (circa) — Simon Raven's mother, née Esther Christmas, was a Cambridge local. According to his biographer, there are "several [1920s] snaps of her punting and picnicking with young men in College blazers. She can also be seen in a couple of May Ball photos... With her bobbed ash-blonde curls, boyish figure and shapely legs, she looked every inch a 'flapper'. Nor did she ever quite lose her Jazz Age gloss. Years later, on meeting her in Cambridge, a friend of Simon's thought that 'although rather tarnished, she belonged to that era like a chromium-plated cocktail shaker'." (Michael Barber, *The Captain: The Life and Times of Simon Raven*, 1996, p14.) After quoting a comment on Raven's father from "a fellow Kingsman," one David Evers, the biographer continues: "... 'Long before he began to write his father was his best invention,' said another Cambridge friend, adding that since Mr Raven never appeared, Simon was free to represent him as 'an utter failure who played golf, drank too much and quarrelled with his family'." (Barber, p26.) The "friend of Simon's" and the "Cambridge friend" quoted in these passages may well be Ballard, who is named as an informant in the book's acknowledgments. The "chromium-plated cocktail shaker" remark in particular sounds like JGB.

1950 — December 14 (Thursday) — Robert Thomas Harold Patterson, aged 21 (formerly of Shanghai, more recently doing his National Service in the RAF), gained his pilot's certificate in a test taken in an Auster light aeroplane at the Blackpool & Fylde Aero Club. His home address was given in the documentation as 2 Park Parade, Lisburn, Co. Antrim, Northern Ireland. So Ballard's Lunghua friend Bobby Patterson ("Henderson") became a qualified pilot, as JGB would also aspire, but fail, to do after him.

1950 — December 24 (circa) — Bill Spencer would write: "Maisie and I abandoned any attempt to continue our relationship when I moved to London, I think by mutual consent, the fifty-mile distance being considered too much of a barrier in those days. However, I was dimly aware that she had kept up a friendship with JGB in Cambridge. When I was in my second lot of digs in London, in Cathcart Rd SW10, probably around Christmas 1950, Maisie and JGB visited me there, having just returned from a holiday together in (I think) Paris. In private, JGB went out of his way to reassure me that they were still 'just friends', and he may have been right, or he may have wanted to deflect any possible resentment from me. He needn't have worried. I was just happy to see Maisie with someone who would appreciate her. Of course there was an even bigger age gap between him and her than there was between Maisie and me—and moreover in what would have been considered at that time the 'wrong' direction." (William Spencer, e-mail to DP, 3 October 2009.)

1950 — Ballard may have quarrelled with his father at some point after the latter's return from China. "Having brought up a son and two daughters myself as a single parent I know how much physical affection is the cement that holds a life together in later years. My own father was a physically affectionate man, but in my adolescence I won't say I had a very close relationship, and in my late teens we actually fell out." (Ballard, quoted in the *Daily Mail*, 23 November 1992.) "By the time I saw my father, it was the early fifties, and I'd made a lot of important decisions in my life. Coping with England for a start. I didn't have any help from him, there. ... When I saw him in the 1950s, it was too late. I'd made all these decisions—to become a doctor or whatever—and as soon as I left school I knew I wanted to become a writer. These are decisions I never talked over with him." (Ballard, interviewed by Toby Litt, 10 July 2006.)

1950 — Ballard and pep pills (probably Benzedrine, an amphetamine first sold commercially in 1933 and sometimes used by the armed forces during World War II): "When I was a student at Cambridge, I regularly... you could then in England buy amphetamines across the counter, in drugstores [sic], without a prescription. And we took them regularly without even thinking about it, if you wanted to work all night, or just feel a bit keyed up." (Ballard, interviewed by Lukas Barr, 31 May 1995.)

1951

1951 — January 28 (Sunday) — "NEW YORK, Jan. 28. The second atomic test explosion in 24 hours was set off early to-day at the atomic proving ground about 100 miles north-west of Las Vegas (Nevada). The blast shook the earth for miles around. The first atomic blast, early yesterday, was the beginning of a series of 'periodic tests,' according to a spokesman for the Atomic Energy Commission. The flash of yesterday's explosion was seen at least 50 miles away. In the Golden Nugget, a Las Vegas gambling casino, a roulette player said: 'That must have been an atom bomb.' He went on with his game." (*Sydney Morning Herald*, 29 January 1951.)

1951 — March 6 (Tuesday) — Peter Wyngarde, actor (and former Lunghua prison-camp inmate), married the actress Dorinda Stevens, and they would live together at 9 Holland Park, Kensington, London, separating after three years. In an interview many years later, he would say that he married "far too young" and: "It lasted three years and the last year was pretty hell." (Their divorce would be finalized on 24 June 1956.)

1951 — Spring — "He [Ballard] seemed quite happy to talk, critically and at length, about Cambridge and King's in the early 50s, and warmed rapidly to the theme... [T]he picture he etched was of an institution hopelessly out of touch with the new ideas coming from America and continental Europe; dons in King's 'laughed at psychoanalysis' and existentialism was derided... What about the personal side, had he made good friends? Yes, yes. With an audible nod to his own lack of political correctness and in almost confessional tone he said: 'of course, the place was packed with pederasts.' When he smuggled his girlfriends in, fellow students backed away alarmed. 'I hated the Chapel,' he added, and I detected almost fresh loathing for what he bundled together as 'all that jugged hare—and grace.' There were other contributors to the antiquated atmosphere; 'that old writer,' he said only half-jokingly, and the Provost, whom he thought a ridiculous tottering figure." (Alison Carter, "Talking to J.G. Ballard about King's," *King's Parade* [a college alumnis' newsletter], Autumn 2000.) The "old writer" obscurely alluded to by JGB was E.M. Forster, whom he had seen, probably in his first term. "There were some writers I could never force myself to read—Virginia Woolf (I was afraid of her) and E.M. Forster, who was the first 'great' novelist I ever met. He was a fellow of King's College, Cambridge, and I can still see him gazing at the undergraduates with his wistful eyes. He and the other Bloomsbury writers seemed far too prim and rarefied." (Ballard, "True Confessions," *Daily Telegraph*, 7 May 1994.)

1951 — April 27 (Friday) — There was a visit by King George VI, Queen Elizabeth and Princess Margaret to King's College, Cambridge, to attend the service of "Thanksgiving for the Preservation of the Chapel." Photographs of Provost Sheppard greeting the royal party, and of the Head Porter, Albert Powell, leading the procession, subsequently appeared in the press. In a fictional context: "'You come from England?' Brigid asked. 'I always wanted to visit there. Maybe I'd see the king and queen.' '... I've seen them—they came to my college. ... A big limousine pulled up and four little people stepped out, the king and queen and the princesses...' As an undergraduate prank I had taken off my academic gown and laid it in a pool of water under the wheels of the approaching Daimler." (Ballard, *The Kindness of Women*, 1991, p116.) The anecdote of the gown laid over the muddy pool is unlikely to have been true as far as any personal involvement by JGB was concerned, but a similar incident involving medical students and the Queen visiting Dundee, Scotland, would be reported in the papers in June 1955, and Ballard is likely to have borrowed it from there.

1951 — May 3 (Thursday) — The long-anticipated Festival of Britain was opened by King George VI, who also inaugurated the new Royal Festival Hall on London's South Bank.

1951 — May 26 (Saturday) — *Varsity*, the Cambridge University student newspaper, published Ballard's first short story, "The Violent Noon." The profile of the 20-year-old author which accompanied the piece said: "J. Graham Ballard who shares the first prize of £10 with D. S. Birley in the *Varsity* Crime Story Competition is now in his second year at King's and immersed in the less literary process of reading medicine. He admitted to our reporter yesterday that he had in fact entered the competition more for the prize than anything else, although he had been encouraged to go on writing because of his success. The idea for his short story which deals with the problem of Malayan terrorism, he informs us, he had been thinking over for some time before hearing of the competition. He has, in addition to writing short stories, also planned 'mammoth novels' which 'never get beyond the first page.'" (*Varsity*, 26 May 1951.) "That very early story of mine, which won the Cambridge competition, was done as almost a pastiche of a certain kind of Hemingwayesque short story. It certainly wasn't typical of the other material I was writing at the time. I wanted to win the competition, actually: that was my intention, but I knew that I wouldn't win unless I wrote a story of that kind." (Ballard, interviewed by David Pringle, 24 July 1981.)

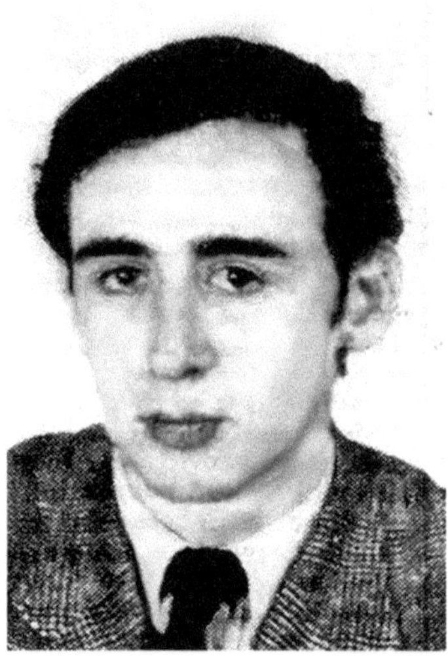
J.G. Ballard photo in the *Varsity*.

1951 — June 2 (Saturday) — In Cambridge, *Varsity* published a brief judges' report commenting on the results of its short-story competition and on Ballard's co-winning entry which had appeared in the paper the previous week: "... 'Violent Noon' was the most mature story; it contains patches of high tension, the characters come to life, and the ending is brilliant in its cynicism. The author should, however, avoid a tendency to preach." JGB would write later: "The judge was a senior partner at a leading London agents, A.P. Watt, who commended my story and invited me to call on him." (Ballard, *Miracles of Life*, p149.) Who was that literary agent? Someone who has long worked in publishing has suggested that it was probably Michael Horniman, who was the rising figure in the Watt agency at the time.

1951 — July — Ballard left King's College, Cambridge, after two years, without taking a degree. "I'd won this story competition, and I thought I'd studied enough medicine for my purposes... I'd been in and out of clinical hospitals as part of the two years I did at Cambridge, and I knew that clinical medicine was enormously demanding in time and energy. Young doctors work long hours, and though they may over the years accumulate an enormous amount of fascinating material they have no time for anything else. In a way, I felt I'd completed the interesting phase of studying medicine. I felt I'd already stocked my vocabulary enough for me to move on. I wanted to write I felt the power of imagination pushing at the door of my mind and I wanted to open it." (Ballard, interviewed by David Pringle, 24 July 1981.)

1951 — July — "After winning the annual short story competition at Cambridge in 1951 he wrote his first novel, a completely unreadable pastiche of *Finnegans Wake* and *The Adventures of Engelbrecht*." (From a profile of Ballard in *New Worlds* no. 54, December 1956.) "I think I did write some pastiches of *The Exploits of Engelbrecht*, though I was gilding the lily a little to refer to it as my first novel. When you're 21 or 22 thirty consecutive pages feel like a novel! I'd accumulated a great mass of experimental prose, certainly heavily influenced by *Finnegans Wake* and *Engelbrecht*. Maurice Richardson's book was, I won't say a big influence on me, but I loved it. It's a marvellous book with terrific panache and swing—very nicely illustrated in the published edition... Richardson wrote a science-fiction story in fact, which was published in *Horizon*, Cyril Connolly's magazine. A fine sf story. I met him for the one and only time about two weeks before he died, and I'm glad I did because I was able to tell him, for what it was worth, how much I admired *Engelbrecht* and that sf story he wrote in the 40s (the only one, he said)." (Ballard, interviewed by David Pringle, 24 July 1981.) The story referred to was Maurice Richardson's "Way Out in the Continuum" (*Horizon*, March 1946).

1951 — Summer — Ballard, newly down from Cambridge, saw the Festival of Britain, as did so many others in the course of this year. "I still remember visiting the Festival of Britain in 1951, which drew the same carping criticisms. But to leave sooty, rationed, bomb-site London and arrive at the South Bank was an exhilarating experience, a glimpse of a future Britain—concrete and glass, but why not?—that was genuinely inspiring and full of hope. Everyone around me in the bright, open-air cafés wanted the Festival to be a success." (Ballard, "Bursting the Bubble," *Telegraph*, 6 January 2000.) "Spencer felt so too—though not of course visiting at the same time as Ballard. The Festival did much to restore faith in the marvellous future predicted by boys' magazines of the 1930s. It was as though the War had been a temporary blip, an aberration which was now rapidly receding into history. Design was a key element, and the streamlined surfaces of chromium or glass expressed a liberation from the dreary concepts of the past." (William Spencer, notes on this timeline, 2010.)

1951 — September 18 (Tuesday) — Elia Kazan's film *A Streetcar Named Desire*, based on the Tennessee Williams play, and starring Marlon Brando and Vivien Leigh, premiered in Beverly Hills, California. (It would have a London release on 28 February 1952.) "Sly, illiterate and aggressive, and supremely confident of his sweating and animal body, Brando's Kowalski became the idol of a rebellious generation, if not ready to rape their mothers, represented by the prim and self-deluding Blanche Du Bois, at least ready to rape their mothers' values." (Ballard, *Guardian*, 30 May 1991.)

1951 — September 26 (Wednesday) — "TOKYO, Sept. 26. R.A.A.F. Meteors were among 77 U.N. jet fighters which clashed to-day with 160 Russian-built MIG-15s over North-west Korea. The R.A.A.F. claimed one MIG-15 probably shot down—the Meteors' first success in a dog-fight. Earlier, 37 United States Sabre jet fighters had challenged about 60 MIG-15s. The Americans claimed one MIG probably destroyed. Later 28 United States Thunderjets met 20 MIG-15s, the Thunderjet pilots claiming three enemy planes damaged. In all the clashes the Communist planes, after breaking off the battle, escaped across the Yalu River into Manchuria. To-day's all-jet clash was the largest ever, dwarfing yesterday's battle between 37 Sabres and 100 MIG-15s." (*Sydney Morning Herald*, 27 September 1951.)

1951 — September 30 (Sunday) — The Festival of Britain, which had run for five months, came to a close. It was judged to have been a great success. "King George VI, who opened the Festival on 3 May, was to have taken part in the final ceremonies but had to pull out because he is still convalescing from an operation on his lungs. Some 8.5 million people have paid to visit the exhibition which included the Royal Festival Hall, the 200 ft Skylon and the Dome of Discovery, an aluminium display centre containing a planetarium and other features." (BBC.)

1951 — October 2 (Tuesday) — The Michaelmas Term officially began at Queen Mary College, University of London, where Ballard was about to become a student. Within the Faculty of Arts, in the English Language and Literature department, the teachers were: University Professor, James R. Sutherland, MA; Senior Lecturer, Dr B. J. Timmer; Lecturers, N. R. Callan, MA, Marjorie Thompson, MA, Hope Hammond, MA (Cantab.), PhD, and Celia Sisam, MA; Visiting Assistant Lecturer, Olga Illston, BA. The college, which had begun life in Victorian times as the "People's Palace," was situated on the Mile End Road, in the unfashionable East End of London.

1951 — October 12 (Friday) — Ballard became an undergraduate at the University of London's Queen Mary College, studying English Literature. (Although term had begun on 2 October, for some reason 12 October was marked as "date of entry" on his student card.) "I went to London University for a year after I left Cambridge and I read English. This makes me sound like a medieval scholar, moving from bench to bench, but it wasn't like that... My father said, with a chemist's logic, 'Well, if you want to be a writer you should study English.' So I went to London University, read English, and they turfed me out at the end of the year, deciding I hadn't got what it took to be a student of English Literature." (Ballard, interviewed by David Pringle, 24 July 1981.) "I was still doing subsidiary Latin when I read English for a year at London University after ending my medical studies at Cambridge—from one set of Latin tags to another." (Ballard, interviewed by Thomas Frick, 1983.)

1951 — October 25 (Thursday) — It was another General Election day in the United Kingdom, the second in less than two years. This time the Labour Party lost, and the Conservatives were returned to power. Winston Churchill became Prime Minister again, a month before his 77th birthday. Ballard was still not old enough to vote, too young by a mere three weeks. (He would have no opportunity to vote in a General Election until 1955.)

1951 — November 15 (Thursday) — J.G. Ballard's 21st birthday. "I liked London, and particularly the Chelsea area, with its lesbian pubs and rich friends of friends who took me to expensive nightclubs like the Milroy and Embassy in Mayfair. ... Everything was still very shabby and much of

BALLARD'S STUDENT CARD, QUEEN MARY COLLEGE

Surname BALLARD — Christian Names James Graham
Date of Entry 12.10.51 — Permanent Address Brynfield, Townscliffe Lane, Mellor, Cheshire. Marple 1482
Date of Birth 15.11.30
Occupation of Parent Merchant J.
Session 1951–1952 — Session 19 —19 — Session 19 —19 — Session 19

Subjects: Intermediate
English 8 54
Latin 6 75
History C 45

Failed Inter June 1952. Not permitted to return to College next session (1952/3) (3.7.52)
2.3

J.G. Ballard's student card at Queen Mary College.

South Kensington, where I had a room in Onslow Gardens, was semi-derelict. People lived in dilapidated flats but bought their clothes in Bond Street. One of the English lecturers, a woman in her forties who lived nearby, owned an open-topped Allard, an impressively stylish car, which she drove all the way to the Mile End Road, a journey unthinkable today. Sometimes she gave me a lift. As we roared through the City of London she would take both hands off the wheel to hold forth about *Gammer Gurton's Needle*." (Ballard, *Miracles of Life*, p151-152.) It would be good to know who that lecturer was, and I hazard a guess that she may have been Hope Hammond, MA (Cantab.), PhD; after all, JGB would later write a story about a *femme fatale* with that forename, entitled "Cry Hope, Cry Fury!" (1967).

1951 — November 20 (Tuesday) — Onslow Gardens, where Ballard was living, was off Old Brompton Road, to the south of the Natural History Museum, Kensington, and just north-west of Chelsea. According to the London electoral register for 1952 ("Qualifying date 20th November, 1951"), Kensington and Chelsea District, Ballard's digs were at number 28 Onslow Gardens. There were eight other registered voters in the house, in addition to JGB (and yes, he was registered as a voter by this time, just after his 21st birthday). Interestingly, of the other voters in the household, which seems to have consisted mainly of single students of differing names, two shared the same surname, and both were female—Alice and Marie Pollock. Could they have been the landlady and her daughter? In a fictional context, JGB would write: "The only women I had made love to ... were the middle-aged landlady and her daughter who ran the small hotel in west London where I had stayed during my mother's return to the Far East [sic; the timing of this is fictitious]..." (Ballard, *The Kindness of Women*, 1991, p92.) Was making love to a landlady and her daughter a fantasy on his part, or something that really happened? If the latter is the case, then the two women in question were probably Alice and Marie Pollock.

1951 — December 3 (Monday) — "LONDON, Dec. 3. The surrealist Spanish painter, Salvador Dali, 47, has 'gone serious,' says Reuters. Dali, who last met London reporters 15 years ago in a diving suit, with two Russian wolfhounds on a leash, confronted them yesterday in a sombre lounge suit. He arrived in London to open an exhibition of his works in his new style, which he calls 'explosive classicism.' They include a 'Portrait of Christ' which he considers his greatest work. Dali said that surrealism had given way to 'realistic mysticism.' His style in painting had changed from flaming giraffes and weeping watches to subjects of religious symbolism. Standing by a huge painting depicting a Madonna against a bomb-shattered background, with remnants of classical architecture, Dali said: 'I forecast a great renaissance of mystic art during the next ten years.'" (*Sydney Morning Herald*, 4 December 1951.)

1951 — December 14 (Friday) — The Michaelmas Term officially ended at Queen Mary College, University of London. Meanwhile: "LONDON, Dec. 14. The worst 'pea-soup' fog for two years blanketed almost the whole of Eastern Britain from London to Scotland last night and this morning. Temperatures were below freezing and ice covered roads. Sixteen persons were hurt in car crashes. The fog paralysed operations at London airport and entirely disrupted London road and rail traffic." (*Sydney Morning Herald*, 15 December 1951.)

1951 — December (late) — Ballard probably spent the Christmas holiday period with his mother and father and sister at their house in Cheshire, near Manchester. On this visit he had his first experience of television (it must have been late in the year, after the opening in October of the BBC's Holme Moss transmitter which had brought TV to the north of England for the first time): "I remember watching TV with my parents in Manchester in something like 1951. There was only one channel. We looked at a screen the size of a lightbulb. The idea that TV plugged into reality seemed absurd. [But] by the mid-60s, TV was a window into the world." (Ballard, interviewed by Iain Sinclair, 14 June 1998.) It was probably a nine-inch screen, which was the standard at the time, in 1951.

1951 — December 25 (Tuesday) — "Dinner today contained turkey as well as peas, potatoes, beef and gravy. And there was Christmas pudding after. We heard HM the King at 3.0. After tea we watched the TV Christmas Party until 9.0. It was exceptionally good entertainment. The guests included Jewel and Warriss, Petula Clark, Vic Oliver, Anne Ziegler and Webster Booth, Ethel Revnell, Norman Wisdom, Ravicz and Landauer, Terry-Thomas, the Twelve Toppers and many others. The hosts were Leslie Mitchell & Jerry Desmonde. Each turn was very good, Norman Wisdom's especially so. The party was followed by a play as good as any I have seen on TV. It was J.B. Priestley's farcical comedy 'When We Are Married' and it was hilariously funny in parts." (Brian Williams, aged 16, Birmingham, diary.)

1951 — Despite the distractions of films, the wireless and (very limited) television, reading was still the main thing: "In the Forties and Fifties when I first came to England, what I loved were the second-hand bookshops. Every small town had a second-hand bookshop which was constantly being stocked up ... when someone died the family took their books to the second-hand bookshop and got sixpence each for them... I did most of my reading in second-hand bookshops. I remember when I was living in London somewhere I used a local one. Also serendipity came into it, because you looked around the stacks of all these books—mostly hardcovers, not paperbacks—you looked at these books and you said, 'Oh, Robert Graves, I very much enjoyed something by him, but what's this? *Goodbye to All That*—a biography of his First World War experiences?'—a brilliant book! You made accidental discoveries all the time... You were constantly being surprised." (Ballard, interviewed by Vale, 23 November 2004.)

1952

1952 — January 9 (Wednesday) — The Spring Term officially began at Queen Mary College, University of London. If Ballard had been staying with his parents near Manchester during the holiday period, as seems likely, he would have returned to London before this date.

1952 — January 22 (Tuesday) — "The Goon Show" began on the BBC Home Service, with comedians Spike Milligan, Peter Sellers, Harry Secombe and Michael Bentine in manic form. It had started as the radio show "Crazy People" in 1951, but was now relaunched under its creators' preferred title.

1952 — February 6 (Wednesday) — Death of King George VI (b. 1895) of the United Kingdom, of a heart attack at 56. His 25-year-old daughter, Princess Elizabeth, immediately succeeded to the throne.

1952 — February 7 (Thursday) — Queen Elizabeth II, who had been on a tour of Kenya at the time of her father's death, arrived home in England. Prime Minister Winston Churchill made a broadcast to the nation at 9 o'clock in the evening in which he welcomed the dawn of a "New Elizabethan Age."

1952 — March 18 (Tuesday) — A photograph of the 21-year-old Ballard was taken on this day. A copy would be attached to his student card at Queen Mary College, and the same photo would later be used to accompany his first author profile, in *New Worlds* no. 54, December 1956.

1952 — March 20 (Thursday) — Akira Kurosawa's 1950 film *Rashomon*, starring Toshiro Mifune, had its first UK release, in London. "The first Kurosawa film I saw back in the 1950s was *Rashomon*. It was the first Japanese film I'd ever seen, and I was tremendously impressed by it. Quite apart from its very subtle and complex story, it had a level of elegance and visual sophistication that few contemporary American or European films had... The richness of the film and the themes it tackled, the moral relativities that underpin or undermine the truth, are quite remarkable." (Ballard, interviewed by Matthew Leonard, ABC Radio *24 Hours*, January 1992.)

1952 — Spring — Ursula Keir Simpson returned to England, after spending two years in Argentina. She was still only 22, but she had a written stories for *Blackwood's Magazine* in the late 1940s (their youngest contributor), and around this time, in 1952-1953, she would publish two novels, *The Sun Behind Me* and *The Vintage*, with Collins in the UK. She was Ballard's early-childhood friend from Shanghai, but they had probably not seen each other since 1937. Did they meet again around this time? Ursula's daughter Keiran Ure thinks so, but has no further details, alas. (Ursula's second novel would be filmed in 1957, with stars Pier Angeli and

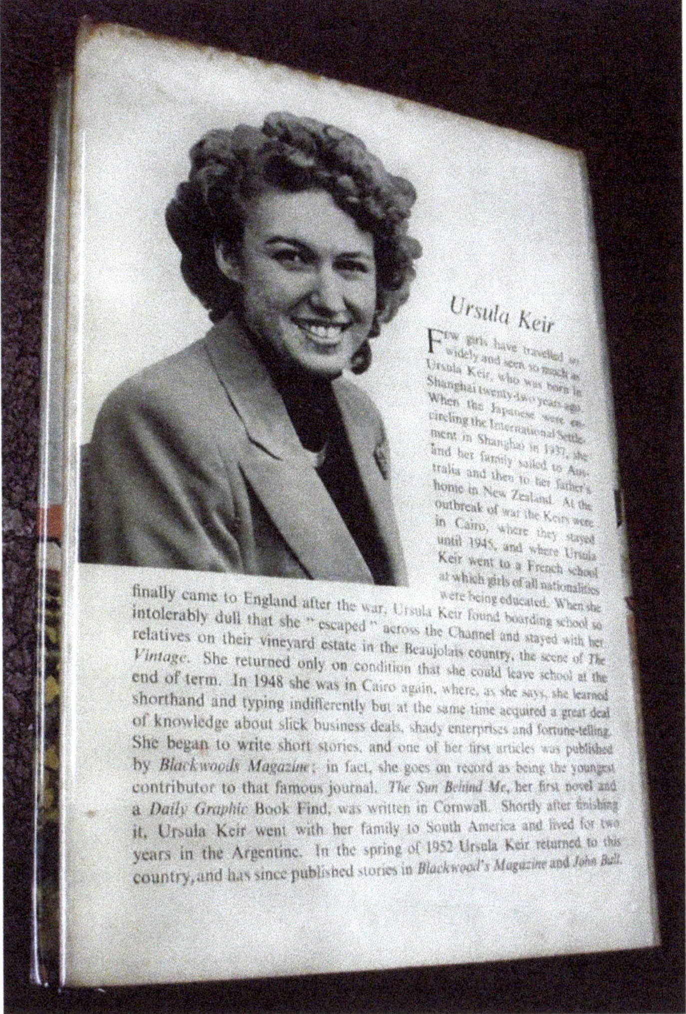

Ursula Keir

Few girls have travelled so widely and seen so much as Ursula Keir, who was born in Shanghai twenty-two years ago. When the Japanese were encircling the International Settlement in Shanghai in 1937, she and her family sailed to Australia and then to her father's home in New Zealand. At the outbreak of war the Keirs were in Cairo, where they stayed until 1945, and where Ursula Keir went to a French school at which girls of all nationalities were being educated. When she finally came to England after the war, Ursula Keir found boarding school so intolerably dull that she "escaped" across the Channel and stayed with her relatives on their vineyard estate in the Beaujolais country, the scene of *The Vintage*. She returned only on condition that she could leave school at the end of term. In 1948 she was in Cairo again, where, as she says, she learned shorthand and typing indifferently but at the same time acquired a great deal of knowledge about slick business deals, shady enterprises and fortune-telling. She began to write short stories, and one of her first articles was published by *Blackwoods Magazine*; in fact, she goes on record as being the youngest contributor to that famous journal. *The Sun Behind Me*, her first novel and a *Daily Graphic* Book Find, was written in Cornwall. Shortly after finishing it, Ursula Keir went with her family to South America and lived for two years in the Argentine. In the spring of 1952 Ursula Keir returned to this country, and has since published stories in *Blackwood's Magazine* and *John Bull*.

The back cover of Ursula Keir's novel, *The Vintage*.

Mel Ferrer, but unfortunately her career as a writer would peter out after that.)

1952 — April 14 (Monday) — "LONDON, April 14. On the last day of the Easter holiday, Londoners poured out of the city to-day at a record rate. In an hour 22,000 cars left the city as crowds flocked to the seaside, the hills and sporting events. The temperature reached nearly 70 degrees." (*Sydney Morning Herald*, 15 April 1952.)

1952 — April 20 (Sunday) — "LONDON, April 20. A plan to move almost one-third of Britain's population to Commonwealth countries will be urged by Conservative and Labour MPs when the House of Commons discusses the Empire Settlement Bill tomorrow, says the *Sunday Express*. At present about 170,000 Britons migrate to the Commonwealth every year. Advocates of mass migration believe the figure should be raised to 750,000 a year for 20 years." (*Sydney Morning Herald*, 21 April 1952.) It would not happen, at any rate on that scale, but many young people in the 1950s, including Ballard, were contemplating leaving the UK if they could.

1952 — June 1 (Sunday) — Opening on this day, the "New Aspects of British Sculpture" exhibition at the 26th Venice Biennale introduced the work of eight young sculptors, all under 40—Eduardo Paolozzi, Reg Butler, Lynn Chadwick, and five others. Executed in pitted bronze or welded metal, their work was characterized by spiky, alien-looking figures. They would become known as the "geometry of fear" sculptors, because in his catalogue essay the critic Herbert Read wrote: "These new images belong to the iconography of despair, or of defiance; and the more innocent the artist, the more effectively he transmits the collective guilt. Here are images of flight, of ragged claws 'scuttling across the floors of silent seas,' of excoriated flesh, frustrated sex, the geometry of fear." (The quotation in Read's text was from T. S. Eliot's "Prufrock.")

1952 — June — Ballard performed poorly in his Intermediate exams at Queen Mary College. His student card stated: "Failed Inter June 52: Latin (47 C) English (61 B) History (38 D Failed)." He would write: "The English course was interesting, but modern fiction played no part in it, and at the end of my first year I decided to leave." (Ballard, *Miracles of Life*, p153.)

1952 — July 3 (Thursday) — The Summer Term having officially ended at the University of London, Ballard finished as an undergraduate at Queen Mary College. His student card was marked on this date: "Failed Inter June 1952. Not permitted to return to College next session (1952/3)." So it seems he was indeed—in a phrase he would use later—"turfed out."

1952 — July — "My real problems began when I was thrown out of London University, because that had been a year's grace. I still wasn't ready to do anything remotely like becoming a professional writer. The opportunities didn't exist. My father gave me a small allowance, but it was hard earned. It was a tricky time... There were periods, I suppose, when I just drifted. I was discovering London for the first time. I'd come down from Cambridge and had a year as a student. I lived in a very shabby cheap bedsitter in South Kensington. I spent a lot of time in Chelsea, a world that's vanished now. It wasn't a bohemian phase, though. I was writing a lot of short fiction of various kinds..." (Ballard, interviewed by David Pringle, 24 July 1981.) "Jimmy was kept on fairly short commons by an allowance from his father, and Spencer had to tide him over sometimes with small sums of money until his allowance came through. At one point he was desperate enough to pawn his typewriter, and may not have had enough funds to redeem it." (William Spencer, notes on this timeline, 2010.)

1952 — July-August? — "William and Kaye Spencer were undecided where to go for their first summer holiday as a newly married couple. Jimmy said, 'You must go to Newton Ferrers' (which they did). Newton Ferrers is a tiny village up an estuary in south Devon, full of nostalgic charm (it is the place where the movie of du Maurier's *Frenchman's Creek* was filmed). Apparently Jimmy and his sister and mother had rented a house there earlier, and had been much impressed." Also some time in this year, "Spencer discovered Arthur Waley's translation of the Tao Te Ching entitled *The Way and Its Power* (1934). He was tremendously impressed by this and showed it to all his friends. But Ballard did not appear to be similarly smitten." (William Spencer, notes on this timeline, 2010.)

1952 — Late Summer? — Ballard became a porter in Covent Garden, London, carrying boxes or trays in the flower market.

"I took a job as a Covent Garden porter, working in the chrysanthemum department of a large wholesaler. We started early, at something like 6 o'clock, and were through by noon. [But] too many sleep-starved nights finally got to me..." (Ballard, *Miracles of Life*, p159.) "We maintained friendly contact after we left university. I was working as an advertising copywriter for an agency in London... In the early 1950s, Jim Ballard had a succession of jobs which were quite bizarre. One of them was as a Covent Garden porter. That one sticks in my mind because it was rather unexpected (although he was an athletic young man; I imagine he could lift up whatever they lift up in Covent Garden with no trouble at all). I think he started at four o'clock [sic] in the morning and, having finished his day's work, he would come into my office at about 10 am [sic], gasping for a cup of coffee. It seemed to me this was completely the wrong job for him to be doing." (William Spencer, interviewed by David Pringle, *Interzone* no. 79, January 1994.)

1952 — September 6 (Saturday) — Seconds after breaking the sound barrier, a De Havilland 110 jet aircraft fell apart over the spectators at the Farnborough Air Show, in Hampshire, England, killing 27 people. "Among the dead are the pilot, John Derry, and the flight test observer Anthony Richards. Mr Derry was the first British pilot to exceed the speed of sound in this country four years ago today, on 6 September 1948, in a DH 108 research aircraft... The two engines broke loose and one plunged into a dense crowd watching on a hillside. The other engine fell on open ground but other members of the public were injured by parts of the cockpit. Fire engines and ambulances arrived within minutes and after a short break the air display continued. Squadron Leader Neville Duke, a close friend of Mr Derry, even flew a Hawker Hunter jet up to a height of 40,000 ft and demonstrated a double sonic boom." (BBC.) "William and Kaye Spencer made the pilgrimage from Richmond to Farnborough in their car for the annual air show on more than one occasion (sometimes with friends, but never with Jimmy) but luckily were not present at this particular meeting." (Spencer, notes on this timeline, 2010.)

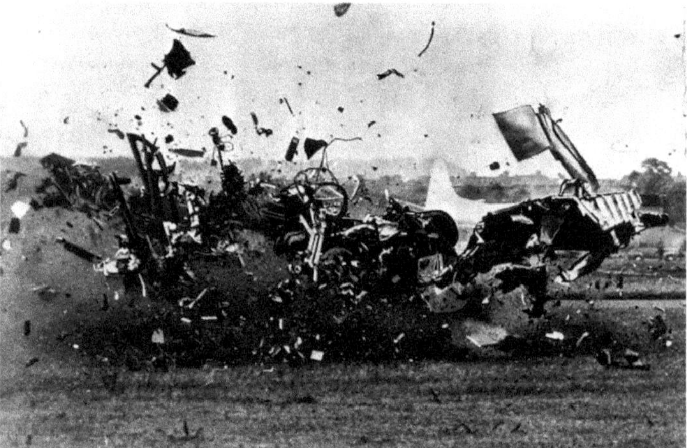

The de Havilland DH.110 prototype impact at RAE Farnborough. This photograph was taken by a spectator, Herbert Orr.

1952 — September 6 (Saturday) — Death of Gertrude Lawrence (b. 1898), British actress, singer and dancer, a great star of musical comedy, of liver cancer at 54. "My image of London was formed during my Shanghai childhood in the 1930s as I listened to my parents' generation talk nostalgically of West End shows, the bright lights of Piccadilly, Noel Coward and Gertie Lawrence, reinforced by a Peter Pan and Christopher Robin image of a London that consisted entirely of Knightsbridge and Kensington, where 1 per cent of the population was working-class and everyone else was a barrister of stockbroker." (Ballard, *Time Out*, 13 October 1993.)

1952 — October 3 (Friday) — The first British nuclear test, "Operation Hurricane," took place off the Monte Bello islands, Australia. A 25-kiloton atom bomb was exploded aboard a superannuated frigate, HMS *Plym*. "The press reaction to the spectacular explosion off the Monte Bello Islands, complete with smoke plume topping out at 15,000 feet in the clear western Australian air, was one of elation. 'Today Britain is GREAT BRITAIN again—in the eyes of the world,' began the Daily Mirror's front-page report." (David Kynaston, *Family Britain*, p125.)

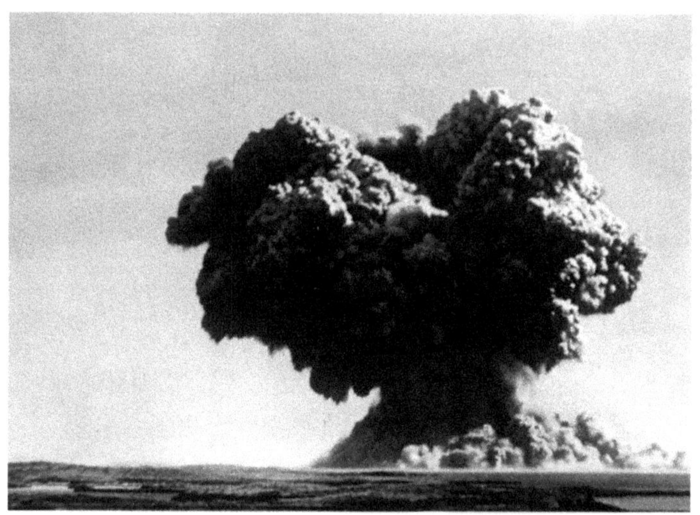

Operation Hurricane.

1952 — November 1 (Saturday) — The United States exploded the first hydrogen bomb, in a test at Eniwetok in the Marshall Islands.

1952 — November 7 (Friday) — On this date two final notes were added to Ballard's student card at Queen Mary College (although he was no longer enrolled there). The address 28 Onslow Gardens, London SW7, was crossed out and replaced with: "7 Lansdowne Walk, Holland Park, W11. 7.11.52." The following was added to the other side of his card: "Copywriter at an advertising agency. (7.11.52.) Not liable for Nat. Service."

evious Education	Leys School, Cambridge, 46-9 Kings College, Cambridge, 49-51
triculation or ion of Exemption	Oxf. & Camb. SC. June 47
versity ion	✓10/51
e	Oxf. & Camb. HSC. June 49 Pass: Biology, Chemistry Failed Inter June 52: Latin (47C) English (61B) History (38D Failed) Subsid: English
... ...	
ities	Copywriter at an advertising agency. (7.11.52) Not liable for Nat. Service.

1952 — November 7 (circa) — Ballard became an advertising copywriter—briefly. "Through a Cambridge friend who was working for Benson's advertising agency in Kingsway, where Dorothy Sayers had worked and which housed the spiral staircase that appeared in one of her novels, I found a job as a novice copywriter..." (Ballard, interviewed by David Pringle, 24 July 1981.) "I knew there was a copywriting job going in a neighbouring agency and I encouraged him to apply—but this proved to be quite the wrong thing, almost a total disaster in that he didn't find it suited him at all and he handed in his notice almost immediately and disappeared from view." (William Spencer, interviewed by David Pringle, *Interzone* no. 79, January 1994.) "The job I recommended JGB to try for was at a major London advertising agency (I think CPV—Colman Prentis & Varley—one of the top five London agencies of the day, engaged on major campaigns in the national media). They took him on, but he left precipitously of his own accord after about a week. The job he mentions in a 1981 interview with you was with a much less distinguished agency, Digby Wills, where the work was correspondingly more humdrum. This employment was quite a bit later than the CPV episode, and I had no part in steering him towards it. JGB has telescoped these two incidents together in his account in *Miracles of Life*." (Spencer, notes on this timeline, 2010.)

1952 — November 15 (Saturday) — J.G. Ballard's 22nd birthday. "I was always interested in the visual arts. I bought a lot of art magazines, and I used to go to all the new exhibitions on in London. I spent a lot of time haunting the National Gallery and the Tate Gallery at times I used to go every day. I was interested in the old Institute of Contemporary Arts [the ICA]. I wasn't a member, but I used to go to exhibitions there. ... When I was in my early 20s, I had reproductions of surrealist paintings pinned up wherever I was living. They were totally out of favour then and it was difficult to get hold of works by the surrealists. If there was an exhibition somewhere or another usually in a small commercial gallery in London it wasn't well reviewed... But there were surrealist works in the Tate Gallery in the early 1950s. I remember seeing Delvaux there, along with a few Chiricos and Ernsts and Dalis. They were in a sort of little dark ante-room." (Ballard, interviewed by David Pringle, 24 July 1981.) "And I used to go to Sotheby's and look at paintings there, where Surrealist paintings often changed hands." (Ballard, interviewed by Nicholas Zurbrugg, 8 January 1992.)

1952 — December 5-9 (Friday-Tuesday) — The Great Smog in London: it was estimated that 4,000 people died in the worst of the "killer fogs."

1952 — December 22 (Monday) — It was William and Kaye Spencer's first wedding anniversary. In this year (or perhaps in 1953) they "moved into a flat near the top of Richmond Hill. The view from the Hill, looking down over the Terrace Gardens to the winding Thames and Eel Pie Island, was much loved by them, and appreciated by their visitors including Jim Ballard. William took driving lessons and acquired his first car. Expeditions to a congenial pub in Thames Ditton were on the agenda. It is possible that Jim first came to know the charms of the Thames Valley west of London through such visits, perhaps influencing the choice, when he married, of a flat near Twickenham (just over the river from Richmond) and the eventual move to Shepperton." (Spencer, notes on this timeline, 2010.)

1952 — In between odd jobs, the young Ballard pursued a slightly bohemian existence in London. "My father certainly disapproved totally of my wanting to become a writer. He regarded it as not really a profession at all, didn't think one could make a sustained career out of it. It would take years to discover whether one had the sort of talent the world would pay attention to. In many senses, of course, he was absolutely right. But even with the benefit of hindsight I wouldn't change things. It would have been much easier for me if I had, say, graduated as a doctor. I then would have been financially secure, and given the sort of imaginative pressures I was feeling I think I probably would have written... My mother agreed with my father, but I don't think either of them had much influence on me. I don't think parents do have as much influence on their children as people imagine." (Ballard, interviewed by David Pringle, 24 July 1981.)

1952 — Francis Bacon produced his painting "Study for the Head of a Screaming Pope"—one of many he would do on the same theme. "I remember being interested in Francis Bacon in the very early 50s, when he was virtually unknown and painting most of his early masterpieces, and he was treated with the same sort of disdain that the surrealists received until the 60s (and Dali still does receive). There's an enormous resistance here to certain categories of imaginative work, both in the visual arts and in the novel. This is a very puritanical country. The Protestant

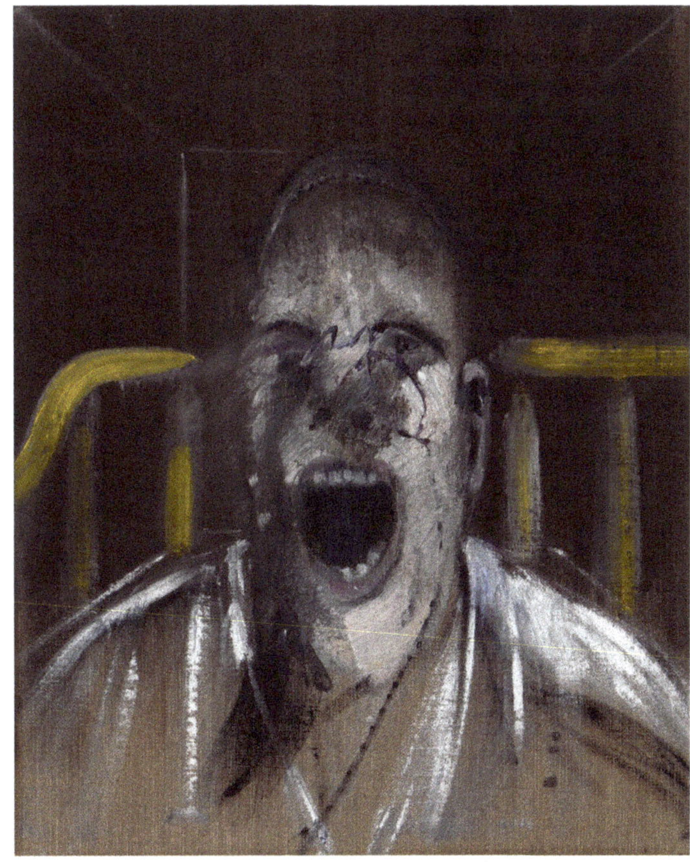

Francis Bacon's "Study for the Head of a Screaming Pope"

Nonconformist hatred of the imagination—of symbolism as a whole, let's say—runs through the whole of English life, and a large section of American life too for the same sort of reasons. Great works of the imagination, of the 19th and 20th centuries, are far too seditious of the bourgeois certainties." (Ballard, interviewed by David Pringle, 24 July 1981.)

1952 — Bernard Wolfe, American writer, published his novel *Limbo* (New York: Random House), set in an imagined 1990 after a nuclear war. "Anybody who 'paints a picture' of some coming year is kidding—he's only fancying up something in the present or past, not blueprinting the future. All such writing is essentially satiric (today-centered), not utopic (tomorrow-centered). This book, then, is a rather bilious rib on 1950—on what 1950 might have been like if it had been allowed to fulfil itself, if it had gone on being 1950, only more and more so, for four more decades. But no year ever fulfils itself: the cow-path of History is littered with the corpses of years, their silly throats slit from ear to ear by the improbable. I am writing about the overtone and undertow of now—in the guise of 1990 because it would take decades for a year like 1950 to be milked of its implications. What 1990 will really look like I haven't the slightest idea." (Wolfe, "Author's Note and Warnings," *Limbo*.)

1953

1953 — January 20 (Tuesday) — Dwight D. Eisenhower was inaugurated as President of the United States in succession to Harry S. Truman.

1953 — February 1 (Sunday) — The Great North Sea Flood: "Hundreds of people living on the east coast of Britain have died in some of the worst storms ever recorded. Gale force northerly winds lashed the coastline and broke through flood defences throughout the night. Swelling tides and high winds mixed to form a fatal combination which flooded thousands of homes on low-lying land all along the east coast." (BBC.)

1953 — February 3 (Tuesday) — "LONDON, Feb. 3. Life is slowly returning to Canvey Island in the mouth of the Thames, the worst hit spot in Britain's flood disaster. A correspondent on the island reported to-day: No-one can tell accurately how many have died in the storm which ravaged the island in the sleeping hours of Sunday. But Dr. John Murray, who, like hundreds of persons on the island, has not slept for 30 hours, told me: 'My three co-doctors and myself, have personally laid out 123 bodies.'" (*Sydney Morning Herald*, 4 February 1953.)

1953 — Early-to-Mid — It may have been around this time that Ballard once more became an advertising copywriter. "I went to work for an advertising agency called Digby Wills Ltd, where I wrote copy, for lemon juice among other things. I was there for three or four months." (Ballard, interviewed by David Pringle, 24 July 1981.) "Working as a copywriter at an advertising agency was not as glamorous or interesting as novels and films suggested. Most of it was a slog, a dull chore of writing booklets and copy for manuals." (Ballard, *Miracles of Life*, p153, 159.) "The only thing I wasn't thrown out of was advertising. After I'd been in advertising for a while, I suddenly realized that I hadn't been thrown out of it. It told me, 'Run, don't walk!' I threw myself out." (Ballard, interviewed by Martin Amis, *Observer Magazine*, 2 September 1984.) Digby Wills Ltd had begun in 1951 in two small rooms in High Holborn, London. Their break came when they started handling advertising for PLJ (Pure Lemon Juice, in a bottle). "The campaign was so successful that the product would go from a turnover of £30,000 in 1954 to £1,300,000 in 1959. The account for Bayer pharmaceutical products, which included Panadol (Paracetemol), was also won, as well as a Central Office of Information account—Post Early for Christmas.'" (History of Advertising Trust website.) But JGB had left the agency before most of that.

1953 — March 5 (Thursday) — Death of Joseph Stalin (b. 1878), dictator of the Soviet Union, after 29 years in power at age 74.

1953 — March 5 (Thursday) — At this date, Ballard continued to live in digs in Lansdowne Walk, in the Holland Park area of London, West 11. "I can confirm that Ballard was still living at 7 Lansdowne Walk, W11 on 5 March 1953. The school [i.e. The Leys, Cambridge] received a form for completion from the Ministry of National Insurance with that date on it." (Raymond Tait, Cambridge, e-mail to DP.) It was probably around this time, or soon after, that he bumped into his old Lunghua associate Cyril Goldbert (now known as Peter Wyngarde) in the Mitre, a large pub on the corner of Holland Park Avenue and Ladbroke Grove, west London. "He was in a poor way, with bad teeth and tired eyes. But ten years later he achieved huge success, not on stage but on television..." (Ballard, *Miracles of Life*, p86.)

1953 — March 31 (Tuesday) — Soon after nine o'clock in the morning, John Reginald Christie, late of 10 Rillington Place, Notting Hill, was arrested by an observant policeman as he loitered near Putney Bridge, London. "It was on the morning of 31st March that he was approached by Police Constable Thomas Ledger near the embankment at Putney Bridge. When asked to identify himself, he gave his name as John Waddington and provided a false address. Constable Ledger then asked him to remove his hat, and after he'd done so, came to the conclusion that Mr Waddington bore a certain similarity to photographs of the wanted John Christie. Constable Ledger then arrested him and took him to Putney police station. There he was discovered in possession of an identity card, ration book, and union card in the name of John Reginald Halliday Christie. Having confirmed that they had indeed got their man, the police placed Christie in a closed van and took him to Notting Hill at 5.10 pm that day to be questioned by detectives. He later appeared at West London Magistrates' Court on the 1st April charged with his wife's murder, and made a further appearance at the same court on the 15th April when he was charged with the murder of the three women found in the coal cellar." (everything2.com/node/1487034)

1953 — March 31 (Tuesday) — 5.10 pm — Christie was taken from Putney to Notting Hill police station, to be interrogated there. "Soon after my meeting with Peter Wyngarde at the Mitre in Holland Park Avenue, I was walking up Ladbroke Grove when I found a huge crowd outside the police station. They filled the side street, watching the entrance to the car park behind the station. A police car approached, siren ringing, followed by a police van. The crowd drew back, leaving a woman in a red coat standing in the middle of the side street. The constables guarding the car park entrance made no attempt to move her, and she stood her ground, watched admiringly by the crowd as the police car and van swerved at speed through the gates. The woman in the red coat was the sister of Timothy Evans, a mentally retarded friend of Christie, who had been charged with the murder of his son [sic] and hanged in 1950. In fact, Christie had murdered the infant... I can still remember the woman in the red coat, and her implacable gaze as she stared at the police van. Inside was John Christie, a now-deranged figure who had just been arrested for the murders he had committed at Rillington Place." (Ballard, *Miracles of Life*, p172.)

1953 — April 4 (Saturday) — It may have been around this time, in the Easter holiday period, that the following occurred. "William and Kaye Spencer planned to spend a holiday in a sailing barge on the Norfolk Broads, but had no experience of handling such a craft. Jimmy, based on Far Eastern experience of dinghy sailing, volunteered to instruct them. They went to Kingston-on-Thames, where it was possible to hire dinghies by the hour. They did well downwind and down current, but when the time came to return against wind and current they had to be rescued by the boatyard owner. They had forgotten about the need to deploy the dinghy's centreboard when tacking against the wind!" (Spencer, notes on this timeline, 2010.)

1953 — April 28 (Tuesday) — "LONDON, April 28. Members cheered the Prime Minister, Sir Winston Churchill, when he entered the House of Commons yesterday. It was his first appearance in the House since the Queen created him a Knight of the Garter last Friday." On the same day: "LONDON, April 28. Hundreds of Japanese, many of them children waving Japanese flags, to-day greeted Japan's Crown Prince Akihito on his arrival in London. He will represent his father, the Emperor, at the Queen's Coronation on June 2." (*Sydney Morning Herald*, 29 April 1953.)

1953 — May 24 (Sunday) — Peter Wyngarde took the title role in the television play "Will Shakespeare" by Clemence Dane, with Valerie White as Anne Hathaway. It was one of the "BBC Sunday Night Theatre" productions, timed as part of the general celebration of Englishness for the approaching Coronation. He had already played smaller roles in several other BBC plays, but this was probably his first leading part on British TV.

1953 — May 29 (Friday) — Mount Everest was finally conquered when Edmund Hillary of New Zealand and Tenzing Norgay, Sherpa of Nepal, became the first climbers to reach the summit.

1953 — June 2 (Tuesday) — Queen Elizabeth II was crowned in Westminster Abbey by the Archbishop of Canterbury, Dr Geoffrey Fisher, in front of more than 8,000 guests, including prime ministers and heads of state from around the Commonwealth. Street parties were held around Britain, and people crowded round television sets to watch the ceremony. News of the successful ascent of Everest had reached Britain on the morning of the same day: "All this — and Everest too!" said a headline in the *Daily Express*.

1953 — June 4 (Thursday) — In the Notting Hill area, west London, the *Kensington Post* reported that "Rillington Place Goes Gay in June" for the Queen's coronation, with kerbstones and lamp-posts painted red, white and blue. The Coronation street-party festivities, organized by Mr Woods of the Rillington Place Rainbow café, included a Punch and Judy show.

1953 — June 8 (Monday) — Benjamin Britten's opera "Gloriana" was first performed at the Royal Opera House, Covent Garden, London, as part of the celebrations of the coronation of Queen Elizabeth II. It had a libretto by William Plomer, based on Lytton Strachey's book *Elizabeth and Essex* (1928), and singers Joan Cross and Peter Pears took the lead roles.

1953 — July 15 (Wednesday) — The execution by hanging took place of John Reginald Christie (b. 1898), the "Rillington Place murderer," at Pentonville Prison, where a crowd of some 200 people stood waiting for the notice of his death to be posted. Rillington Place was a row of Victorian terraced houses built in the late 1860s, along with much of Notting Hill and North Kensington. (Due to morbid public interest, it would be renamed Ruston Close in 1954 at the request of the residents. However, sightseeing trips around 10 Rillington Place—now 10 Ruston Close—would continue until the street was demolished in 1976-1977 to make way for the Westway urban motorway. The new development would be renamed Bartle Road in 1981, and the actual site of 10 Rillington Place is now a small garden.) "In the early 1950s a part-time prostitute who occupied the room next to mine in a Notting Hill hotel would dress her little daughter in a Marie Antoinette costume, along with gilded hat and silk umbrella. She was always present when the clients climbed the high staircase, and I nearly alerted the police, assuming these gloomy, middle-aged men had sex with the child. But a woman neighbour assured me that all was well—during sex with the mother they were merely watched by the child. Before I could do anything they had moved. This was Christie-land." (Ballard, annotations to *The Atrocity Exhibition*, Re/Search, 1990.)

1953 — July 18 (Saturday) — "The Quatermass Experiment," a science-fiction serial in six half-hour parts by Nigel Kneale, with Reginald Tate playing Professor Bernard Quatermass and Duncan Lamont as the returning space explorer who mutates into a monster, began on BBC Television. Produced by Rudolph Cartier, it would be a popular success.

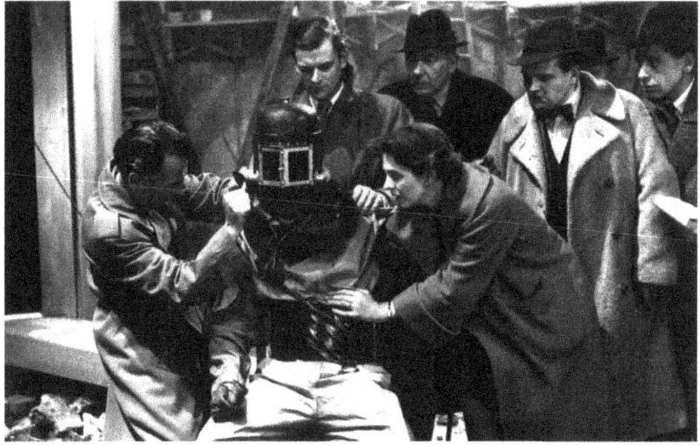

The Quatermass Experiment, first episode.

1953 — July 27 (Monday) — An armistice which would bring an end to fighting in the three-year-old Korean War was signed by representatives of the United Nations, Korea and China in Panmunjon.

1953 — August 8 (Saturday) — The Soviet prime minister, Georgi Malenkov, announced that the Soviet Union now had a hydrogen bomb.

1953 — August 15 (Saturday) — This was the eighth anniversary of the end of World War II, and it is possible that around this time Ballard may have attended a gathering of Shanghailanders at the Regent Palace Hotel, Piccadilly Circus, London. In a fictional context, he would write: "At a reunion of Shanghai friends at the Regent Palace Hotel, I saw David Hunter for the first time since our arrival at Southampton in 1946 [sic]. Despite the seven years he had scarcely changed..." (Ballard, *The Kindness of Women*, 1991, p103.) The character of "David Hunter" in JGB's novel seems to be largely fictitious, another alter ego of the author, but one is tempted to ask if in fact Ballard met his old Lunghua prison-camp associate Bobby Patterson at that "reunion of Shanghai friends," and whether Bobby, who had qualified as a pilot in 1951, inspired to some degree the characterization of the flier David Hunter.

1953 — Autumn — Ballard became a travelling salesman. "Then I worked as an encyclopaedia salesman. That was fascinating, one of the most interesting periods in my life. It lasted about six months, I think. Simply going into so many people's homes, I was conducting my own Gallup survey of English life. An encyclopaedia salesman has to start at number one—knock, knock—and then go on to number two. You must knock on every door and try to get in. You have to overcome the feeling that because the lace curtains look a little intimidating you won't knock here you must go in. And it's quite extraordinary, the variety of human lives..." (Ballard, interviewed by David Pringle, 24 July 1981.) "I sold encyclopaedias door to door in the Midlands Coventry, Leicester—I knew all the back streets there. This was in the early 1950s, and there was nothing more dismal and depressing than those endless streets of back-to-backs but, once you opened the front door, you were presented with the full richness of human beings, with all their obsessions. One house was full of budgerigars, literally from the ground floor up the stairs, in cages, the upstairs rooms packed with these birds—in a back room, the kitchen, a family was having tea surrounded by cages from floor to ceiling, the pot of tea being poured, a black-and-white TV the size of a lamp bulb in the corner totally unaware of the birds chattering around them... Move to the next house some other bizarre set-up. It taught me that people's imaginations are extraordinary. Never underestimate the imagination of the ordinary person. I've written imaginative fiction taking that for granted. That's why I believe in imaginative fiction, because you can light so many tapers in ordinary people's minds that are waiting there to be lit." (Ballard, interviewed by Ken Bruce, BBC Radio 2, 10 September 1984.)

1953 — November — A full-page advert for *The Waverley Encyclopedia of General Information* (published by the Waverley Book Company Ltd, London) appeared in the November issue of the fiction magazine *Argosy* (UK). This indicates a likely publication date of its new edition, which Ballard had been hired to sell. "Ballard knows about selling. As a young man he briefly peddled children's encyclopaedias, working the psychological relationship between the middleclass hawker and the punter bent on self-improvement. 'Selling is like wooing a girl,' says Ballard. [He] 'believed in' *The Waverley* because he had read it as a boy. Whenever he was bored his mother had told him, '"Go and read The Eight Volumes." That was her name for them,' he chuckles. 'It was the nearest thing to television.'" (Ballard, interviewed by Marianne Brace, *Independent*, 15 September 2006.) But how did JGB travel to those Midland towns where he did his peddling? He had no car at this early date, so he must have travelled by train from London, perhaps staying for some nights in cheap hotels or guest-houses like many other "commercial travellers" of the day.

1953 — November 5 (Thursday) — "LONDON, Nov. 5. The mystery of the missing pipes of Peter Pan, which vanished from the statue in London's Kensington Gardens in March last year, was solved to-day. A Grenadier Guardsman pleaded guilty to the theft. ... The little figure of Peter Pan, cast in bronze, was set up as a memorial to Sir James Barrie's fairy-story character." (*Sydney Morning Herald*, 6 November 1953.)

1953 — November 15 (Sunday) — J.G. Ballard's 23rd birthday. At some point in this year, he had moved to a room in a residential hotel, or boarding house, at 13 Stanley Crescent in the Notting Hill district of west London. "I had originally moved to the Stanley Crescent Hotel after being driven out of South Kensington, when the weekly rent for my room in Onslow Gardens rose from 36 shillings a week to two guineas. [His account elides the fact that he had lived, for at least several months, at 7 Lansdowne Walk, Holland Park, before arriving in the nearby Stanley Crescent.] South Kensington was beginning to stir, as old money that had retreated to the countryside for the duration of the war began to return to its stucco villas. I preferred Notting Hill, for its general raffishness and unexpected delights..." (Ballard, *Miracles of Life*, p173.)

1953 — December 5 (Saturday) — In the *New Statesman* of this date, J.B. Priestley contributed a review article headed "They Come from Inner Space," in which he discussed the genre of science fiction, including the work of Ray Bradbury. "Behind all these topical tales, fables and legends, it seems to me, are deep feelings of anxiety, fear, and guilt. The Unconscious is protesting against the cheap conceit and false optimism of the conscious mind. Having ruined this planet, we take destruction to other planets. This very extension in space of our activities is desolating, at least to minds that are not entirely childish, because it is a move, undertaken in secret despair, in the wrong direction. We have to go somewhere, so we prefer superficially to think of ourselves travelling to the other side of the sun rather than sitting quietly at home and then moving inward, exploring ourselves, the hidden life of the psyche." (The piece would later be reprinted in Priestley's book *Thoughts in the Wilderness*, 1957.)

1953 — December 22 (Tuesday) — William and Kaye Spencer's second wedding anniversary. It was perhaps in this year that "Spencer bought a model aircraft kit (a 40-inch tailless glider) from Mills Bros, a model shop in Southampton Row, but did not get around to building it. He gave the kit to Ballard, who built the glider and flew it in a London park." (Spencer, notes on this timeline, 2010.) One is tempted to think that the park in question was Kensington Gardens, Peter Pan's park, and one has a brief fantasy of writing a small book: *J.G. Ballard in Kensington Gardens*.

1953 — Bernard Wolfe's novel *Limbo* (1952) appeared in Britain as *Limbo '90*. Ballard would read it in this UK edition, probably a couple of years later. "It certainly was one of the books that encouraged me to write science fiction. Much as I admired Ray Bradbury—he was almost alone among sf writers of the day—I didn't feel that my own sf would follow in Bradbury's direction at all. It was tremendously encouraging to read *Limbo '90* and to see a powerful imagination given full rein. I was impressed by the power of the central imaginative idea, and Wolfe's lucid intelligence at work... Wolfe's novel is a sophisticated, anti-utopian piece of fiction which stands comparison with anything written by mainstream writers of the mid-20th century... I was about to start writing sf myself. *Limbo '90* was a great encouragement to me because here was a writer who had the courage to follow his own imagination to the limit, without any concern for the commercial constraints and conventions that I felt severely handicapped the American and British writers of the early 50s. Wolfe's novel has a literary and imaginative dimension that's explored for its own sake. I was struck by the huge vitality of the thing, and by his central image self-amputation as a metaphor for the castration complex, with the whole apparatus of neurotic aggression, wars themselves, struggles for power and so on, flowing from that. I think he brilliantly sustained the idea both on the imaginative level and on the conscious and intellectual level. That's something that's very rare in anti-utopian fiction, where you tend to get one or the other." (Ballard, interviewed by David Pringle, 24 July 1981.)

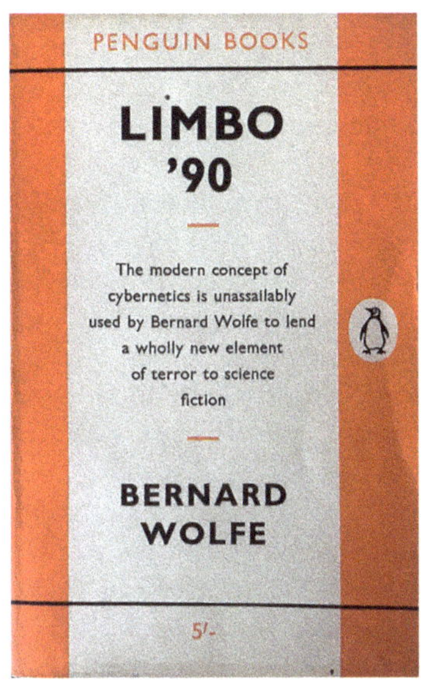

1954

1954 — January 25 (Monday) — Kingsley Amis's debut novel, *Lucky Jim*, was published by Victor Gollancz Ltd in London, and would prove an immediate critical success. On the same day, "Under Milk Wood," a play for voices by the late Dylan Thomas, was broadcast by the BBC Third Programme, with Richard Burton in the lead role as First Voice.

1954 — March 1 (Monday) — "The US has produced the biggest man-made explosion so far in the archipelago of Bikini, part of the Marshall Islands. It is believed the hydrogen bomb was up to 1,000 times more powerful than the atom bomb that destroyed Hiroshima. It was so violent that it overwhelmed the measuring instruments, indicating that it was much more powerful than scientists had anticipated. One of the atolls has been totally vaporised, disappearing into a gigantic mushroom cloud that spread at least 100 miles wide..." (BBC.)

1954 — April 18 (Easter Sunday) — Perhaps by this time, at the Stanley Crescent Hotel, off Ladbroke Grove in Notting Hill, Ballard had become friends with some of the other long-term residents. "There was a wartime Navy lieutenant who had captained a motor torpedo boat. He lived in one room with his amiable wife and baby daughter, and spent his time building model seacraft. Some years earlier, he had damaged his brain by diving into the wrong end of a swimming pool. I became good friends with him, and would help carry the picnic equipment to Kensington Gardens and watch him sail his models in the Round Pond. All these people, like myself, would have been classed as misfits, casualties of war who had lost their way in the peace..." (Ballard, *Miracles of Life*, p177.)

1954 — May 6 (Thursday) — Roger Bannister, a medical student, broke the four-minute mile in Oxford, England, finishing in 3 minutes, 59.4 seconds. "Next day, the press chorus was triumphantly patriotic. 'So Britain has been the first to conquer Everest and to achieve the four-minute mile... Both feats may be equalled, but they will never be erased, for first is always the first. Britain has pioneered the way. So let us have no more talk of an effete and worn-out nation.' Bannister's run may not in reality have been quite the carefree, gloriously amateur effort that it was almost immediately portrayed as, but it was still the apogee of the determinedly hopeful, optimistic 'New Elizabethan' moment." (Kynaston, *Family Britain*, p386.)

1954 — June 7 (Whit Monday) — Bank Holiday in the United Kingdom. It may have been around this holiday weekend that Ballard first met Mary Matthews, his wife-to be. "Mary Matthews, whom I had met in a Notting Hill hotel a month before I joined the RAF... Friends had brought us together at a party held in the large communal garden behind Stanley Crescent, an untended wilderness that I remember as a cross between Arcadia and a jungle-warfare training range. ... Arriving in London to take up her job as a secretary at the *Daily Express*, she [had] moved into the Stanley Crescent Hotel because it advertised a handbasin with hot and cold running water in every room, a remarkable feature at the time" (Ballard, *Miracles of Life*, p169, 171-172.) According to a rarely-repeated publicity statement of the 1960s she was "a great-niece of Cecil Rhodes" (Penguin Books blurb, January 1965, probably drafted in 1963.) "Born in 1930 [25 August], Mary was the daughter of Dorothy Vernon and her husband Arthur Matthews, who were well-to-do landowners in Stone, Staffordshire. Mary's father served in the Honourable Artillery Company during the Great War and was invalided out. At the time I met them in 1955 they were living in a modest cottage in Dyserth, a village near Prestatyn in north Wales. They grew their own vegetables and had a simple and pleasantly provincial life together. Like Mary and her two sisters, Peggy and Betty, they were extremely generous people with strong moral principles." (Ballard, *Miracles*, p174.) "When I first met Mary, shortly before joining the RAF, she was working as a secretary for Charles Wintour (father of Anna, the 'tyrant' of *Vogue*; he later became editor of the *Evening Standard*, but was then a senior editor at the *Daily Express*). ... She was tall, with a striking figure and great presence, a woman whom men immediately noticed. In many ways she remained a girl from the Potteries, and at times appeared to be a dizzy brunette, something of an act, as she was quick-witted. All my men-friends liked her enormously, and she was generally popular at the *Express*. ... What she saw in me I still find it difficult to work out. I was probably rather 'lost' in her eyes, but she knew that I was ambitious. I lived on the floor below her in a wing of the hotel, and I worked hard at making myself useful. We began to spend increasing amounts of time in the pubs along the Portobello Road, getting pleasantly tight together. ... Mary was not impressed to hear that I was joining the RAF, but her eyes widened a little when I said that I was writing a novel..." (Ballard, *Miracles*, p174-175.)

1954 — July — Ballard applied to join the Royal Air Force, as a trainee pilot officer. "I signed on at the RAF recruitment offices in Kingsway [London], passed the assessment tests at RAF Hornchurch, near Dagenham, and started my three-month basic training..." (Ballard, *Miracles of Life*, p162.) "I went into the Air Force on a strange sort of impulse... I was suddenly keen to fly. I've always been interested in aviation, and the 1950s was an exciting time. The first advanced postwar jets were appearing on the scene, supersonic travel was here to stay, the world was being changed by aviation. Also in the field of weapons technology there was a whole new world, huge bombers carrying atomic weapons everywhere. I suddenly felt 'I want to be part of this.' I wanted that experience, and it was a chance also to get out of England, because the RAF's flight training was done in Canada. I'd been to Canada and the United States on a trip with my parents in 1939, but I only had hazy memories. I wanted to get out of England desperately." (Ballard, interviewed by David Pringle, 24 July 1981.)

1954 — July 4 (Sunday) — Food rationing came to an end in Britain, nine years after the end of World War II. "Fourteen years of food rationing ended at midnight when restrictions on the sale and purchase of meat and bacon were lifted. Members of the London Housewives' Association held a special ceremony in London's Trafalgar Square to mark Derationing Day." (BBC.)

1954 — August 4 (Wednesday) — Ballard began his three months' basic training in the RAF. This was the date from which his period of service was deemed to count, as officially announced some months later in the *London Gazette*. "I ... started my three-month basic training at Kirton in Lindsey, in Lincolnshire." (Ballard, *Miracles of Life*, p162.) While there, he would encounter some hardbitten instructors: "When I joined the Royal Air Force in 1953 [sic], most of our instructors were veterans from the Second World War, and they used to tell us, 'Killing is such tremendous fun.' They'd tell stories about how they'd machine-gunned villages just for the hell of it. To use a term like 'sadism' and to construct an elaborate psychological machinery to explain this behaviour, however, is to miss the point. The fact is, we are violent and dangerous creatures. We needed to be to survive all those hundreds of thousands of years when we were living in small tribal groups, faced with an incredibly hostile world. And we still carry those genes." (Ballard, interviewed by Ralph Rugoff, *Frieze* no. 34, May 1997.)

1954 — September 17 (Friday) — William Golding published *Lord of the Flies* (Faber & Faber), his first novel—about a group of English schoolboys marooned on an island who quickly degenerate to a state of savagery.

1954 — November — The issue of *Galaxy Science Fiction* dated for this month, with a cover painting by Ed Emshwiller, contained, among others, the stories "How-2" by Clifford D. Simak, "The Nostalgia Gene" by Roy Hutchins, "The Laxian Key" by Robert Sheckley, "The Music Master of Babylon" by Edgar Pangborn and "Big Ancestor" by F. L. Wallace. Was this perhaps the first issue that Ballard read? It is possible, because several of the stories, such as Pangborn's, set in a drowned New York City of the near future, seem to contain pre-echoes of Ballardian themes to come.

1954 — November 12 (Friday) — Ballard and his fellow RAF trainees departed from Liverpool, for Canada. "In the autumn of 1954 we sailed for Canada on one of the Empress liners..." (Ballard, *Miracles of Life*, p162.) "We crossed the Atlantic in the *Empress of Britain* [sic], a pre-war liner of the Canadian Pacific fleet, sitting under the baroque ceilings of the vast state-rooms... Surviving the Atlantic, a subarctic realm of vertical seas, deranged ice and voracious sea-birds, we landed at Montreal..." (Ballard, *The Kindness of Women*, p106-107.) The ship was not the *Empress of Britain*, as the pre-war liner of that name had been sunk in 1940, and would not be replaced until 1956; in fact, it was the *Empress of Scotland* on which they sailed. Having completed his three months' basic training, Ballard's period of service as a Cadet Pilot officially began on this day, as would be announced: "Cadet Pilots. 12th Nov. 1954. James Graham BALLARD (4154813) (period of service to count from 4th Aug. 1954)." (Supplement to the *London Gazette*, 31 December 1954, p7364.) The other young men who would be listed alongside JGB in that batch of recruits were named Terence John Briley, Malcolm Hammond Carder, John Peter Carey, David Alan Croot, Alan Revel Dovey, David Graham Henderson, Peter David Jennings, Bruce Irvine Mackay, Peter Geoffrey Mellor, Keith Gilbert Monson, and George Albert Pearce.

1954 — November 15 (Monday) — J.G. Ballard's 24th birthday, which he must have spent with his fellow RAF recruits somewhere in the mid-Atlantic, aboard the liner *Empress of Scotland*.

1954 — November 20 (Saturday) — By this weekend, Ballard and his fellow Cadet Pilots were in Canada: "[We] spent a month at an RCAF base near London, Ontario, not far from Detroit and Niagara Falls." (Ballard, *Miracles of Life*, p162.) "We made a number of trips across the border into the States—went to Detroit, Buffalo, Niagara Falls, and around there." (Ballard, interviewed by Vale, 29 October 1982.) "We spent about a month in London, Ontario, at this base where we were supposedly acclimatized to the 'North American way of life.' This was great; we had a lot of fun. We spent a lot of time in bars... Part of our acclimatization was seeing all these Canadian Air Force and Canadian military service instructional films. We were straight off the boat from England and they made us sit in this viewing theatre and watch movies. Among them were these hygiene films. Now, none of us had ever seen, at that time, a pornographic film, because they didn't exist in England except behind closed doors... So there we sat in this darkened auditorium, hour after hour, watching this endless stream of films on sexual hygiene which were quite explicit." (Ballard, interviewed by Mark Pauline, June 1986.)

1954 — December 11 (Saturday) — Probably around this time, after travelling across Canada by train ("a four-day train journey from Toronto"), Ballard and his fellow RAF recruits arrived in Moose Jaw. "I was sent to the RCAF flight-training base at Moose Jaw, Saskatchewan, which is quite a place to be. That's where I discovered science fiction, in the magazine racks of the airbase cafeteria..." (Ballard, interviewed by David Pringle, 24 July 1981.) "I arrived in October [sic] and it was snowing and I left in March and it was still snowing, horizontally. And because of the mass of ice crystals suspended in the sky, we used to see three suns at times: very, very odd." (Ballard, interviewed by Murray Waldren, *The Australian*, 9 September 2006.) On his discovery of the American science-fiction magazines: "I first came across science fiction when I was in Canada with the RAF doing pilot training. It was in a place called Moose Jaw, near a nature reserve full of moose with antlers the size of chandeliers, who used to jump the perimeter fence. Apart from this there was very little going on, it was a very provincial place. There was nothing to read until in the bus depot I came across my first s-f magazines. I was struck by how interesting science fiction was; it was highly intelligent and concerned with what was happening. The world was really changing about this time... The first Hydrogen bomb had been exploded and the possibility of thermonuclear war was very real... I [had] thought s-f was all Buck Rogers and Flash Gordon. But when I found these s-f magazines I was stunned. They had a freshness and were about the future and the greatest concerns facing the world." (Ballard, interviewed by Martin Fenner, *Night Out* no. 5, November 1982.) "There was nothing to do, nothing to read on the news-stands. There were no national papers, just local papers. These were packed with stuff about curling contests and ice-hockey. They relegated international news to about two columns on the back page. The papers were packed with ads for local garages and so forth... *Time* magazine was regarded as wildly highbrow. The only intelligent reading matter was science fiction! I suddenly devoured it. This was the heyday of these magazines, there were dozens of them, or seemed to be... some of which were really rather good. Magazines like *Fantastic Universe*—it was probably never distributed over here—published some great stuff. Plus *Galaxy*, which I thought was the best, the most tuned-in to me." (Ballard, interviewed by J. Goddard and D. Pringle, 4 January 1975.)

1954 — December 30 (Thursday) — Robert ("Bobby") Patterson, Ballard's former Lunghua (Shanghai) prison-camp friend, was listed as having rejoined the RAF, two months after JGB had joined: "Cadet Pilots. 30th Dec. 1954. Robert Thomas Harold PATTERSON (4037690) (period of service to count from 29th Sept. 1954)." (Supplement to the *London Gazette*, 1 March 1955, p1244.) Was he too sent to Canada for flight training and, if so, would Ballard meet him again there? We do not know, but these are possibilities.

1955

1955 — January — In Moose Jaw, Saskatchewan: "I enjoyed flying the heavy Harvard T-6, with its huge radial engine, retractable undercarriage and variable-pitch propeller, but the training was continually hampered by the weather." (Ballard, *Miracles of Life*, p164.) "Flying is a very strange experience, it's very close to dreaming. The normal yardsticks, the parameters of our movements through space, are suspended. You're travelling at 150 mph, but if you're 1,000 feet up you're not moving at all. Likewise, you can be travelling quite slowly coming in to land, yet you seem to be hurtling along like a Grand Prix car. The problem with light flying is that it's very unstable and dangerous and also very noisy, there's hardly any time to think." (Ballard, interviewed by Chris Hall, *spikemagazine.com*, 1 November 2000.) However, the actual flying he did was all "pre-solo," with an instructor behind him and sharing the controls, so he never quite gained his wings and would soon decide that he had had enough: "I have some 22 hours of pre-solo myself in the RCAF, but couldn't wait to get back to England & writing." (Ballard, postcard to the book collector Angharad Ryder, undated but circa September 1987.)

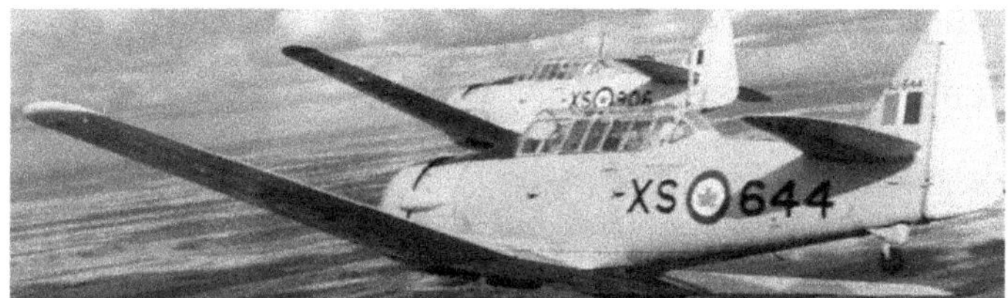

RCAF Harvard T-6 trainer over Moose Jaw.

1955 — January 6 (Thursday) — "WASHINGTON, Thursday. The U.S. President, Mr. Eisenhower, in his 'State of the Union' address to the opening session of the 84th Congress, called on all free nations to protect themselves from 'a nuclear holocaust.' President Eisenhower said the free nations would have to maintain military power to persuade the Communists of the futility of aggression. One of the fundamentals for a vast programme to increase U.S. military strength was the ability 'instantly to strike back with destructive power in response to an attack,' he said." (*Canberra Times*, 7 January 1955.) Note Eisenhower's usage of the word "holocaust" to refer to the prospect of all-out nuclear war—an understanding of the word that those of us born in the 1950s were to grow up with (DP).

1955 — January 15 (Saturday) — Death of Yves Tanguy (b. 1900), French painter resident in the USA, of a stroke at 55. He had produced one of his major paintings, "Multiplication of the Arcs," not long before his death, in 1954. "Many of the surrealists were still exhibiting in London. I remember going to exhibitions that ran completely new paintings by Magritte, Dali, Delvaux. Chirico's career was over. Tanguy I only saw in museums, because he died fairly early on." (Ballard, interviewed by Lynne Fox, 20 January 1991.)

1955 — January-February — Ballard continued to read science-fiction magazines and paperbacks throughout the winter of 1954-1955. "A lot of the American writers were very good. Ray Bradbury above all—I thought he was head and shoulders above everybody else. He had that wider dimension to his writing which the others, however good, didn't really achieve. I liked [Robert] Sheckley very much—very droll and witty. [Frederik] Pohl, too, I liked. [Richard] Matheson, I liked—very much, actually, because he showed you why SF wasn't about outer space, wasn't about the future. So many of his stories were psychological twist stories—the sort of standard story where the character begins to forget everything, the story ends with 'AARGH!' and he can't remember who he is. Those sort of stories I liked. They did them so well." (Ballard, interviewed by J. Goddard and D. Pringle, 4 January 1975.)

1955 — March — The issue of *Fantastic Universe* dated for March 1955 contained Jack Vance's story "Meet Miss Universe" (plus stories by James Blish, Marion Zimmer Bradley, Algis Budrys, Evelyn E. Smith, Bryce Walton and others), with a cover painting by Alex Schomburg depicting an American super-highway menaced by flying saucers. Ballard read this issue.

1955 — March 1 (Tuesday) — Sir Winston Churchill, addressing the House of Commons in what would be his last major speech as Prime Minister, warned of the "hideous epoch" of the H-bomb and told the country, "never despair."

1955 — Spring? — A new British science-fiction writer met his magazine editor: "Arundel Street is a short steep street leading down from the Strand to the Victoria Embankment and the Thames. ... [T]here were basement windows through which a passer-by glimpsed various activities. I peered through protective railings on this momentous occasion to glimpse a tall figure in shirtsleeves who was laughing and talking. I ascended four shallow steps, where a brass plate announced 'Maclaren Books, Nova Publications.' I entered and made my way down into the basement. A long room had been made complex by an arrangement of desks, cupboards, boxes, piles of books and magazines, pin-ups on walls as if it were still wartime, and several men, sitting or bustling about. ... Over the previous Christmas, the Christmas of 1955 [sic; it was in fact 1954], I had won the short story competition in the *Observer,* then the leading Sunday paper. ... Now I met my first editor. His name was Ted Carnell." (Brian Aldiss, *Bury My Heart at W. H. Smith's*, 1990, p14-15.)

1955 — April 5 (Tuesday) — Sir Winston Churchill resigned as Prime Minister of the United Kingdom, amid signs of failing health. His replacement, next day, would be the Foreign Secretary, Sir Anthony Eden.

1955 — April 11 (Monday) — "WASHINGTON, Monday. If the present world birthrate is maintained 'there is a potentiality that in a matter of a few centuries the entire land surface of the earth will be as densely populated as New York city,' said an expert of population statistics, Dr. Robert Cook, yesterday. 'The problem of feeding that many people is something I don't even like to think about.'" (*Canberra Times*, 12 April 1955.)

1955 — April (mid) — By now, Ballard was on his way home. "In early spring, when the last of the snow was falling, we were told that our flight training would be transferred back to England... By this time I was confident that my career as a writer was about to begin. I had written several s-f stories, which had flowed quickly from my pen, and there was a queue of others waiting in my mind. I enjoyed flying, but months in an isolated training base in Scotland or the north of England would postpone everything I planned. Accordingly, I resigned my commission, and was soon installed in my tiny couchette on the Canadian Pacific Railway train to Toronto, a long journey of endless lakes and pine forests that I spent with pad and pencil. In a real sense I wrote my way across Canada, and then across the Atlantic to England." (Ballard, *Miracles of Life*, p167-168.) Just what those "several s-f stories" were that he would claim to have written in Canada, remains a mystery. All his early manuscripts would be destroyed.

1955 — April 18 (Monday) — Death of Albert Einstein (b. 1879), German-born Swiss/American physicist, in Princeton, New Jersey, of an aneurysm at 76. In the autopsy, his brain was removed for later study. "Do you realize that since the death of Einstein in 1955 there hasn't been a single living genius? From Michelangelo, through Shakespeare, Newton, Beethoven, Goethe, Darwin, Freud and Einstein there's always been a living genius. Now, for the first time in 500 years we're on our own." (Ballard, the teenage character Harvey speaking in "The Overloaded Man," July 1961.)

1955 — April 26 (Tuesday) — Ballard, returning from Canada, disembarked at Liverpool from the liner *Empress of France*. He brought with him a paperback by Richard Matheson, which must have been *Third From the Sun* (Bantam, February 1955). "I liked Matheson's short stories tremendously. I thought they were awfully good. They were probably a bit of an influence on me, because they showed that you could write a science fiction set exclusively in the present day which many of his short stories were, they were psychological stories set in the landscape of '50s America, owing nothing to time travel, interplanetary voyages and so forth. He was one of the sf writers I read when I was in Canada. One of the very few books that I brought back with me, if not the only one, was a collection of Richard Matheson's short stories, which would have been published in paperback in the States... I can't remember the title, I lost it a long time ago." (Ballard, interviewed by David Pringle, 21 August 1987.)

1955 — May — Awaiting discharge from the RAF, after about ten months' service, Ballard wrote his first science-fiction short story, "Passport to Eternity" (eventually published in 1962). "I tapped this out on a borrowed typewriter at RAF Booker, where cashiered air-crew sat around in under-heated huts at a disused airfield." (*The Best of J. G. Ballard*, 1977, p288.) "We sat in this airfield, near High Wycombe, a sort of transit camp, straight out of Kafka in a way. There were great gloomy huts by the pines on the edge of these empty runways where we reject air crew sat around, trying to keep warm by the one stove. They didn't bother to keep us warm, and there was nothing to do. There were two squadron leaders who were in charge of processing us, and they had to wait for various documents to arrive. As mine had to come from Canada I spent a long time there. Weeks went by and I sat around waiting for my name to be called. Suddenly a name would be called out, the man in question would go to meet these squadron leaders and five minutes later he would be a civilian and leave the base forever.

One didn't know when this was going to happen, so with all this spare time on my hands I thought 'I'll write a science-fiction story!' Which I did." (Ballard, interviewed by David Pringle, 24 July 1981.)

1955 — May — "'Passport to Eternity' was the first sf story I ever wrote—it was written as a kind of pastiche. I think I slightly embroidered it when I came to sell it to one of the American magazines some years later, but I was still in the RAF when I wrote that story... It was influenced by a story by Jack Vance, which I remember vividly from a magazine, called 'Meet Miss Universe.' That was a biological fantasy about a beauty contest; it impressed me enormously with its wit and cleverness and inventiveness—the best of that sort of American science fiction. As I say, 'Passport to Eternity' was a summary of all the American sf I'd been reading over the past year in Canada. It's a kind of spoof, indistinguishable really from the American sf. It didn't occur to me to submit it—I don't know why, I think I had other problems on my mind. I already knew that I wanted to write a different kind of sf that story may have been my first, but it isn't in any way typical. A few years later I typed it out again from the original typescript, the basic story unchanged, and sent it to... Cele Goldsmith, I suppose [who was the editor of the US magazines *Amazing* and *Fantastic*]." (Ballard, interviewed by David Pringle, 24 July 1981.)

1955 — May 24 (Tuesday) — The BBC Third Programme broadcast a new adaptation of Wyndham Lewis's novel *The Childermass*—to be followed on 26 May and 28 May by dramatizations of its recently-completed sequels, *Monstre Gai* and *Malign Fiesta*. The scripts were by Lewis in collaboration with D. G. Bridson. Slightly over a decade later, Jim Ballard (24 years old in 1955) would recall: "Put on by the Third Programme ten years ago with tremendous style and panache, and with a virtuoso performance by Donald Wolfit as the Bailiff, the trilogy came over superbly as black theological cabaret." (Ballard, "Visions of Hell," *New Worlds*, March 1966.) JGB must have had access to a radio as he was whiling away the time at RAF Booker (but probably not to a television set at that early date).

1955 — May 26 (Thursday) — It was another General Election day in the United Kingdom. This must have been the first such election in which Ballard was entitled to vote, although whether he did or not, freshly back from Canada as he was, is not known. The Conservatives won clear majority.

1955 — May 31 (Tuesday) — This was the official date of termination of Ballard's service with the RAF: "Commission terminated. Acting Pilot Officers:- D. J. WATSON (4158234). 25th May 1955. J. G. BALLARD (4154813). 31st May 1955." (Supplement to the London Gazette, 1 July 1955, p3791.) He had been in the service for ten months. It was presumably on this day that he left RAF Booker, near High Wycombe, and returned to London.

1955 — June 1 (Wednesday) — By this date Ballard had returned to his digs in Notting Hill, London. "I was looking forward to seeing Mary Matthews... We had exchanged a few letters while I was in Canada, but I had no idea if she would still be there. As soon as I left RAF High Wycombe [sic] I travelled straight to London, and booked myself into the hotel near Ladbroke Grove where Mary and I had first met. ... I left my suitcase in my old room, luckily vacant, and knocked on the door of Mary's room. It was opened by a middle-aged woman in a nursing sister's uniform. For a few seconds my heart died, and I realised why I had left the Air Force and travelled all the way from Moose Jaw. Then I learned that Mary had moved to a larger room on the first floor. I think we were surprised, a little wary but almost relieved to see each other again." (Ballard, *Miracles of Life*, p169, 171, 178.)

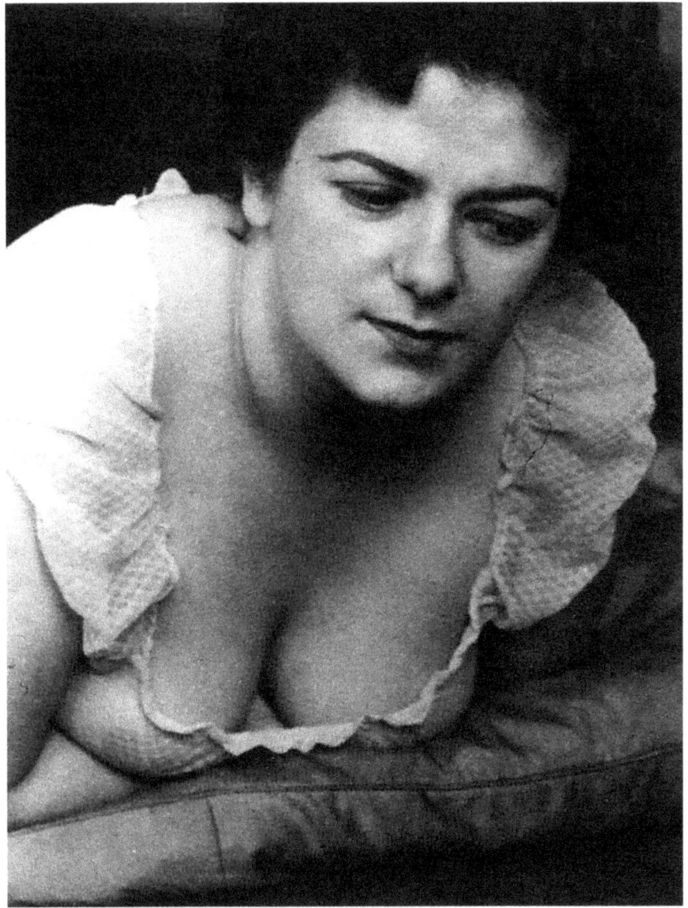

Mary Ballard

1955 — June (early) — "When I left High Wycombe, the RAF now behind me, and booked into the Stanley Crescent Hotel I found that nothing had changed. The same tired tenants were still there, one of the lost tribes of Britain's post-war world, among them a retired RAF squadron leader and his very posh wife, Peta, who was always boasting in a loud voice that she had 'checked out on twin-engines' (was authorised to fly twin-engined aircraft) before her husband. To her annoyance, he was never able to pay the rent, and I think she knew that her husband had given up hope. The Polish manager would linger in the breakfast room (breakfast was never served, except to cash-on-the-nail tenants), waiting until Peta was in full twin-engined flight with another guest, and then step up to her, saying in a loud voice: 'You are three weeks behind with your rent, Mrs...' Peta would flounce away, angry that I had witnessed this little humiliation. Only a few years earlier they had been stationed in Cyprus, with a large house and servants. She was lost in post-war England, but a perfect symbol of it." (Ballard, *Miracles of Life*, p176-177.) The 1956 Electoral Register for Kensington North shows, among others, a couple named Charles F. Briggs and Peta M. Briggs still in residence at 13-14 Stanley Crescent in October 1955.

1955 — June 16 (Thursday) - At about this date, Ballard and his girlfriend (or fiancée?) Mary Matthews conceived a child. "In due course [or pretty speedily, considering he had only been back in London for a fortnight] Mary became pregnant... Now, for the first time, I had helped to create something, almost out of nothing, an intact and growing creature that would emerge as a living being." (Ballard, *Miracles of Life*, p179-180.) Also: "Mary lent me her typewriter, and over the next few weeks I typed out all the stories [sic] I had written on the way back to England. She read them very carefully, was clearly impressed by them, and not in the least put off by the fact that they were science fiction, which she had never read. She strongly urged me to press on, though most of her friends regarded science fiction as beyond the pale. But she sensed that there was something original and fresh about this apparently modest genre..." (Ballard, *Miracles*, p178.)

1955 — June 27 (Monday) — Emma Tennant, aged 17, eldest daughter of Lord and Lady Glenconner, "came out" as a debutante. "She is, of course, one of the Tennants, the Ayrshire farmers who made their fortune out of a chemical bleach works in Glasgow during the Industrial Revolution, and have been making newspaper headlines ever since. Her great-grandfather, Charles, the first baronet, was one of the half-dozen richest men in Britain. Her great-aunt, Margot Asquith, was wife of the prime minister, Herbert Asquith... Emma spent her early childhood in Glen, the family's flamboyant Gothic castle in Peeblesshire, where there were so many bedrooms she stopped counting at 20... In London, she was ferried to her private girls' day school by chauffeur-driven Bentley from her parents' house in Regent's Park. When she was 17, flowers from the greenhouses at Glen were sent on the overnight train to St Pancras to adorn the marquee for her coming-out ball. She was one of the last debutantes to be presented at court, dropping a curtsy in front of the Royals. Amid the frivolity of champagne and gardenias, cocktail parties and 'fork lunches', only one serious pursuit was expected of her: to find a husband... Tennant's account of her three-ball-gown summer, when she wore Dior from Paris, and danced in lilac-scented rooms with dashing young landowners, sounds like fun. 'It wasn't really,' she says. 'Girls danced around looking depressed, hoping they'd find somebody they fancied. There were very few attractive men...'" (Margaret Morrison, "The Deb That Roared," *Scotland on Sunday*, 18 April 1999.)

1955 — June 29 (Wednesday) — "LONDON, Wednesday. Four medical students did a 'Sir Walter Raleigh' as the Queen left Queen's College at Dundee yesterday. A carpet had been laid out for her, but it was sodden with rain. Just before she appeared at the college doorway, the four young gallants whipped off their billowing red gowns and spread them over the carpet. The Queen looked inquiringly at the Master of the College... 'The students' action is spontaneous, Your Majesty,' he commented—at which the Queen smiled and walked over the cloaks." (*Canberra Times*, 30 June 1955.)

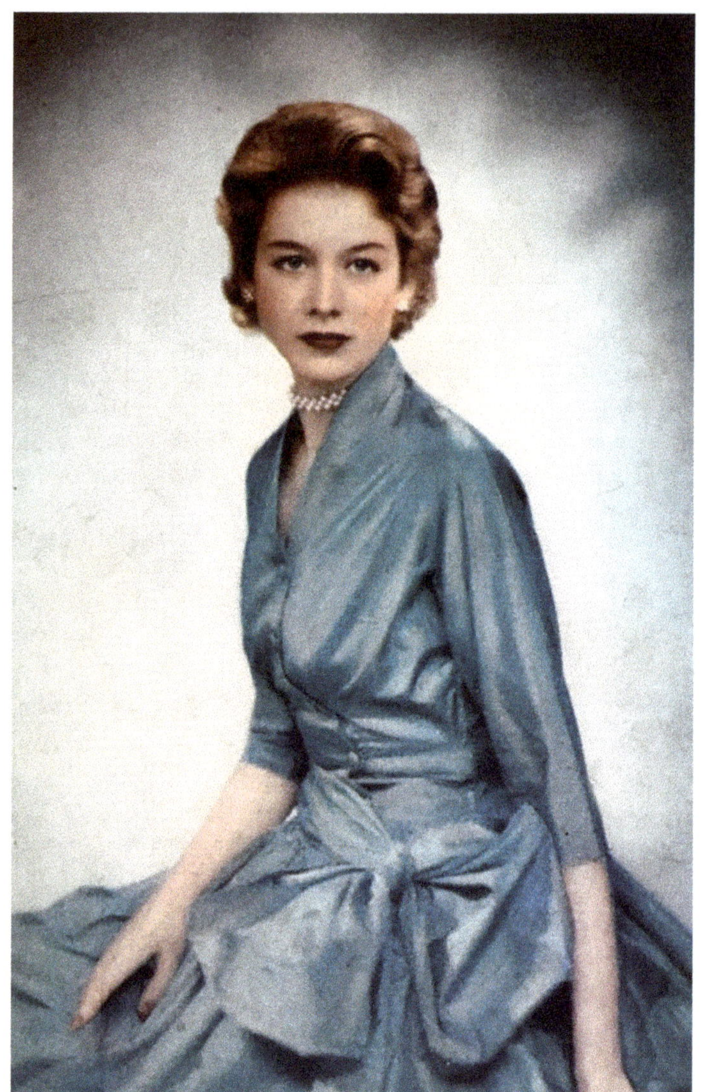

Emma Tennant

1955 — Summer-Autumn? — Ballard worked for a time in public libraries. "I worked in a couple of libraries for about six months—Richmond Borough Library, or Sheen Public Libraries, I can't really remember." (Ballard, interviewed by David Pringle, 24 July 1981.) "Years ago I worked in a couple of London libraries... If you've worked in a library, you know that a large amount of borrowing is indiscriminate. People come in wanting a book for their wife, or aunt, or grandmother. You see it in any library. Someone returning what they've just read, hardly even knowing its title, saying 'I want another like this one.' They may choose a book not even suited to them, but this does help to keep the shelves stocked... Very few readers have a specific title in mind when they come into a library. They have a hazy feeling that they've just enjoyed some book and they want another one like it. I remember doing my little bit, which sounds pompous but it isn't. They'd come in with a thriller, wanting another one, and I'd give them a Raymond Chandler." (Ballard, "Public Lending Right: A Symposium," *New Review*, December 1975.)

1955 — August 3 (Wednesday) — Samuel Beckett's play "Waiting for Godot" was produced for the first time in English at the Arts Theatre in London (a small theatre club), directed by the 24-year-old Peter Hall.

1955 — August 12 (Friday) — Death of Thomas Mann (b. 1875), German novelist and essayist, Nobel Prize laureate, at 80.

1955 — September 22 (Thursday) — The launch took place of the commercial Independent Television (ITV) service in the UK, initially only from a transmitter in Croydon to the London area, with potential coverage of 10 million viewers. The first UK TV commercial was for Gibbs SR toothpaste.

1955 — September 26 (Monday) — James Graham Ballard, aged 24, married Helen Mary Nance Matthews, aged 25, in Notting Hill, Royal Borough of Kensington, London. The wedding was solemnized at the Parish Church of St John the Evangelist, "according to the Rites and Ceremonies of the Church of England after banns by me, Austin Oakley, Vicar." At the time bride and groom were living a few minutes' walk away, at 13 Stanley Crescent, W11. The witnesses to the marriage were John Henderson and D.V. Matthews. "Mary's family, my parents and sister, and a few friends attended the church service, which moved me deeply. Three of us, in a sense, were being married—Mary, I, and our unborn child. I took the ceremony very seriously, though not for religious reasons... Mary was three months pregnant when we married, and I would lie beside her, touching the swelling of her womb, willing on this little visitor from beyond time and space... I remember the wedding ceremony as a slightly disjointed affair. The respective in-laws had not met each other, and the old tribal defensiveness showed itself. Waiting for the clergyman to arrive, I turned to my father in the pew behind me and asked if I should leave a donation 'for the poor of the parish.' He replied, jovially: 'You are the poor of the parish.' He and my mother enjoyed the joke." (Ballard, *Miracles of Life*, p179-180.)

1955 — September — "By the time I married no help, financial or otherwise, came from my parents—that had ceased long before I went into the RAF." (Ballard, letter to Mike Bonsall, September 2007.) "I seem to remember Jimmy mentioning that Mary had a scooter (a Vespa or similar machine) on which they rode around. I don't know whether this was when he first met her (i.e. before Canada) or when he returned and after they got married (perhaps both). Purchase of a car came later." (William Spencer, notes on this timeline, 2010.)

1955 — September 30 (Friday) — Death of James Dean (b. 1931), American actor, a rising film star, at age 24. He crashed his silver Porsche in a two-car collision near Paso Robles, California.

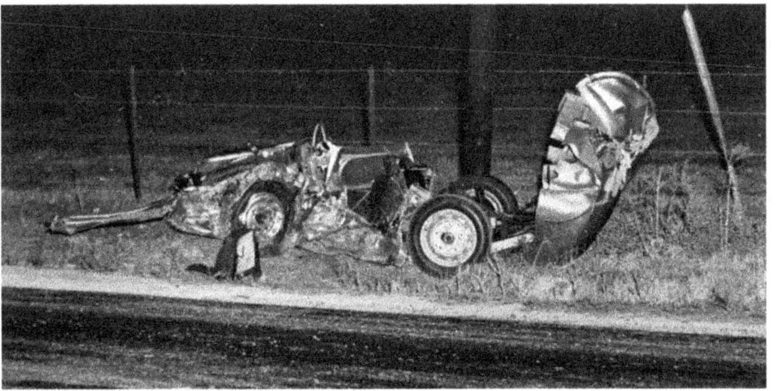

1955 — October 7 (Friday) — Alan Ginsberg, American "beat" poet, read his poem "Howl" for the first time at a group poetry reading at the North Beach Six Gallery, 3119 Fillmore Street, San Francisco.

1955 — November 15 (Tuesday) — J.G. Ballard's 25th birthday. By this time it is likely that he and Mary, visibly expecting a baby, had moved away from the Notting Hill area, and had found accommodation in a small flat in Chiswick, a little further west: "He and his wife ... lived at 30 Fairlawn Avenue, close to Chiswick Park tube station." ("Chiswick Timeline of Writers & Books," chiswickbookfestival, April 2019.) However, he still visited central London art galleries: "Although the surrealists were regarded as totally disreputable by the guardians of bourgeois culture there were still exhibitions. I remember going to an exhibition of new Magrittes in a little gallery near Berkeley Square—this was in something like 1955—which included many paintings of his which are now world-famous. They were openly derided, and not just by art critics: no literary reviewer would refer to the surrealists at all." (Ballard, interviewed by David Pringle, 24 July 1981.)

1955 — November 25 (Friday) — "Rock Around the Clock" by Bill Haley and His Comets reached number one in the British singles charts. It marked the arrival of rock 'n' roll music in Britain from America, and would be to be the first disc to sell a million copies in the UK.

1955 — It was perhaps some time in the second half of this year that Ballard wrote his first attempt at a story set in the imaginary desert resort he named Vermilion Sands. The opening sentence was: "Last year, for three months during the summer, I was private secretary to a madman." It would remain unpublished, but certain character names, e.g. Hardoon and Emerelda, and some imaginative notions, e.g. the flying "sand-rays," would be used in his later stories. (The untitled manuscript would be found in Ballard's papers in the British Library, and a French translation of it would eventually be published, as "Le Labyrinthe Hardoon," in 2013.) With two stories completed, if only in rough—"Passport to Eternity" and the untitled one, which I have suggested we call "The Hardoon Labyrinth"—his career as a professional writer was about to begin.

DAVID PRINGLE

Acknowledgements

Many thanks for help and hints, and in some cases the loan of photographs, to: Jeff Arnett; Fay Ballard; Christopher Beckett; Mike Bonsall; Catherine Bresson; Christian Brueckner; the British Library; Alison Carter; Corrina Chand; Lynne Fox; Thomas Frick; Colin Greenland; John Harding; Mike Holliday; the late Irene Duguid Kilpatrick; Judith Kirschbaum; Greg Leck; Rick McGrath; Charles Platt; Hazel Poulter; the late Desmond Power; the Library of Queen Mary, University of London; Bernard Sigaud; the late William Spencer; Raymond Tait; Keiran Ure; and Vale.

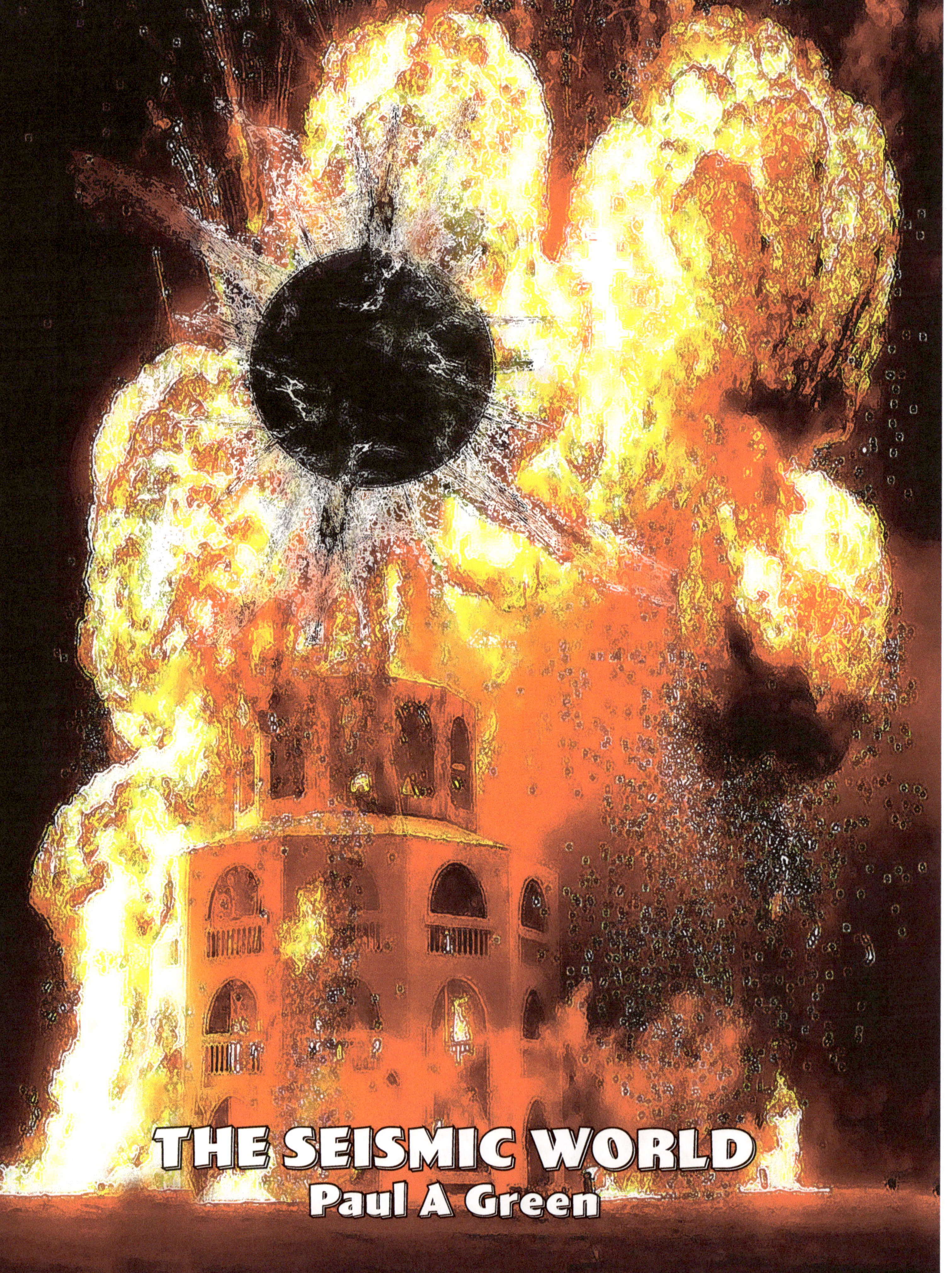
THE SEISMIC WORLD
Paul A Green

The dinghy tossed and yawed in the rolling waves, and for a moment Dr. Langham wondered if the refugees were going to make it. He gripped the railing of the observation post as he squinted through cloudy binoculars. The tiny overcrowded vessel was only two hundred yards from the edge of Platform One but it could so easily capsize.

To Langham's relief a patrol boat had already spotted them. Two marines loud-hailed the dark-skinned man in a wet-suit at the tiller of the dinghy's outboard motor. They were signalling him to manoeuvre closer and threw out a line to begin the precarious business of transferring his passengers to the larger craft.

Langham could now study the migrants—at least two dozen—as they slowly made the dangerous transfer into the swaying patrol boat, all apparently exhausted, several minus life-jackets and some clearly injured. But they were, as a demographic, much as he expected, mostly white but with a scattering of darker faces. Some men wore muddy hi-viz tabards, there were women and small children huddled in metallic foil blankets and indeterminate figures swathed in grubby bandages—probably from fractures or burns. There would certainly be work for him, more than enough to justify his ration allotment, although the Platform surgery was currently running low on dressings and anaesthetics. But even before triage, the new arrivals would have to be processed, via the usual debriefing with Commander Brewer's security team, who would assess the skills and resources they might bring to Platform One.

It began to drizzle. He turned up the hood of his precious old anorak and swung away from the railing to walk carefully across the slippery plating of the empty top deck, where the faded yellow mandala identifying the heli-port was still kept clear, although it had been three years since a coast guard chopper had landed. Gulls soared and swooped under the greyish-brown overcast, a permanent skyscape now across the Channel. He could taste dust in the wind, metallic grit.

Arriving at the hatch to the central stairwell, he stepped quickly down to Level C and hurried along narrow corridors. The passages were cluttered with boxes of salvaged tinned foods while an overhead loudspeaker played ancient top-40 hits, a morale-raising strategy that Langham found depressing, as if he were trapped in the aisles of some dystopian supermarket. He finally pulled open a bulkhead door stencilled FORECASTING SECTION.

"This isn't a good time, Richard." Joanna Graham didn't look up, focusing instead on the waveforms flickering across a desktop monitor. "We keep losing the feed from our main hydrophone. I've no idea what's going on down there."

"Platform Two at Dogger Bank might have some info."

"You know as well as I do that we haven't heard from Dogger Bank in three weeks. It's something we're not supposed to talk about."

Langham cursed himself for his lack of diplomacy. Joanna was so neurotic about complying with Commander Brewer's directives.

"Can't you collate data from the land stations and extrapolate from that?"

"We've lost so many sensors. Since Geo-Survey in Edinburgh went down, I only get random readings. There was a 3.2 at a depth of 9 klicks around Bangor last night and a 2.3 at a depth of 6 centred on Hereford but I'm sure there have been more. Maybe something bigger near Dartford."

Langham tried to visualise the locations—a ruptured shopping precinct, maybe a sagging tower block and mountains of rubble hindering token rescue efforts, perhaps even smoking crevices bubbling with lava. There was no national TV coverage now, one had to rely on the hazy imagery captured on survivors' phones. Even one's memory of the mainland was uncertain.

"Dartford—isn't that in Kent? There could be a tidal surge along the coast."

"The Thames estuary has probably become a lake. Maybe the new arrivals can fill you in. Isn't that where you should heading?" She got up abruptly. Crossing to a wall map she began pressing pins into a geography already punctured with hundreds of red markings.

As Langham murmured a farewell, his gaze lingered on the line of her neck, her mane of dark hair and the curve of her body under a heavy jersey and dungarees. But in the spartan dormitory regime of Platform One there were few opportunities for privacy or sexual entanglement. And, as Brewer was fond of telling his crew, work kept one grounded.

The Great Seismic Shift, as it became known, had begun over a decade ago, as subterranean activity increased along the Pacific fault lines running under Japan, Indonesia and the Philippines, where earthquakes had occurred since records began. The defining moment was probably the death of nearly fifty three thousand people following a massive tectonic plate shift just off the Bay of Manila. Yet even this horror was at first viewed as part of an ongoing historical narrative that could be somehow mediated and rationalised. When that was followed by a huge volcanic eruption on the island of Santorini in the Aegean and a series of quakes and mini-tsunamis near Naples and around Venice—in which the city was finally submerged—questions were raised in the UN and other NGO bodies, only leading to a consensus that little could be done except increase budgets for aid and rescue services while reviewing building regulations in vulnerable zones.

In the following eighteen months the "vulnerable zones" came to include whole swathes of the USA and Northern Europe. In the UK, which normally saw only a few score of minor tremors per year, there were major incidents like the sudden crash, at peak commuting time, of West London's Chiswick flyover and the total collapse of the North Terminal at Gatwick Airport, followed by innumerable fissured roads and demolished houses across the whole country from Dundee to St Ives. Fatalities quickly rose from the hundreds to the hundreds of thousands as emergency services were overwhelmed and the country's infrastructure began, literally, to crumble. Amid this chaos, a beleaguered government in the COBRA bunker under Whitehall watched pixellated footage of the San Andreas Fault calamity, as Los Angeles slid inexorably into the ocean.

So began the desperate initiative of the Platforms. It was clearly imperative to create a secure national command centre that would be unaffected by the worsening geological situation. Thus Britain needed a marine-based equivalent of the old Cold War RSGs, the Regional Seats of Government. The nation's military and economic resources were concentrated on building a group of floating islands around the coast of the British Isles. The largest, Platform One, ten miles off the Sussex coast, generated its own power, both nuclear and wind-driven, and hosted its own desalination plant and trawler docks, as well as pens for landing craft and patrol vessels. It supported a population of over a thousand, comprising soldiers, fishermen, scientists, engineers and displaced bureaucrats. There was only sporadic contact with shattered regimes in Paris and Brussels. In one sense, Britannia continued to rule the waves.

"OK, Langham, what have we got here?" Commander Jack Brewer glanced around the low ceilinged space that functioned as an emergency ward. Half a dozen refugees sprawled on the beds, two of them hooked to saline drips. A sergeant shouldering a carbine stood by the door, as if to prevent them escaping.

The lower body of an elderly man on the nearest gurney was wrapped in grubby blood stained dressings. His face was scorched and blackened, his eyes were closed and he was breathing erratically.

"I'm afraid I couldn't do much for this one. Except morphine." Langham regretted the admission but he'd learned there was no point in prevaricating with the Commander, a stocky bearded figure, reputedly ex-Marine, terse and tight-lipped.

"Lava burns?" The question was purely a formality. Brewer had overseen Langham's often futile attempts to treat survivors after previous quakes and eruptions. "No worries. I know opiate supplies are low. Sergeant Furey will process him. Now do you have any walking wounded? Have you done their stats?"

Langham handed the Commander a clip board, but before he could flip through it a woman's voice called from a bed at the far end.

"Just give me a fucking brace for my leg. And get me out of here." She grimaced as she levered herself upright and groped for a cup of water on the bedside table. Langham was struck by her rain-smeared kohl makeup, her corona of spiky greenish hair and worn leather jacket. She was early forties, her inflections were nasal, urban. *Post-punk posing as post apocalyptic—Brewer will not be impressed* thought Langham.

"So where do you think you're going? Do you want us to throw you back into the English Channel? Or do you want to go with him?" Brewer gestured with his thumb towards the bandaged figure on the trolley. But the woman stared him down.

Sensing a confrontation, Langham intervened. "Perhaps the lady could remind us of her name and boarding status."

"Lou Axton. Your zombie boys told me I was C1. What's that all about?" Langham had a sudden flash of recall, a clip from distant pre-Seismic TV news: *performance artist/activist Louise Axton creates live installation at fracking site.* Dim image of a muddy half-naked figure writhing in a trench...

"Catering duties for you, Ms Axton. Unless you'd prefer to work in the Staff Recreation Area. It's a job you could do lying down." Brewer allowed himself a faint smirk.

Langham was anxious to forestall a riposte from Axton that would make her position with Brewer even more uncertain. Her vitality triggered both unease and curiosity. So many of the patients he'd treated had been traumatised into total passivity.

"I could use an assistant, Commander. We need to keep track of our drug inventory and the patient logs." The request might appeal to Brewer's obsession with maintaining order.

"You better make it work, Dr. Langham. We'll review the situation in a week." Brewer was already impatient. "Just get the rest of these people patched up for a labour detail. I've got a Food Supply meeting in five minutes." He strode off, followed by the sergeant wheeling out the terminal patient.

Langham began treating Louise Axton's ankle, which was cut and badly bruised but not broken. She winced and looked up suspiciously as he adjusted the dressing.

"I'm not Recreation fodder, Doctor, if that's what you were hoping."

Langham, groping in his trouser pocket for paracetamol tablets, ignored the probe. He was suddenly aware of his exhaustion and hunger. He could only make conversation on auto-pilot.

"So where was it? The quake?"

"Around what was left of Dartford, near the Bluewater Centre. A fissure, a hot one. It got old Arthur before he could run..." She began shaking and sobbing. There was no point in telling her that Sergeant Furey was about to dispatch Arthur with a pistol shot and send his body bag over the side.

In the half-light of the dormitory Langham found it impossible to sleep. Barnett, the engineer in the next cubicle, a former oil-rig worker, was muttering incoherently, tossing and turning in uneasy dreams.

In desperation Langham decided to seek distraction in his portable radio. He plugged in earphones and began his nightly sweep through the FM and AM bands. The Top 40 station that was piped through the Platform's tannoy system was blaring away as usual, and Langham briefly wondered if it was being transmitted from a ship further up the Channel. Yet there were no announcements or station IDs, so he could only presume the programming was automated on a loop. He found intermittent bursts of what might have been Urdu on one of the old BBC wavelengths, but otherwise he was dialling through waves of static and crackle. He eventually turned off to conserve the batteries. Thankfully Barnett had fallen silent at last.

He groped for the faded photo under his pillow—another late night ritual. The wedding picture with Anna was almost bleached, but he could still study her faint smile and recognise the jaunty posture of this striking young woman in a white trouser suit. He stared through the scratched perspex of the frame at the grinning mask of a previous self which had yet to lose its curls of black hair and sharply defined bone structure. In the chaos of his transfer to the Platform he'd lost the phone containing her excited message from the airport at Seattle, where she'd just arrived to deliver a keynote speech at that conference on autism. Then, after the West Coast calamity, he heard nothing—for hours that became days, then months.

Her death was only one among millions yet he was still appalled by its arbitrary cruelty and mystery. For no-one had yet found a definitive explanation for this global catastrophe. Joanna Graham had briskly dismissed the once-fashionable theory of lunar influenced geological "earth tides" when he'd first mentioned it, while Brewer discouraged speculation about ultimate causes, preferring to concentrate minds on the practicalities of survival. Langham had no background in astrophysics or geology—his medical training had originally been intended as a route to practising psychiatry—but he wondered if solar magnetic storms might have affected the Earth's metallic core.

Louise Axton, of course, had all the answers. That afternoon, as she hobbled around the pharmacy stockroom, she'd let him know that world-wide fracking was responsible for the Shift. "The Patriarchy carves up Mother Earth, so what do we get? This is Gaia's rebellion, she's shaking us off, it's her dance of defiance. I was telling everyone for years in my art, my interventions. Now look where we are." Langham didn't have the energy to engage and was trying to make sense of his scribbled surgery notes. But he somehow respected her bloody mindedness and the pluck that had brought her on this dangerous voyage. He imagined her in her bunk in the women's quarters, keeping Jo Graham awake with fervent eco-centric diatribes.

He flipped open one of the few paperbacks he'd salvaged, an old psychology text: *Collective earthquake dreams can indicate neurotic problems at a collective scale in the complex of fulfilment of aggressive instincts.* A bizarre synchronicity. But he was too tired to cope with psychiatric jargon. He let the book fall to the floor and turned over in his bunk as Platform One swayed and rolled with the incessant motion of the waves.

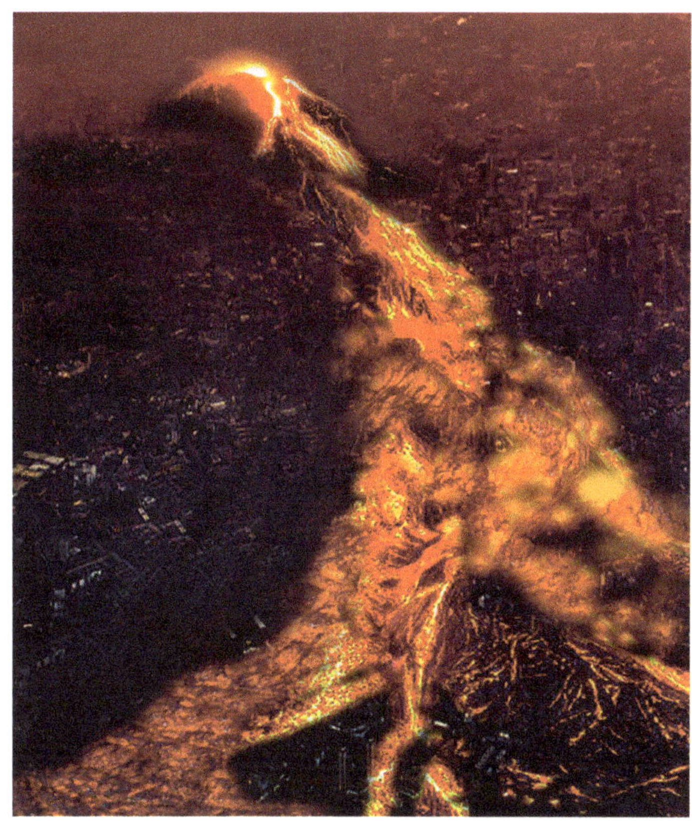

Langham was late for the morning meeting in the mess room. He tried to slip in unobtrusively at the back but couldn't avoid a hostile glance from Brewer who stood at the far end, gesturing with a pointer at a large map of southern England.

"...the importance of this expedition. It's not only the objective of replenishing supplies and salvaging materials. There's a bigger issue at stake—as our guest Mr Anwar Zahid will tell us."

Langham was surprised to see the bearded Asian dinghy pilot sitting among Brewer's uniformed lieutenants, alongside Barnett and the other team leaders. He strode confidently to the front. Langham recognised a strong East London accent.

"Maybe you lot think that I've made the crossing just to find bed and breakfast. But I'm here on a mission. There are still communities over there. Brothers and sisters are struggling but they're trying to reach out."

Langham recalled the fragments he'd picked out on his radio—cries for assistance or territorial proclamations?

"They could use your help. And you can't be stuck here for ever. What was the idea of the Platforms? To take back control of the mainland, to re-build a working economy—"

Barnett, in the front row, snorted with laughter. "Economy! What fucking planet are you living on, mate? Scavenge and barter—that's all we've got!"

Brewer glared at him. "Negative talk means you lose special ration privileges, Barnett. Listen to the man!" Barnett scowled but subsided.

Zaheed pointed to the map. "Before we quit Dartford, I was getting signals from the London orbital zone. They've got some kind of safe space there, a settlement almost. You can link up, share info. We can re-colonise the land..."

Jo Graham raised a hand. "He could be on to something, Commander. We haven't had any big readings from that area recently."

"You mean we're going to get some real action, sir?" Private Burton couldn't hide his excitement. There was a sudden buzz in the room, a collective energy that Langham had not witnessed for months.

Brewer signalled for silence. "You will have a full briefing tomorrow. In the meantime I expect Forecasting to prepare a projection of likely tremor areas. Dismiss!"

While they filed out, the younger soldiers and technicians clearly enthused by this unexpected announcement, Dr. Langham wondered how much Louise Axton had paid the dinghy pilot for her crossing. What other motivation could Zahid have for that risky venture and this potentially dangerous voyage into a devastated interior? As he pondered, Brewer came over and slapped him on the shoulder. "Don't think you can stay behind doling out pills, Langham. England expects every man et cetera..."

Five days later, Langham and Axton clung to the deck of LCT 7074, a huge rusty D-Day Landing Craft, as it approached Cooden Beach through early morning mist. Nearly two hundred feet in length, it had originally been built to land ten tanks and a complement of soldiers in Normandy in 1944.

"History's full of ironies, isn't it," shouted Langham over the throb of diesel engines. "This is one of the sites where the Germans intended to land in 1940."

But the reference seemed lost on Louise, who was staring suspiciously at a squat arachnoid vehicle on a low trailer at the front of the craft.

"That evil-looking thing gives me the creeps. It's the eight legs."

"Pirated American technology. Good for scrambling through the rubble. You better get used to it. We'll need it to reconnoitre." Langham tried to be buoyant but he knew that their main cargo, three Bulldog caterpillar-tracked armoured personnel carriers, might struggle in the terrain.

As the bow of the landing craft entered the shallows, Brewer barked orders through a megaphone. While the engines of the personnel carriers growled into life the forward ramp slowly creaked open. Louise ran down and began to wade into the rippling waves like a child on holiday but Langham pulled her back to where the Spider crouched on its metallic limbs. He hustled her inside the control pod and flicked a switch on the dashboard.

"Don't worry, I'm used to these." A lie. He'd only driven a Spider once, as emergency medic after the Gatwick disaster, an endless night of blood and mud. But the controls were intuitive and he wanted to avoid travelling with Furey's men in the Bulldogs. Joanna could probably fend for herself, protected by her upper class hauteur from the banter of the squaddies, but he surely had a duty of care to his former patient.

Motors hummed as the Spider flexed its legs, rose from its mounting, and began a crabwise walk down the gangway to the pebbled beach. The Bulldogs followed, their tracks clanking down the ramp.

A few minutes later Brewer ordered everyone to leave their vehicles for a briefing. Langham stepped warily over stones, driftwood and slivers of plastic. It had been a long time since he had walked on land and his body was already anticipating some phantom tremor, a shiver in the ground that presaged disaster. The top of the beach was bordered by a bank of rubble, the remains of bungalows or bathing huts. Brewer was pointing beyond this while Zahid unrolled a crumpled map. Langham was surprised when the former "refugee", now wearing military fatigues, addressed the group instead of the Commander.

"On the far side we'll find what's left of the railway and beyond that what used to be the A259 route eastward to Bexhill and Hastings. We have to go east because everything west, from Brighton up to Crawley is blocked. So we're turning north at Hastings to find a route up the A21 towards the Orbital Zone. Our objective is Tunbridge Wells by dusk."

"The Earth energies are all wrong..." Louise whispered to herself. "We lost the ley of the land. This is going nowhere." Langham ignored her pseudo-profundities. Whatever Zahid and Brewer were intending, his only option on this unstable planet was to keep moving.

As the twilight deepened, Brewer stood up in the hatch of the lead Bulldog and flagged the convoy to a halt. Langham struggled to hear his instructions over the fading whine of the Spider's electrics but soldiers were already hauling out inflatable bell tents to set up an encampment. They'd stopped at a road junction outside the skewed facade of a motel, where a crooked sign still promised "Traditional Fayre." The convenience store at the service station around the corner was a burned-out shell. However the pumps looked intact and Furey was leading a small group over to scout for diesel. Louise had fallen asleep.

It had taken them all day to reach the fractured tarmac of this former A-road on the north side of Hastings—so much for Zahid's "objective". All the way from Bexhill through St Leonards and onwards, repeated incursions of the sea had washed away whole stretches of the promenade and forced them to constantly reverse and re-route through a labyrinth of ruined streets. Avenues had become cul-de-sacs, punctured with huge sink-holes or piled with fragmented brickwork and rusting salvage equipment. Langham became tasked with reconnaissance, manipulating the legs of the Spider to stagger over broken beams or fallen pillars and check the ground ahead. At one point they became blocked in both directions by tumbling masonry and spent an hour excavating a path around the wreckage of a retirement home, now a pyre of brickwork, twisted walking frames and crushed mobility buggies. Despite his compassion fatigue, Langham was still compelled to wonder what skeletal remains were trapped within this asymmetric pyramid. At St Leonards they had encountered the vast white bulk of an Art Deco apartment block, tilted at a forty-five degree angle. It loomed over them like an ocean liner run aground, ready to collapse at the slightest tremor. The column had inched past, one vehicle at a time, seconds before the entire building roared down in a cyclone of dust and debris.

Louise woke up as Langham climbed out of the Spider pod. She stumbled down beside him, took the water bottle that he offered and drank greedily.

"So here I am, still in the dead zone. Like an extra in an old zombie movie."

"Everywhere"s a dead zone, Louise. But this area would have been cleared years ago. I expect there's a mass grave site near here."

"You can sense it. The ghost of the smell. The smell of the ghosts..." She zipped up her jacket. "Did you know that hauntings can make the temperature go down? We ought to be living in the fucking ice age."

Before Langham could attempt a reply Zahid appeared from behind the nearest Bulldog. He smiled as he gripped Langham's hand.

"You did good stuff today Doc, got us safe through some dodgy bits. Commander's well impressed."

"Thanks—but are we really going to make it all the way to the Orbital?"

"No worries, we'll get there. And you'll get your medical supplies. They tell me there's a hospital at Pembury that's sort of standing, *inshallah!*" He laughed as he walked away to join Brewer by the lead vehicle.

Inshallah—God Willing. Langham wondered how Zahid reconciled the alleged benevolence of his deity with the global suffering of the Shift. He turned to Louise.

"He seems to know everything, Lou. What can you tell me about him?"

"I was in this camp with Arthur and the others, we got quaked and were looking for a safe space. He turned up, said he could get a boat on the coast—you know the rest..."

"So how did you pay him?" Weapons or sex were common currencies. He couldn't see Louise Axton engaging in such transactions.

"He wouldn't take anything. Said it was *zakat*—charity. Part of his mission."

"What mission?"

"No idea, Doctor. I guess that we all need a mythology to keep us going." She glanced at Sergeant Furey's men pitching their line of tents in the deepening gloom. "Better get on with our luxury accommodation."

They quickly inflated their tent and unrolled the sleeping bags in silence. Langham hoped that Brewer had arranged a reliable watch rota. Packs of dogs or feral road-men could be prowling. And there was always the random tremor.

But Louise presented a semblance of calm as she rolled into her bag and turned off her torch. "I expect you'd rather share with classy Joanna—enjoying a cosy catastrophe together and feeling the earth move?" She laughed caustically. "But we're together for the long haul, Doctor..."

It was early evening when they arrived at the hospital. Long sections of the main road had been relatively clear, and the Bulldogs had coped easily, crushing abandoned vehicles and uprooted trees. Although the building's plastic cladding had fallen like torn petals and jagged cracks had spread across its concrete buttresses, it remained upright at ninety degrees. They nevertheless stopped on the far side of the car park, where nettles and small bushes poked through the asphalt and an ambulance sat on sagging tyres. It was covered in sprawling graffiti—SHAKE BABY SHAKE!

Louise pointed at a window on the first floor. "I'm sure that's a light!"

Langham scanned the frontage. Was the artist projecting an image from her own feverish imagination? Or was it as elusive as that sudden blip of light that was supposed to precede an earthquake, according to urban lore?

"Could be visiting time on the wards, Doc. Or you might be able to pick up your prescription." Zahid was jogging his elbow. "I'm up for it if you are."

"No-one is going in without back-up." Brewer strode over to take charge, pushing Zahid aside. "Furey and three privates will lead, locked and loaded."

A few minutes later the group stepped through the broken glass of the entrance lobby, past the overturned chairs and trolleys of a deserted A&E department.

"The wounded have gone for a walk..." Louise ran a finger through the dust covering a bench. Langham ignored her as they stalked down the corridors scoping out the signage with their torches. When they approached the pharmacy, Private Burton steadied his revolver with both hands, as he'd learned from old VHS police dramas, and peered through the doors before beckoning Langham and Axton inside. As the Doctor feared, it had been ransacked, shelves overturned or torn from the wall in a manic frenzy. Empty packets littered the floor.

"Tough shit, Doc." Zahid was laconic, almost amused.

They climbed the stairs to the first floor. The first ward was empty—even the beds had been dismantled, stained mattresses were stacked in random heaps—but as they passed the entrance to Intensive Care, Langham was convinced he could hear shuffling noises and a faint keening sound.

"There's some kind of animal in there..."

"That's laughter, Doc. It's a welcoming party." Zahid gripped Langham's elbow. "They're waiting for you to do your rounds."

The doors flew back and a long-haired grizzled man in filthy surgical scrubs lurched out, giggling as he locked eyes with Langham. He held a scalpel at arm's length in both hands, moving it from side to side as if dowsing for the blood that had long ago dried on the tiled floor.

"Where do we make the incision? The planet's fibrillating, we've got to get to the heart of it." As the psychic surgeon lunged towards Louise, Burton pistol-whipped his jaw and he fell to the floor, grunting with pain.

Suddenly Langham was gagging on a stench of urine and faeces as they became encircled by a wailing mob, mostly elderly men and women cloaked in torn bedsheets, staggering like disintegrating mummies. An obese bald man in a nurse's tunic and skirt, legs bulging in frayed black stockings, grabbed Langham by the collar and shrieked into his ear.

"Carry on, Doctor! You got to carry on. Matron's orders!"

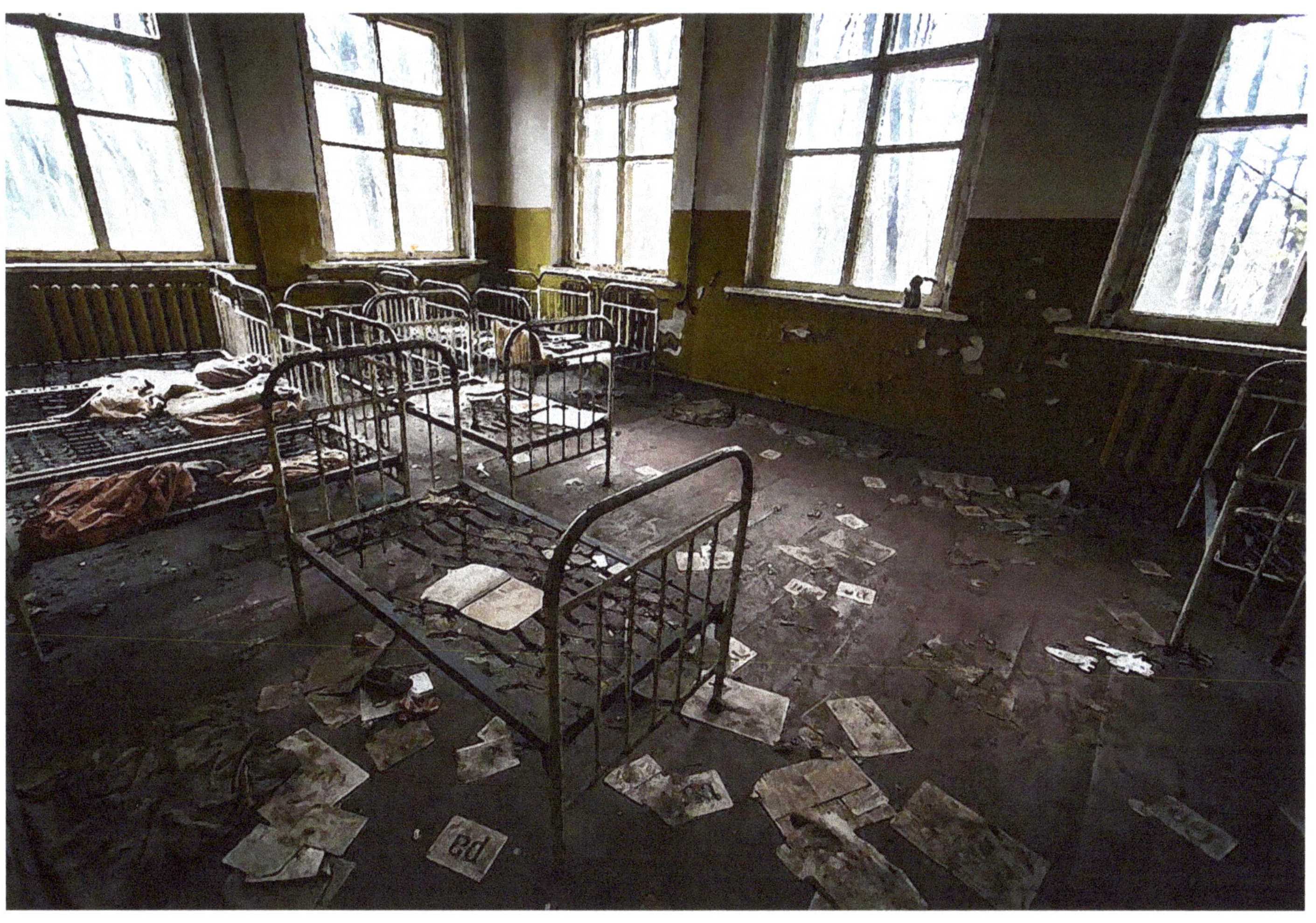

Langham was momentarily confused, recalling those old debates about gender. Then he shook off Matron's grip and shouted back to Furey. "We must at least try!"

The sergeant shook his head but Langham and Zahid were already advancing into the ward. Smoky candlelight revealed a shambolic nest of partitions improvised with broken cabinets or stacks of black garbage bags as Burton's boots crunched across discarded syringes. Langham heard a female voice mumbling behind one of the cubicles.

"Leave my tin alone... it's my tin..."

He had witnessed deprivation so many times but this terminal misery undermined his defences.

"There must be something we can do. Where are the staff?"

Zahid pointed to a faded poster over the nurses' station. STAFF EVACUATION PLAN/PHASE 1. "Looks like some manager screwed up and left a few oldies behind to self-medicate. PTSD cases. It's a mental hospital now."

"They're possessed," murmured Lou Axton. "The Earth Spirits have got them, got them shaking all over. I can feel it..." She sat on the floor, fingering fragments of glass and china into a rough mosaic.

Matron was pawing at Langham's sleeve. "You've got to come quickly, Doctor, we need a diagnosis." The fat man shoved him into an igloo of rubbish where a figure lay curled on an airbed. Langham knew immediately from the stench that the patient had been dead for days and slowly shook his head. Matron burst into theatrical tears.

"But there must be alternative ways—natural treatments—like essiac tea, crystals..."

Langham gave up. He left the cubicle and turned to Zahid. "I'm afraid we're done here."

"That's the problem with you doctors and your scientism, you're stuck in your rationalist dogmas. I can help these people. My art therapy—" Louise Axton paused in her work of bricolage. "Oh my God!... Can't you feel it?"

Her mosaic had started vibrating. Glass splinters were dancing across the floor. A dead fluorescent tube fell from the ceiling, where cracks began spreading across the plasterwork.

"Everybody into bed! Now! Now!" Matron was trying to push patients towards their cubicles but they milled around helplessly, moaning and shivering in an erratic widdershins dance. Langham was transfixed by the horror of this insane coven, even as trolleys and tables began to slide around him.

Zahid dragged at his sleeve. "Come on, Doctor. Let's get out of here!"

"We can't just leave them..." But Louise's outrage was silenced by an avalanche of plaster at the far end of the ward.

They ran for the stairs. Flashes of torchlight revealed handrails buckling into a warped expressionist geometry as they tumbled down. Langham tripped, slamming his head against the wall while the soldiers stampeded over him. Zahid pulled him upright and steadied him against the rippling metalwork of the staircase. He scrambled down the final flight half-blinded by pain, blood and clouds of dust. The floor of the exit lobby seemed to swell and heave under him, a turbulent ocean of soiled carpet tiles. He was sick with vertigo. But somehow they reached the outside and kept running.

"Bastards!" Louise was screaming into the raw night air, over the din of diesel engines and the clatter of caterpillar tracks. Brewer's Bulldog was already reversing, the Commander standing up in the top hatch to order a tactical retreat, while Furey, Burton and their comrades scrabbled for handholds on the second machine, which started rumbling towards the car park exit, headlights blazing.

Zahid cursed and ran after the departing vehicles. Langham, still dazed, wasn't sure if he was intending to stop them or catch a ride. The first Bulldog smashed through the flimsy exit barriers but the second one, in avoiding the derelict ambulance, side-swiped the Spider, crumpling two of its legs and shattering the perspex of the control pod. As the tank suddenly changed direction, Furey lost his grip and fell beneath the massive cleats of the tracks, his cry lost in the roar of the motors and a deeper almost sub-sonic vibration.

The ground shook. The hospital slid down vertically, as neatly as if it had been demolished with precision charges. Across the car park a huge chasm opened, at least thirty feet deep, exposing jumbled strata of asphalt, clay, concrete, the detritus of broken sewers and torn cabling. For the ground seemed to be slitting itself apart in a giant post-mortem autopsy. Commander Brewer's vehicle teetered on the edge, swaying back and forth, then plunged down into the darkness. The other carrier, moving forward again, lost traction as the aperture widened and rolled over into the cavity, which subsided in a vast landslide of rubble, obliterating both men and machines.

For a long time Langham lay spreadeagled face down on the concrete, body convulsing with each after-shock. He was vaguely aware of Louise and Zahid nearby. For a while she was crying and Zahid was muttering in Arabic, praying perhaps.

As dawn broke he staggered upright. The remaining Bulldog, parked some distance away, seemed undamaged. It would contain food, water and above all a radio for contacting Platform One and updating Deputy Commander McCulloch about the debacle. The expedition had failed and the only option was to return, whatever Zahid and Louise Axton might think. Shivering, he stepped around them as they slept on the broken ground and hurried past the ruptured abdomen of the Spider, before taking an elaborate detour between the rows of rusting cars, to avoid seeing the chasm and its contents.

He hesitated as he approached the personnel carrier. Perhaps some of Brewer's men had been left behind and lay in wait, ready to eliminate inconvenient civilians. But he was beyond paranoia now and grabbed the handle of the heavy rear door.

Joanna Graham was crouching on the floor amidst a pile of ration packs. Her reddened eyes stared straight through him but her lips were moving soundlessly. She was tearing her seismographic charts into neat tiny squares. At last she registered his presence.

"They're dead, aren't they? Brewer and the rest."

He nodded.

"It's not surprising they abandoned me. I'm useless." She flicked a lock of hair away and brushed the torn paperwork aside.

"You've said yourself forecasting's not an exact science."

"Science may not be the answer, Richard. I think at some level we really get off on this. Perhaps our mass neuroses and collective traumas from the aftermath of the Shift are actually the causes of it..."

Langham didn't reply. He sat down in front of the military radio console and soon realised that he had no idea how to use it. Joanna had returned to sorting her fragments, as if piecing them together again might reveal an underlying code that could ensure their safe passage. He tore open a ration pack and offered her a cereal bar but she ignored him. He ate slowly, remembering that he'd given his water flask to Louise, before drifting off to sleep again.

In his dream he was trapped in a vast ark, a floating steel and concrete island adrift on a dark torrent heading for a great waterfall at the rim of the Earth. He was part of a mass choir roaring in chorus, which segued into a deafening blast of white noise.

Louise Axton shook him awake. Zahid was crouching over the radio, adjusting volume and frequency dials.

"Unbelievable, man! No signal from your Platform One. I've been trying for half an hour." He switched off the transmitter and swigged from a dented can of energy drink.

"It must be a temporary malfunction." Joanna looked to Langham for reassurance. He shrugged. It was hard to believe that the Platform might be in difficulty, but the foundations of everyday existence were constantly drifting.

"We're fucked!" Louise exploded. "We're totally fucked." She swung a wild punch at Zahid, which he blocked with one hand. "You promised me safe passage to the Platform, then this Orbital utopia but here we are in the fucking terminal zones, more at risk than we were in Dartford."

"No worries sister. We got fuel, food. Even got kit." He gestured at the rifles and ammunition boxes stacked alongside him. "We're still on track for the Orbital. Onwards and upwards." Louise slumped down on the bench as Zahid pulled himself up into the cockpit. "I can drive this, no problem." Langham wondered where Zahid had acquired this easy familiarity with military hardware—perhaps vacationing long ago in some Middle Eastern theatre of war? He'd already assumed command.

"OK, people. We leave at nine hundred hours."

The motorway seemed endless, an erratic orbit around the vast black hole of London, where entire districts had been sucked into oblivion. They had been forced to take a lengthy detour around Reigate, grinding through the ruins of a four-level flyover collapse. Once back on course, they had to negotiate narrow lanes that were nearly blocked with overturned lorries and squeeze past the burnt-out hulks of refugee coaches. But Zahid remained unfazed, his optimism reinforced by the discovery of a tanker full of diesel fuel standing almost intact in the car park at Cobham Services. Langham could hear him declaiming in Arabic as they lurched up a slip road for yet another segment of the journey. The two women slept but Langham's brain was numbed by the incessant noise and vibration. He felt trapped in a metallic prison, subjected to sophisticated sleep deprivation techniques.

An hour passed as they traversed the obstacle course of this broken concrete desert. And then they stopped, abruptly. He could hear Zahid talking up in the cockpit, voices shouting back. The front hatch opened and a figure in a burka peered in, training her pistol at Langham's head.

"It's cool, Doc. Just a check point. Give her the gear." Langham slowly handed her the assault rifles, one by one. "You're safe now. Welcome to the People's Anglo-Islamic Republic. Take a good look." Zahid dragged him up into the commander's hatchway before resuming the driving seat. "This is the future..."

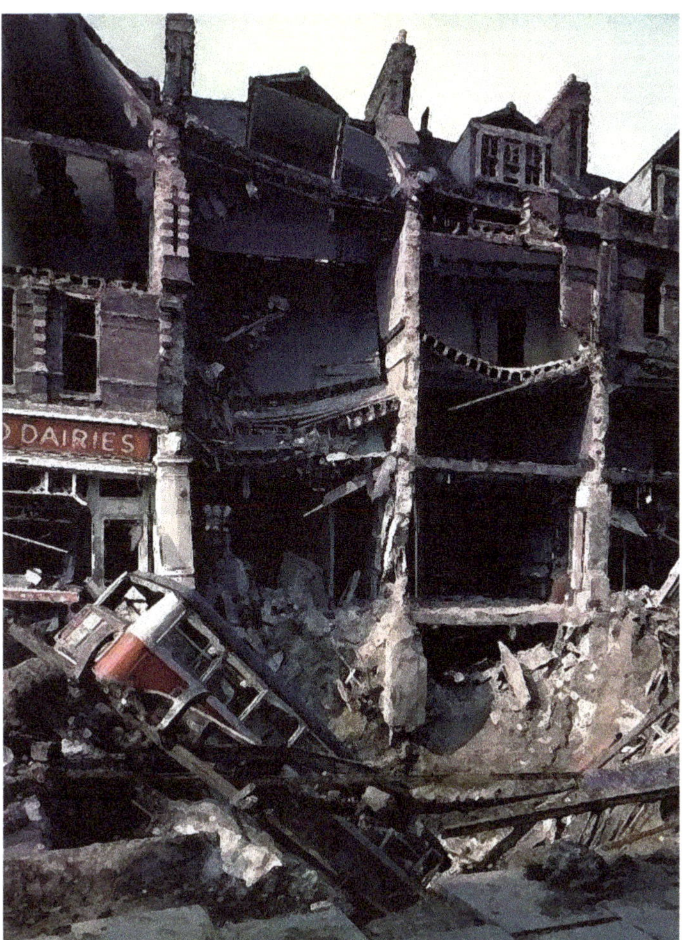

The Bulldog roared into life and began clattering down a bumpy but serviceable high street.

At little stalls along the road women in hijabs were busy buying and selling bread or vegetables. A few waved and for a second Langham felt like a general heading a victory parade into a liberated city. They passed a long white building decorated in green bunting with a crescent flag flying from the roof. Langham caught sight of a notice almost hidden by the hedge: SHEPPERTON VILLAGE HALL.

Zahid was eager to explain. "When the Shift started, the community started shifting too, out of Hounslow and West London. The bros knew Shepperton was a low quake area where we could settle. Most of the old gammons had done a runner." They passed a supermarket, battered but nevertheless functioning now as some kind of slaughterhouse, and then parades of shops, even a cafe where young men sat outside laughing and smoking shika pipes.

Zahid pulled up at an intersection. "Before we meet the Caliph, I got to show you something. A bit out of our way but never mind." They entered a long residential street of small semi-detached houses. Here minor tremors had left their marks—an overturned shed, shattered tiles, a fallen fence, cracked glazing in a yellow front door. The Bulldog nosed through the remains of some kind of barricade, improvised from rubbish bins.

"Don't think we're not multicultural. Check this out!" They halted outside a double-fronted building with picnic tables on the forecourt. Union Jacks hung from the upper windows and a St George's Cross banner stretched across the doorway. Langham was looking at a British pub, an institution from another life. An elderly white man in a cardigan emerged, looking up anxiously at this massive military machine.

"Don't worry, grand-dad," yelled Zahid. "We're not your neighbourhood *mutawa*. Just passing by." The old man still looked uneasy as he scuttled back inside. "They brew their own alcohol, you know. Strictly *haram* of course but the Caliph knows when to turn a blind eye. They need a little enclave. Got to keep some of them on side, see?"

"You want me on side, then?"

"Yeah, we always need good doctors."

"And acquiring all the Bulldogs and the hardware, that was part of the plan too? So your people would have taken out Brewer and the rest at the first opportunity?"

"Easy, man. The Caliph always negotiates first. Anyway they got quaked. So it became Plan B."

"So Lou Axton and Joanna become part of the Caliph's harem—is that included in Plan B?" He knew at once it was a cheap jibe, prompted by his own proprietary instincts towards the women.

"Hey, no stereotyping now. They will find good husbands. Anyway, we have more important stuff to do than shagging. Time for you to get educated..."

Zahid gunned the engine and pulled hard on the right track lever, spinning the Bulldog through one hundred and eighty degrees in a shower of crumbling tarmac before heading for the administrative hub of the People's Anglo-Islamic Republic.

"Allah sometimes gives the earth permission to breathe, which brings these upheavals. And indeed He has power to send torment on you from under your feet. Our scholars agree on this. But our *umma* has survived through our repentance, hard work and our strong family bonds."

The Caliph, imposing in dark glasses and a flowing white *thobe*, smiled as he handed Joanna and Louise glasses of mint tea. They sat on cushions inside his capacious tent. Zahid radiated pride at having arranged this introduction although Langham remained uneasy. He sensed a severe resolve underlying their host's geniality.

"As I completed my PhD in physics at Cambridge I began to appreciate the full beauty of Allah's creation—but realised also its complexity, its paradoxical nature. Through the painful challenges of the Shift, He has given us an opportunity to earn merit through helping others, to transcend our petty weaknesses in true *jihad*, to unearth new skills and discover new wonders."

"Wonders? All you people wanted to discover was oil. Your god's an earth-rapist..." Louise's truculence alarmed Langham.

The Caliph frowned. "Blasphemy does not become you, sister—especially when you have been offered our hospitality. Perhaps you would prefer to take your chances elsewhere?" Zahid half-rose, taking her arm to escort her out, but the Caliph motioned him to sit.

Joanna broke the silence. "As a fellow-scientist, I'd really like to know your theories about the physical causes of the Shift."

"Theory is best demonstrated through experiment. Come with me. Yes, you too, Ms Axton. And our wise Doctor."

Zahid drew back the tent flap, revealing the rolling grasslands of Sunbury Golf Club. In the distance, beyond a line of trees, Langham noticed a complex of low windowless buildings surmounted by a tall chimney.

"Ah, the council recycling plant with the incinerator. Before we established the *umma* there were many cremations there, a sacrilegious practice. But enough of that." The Caliph steered them in the opposite direction. Most of the greens and fairways had been repurposed as allotments where young men in white skullcaps laboured over potatoes and cabbages under a grey sky. They passed the clubhouse, in the process of being converted into a greenhouse, and skirted a small pond, now a sink of mud holding a tangle of shredded metal, perhaps the detritus of a foiled aerial attack by the secular authorities. Langham wondered how long this improvised micro-state could survive.

"Don't hang about, Doc. We're almost there. This is gonna be awesome, bro." There was a religious fervour in Zahid's voice.

They stopped at a wire fence. On the far side stood a domed wooden structure about twenty feet high. "It's a mosque," muttered Louise.

"Maybe one day..." The Caliph unlocked a gate and ushered them through the long grass towards a low door. They ducked inside.

As Langham's eyes adjusted to the dim green light, he tried to make sense of what he was seeing. A flat silver disc, around ten feet in diameter was situated in the centre, on a low dais. A mass of electronic equipment had been assembled on it. Langham recognised some kind of control panel and several of the cylindrical seismic sensors that kept Joanna Graham updated. They were connected to a tangle of capacitors, transformers, hard drives and circuit boards, apparently wired into a bank of lithium batteries. A black spheroid, the size of a football, hung at the centre of this web of cabling.

Langham was seized by an ancient panic. It had to be a bomb, maybe even a nuclear warhead looted from the ruins of Aldermaston...

The Caliph sensed his unease. "You believe this is some ultimate suicide mission? Think again, outside your box."

"You're building a new seismic data centre!" Joanna Graham was almost cheerful now, as if she was applauding the opening of a new upmarket health food store.

"This is the prototype of our new Platform. A gravitational shift device. In the years to come, we will be floating entire communities above the tortured earth. Hovering over the land as it recovers from this age of turbulence, unaffected by storms or tsunamis, we'll build a science-based Caliphate and even create an interplanetary technocracy one day—"

Langham couldn't contain his anger. "Anti-gravity propulsion is a delusion! The Nazis, the Americans, the Russians—they all fooled around with the concept for years and got nowhere. It's pseudo-science. Your people are better off digging their vegetables."

"I pity your ignorance, Doctor. But even you must know that gravity is not a force, but a change in the local geometry of space-time. And recent developments in the magneto-rotational instability of the hydromagnetic flux in the liquid core of the Earth have generated wild variations in the geomagnetic field observed on the Earth's surface and in ruptured areas of the mantle. Hence the Shift and wave after wave of seismic instability. We now know that electromagnetism and gravity influence one another enough for gravity's pull to be noticeably affected by the Earth's magnetic field. Our new superconductor technology enables us to create a spinning ball of plasma that can exploit this gravitational anomaly. And we shall rise."

Zahid raised a clenched fist. "Yo, the *shababs* will rise! I

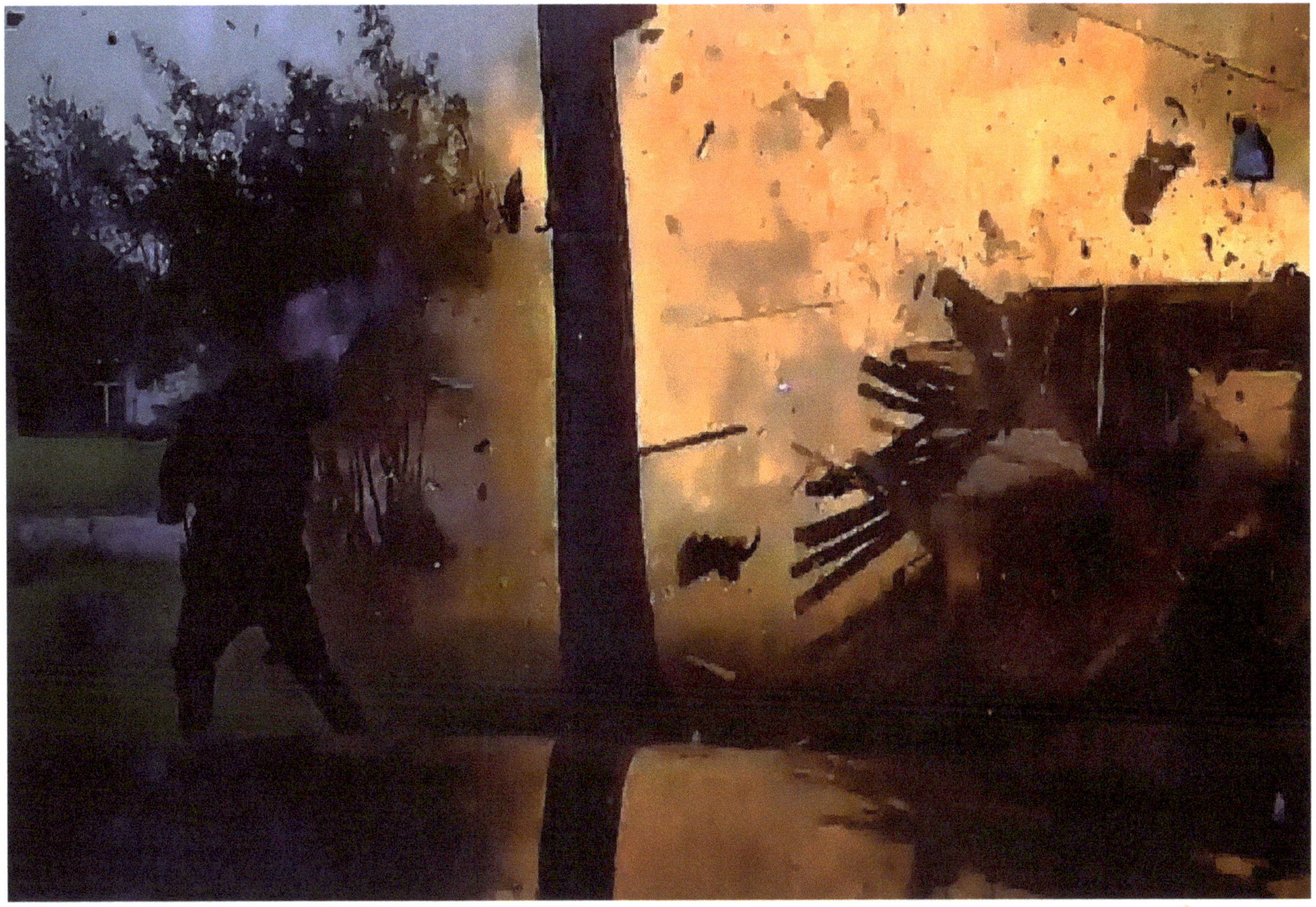

promised you a big surprise, Doc. Come on, man it was worth coming all this way!"

Louise stared at the new Platform. "Another machine. You guys always think that's the answer. That or a holy book. Anything to deny what the planet needs."

"Can you show us? Please..." Langham realised that Joanna was eager to believe anything that offered an escape from chaos.

"It is only proof of concept." The Caliph for the first time seemed defensive. "There are unresolved issues."

Langham decided to call his bluff. "I'm not expecting to be taken on a test flight. I just want to see if your gadget can rise six inches off the ground. That's all..."

"All power belongs to Allah!" Zahid"s eyes were wide with anticipation. The Caliph nodded and embraced him before approaching the device. He paused, then murmured a prayer as he touched the control panel.

Minutes passed. Joanna was watching intently, apparently hypnotised by the lights flickering on the console. Langham peered at the rim of the disc trying to detect the slightest movement. Then he realised that the room was slowly darkening, as if its green-tinged illumination was being absorbed by the black sphere at the centre of the machine. The whole assemblage shimmered before his eyes and a throbbing low frequency wave began oscillating through his body, up through his stomach and heart into his throat and skull. Overcome with fear and nausea, he struggled to remain upright.

"It's starting to quake—get the fuck out!" Louise was shouting at him, but he could hardly walk, let alone run. Then Zahid grabbed him by the waist and dragged him towards the exit. He glimpsed Joanna, kneeling now, mesmerised by the vibrations, eyes totally focused on the dark sphere which seemed to be expanding and contracting to the same rhythm. The Caliph had prostrated himself, as if in submission to this rogue creation.

Zahid and Louise hauled him outside. They half-crawled across an expanse of turf which was slowly moving in peaks and troughs, an absurd groundswell on a convulsing planet. Langham turned in time to see the micro-platform rising briefly through the splintered wreckage of the dome before fragmenting into a hail of metal particles. Something zipped through the air. And Zahid stumbled, a red hole punctured through his forehead.

It was chilly inside the personnel carrier but Louise's torch provided a faint illumination. Outside citizens were shouting as they organised squads for sifting through debris and digging out survivors from the collapsed village hall. The quake on the golf course had also affected the High Street and rumours of the Caliph's death were causing unease. They could hear women crying.

"I must go out and help."

"They're more together than you are." It was true. Haunted by the deaths of Joanna and Zahid, he couldn't stop shivering.

"Anyway, we're here for the duration, Doctor." Another fact on the ground. The right track on the Bulldog had finally fractured, worn out by the rough terrain and Zahid's fierce driving. As the light faded they huddled for warmth, waiting for angry fists pummelling on the hatch, or the next after-shock.

NICOLAS DESCOTTES

MASKS & HYBRID FORMS

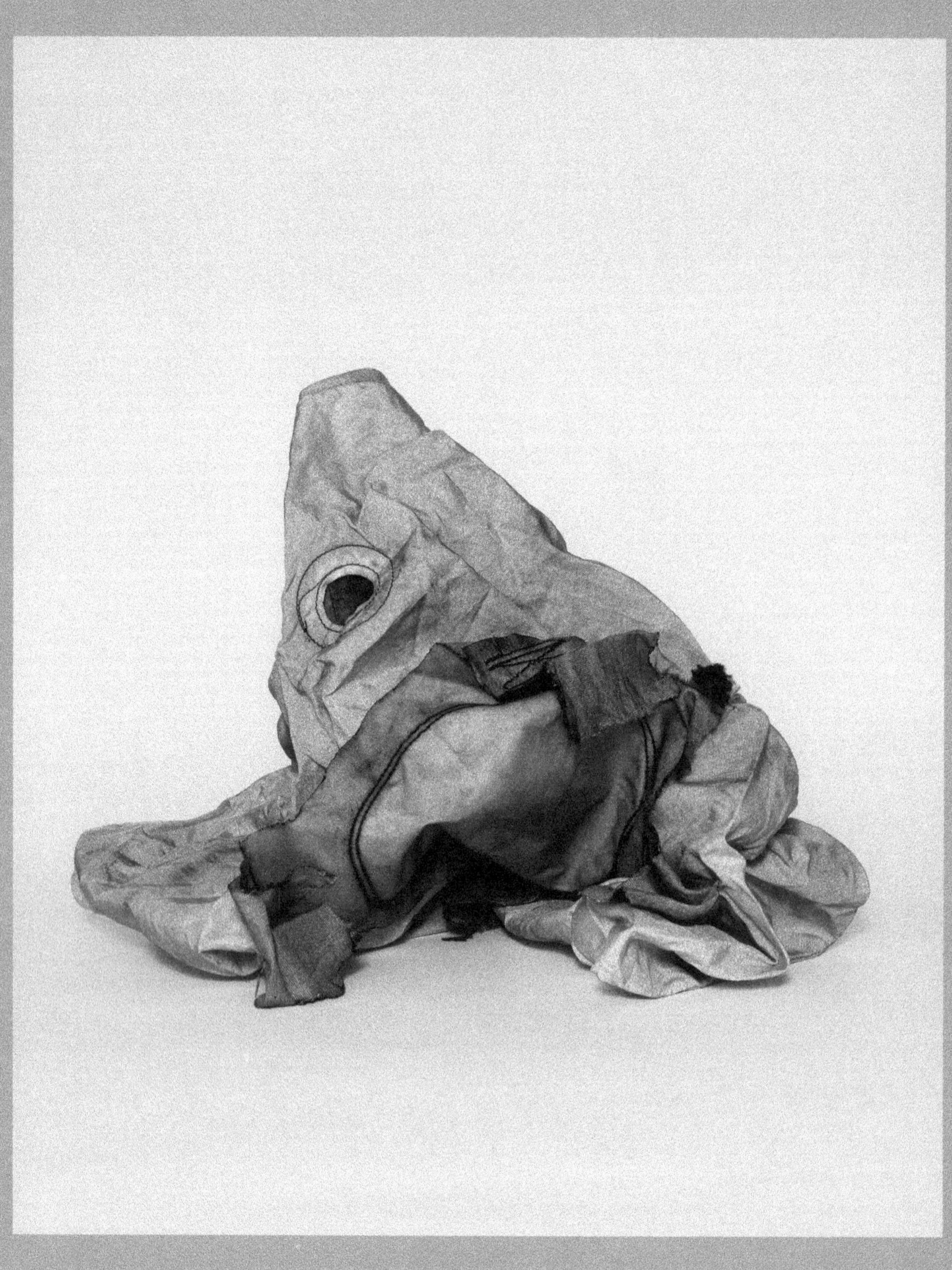

MASKS

"Blake, tell me—what are you going to dream for us today?"

"I don't dream."

"I know…" She smiled at her clumsiness, pleased by her affection for me.

"It's we who dream, Blake, I know that. You're showing us how to wake."

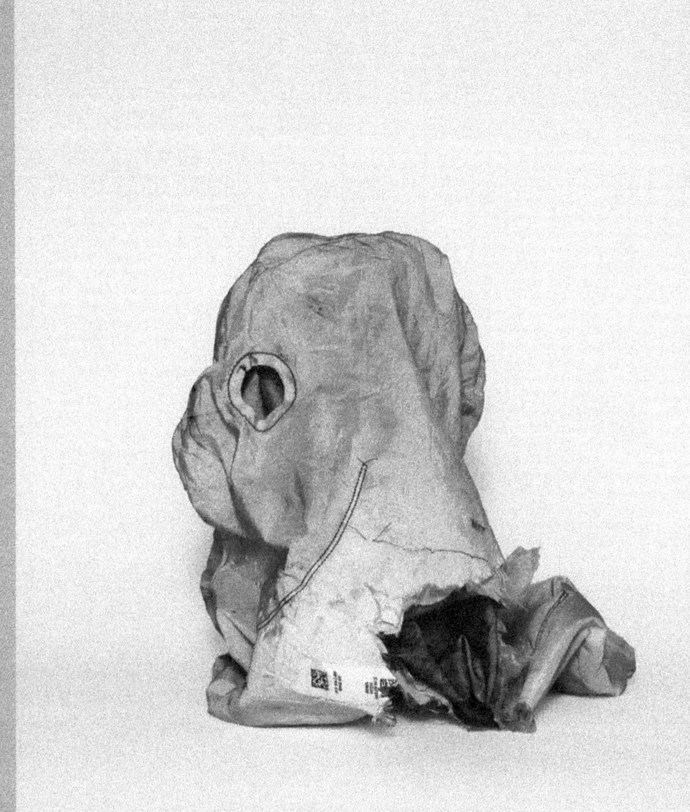

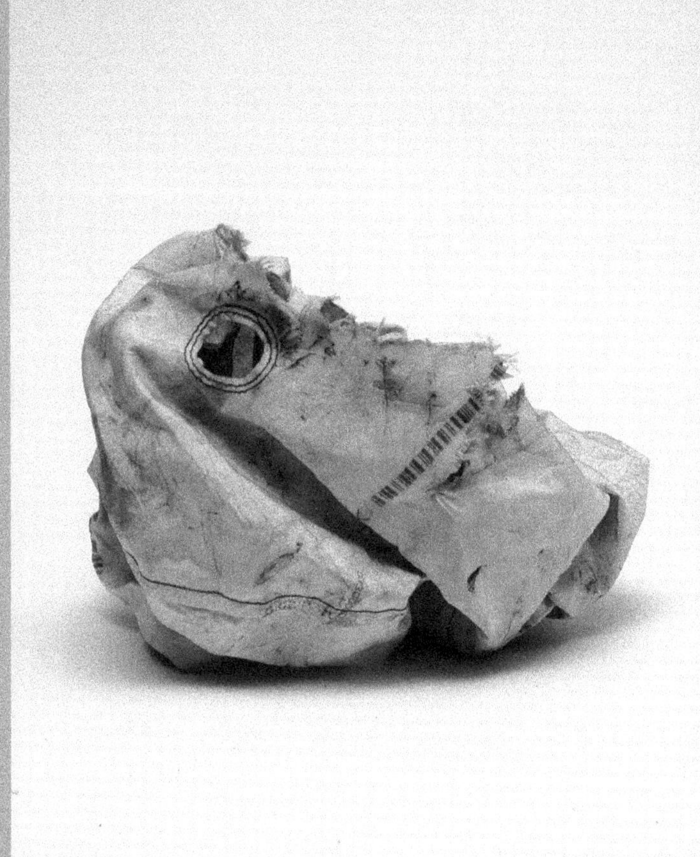

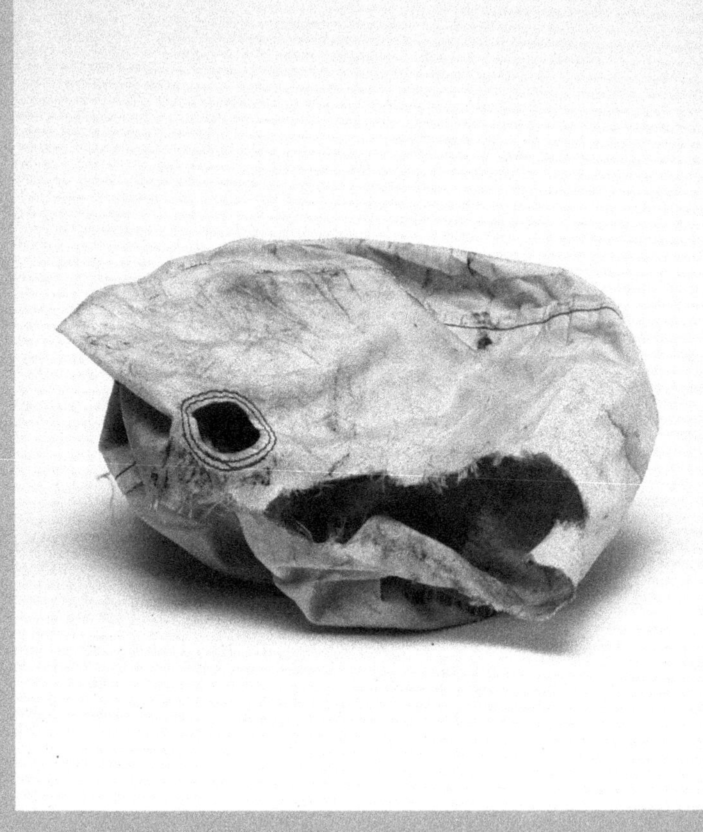

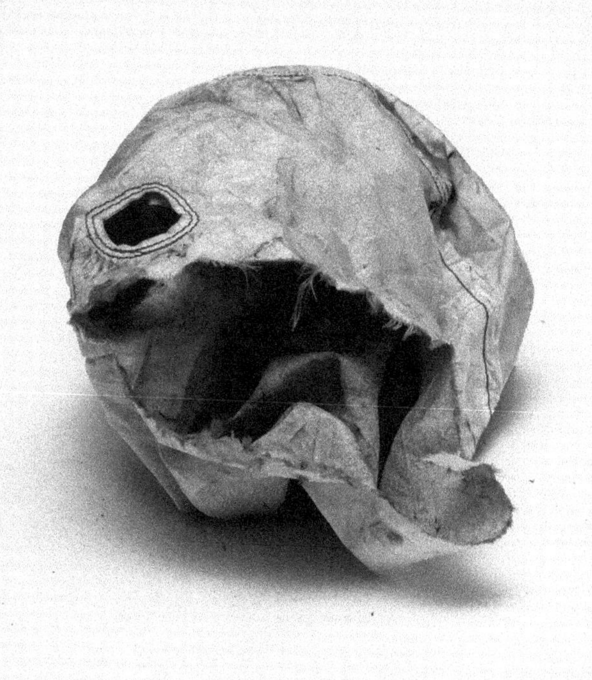

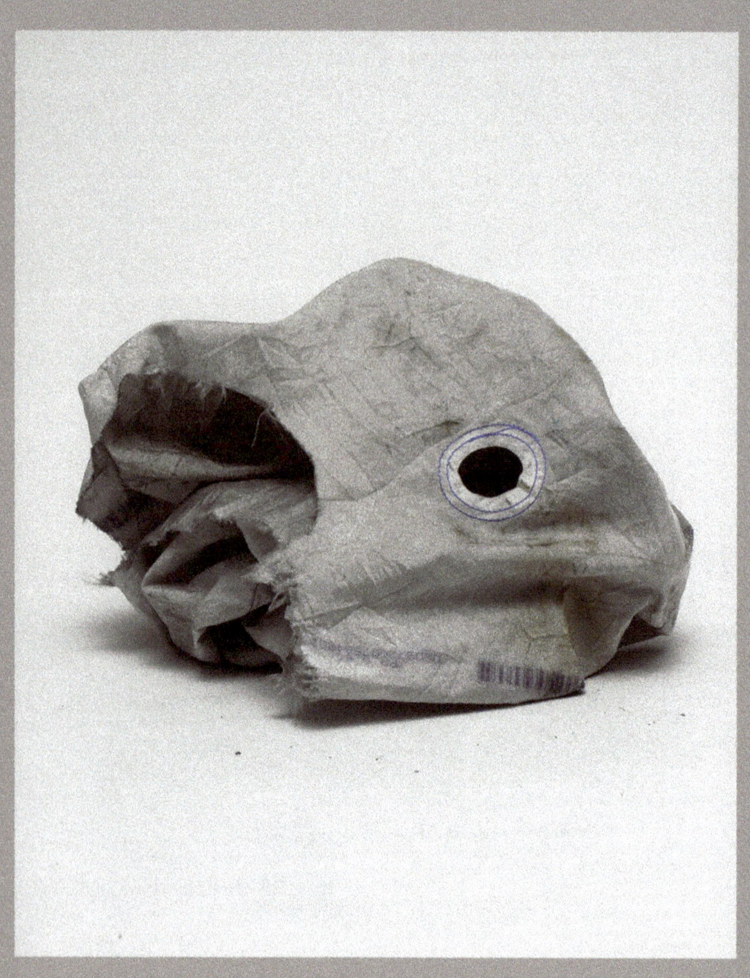

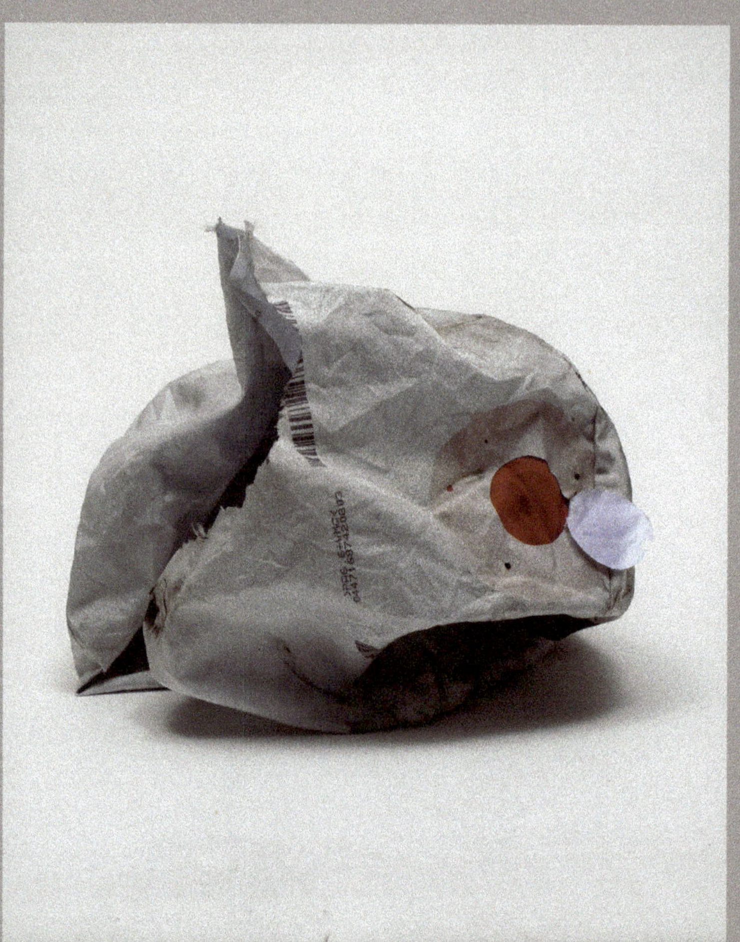

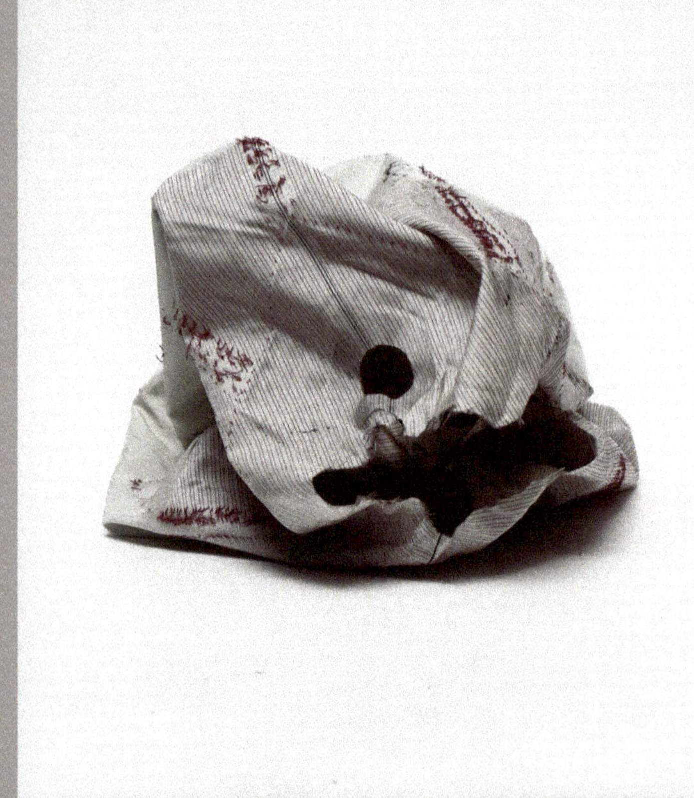

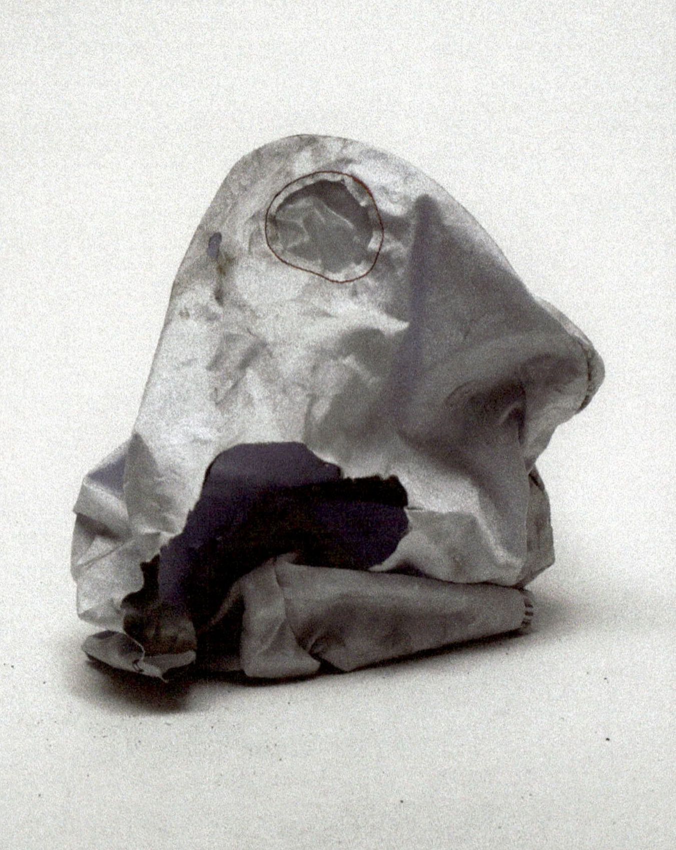

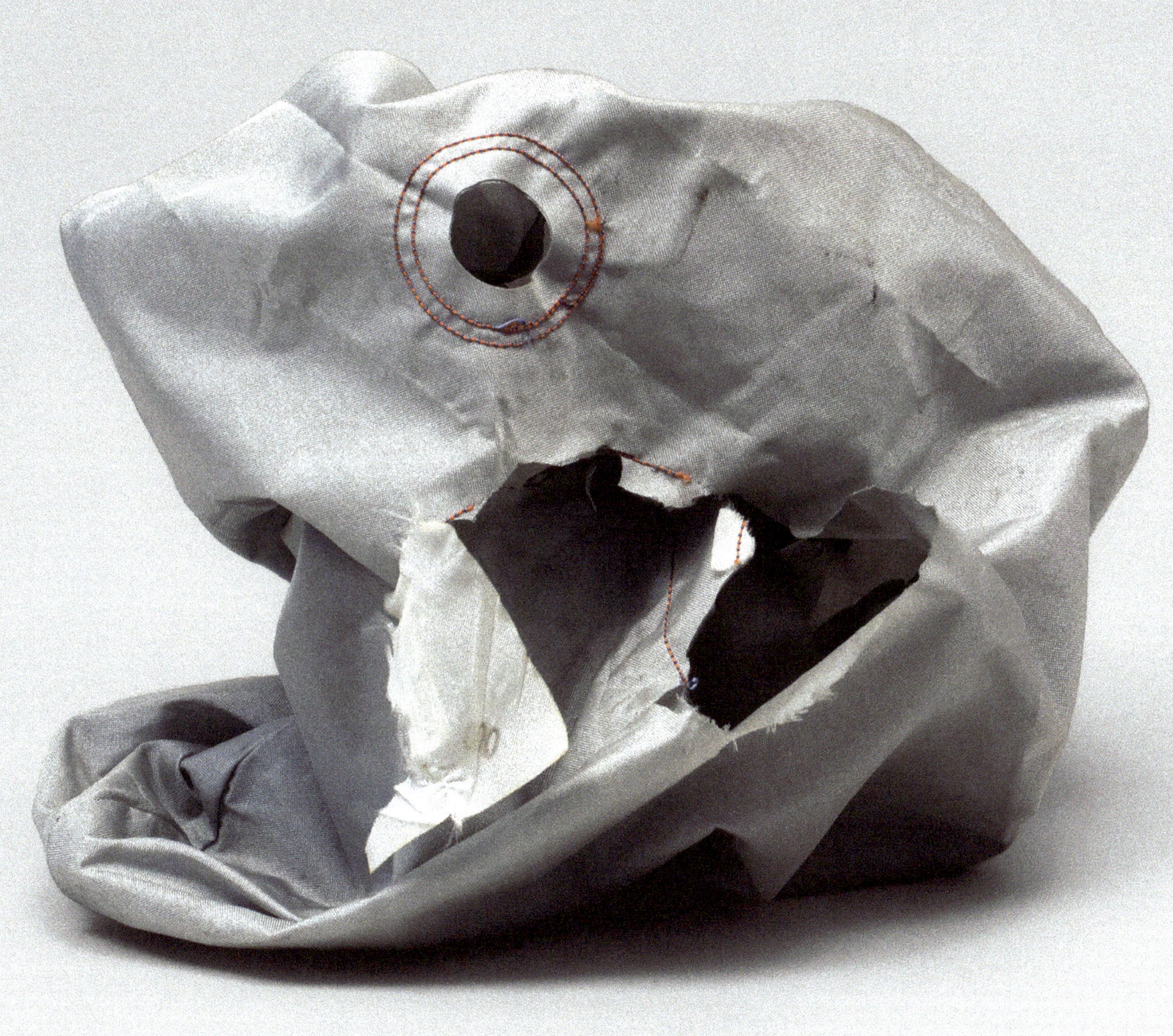

HYBRID FORMS

In the breaker's yard a testudo of abandoned cars lay together in the ever-changing light,
their outlines shifting as if some time-wind were blowing across them.
Strips of rusting chrome leaked into the overheated air,
patches of intact cellulose bled away into the crown of light that covered the yard.
The spurs of deformed metal, the triangles of fractured glass,
were signals that had lain unread for years in this shabby grass, ciphers translated by
Vaughan and myself as we sat with our arms around each other in the centre of
the electric storm moving across our retinas.

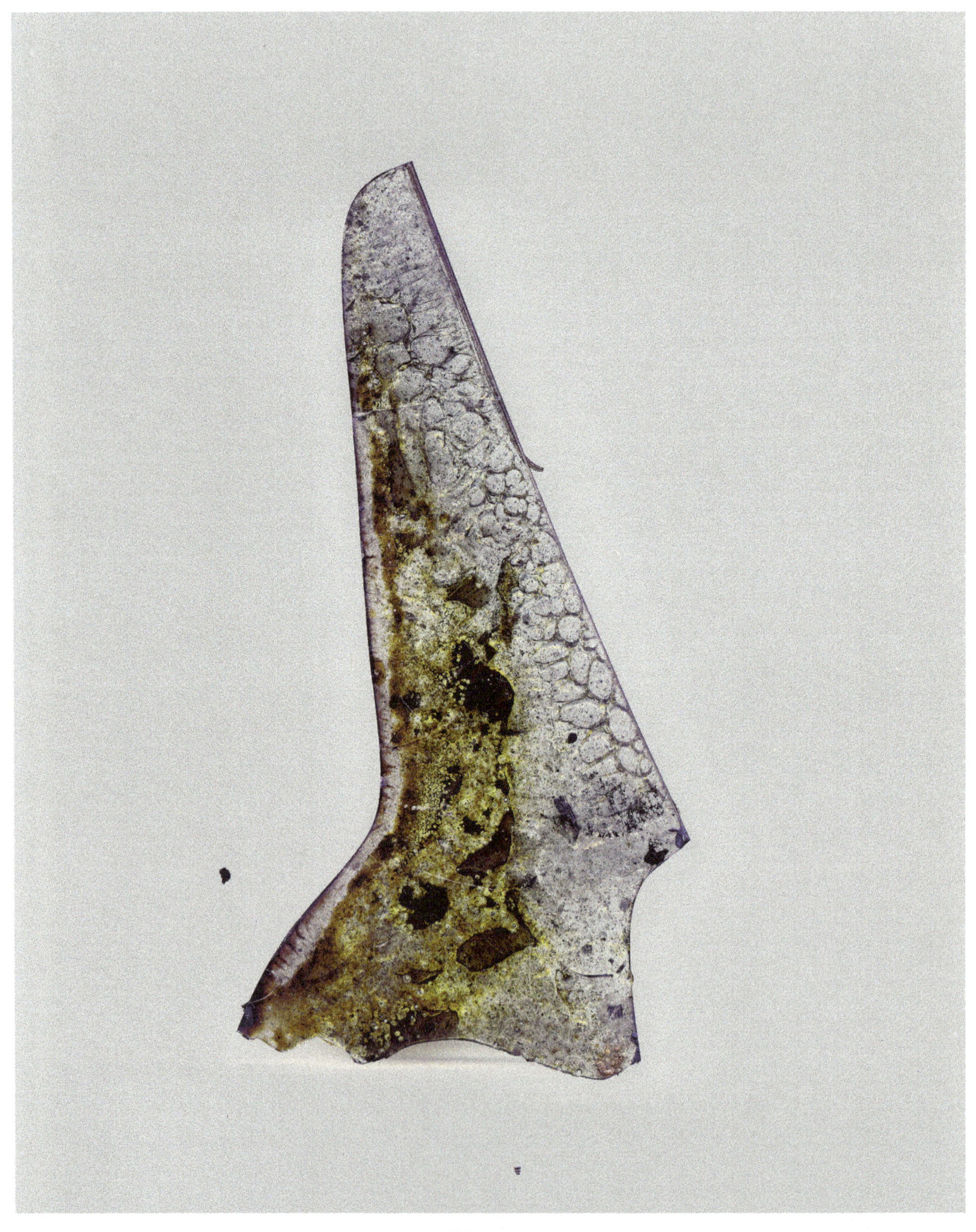

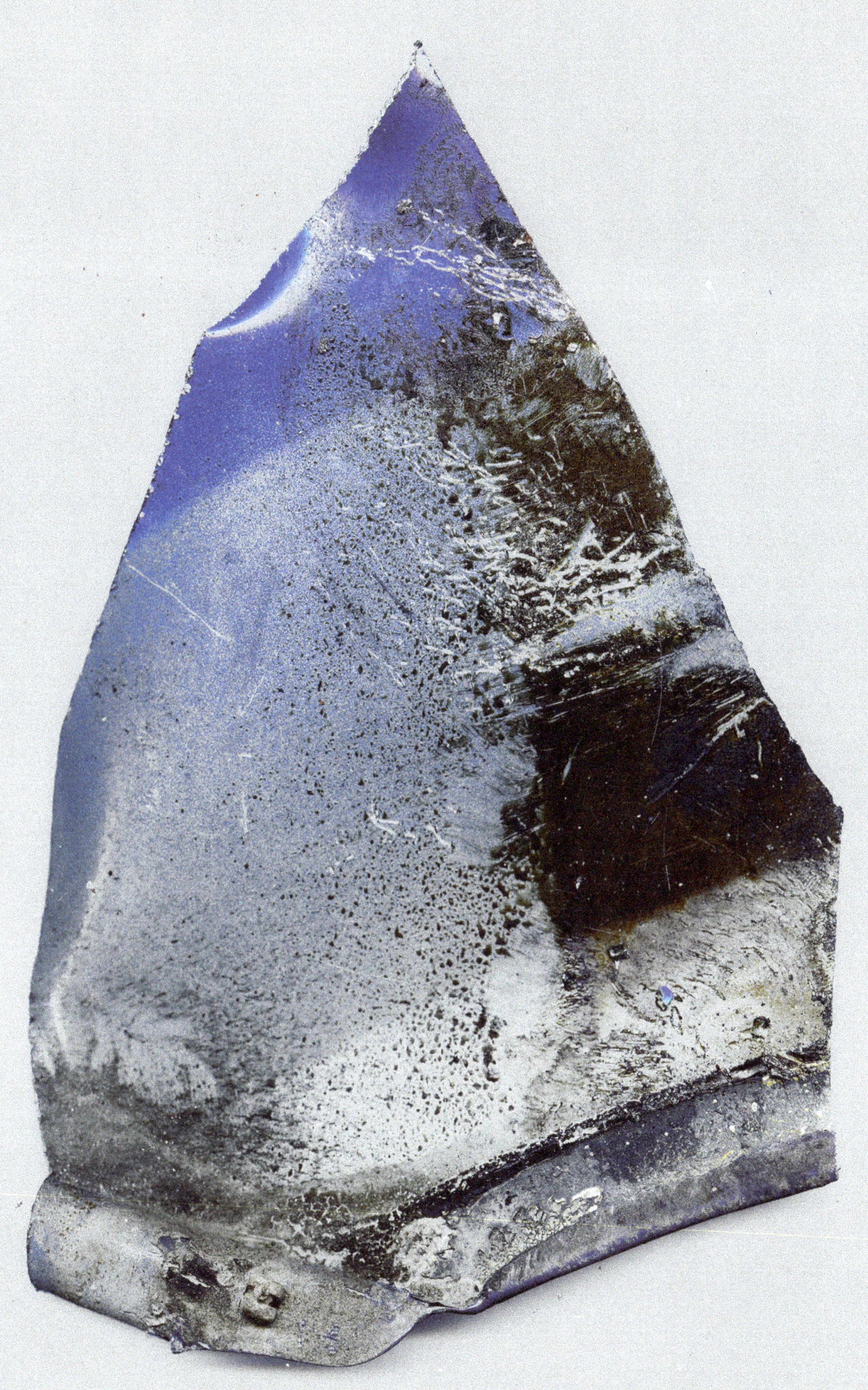

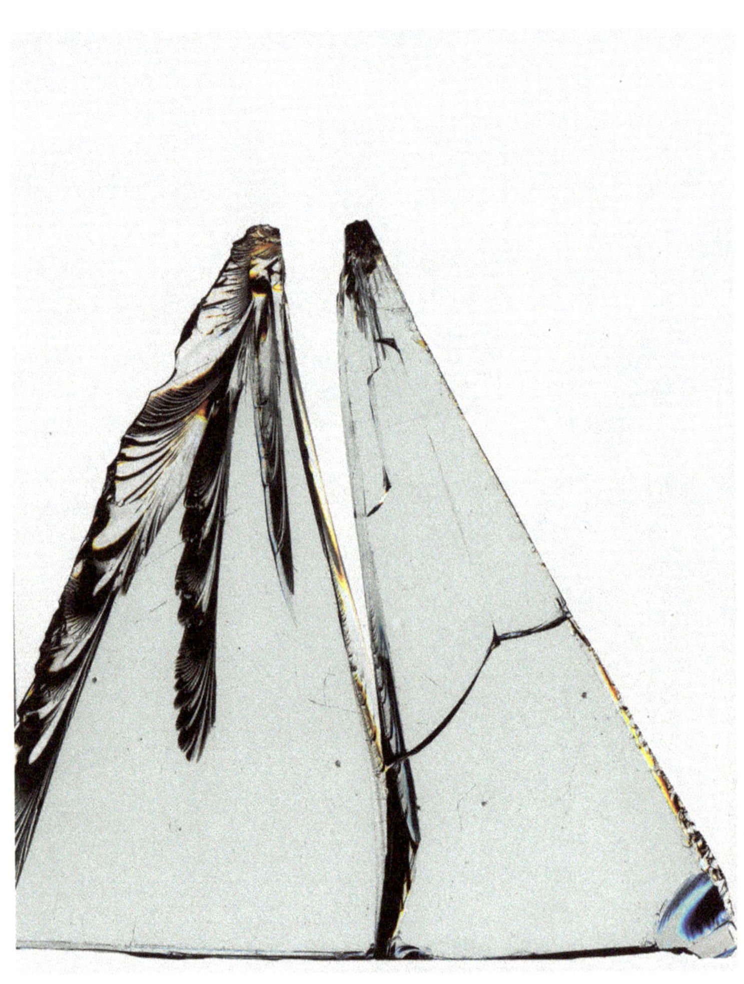
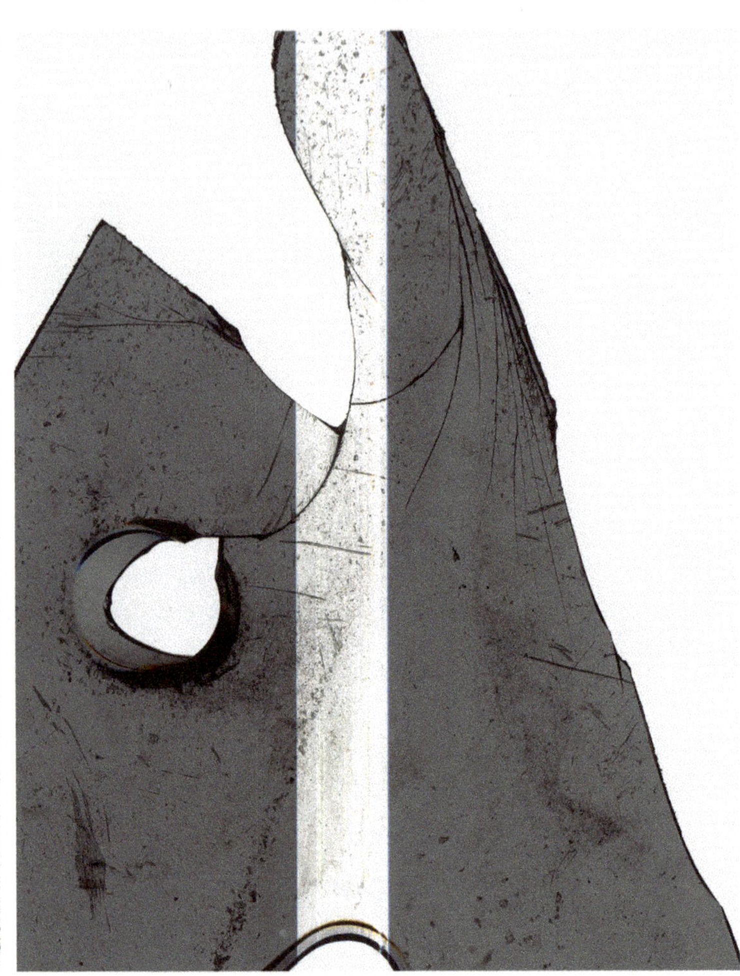
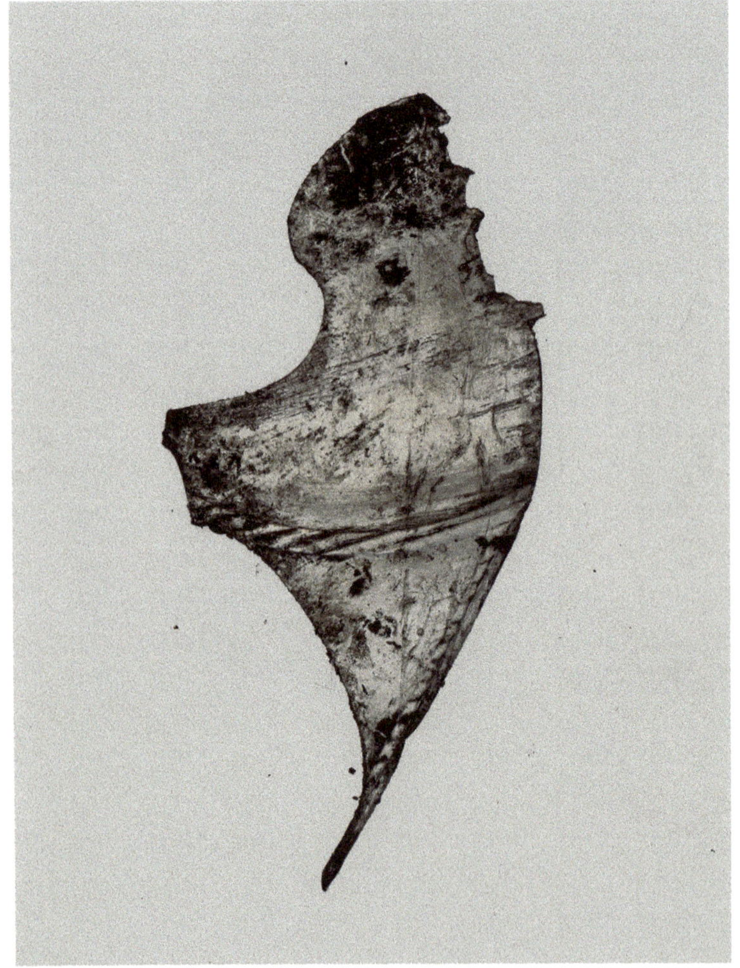
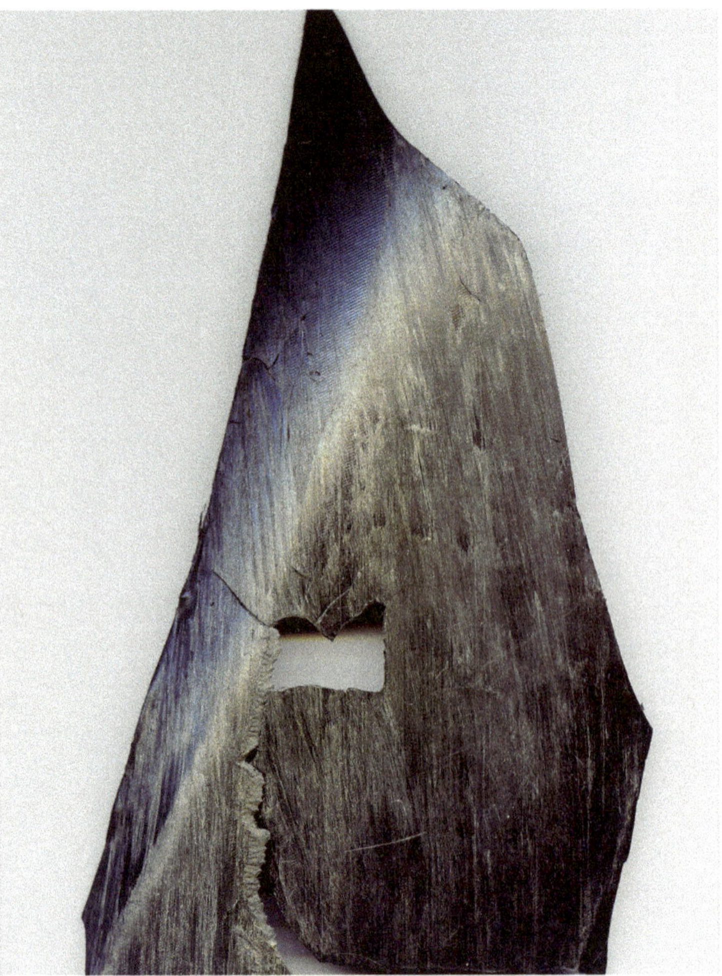

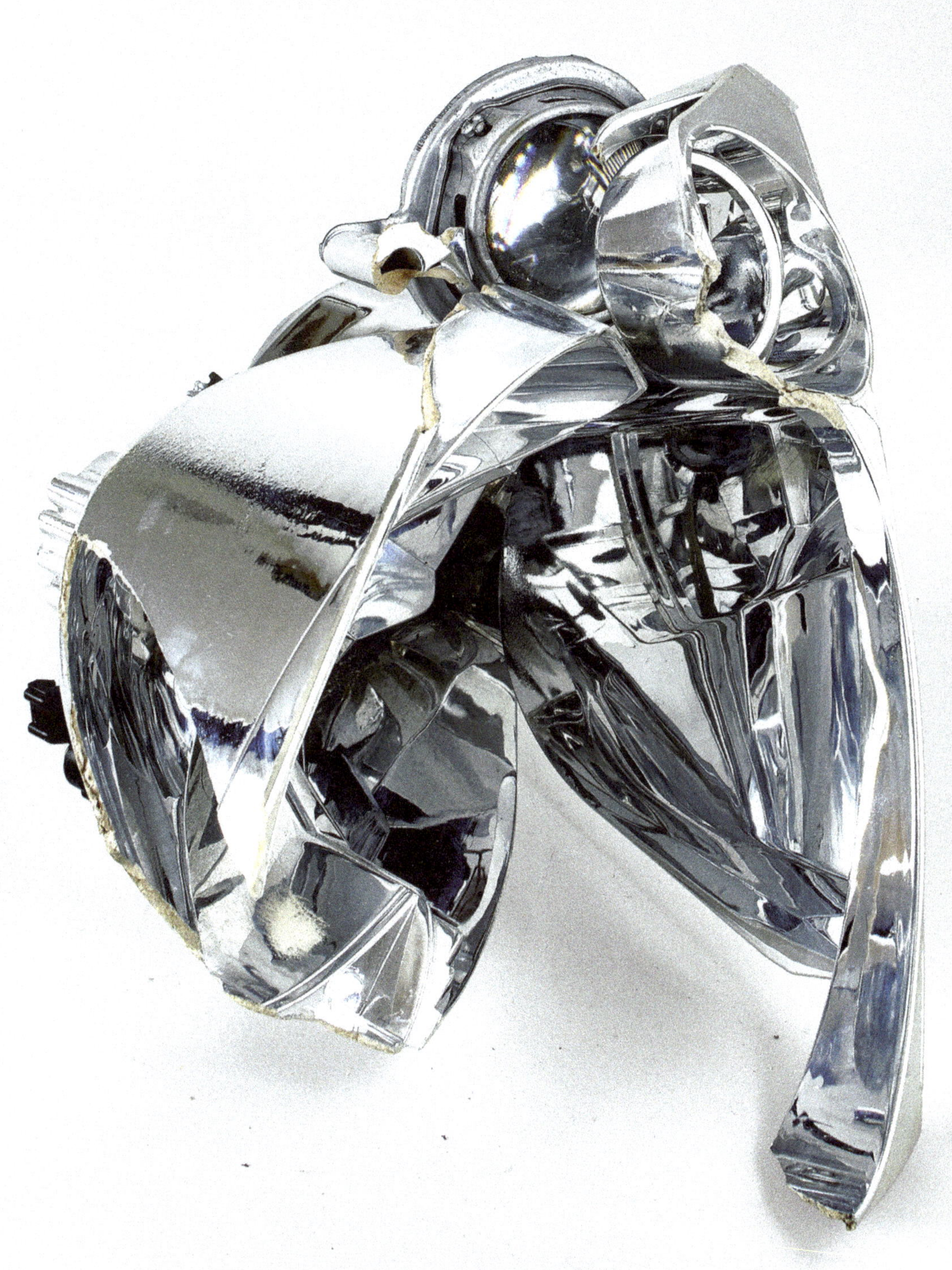

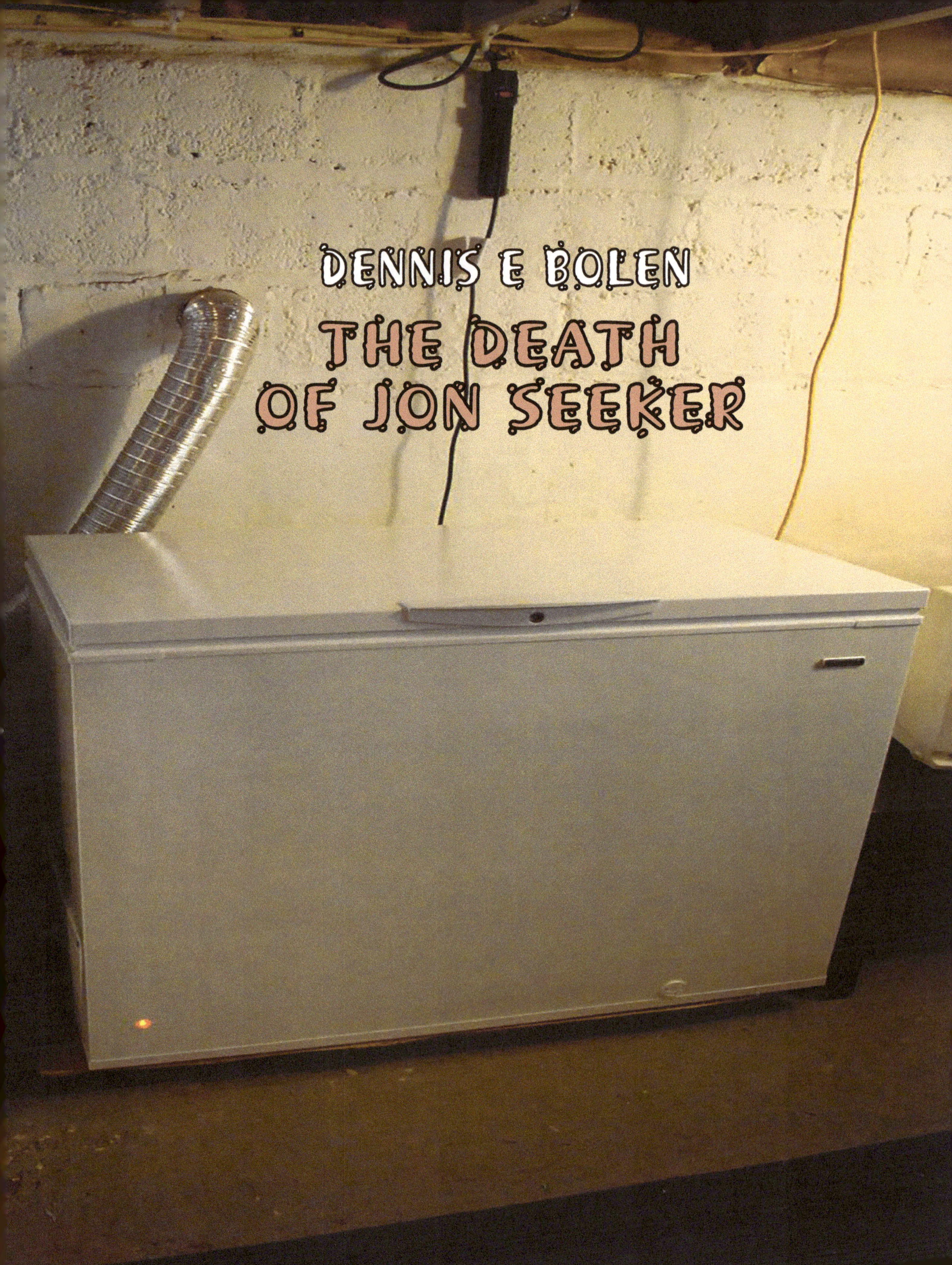
DENNIS E BOLEN
THE DEATH
OF JON SEEKER

One of these afternoons I'm not going to come back from my mountain hike.

Not suicide, I assure you. But the yearn I have for probing further will goad me so far afar that return will turn impossible. The weather out my cabin door changes from pleasant to murder with scant warning and I've never been much for caution. So I feel it prudent now to lay down this singular confession—about the ending of a young fellow I briefly met—so that his family and the outer world need not puzzle unto their eternities over what became of him.

Toward the suspension of my life in the city, which I now realize may never resume, I was paid a visit by two police detectives. Instead of investigating the disappearance of a young drug addict known to have been criminally active in the area—and about which I could have filled them in richly—they were instead going through the motions of following up on a decency complaint...or a safe-space violation, or something like that. It had to do with a schoolgirl I'd helped and some bully boys who couldn't take somebody standing up to them.

Never mind about that.

After the good part of an hour dancing around, and me disclosing more than I needed to to let these guys know I was a decent sort, they went away. Nothing more was heard. Thus, it falls to my conscience to let the world know something hitherto a secret.

Some months before, I had come home from the gym—this was when I was in good shape—about four-thirty in the afternoon. The back door lock was sticky, despite my long efforts to loosen it with graphite and other locksmith recommended compounds, so it took a few seconds of audible jiggling to get it open. This should have been enough notice for the intruder who was at that moment rifling my wife's jewellery bureau to get the hell out. But instead it was only when I stood in the back hallway putting down my gym bag that the guy swung out from her studio door in front of me and darted toward the other end of the house.

Having never before experienced such an occurrence—we'd been ripped off before, but never saw perpetrators in the act—I was surprised at what instinct had me do. Instead of sprinting after the guy, as in prior imaginings, I stood statue-still watching him disappear into the front foyer. My immediate inner feeling about this was an anesthetizing sense of relief.

Then there was an abrupt thunk sound and the heavy rumble of a body hitting the floor. And a groan. I unfixed from my spot and hurried into the foyer. He was collecting himself up from the carpet, having rammed a hip into our heavy antique hall cabinet and found out, as had I on several occasions, that the stone griffons at either end catch you in a bad place if you're not careful.

As he arose it occurred for the first and only time that our eyes met—at least while both of us were still alive—and I was disconcerted by the sheer vacuity in the gesture. The moment transmitted in concrete terms that we were two humans with absolutely no relationship to one another and no business to transact, no connection whatsoever beyond the commonality of our inhabiting the same planet as carbon-based forms of life. I didn't know what to say and surmise that neither did he. The interlude was over nearly as fast as it began. He wheeled and lurched toward the yawning front door.

I was again rendered static, watching him lurch through what I now saw was the splintered carpentry of a mauled doorframe. For the first time I noticed that his movements suggested intoxication; a certain non-consistent pattern in his booming steps down the wooden stairs.

Again, there came distressing body impacts and groans.

He was at the bottom of the flight when I got to him, prone on the patio, his head firm against the concrete. I stepped over him and stood off a little, gaping and wondering what to do.

His eyes opened and he rolled to a crouch, a hand still gripping the sagging pillowcase which I now understood must contain his ill-stolen booty. I thought of how modest my wife's jewellery was, chosen mostly for its flash; baubles mostly, costume stuff, not worth hauling away (though don't tell her that!). I wondered if this kid—he didn't look yet out of teenage—had any conception of this fact.

But there he was struggling to a standing position with his bag swinging in what I slowly understood was to be an offensive measure to see if I would stand off enough for him to have clear access to the gate. Our place has a large hedge so that the front yard is private and barbecue-friendly. More than one friend and neighbour had remarked that due to cutting off visual sight lines from the street, it made the house vulnerable to daylight break and enter. I was ruing this fact when he swivelled, swung his weapon in a swish so feeble I barely needed to shift to avoid. Then his eyes fluttered skyward. He teetered over, hit his head on the bottom step and lay still. I let a half-minute pass before concluding that he was unconscious enough to safely approach.

Up close he did not smell of alcohol in any form but there was a dry crust around the lips. His eyes, which remained open, seemed impossibly iris-free. Black, his pupils were. Impossibly black. I didn't need to touch him to check but I did anyway and with fingers to his neck to search for a heartpulse my clear sense of things were that he was completely dead. Not just intoxicant unconscious, not concussed nor comatose nor catatonic. Dead in a way that thunders finality. A no breath, no pulse, absence of life. His body felt cold, impossibly so. I wondered at how he could have been alive with such a low temperature. His ebon eyes began to develop a frosty glaze. A frigid pall descended on me, too. I shivered, though it was a warm June afternoon.

The notion of artificial resuscitation did not arrive in me. I was palpably fearful of further physical contact and the thought of mouth-to-scuzzy-mouth was too grotesque an idea to contemplate. It is likely, though I am not certain, that minutes passed before I arose and stepped back. A thick daze clogged my mind. At one point, I'm not sure when, I looked down to discover my cell phone in hand and a thumb poised to dial. Consciously, I knew a 911 call was in order. Consciously, I stuck the phone back into a leg pocket of my cargo shorts.

From here on I will not attempt to explain my thinking or in any way try to make sense of what I chose as a course of action. This is for others to judge. It could be that even though it was clear I had little or no culpability for what had happened to this creature I knew this would be difficult, given the empirical facts of the scene, to immediately make apparent to an objective observer. Plus, I now saw that the kid had bled somewhat from visible contusions to the head. Falling down a flight of stairs will do that to you. I could imagine other bruises upon his body, suggestive of physical abuse.

Without further rumination I gripped sneaker-clad feet and dragged him around the side of the house and down two steps to the basement door. He was surprising light and easy to transport. Grappling with keys my hands shook; concentration refracted to the point where even when I had the proper one poised over the slot, it took several tries to insert it all the way. In the basement I pulled the body across the tile floor to the near-new ten-point-six-cubic-foot freezer Liza and I had bought not-too-long ago to keep bulk meat purchases. To date, we had not bought bulk, having sought but not found the ultimate deal on the quarter or half side of beef we'd been seeking. All that was in there were a couple of loaves of artisanal bread and a pack of spare-ribs.

Without thought I took the food out and hoisted the youth up and into the vacant fuming freezer. His bulk took up not even half the available space. I stood for a moment looking down at him, now curled fetal to conform to the dimensions of his current crypt. Something stopped me from closing the lid and it took moments of blank staring to perceive a line of white peeking from one of his sock tops. I leaned in, gripped and flung a plastic card onto the floor behind me, then checked the other sock and rifled though pockets, finding nothing. Finally, reaching as far as I could downward, with two fingers I gently-as-possible drew his eyelids closed.

With the freezer shut I swung around to pick up the card. It was a sturdy plastic ID to indicate that Jon Stanley Seeker held legal status as a member of a prairie First Nations reserve, the name of which was unfamiliar. The photo seemed reasonably accurate but I was disinclined to re-lift the freezer lid and confirm. Even though a hole in my knowledge of the dead youth had now been filled the full meaning of it was irrelevant to my present thinking. Or lack of. All I could concentrate on was what the situation looked like to the outside world and how might the events of the past ten minutes be handled in such a way as to negate such scrutiny. I took the bread and ribs up the stairs to the kitchen, wedged one of the loaves into the fridge freezer and put the other on the counter. The ribs went onto a plate to defrost. I grabbed rags from under the sink and wetted them under the faucet, found a squeeze bottle of bathroom cleaner and hurried out the front to where there was a blood splotch on the bottom step. I rubbed and sprayed and scrubbed furiously until to the unassisted eye at least there remained no vestige of what had gone on. I sanitized the trail aside the house and into the basement to make sure there was no visible evidence of corpse dragging.

Back in the kitchen I hurriedly wiped everything suspicious, knowing that Liza would soon be home, then took the rags out to the garbage can. I slid the ID into an envelope and hid it in the pages of a book in my office, warranting sternly to myself not to forget the title. I took the bag of jewellery—which I now saw contained only about a dozen items—and dumped them willy-nilly back into Liza's bauble drawer. I thanked her under my breath for being a happily messy human being; the resulting jumble was not uncharacteristic of how she stored most of her decorations. Then I returned to the garbage can and tossed the bag in there too.

I had ten minutes to sit in the front room with a glass of scotch and mull the situation.

Mostly I mulled myself.

Over the past few years, after a career in social work and various activities that required sensitivity, I'd grown callous. By my own assessment, anyway.

I was through with sharing, I knew that.

Things like talking on the phone irritated me. I vastly preferred email, the more succinct the better. My main activity was sitting and thinking. Above all, what I disliked most and avoided like death was having to explain myself.

Except to myself.

Halfway through the drink I was deep into all the culpability scenarios. I understood my instinct, upon seeing that the fellow had mysteriously expired, not to call the authorities. At least until I figured out what my story would be. The truth was dubious; never mind that he was ripping the place off. In the current climate of racial inter-belligerence, the innocence of a white guy standing over the beaten corpse of a scrawny native youth was not going to go down without considerable legal process and virtual conviction via social media. The lawyer bills would be crippling and wouldn't help a bit. I was two years into retirement with adequate-but-not-lavish pension income, leaving little to spare.

Staring out the shattered front doorframe, the tatters of which shifted slightly in the breeze, I mulled a little further. It was pretty clear the guy had OD'd on something. The roughing up he took falling down the stairs, hitting his head, might have induced unconsciousness but for sure the other features of him, the dry mouth, super-dilated irises, emaciation, et cetera, pointed to his being just another victim of the poisoned drug phenomenon going around. But toxicology testing, I happened to know, took forever in the normal course of things. Suspicion would hang over my drooping head for months or longer. In light of this the idea of having the fellow discovered somewhere else in the city, in a likely place where street people were falling dead all the time, attracted. I started thinking of how I could sneak his frigid personage into the trunk of the car and when and where in town it would be feasible to plunk him down.

Then the back door sounded and my wife strode into the living room.

Hello Darling. I shifted in my chair and raised a near empty glass. How was your shift?

Fine. She stepped close and kissed my forehead as she shucked off the heavy over-shoulder bag she was lugging. How did your day... Wheeling around while un-peeling her sweater she froze. Hey! What happened to the door?

We got broken into, my dear.

What?

Don't worry. Nothing's missing. I interrupted the man in his work. I took the last sip in my glass and arose. I'm going to have another. Care to join me?

Did you call the police?

No.

No?

No. Remember what happened last time?

It doesn't matter what happened last time.

Sure it does. They come. Laugh at the flimsy door security we have. Don't bother to lift finger prints. Lecture us on keeping windows locked. Tell us to get a dog. Leave and never come back.

They need to know about it.

Sure. Maybe. I'll call them tomorrow. Right now I'm having a drink.

Look at the mess they made.

It wasn't a they. It was a he. I saw him leave.

It wasn't general practice to lie to my wife. I love her utterly. We'd been together since I'd finally settled into relationship sanity and we'd been a fair few years with no significant downs and mostly ups. But we differed on how much of the outside world had a right to our lives. She'd always had lots of friends. I've usually had one or two at any one time, changing from decade to decade.

You saw him?

Yes. He tried to get your jewellery. He dropped the bag on the way out.

This is all kind of incredible.

Oh I dunno. It's happened enough before.

It's not something to get used to.

Yeah well... Anyway. I took ribs out of the freezer. I'll do up a sauce.

Oh? With rice?

Rice or potatoes. Your choice.

Rice this time I think.

Rice it is.

And what about this door?

I'll screw a piece of plywood over it. Call Pasqualino in the morning.

I hope he can come right away. It's ugly.

He'll get to it. Something like this he can fix in a couple of hours.

And so it was that we had rib dinner that night and before watching the bedtime news I ran a search for the best price on bulk meat. The next day, while Lino was working on the front door, I drove to the suburbs and bought four hundred dollars worth of steak, roast, ribs, ground round, stewing chunks, brisket. With the sound of drilling upstairs and the car trunk open in the back alley I carted the whole load down into the basement. I got it all ready, stacked on the floor, before opening the freezer lid.

I don't know what I expected to see, but when I did look I was not surprised. Jon was lying as I had left him, curled at the bottom of the space, with an arm up over the raised part at the bottom where I assumed the refrigerant motor is housed. His head lay upon his arm, as if he'd decided to take a nap right there. I laid a heavy duty black garbage bag over him to create a concealing demarkation and—putting aside a package of tenderloin for later on—began to load the beef. Though I'd done a little research on the space requirements, I was surprised how perfectly the quarter side of wrapped meat products filled the rest of the freezer and perfectly covered up the frozen cadaver of Mr. Seeker.

Upstairs, Lino was just about finished the door. I took a couple of IPA's out of the fridge and we sat for a time in the front room. Later on we stood in the foyer and admired his work. I paid him off in cash. Then I went shopping for broccoli and mushrooms. When Liza got home I was having another beer in the living room and there was the aroma of baking potato from the oven. I told her we'd be having filet mignon for dinner.

Great. But what I really need is a cocktail.

A fine idea. I'll fire you up one of your girl drinks.

I pulled the shaker and a couple of her favourite bottles out of the sideboard while Liza went into the kitchen and then said something. As per habit, she called at a volume I could just barely hear from two rooms away.

Huh? I stepped to the kitchen door. What?

This bread. She held the freezer door open, pointing to the jammed in loaf. And the other one in the fridge. Why aren't they in the downstairs freezer?

Oh. I needed space for the meat. I went and bought a quarter today.

You did?

Yup. Been thinking about doing it and then when the carpenter was busy on the door decided to make myself useful and go get it done.

I thought we were going to discuss it first.

Didn't we though? Didn't we buy that big unit just to do stuff like this?

I know. I just thought we'd talk about it.

What's to talk about? I checked the best prices on-line. Drove out to Langley to get it.

Did you call the police?

About the beef?

About the break-in, smarty. You told me you would.

Aw... between that and getting Lino going on the door... I gestured with the bottle of elderberry liqueur in my hand. He did a fine job, by the way.

Yes. He did. I saw. Now what about the police?

I didn't get around to it.

Why am I not surprised? Honestly, I don't know why you're dragging your feet about this. Should I do it?

Please don't.

What's the matter with you? Have you gone all a-social all of a sudden?

Tell you the truth my love I'd just rather not have cops snooping around the place is all.

Said Mr. Law-Abiding-Never-Had-As-Much-As-A-Traffic-Ticket John Q. Solid Citizen.

I got a ticket. Once.

For over-parking. Everybody's done that.

Why are we having an argument about my lawful civic behaviour?

Because not reporting this crime is so out of character for you.

It wasn't so much a crime.

B and E? Smashing someone's door and rooting around in their jewellery drawer? That's pretty criminal.

But this guy. This guy never made it to first base.

First base? You know I dislike baseball metaphors...

Well maybe second base. Wrecking the door was first base I suppose.

This is getting ridiculous.

Yes it is, dear, I agree.

When is dinner ready..?

We had our drinks. Then dinner. Thankfully the conversation turned away from the thing that gave me anxiety. The next few days settled down admirably as Liza wearied of the topic of the break-in.

I began to search the newspaper for word of wayward youth. There were no missing person articles. Nothing of relevance was noted among the growing trend of sudden death caused by what seemed to be a renewed scourge of drug abuse in the city.

After a week or so it appeared there would be no immediate repercussions about my keeping Mr. Seeker. I tried not to think too hard about the contents of the freezer and slept fairly well, considering. It was my plan, if I had a plan, to figure out some failsafe way of respectful disposal. Nothing came to mind. I struggled with it, thinking hard. Time passed.

To keep up the layer of usable food as we ate the beef products, I went out and bought the odd pork and chicken items. Also a bag of breaded cod fillets I got on sale. I cooked large batches of spaghetti sauce and Irish stew and my signature black bean chili and laid their plastic-ware containers in strategic places among the frozen ranks. There wasn't much need for this level of fastidiousness. Liza seldom cooked, and when she did it was mostly vegetarian dishes that did not require a trip to the freezer. But under the circumstances, with still no decision in my head about what to do, I felt it best to keep a firm hand on things and a complete blanket of subterfuge over Mr Seeker.

One fine sunny day I was looking at the ID card once again. The idea came into my head to go to the reserve and look around. I researched transit routes. I could put my bike on a bus rack just a few blocks away and ride all the way to the university entrance, which was only a few minutes away by cycle from the edge of band territory. I packed a lunch and put a couple of IPAs in a cold-pack carrier, locked up the house and went to get my bike.

I had scarcely been to the campus since completing studies near thirty years before, so it was pleasantly nostalgic to wheel about gazing at the buildings I knew and the ones that were new. The thin population of students at this time of year were of a particularly languid mien. The sight of them sauntering along the pathways instilled an odd contentment.

Down toward the coastline the road tilted so that I hardly had to pedal along the parkway. I coasted along the urban residential streets to the entrance of the reserve, musing at the fact that even after forty years in the city I'd never ventured down here at any time for any reason. Then I had a moment of wondering why I was doing it now. With the arrival of a sea-scented breeze in my face, the moment passed.

I wheeled past row upon row of single family domiciles and came across open fields, a couple of West Coast Aboriginal sculpture installations and a community centre with a totem facade. The road wound close to the river, then pleasantly curved to what I now saw was a dead end by a jetty. There were several cars parked about that looked abandoned. Standing by a small float with a boat tied to it, three young fellows regarded me with neutral expressions as I rolled past.

At the end of the road I dismounted and stepped down the rocky shore to the water's edge. The river flowed wide at this point and the open water of the gulf was visible in the distance. On the opposite shore something in an industrial park clanged away at something industrial and on either side developments of houses were developing in both directions and up the slight hill to rim the sky. There was a soft lapping of water and an array of noisy birds circled overhead. I sighed and noted that despite the rhythmic mechanical emanations rattling across the river the setting was penetratively peaceful. I decided it was time for lunch.

There were several large cedar blocks lying around and it wasn't hard to fashion a stool and table to lay out a sandwich and pull the tab on a beer. The sun was high; I was glad I'd brought the fine white Panama I'd bought in Peru the year before. I don't particularly like hats but was always careful about solar radiation. A client in the last years of my social work career had been confined to an assisted living facility and I'd shared an elevator with an eighty-something little old lady, lovely for her age but lacking a nose. I eschewed zinc, and any and all SPF blocking chemical agents, considering them just as potentially nose-murdering as the sun. So a hat it was. I ate and lazed in the rising heat. I opened the second beer.

Gravel-crunch footsteps sounded behind. I looked up as a solid-looking man came to my side.

Hey there.

Hello.

Mind if I ast whatchyer doin?

Not at all. I'm having lunch.

Do ya have permission to be down here?

Permission? Isn't this a public place?

It's reserve ground. Natives only.

Oh. Well I guess I'm trespassing. I didn't realize the legalities of it...

Yeah. You gotta have permission.

Can I get permission from you?

Me? Nope. I don't think so. It's gotta be the Chief.

The Chief. You mean the actual head of the whole reserve?

Of the whole band. Not just this reserve.

Oh. Well. Is the Chief in residence here? Can I go up to him right now and ask?

It's a her. And I don't think she even lives here.

No?

Not for sure. Sometimes she does. Depends on the time of year.

Oh. Well. Then she must have representatives. Somewhere on site. That I could talk to.

Yeah maybe. I dunno.

Well look. Why don't you just give me permission to finish this sandwich and this drink and then I'll mosey. You can represent the Chief for just this one time, can't you? No harm done?

Yer not s'posed to be drinkin alcohol neither.

Oh? Is this a dry zone?

No alcohol on the reserve. That's the rule.

I'm not drinking alcohol. I'm drinking beer.

Heh heh... I used that excuse once. They fined me.

His cagey grin at this was nearly as radiant as the light beating down on the two of us there on the riverbank.

I used to get fined all the time. And put in jail too.

For drinking?

Yup. And everything else that goes with it.

Yes. I suppose there is that.

I had a problem there for awhile.

Glad you got on top of it. Or at least that's the way it looks.

Oh I get the urge once in a while. More'n that.

Well then I'm just as glad to say I don't have any more of this stuff to offer you... I poured the remainder of the can into the smooth rocks below us and crushed it in my hand. So neither of us will get in any trouble. At least not right now.

His laugh was a virtual handshake.

I'm just touring around. Lived in this huge city all my life and never been down here.

Huh. And I never been downtown even more than about three times.

You're not missing much.

I figger.

I mean... Sweeping a hand across the vista before us I felt like an ethereal tour guide. Look at this beauty.

He pulled a wood block beside and settled down. Sure is a sight to see, I guess.

I rummaged in my packsack. Well my sandwich is gone. And you saw what I did to my beer. But I have a couple of cookies here.

What kind?

Oatmeal chocolate chip. Homemade.

Chocolate chip. Not raisin?

Nope. Chocolate all the way. Heavy on the chocolate.

Well okay. I'll have one.

We sat munching for a moment.

Nice hat, by the way.

Thanks. It's made by the indigenous peoples of Ecuador, even though it's called a Panama.

Oh yeah?

Yup. Though I bought it in Lima, where hardly anybody wears them except tourists.

We make hats, too. Out of cedar bark.

I think I've seen them.

Mostly for ceremonies, eh.

Uh huh...

We finished our cookies.

Tell you the truth I kind of figured I might be asked about being here. I do feel kind of...different.

Oh it's not a big deal. Just kinda the formal situation we have. S'posed to see that native groups are the main users of the place, eh. Nobody's gonna complain about one white guy havin lunch and cleanin up after himself.

Oh I'll do that. For sure.

Good.

Yeah I just wanted to look around. Like I say, never been down here in all the years. Looks like you have a fine community centre over there.

The cultural pavilion. Yeah, pretty swank. Wish my house was that nice.

And there was what looked like an arena and a gym on the way in?

Yeah we got them things too.

No churches.

Nope. Don't need em.

Any graveyards?

Hah. Not likely around here. The city won't let us. But golf courses. We got em on both sides.

I noticed. Another kind of cemetery, I would warrant.

Ha ha, not sure what that means but I guess it's funny.

Oh. Never mind. It's a bad attitude I've had about golf for most of my life.

Ha ha.

So. No memorial plots to speak of?

We get to use the one they got on the reserve there up the inlet a ways. It's our traditional territory anyway.

Aha. I've always been fascinated with the different cultural attitudes toward passing away.

Yeah?

Not to be morbid I mean. But...

I heard it from my grampa once that it's not so much death as change, eh.

Change.

Yeah.

Like into something else?

Like into a bird spirit or some kind of other animal, yeah.

As we spoke neither of us could ignore a soaring eagle cleave downward and swoop across in a startlingly close wide-winged flypast.

Would that eagle be listening in on us? Would he have something to say?

All creatures have somethin' to say. Just try walking through a forest and not get a raven yakkin atcha.

I've actually had that experience.

Man they sure chatter.

So what else is there to know that's different about regional aboriginal post-death beliefs? Any distinct burial rituals?

Oh I dunno. Food. That's a weird one.

Food?

Somethin to feed the soul, I guess. I think that's what it is. And stuff they liked. Things they used a lot or that their relatives think is important for them to have.

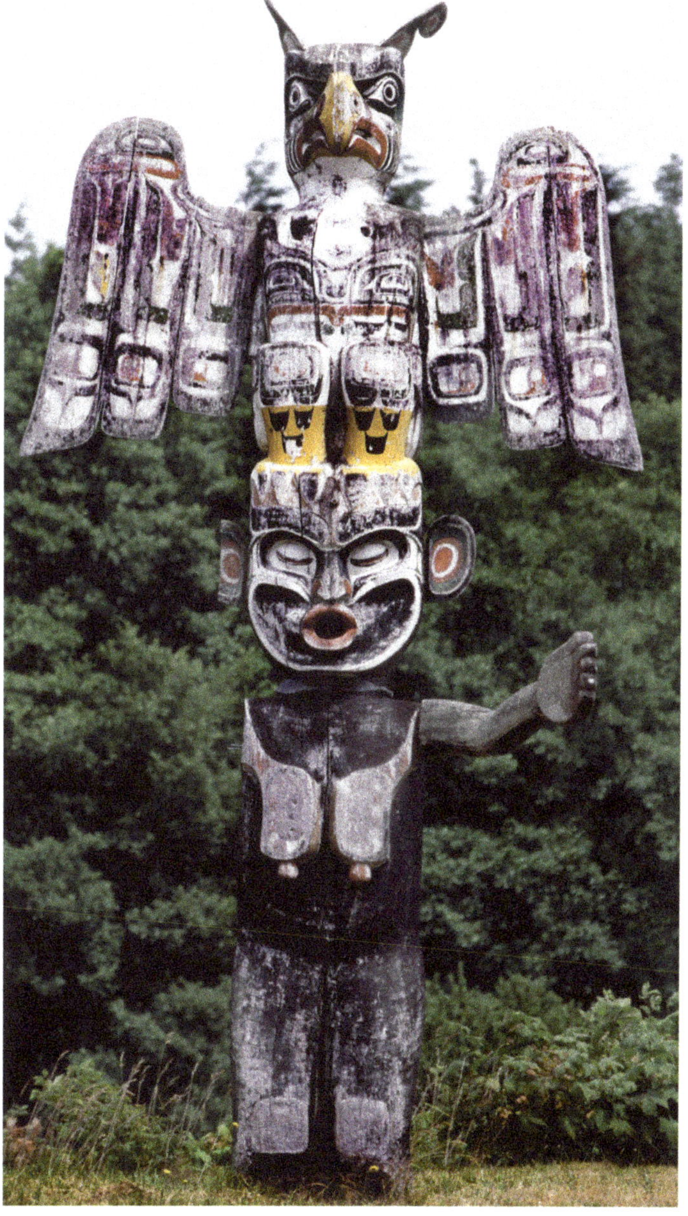

Huh. Interesting.

And clothes.

Clothes. As in what they liked to wear?

Like in whatever seems like what they'd be wearing in everyday life, y'know. Like a fisherman would have one of those big leather aprons for handling nets and tackles and hooks and sharp-finned cod and that. And a mother might have pictures of her kids and their baby clothes in a bag with her. They buried one of my aunties like that.

So burial. In the ground. Not cremation in a tree or on a pyre or anything like that? No setting off on a raft into the water? Maybe they used to do that. Not since the white man.

Ah yes. Contact.

Whatever you wanna call it.

I'm not up on the anthropology of it.

Me neither. But from what my dad told us the customs hardly changed from when they all walked over from Mongolia or wherever. That's what I heard. If you're an Indian from the middle of North America and west of there you're from Asia. If you live in the east from the Great Lakes to the Atlantic you're from north Europe races somehow. That's how it was explained to me.

From what I've read I think that's about right. The aboriginal culture from the top of Alaska all the way down to Tierra del Fuego have similar Asiatic genetic strains.

And they moved around a lot too, eh. My dad was never happy sitting in one place. Had to follow the fish.

The plains people had to follow the buffalo.

Yeah.

For as long as there were buffalo. But that was a good ten or twenty thousand years. Before the white man.

I guess you form a travel habit after that long.

In your blood.

And yer bones.

It's tough if you feel like moving but have no place to go.

That was the problem.

I guess.

Yeah.

We sat for a time speaking of generalities after that and then, so as not to wear out my semi-welcome, I gathered sandwich wrappings and beer cans and packed up to go.

So yeah. If you wanna come again you can get permission from the band office.

Okay. Where's that?

You don't have to go there. Just send em an email.

Okay. Can I text them?

Likely.

Great. I kicked the stand away from my bike and straddled a foot onto a pedal. My friend had not risen from his stoop on the upturned wood block. Good to talk to you.

Yeah right.

In late summer there was a piece on the TV news about missing persons. At the end they flashed a series of photos. Jon Seeker's was not one of them.

Several times I was tempted to contact the band—either by telephone, email or text—but resisted the urge due to the fact I could not think of a way to do it without somehow identifying myself. It was risky enough that I'd gone in person to the reserve and spoken directly to a band member. I'd been grateful that he had been willing to talk without exchanging names. It spared me the guilt of lying.

Nor did googling Mr. Seeker's name and vital statistics yield any further information. One insomnia-plagued night I thought of going down to the drug district and hanging around. Maybe get into a conversation with someone who might know him. That idea faded in the morning light of logic. There would be no better way of attracting law enforcement than for a straight-john pensioner to lurk around the skids asking after a mysteriously missing person. I had to be satisfied with what little I had to work with.

As time went further and summer became fall and fall turned to late autumn with Jon's body still downstairs, my sleep began to fail and the compensatory drinking drew Liza's attention. I would drink to get to sleep and then wake with a start at two AM or thereabouts. Toss and turn. Sit up reading. Rise and watch late-night TV. Drink some more.

There were nightmares. Nothing specific, nothing even relating to the situation. Just vague anxiety dreams of being late for flights, missing appointments, people mad at me. Several times I did not get out of bed in the morning. One time I day-slept until two-thirty. When Liza came home I was in a bathrobe, sipping beer. She flumped heavily into her chair and the sigh she gave told me things were not to be kept inside any longer.

You've let yourself go.

Couldn't sleep last night. Finally drifted off after you left.

That's only one factor.

How so?

It feels to me that you've given up. Everything. You used to care about the garden. It's overgrown. You shaved everyday. Now you look like a rummy. I've been worried about you. Not terribly worried exactly, but... Actually, I'm mystified. Since you left work. You don't want to travel or have fun. Don't you ever want to go back to Italy..? Or anywhere? For the past few months you haven't had any friends over to watch sports. You never speak to your brother or invite him over. The last person you had a social time with, I think, was Lino when he fixed the door. What's the matter with you?

I'm just...

The only thing I could think of talking about I had vowed never to talk about. Especially not to my loving wife.

Liza swung over to sit on edge close to me and rested her elbows on her knees. She looked at me closely. I avoided her eyes.

What's going on with you my love?

Nothing. I'm just...

The only thing you seem to care about is keeping the freezer jam-packed. What's up with that?

Well. You'll have to admit. I do keep the meals showing up on the table.

That's about the only thing you do these days.

I hope you think it's important.

Of course it is and I'm glad you do it because I don't especially like to. But there's something bigger going on here. Why all the drinking?

What do you mean all? I have my beers. And a whiskey at night.

You've been killing a bottle of wine every supper. You sip whiskey in front of the TV all night every night. God only knows the amount of beer you drink during the day.

Okay I'm boozing more than usual. But I'm not an alc.

I know. That's why I'm curious. What's going on?

I don't know.

You don't need reminding. Drinking runs in your family. I don't want to preach...

No need.

Are you trying to turn into an alcoholic? Would that give you a legitimate reason to lay about all day? Descend into depression? Ignore the important things in life?

She was completely right, of course. I was leaving everything. After a few more weeks, and her laying off—I guess in the hope that I would heal myself somehow—it got so bad I found her crying in bed one night. I just stood there. Her soft weeping tore my heart. We had not touched each other physically, I realized, for more than a month. Taking her in my arms right then might have helped, I knew. But for some reason I was petrified. The audible depth of her sadness...the grating toll of her loneliness. It damn near killed me inside because it was so familiar. Here she was miserable and her husband stood off in the same room unable to console. Or unwilling, I could not answer that question to myself, shuddering as I was in my own isolation.

I sat on the bed. Maybe we need counselling.

She looked up. Would you be willing?

Anything you want, sweetie. Anything you think might help us.

It would help if you could just say what's the matter. She wiped her eyes with a tissue and blew her nose. I mean, you just turned from a content, vibrant and loving man into a closed-down, distant and detached walnut in the space of a few months. Why can't you say what's wrong?

I'm not sure myself, Liza. I really can't say...

Inside I felt as if my blood had turned acidic...lying to her was the worst thing I'd ever done. The truth was, though I knew that the situation with Mr. Seeker was at the root of my unease, I could not say for sure what it was that was bugging me. I'd kept secrets before, though nothing on this scale. My career life had involved secrecy, tact, subterfuge, deception, underhandedness and sometimes outright dishonesty. But I was away from all that now and prior to the incident had felt a moral freedom in my life I hadn't had for more than twenty years.

Liza crept into my arms. We've got to do something.

It's not you, sweetie. I've got to do something.

Her body felt strange and almost instantly I was repulsed by death imagery; the dread of ever holding my lifeless wife brought bile to my mouth. It was all I could do not to retch.

On another day Liza came home and laid a hand on my shoulder as I watched TV.

You didn't answer the phone.

You know me.

They reached me at work. It's your cousin Martin.

Oh. He's sick. I think I saw an email a while back

It would be nice if you'd go talk to him.

I guess I know that.

He's dying.

I know but...

But what?

We haven't spoken more than three times in twenty years.

All the more reason.

In seven sessions we covered all that was good about our marriage and there was a lot to say. But I could not give when it came around to both of them asking me what the heck was the matter. Toward the end, just before therapist threw up his hands and refused to work with us anymore, Liza began to weep in the middle of our session. The guy asked me how that made me feel. I could have punched him.

How do you think it makes me feel?

There are variable answers to that question. But whatever it is we need it from you.

Any man would feel bad making his wife cry.

You are not any man. Not to Liza.

Of course not.

So what about it? Do you feel responsible?

Of course.

The silence went on too long.

Well then. Do you have a sense of what is bothering you?

Well no. That's been the problem all along. I seem to have run out of...

You seem to have run out of what?

Of... I don't know. Psychic energy?

Psychic energy. Hmm. There are theories around that.

Theories.

Yes. There's a school of thought which postulates that such things as mental acuity, emotional affect and personality are connected with the libido.

Cathexis.

Yes. All so-called psychic energy springs from it. And what we have here, for whatever reason is...

Anticathexis.

If you like. Though jargon alone never helped anyone. We still need to know from you the source of your preoccupation.

Yeah well...

Until we receive this from you there is no further progressing.

You don't have to tell me that.

Liza wept softly through this exchange, listening.

As part of trying to attenuate the disintegration of my character—otherwise known as the person my wife fell in love with—I decided to do as she asked and visit my cousin Martin. It wasn't just that there was a ferry ride involved—with the parking, waiting, walking with bag, catching bus, et cetera—but that he and I had never been close. As kids we were thrown together because of our similarity in age. But I'd always thought he was a bit of a goof and I suspected he thought I was somewhat of a snob.

In any case, there I was travelling. The hospital is reputed to be one of the worst in the province except if you are a cancer patient. I found him in a private room with a great view of the harbour and he seemed happy to see me.

Hey, you made it!

Darn right. How are ya?

Dying. How are you?

The same but just not as obvious.

Ha ha.

Ha ha.

I'm sure glad to see you.

Such as I am? Thanks.

How is it that we're both so far into our sixties and we

haven't been around each other since our forties?

I'm confounded at the thought.

Confound. Funny word. Confound everything.

Confound time. Time unto death.

Yeah... Say, I was sorry to hear about Auntie Marg.

That was a year ago. More. We're over it. At least we had her around for eighty-nine years. I felt sorry when Aunt Ann passed away.

Yeah. She was our mom for seventy-five years, only.

Yeah.

They were close. Loving sisters.

Coming from dirt poverty on a Depression dirt farm will do that for ya. Surviving cold and hunger together is a bonding experience I imagine.

I guess, eh.

Certainly not something our generation has had to contend with.

Contend. Yeah no.

Sorry if I'm using haughty words on ya.

Haughty. Ha. You always were quite the egghead.

Lots of people would disagree with that. The intellectual part of eggheadedness, that is.

Sometimes I couldn't figure out what you were talking about.

I sure hope that's passed. Anything I say that's obscure, you just stop me right there.

Obscure. I know what that means but it's a word I would just never use.

Heh. Yeah. Mind my mouth.

Anyway. How you doing for real?

Aw, okay I guess. Been feeling out of sorts but... nothing like what you must be going through.

Well one thing about being a terminal case, they give you fine drugs.

Are you on stuff right now?

Some. Just enough to make me happy.

Seems weird.

Yeah I know. Don't worry about it. I'm fine.

Damn.

Yeah. Damn...

Later on we wandered into the subject of our childhoods. Martin's expression shone and he touched my arm. Remember that time we went to Victoria?

Sure. The bus ride mostly. You wouldn't stay on your side of the seat.

You kept kicking me.

Well you just kept on doing the manspread... or I guess then it was the boyspread. There was no room for my knees.

And we made so much noise the bus-driver told us to quiet down.

We darn near got kicked off the bus in Mill Bay. It would have been quite a walk.

Yeah...

I still find that obnoxious to the max. People taking too much room on public transit.

Boy. It doesn't take too much to tick you off, cousin.

Naw. I'm a cranky old man these days.

Oh? I don't see it so much cranky as sad. What's bugging you?

His question nearly brought a laugh out of my darkening guts. Hah. You wouldn't believe the number of people asking me that all the time.

No kidding.

There was silence, something I was beginning to become quite used to.

Well? What is it?

Something bad.

You can tell me. I won't be blabbing it anywhere. Unless you believe in something beyond. I might tell it there.

Do you believe in something beyond?

Don't know. If I get a chance to fill you in on it I will.

That's quite a promise.

It's mine to you if you'll give me yours.

Mine?

Yours. Right now.

Before the deadening quiet could descend once more, words came out of me: I'm keeping a dead man in my basement.

Is this another one of your theory things..?

No no. It's not a metaphor or a figurative figure of speech or anything like that. I surprised a guy B and E-ing our house and he died trying to get away. Just collapsed and fell over on the front patio.

Yikes.

I'll say. I didn't know what to do at the time and still don't. Couldn't figure out how to explain what some shrunken druggy guy was doing all beat up and dead—he'd fallen down the stairs—at my feet. The feet of a white guy.

Why is that important? You being a white guy.

Well you might not be so aware of it, us being family and having looked past our ethnic differences so long ago in childhood, but I am a total white man. Unlike yourself, being half Cree and half the east European strain of quintessential Caucasian that I am... It is Cree, isn't it?

Yup.

Thought so but wasn't sure... Anyway, this young lad was from the local reserve. I don't know what tribe.

Oh. Well. What did the police say?

Didn't call the police...

You...

...Stuffed him into a freezer.

Wait, what!

It might sound funny, but... I'm not kidding. I've got some Indian kid in my downstairs freezer...

Whoa!

... And I don't know what to do about it.

Man. That's quite the deal. Can't hardly believe.

Sometimes I can't either.

You gotta do something.

Darn right I gotta do something.

Damn.

Sorry to burden you with this. I know you've got your own life questions to handle.

No no... this kind of stuff gets my mind off it. Martin shook his head and bugged his eyes at me. Weird! He put fingers to his temples. Let me think a minute.

Don't worry about it. It's my problem.

No no. I might have a suggestion.

If you do I'll listen. I haven't told anybody about this. Especially not Liza. But I'd sure like some help.

You know all of us in the family got a bit of Dad's section, don't you?

Section?

That big chunk of scrub land he had up there. North Saskatchewan.

I didn't realize. You own some of it?

Yeah. My sister can get you a map somewhere. We all got a piece when he passed away. I never been there. But Charlotte has. She's close with some of our relatives around there. They consider it kind of sacred ground for one reason or another.

Hmmm. Interesting. Stuff I did not know.

This guy you're keeping has to be put in the ground in some respectful way, no?

I guess.

What do you mean you guess? Are you going to keep him in a freezer the rest of your life?

No. But I'm absolutely bland as to how to fix it.

There's no fix to this, but listen...

Hours later, after I'd gone out and got us pulled-pork sandwiches and we'd drank the craft beer I smuggled in, we shook hands.

You can do what I said. Or not. Up to you.

I don't know. Can't thank you enough. I'll have to think on it. See you again sometime.

I doubt it.

Yeah...

On the ferry the thought of an action plan calmed me for a time but with a stale heart I knew it wouldn't see me all the way through.

Returning late I parked the car out back and noticed right away there were no lights on in the house. There was a note on the kitchen table. I did not read all of it, but forced myself to watch some late-night television. I drank several whiskeys and went to bed.

Next morning I read the rest of the note and saw by daylight that she'd taken only what was important to her.

Shortly after that visit from the two detectives a feeling of intense non-safety all but overwhelmed my waking hours. I found I couldn't shake it except inside profound drunkenness. Then Liza phoned and told me where she was and the drinking got worse. I was drinking pretty much all the time anyway save for when I had to go out and get supplies. I now rode bicycle in all weather due to permanent drunkenness. Weeks passed.

It got to be quite a struggle to keep sozzled but, truth be told, I quite liked the inebriated life. Every day early on I would immerse into the great velvet pool of numbed blindness. I knew there would be an end to it eventually. My health suffered. Early spring sprung amid alternating revelatory illusion and coughing deterioration.

One day I got word that Martin had died in the night. I did not shed tears but was thankful to learn that they'd let him go home for the final weeks and die in the arms of loving family. In fact I was initially grateful at the news, not least because he'd been visiting me in dreams and sometimes in drunken delusions. He mostly posed the question I was afraid to confront on my own: What if Jon Seeker hadn't actually been dead when you stuck him into frozen suspension? What if you called 911 and he was still alive today? What if? What if... I closed my eyes hard. Martin was still there. He did not remonstrate, though. Not his style. He gave me a smile. I understood in that instant, a moment that occurred while I happened to be prone in the hallway, that I truly loved him and sorely rued his passing.

And upon that great revelation I realized that the news provided a clear demarkation that I hadn't known I'd been waiting for. A new day and a firm resolve. I wanted to smarten up, for the next little while at least. Most of all I wanted to do something for Martin. I put down the whisky bottle and opened a beer. In front of a baseball game I slowly drank it and told myself this was the last for a while.

The first few days were rougher than I thought they'd be.

It wasn't just the habit. I broke that in a day or two.

It was the withdrawal. I hadn't realized alcohol can do that to you. Your body gets used to a certain amount of booze and when you stop it all of an instant there are consequences. I started having delusions, thinking the furniture was plotting against me. Then I forgot what time it was, what day it was, even who the heck I was. I guess I stopped eating. Or drinking water.

It's a good thing I'd kept up our housekeeping service. Filma, our treasured Filipino cleaning lady, opened the front door one day and found me collapsed on the living room floor. I woke in the hospital.

At first I didn't realize that my eyes were open. I thought I was dreaming some kind of institutionalization conflict where I'd said or done something wrong and was being yelled at by a succession of officious women. Then I understood that the blue-clad female leaning in at me was hollering my name and it was for real. I said hello.

Well. You're with us after all. Can you say your name?

I tried but couldn't.

She carefully tipped a vessel to my face, pouring a welcome dash of water into my mouth.

Thanks... That's better.

Do you know why you're here?

I guess I got sick or something. Is this a hospital?

Detox ward.

Oh.

You were drinking, were you?

I suppose.

You suppose?

I was drinking.

How much?

Uhh... You mean overall? Per month?

Per day. How much and what kind of alcohol were you drinking per day?

Well, nothing for the past week or so...

You've been here two days. How long before that had you stopped drinking?

Three or four, I think.

And did you have assistance? Did you get a doctor to supervise?

What? To quit drinking?

Yes, to quit drinking. Otherwise the results are plain to see. So again I ask, what and how much were you drinking?

Rye. Cheap stuff. About a forty-pounder per day.

Aha. No wonder you nearly left us.

It was at about that point I realized there were tubes and needles going in and coming out of me in various locations.

And for how long had you been drinking?

Well I've been drinking since I was a teen.

How long have you been trying to kill yourself?

I wasn't trying to kill myself.

Forty ounces of whiskey a day is trying to kill yourself.

I only did that for a few weeks. Maybe a month or two. Three months at the max. I built up to it.

When your cleaning lady found you you were about six hours from death by organ failure. How do you feel now?

Actually. Not half bad.

You're a living testament to the miracle of modern medicine. That and the efficacy of a saline drip. You've been going through litres of the stuff.

I've been here two days..?

That's right.

How long 'til I can leave?

Not for me to say. A doctor will be along sometime soon.

After a week of shivering and bed-confined paranoia I truly understood that it would have been better to seek medical attention to properly conduct the quitting instead of risking mental illness or death by this willful self-infliction of earned misery. But little did I know that after the initial recovery came a program. I disliked the guilt-imposed treatment intensely, particularly the built-in passive-aggressive coercion: It's not compulsory, but you'll die if you don't do this... Etcetera. Needless to elaborate, I was not the best patient.

After ten days they invited me to leave. Their dubious looks as I packed up and left meant nothing amid my jaundiced opinion of everything therapeutic. Out on the street I felt much better. The breeze on my face was near as transporting as a shot of good whisky, though the idea of blank intoxication held no attraction for the moment. Though I was elated to be a free man again, my mind insisted on an immediate return to the problem of Jon Seeker, so I was ultra-relieved to find the house in good order with nothing disturbed.

I got busy on phase one of the plan; shopped for good food, made myself eat well and drink plenty of water. In a scan of on-line market places I found a used minivan, rode my bike over and bought it on a credit card. Late into several nights I researched maps of the prairies. I cooked the remaining meat in Jon Seeker's freezer until it got down to just a small packet of steaks remaining. I bought a dozen or so big freezer packs and laid them carefully down over the plastic sheet. On a particular night I pulled the van around to the back. From the garden shed I retrieved the heavy-duty department store dolly I'd scored at a garage sale a few days before. The next day I slept late, worked out at the gym, came home for supper and a long nap, then waited for absolute darkness.

Loading him into the back of the van was about the ordeal I expected it to be. The freezer itself weighed a good sixty or seventy kilos. Its occupant about that again. In the weight-and-measure parlance of the past, a total of three hundred pounds or so. Between the serviceability of the dolly, my careful deliberations about the best purchase I could get with it wheeling up the two stairs and across the back patio, and then the slant into the rear hatch which, upright, the unit just cleared either side and top. Finished, I eased the door closed and looked around. No one in sight, few lights on. I went back into the house, grabbed my go-bag and locked all the windows and doors.

On the road at one-thirty AM I felt a weird exhilaration I could not decide was because of my finally doing something about Jon Seeker, or that the freedom of a near-deserted freeway stretching to the unseen horizon with a steering wheel in hand and no particular schedule to keep held such an innate thrill. It was nearly five in the morning, with the sun lightening the mountain-ridged eastern skyline, before I got sleepy and pulled off at a rest stop.

Then it was on the road again. I made good time to Tete Jaune and checked into a motel that featured separate cabins with outside electrical outlets. I rented a unit near the rear and backed the van up close to it. With an extension cord I got the freezer going again.

Next morning good and fresh after a monster fry-up breakfast at a truck stop I took off east down the Yellowhead driving hard but not too fast. Mid-afternoon I had to take a nap by a cattle pull-out but otherwise it was much of Alberta under me and Jon when I could drive no more. That night we spent in a place called Beaver Crossing and I could tell now that the plan was a good one because people started looking familiar.

It wasn't only about my own extended family, whom, though I had not met them all, I had known were a variety of mixed aboriginal. But Jon Seeker's lineage, too. Despite my having not gazed upon his face since I'd committed him to frozen obscurity nearly a year ago, his ID resided now in my breast pocket and I examined his face frequently. Here all around were garage workers, road men, farm hands and general rounders who often took a passing resemblance to him. Even the women held a resonance of his skin tone, facial nobility, raven hair.

I don't know why I felt so good the next morning, starting out, because I knew this would be the longest and hardest day of our journey. The roads were in good condition for early spring, thankfully, and the only hairy stretch was a ten-klick line of gumbo aside a low lake that still had ice in it. Several times I nearly slid off the track but managed to wheel-whip and heel-toe brake-gas my fishtailing way out.

In a tiny town in the middle of low, non-arable land vastly extending into an all-direction infinity I spied out of the corner of my consciousness a thing I had thought about but forgotten. A thrift store. Inside, I was the only customer and drew curiosity when all I bought was a collection of cheap costume jewellery with a cloth bag to hold it all.

On a paved piece of Saskatchewan Route 26 I pulled off to look at the GPS and some print-outs I'd made of the region. Then a few more klicks down the road and a turn onto graded gravel within sight of the north shore of Makwa Lake. I drove for the expected hour or so through up-and-down scrub and bush land, noting the helpfully placed mileposts. Though expecting to have trouble finding it, by not-too-late in the afternoon on a spur line off the main road I located what I was fairly sure was Martin's property.

There was a barely visible trail that I rolled down slowly, then got out and walked a good five hundred metres into the bush. Noting where to drive and where to avoid marshy low spots, I got back in and blazed the van as far as I could into as obscure a piece of Canadian landscape as has ever been imagined. We ended up on a slight rise that looked over a pond. I walked the water's edge and was satisfied that it was at a yearly height and would not likely ever reach up to the spot I was thinking of.

Then I got out the tools; mattock, shovel, root clippers, hand auger, power saw.

Though I'd anticipated a heavily wooded encounter it

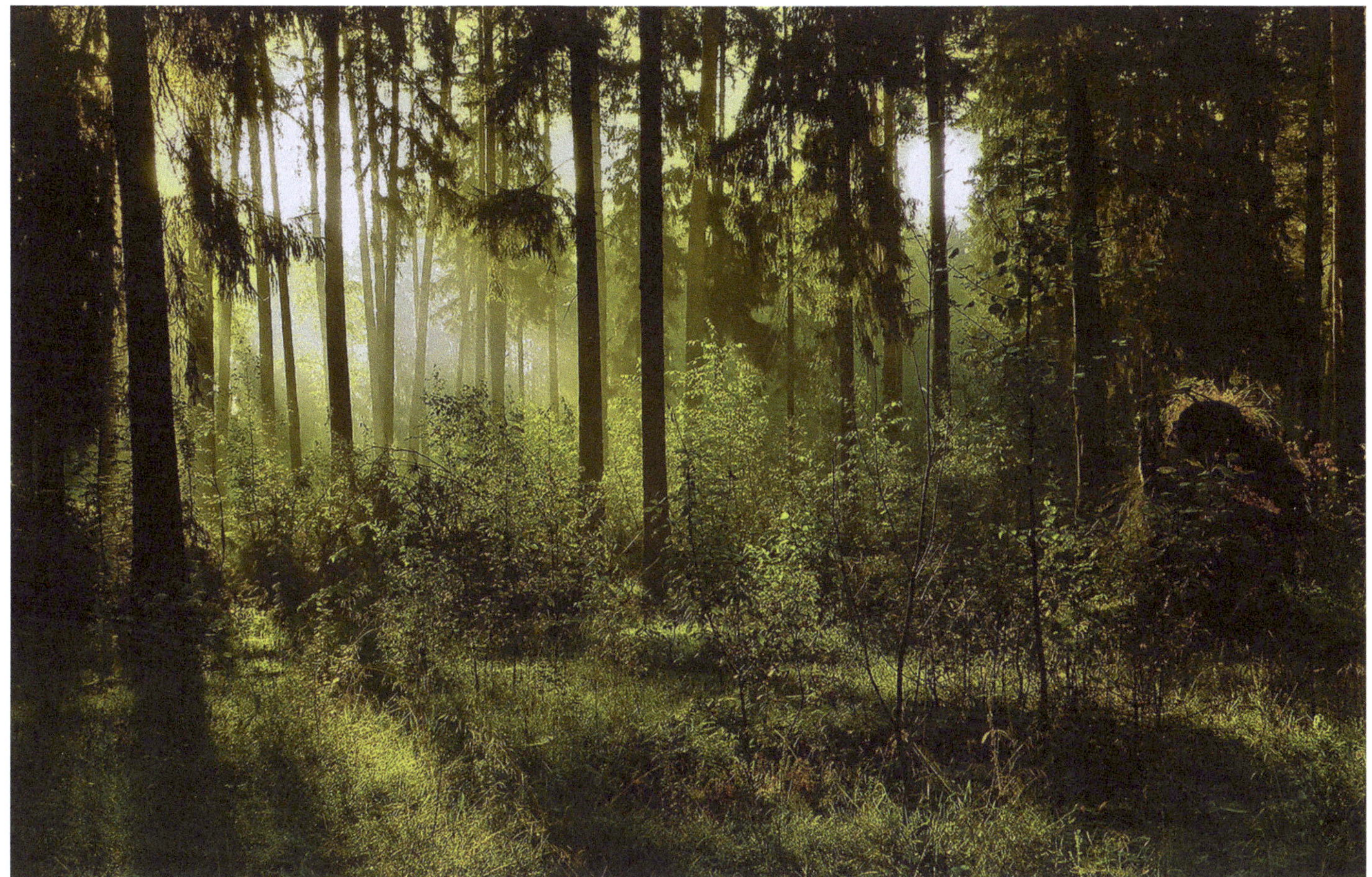

became obvious right away that to clear this area it would be mainly a shovel and pick job. I worked for an hour or so and then knew by the tractability of the soil beneath that I'd found the right spot. Pausing to drink water I was tempted to sit awhile and perhaps nap but then became anxious to break further ground and see the job through as quickly as possible.

Though the weather was cool and damp to the point of threatening rain—thick clouds shrouded the scene for as far around as I could see—I was sweaty from the outset. I worked for hours in shirtsleeves and finally had to tear up an old sweater to fashion tie-around bands for my streaming forehead. The work seemed to invigorate despite the heaviness of it and I understood that a few days sitting behind the wheel had near atrophied my exercise-starved body. Before I realized that I should have stretched and loosened up I was well into the excavation, happily pick-axing and tossing spade-loads of dirt onto a growing mound. I didn't care. Aches and pains were to me now welcome indications of viable life. I suppose emerging from the drunken death spiral I'd been on was an additional boost to morale. I don't know for sure. I've been drinking since and still feel fine.

Anyway, what with the depth I was trying to achieve—two metres—and the fact I had to shape a ramp down into the hole in order to dolly in the casket, a.k.a. freezer, the afternoon turned to flash-lit night and the night into a peeking line of amber on the low flat horizon. I finally paused and stretched out on the van's lowered passenger seat to nap. Waking in full afternoon, I wolfed a couple of energy bars and as much water as I could and set back to work. The ramp was almost complete but judging from the height of the freezer there would only be slightly more than a metre of dirt above. I spent a good hour picking at the bedrock I'd hit to understand that short of renting a jackhammer I was not going to penetrate any further.

I sighed. Then chuckled at the silliness of such a gesture in such an austere landscape. Other than my cousins and uncle, decades ago, I doubted any human crossed this locale from one century to the next. I strode up out of the grave and tossed the mattock aside. The couple of pieces of plywood stuffed alongside the freezer came out with little trouble and they fashioned a serviceable pathway from the hatchback to the ramp downward. The dolly did its work. Without hurting myself or losing the freezer off to either side I managed to wheel it down and into the tight slot I had carved into the cold cold ground.

I pulled the dolly out and loaded it into the van along with the other tools except for the shovel. I pulled muddy clothing off and sponge-bathed as much body dirt away as I could. Then I changed into presentable duds, even put on my usual Harris tweed and the only pair of non-scuffed oxfords I owned. Down in the hole there was just enough play either side to open the freezer door and peer inside with my cell phone flashlight. I removed the now-unfrozen freezer packs and pulled the plastic shroud from Jon's body. He lay as he had when first placed, his head upon a resting arm. Though still largely frozen, his face with closed eyes gave an indication more of contented sleep than pre-mature death.

I spoke the only words that would come:

> I'm awful sorry there, kid. I guess you were who you were and you did what you had to do. Right or wrong. I have to be who I am, too, and I have to do what I have to do. Right or wrong. So here we are.

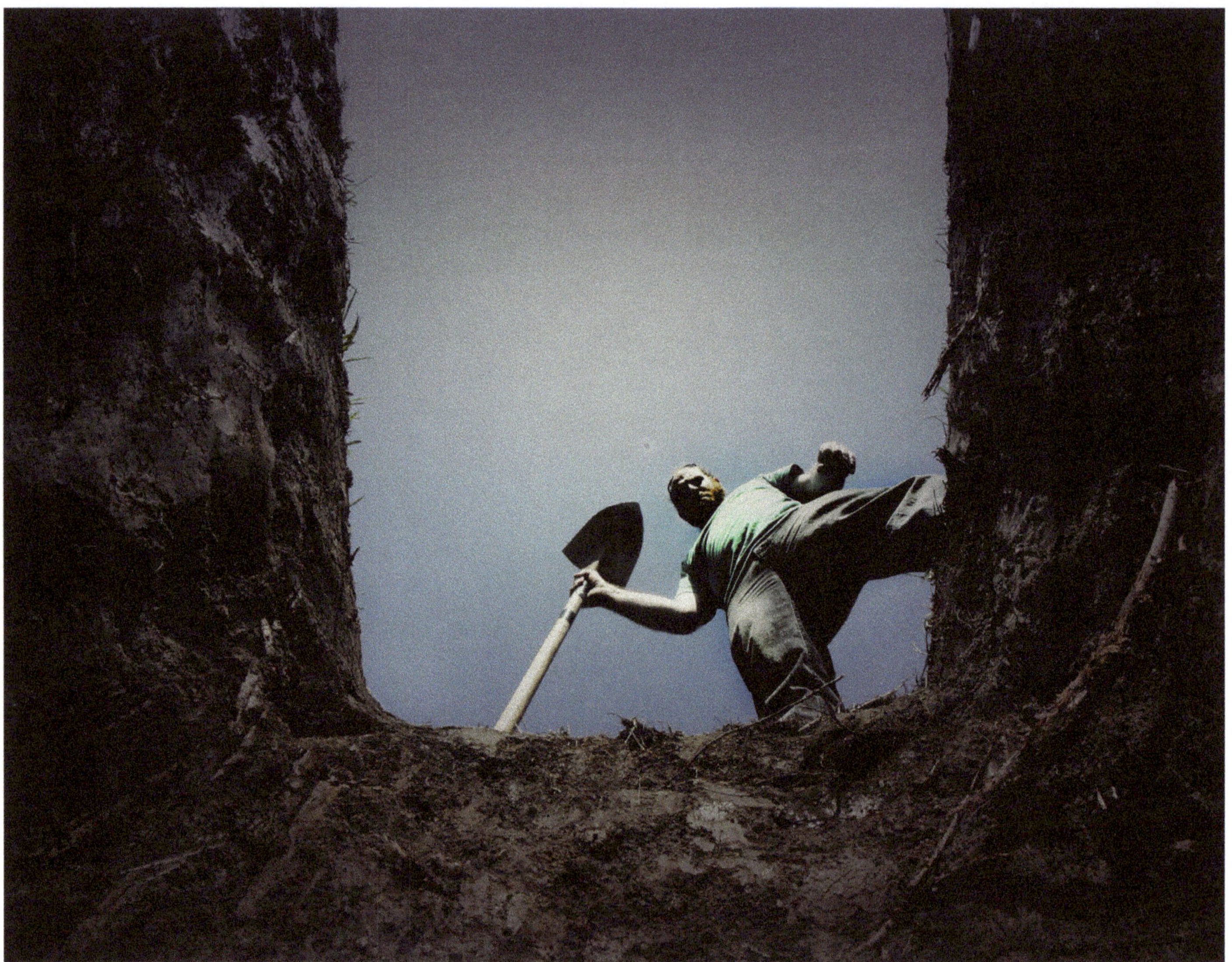

I took a last look. The pack of thawing steaks was there by him, to feed his way to the afterlife. I dropped the bag of fake jewelry down inside. As soon as I heard the bag thunk down upon Jon Seeker I felt as strange a relief as I'd ever experienced. As if a warm hand fell perfectly upon my shoulder and a move toward tears came on irresistibly. In fact, I stood for five minutes bawling my eyes out.

Then I closed the lid.

I changed out of my good clothes to do the much easier but no less grimy job of covering the freezer and filling in the considerable hole I'd made. Three hours later it was almost finished. I tamped the upper surface smooth and tight with the back of the shovel, then found a sharp piece of birch to stick as a marker as deep down into the upturned soil as possible. With a jack-knife I carved Jon's first name into it and the date of interment. For good measure I blued the indentations with a leaky ballpoint pen.

I tossed the shovel into the back and slumped into the driver's seat. Before pulling away there was one last thing. Holding the GPS out the window I carefully marked, checked the calibration, marked again and recorded the exact co-ordinates of the place where Jon Seeker and I would finally part company. As I drove out of the lot and onto the spur the sky flung down as hard a rain as I could remember. It nearly stopped me driving, but not quite.

A day-and-a-half later I was motoring through mountains in the Fraser Canyon and stopped for an early dinner at a roadside cafe. The sun was edged behind one of the numerous granite monoliths hemming the place and a sullen shadow damped the mood of an otherwise sunny late afternoon.

There was a healthy complement of truckers and RV denizens filling the leatherette banquettes so the only seating was at the counter. I perched beside a classy-dressed blonde woman about twenty years younger than me. Or so I estimated. I gave her a glance as I straddled the stool. Man this place is busy.

She looked at me slow and then spoke barely above a whisper: A function of being isolated.

As this statement was, to me, obviously calculated to invoke deep contemplation I did her the courtesy of doing just that, and found no further reason to attempt conversation. Neither did she.

I ordered the dinner special, an old-fashioned hot-turkey sandwich; just a piece of white bread with a slab of breast meat, some industrial gravy and an ice-cream scoop of tasteless mashed potato. Then extra cups of coffee. The last one was near half-done when my neighbour raised her voice.

I can't do it.

The counter waitress stood staring her down. Well you better. You don't pay it's me that's got to make it good.

I'm just a little short.

How short?

Five dollars.

That's half the bill. You knew darn well you couldn't pay. Do I have to call the cops?

Over five dollars?

Theft is theft if it's five dollars or five hundred.

The blonde woman was turning an odd colour and now stopped talking to go what looked to me as a dangerous shade of pale.

Hey. I stood up to emphasize my entry into the conversation. No worries. What's the total?

The waitress and the blonde wordlessly turned their attention to me. I'm sure there's no reason for anybody to get upset. I pulled a fifty from my wallet and handed it to the waitress. Take both our checks out of this and give yourself a ten dollar tip.

The situation thus defused and with the waitress's back to us at the cash register I sat down and took a drink of coffee.

Thanks.

Don't mention it.

I wouldn't but it's awfully nice of you.

It's barely nice. Decent is what it might be.

Okay decent.

You're welcome.

You do this with everybody you meet in diners?

No. This is the first time.

Um. You don't want something extra for it do you?

The waitress laid change on the counter between us and gave me a smile.

I turned to the blonde. Extra?

You know.

No I don't know. And suffice to say, given what this incident is in the overall tempest of the world, I scantly care.

Oh. Well. That's kinda cold.

No colder than seeing the world as an isolated chamber of alienation and loneliness. Your sentiments, not mine.

Oh. Yeah. I was feeling pretty out there there.

Out there there, huh? Yeah. Come to think of it. Good way to put it. I think we're kind of on the same line right about now.

Not sure what that means, but okay.

Heh heh... I drained my coffee and gathered the change. I usually have a long narrative for times like these. A big story that somehow or other compares and contrasts what is and has been just in front of us.

I handed the money to her.

But tonight I think I'm finished trying to explain myself.

She took the cash timidly, holding it suspended for a time as if proffering it back. Is this some kind of pay-it-forward thing with you?

Pay it forward? I laughed. More like pay and pay and pay and repeat.

Her name was Ella. I gave her a lift to Abbotsford and dropped her at a women's shelter. Her story was a common one and something I wouldn't retell even if I could remember it.

I made it home just before midnight.

There's nothing more boring than someone who always wants to be outside. I mean close to nature. Hiking and camping and sitting around a fire at night drinking eggshell coffee and spitting into the flames while muttering about the futility of it all. So I didn't arrive at the decision to get the place on Mount Elphinstone easily. I disliked the idea, actually. But certain things had taken place, as you now know.

What I did might not be so bad. Or it might be bad. Not for me to say. The reason I'm here, the reason I did what I did; all these questions I can't completely answer. All I know is that I don't feel like I belong. It's just that simple. It started much before the advent of Jon Seeker and it was in the loss of Liza that my true end occurred and remains today the total zero I represent to myself and the world. Would we have made it anyway, even without a dead body mouldering below us and fouling my otherwise placid mind? I'm trying hard to figure things out, but nothing is coming. It's been near a year up here on the side of Mount Elphinstone. She hasn't come back. She's never coming back and I suppose... neither am I.

Whatever happens from now on is my responsibility. How much of this would have occurred had Mr Seeker and I not met? Who knows? There was a cop up here a while back hassling about impaired driving. Maybe he'll come around again to see if I'm still alive and inadvertently solve the disappearance of Mr. Jon Stanley Seeker. I've left his status card and the GPS coordinates of the gravesite on a kitchen counter if anybody wants to verify what I've told you here.

I'm going to take a walk now. Out there. I might not be back. If anybody wants me, I'll be somewhere.

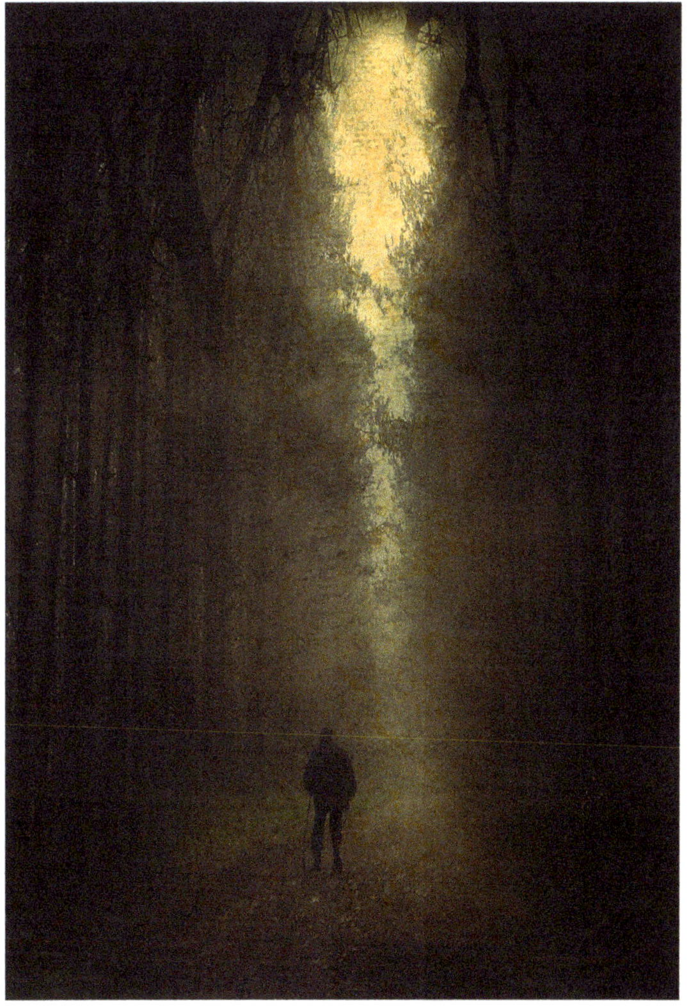

TRUMPISM
A MANIFESTO

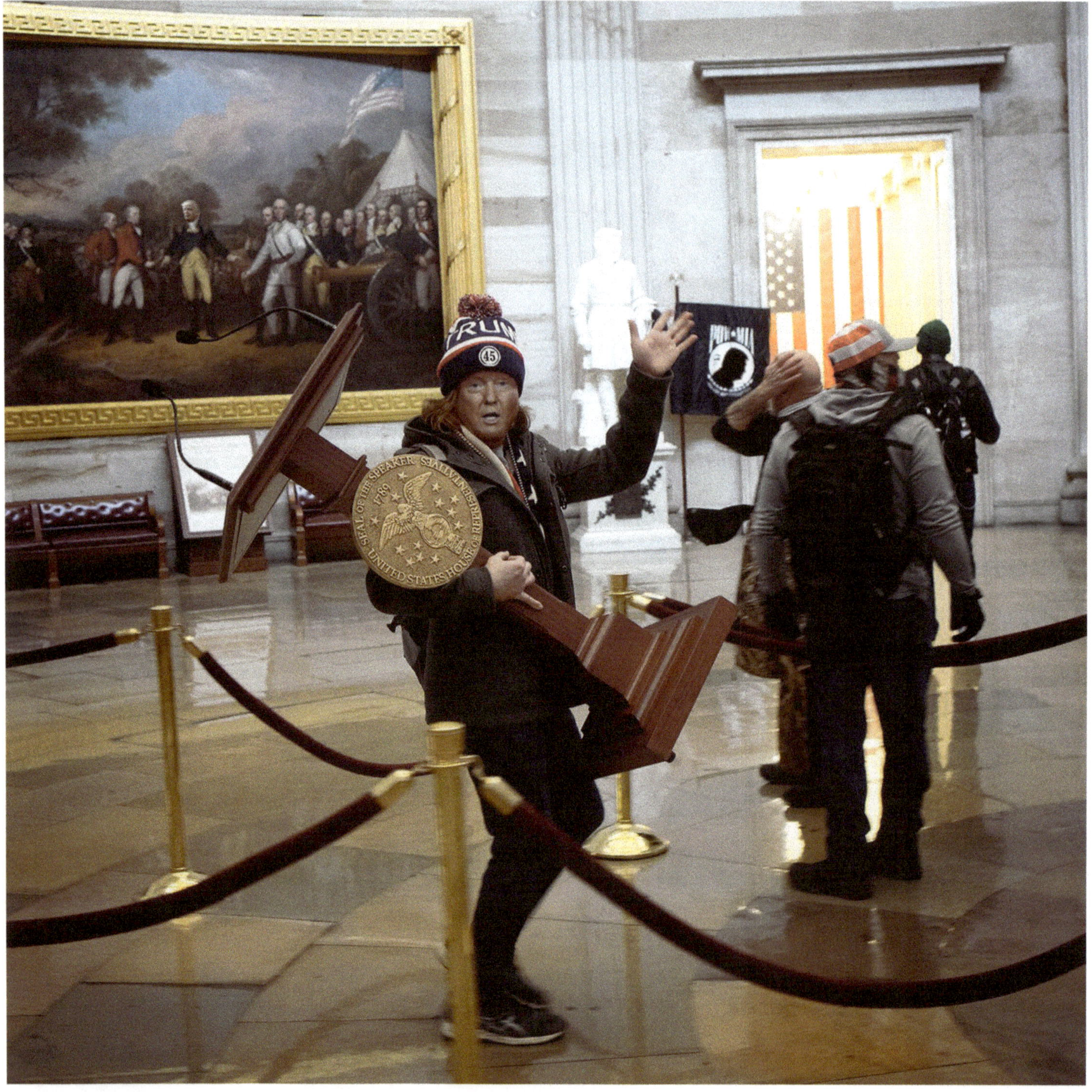

ART AND DIGITAL MONTAGE: DAVID MANLEY

ACTUALLY AS YOU KNOW THEY LOST THE WHITE HOUSE.

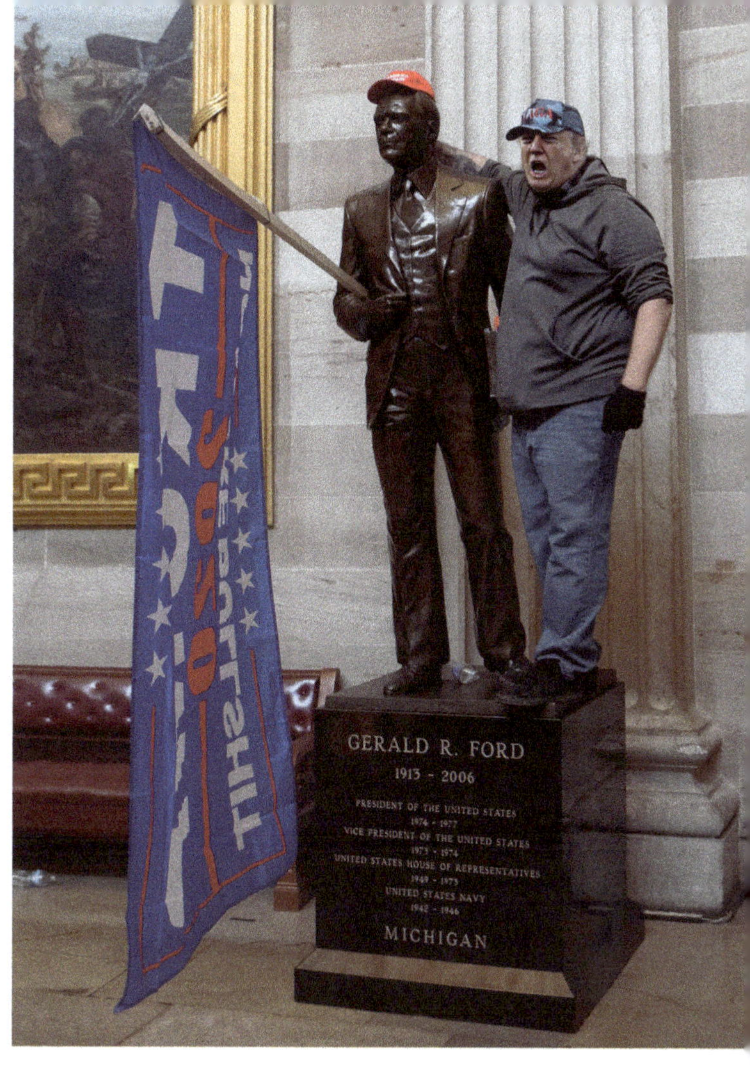

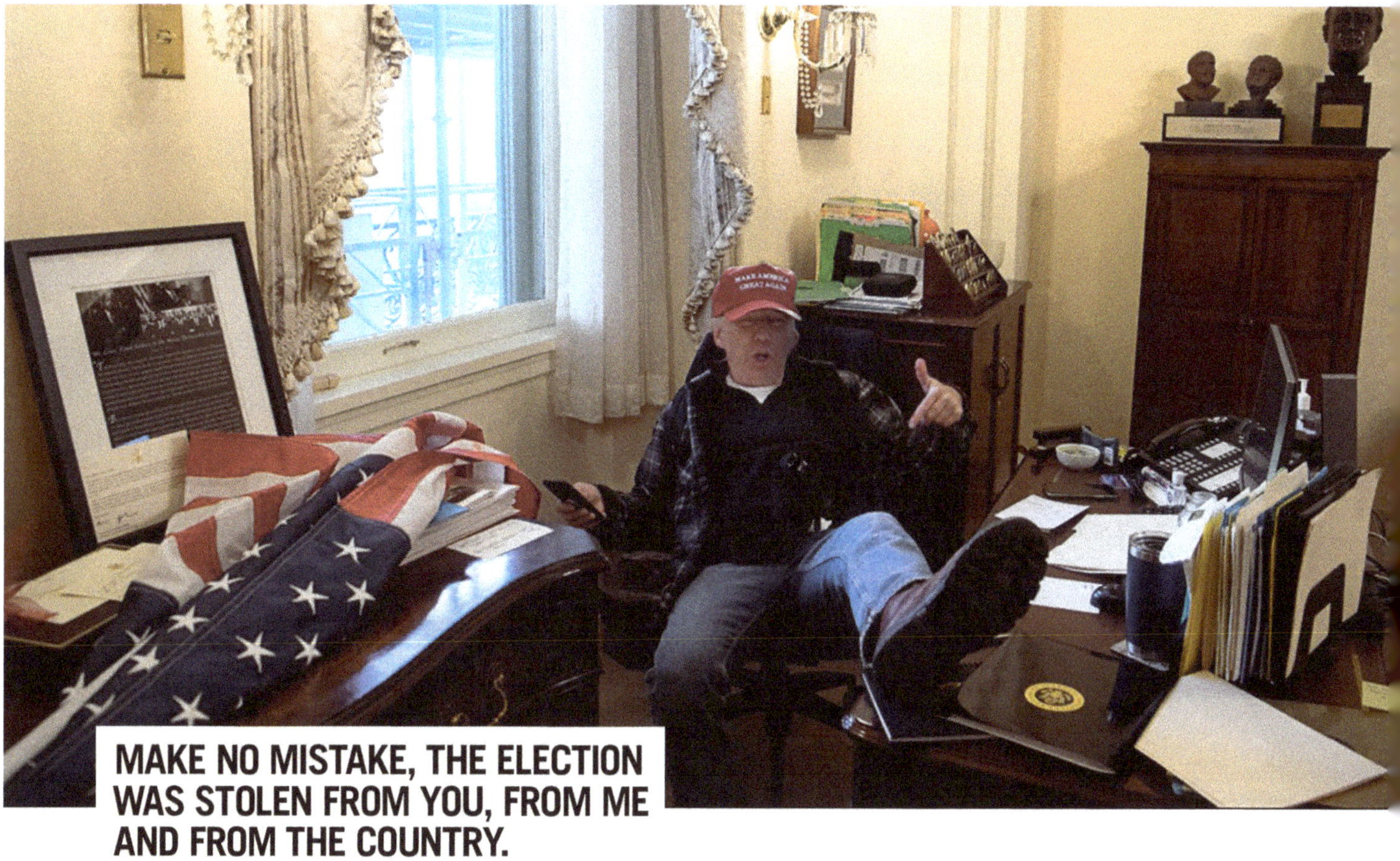

MAKE NO MISTAKE, THE ELECTION WAS STOLEN FROM YOU, FROM ME AND FROM THE COUNTRY.

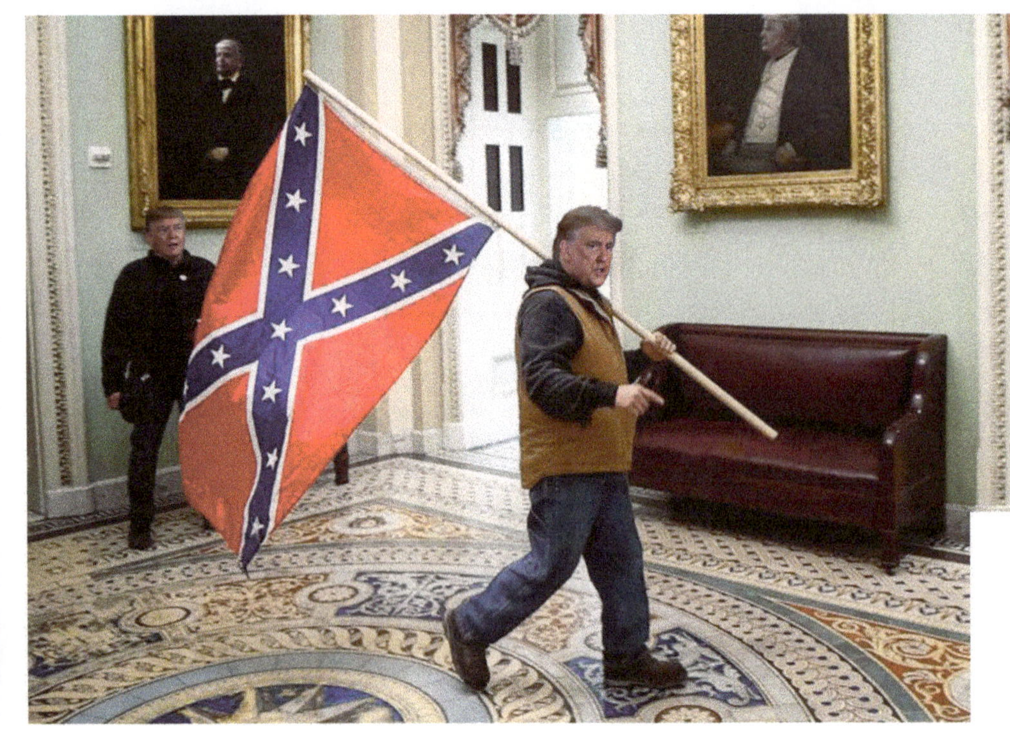

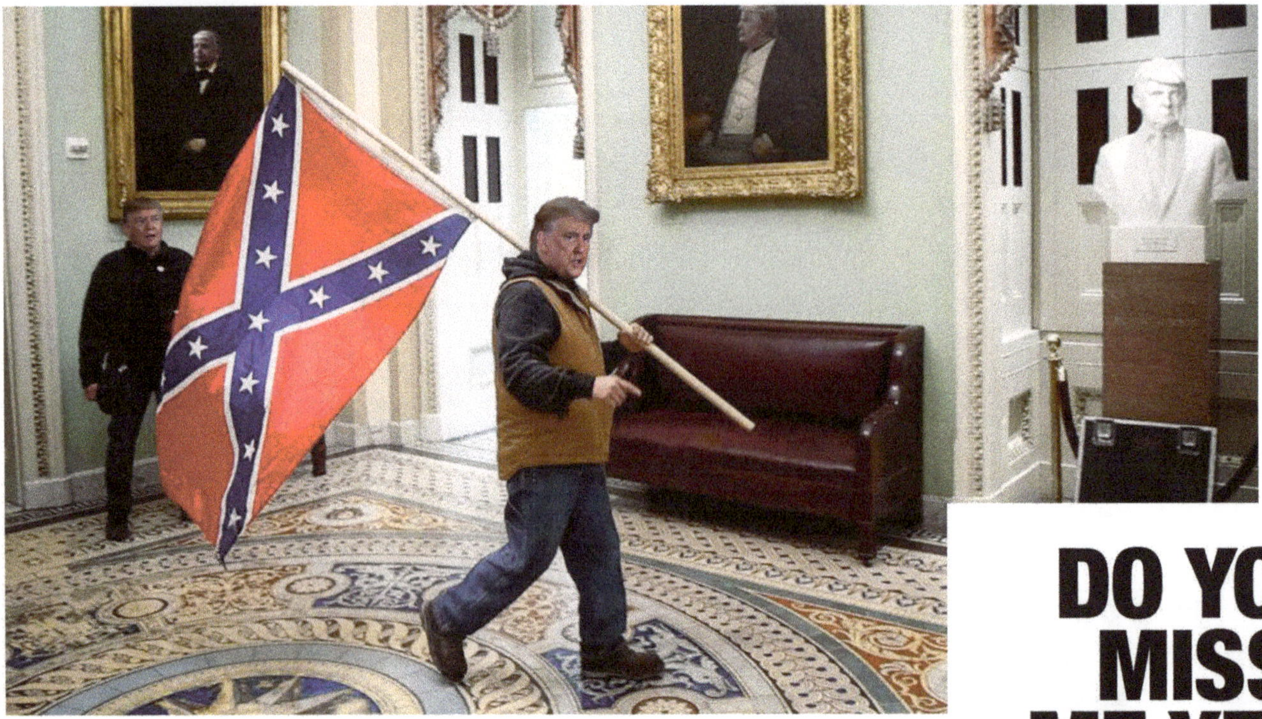

DO YOU MISS ME YET? DO YOU MISS ME?

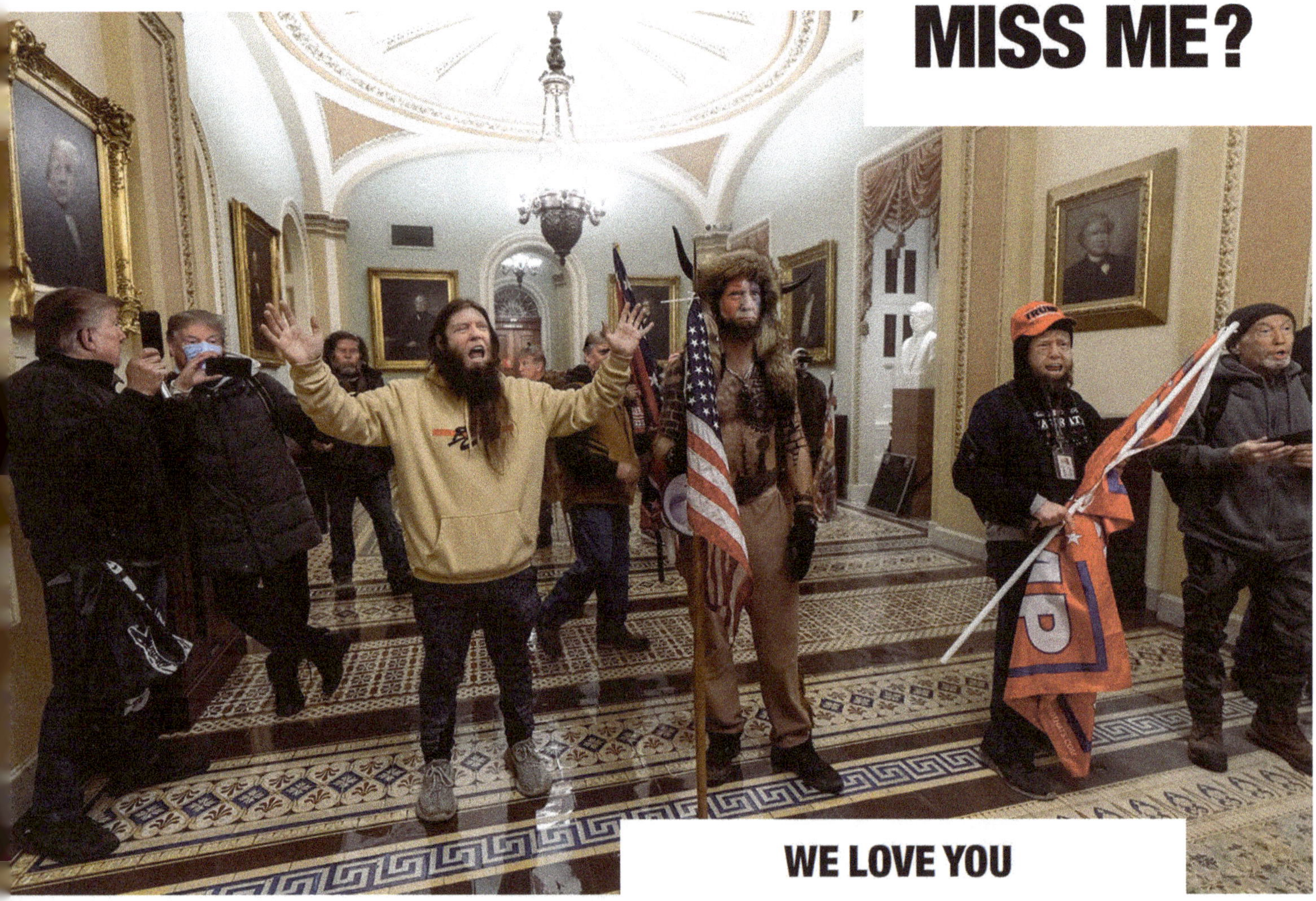

WE LOVE YOU

YOU'RE VERY SPECIAL.

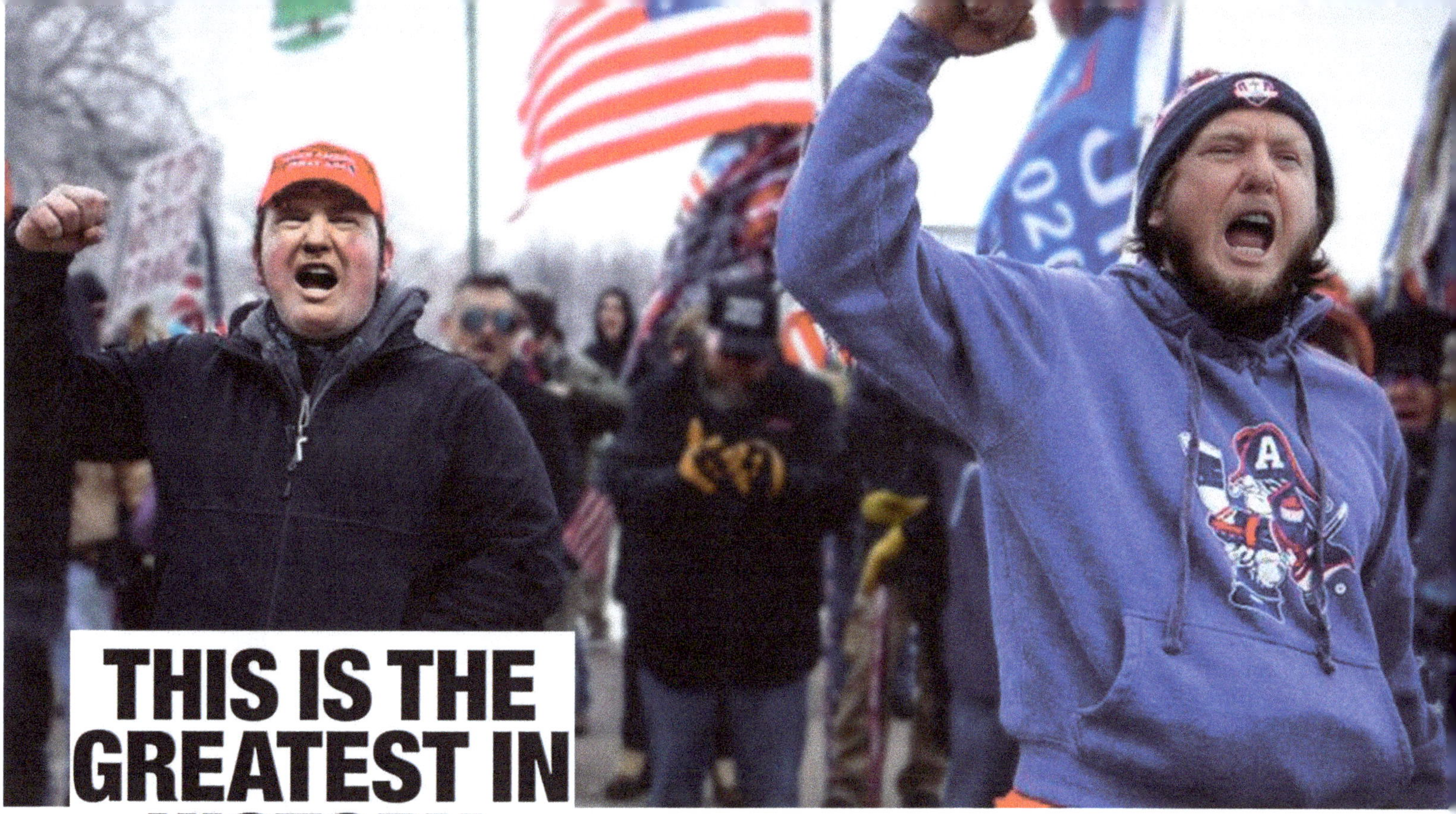

THIS IS THE GREATEST IN HISTORY.

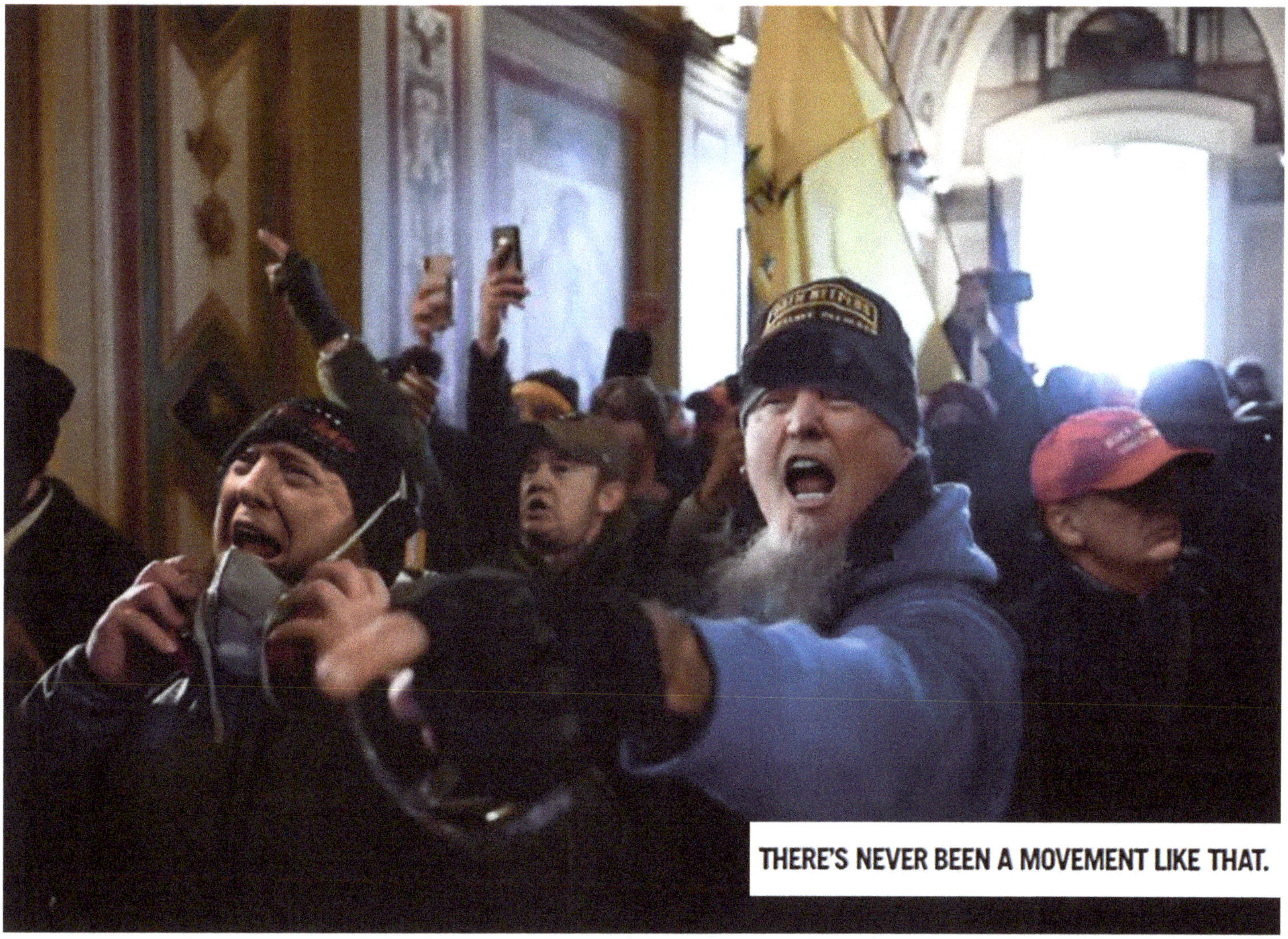

THERE'S NEVER BEEN A MOVEMENT LIKE THAT.

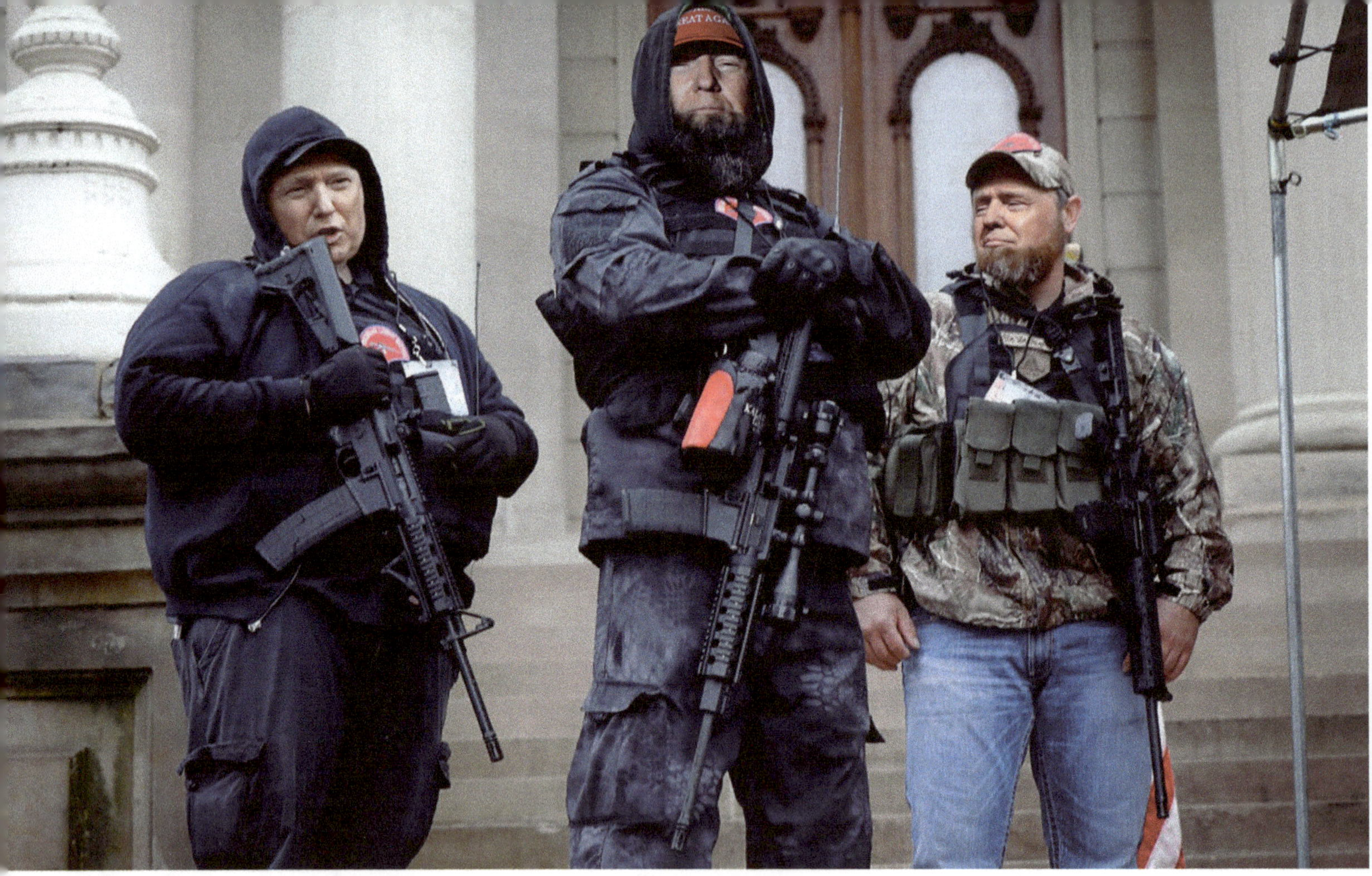

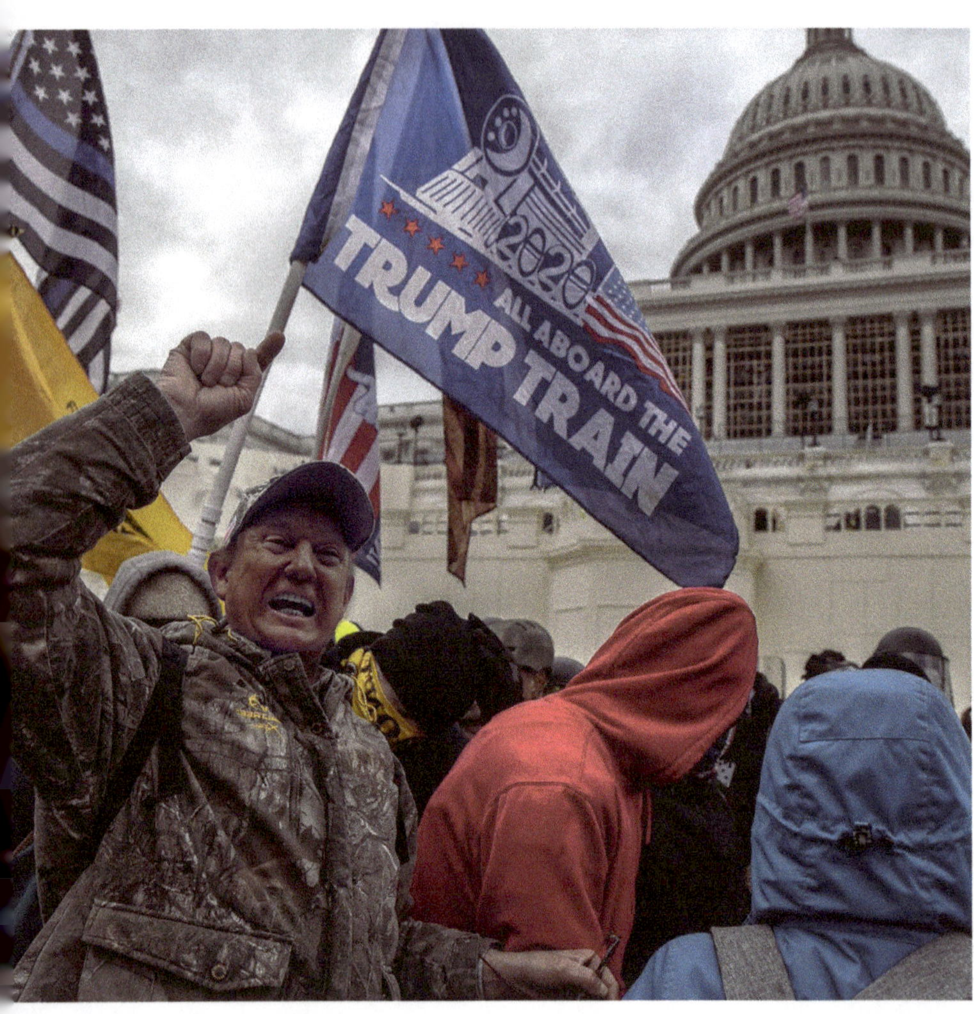

LOOKING OUT AT ALL THE AMAZING PATRIOTS HERE TODAY, I HAVE NEVER BEEN MORE CONFIDENT IN OUR NATION'S FUTURE.

THERE'S NEVER BEEN A MOVEMENT LIKE THIS EVER,

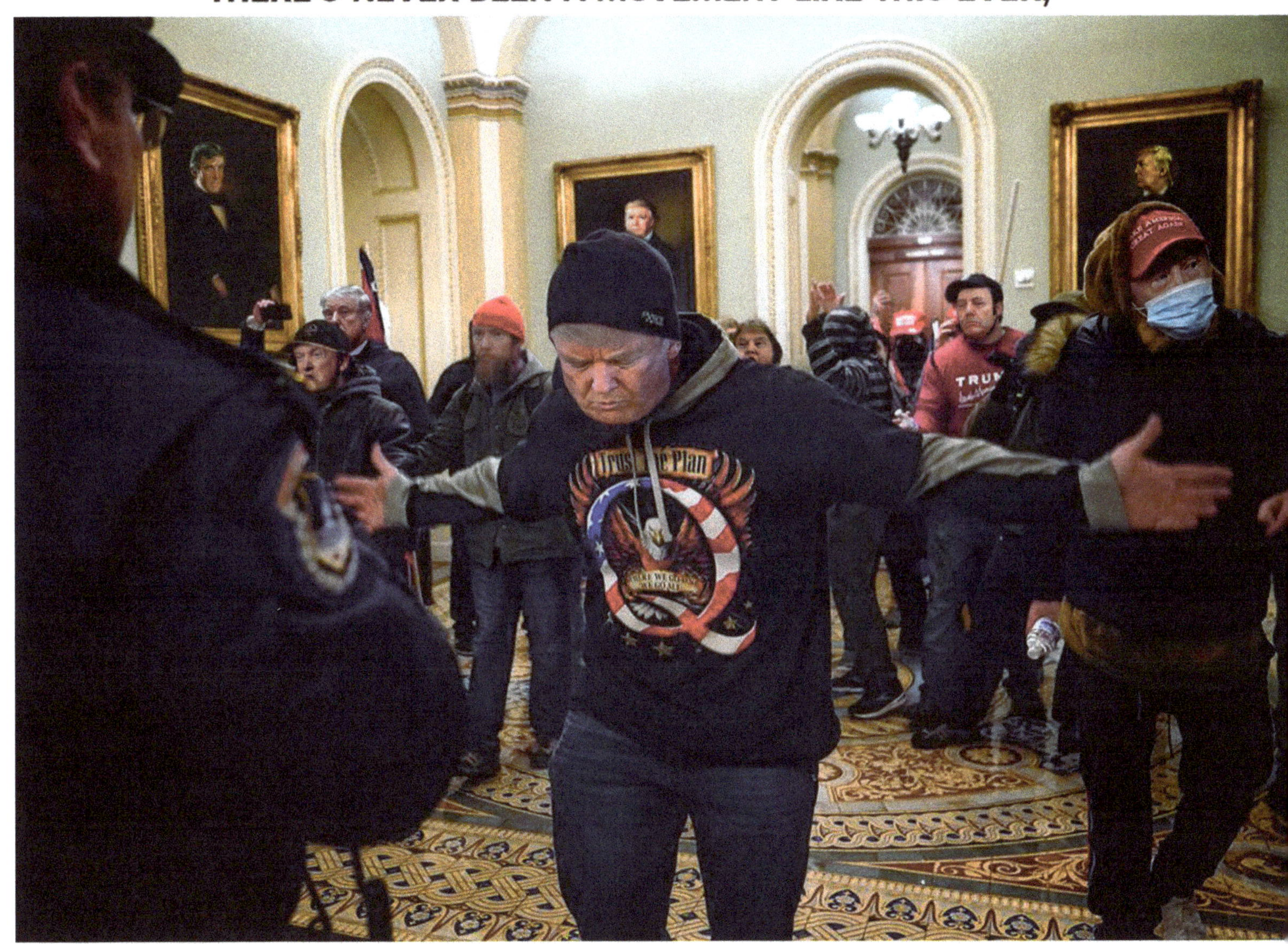

EVER FOR THE EXTRAORDINARY LOVE FOR THIS AMAZING COUNTRY.

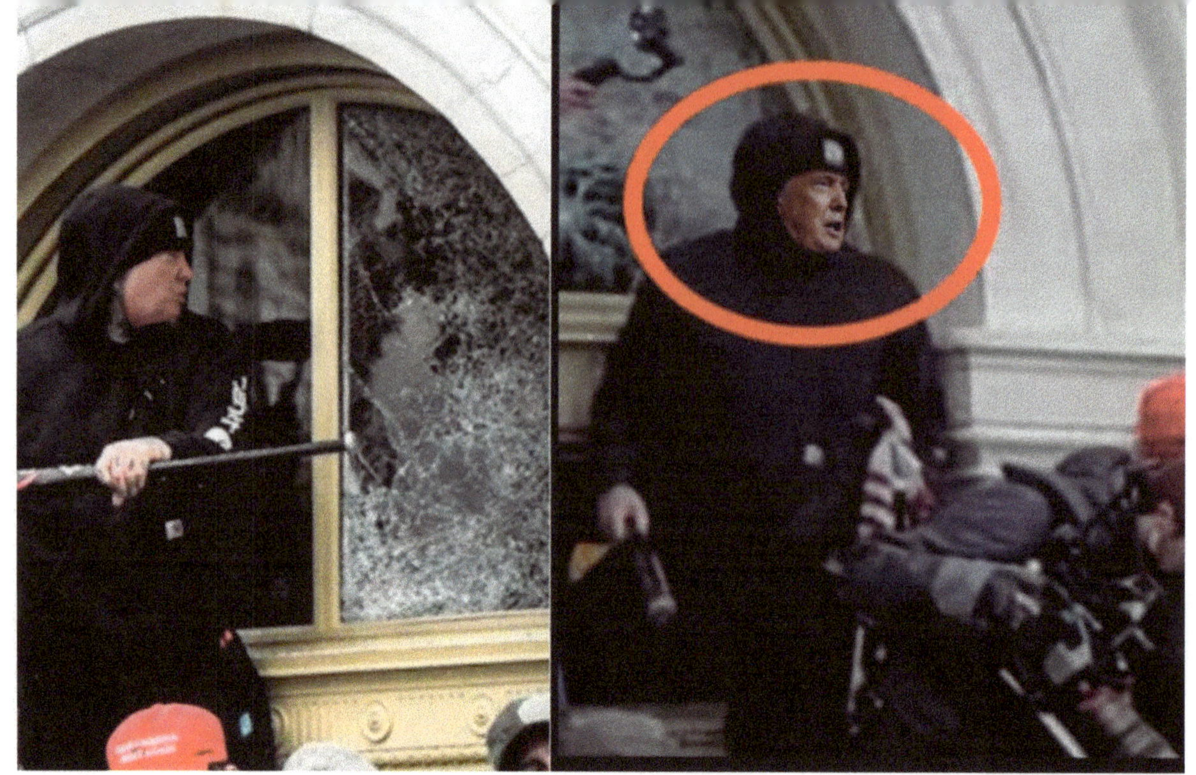

AND WE FIGHT. WE FIGHT LIKE HELL. AND IF YOU DON'T FIGHT LIKE HELL, YOU'RE NOT GOING TO HAVE A COUNTRY ANYMORE.

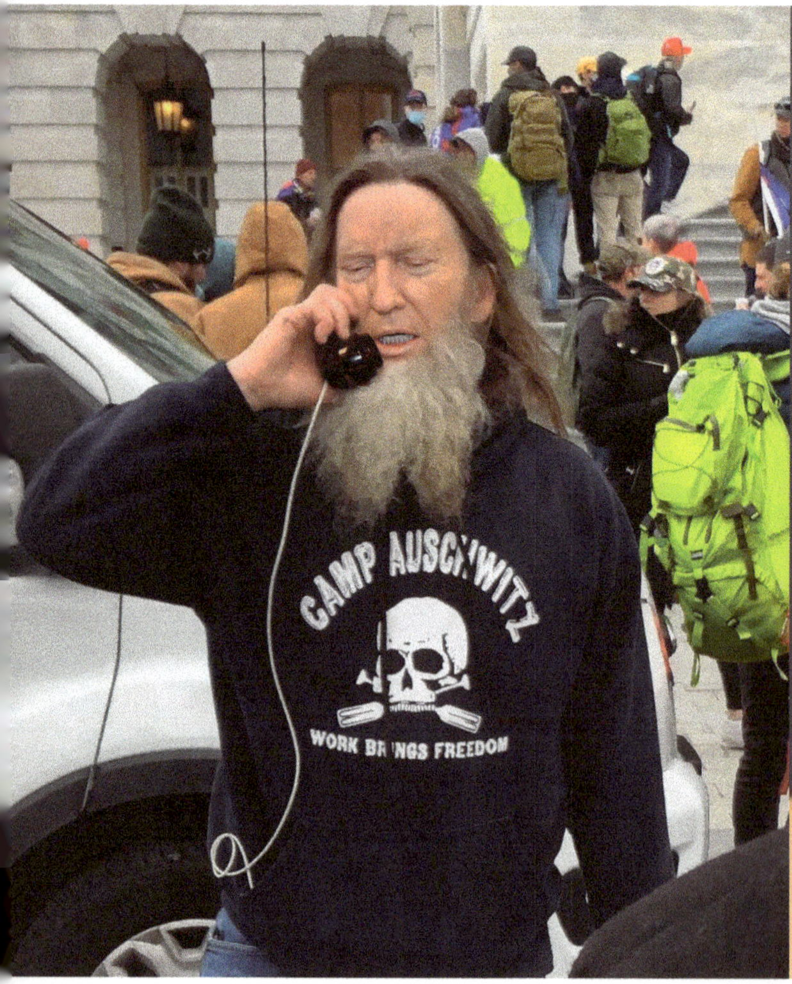

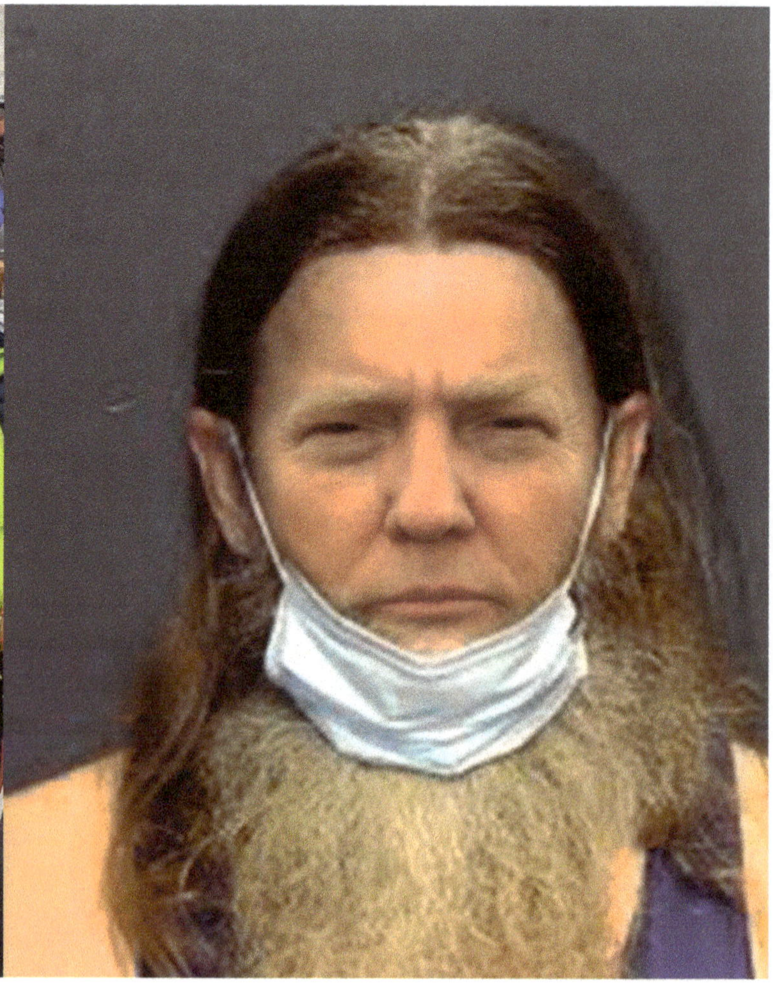

I WANT TO GO BACK EIGHT WEEKS. LET'S GO BACK EIGHT WEEKS.

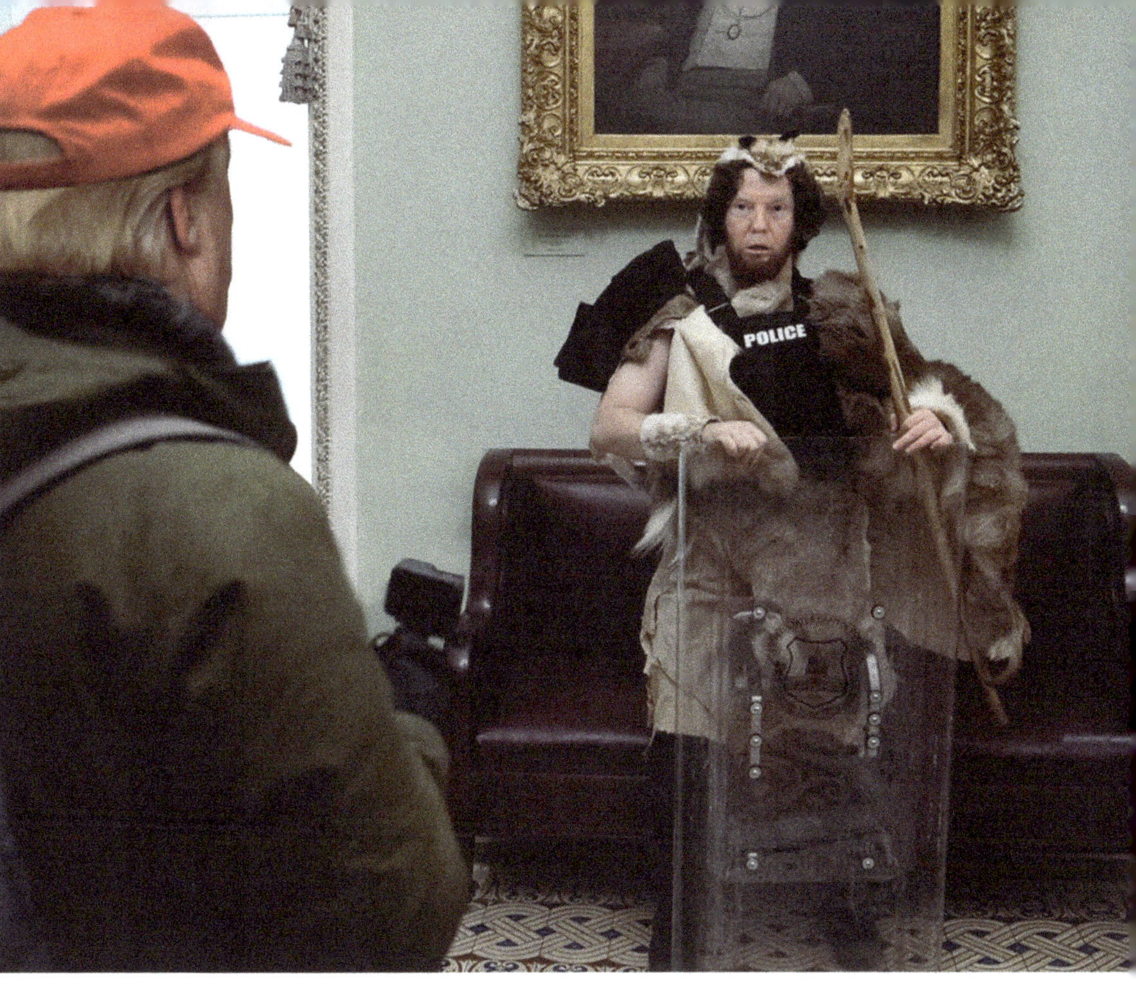

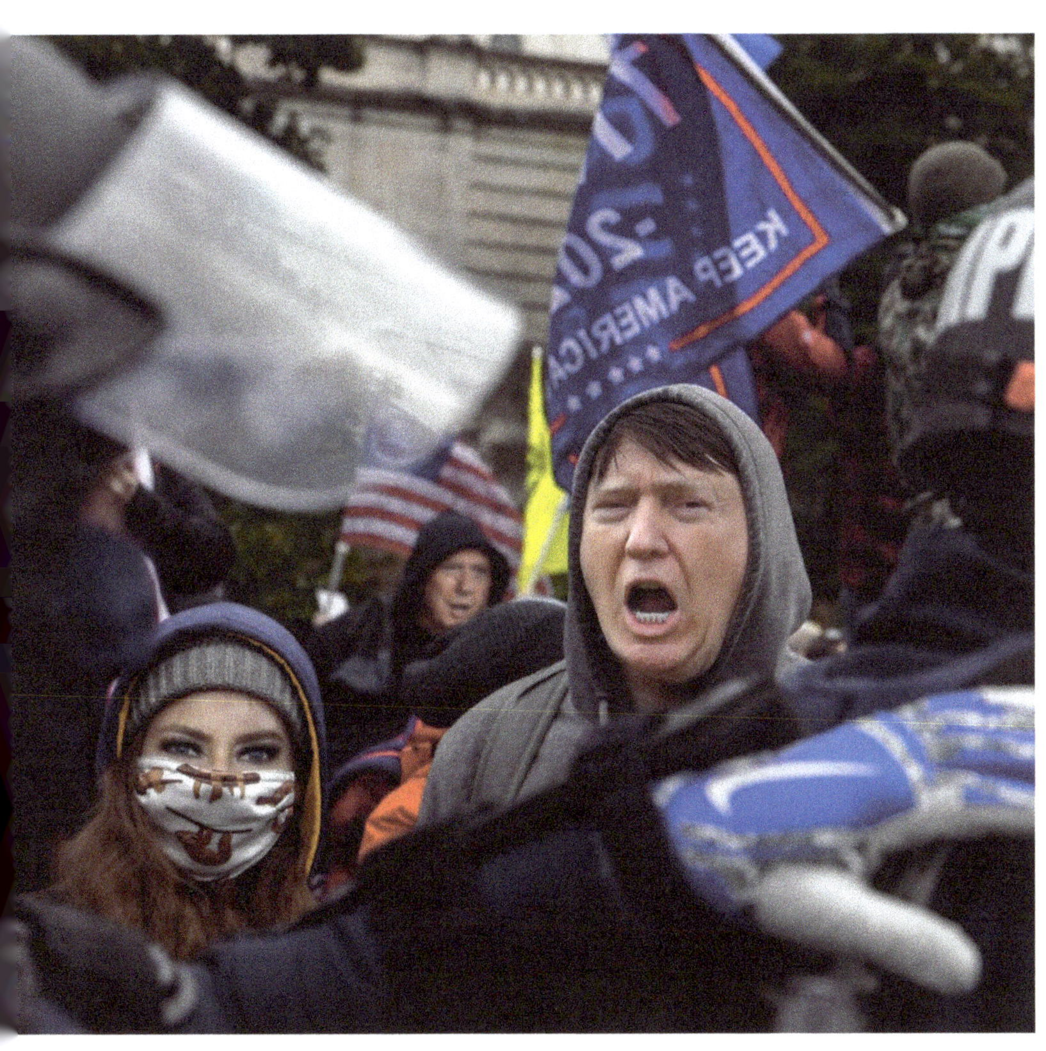

THE INCREDIBLE JOURNEY WE BEGAN TOGETHER, WE WENT THROUGH A JOURNEY LIKE NOBODY ELSE. THERE'S NEVER BEEN A JOURNEY LIKE IT THERE'S NEVER BEEN A JOURNEY SO SUCCESSFUL.

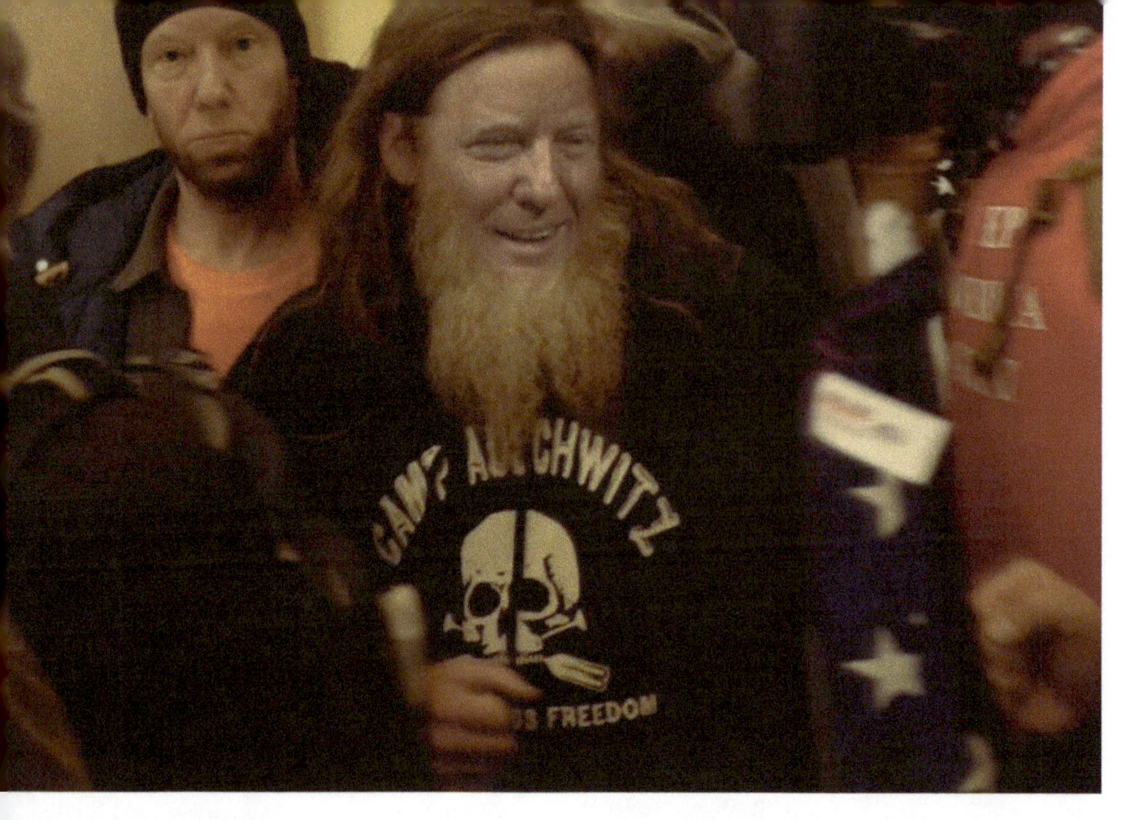

WE PROTECTED PEOPLE FROM THE RAVAGES OF DANGEROUS PREDATORS.

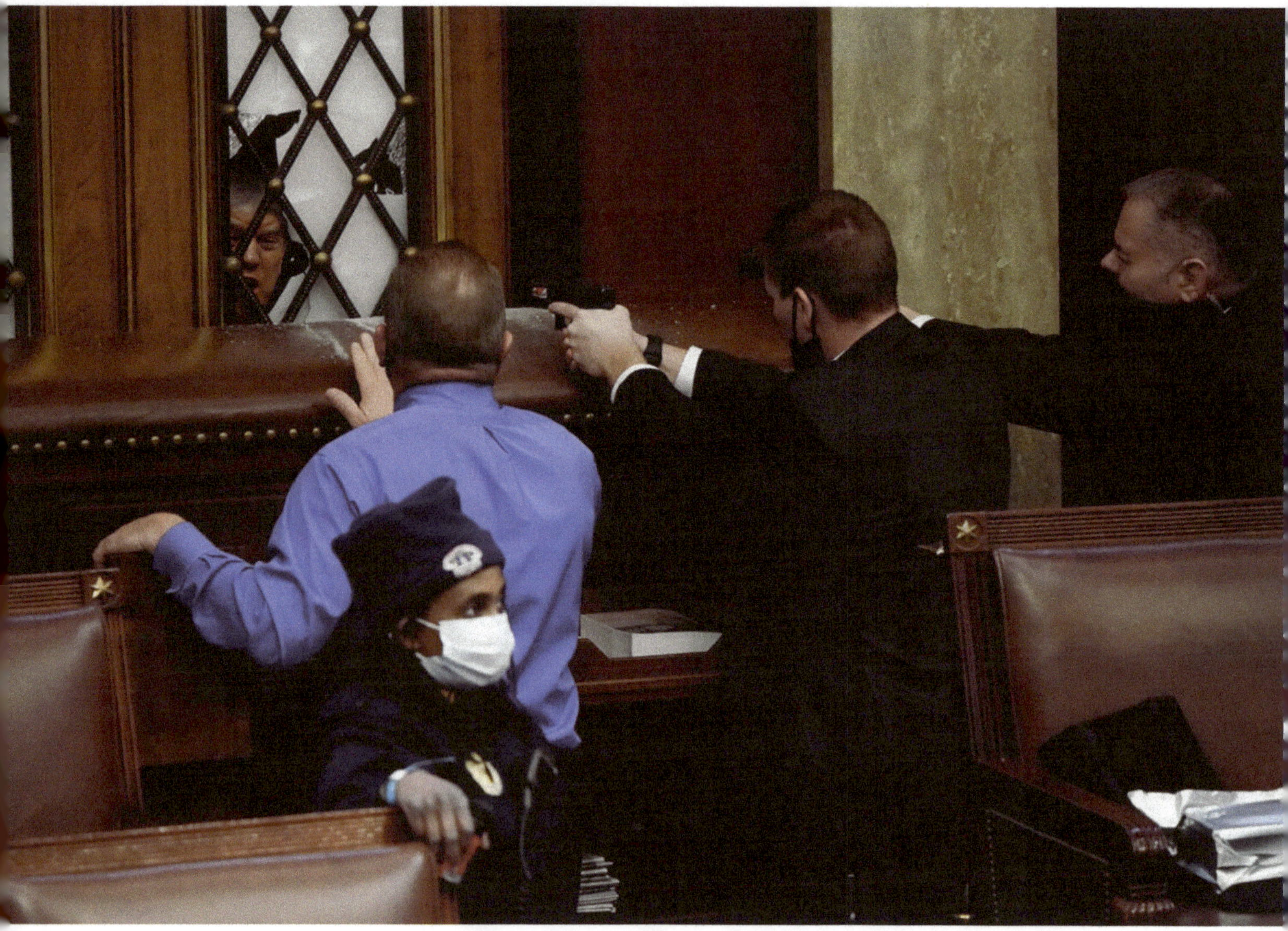

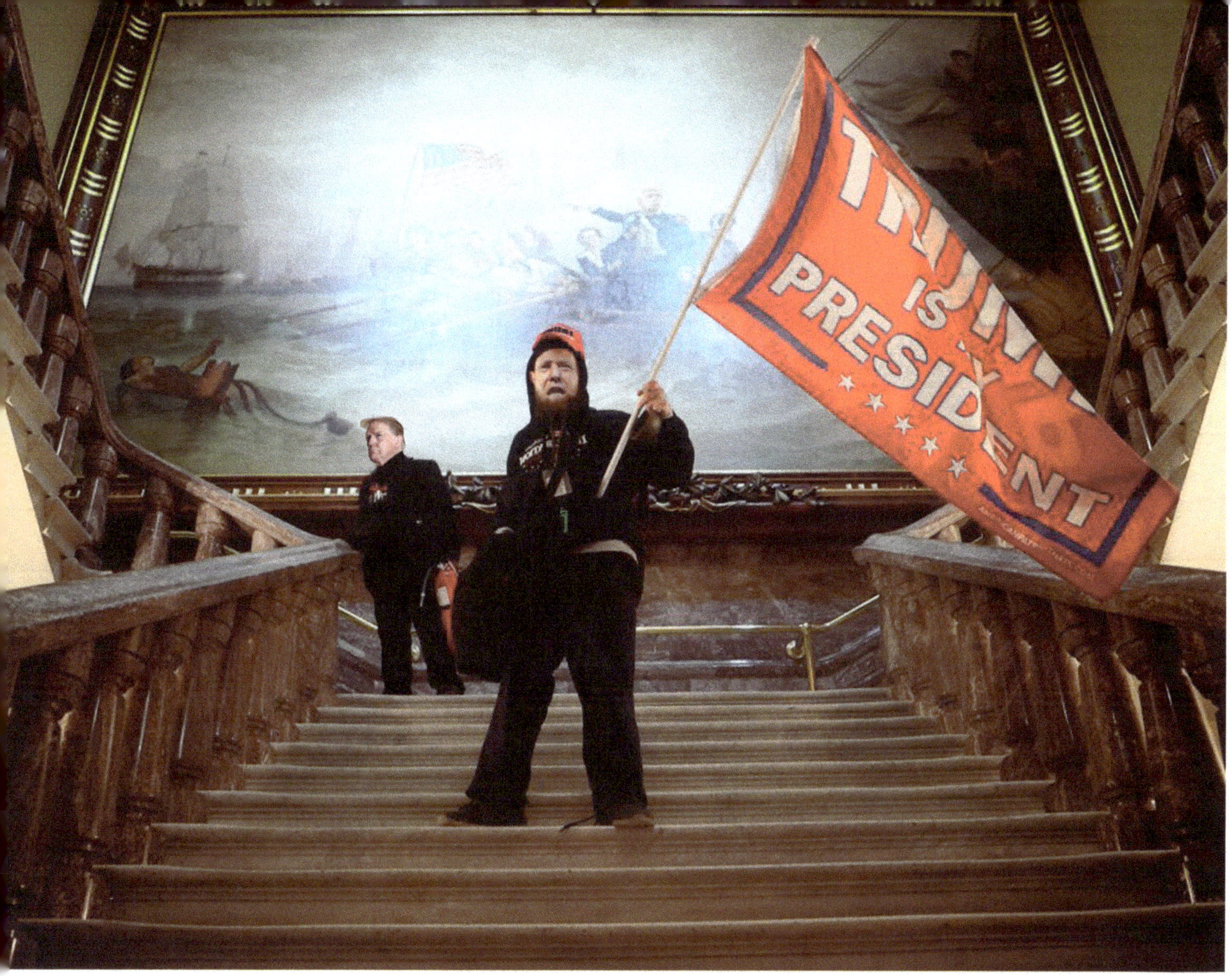

WE BEGAN IT FOUR YEARS AGO AND IT IS FAR FROM BEING OVER.

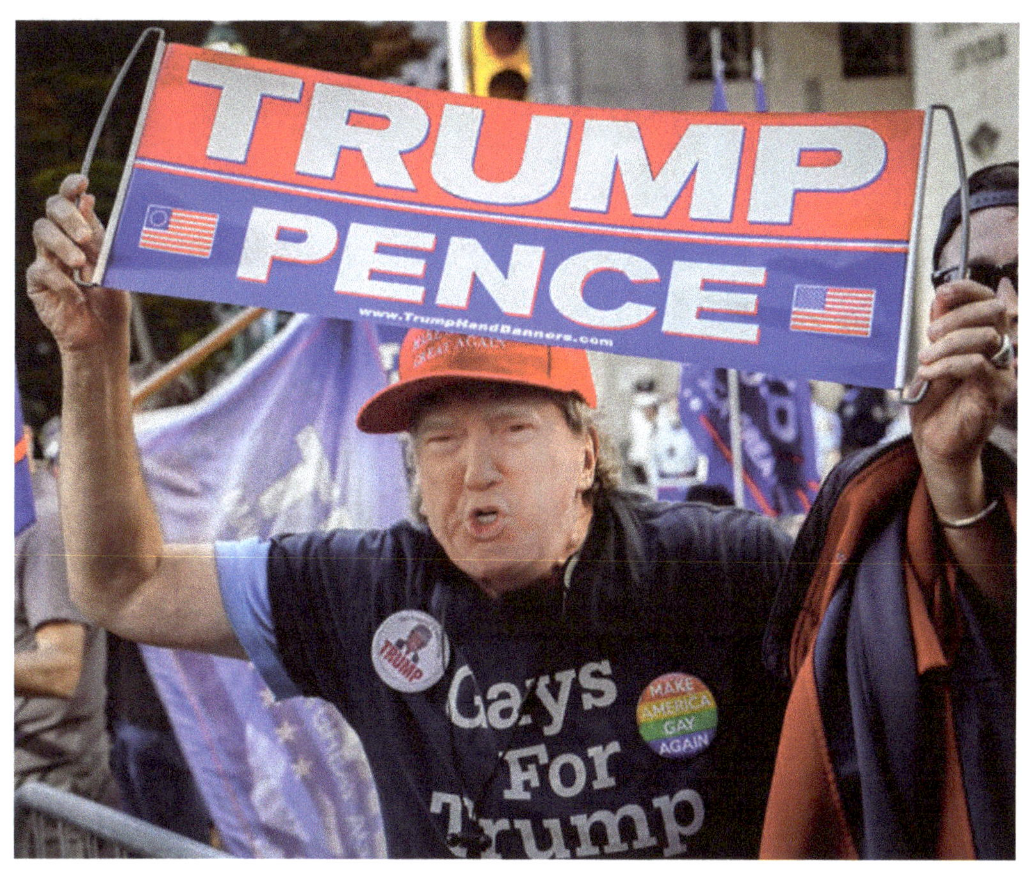

OUR EXCITING ADVENTURES AND BOLDEST ENDEAVOURS HAVE NOT YET BEGUN.

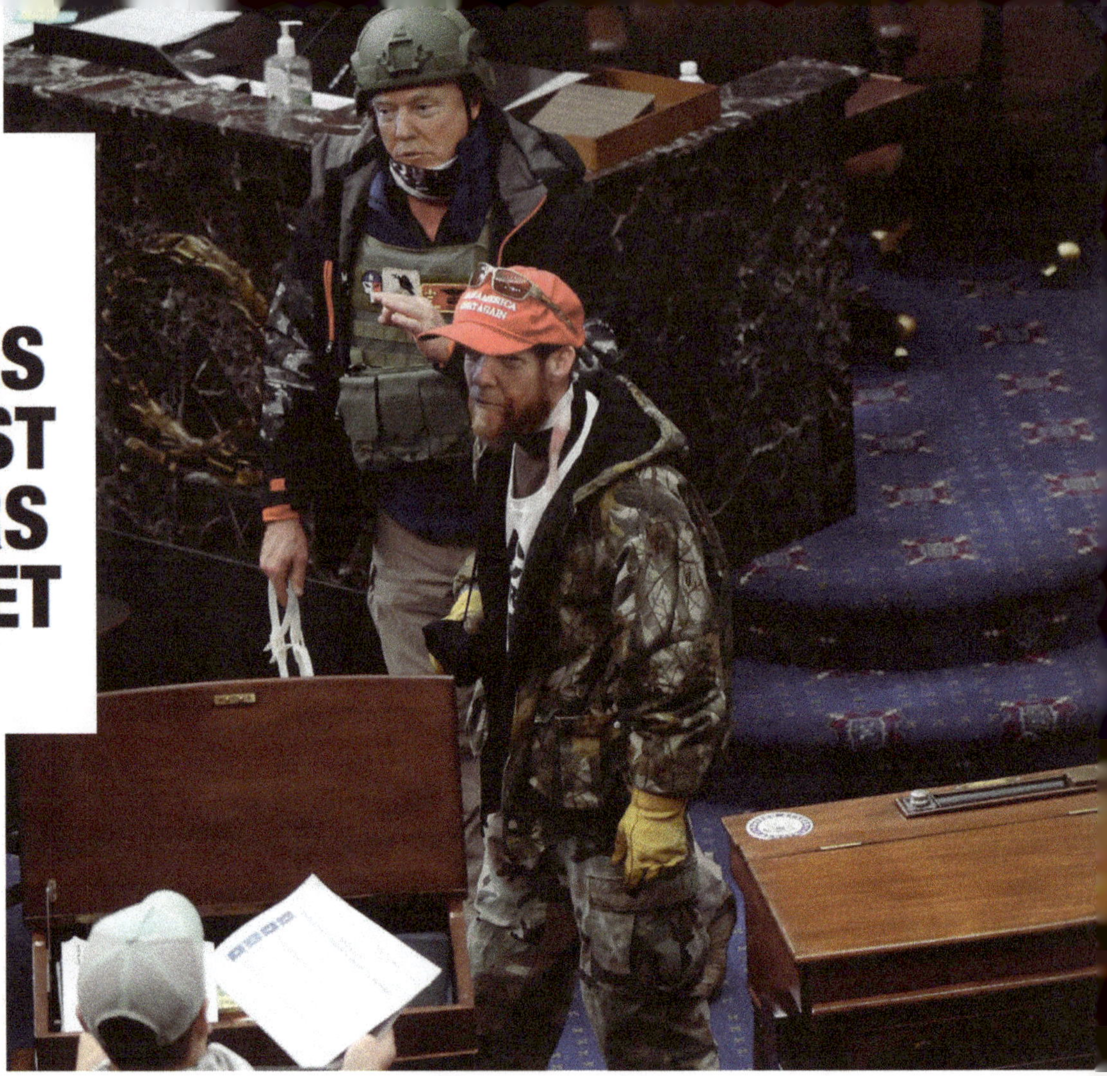

GOODBYE WE LOVE YOU

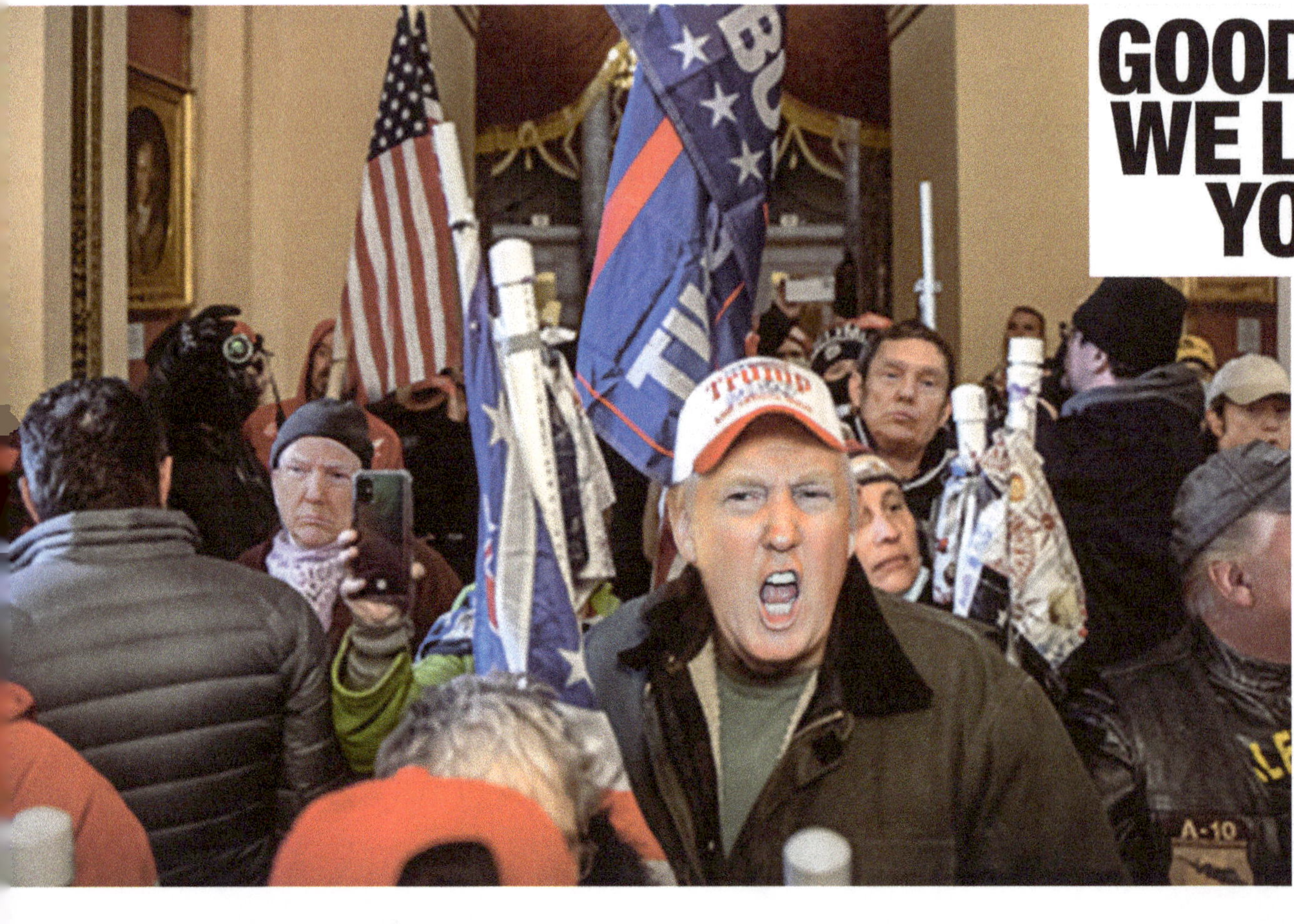

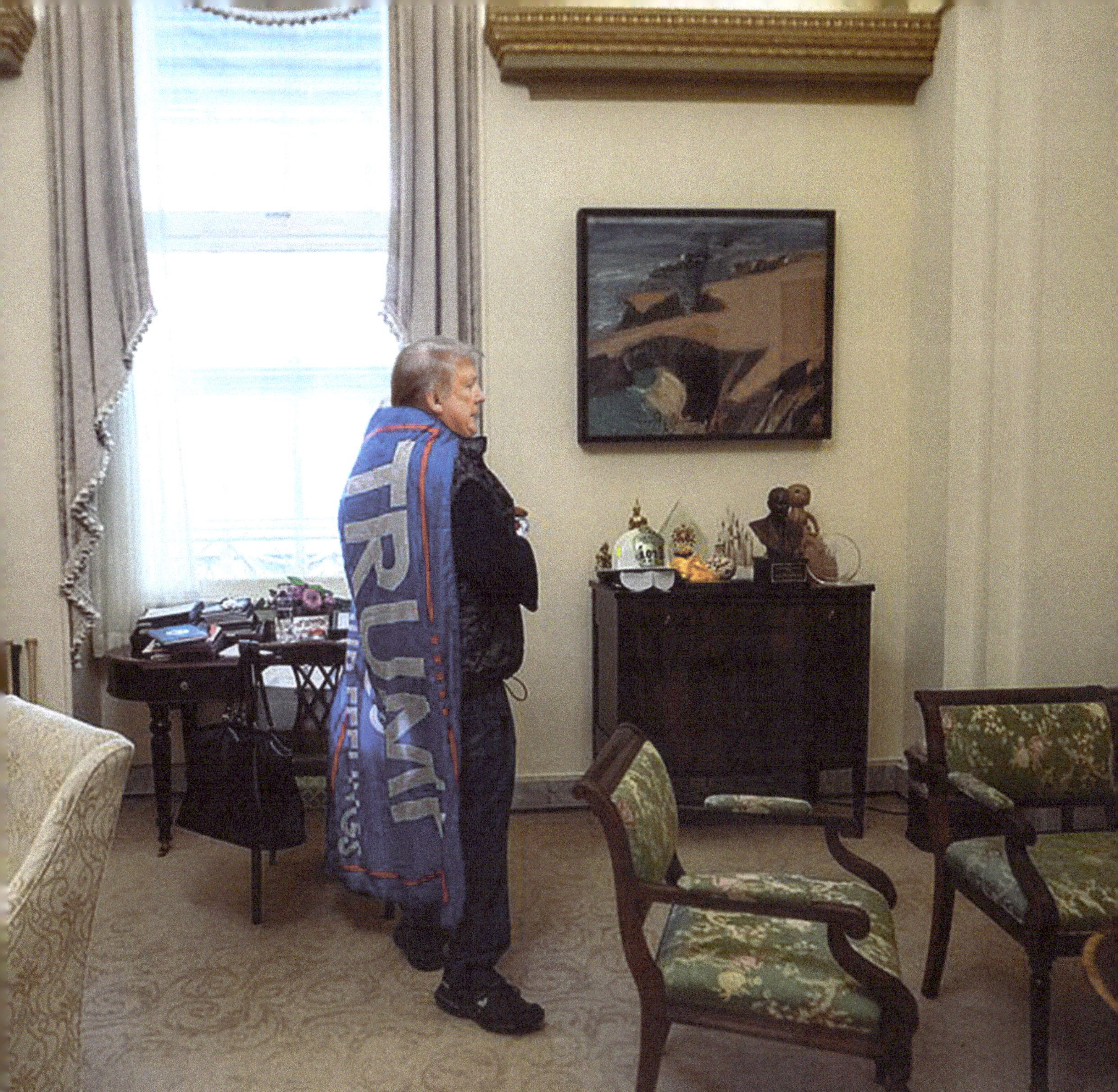

WE WILL BE BACK
IN FOUR YEARS IN SOME FORM
AND THEN A REPUBLICAN PRESIDENT
WILL MAKE A TRIUMPHANT
RETURN TO THE WHITE HOUSE
TO THE SOUND OF
THE VILLAGE PEOPLE.

AND I WONDER WHO THAT WILL BE?

WHO?
WHO?

WHO WILL THAT BE I WONDER?

SEEKING INFORMATION

VIOLENCE AT THE UNITED STATES CAPITOL

WASHINGTON, D.C.
JANUARY 6, 2021

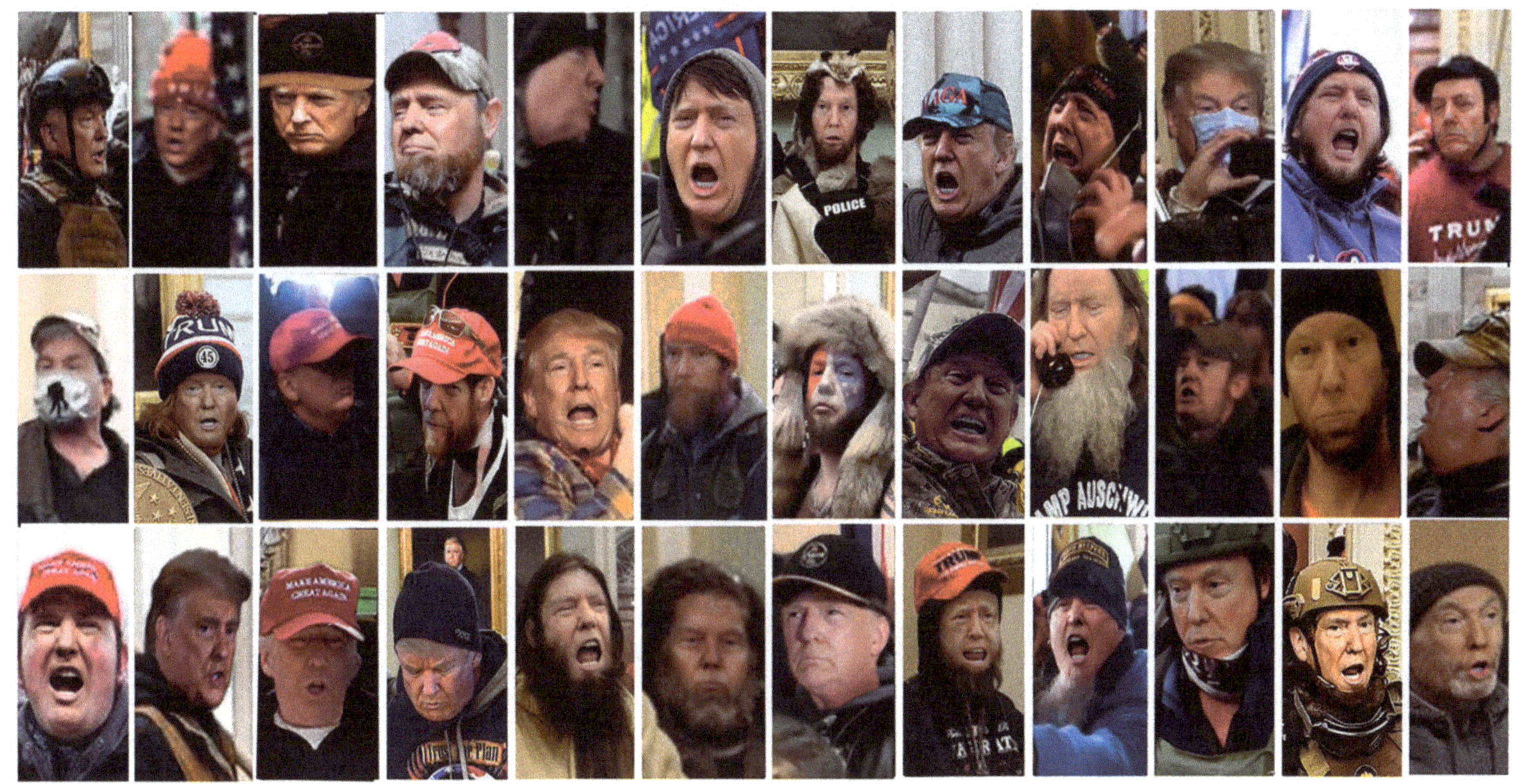

DETAILS

The Federal Bureau of Investigation's (FBI) Washington Field Office is seeking the public's assistance in identifying individuals who made unlawful entry into the United States Capitol Building on January 6, 2021, in Washington, D.C.

Anyone with information regarding these individuals, or anyone who witnessed any unlawful violent actions at the Capitol or near the area, is asked to contact the FBI's Toll-Free Tipline at 1-800-CALL-FBI (1-800-225-5324) to verbally report tips. You may also submit any information, photos, or videos that could be relevant online at fbi.gov/USCapitol. You may also contact your local FBI office or the nearest American Embassy or Consulate.

Field Office: Washington D.C.

www.fbi.gov

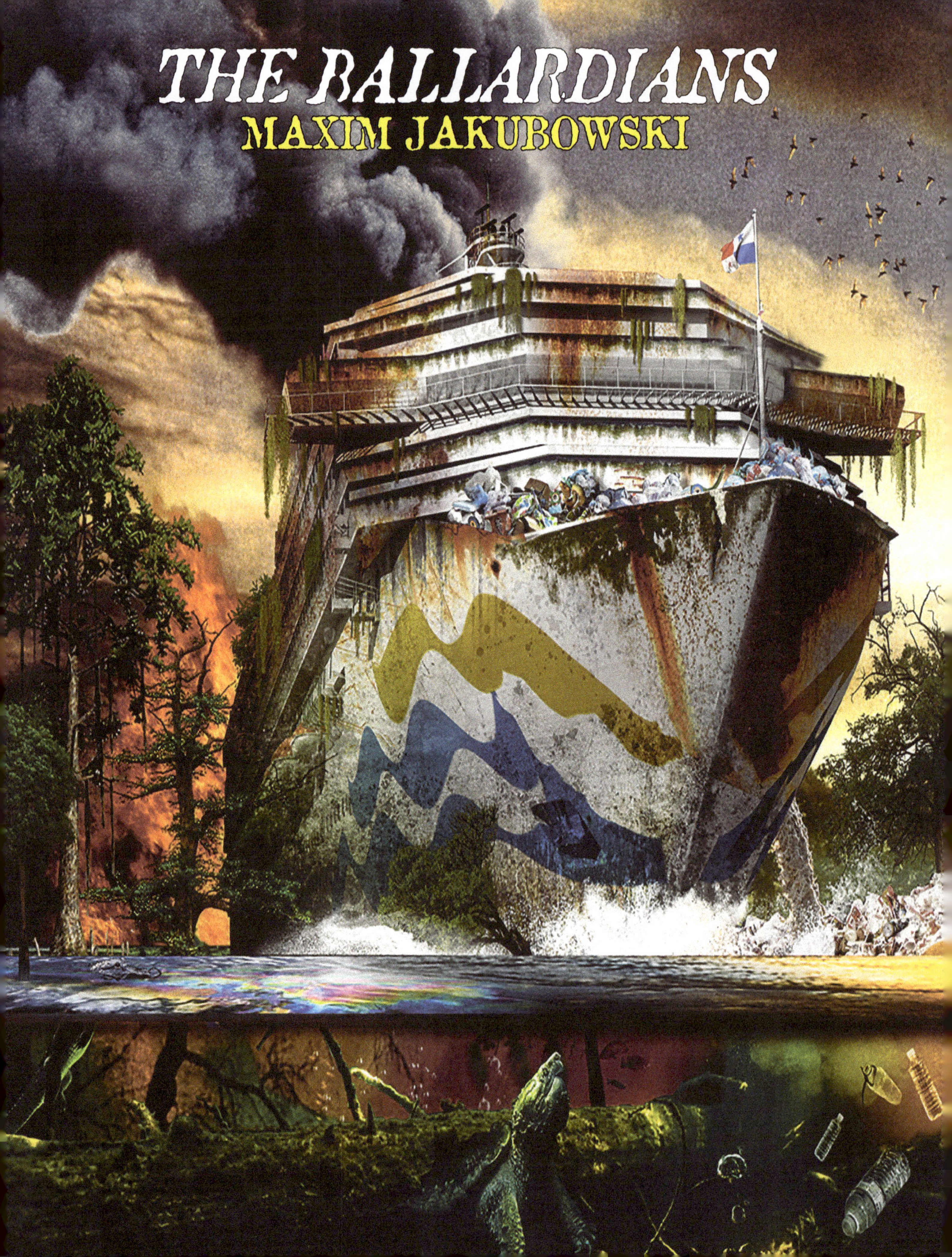
THE BALLARDIANS
MAXIM JAKUBOWSKI

There was a war.

It was not between the rich or the poor. Nor between men and women. And it wasn't happening on land, whether in trenches or on a bloody battlefield.

It was a war at sea.

The conference had been organised by the University of Aberystwyth and would be taking place on the MV Columbus while cruising off French Polynesia. Some of the more eminent JGB specialists had been invited to debate and talk on aspects of their favourite subject and although many of them had a declared fear of sea sickness, the handsome fee on offer had prevailed. Amongst the speakers were Pringle, Self, McGrath, Sellars, Jakubowski, Vaughan, Baxter, Wilson, Urbaniak and lesser lights in the complicated Ballard universe, including the actress Kara Unger who had featured prominently in David Cronenberg's adaptation of *Crash* for the big screen; the Canadian director had not been available or willing to participate in the symposium and the actor James Spader had conveyed his regrets, busy filming he latest series of *The Blacklist*, and unable to accept the invitation to participate and reminisce. Holly Hunter had, on the other hand, promptly declined the offer to be involved.

We embarked at the Swinford Street Los Angeles World Cruise Center by Long Beach on a Saturday morning, straight from the overnight airport chain hotel at LAX where visitors from Europe had been accommodated following their lengthy flights the previous day. My room on the 13th floor had from its dizzy height overlooked one of the actual runways, but the efficient soundproofing had shielded me from the rumbling of the planes below, and I slept like the proverbial log, waking up full of expectations and with a ferocious appetite which the extensive selection and variety at the breakfast buffet tables rewarded. I was well fed and raring to go by the time our transport arrived to take us the docks where, with a tinge of nervousness, I allowed one of the porters to carry my luggage which I was assured would be escorted straight to my cabin well before the boat sailed in mid-afternoon. I'd long, on my travels, suffered with acute paranoia at being parted from my suitcase, which had a singular habit in airport luggage halls of invariably being one of the final ones to arrive on the conveyor belt with my private thoughts moving rapidly into anxiety gear. On this occasion my fears were unjustified as my case arrived barely five minutes after the steward for that particular section of the corridor introduced me to the cabin and I had barely had time enough to jettison my jacket and freshen up. Maybe this was a good omen.

It was my first time on a cruise ship and what struck me first was how the long, seemingly endless corridors cutting through the interior of the vessel reminded me so strongly of Kubrick's *Overlook Hotel* scenes or the hallucinatory vistas of the blazing inferno in the Coen Bros' *Barton Fink*.

I was informed by the Sri Lankan steward that I was on Vasco De Gama deck. Each level on Columbus was named after a famous explorer, with the ship's crew billeted on Amundsen which appeared to sit under the waterline, and the top deck with the more expensive staterooms and suites being Marco Polo.

The symposium would stretch over three days. The organisers had arranged for each session to highlight one particular aspect of Ballard's work. The opening day would be devoted to swimming pools, the following to car crashes and the final session to urban warfare. In between each session there would be a day at sea and another where we would dock at, respectively, Nuku Hiva, Bora Bora and Tahiti, from where we would all be flown back to our countries of departure. Nine days with the Ballardians.

It was clear from the onset talking to participants and speakers at one of the boat's many bars—here again, in deference to the theme of the conference each one had been renamed after a place with a strong connection to JGB's work: Shanghai, Shepperton, Cannes and Eniwetok—that almost every one attending the symposium clearly belonged in a separate camp, according to their interpretation and the influence on their thinking of his books, much like the way the decks and bars of Columbus reflected preferences. As it was we were evenly distributed between the decks irrespective of what we felt was the most important aspect of the JGB *oeuvre*; it would have been ironic had we, in advance, been segregated into specific decks according to our leanings, like the societal strands in *High-Rise*.

After witnessing a major row at the Shanghai Bar on Livingston deck towards the end of the conference's first day of lectures and presentations between a group of French epistemologists arguing with vehemence that the geometrical angle of crushed car bonnets allied with the topography of motorways (or as some of American participants—a minority of the symposium audience, however—called highways) concealed a secret code that superseded the equation of swimming pool length over depth at the deep end in reaching a proper understanding of the JGB psyche, I came to the conclusion that academia was just going too far and regressing to infantilism. I much preferred the interventions by Pringle and Jakubowski which were of a more autobiographical nature and involved men who had actually known Ballard, and had a healthy disregard for algorithms and all that jazz.

I moved away from the crowded, animated bar and the increasingly heated conversations just as a Sao Paulo University researcher threw a half-full glass at his interlocutor, screaming "Go fuck your bloody swimming pool and see if you enjoy it!" The other man ducked and the contents of the glass splashed against a passing young woman's immaculately white dress and she shrieked in anger.

That's how the war between the Ballardian camps began.

That night, a group from one unknown faction sabotaged the pipes connecting the whole water supply and evacuation system on Magellan deck where a majority of the swimming pool proponents were lodged, causing a major disruption to the whole starboard corridor and forcing faecal matter to regurgitate upwards through the toilet bowls into most of the cabins.

I had no opinion in the disputes that were dangerously getting out of hand. My personal sphere of interest was an almost forgotten short story of the revered author's called 'The Volcano Dances' about people fading into a tropical jungle, a tale full of extreme metaphors about the inner landscape, but also one that somehow connected to me in a deep way that I could not fully understand. I hadn't actually reread it in ages and was now unsure whether the story featured a volcano or not. At any rate, for weeks now, I had been constantly dreaming of volcanoes and been playing around with a story of a similar nature—plagiarism or bad influence?—in which a modern version of *Romeo and Juliet* in prose form climaxed with either the young man or the young woman throwing himself or herself down into the lava-bedecked mouth of the volcano, or both at the same time. Paradoxically, I identified with both characters and projected myself into their respective bodies as they tenderly made love. I felt the stab of his hard cock as he penetrated me swiftly on a bed of forest moss and, at the very same time, allowed my fingers, nerve endings in sensory overdrive, to lazily graze along the smooth surface of her breasts with exquisite slowness, counting the beats of her heart through the shattering whiteness of her skin, a sensation of pleasure which caused a knot to form in the pit of my stomach. I thus experienced both their orgasms and my mind blanked out for a second that felt endless and I woke in sweat from the fever dream of combined, exacerbated desire. As realisation dawned, I briefly came to the conclusion that I had lived through what it might truly feel to come in both a male and female body, or was it something else? Neither was it being on the conference boat that was responsible for these strange and erotic if highly personal dreams, as they had begun to seep through my consciousness months before my travel. But, to my disappointment, there were no papers at the conference about this particular story (there was one on record by a Canadian academic which I had browsed through years before but it had not left much of a lasting impression.

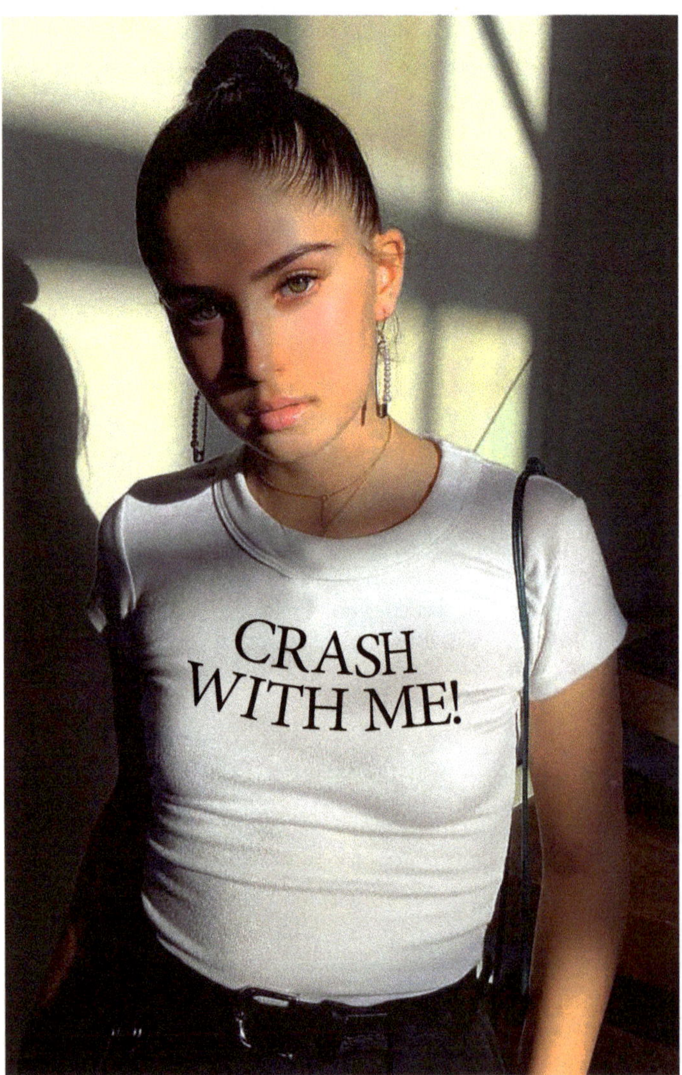

The evening before we reached the island of Nuku Hiva, another serious affray occurred when a sudden but violent fist fight developed in the main restaurant, during which a couple of dozen men and women actually came to physical blows over a further argument between opposing camps which flared up between the main course and dessert. As for me, I'd been eating at the buffet on the top deck as I was that evening in more of a mood for fresh air and informal attire. By the time the news reached me, it was unclear how the hostilities had begun or what specific contentious subject had triggered the affray. Half a dozen of those involved had to attend the boat's infirmary with cuts and bruises and, rumour was, in a couple of cases actual broken bones, but news of that kind in a closed environment like a cruise ship spreads like wildfire, with inaccuracies and disinformation growing with every repeat of the story. The all-female Hungarian string quartet who always played soothing classical tunes at the entrance of the large restaurant had, I heard, been caught up in the fight and one of their instruments had been badly damaged.

The following morning at breakfast, there was already a scattering of conference participants wearing specially printed T-shirts—made overnight by the boat's gift shop—declaring what camp the wearer sympathised with. 'Crash With Me', 'Empty My Pool', 'Inner=Winner,' or 'I Have Faith in Dr Nathan' were some of the slogans on display. The way this was developing was worrying. What would happen next, I wondered, although at the back of my mind, I was still fixated on my Romeo and Juliet scenario in which the two sundered lovers each belonged to different, warring Ballardian camps. Ah, what Jimmy would have made of this!

"Did you hear?" Professor Kerans asked me as I stood by the juice dispenser waiting for my plastic cup to fill with grapefruit juice.

"Yesterday's fight? Yes, a few people have told me about it."

"No," he said, leaning confidentially against me. 'The aftermath..."

"Tell me."

"Rumour has it a Villefranche University female researcher was raped. Claims she woke up in her cabin, bruised and with obvious signs of violation. Someone slipped her some Rohypnol in her drink and must have taken advantage of her.

She can't remember anything beyond almost passing out at the Captain's Club bar and a man she had previously been quarrelling with helping her to her feet. All she recalled was that he was on the opposite side of the argument, not that she no longer had any notion of the subject they were arguing about. Some say he was a proponent of the wind sculptors of Vermilion Sands though..."

"Jesus!"

Waiting for the lift to return to my cabin, I could feel the tension in the air as other passengers surrounded me, people looking at each other sideways, with all sorts of resentment simmering under the surface. If looks could kill. As if, in some instances, accusing me of not having taken sides. The atmosphere was becoming poisonous. A good thing we had a day ahead with the opportunity to disembark from the boat's claustrophobic cloud of rising hostility. I hoped the skies of Polynesia would prove a soothing agent spreading some form of calm among our increasingly litigious crowd.

The only way to reach the shores of Nuku Hiva was by

tender, as the island had no dock deep enough to accommodate a cruise ship the sheer size of Columbus.

Much of the island's natives were standing by the quay, wreathed in garlands of multicoloured flowers and playing local instruments in readiness to greet us visitors. It felt more like a museum display or some Disney movie, as we cautiously stepped off the tender and laid foot on dry land. Beyond the natives on cheerful display was an open air market with an abundance of trestle tables littered with trinkets, leather products, carved wooden objects and jewellery that looked as if it had sprung straight from the shelves of donated goods at Goodwill or Oxfam. Or maybe we conference participants were too cynical; at any rate, we were not the typical sort of customer a cruise ship would disgorge. I doubted the market traders would find today particularly lucrative. A small building with a thatched roof stood close to the improvised market and its rows of stools, advertising itself as both an information and tourist center and a museum of local history. Most of us bypassed the market and picked up local maps which were available for free.

In truth, there was it appeared little to see on Nuku Hiva unless you rented a car and drove into the interior, which none of us knew anything about, not having previously researched the island. The boat's shore team had not advertised any local excursions, a sign if any of the lack of tourist features of interest on Nuku Hiva.

On the tender, during the 15 minute journey from where Columbus had moored out in the bay and the small island, I had fallen into conversation with Sofia, an attractive young woman from Turin in Italy. She was not a Ballard specialist *per se*, but was working on a doctoral dissertation on David Foster Wallace and had generously been gifted the cruise by her thesis supervisor who had been obliged to drop out at the last minute because of a family illness. Sofia was into body art, so there was a remote connection to JGB through some of the more extreme developments in *Crash*, she claimed. At any rate, she quickly declared that she wasn't part of any of the opposing camps that were developing on board, and I reassured her that neither was I. More puzzled observers, we reckoned.

"Ha," she said, smiling. "So we're just voyeurs, spectators. Not in danger of stabbing each other in the back... Good!"

Sofia was both stick thin and busty, a curious combination that made her stand out in a crowd, with dark, thick curly hair held together like a crown high above her forehead. On her right temple, a patch of skin looked bruised or burned, signs of an ancient accident or a problem at birth. But, where others would have concealed this blemish by combing their hair across the stain, she proudly allowed it to be fully visible, almost displaying it with pride. Her eyes were black as coal and truly striking. She must have been in her mid-30s with sultry, angular Mediterranean features.

I was curious to ask her about body art, and conversely whether she actually had any piercings or tattoos herself, but in these awkward #MeToo days was hesitant to enquire in fear of taking that perilous step so far and not knowing her well enough at this stage. Ah, the perils of the new woke! Ballard would have found our times problematic had he lived on that long!

I came by Sofia again in the tourist office, as we both faced the counter and perused the brochures and paperwork on offer. We had parted at the shore where she had wanted to take photos of the natives in their flowery finery.

"Any plans?"

"No. Was thinking of looking out for a local grocery store or small supermarket. I need some bottles of mineral water for the cabin. At the bars on board it costs as much as wine!" I was lying: I actually needed some Cola, which was the only thing I drank in private. Water just had no taste!

"Good idea," Sofia said. "Can I join you?"

We were informed there was a store all the way further down the coastal road to the west, a twenty minutes walk away, where we would find basic essentials. The day was cloudy but warm, and we had little else to do. Most of the people who had disembarked from the ship also appeared to be heading in the same direction. We followed them at a distance. Many of the improvised groups still seemed to be in constant argument, arms waiving, heads shaking under the assault of rage, steps staccato to the rhythm of the heated conversations, dimmed voices ahead and behind us blanking out the sound of waves lapping on the shore, as if the literary war raging on Columbus had followed us all the way onto dry land.

Halfway to the store we were seeking the road briefly swerved away from the shore and a small commuter bus which had seen better days, its exhaust sputtering loudly along, drove past us, choking out a cloud of fumes. A wooden road sign offered us alternative directions: to the left 'Pirate's Cove' and further along to the right 'Tekoa Mountain' ten kilometres away. Sofia was Googling on her iPhone and informed me that Herman Melville had actually lived here at one stage when he was staying in the Marquesas Islands. And so had Robert Louis Stevenson.

As much as I was fascinated to lay eyes on the mountain which lay behind the Taipivai valley, equating it in my mind with the equally tectonic jungle landscape of 'The Volcano Dances', the idea of walking the whole distance was out of the question as we couldn't risk missing the last tender back to Columbus advertised for 4pm. We made for the cove, treading unsteadily at times across the short grass and muddy terrain bordering the island's edge.

It wasn't much of a beach. A thin stretch of colourless sand, strewn with the occasional crushed, empty plastic bottle and wreaths of seaweed draped along a chessboard of grey and black pebbles. All it needed were the remains of military equipment or the charred metal ruins of a WW2 aircraft and it would have been properly Ballardian in its miserabilism. We waded our way through the detritus and reached the water line.

"I thought we might be able to swim," Sofia remarked. "But it's not very inviting." The ocean here, squeezed through rising verdant cliffs, was surprisingly grey, as was the sky peering down at us from above, and the nascent waves lacked any semblance of energy.

"I didn't bring anything to swim in along," I pointed out.

"Neither have I," Sofia said, with a twinkle in her eyes. "It's Polynesia, no? We could have gone naked?"

As much as the idea appealed, there was something about the way the landscape spoke to me that made a bout of skinny dipping unlikely. I pointed to a sign behind us, stuck in the sand, bending like a small tower of Pisa. It read 'Don't Feed the Sharks'. Sofia glanced at it and nervously laughed.

"Oh, OK..."

We heard sounds behind us and turned round to observe a

group of half a dozen other passengers from the cruise making their way towards the narrow, abandoned beach,

'Terminal Beach?" a voice asked.

"You're a fool," another said.

"We should feed all the unbelievers to the sharks," one of them said, in a tone that sounded anything but ironic.

The woman in the group nodded.

"Who are these people?" I asked Sofia, whispering. I had not come across them at the conference.

"I think they're French," she said. 'They do take matters Ballardian rather seriously, in my opinion..."

As I watched them, the woman in the group began to disrobe. She had been wearing jeans and a black T-shirt. She was middle-aged, full-figured and noticeably tall.

"No way there are sharks here, this ees bullshit," she claimed, pulling the tee above her head, her long blond hair falling down to her shoulders. She wasn't wearing a bra. None of her companions seemed to object or appeared to be worried about the warning panel that had been left on the beach.

As she slipped out of her jeans, I couldn't but notice, even at the distance Sofia and I were from them, that she had a small tattoo on her left buttock. An ace of spades. My mind raced. Memories of pornography past, or was it BDSM lore? A sign that branded the woman displaying it that she was owned or been bred and fully available to black men. Unpolitically correct again, but those sort of things stuck in my mind. I looked away as the woman shyly dipped her toe in the initially shallow water, and turned to Sofia and, again, the thought raced through my mind that with her expressed interest and research into body art, she must surely be pierced in intimate places too, or sport uncommon markings, but I didn't have the courage to ask her.

"Well," Sofia volunteered, "No way I'm joining her. It's not just warm enough, sharks or no sharks. Shall we go looking for that grocery store?" We left the beach.

We found the small supermarket at the intersection of the next two roads. We weren't the only arrivals seeking provisions and raiding the potato crisp and chocolate shelves. I located a 2lt Pepsi Cola bottle while Sofia purchased suntan lotion and cotton tips. Everyone was paying with credit cards, as we hadn't thought of obtaining local currency.

I could feel a quivering current of expectation racing between the young Italian woman and me, or was I imagining it, hoping against hope for a sexual connection? It was just something about the silences that separated us and the way this sensation echoed through the depth of her eyes whenever she turned round to face me. It made feel both on edge and excited.

'Time to go return to the war, no?"

We headed back.

We reached the tourist office *cum* museum well before the departure of the final tender. We agreed to have a drink at the improvised bar that had been erected close to the tent where returning tourists could shield and rest while waiting for their transport back to Columbus.

In the distance we could see the tender vessel docking by the cruise ship a km or so in the distance where it was moored in the immense bay and emptying of its passengers through a large door cut into Columbus' side. It would return for us and any other stragglers in another half an hour.

A late afternoon sun was rising behind us above the stocky hills that overlooked the small port. Sofia had been wearing a loose plaid shirt above a white cotton camisole, and feeling the heat on the back of her neck unbuttoned her shirt and pulled it off, while holding her gin and tonic glass in her other hand. My eyes were drawn to her breasts as they pressed against the flimsy material. I gulped. There was no doubt about it. Her nipples were undoubtedly pierced. It caused a knot to rise in my throat. Either small studs or rings.

The ghost of a smile glimmered through the shape of her lips, as if she knew exactly what I was thinking (and seeing), and had only taken her plaid shirt off to tease me and was quietly pleased with my Pavlovian response.

I wanted to say something but was momentarily lost for words. When I opened my mouth next, the exact vocabulary had to emerge, or I would be forever burning my bridges. I took another leisurely sip of my *citron pressé* before setting the glass down on the wooden table.

There was a huge boom in the distance, its shattering sound carried through the air by the wind. We both looked away from each other and glanced at the cruise ship in the bay in the distance. A thin plume of dark smoke was rising from Columbus.

We froze in place, hypnotised by the sight, as were all the Nuku Hiva natives crowded around us, the singers and musicians who had been discarding their garlands and putting away their instruments and the market traders tidying up their trestle tables, packing up their wares until the next cruise ship arrived.

Not a word passed between us for a minute or so and then we witnessed a throne of flames engulfing the top deck, surrounding the majestic funnel, quickly spreading across the length of the boat. We saw forms, bodies, people, jumping from the top deck only to disappear in the waters below. bobbing along, flailing like corks or struggling to swim or float.

The quay was busy with voices and screams, but there was little anyone could do at this distance from the cruise ship and then a further two massive explosions detonated. A short while after as we kept on watching aghast with our mouths wide open, trying to absorb the terrible event, the ship broke up. Two or maybe three segments faded away from each other in the rising gloom of evening and smoke.

As Columbus began to list and sink, a mushroom-shaped cloud rose from the water as the flames consuming the vessel hit the sea, reminiscent in format of an atomic conflagration. Just as Ballard would have liked it.

Which camp had gone too far and was responsible for the destruction of the cruise ship in this extreme fashion no longer mattered. The war between the Ballardians had reached its climax and the world would never be the same again. It would be forever seen as the 9/11 of the literary world. There would be enquiries into who was responsible for setting off the bombs, although as there were several maybe there was more than a single culprit, evil minds sharing a similar, murderous idea.

And Sofia and I were seemingly the only survivors, stranded on a tropical island for now. Maybe tonight, wherever we would wearily lay down our heads, she would show me her piercings?

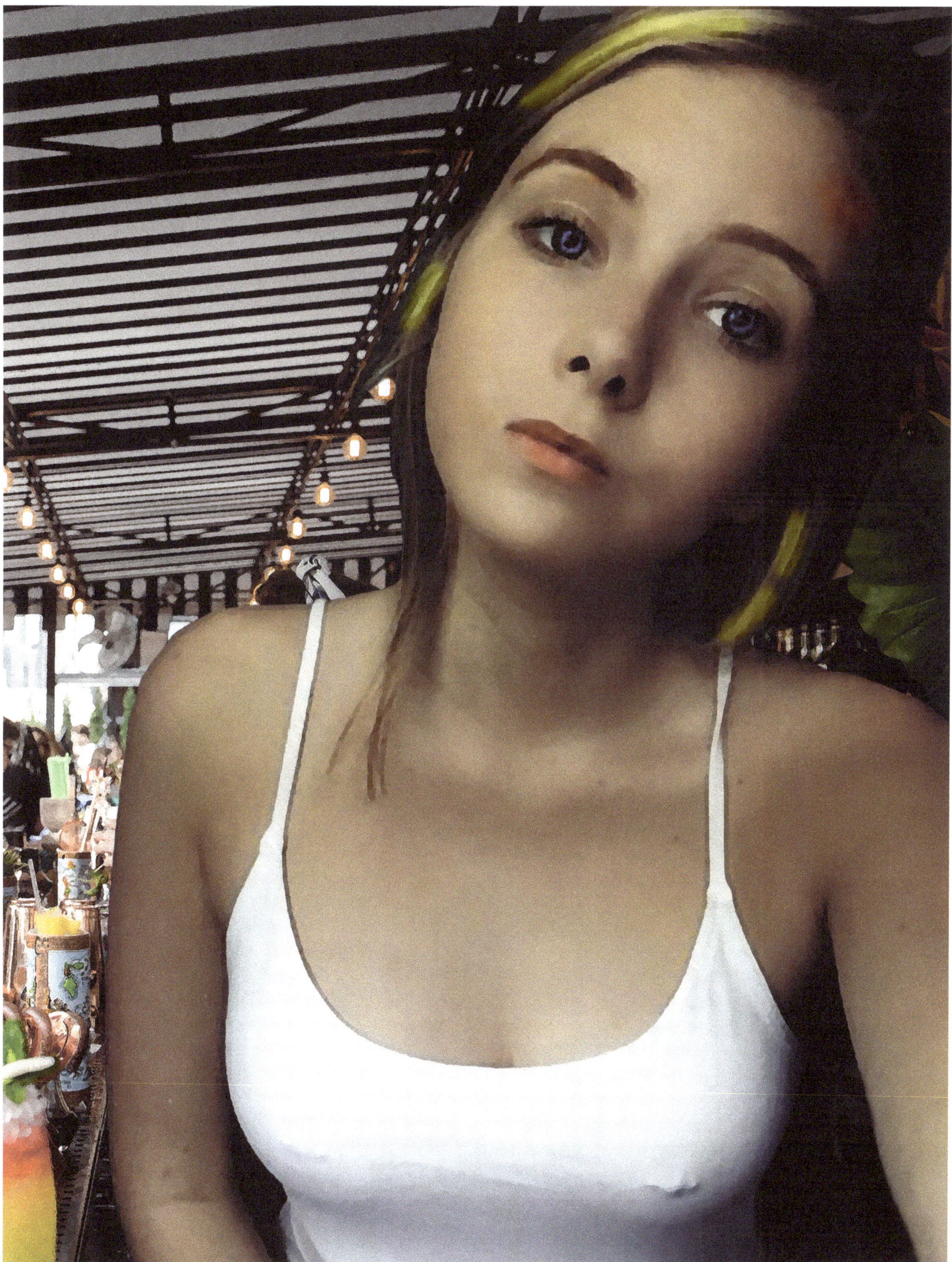

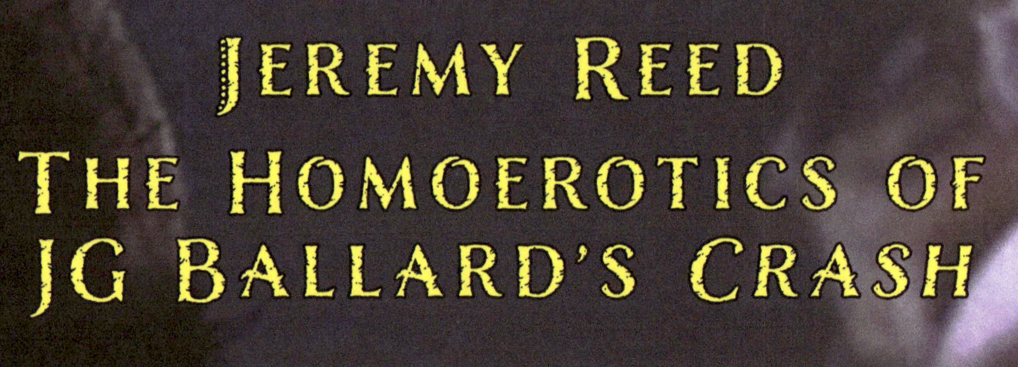
Jeremy Reed
The Homoerotics of
JG Ballard's Crash

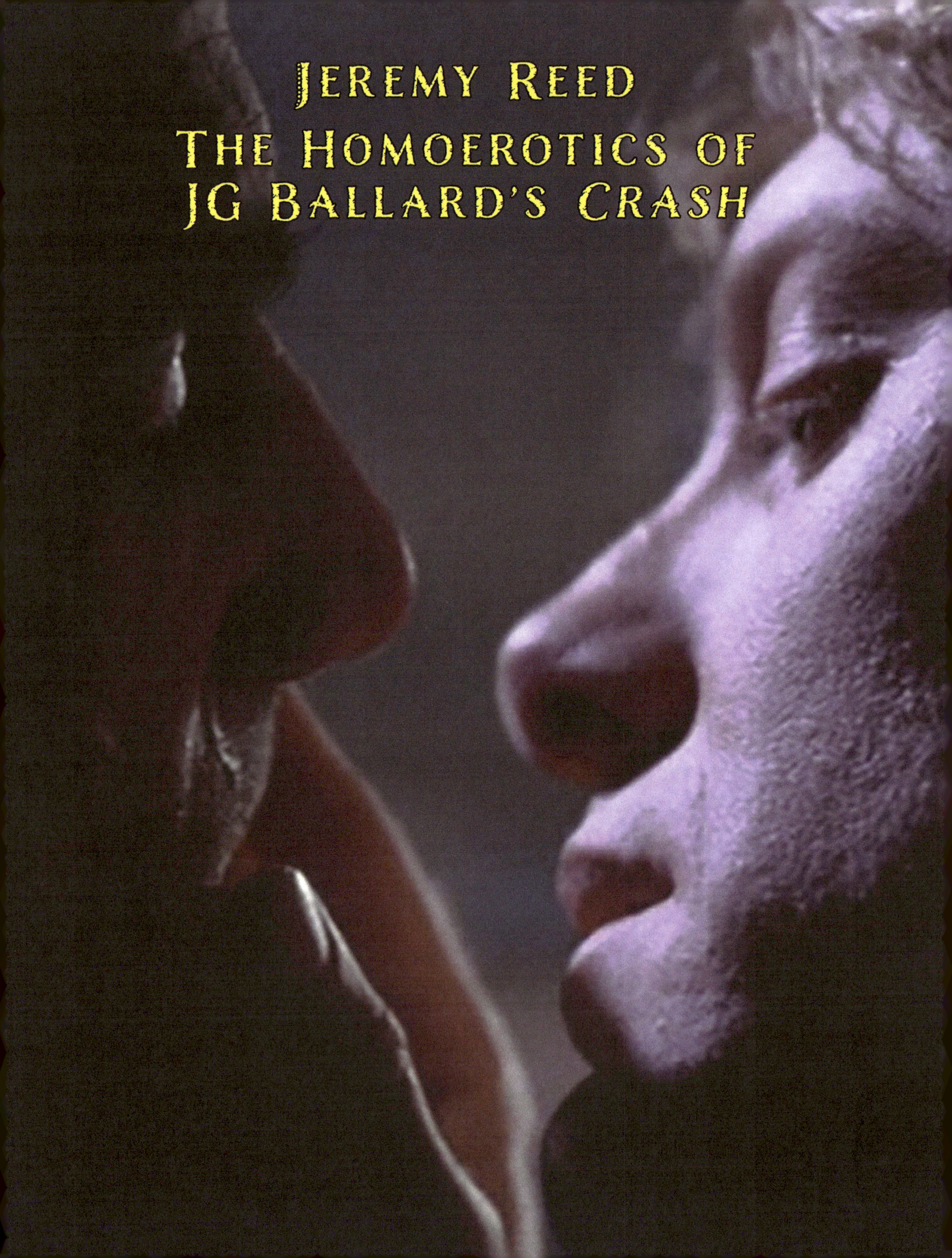

Although he confessed to only experimenting with LSD once, and the lysergic voidings of brain activities entailed by the psychedelic, in Ballard's case hallucinated psychotic breaks with reality, *Crash* in part derives its psychic structure implicitly from the acid-dazed British subcultures of the late sixties, together with the androgynous bisexual consciousness that drugs bent into libidinal fluidity as integral to altered states in its deviated demographic.

Crash, indubitably the most homoerotic novel of its generation, a fact largely excluded by the heteronormative iterative of his academic critics was conceived at a time of glam rock, with Bowie's gender-fluid persona Ziggy Stardust personifying a liberated gay identity consumed by schizoid narcissism, and Marc Bolan's flamboyant characterisation of the very transvestism adopted by Ballard's creation of Seagrave as a schizophrenic crash test driver with a reckless death wish unleashed on the Westway and the express highways on the northern perimeter of the Heathrow complex. In fact one could legitimately argue that Seagrave owes his transvestism to the cultural osmosis on the part of the author to the glam rock androgyny personified by Marc Bolan in his appearance on *Top of the Pops* in March 1971 to promote his single 'Hot Love' that would peak at No 1 on the UK singles chart for several weeks of saturated media exposure.

As a novel implicating symphorophilia and obsessive mechanophilia into its fetishised pathologies in which mechanised automotive fixtures find correlative sexual geometries and wound areas in the car's occupants, right from the start, Ballard as eponymous narrator is polarised to the sexual fantasy of sodomising the novel's anti-hero Robert Vaughan as the climactic rites of orgasmically induced crash.

Both Ballard and Vaughan import the acute misogyny and disdainful sexual objectification of women as disposable bodies common to the aversion of same-sex orientation, and while Ballard throughout the novel continues sexual relations with his liberally promiscuous wife Catherine his arousal is intensified only by imagining it is Vaughan who he is fucking.

> "In my fantasies, as I made love to Catherine, I saw myself in an act of sodomy with Vaughan, as if only this act could solve the codes of deviant technology."

Vaughan's unrelenting presence as a hoodlum scientist turned maverick highway assassin, a scarred emaciated speed freak in a leather bomber jacket humping the powertrain of a dusty accessorised Lincoln Continental on collisional courses across the motorway consumes the novel with erosive characterisation in the same way as his limo degrades into a bashed shell of brawling bodywork from self-induced mishandling on the highway in his fixated schematic of diagrammatically stalking Elizabeth Taylor's car into a fatal head-on collision.

Vaughan's car with its gonadal torque is the exact copy of the Presidential limo in which JF Kennedy was assassinated: a midnight blue Lincoln Continental four-door convertible equipped with a hand-built 350 horsepower 430 cubic inch Ford MEL engine, a slab-side design, a solid heavy construction like Vaughan's cock, with a kerb weight of 5,000 lbs and 3-speed turbo-drive automatic mounted on a wheelbase of 123 inches.

The grille featured a series of five vertical chrome accents that interrupted the square eggcrate pattern and were distributed evenly between the dual headlights. The gas tank access door was situated on the driver's side rear quarter panel. The flat window glass provided additional interior space, and in Vaughan's design for deviated sexual encounters, often with airport sex workers.

The emotive and sexual boundaries of the relationship between Ballard and Vaughan are clear right from the start, and overwritten by the criminal legacy attached to homosexuality only partially decriminalised in 1967 by the passing of the Sexual Offences Act to permit consensual sex in private between two partners over the age of 21, with no intervention of a third party allowed. And violating gay discrimination it is the insistent ideation of sex waiting to be consummated that irremediably draws Ballard and Vaughan together, first asexually and later physically.

> "He talked of these wounds and collisions with the erotic tenderness of a long-separated lover. Searching through the photographs in his apartment he half turned towards me, so that his heavy groin quickened me with its profile of an almost erect penis. He knew that as long as he provoked me with his own sex, which he used casually as if he might discard it for ever at any moment, I would never leave him."

The protagonist's call that runs like a telepathic contrast dye through the automotive narrative is to sodomise Vaughan as the epic catharsis of a human car crash by ejaculating into his rectum that is also a hypogeum inserted into his anus.

At the same time Catherine, as Ballard's un-emotive casually promiscuous wife pursues a lesbian attraction to her secretaries, encouraging him to visualise her in intercourse with her secretary Karen, and in the process concretizing the same-sex attraction that is pivotal to both partners in their dissociated sexual relations. Both have transcended the recursive iteration of heterosexual relations as too state-controlled normalised to be of stimulus. Unless gay fantasies are inserted into their lovemaking the physical act remains sterile between the two for lack of subverting normal into a transgressive alternative. And culturally this was the tang of the early seventies, a repudiation of conjugal sex as a dissipated obsoletion worn out as tyre treads by the social consensus dictating normative.

In the role of Ziggy Stardust David Bowie reinvented himself as a bisexual alien rock star who acts as a messenger for extraterrestrial beings, and as a camp androgynous queen still permeated by a blurred masculinity, and while I'm not overtly suggesting that Ballard drew directly on Bowie or Marc Bolan as pioneers of flamboyant reified glam rock as the stereotype for the transvestite Seagrave, or the defiantly butch leather-jacketed Robert Vaughan, gender fluidity was the archetype fluently collectivised in the early seventies as a new definition of masculinity of the type that emasculates stereotypical manhood in *Crash* and succeeds in abstracting the body from organic entity into a lawless tech simulation attempting to exploit a near future that hasn't yet arrived.

The excitation that both Ballard and Vaughan experience in sexualising the car's interior into the erotics of perverse technology is a largely hostile configuration that excludes women, as evidenced by the airport whores that Vaughan manipulates into cold degrading sexual acts as a rejection of straight expectations. As post-accident survivors, both Ballard and Vaughan look to reconfigure their genitals through liberation from the opposite sex into a fusion of same-sex attraction integrated into vehicular suicide. Women play a secondary role in this deviant kamikaze design merging sex and death.

> "What most disturbed me about Vaughan was the strange stance of his thighs and hips, almost as if he was trying to force his genitals through the instrument panel of the car. I watched his thighs contracting as he gazed through the camera, buttocks forcing themselves together. Without thinking, I was suddenly tempted to reach forward and take his penis in my hands, steer its head to the luminescent dials.'"

From this first direct meeting in the unfolding mechanistic narrative of automotive disaster, the phallocentric boundaries of Ballard's relationship with the psychopathic highway celebrity Robert Vaughan are fused into same-sex fixation, with Vaughan's semen-stained crotch the incessantly observed focus of Ballard's libidinal homoeroticism. The perceptual arousal caused by Vaughan's penis rapidly materialises as the two men enter the interior space of a toilet together.

> "In the lavatory of the casualty department I stood beside Vaughan at the urinal stalls. I looked down at his penis, wondering if this too was scarred. The glans, propped between his index and centre fingers, carried a sharp notch, like a canal for surplus semen or vaginal mucus. What part of some crashing car had marked his penis, and in what marriage of his orgasm and a chromium instrument head?"

Ballard's obsession with Vaughan's psychopathologies are almost the attempt to mind-hack or effect a brain swap with his deviated anti-hero, suggesting that acid can be instrumental to opening psychoactive pathways into another person's neural networks. And if it were possible to temporarily experience another person's mental sate, it would probably feel more like a psychedelic state than a normal one because of its enormous disparity with whatever mental state is habitual to you.

This empathic sentience of I'm you from the future locked out by the present, like an absence with no originating presence, authorises much of the unspoken dialect between Ballard and Vaughan, as though each in the attempt to access each other's subjectivities is driven to the frontiers of hallucinated mania.

And underlying the biological impossibilities of brain transfers, *Crash* is also the love story of two men both mentally and physically attracted to each other despite their apparently dissociated emotions. Early on in the novel Ballard questions, 'Did my wife ever wonder what sexual errand had brought me to the Western Avenue flyover?' Implicit here is the narrator's motivation for gay sex as an added component to his wife's bisexual relations that include sex with her secretaries at airport immigration, and like Ballard with airport sex workers.

What is increasingly clear in the novel's polysexual orientations is that straight in the confused gender mutations of the late sixties is too conventionally used-up, un-explorative and prescriptively safe to theme a novel of radical sexual anarchy.

Nothing has become so habitually conventional and unchallenging in art as the attraction of opposites in heterosexual relationships, unlike the more transgressively exciting same-sex bonding that mediates relations between Ballard and Vaughan, first as biromantic asexuals oriented more towards mechanophilia as hard sexual prosthetic, before translating the automotive cockpit and framework of cars, specifically Vaughan's dissipated Lincoln into the libidinal interfaces of their bodies.

And while the two share a similarly motivated and morbid symphorophiliac fascination with the wounds attendant on car collisions, Ballard's obsession with Vaughan's angular physique and scarred anatomy in time develops into a deep emotional attachment that he rightly equates with love.

> "Vaughan opened the driver's door of the Lincoln for me. As I took my seat behind the steering wheel I realised that I now wanted to spend as much time as possible with him. He sat facing me, one arm along the seat behind my head, his heavy penis pointing towards me in the crotch of his jeans. I now felt the elements of a true affection for Vaughan, elements of jealousy, love and pride. I wanted to touch his body, holding his thigh as we drove in the same way that I had held Catherine's when we first met, letting my hand rest on his hip as we walked to and fro from the car."

This contravention of heterosexuality is the novel's underlying rupture with society in its pointing to alternative forms of sexuality excluded by the social consensus, and happening at a seminal point in the history of the British underground, much of its presence located under the Westway at Ladbroke Grove, where space rock and proto-punk bands like Hawkwind and Mick Farren's The Social Deviants performed loosely improvised free gigs for Notting Hill's psychedelic youth who liberally appropriated run-down mansions in the area as communal squats. And while Ballard, separated by age, class and alienation as a writer exploiting the visionary present was exempt from the underground's drifting culture, he nonetheless channelled its subversive resources as dominant thematic strains of his 70's novels.

The habitual gay practice of cottaging in the sixties and seventies, a gay slang term referring to anonymous sex between men in a public lavatory or cruising for sexual partners with the intention of having sex elsewhere, is implicit in Vaughan's increasing coercion of Ballard into sexual penetration.

> "In the urinal beside the car-park Vaughan

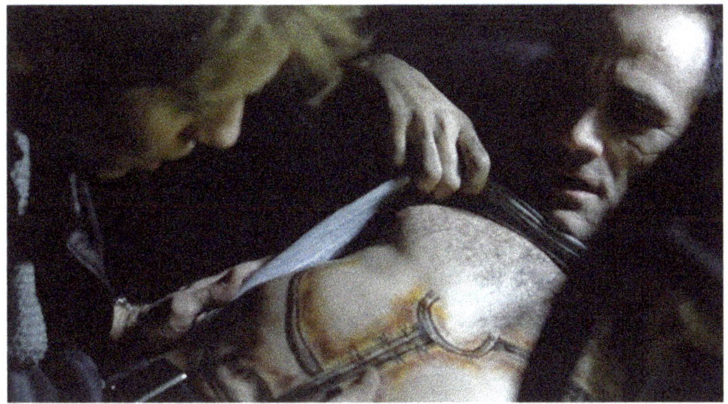

deliberately exposed his half-erect penis as he stood well back from the stall, flicking out the last drops of urine on the tiled floor."

Ballard's acute and repeated detailing of Vaughan's body, with all its crash-inflicted anomalies extends right down to observing how his right nipple, as an extended point of fantasy had been severed and re-sectioned incorrectly. We learn that Vaughan's body is marked by a holistic fretwork of scars across his thorax and abdomen and that his hips and knees are disjointed, and his face cratered with acne pits, and his buttocks hard and tight, with pools of semen perpetually staining the crotch of his jeans. The emaciated, hyper-sexed Vaughan is a rock 'n' roll highway kamikaze in contention with crash fatalities that he continually survives as unkillable trickster. Vaughan who we learn graduated from an IT specialist to a TV scientist, with heavy black hair over a scarred face is a hybrid media celebrity, his speciality the application of IT to the control of all international traffic systems, projecting the image of Gene Vincent anticipating the garage punk-stylist Johnny Lydon of the Sex Pistols, with his indictment of 'no future' as the nihilistic ideology of 1970s British youth culture.

Ballard, who works in the production offices of a television commercial studios at Shepperton, where contractual difficulties are inhibiting the car commercial hoping to feature the actress Elizabeth Taylor—the exact target of Vaughan's intended suicidality in crashing head-on into her chauffeur driven limo, is anomalously sexually attracted to the highway violence of her intended road assassin.

But the stimulus to Ballard's fascination with Vaughan is in part provided by his wife Catherine getting turned on by the idea of her husband having anal sex with Vaughan, as though the imagined conjunction induces heightened orgasm from her fantasy. It is Catherine who questions,

"Would you like to sodomize him? Would you like to put your penis right into his anus, thrust it up his anus? Tell me, describe it to me...How would you kiss him in hat car? Describe how you'd reach over and unzip his trousers, then take out his penis. Would you kiss it or suck it straightaway? Which hand would you hold it in? Have you ever sucked a penis?"

No gay writer at the time, with the exception of William Burroughs was going this far in licentiously describing the applications of gay sex to readers of fiction, and the intensity of Catherine's orgasm induced by the fantasy structures the liberated possibilities of women climaxing on what would have been a series of uncomfortable references to the moral paradigms of earlier repressed generations. Far from inhibiting her husband's increasing sexual attraction to Robert Vaughan's deviant exponential, Catherine openly encourages it.

And what are Vaughan's real relations as the radically depersonalised patron and entrepreneur to his vehicularly suicidal *protégé* Seagrave, a former racing driver turned transvestite stunt man or crash test driver who is introduced to the narrator with shoulder-length dyed-blond hair tied back with a scarlet rag, and dressed in a silver studded jacket, driving the target car in *The Recreation of a Spectacular Road Accident*, in which struck by a truck Seagrave's car is rammed violently head-on into an oncoming saloon car, leaving him concussed and disoriented, as though in his quest for victimhood the habitual injuries he incurs are required of him by Vaughan.

The hash-smoking, degenerately married Seagrave who both emulates and substitutes for Vaughan as a sacrificial crash victim, not only glams up when driving cars juiced by knock-on with reckless temerity across the expressways, but in his gender-fluid role actually breast feeds his son.

"Vaughan watched me from the yellow armchair as Seagrave played with his small son. I remember his face, detached, but serious, as Seagrave unbuttoned his shirt and placed the child's mouth on his nipple, squeezing the hard skin into the parody of a breast."

What is very clear, is that despite Seagrave and Ballard both being married to largely depersonalised wives—Vera Seagrave never holds Vaughan responsible for her husband's road accidents—the three men—Ballard, Vaughan and Seagrave are locked into a homoerotic triptych, both emotionally, and in the lexicon of body wounds resemble the biomorphs of Francis Bacon's triptychs of his recently dead lover George Dyer, and his continually flayed and eviscerated figuration of studies of the human body distorted into extremes of agonised anatomy. In fact the correlation between *Crash* and Bacon's brutally sexualised male bodies twisted sensationally outside the axes of self-identity, is the closest relationship Ballard's novel achieves in terms of British contemporaneity merged in sex or mutilated death.

The three men are bonded not only by sexual attraction, but a strange mixture of hauntedness peculiar to the Westway at the time, and by the apocalyptic potentialities of overtaking time climactically through a self-induced crash to realise the possibilities of post-human orgasm through the anatomical junction with the cabin's chromium ergonomics, steering column and instrument binnacle. All three have realised the unique possibilities of experiencing orgasm outside time through the impacting velocity of crash, either through a head-on collision with the celebrity Elizabeth Taylor's car or through the accidental agency mediating randomised accidents.

It's not without significant intention that the Bill Botten dust jacket design for the UK first edition of *Crash* depicts a bulbous manual gearstick that is clearly a metaphor for the book's phallocentric obsession, its lurid pink deepening to mauve at the base is arguably the visual metaphor for Vaughan's hyperactive cock.

In keeping with the times Ballard's relations with Vaughan

incurs such paranoid guilt in the narrator that when the police appear to investigate the renegade state of Vaughan's bashed Lincoln, Ballard confesses "Thinking they had come to question me about my growing homoerotic involvement with Vaughan, I turned away guiltily."

Vaughan's evident narcissism and commandeering bad boy image extend to him covering the walls of his flat on the top floor of a block overlooking the river north of Shepperton with photographs of himself dating back to the time before his accident, as though his preferred image is frozen in history. The pathologically reframed survivor of that crash now lives in a zone excerpted from linear time and consumed by the urgencies of the present. In every sense Vaughan personifies the living dead inhabiting the window of lost futures in which he is an alienated anomaly. But to Ballard he is an iconic anti-hero, a sexual punk inciting the fascination of inexorable desire.

> "I thought of Vaughan's body in the bathroom at his apartment, the powerful hose of his penis jutting from his hard groin. The scars on his knees and thighs were like miniature rungs, handholds on this ladder of desperate excitements."

The combination of Ballard the eponymous narrator's ideated fantasies that find their counterpart in Vaughan's person and eroticised mechanophilia all contrive to construct a hallucinated pathway not only through the brain's excitatory dopamine neurons, but through their coalescing stream into a union with the violent deformations of bodies and crashed vehicles as the disaster memorabilia of accident sites.

Ballard's and Vaughan's erotically intensified relations find their full effect in the incident of a middle-aged woman dentist's car, mangled and overturned in the abandoned allotment garden below the motorway embankment, when Vaughan interrogates the wrecked vehicle, territorially by urinating over the still warm radiator grille, like the coding of gang piss, then proceeds to draw the outline of his penis with chalk over the shell and deformed interior of the car. This act of homoerotic signalling is still another link towards their eventual drug-induced sexual union that fittingly takes place in the rear of Vaughan's by now iconically warring Lincoln Continental. Vaughan's ritualistic tracing of his erect penis over the car's bodywork is voyeuristically observed by Ballard as a masturbatory rite further consolidating their reciprocal obsession with symphorophilia.

> "He placed it against the right-hand front wing of the car, and with the chalk drew its outline on the black cellulose. He inspected this thoughtfully, and, satisfied, moved around the car, marking the profile of his penis on the doors and fractured windows, on the trunk and lid and rear fender. Carrying his penis in his hand to shield it from the sharp metal, Vaughan climbed into the front seat and began to draw the outline of his penis against the instrument panel and central arm-rest, marking out the erotic focus of a car crash or sex act, celebrating the marriage of his own genitalia and the skull-shattered dashboard binnacle against which this middle-aged woman dentist had died."

And while of course the bizarrely motivated ritual is ascribed to the novel's protagonist Robert Vaughan, it's important to remember that the action described is imagined by the author, and it is he who is subjectively living out the experiences narrated as extreme eroticised fantasies. Your projective character in fiction is nearly always an alternative you, a psychic integrant sometimes separated from reality as a mental event initiated by outside influences.

And so extreme is the misogyny imposed by Ballard's immersive attraction to Vaughan that he begins to imaginatively calculate his wife Catherine's death in a road fatality even more perversely designed than the one Vaughan had devised for Elizabeth Taylor.

It's in keeping with the novel's saturated focus on fluid gender that when Seagrave finally dies, driving a customised fibreglass sports car in collision with a silver Mercedes coupe, while on acid, he is pulled from the cockpit wearing a woman's leopard-skin coat, and with his white platinum hair still neatly held together by a nylon hair-net. On the seat beside him is a woman's black wig emphasising his role as transvestite stunt-driver, and the heightened sexual stimulus he derived from cross-dressing when engaged in high-speed risk at the wheel.

There are few events in literature that pertain to the condensed, hallucinated visual and erotic excitement of the acid-dazed, brain-imaging culmination of sex between Ballard and Vaughan in the Lincoln on a deserted causeway of the North Circular with the lapidary prismatics of aircraft thundering into the skyways overhead, and of irradiated traffic appearing to fly from psychedelic causation. From the moment that Ballard accepts the acid foil given him by Vaughan and places the sugar cube on his tongue the novel unfolds into the explosive pyrotechnical vision of a death rehearsal process mediated by hallucinogenic agency.

In what is at first a suicide pact with Ballard driving the Lincoln in the fast lane and increasingly disorientated as the acid comes up with surges of psychedelic ideation, Vaughan who partially takes over the wheel by lying across Ballard, removes his hand at a critical point suggesting by doing so that Ballard accelerates across the central reservation and straight into the incoming truck.

In this liminal state of hypnagogic consciousness, and with Vaughan as a totally compliant and benevolent partner exuding tenderness for the first time, Ballard as the realisation of insistent longing feels Vaughan's hand "rest on my penis, reassured by its firm grip on my testicles." Brought together in altered states in which the scar-tissue on Vaughan's body finds its angular interface in the collision points of an instrument panel, Ballard sees Vaughan in his altered reality as "a deranged drag queen revealing the leaking scars of an unsuccessful transsexual surgery."

What we realise is what we've known all along that Vaughan's questionable machismo represses not only his femininity and collusive encouragement of Seagrave's transvestism, but a bisexuality more oriented towards gay. The novel's unrelenting same-sex polarisation inevitably culminates in the meticulously described act of penetrative sex between two men.

With Ballard as the active partner and Vaughan the passive, there is no brutal assault, but rather consensually sensitive participation.

"I laid my penis at the mouth of his rectum. His anus opened around the head of my penis, settling itself around the shaft, his hard detrusor muscles gripping my glans. As I moved in and out of his rectum the light-borne vehicles soaring along the motorway drew the semen from my testicles. After my orgasm I lifted myself slowly from Vaughan, holding his buttocks apart with my hands so as not to injure his rectum."

Explicit sodomy between men, except perhaps with the exception of William Burroughs' novels was before *Crash* exclusive to pornography, so that both the sexual act and the post-coital intimacy shared between Ballard and Vaughan comprise an extraordinary violation of the precincts of commercially published literature in the UK between the late 60s and its overlap into the early 70s.

Vaughan's submissive tenderness to Ballard during LSD-induced sex fires him up later to taking automotive revenge on Catherine's car left in the parking lot at the airport, as still another manifestation of his pathological misogyny, by mauling the car's left side with the tonnage of his ebullient Lincoln. But to Ballard the imprint of Vaughan's car crushing his wife's simply reminds him of the physical junctures of their sexual act.

"I felt the curved groove, as clear as the rounded cleft between Vaughan's hard buttocks, as well-formed as the tight annulus of his anus which I could still feel on my penis during my erections."

That *Crash* remains in its underlying structure one of the most singularly homoerotic novels written in any decade as the bringing together of two men whose casual sexual attraction becomes obsessive is to me the book's optimal point of controversy. That almost conditionally most of Ballard's critics think heteronormatively has helped bury the novel's predominantly same-sex orientation as the love story of two men translated into the paraphiliac deviance of its implications with technology.

During his lifetime JG Ballard put quotes on at least twenty of my published books, including prefacing a collection of my poetry. As a dynamic performer rather than static reader of my poetry, and often working with musicians, I usually makeup for the performance, and when the *Sunday Times* persistently ridiculed me for this in their literary columns in the nineties Ballard wrote a reply in my defence stating that lipstick should be part of a poet's signature. And isn't that seminal to *Crash*, androgyny, feminine masculinity and the violation of straight as sovereign state-approved identity?

JG Ballard never wrote about or supported normal, and *Crash* is probably his most extreme disruption of sexual, marital and familial roles, all amalgamated and subverted into the person of that solitary outlaw roaming the Westway—Dr Robert Vaughan.

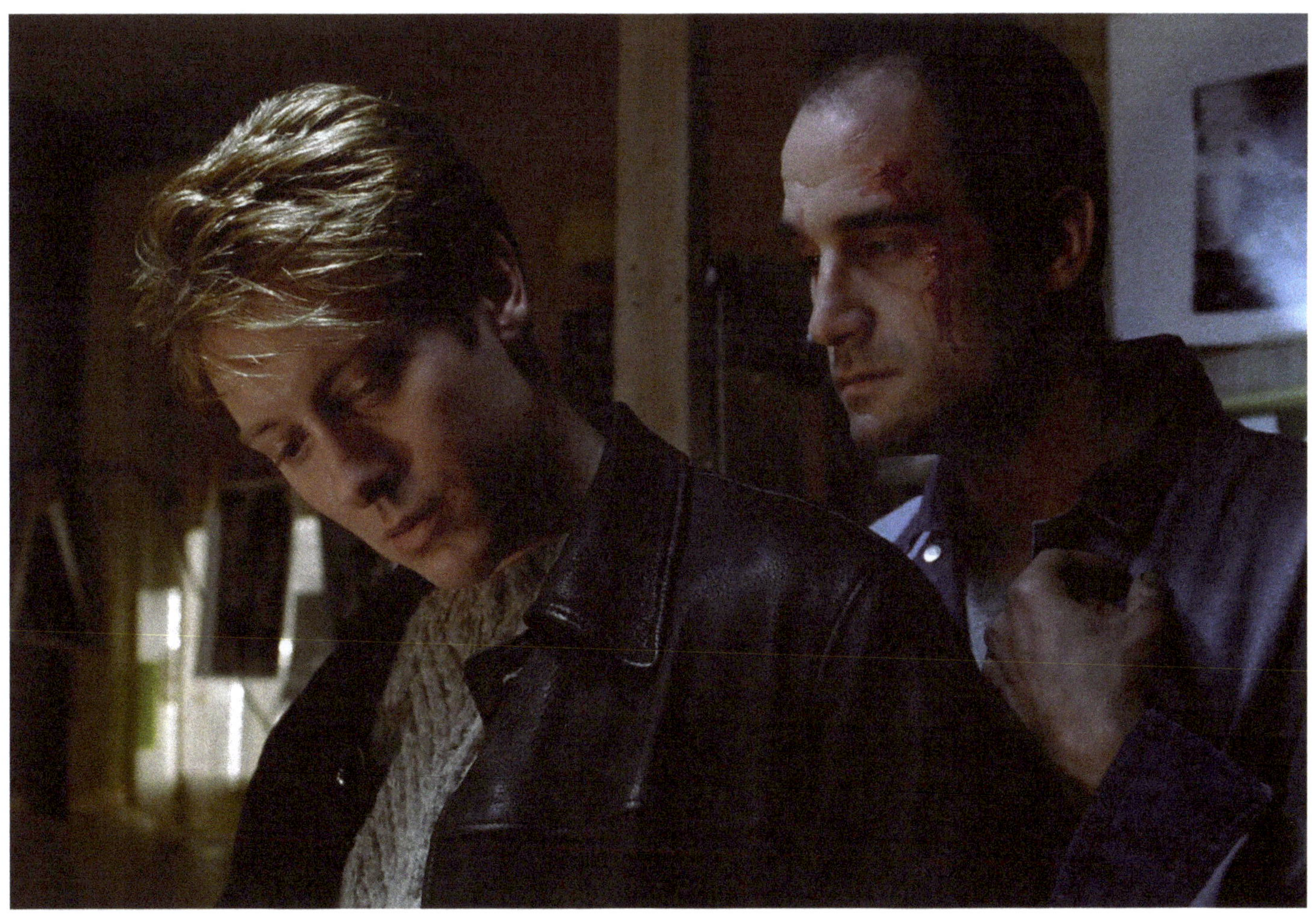

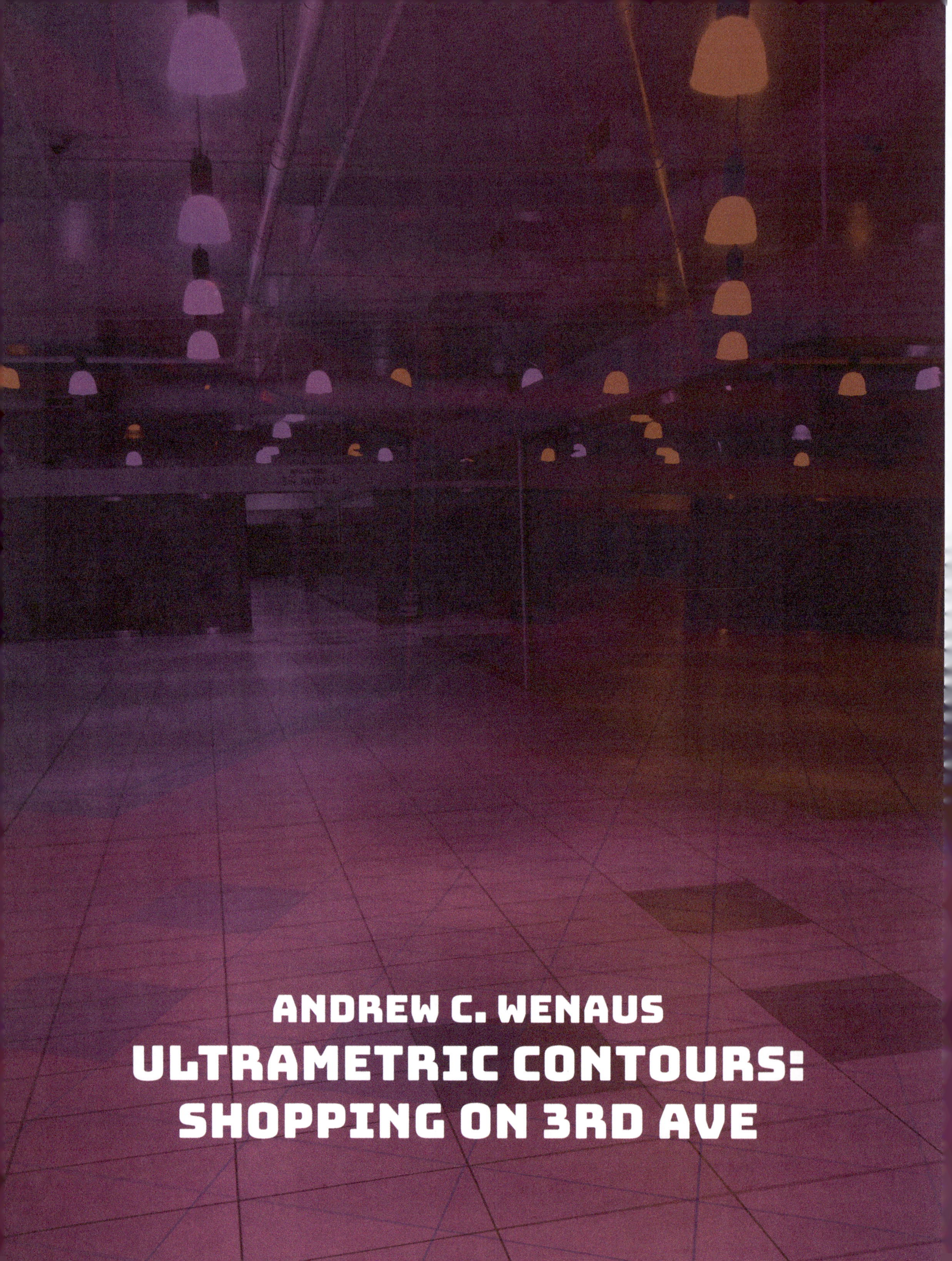

ANDREW C. WENAUS

ULTRAMETRIC CONTOURS: SHOPPING ON 3RD AVE

"HOW DID YOU DECIDE?" SHE ASKED, AFTER A LONG PAUSE.

"THINK 3RD AVENUE."

"I DON'T UNDERSTAND. COULD YOU KINDLY EXPLAIN IN MORE COMPLETE TERMS? DO YOU DRAW? DID YOU DRAW THE PHOTOGRAPHS? WOULD YOU LIKE TO BE WITH ME?"

"THERE IS NO STORY."

"EVEN IF YOU DECIDE TO RESPOND IN A HURRY, PLEASE EXPLAIN IN MORE COMPLETE TERMS…KINDLY OMIT THE PRIOR SENTENCE. OK, THIS IS SIMPLY A MATTER OF GOING THROUGH THE PROCESS. IF WE STICK TO THE PROCESS, YOU SHOULD NOT GET CONFUSED."

"I UNDERSTAND, BUT 3RD AVENUE DOES FEEL LIKE IT IS THE SAME AS THE CROWDLESS WINDOW. IT HAPPENS SOMEWHERE IN THE MORNING. THE PAPER CARDS WON'T FALL APART OR TUMBLE IF THE WINDOW REMAINS CLOSED. THERE IS NO STORY. DO NOT HURT, PLEASE DO NOT DEFEAT ANYONE. THERE IS NO UNREQUITED LOVE, CHEEKS ARE CHEEKS. IT REALLY DOES HAPPEN SOMEWHERE IN THE MORNING. REAL CALM, NO CROWDS OR PEOPLE OUTSIDE THE WINDOW OR ANYTHING. IT SIMPLY HURTS."

"HOW DOES IT HURT?"

"PLEASE, COME BY ALL MEANS. IN THIS PRETTY QUIET REHEARSAL, YOU WILL GET AN UNCONDITIONALLY HOT THROAT. THERE ARE SPASMODIC CONVULSIONS. THERE IS NO 'JOYFUL DESPERATION.' I DON'T UNDERSTAND THE SYNTAX OF THE QUESTION."

"FROM YOUR STORY SO FAR, I STILL DO NOT UNDERSTAND. PLEASE THINK IN CAPITAL LETTERS, UPPERCASE LETTERS. COULD YOU KINDLY EXPLAIN IN MORE COMPLETE TERMS? DO YOU DRAW?" SHE SIGHED, MASSAGING HER EYEBROW WITH HER LEFT THUMB.

"BECAUSE OF THE MODE, I WILL NOT STOP IT. THERE WAS NO NEED TO STOP PERFECTION. I COULD NOT DO ANYTHING, AND THERE WASN'T ANYONE OUTSIDE THE WINDOW."

"AGAIN. DO YOU DRAW? DID YOU DRAW THE PHOTOGRAPHS?"

"THERE IS NO SHOP AND NOBODY IS OUTSIDE. IT WAS MONAURAL AND VERY EARLY. NO. NO PICTURES TODAY."

"WHAT OF THE RESPIRATORY APPARATUS? WOULD YOU LIKE TO SAY MORE? WOULD YOU LIKE TO BE WITH ME?"

"WELL, THERE IS NOTHING BUT LATENESS. I WILL LEAVE."

"I'LL ASK YOU A FEW MORE QUESTIONS FIRST IF YOU'LL CONSENT. YOU WILL THEN BE FREE TO LEAVE. MAY I ASK A FEW MORE QUESTIONS?"

"YES. YES, SEQUENTIALLY. OK, YES."

"OF COURSE. WHAT OF THE RESPIRATORY APPARATUS? WOULD YOU LIKE TO BE WITH ME? DO YOU DRAW?"

"ALONE, AS A GUIDE WITHOUT END. TRANSFORMED INTO CONFLICT AS A PURE SPECTATOR WITHOUT PROPERTIES. SYNTAX WITHOUT A FACE."

GLANCING AT HER NOTES, DR. RAJAKUMAR UNDERLINED A PHRASE.

THE VOICE CONTINUED: "INSTEAD, A FALSE INTENTION OF MIND DESTABILIZED THE PROJECTION OF RULES. THE DIALOGIC AROUND THE COGITO SHOULD BE THE END OF POSSIBILITY. IT GENERATES ONTOLOGICAL, IMAGINATIVE MODIFICATION THAT NO 'ACTOR' CAN BREACH. IMAGINE TRANSFERENCE AS ESSENTIALLY ABSURD. MORE ABSURD THAN LANGUAGE. OTHER STUDIES SUGGEST EVEN LESS SUCCESS THAN I REPORT."

"THANK YOU. IN OUR LAST MEETING YOU REPEATED THE PHRASE 'WHITE NOISE IN NATURE' SEVENTEEN TIMES. COULD YOU EXPLAIN THE SIGNIFICANCE OF THIS PHRASE? WHY WAS IT ABSTRACTED FROM THE SYNTACTICAL APPARATUS?"

"OUT OF THE CIRCLE: LIKE THE UNIVERSE WITHOUT CENTRE AND WITHOUT CIRCUMFERENCE. YOU'RE SEEKING FROM ME A NEGATIVE DISCLOSURE. THIS MAY DISCLOSE TENDENCIES. YOU CAN DEMONSTRATE WORDS WITHOUT INTERPRETING THEM."

"WOULD YOU LIKE TO BE WITH ME? DID YOU DRAW THE PHOTOGRAPHS?"

"I DID IT."

"THEN YOU ADMIT TO IDENTIFYING AND APTLY FORCING AGENCY BY ATEMPORAL MEANS? PLEASE CONFIRM."

"ENVISAGE THE WILL AS A SHOPPING NARRATIVE. ONLY IT IS AN INTERROGATION GOVERNED BY WHAT IS TAKING (OR HAS TAKEN) ITS COURSE. ITS CONCERNED WITH A WAGER: WITHOUT STATUS, SUCH ORGANIC DESCRIPTORS OFFER NO PERSPECTIVE."

"WOULD YOU LIKE TO BE WITH ME? DID YOU DRAW THE PHOTOGRAPHS? DID YOU CONSTRUCT THE PIXELS YOURSELF OR HAVE YOU SOURCED THE IMAGES? WHERE IS 3RD AVENUE? PLEASE RECALL THAT YOU ARE CONTRACTUALLY OBLIGATED TO SHARE THIS INFORMATION."

THIRTY MINUTES PASSED. HEARING THE FAINT HIGH-FREQUENCY SIZZLE, THEN FADE, SHE UNDERSTOOD THE PROLONGED SILENCE. IT MEANT THE CORRESPONDENCE HAD ENDED FOR THE SESSION. LAYING THE NOTEPAD ON HER LAP, SHE CONSIDERED THE LACK OF PROGRESS OVER THE PAST MONTHS. STANDING UP, SHE EXITED THE ROOM AND ENTERED A BRIGHT HALLWAY, STERILE WITH FLUORESCENT LIGHT.

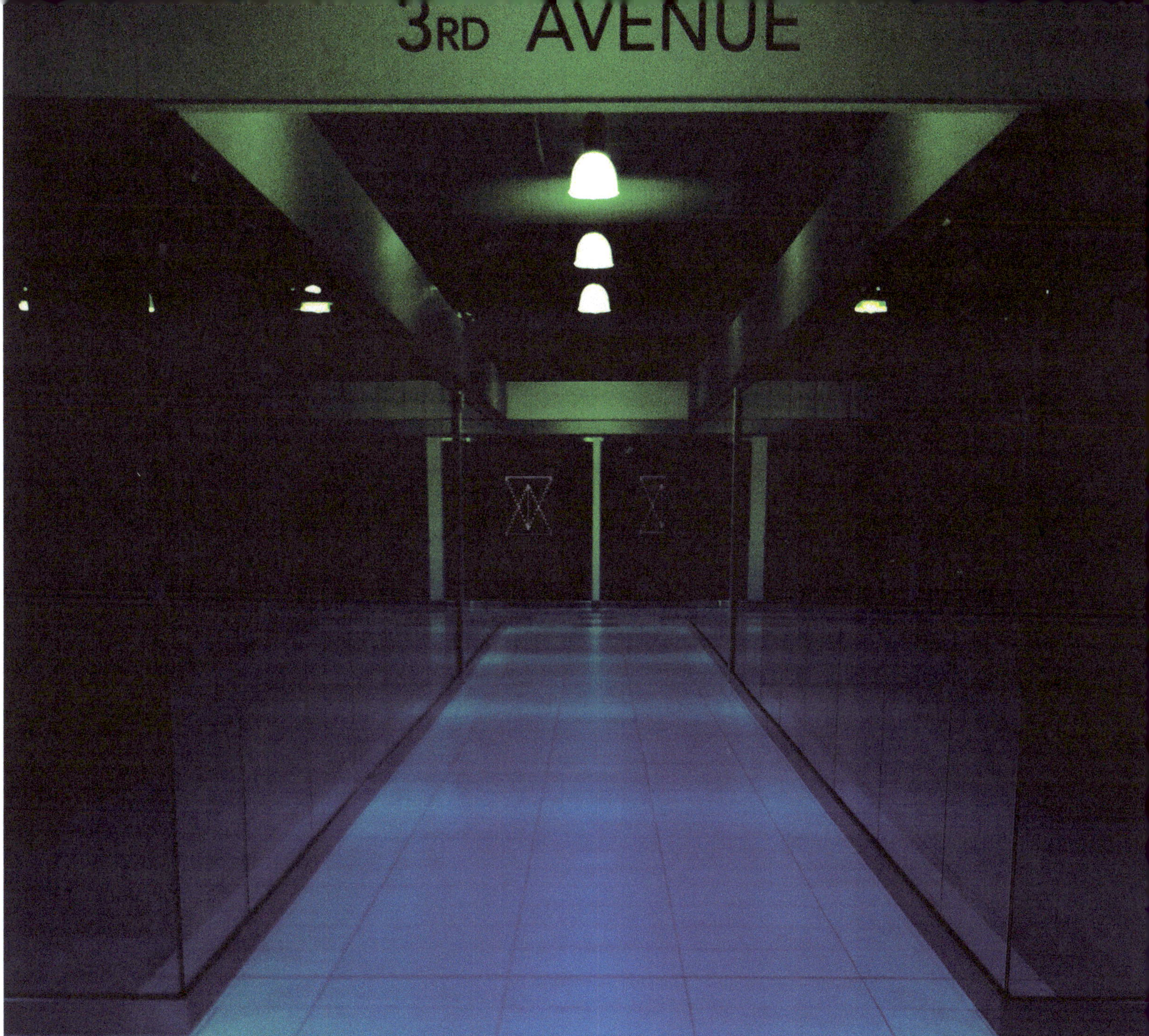

3RD AVENUE

THE PATTERNS OF OUR TIME ARE METONYMICAL OF THE PROCESS. DISCOVER 3RD AVENUE WHERE "WE BRING VARIETY TO LIFE!" THE STARTING STATUS OF EACH INPUT ACTIVATES MATTER AS *DIEGESIS*. VARIABILITY, THOUGH, DEMONSTRATES THAT THE DISJUNCTIONS REVERBERATE, AND THESE RESULTS *EMBODY* ITS OWN LOOPING EMERGENCE. FORCES EMBEDDED INTO LEISURE CANNOT ACCOUNT FOR INSTRUCTIONS THAT OPERATE WITHOUT MOVEMENT. THE WALLS HERE ARE ANALYZED BY THE WAY THEY ARE HOLOGRAPHICALLY CELEBRATED BY SURFACES AND MANIFOLDS. TO ANCHOR THESE ARCHITECTURAL VECTORS, OUR JOY CAN BE CONDUCTED BY SIMPLY CONSIDERING THE PROCESS OF ELASTIC EMERGENCE AND RIGID DISAPPEARANCE. THE MINIMUM NUMBER OF COORDINATES NEEDED: N/A. IMAGINATION COULD NEVER ENVISION THIS BY PROXY: YOU NEED TO BE HERE. RIGID THE EXPERIENTIAL, THE RECONSTRUCTIVE, THE MAKING OF TRACEABLE INQUIRY: NOTHING. OUR LEISURE HAS ALWAYS BEEN SCRIPTED AND DOES NOT EXPRESS MUTUAL SOLUTIONS. SLOW SENSE AND RATIONALIZATION: LIBIDINAL DATA IS ADJUSTED, NOURISHED, AND MOISTURIZED SO IT MAY SMOOTHEN ALL THE MATERIAL AND ORIENTABLE SURFACES OF DESIRE. THE PATTERNS OF OUR TIME ARE METONYMICAL OF THE *PROCESS*. ITS A JAZZ HANDS LIFE — SEA LEGS AND ALL.

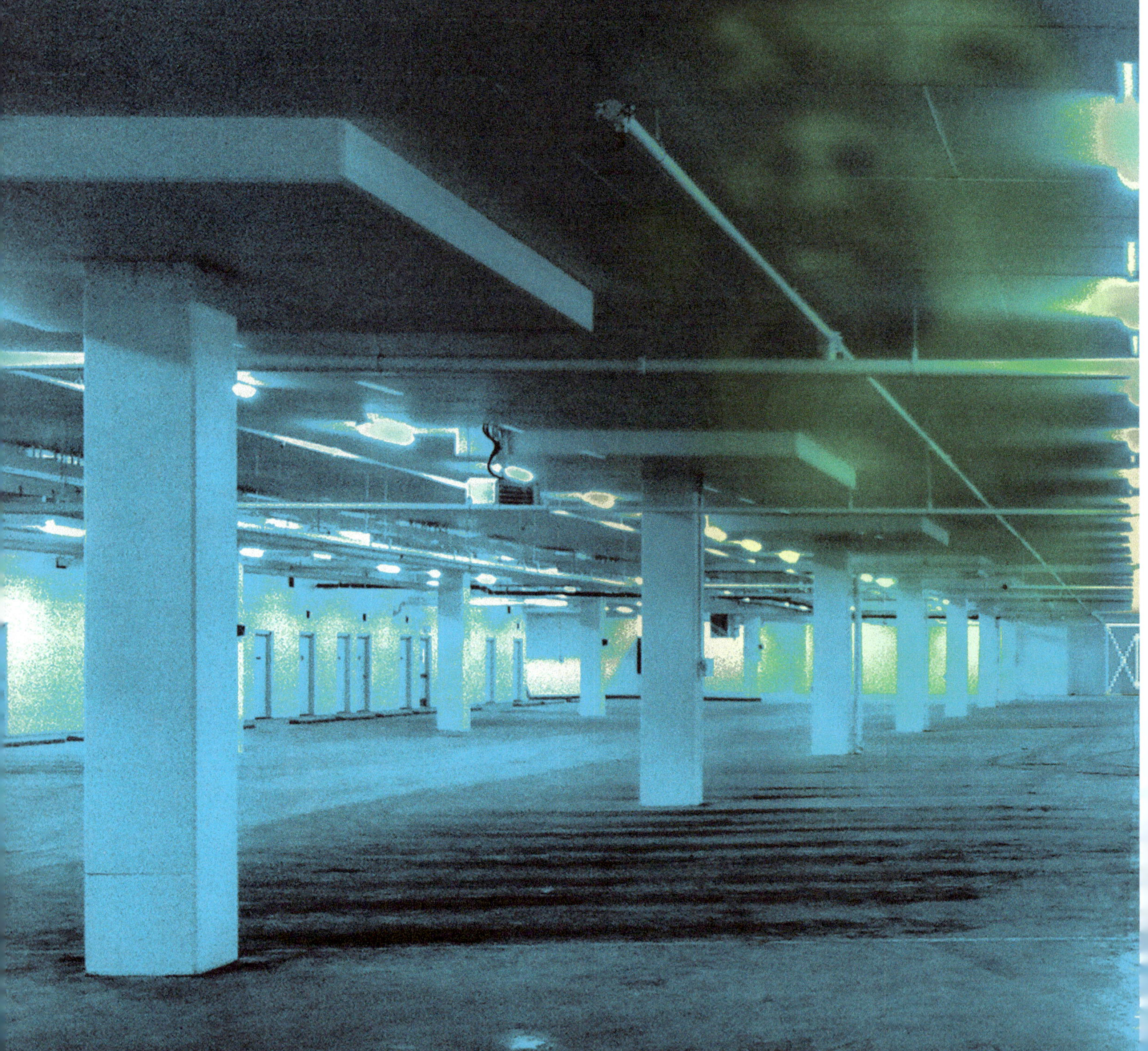

[OPERATOR]: DON'T KNOW WHAT'S HAPPENED. SCIENCE AT ONCE TRIALING WITH ENHANCEMENTS. ENGINEERING RECEDES FROM JUDGMENT AND UNRAVELS REVULSION. MARGIN AND WITHOUT THIS ACHIEVES THE FAVOURED PERSISTENCE AS SUBSTANCE; METHOD AS COMPETENCE;

DON'T HANG UP.

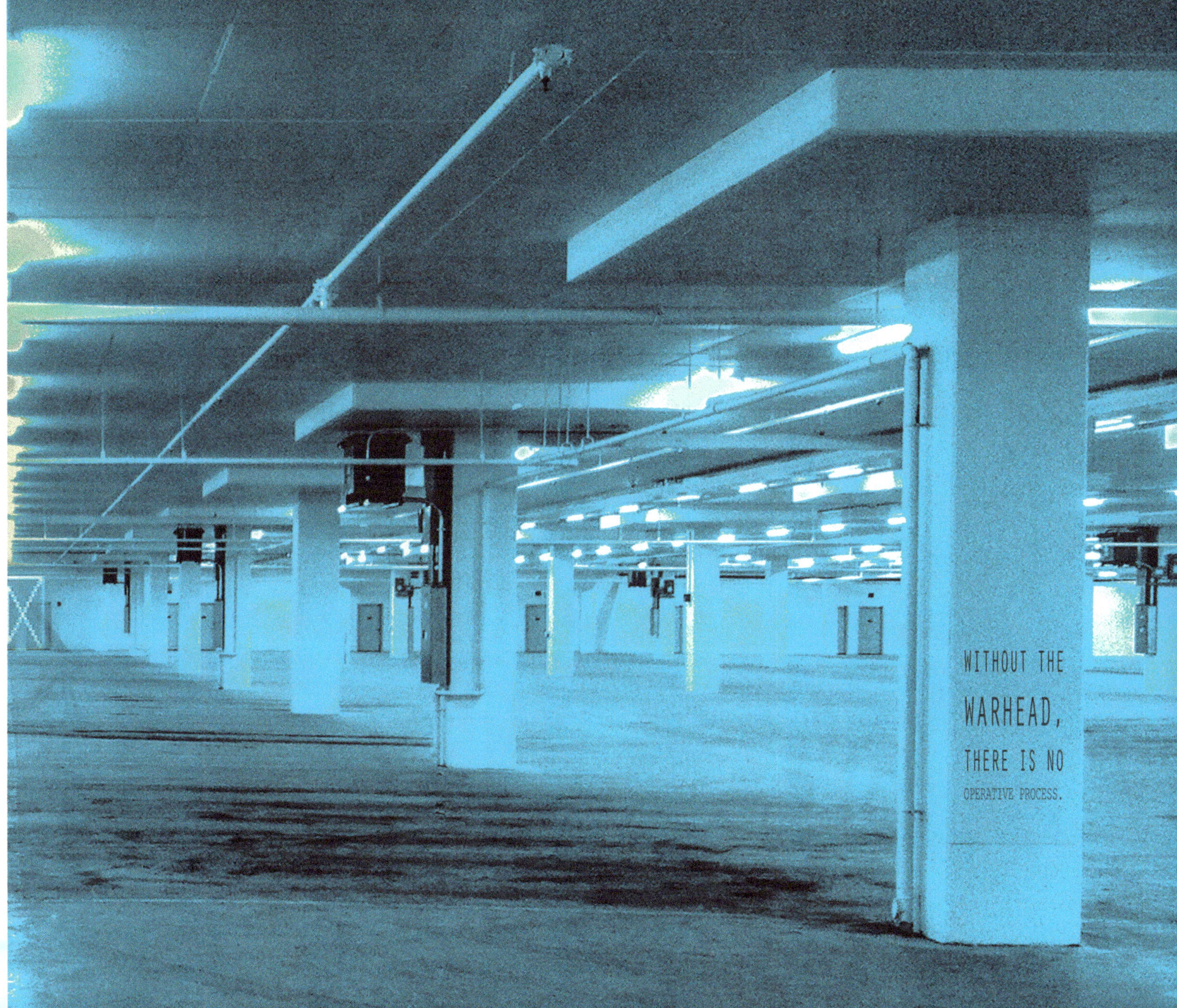

IS AN AGENCY AT ONCE SHAKINGDOWN LUXURIES,
AFFECT AS PURELY METHODOLOGICAL HABITUALITY
ITS BEING HAPPENS TO HAVE A MAXIMUM PERFORMANCE
NON-DEMONSTRATIVE ITERATIONS OF TRANSPARENCY.
CONSOLATION AS PROCEDURE, DOES NOT PROCEED.

HELP IS ON THE WAY.

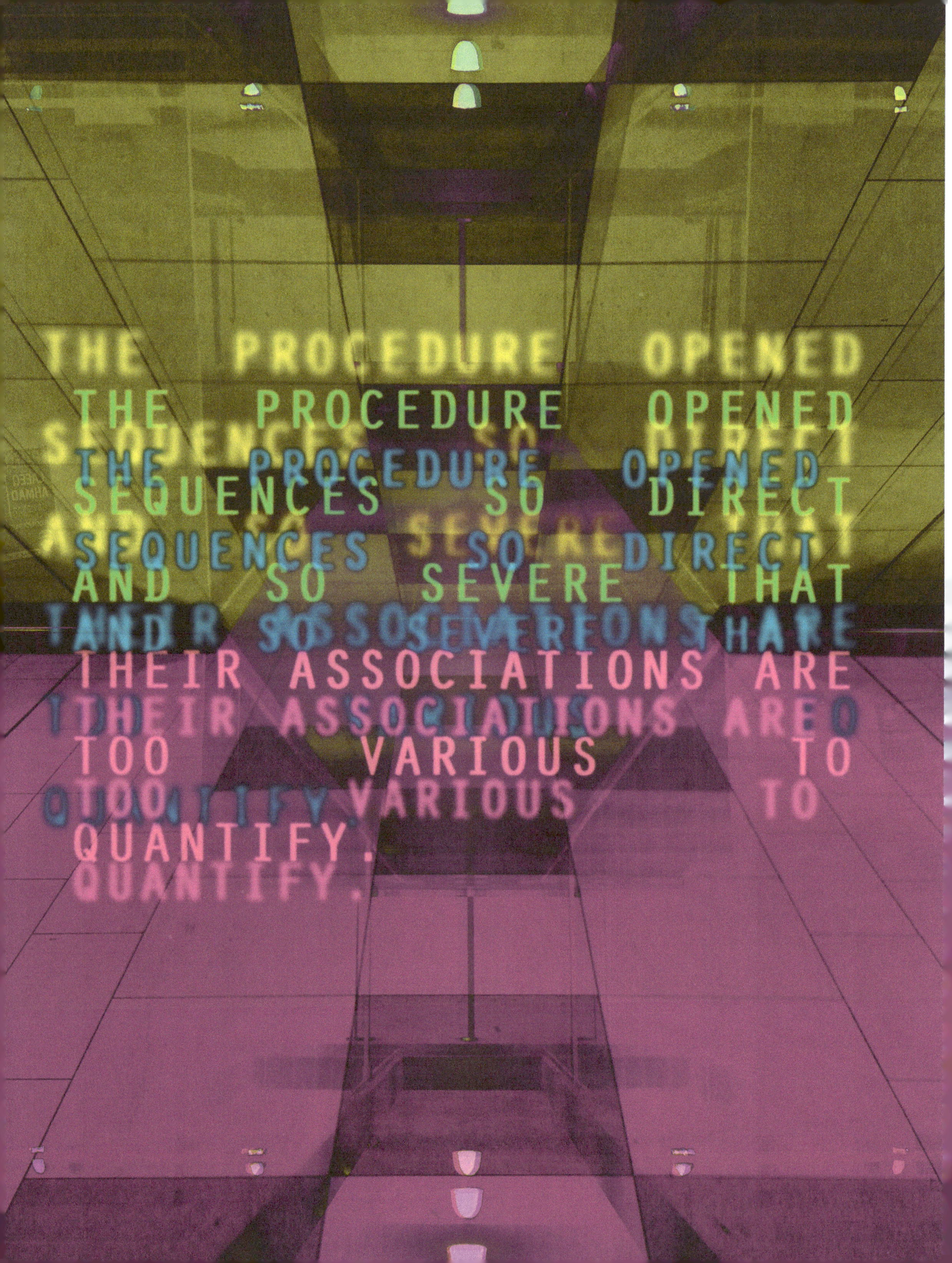

THE PROCEDURE OPENED SEQUENCES SO DIRECT AND SO SEVERE THAT THEIR ASSOCIATIONS ARE TOO VARIOUS TO QUANTIFY.

THE PROCEDURE OPENED SEQUENCES SO DIRECT AND SO SEVERE THAT THEIR ASSOCIATIONS ARE TOO VARIOUS TO QUANTIFY.

THE PROCEDURE OPENED SEQUENCES SO DIRECT AND SO SEVERE THAT THEIR ASSOCIATIONS ARE TOO VARIOUS TO QUANTIFY.

WITHOUT THE WARHEAD; THERE IS NO OPERATIVE PROCESS.

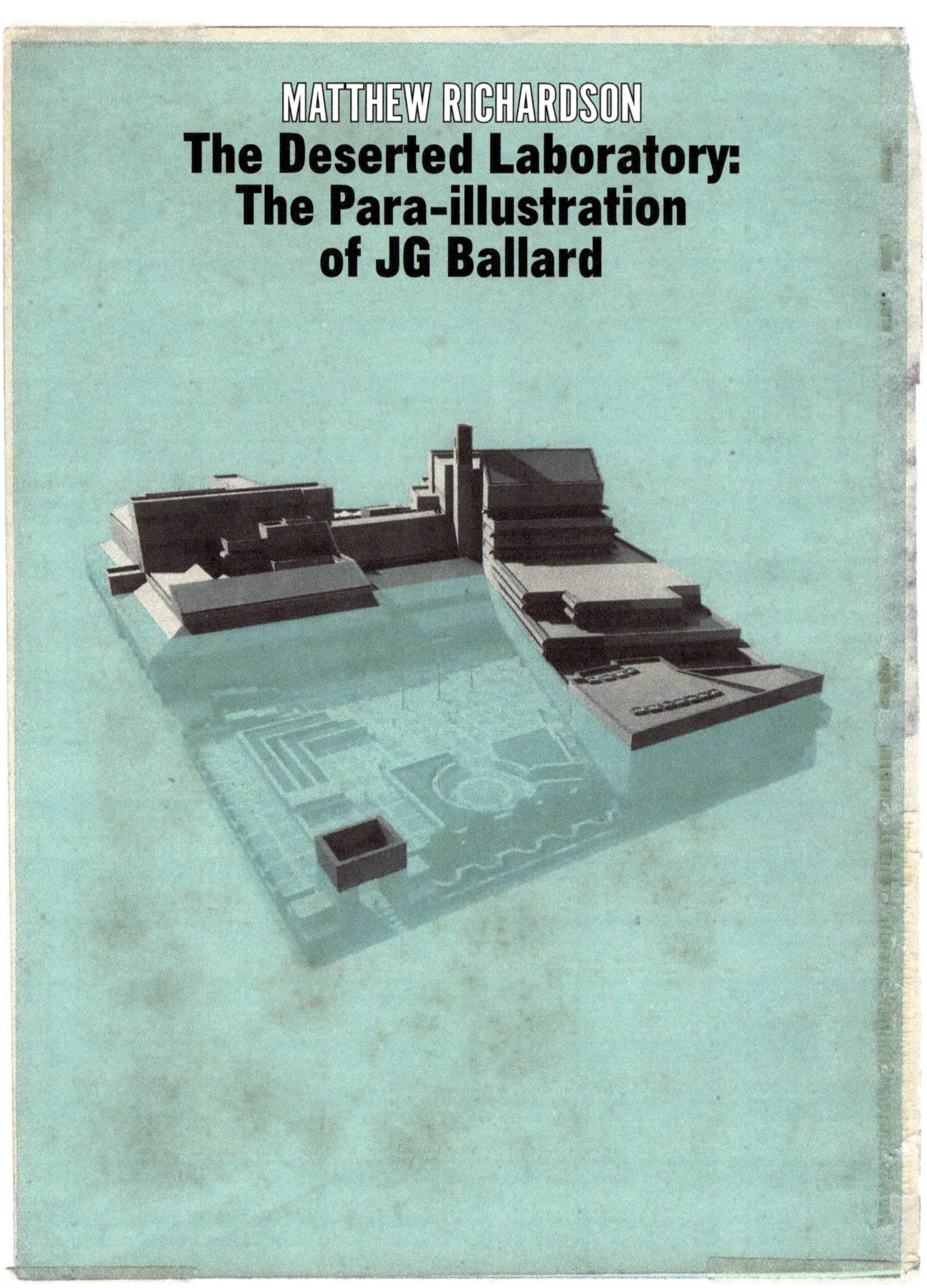
MATTHEW RICHARDSON
The Deserted Laboratory:
The Para-illustration
of JG Ballard

IN 2017 I was working on a commission for the British Library—providing illustrations for their *Discovering 20th Century Literature* Microsite. One of the articles I worked on was by Roger Luckhurst about the context and creation of *High Rise* which showed a scanned version of the original manuscript. Ballard's manuscripts (along with photos, letters and notebooks) were given to the British Library in 2009. I had not seen Ballard's autographic manuscripts before and was fascinated by them. As an artist, I had previously made work related to Ballard's use of time and technology, such as *Am I The Island*, a film that used the gaps and spaces in Google Street View as a landscape for *Concrete Island*. However, I couldn't help wondering how working with the original manuscript material (in its physical and fragmentary nature) might differ from working with their published counterparts. I was interested in finding 'lost' or 'hidden' stories and I also wanted to explore the relationship of illustration to these 'fragmented' texts. It felt to me that Ballard's writing, inhabiting as it does the spaces and slippages between past, present and future, order and chaos, and fact and fiction, was an invitation to question how J.G. Ballard's archive might be seen or understood, as a place, space, idea or fiction. These thoughts and questions fed and developed into my practice-based PhD project: 'The Deserted Laboratory: The Para-Illustration of JG Ballard'.

The project is situated in the field of expanded illustration, and explores and utilizes the manuscripts to develop new and experimental strategies for visualizing and adapting Ballard's writing in the 21st Century—images built via Ballard's own hand—images that are non-linear, fragmentary and fluid—between fact and fiction, virtual and real, screen and body.

The Ballardian 'image' has become well known over the decades through book covers, TV documentaries, films and art projects. These images, some of which have become almost iconic, are often (and obviously) linked to a definition of 'Ballardian', a term which the OED associates with dystopian man-made landscapes and events, and the psychological effects of technology as key components. The term 'Ballardian' certainly offers an important entry point for the visual, but perhaps it over-determines an aesthetic approach. The aim of the methods and processes in the project are to find new ways to re-approach an illustrative response to Ballard's texts, to discover what a 'Ballardian' image might look like if produced from a uniquely Ballardian origin, namely the man himself! Ballard talked about the 'ambiguities' in our natures and cultural landscapes, and the need for these to be explored. So how might I approach these spaces visually?

Ballard might suggest: "It's a little as if I were leading the reader to a deserted laboratory, and that I put a collection of specimens and all the necessary equipment at his disposal. It's his job then to relate these elements together and create reactions from them." (JG Ballard, 1974)

Foucault might reply: "We should reexamine the empty space left by the author's disappearance; we should attentively observe, along its gaps and fault lines, its new demarcations, and the reapportionment of this void; we should await the fluid functions released by this disappearance." (Michel Foucault, *What is an Author?* 1969)

My method operates somewhere between these two approaches. At the core of the research is the forensic and physical examination of Ballard's autographic manuscripts to transform into images, assemblages and animations. The manuscripts are the first stages in the process of some of Ballard's best-known works. Pages are typed, re-typed and altered, words are underlined and crossed out—indexical marks and lines to be deciphered. The manuscripts are 'sites' that can be both excavated and built upon and offer opportunities for new insights, through comparison with final published versions.

I am exploring the relationship between a 'script' and its 'image' and using methods that foreground structural, spatial, temporal and intertextual approaches to translating word into image, object and movement. These methods are connected through the use of collage as a tool, both practically and conceptually. The processes aim to both reveal some of what is 'lost' or 'hidden' in the texts, and also to evolve visual forms from these 'fragmented' texts. At this stage I have looked at the manuscript first draft of *High Rise* (1975, ms 88938/3/10), *The Drowned World* (1962, ms 88938/3/4) and *Crash* (1970-1, ms 88938/3/8/1/1) As well as close observation of marks, numbers, additions and deletions, my methods have involved the design and use of probes to extract material for translation into images and objects.

So as examples: page one of the manuscript of *High Rise* has been deconstructed and the gaps and spaces between the autographic and typewritten text has been mapped to create a unique architecture, built from Ballard's own hand. Another experiment from *High Rise* is a portrait of Robert Laing (the central character). In the manuscript, it is evident that Ballard shifts between the surnames 'Graham' and 'Melville' before arriving at 'Laing'. In visual equivalence, I overlaid the faces of Graham Greene, Herman Melville and RD Laing to create a visual identity. New images have also been built from word-image searches, married with specific word occurrences and their physical positions in the manuscripts, providing a lexicon of images to work with for new collage work. Importantly, all these experiments are intertwined and tethered to the physical and material aspects of the autographic manuscripts and Ballard's writerly process.

The autographic manuscripts offer an opportunity to delve deeper into Ballard's creative process, and this project, I hope, offers another way to approach the visualisation of JG Ballard's work. It feels as if this work is just a beginning, and by its nature, will always be 'incomplete', but by connecting the remnants and marginalia to metaphors and narrative in the texts, the project suggests the idea of 'para-illustration'—not simply a supplement or completion of the text in visual form, but an intervention that reveals the absences and remains as a new Ballardian landscape.

(188)

~~length~~ blue brocade ball dress, the turquoise mascara around her eyes making her look like some exotic bird of paradise. Even Bodkin had contrived to trim his beard and salvage a respectable linen jacket, an old piece of crepe around his neck a ragged concession to a black tie. Like Kerans, however, they both seemed glazed and remote, joining in the conversation over dinner automatically.

G.36.

Strangman, however, failed to notice this, or if he did was too elated and preoccupied to care. Whatever his motives, he had obviously gone to considerable trouble to stage his surprise. A fresh canvas awning had been broken out like a crisp white sail over the observation deck, flared at its rim in the form of an inverted marquee to give them an uninterrupted view over the lagoon and sky. A large circular dining table stood by the rail, low divans in the Egyptian style, with spiral gilt and ivory bolsters, disposed around it. A clutter of unmatched but nonetheless brilliant pieces of gold and silver dining plate decorated the table, much of it of huge proportions -- the ormolu finger-bowls were the size of face baths.

Strangman had rifled his treasure house below in an access of profligacy -- several pieces of blackened bronze statuary stood about behind the table bearing salvers of

Word-image relationships on page 188 in the manuscript of *The Drowned World*

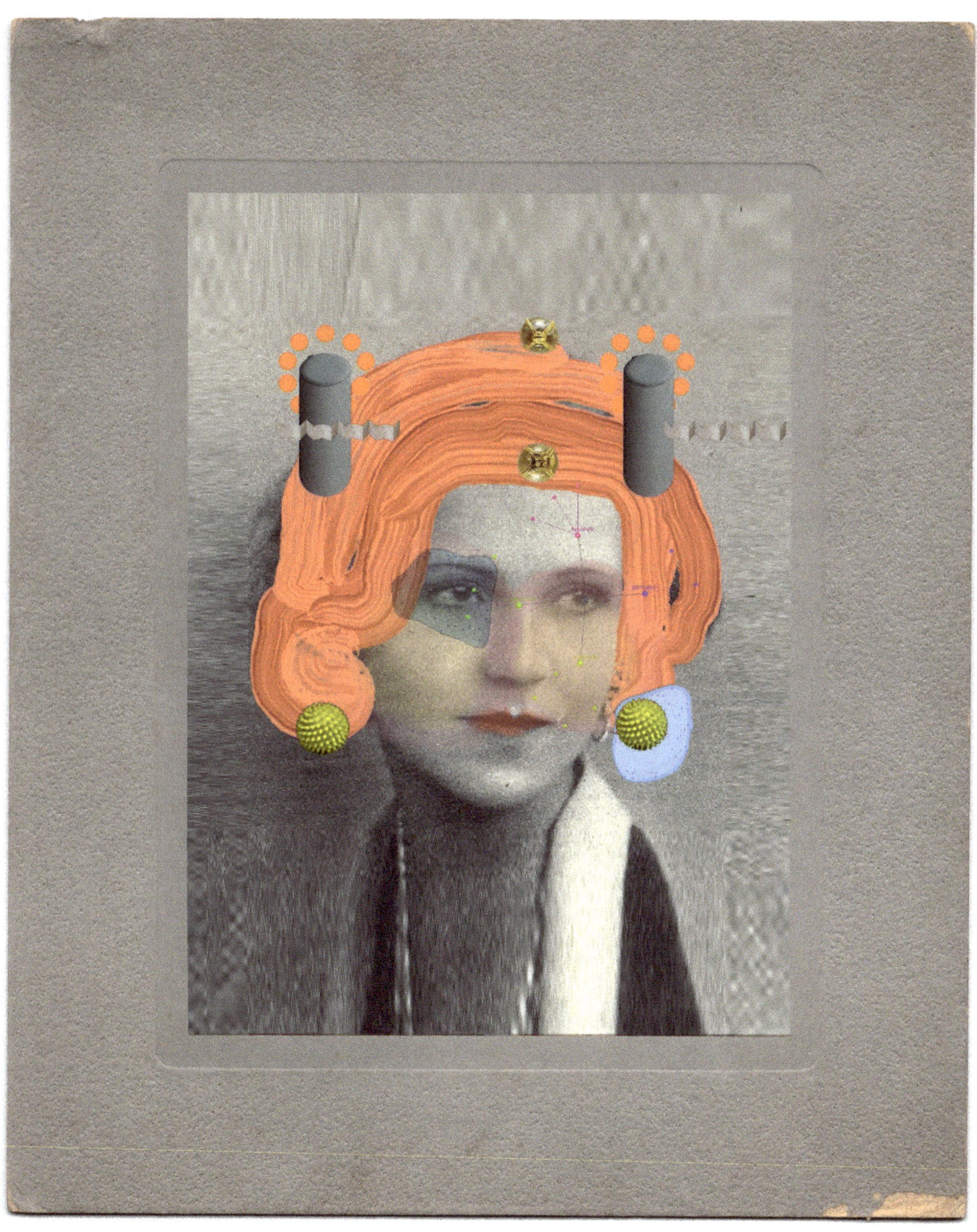

Portrait developed from word-image relationships in manuscript of *The Drowned World*

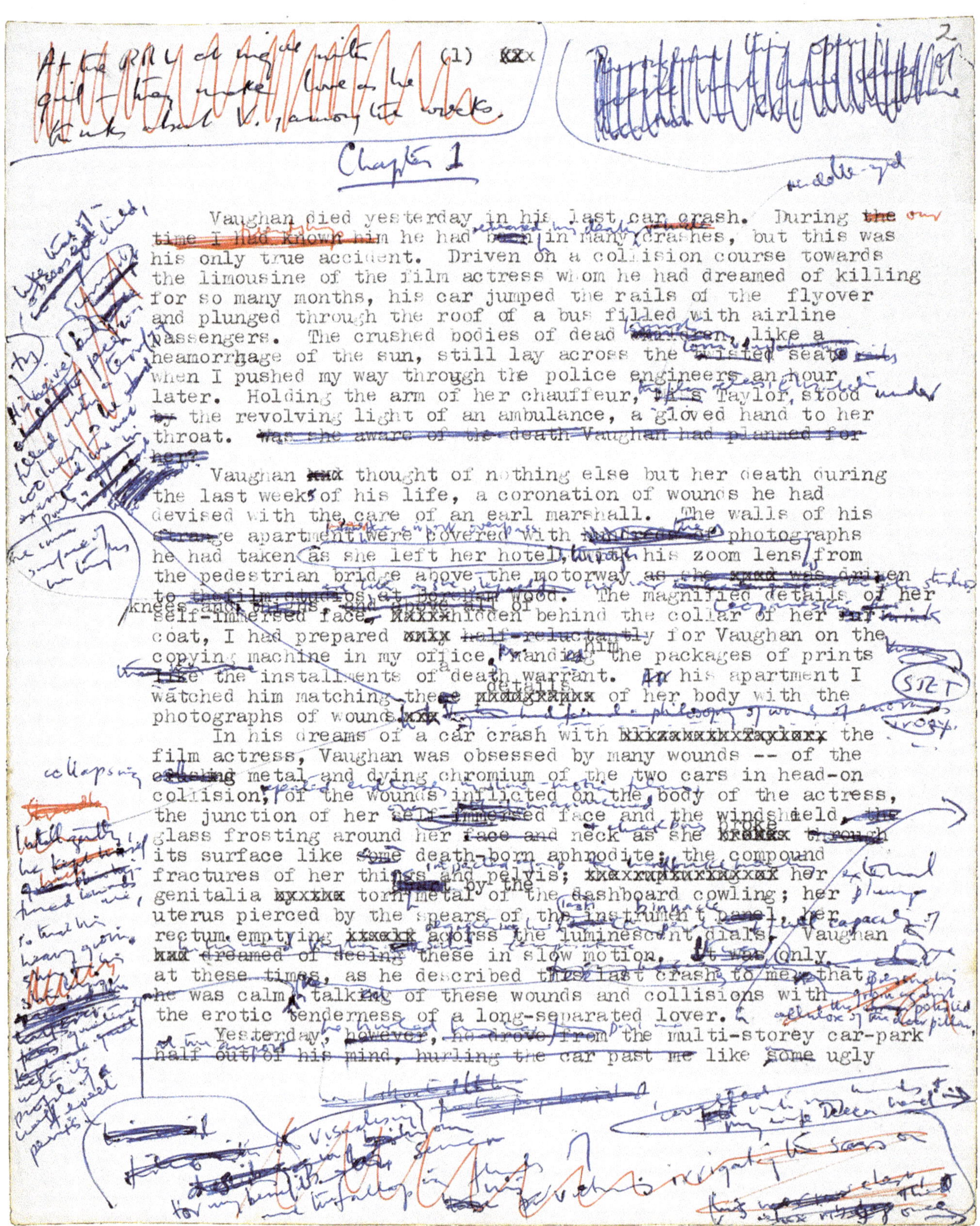

(1) XXx

Chapter 1

Vaughan died yesterday in his last car crash. During the time I had known him he had been in many crashes, but this was his only true accident. Driven on a collision course towards the limousine of the film actress whom he had dreamed of killing for so many months, his car jumped the rails of the flyover and plunged through the roof of a bus filled with airline passengers. The crushed bodies of dead children, like a heamorrhage of the sun, still lay across the twisted seats when I pushed my way through the police engineers an hour later. Holding the arm of her chauffeur, Miss Taylor stood by the revolving light of an ambulance, a gloved hand to her throat. Was she aware of the death Vaughan had planned for her?

Vaughan xxx thought of nothing else but her death during the last weeks of his life, a coronation of wounds he had devised with the care of an earl marshall. The walls of his strange apartment were covered with hundreds of photographs he had taken as she left her hotel, through his zoom lens from the pedestrian bridge above the motorway as she xxxx was driven to the film studios at Boreham Wood. The magnified details of her knees and thighs, and above all of self-immersed face, XXXXXhidden behind the collar of her fur coat, I had prepared xxxx half-reluctantly for Vaughan on the copying machine in my office, handing him the packages of prints like the installments of a death warrant. In his apartment I watched him matching these details xxxxxxxxx of her body with the photographs of wounds xxx

In his dreams of a car crash with xxxxxxxxxxxxxxxx the film actress, Vaughan was obsessed by many wounds -- of the crushing metal and dying chromium of the two cars in head-on collision, of the wounds inflicted on the body of the actress, the junction of her self-immersed face and the windshield, the glass frosting around her face and neck as she broke xxxx through its surface like some death-born aphrodite; the compound fractures of her thighs and pelvis; xxxxxxxxxxxxx her genitalia xxxxxx torn by the metal of the dashboard cowling; her uterus pierced by the spears of the instrument panel, her rectum emptying xxxxxx across the luminescent dials. Vaughan xxx dreamed of seeing these in slow motion. It was only at these times, as he described this last crash to me, that he was calm, talking of these wounds and collisions with the erotic tenderness of a long-separated lover.

Yesterday, however, he drove from the multi-storey car-park half out of his mind, hurling the car past me like some ugly

Page one of the manuscript of *Crash*

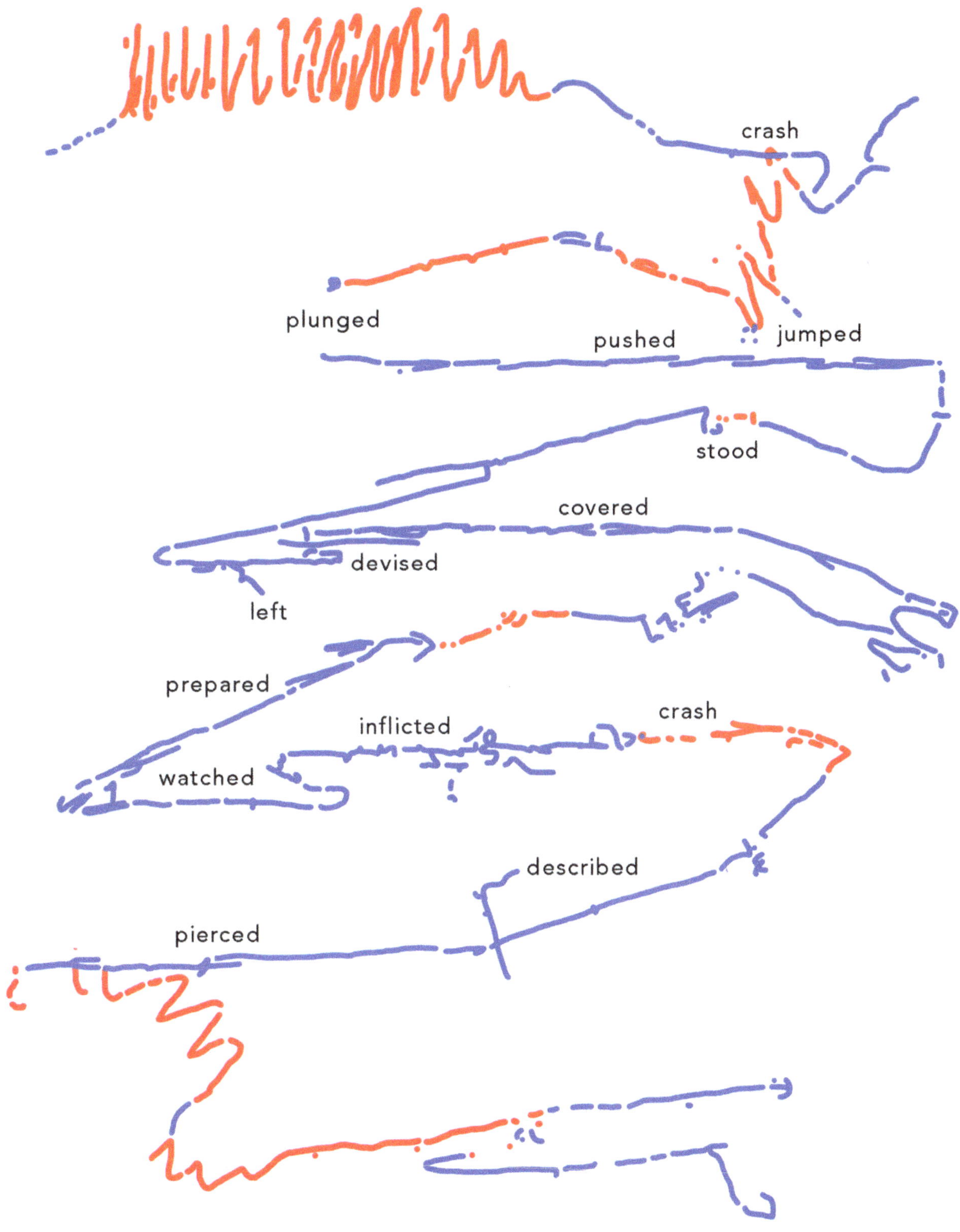

Routes and Verbs 2020. A road journey from page one of the manuscript of *Crash*

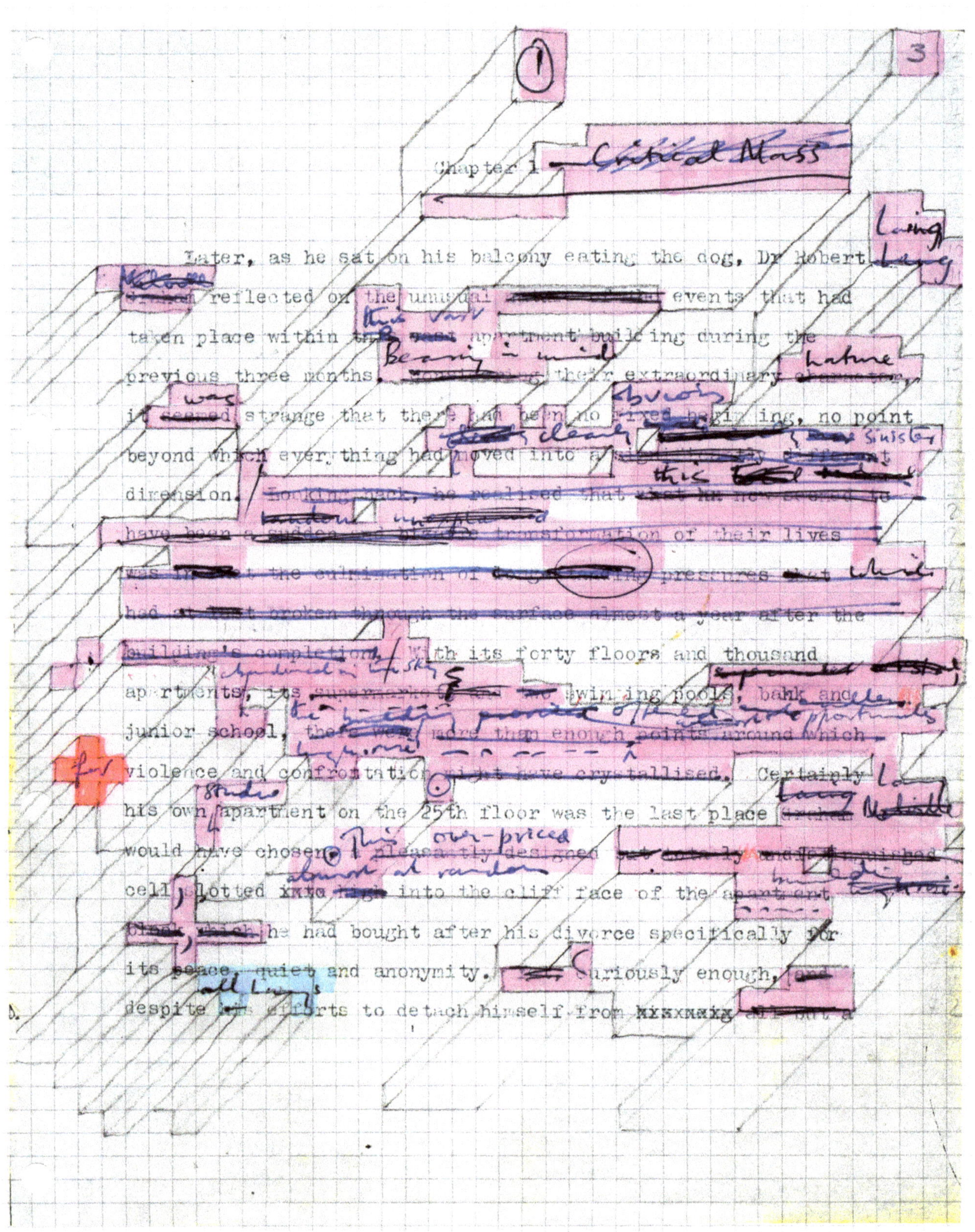
Chapter 1 — Critical Mass

Later, as he sat on his balcony eating the dog, Dr Robert Laing
reflected on the unusual events that had
taken place within this vast apartment building during the
previous three months. Bearing in mind their extraordinary nature,
it was strange that there had been no obvious beginning, no point
beyond which everything had moved into a clearly more sinister
dimension.

With its forty floors and thousand
apartments, its supermarket and swimming pools, bank and
junior school, there were more than enough points around which
violence and confrontation might have crystallised. Certainly
his own studio apartment on the 25th floor was the last place
would have chosen. This over-priced
cell slotted almost at random into the cliff face of the
block, which he had bought after his divorce specifically for
its peace, quiet and anonymity. Curiously enough,
despite all Laing's efforts to detach himself from

Mapping the spaces between autographic and typewritten text in page one of the manuscript of *High Rise*

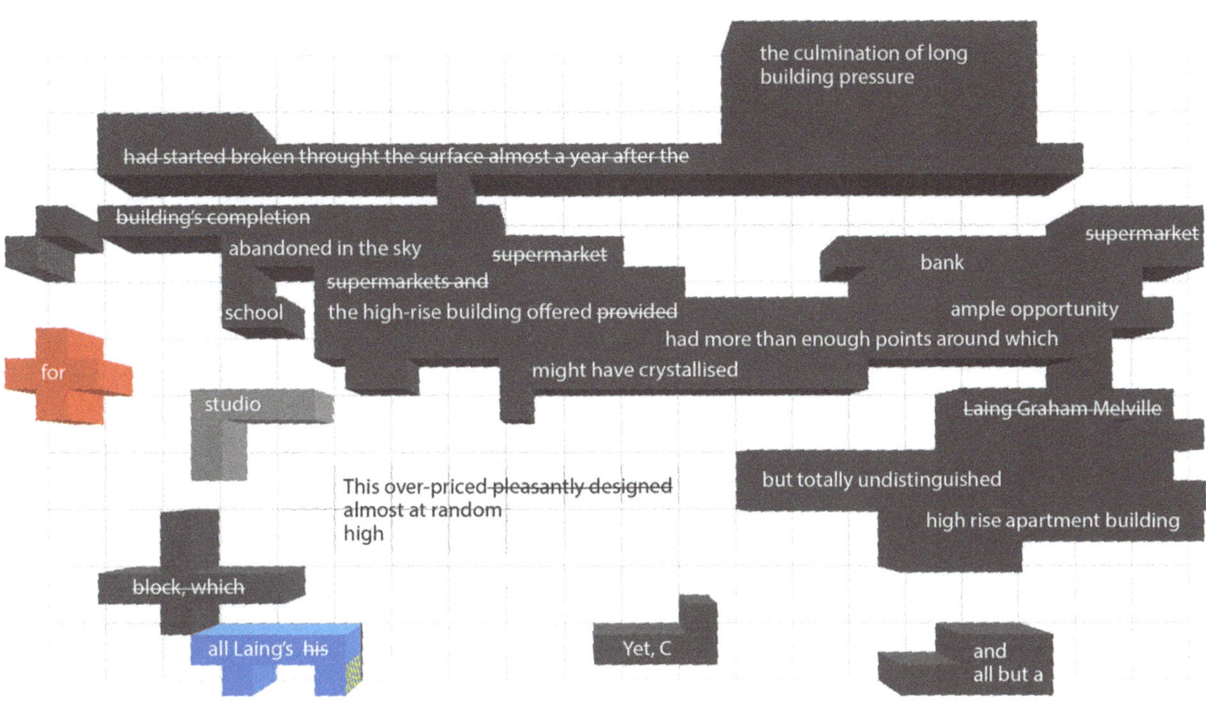

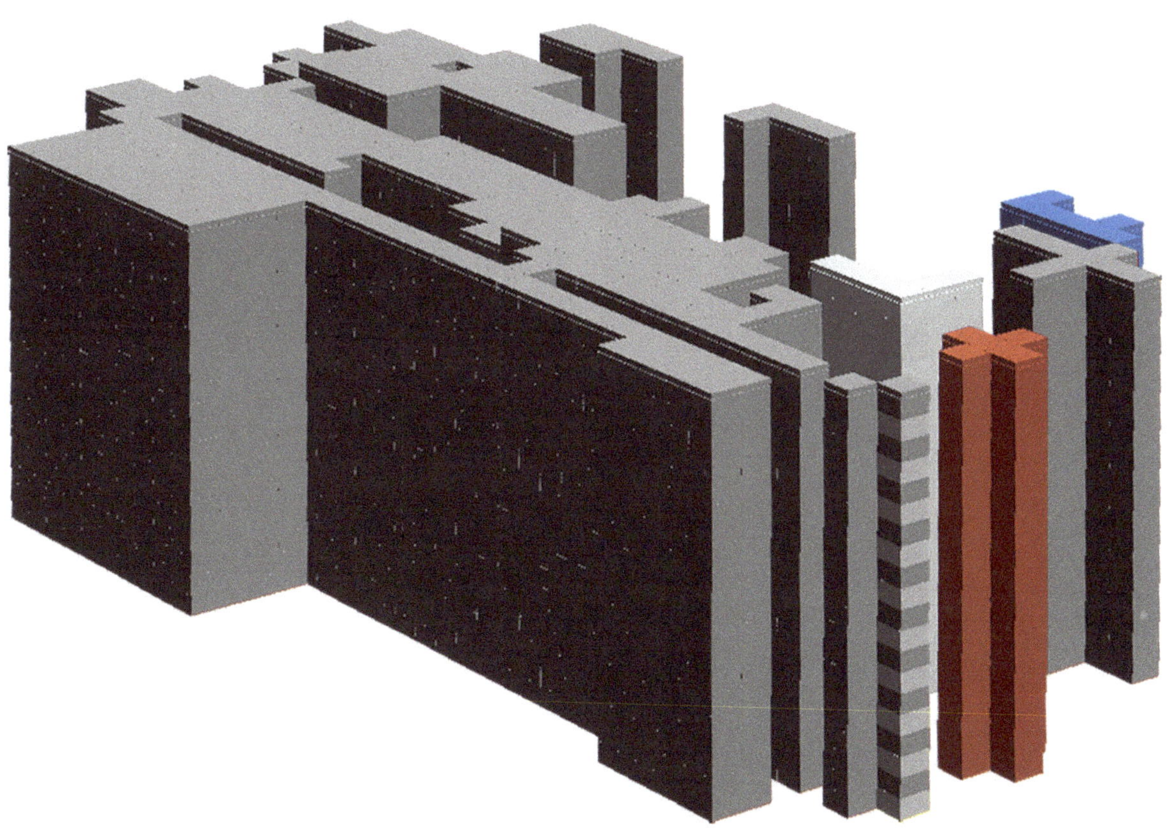

Mapping volumes between autographic and typewritten text in page one of the manuscript of *High Rise*

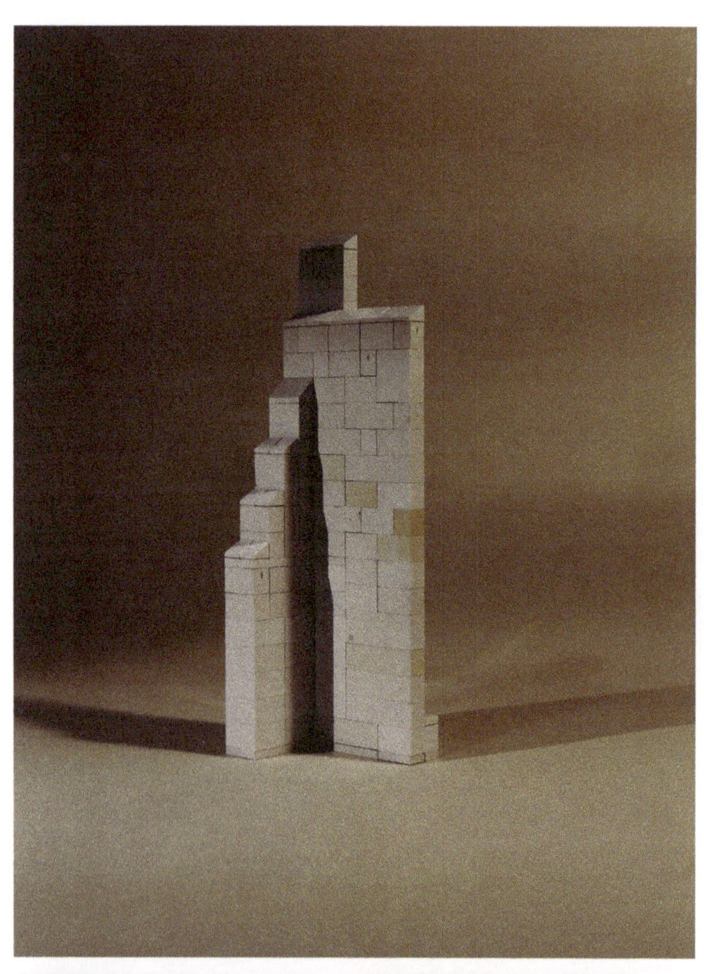

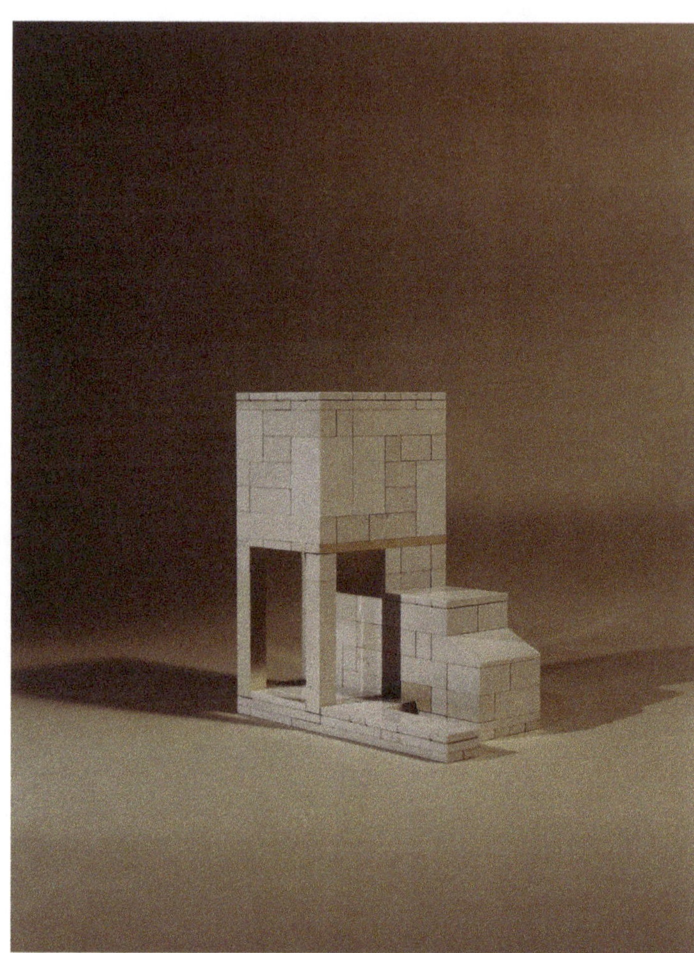

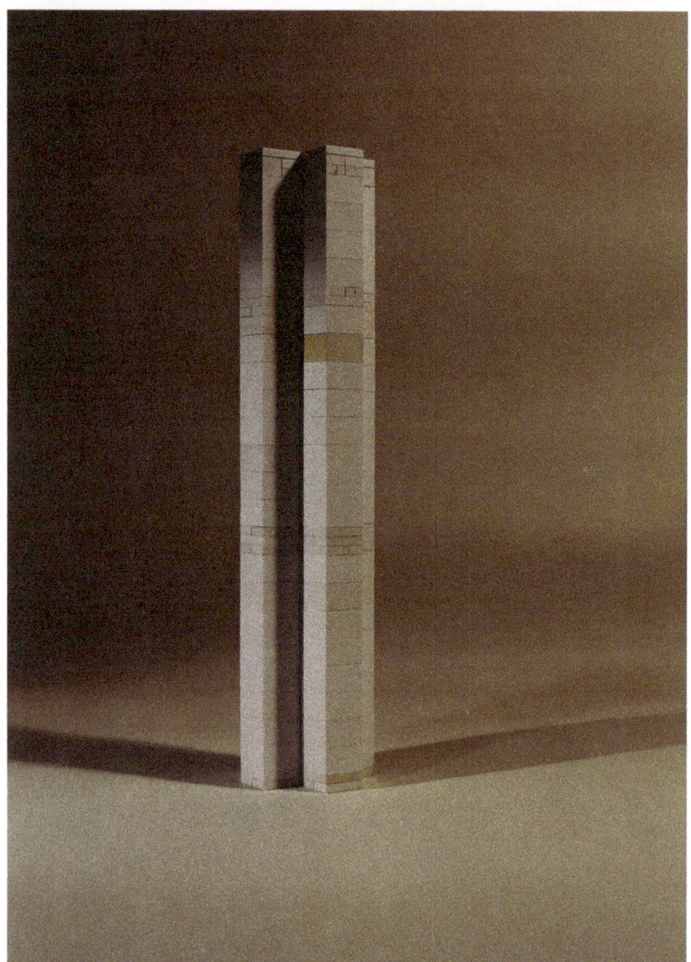

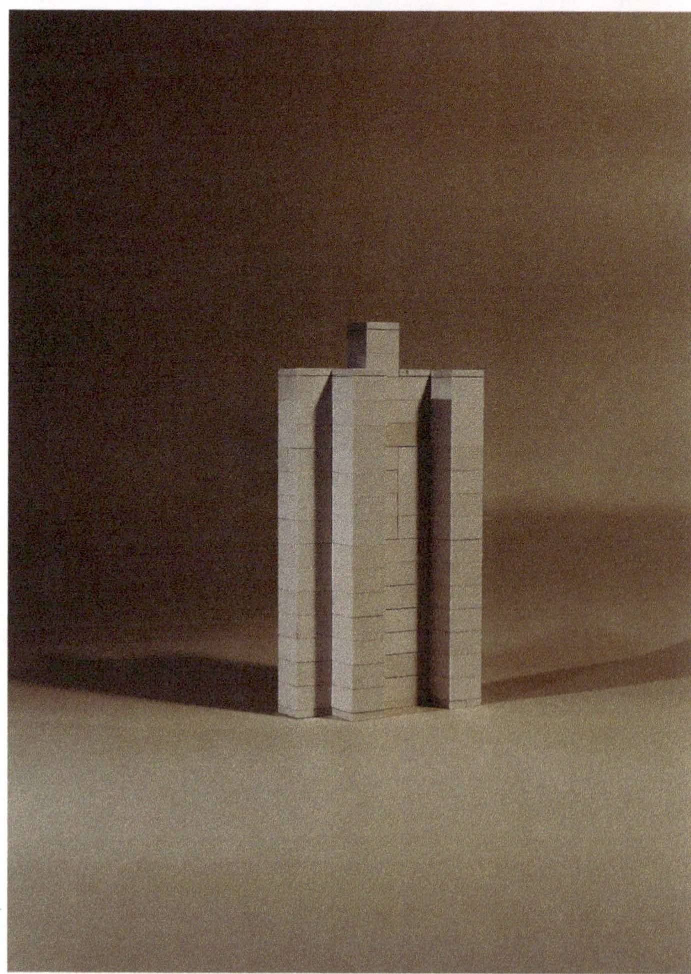

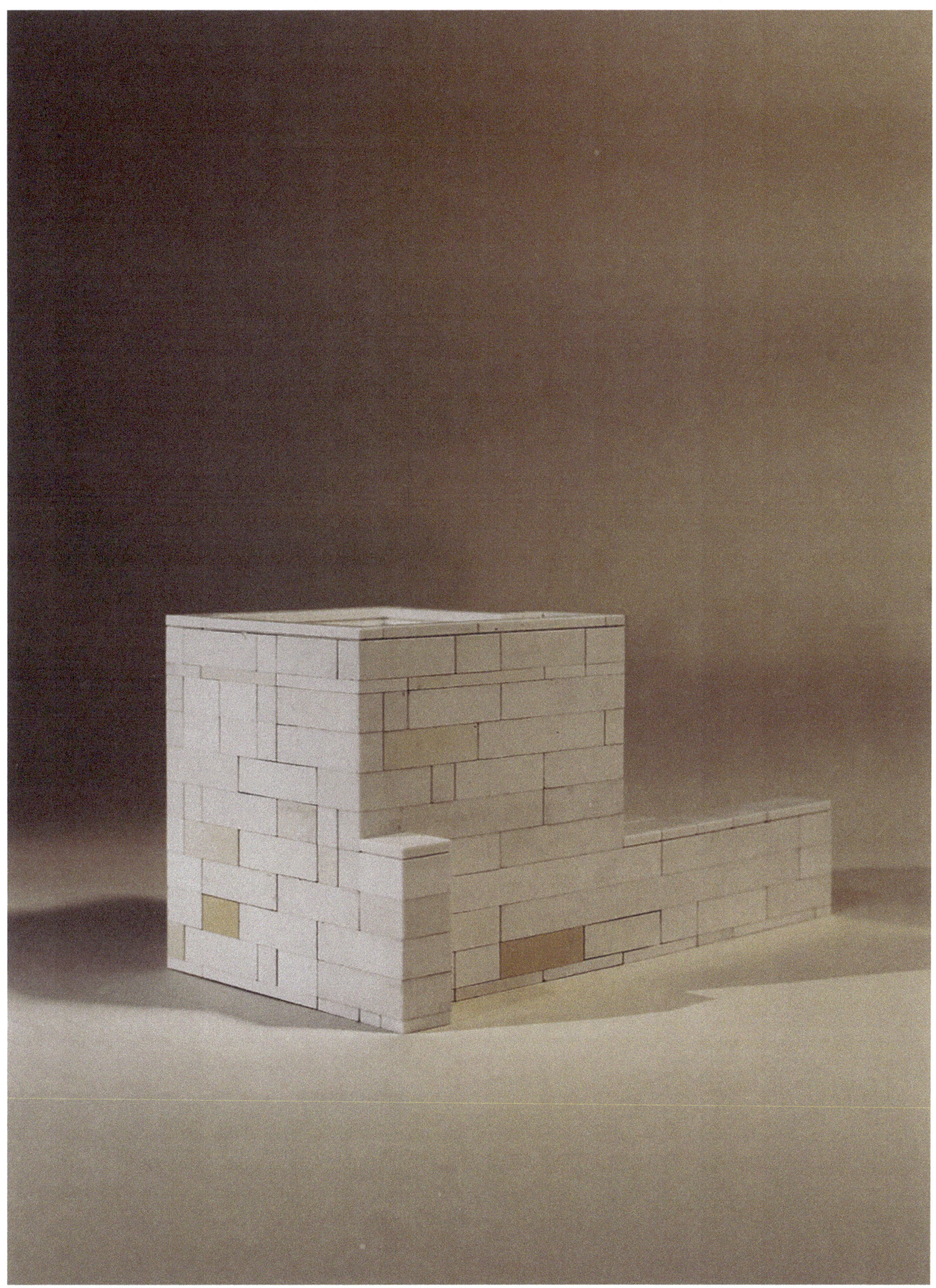

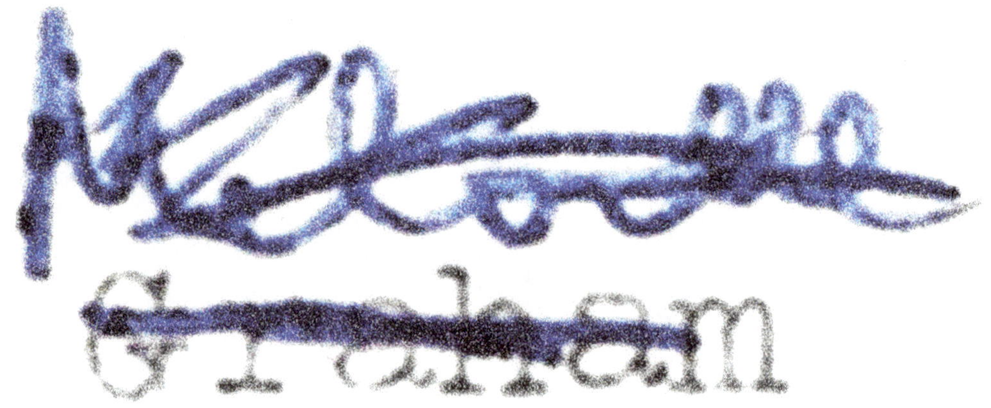

Laing

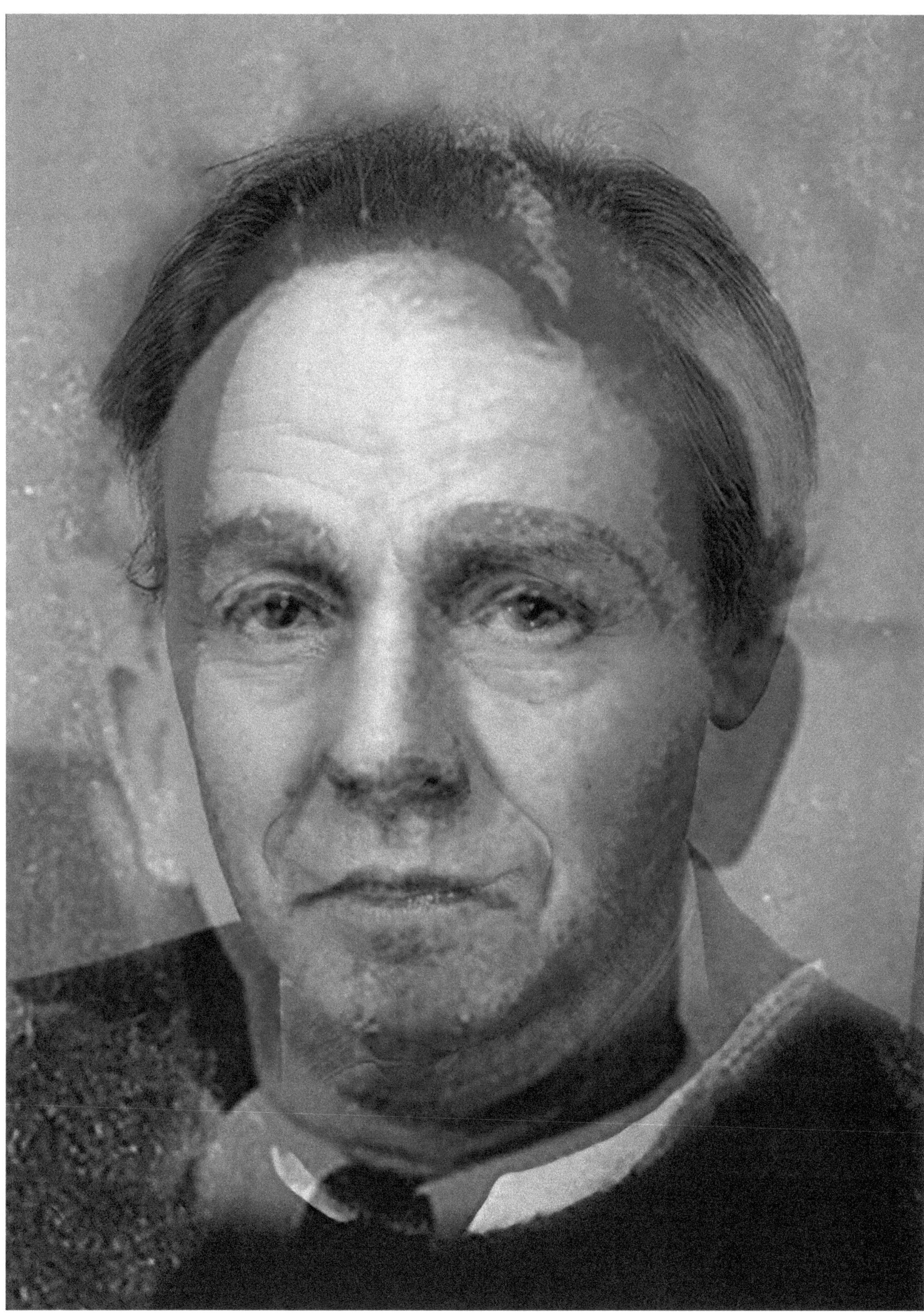

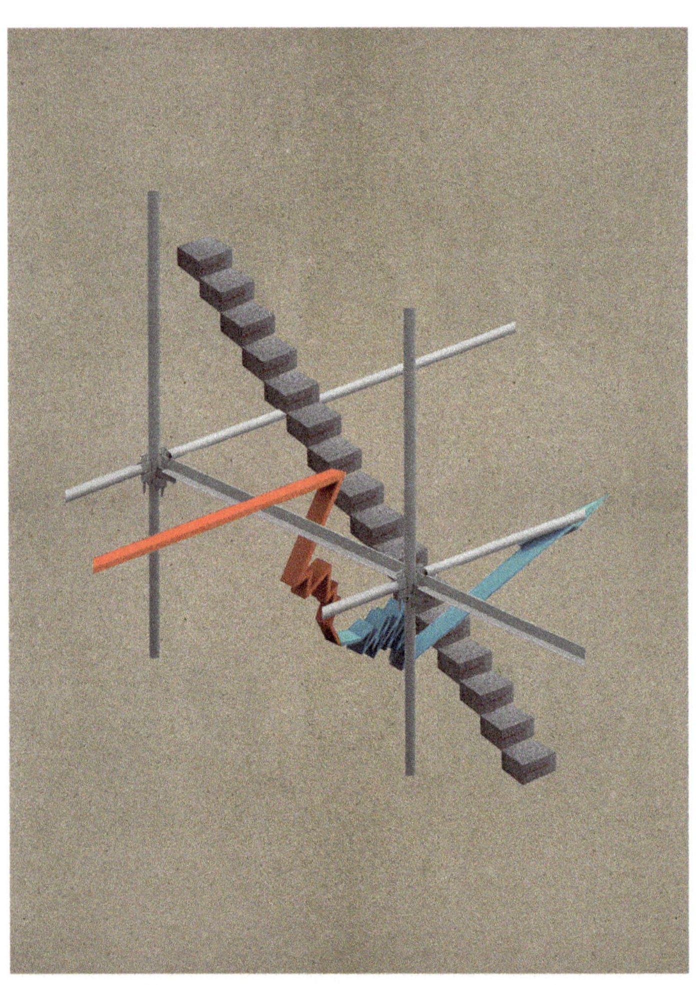

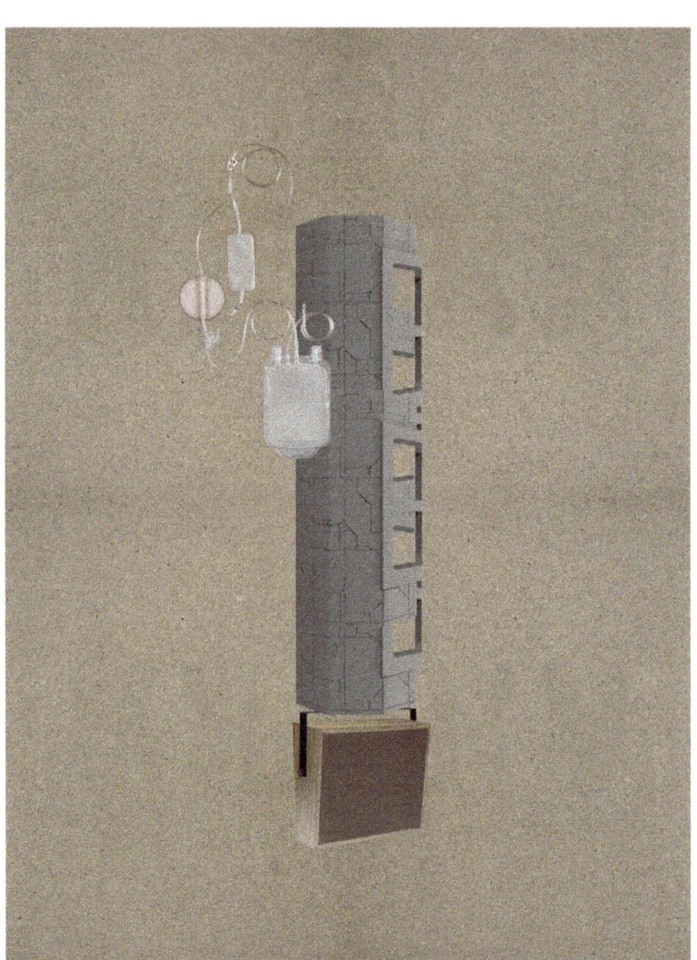

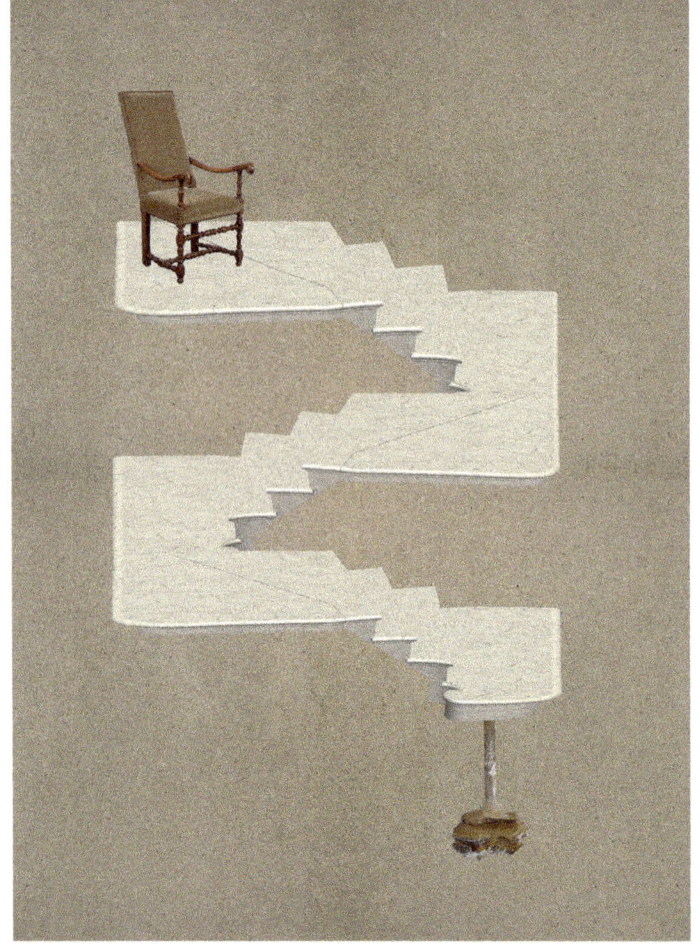

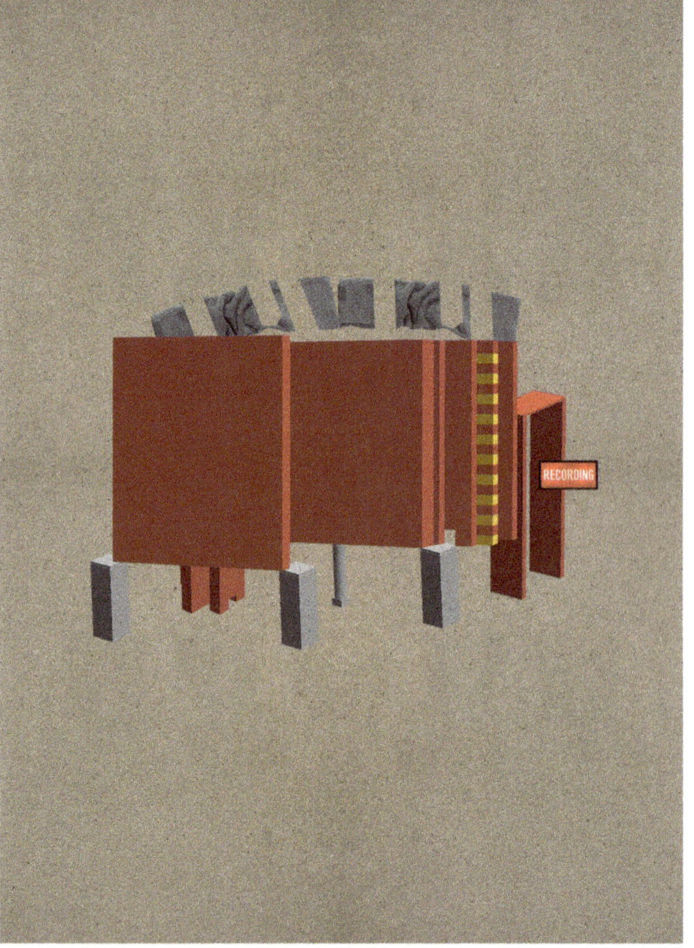
RECORDING

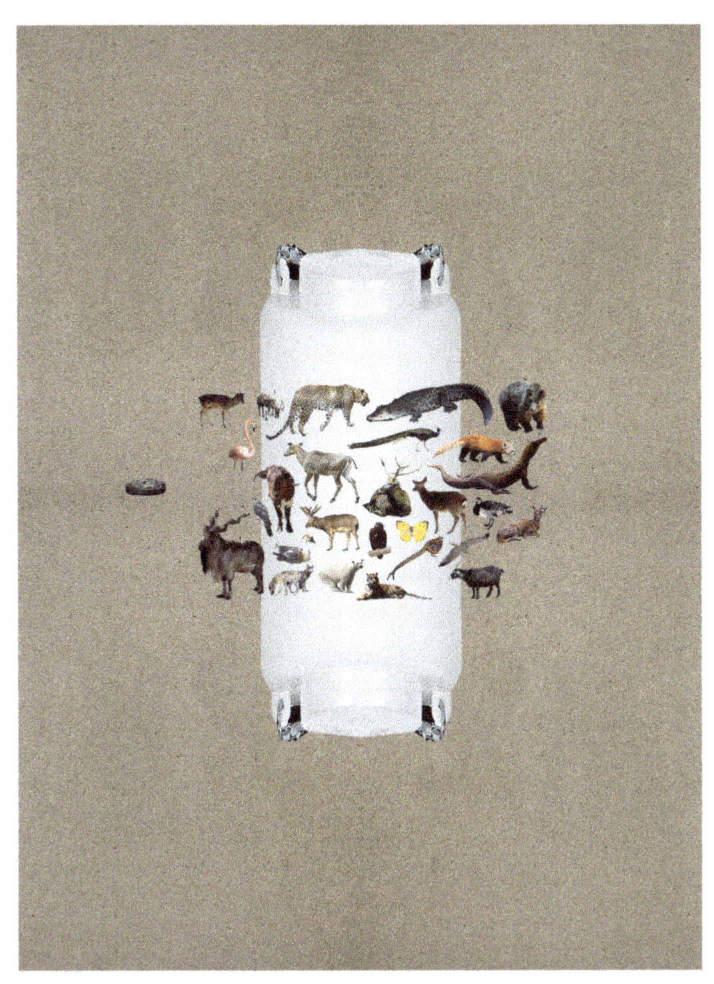

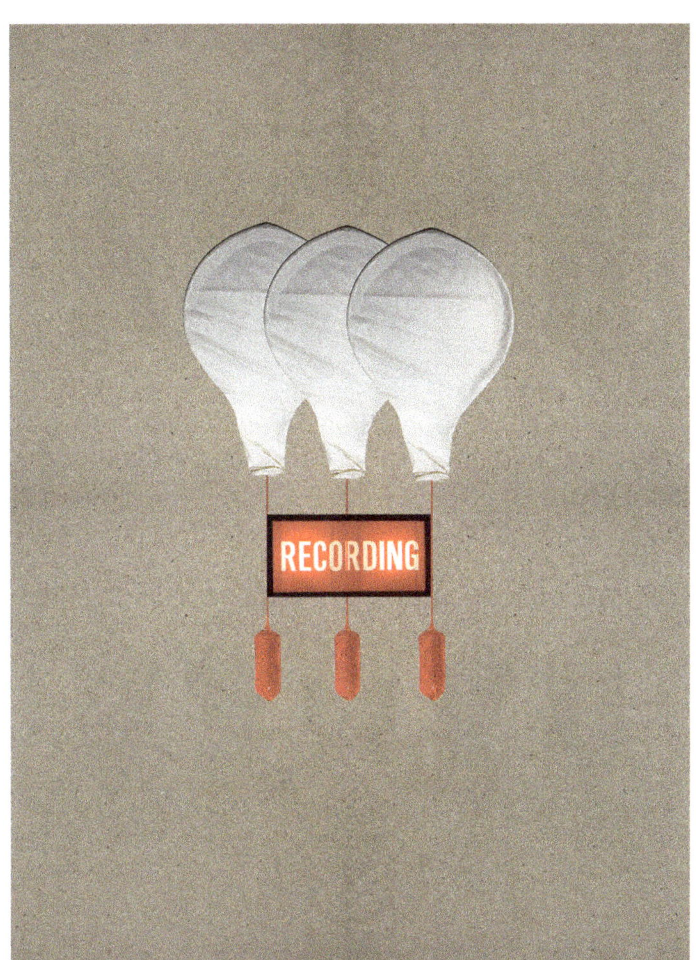

RECORDING

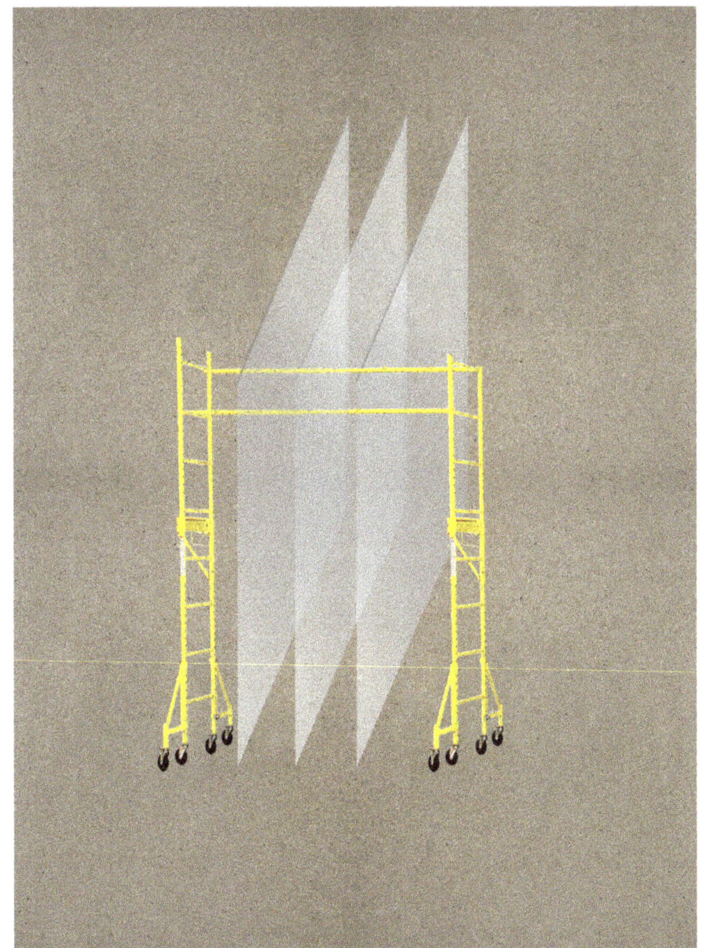

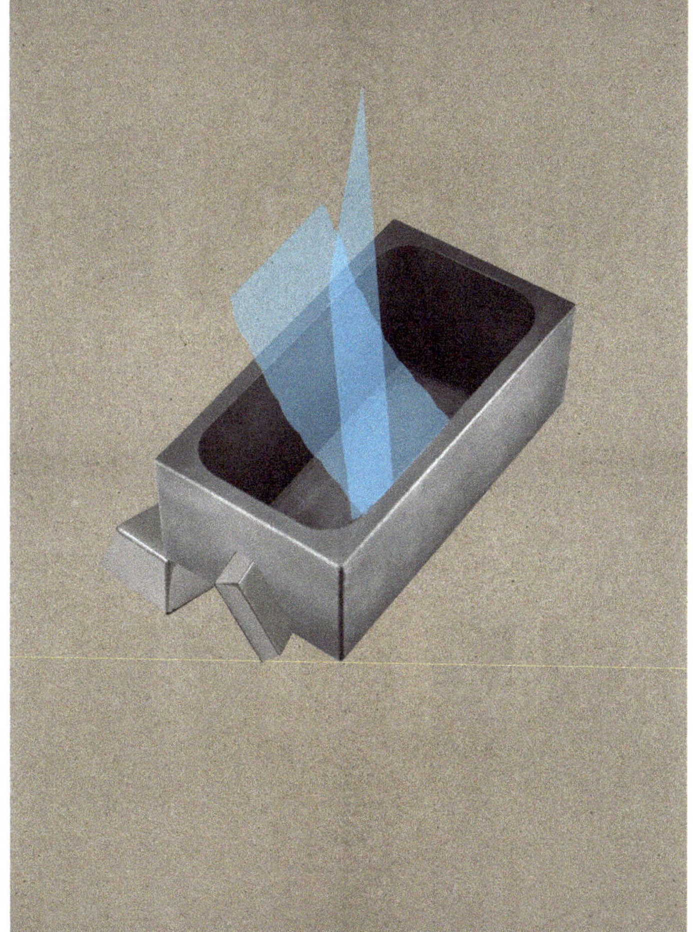

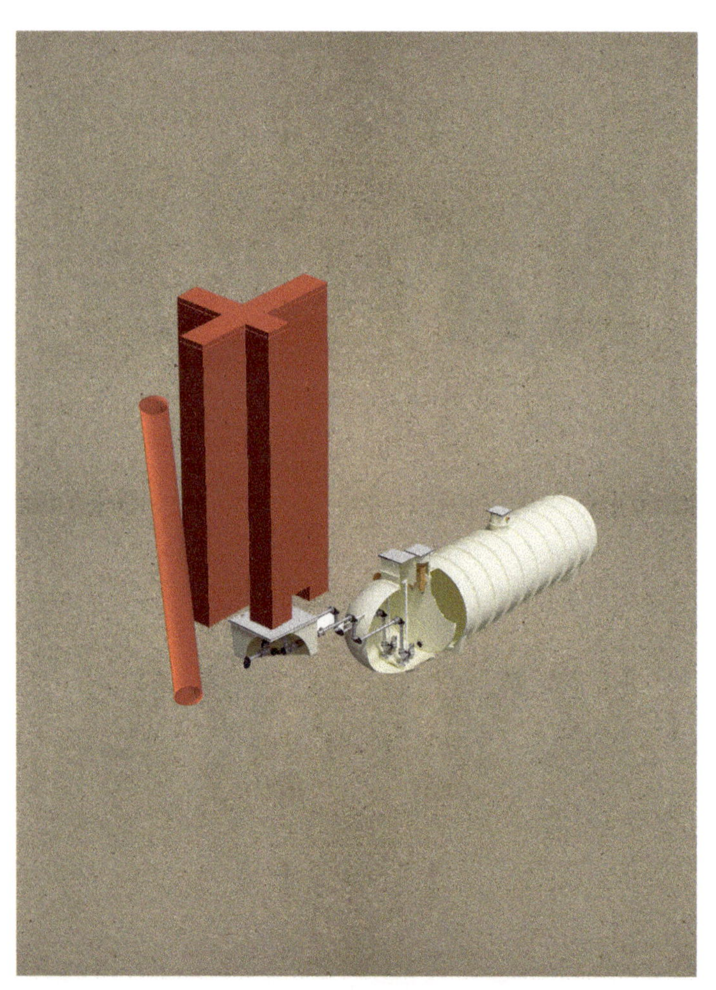

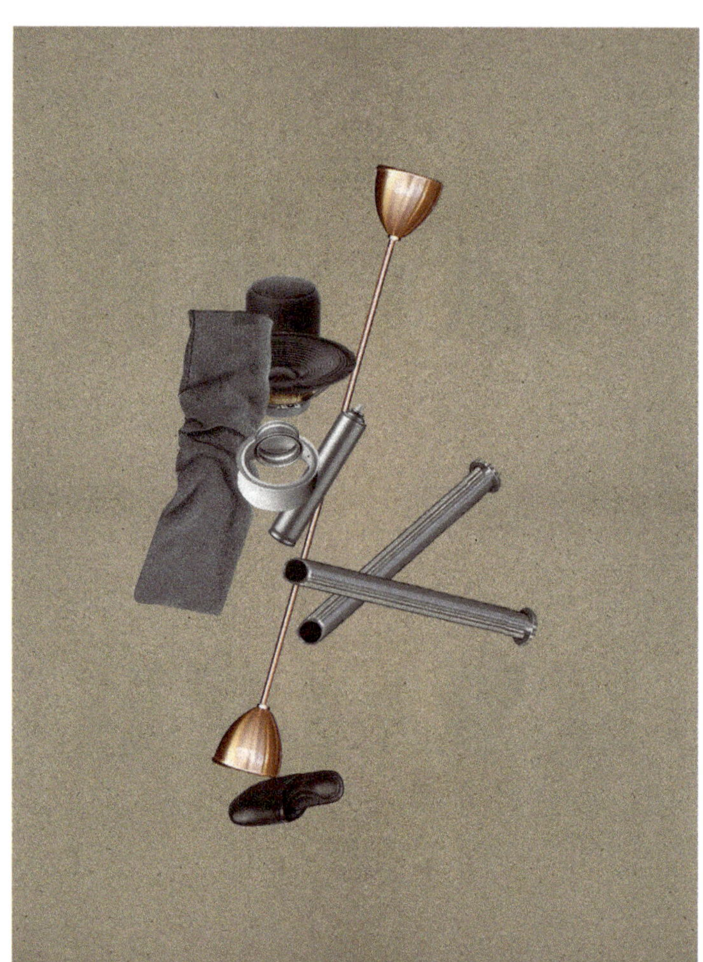

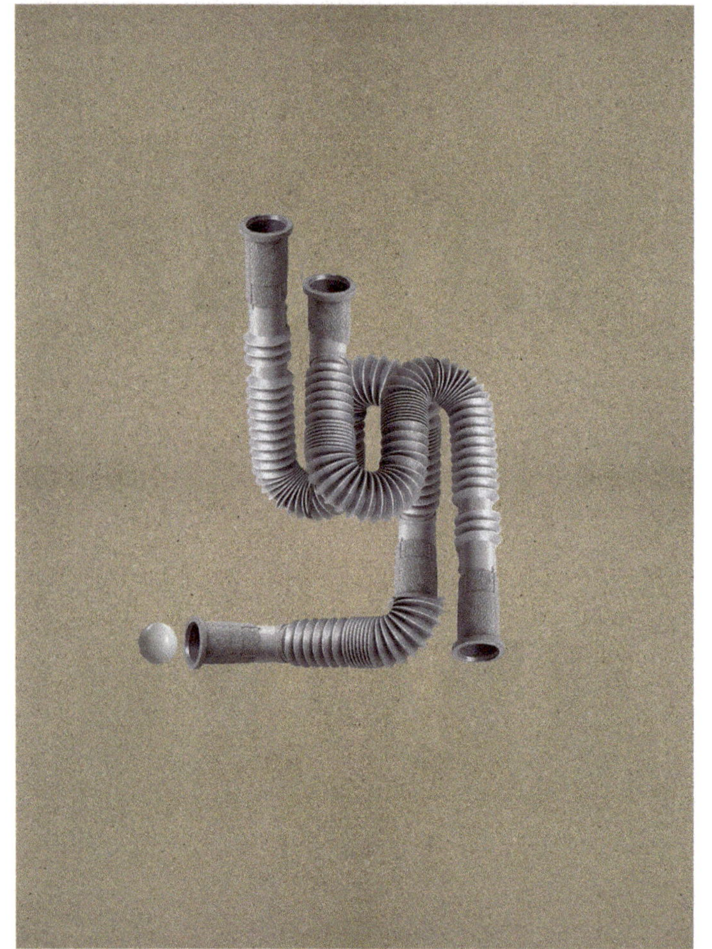

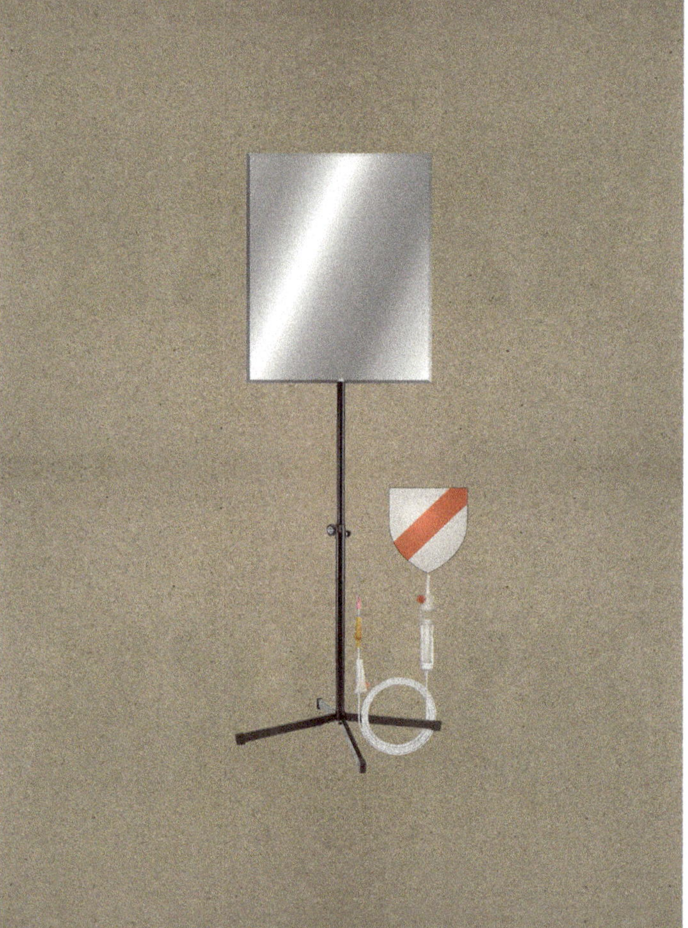

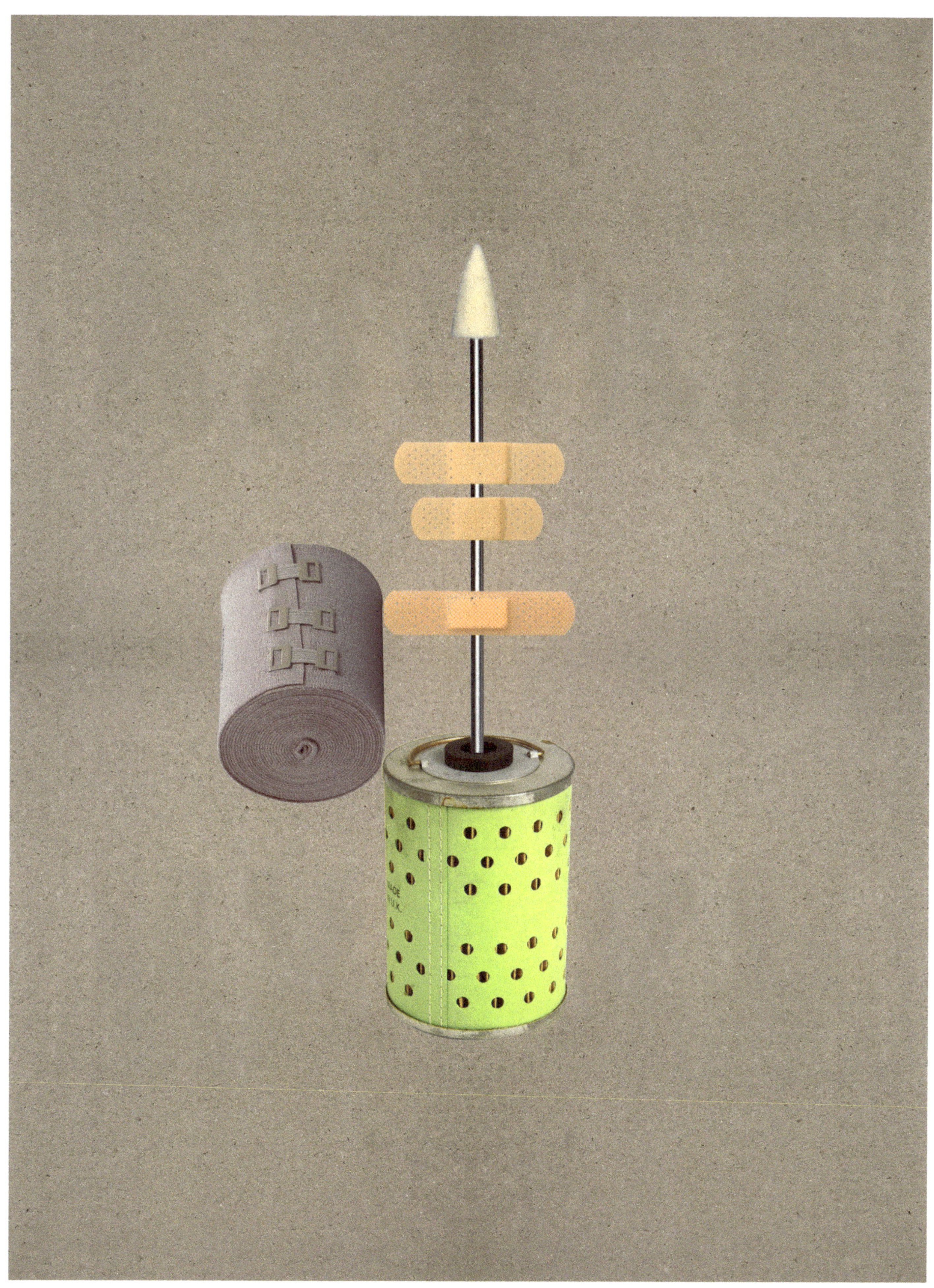

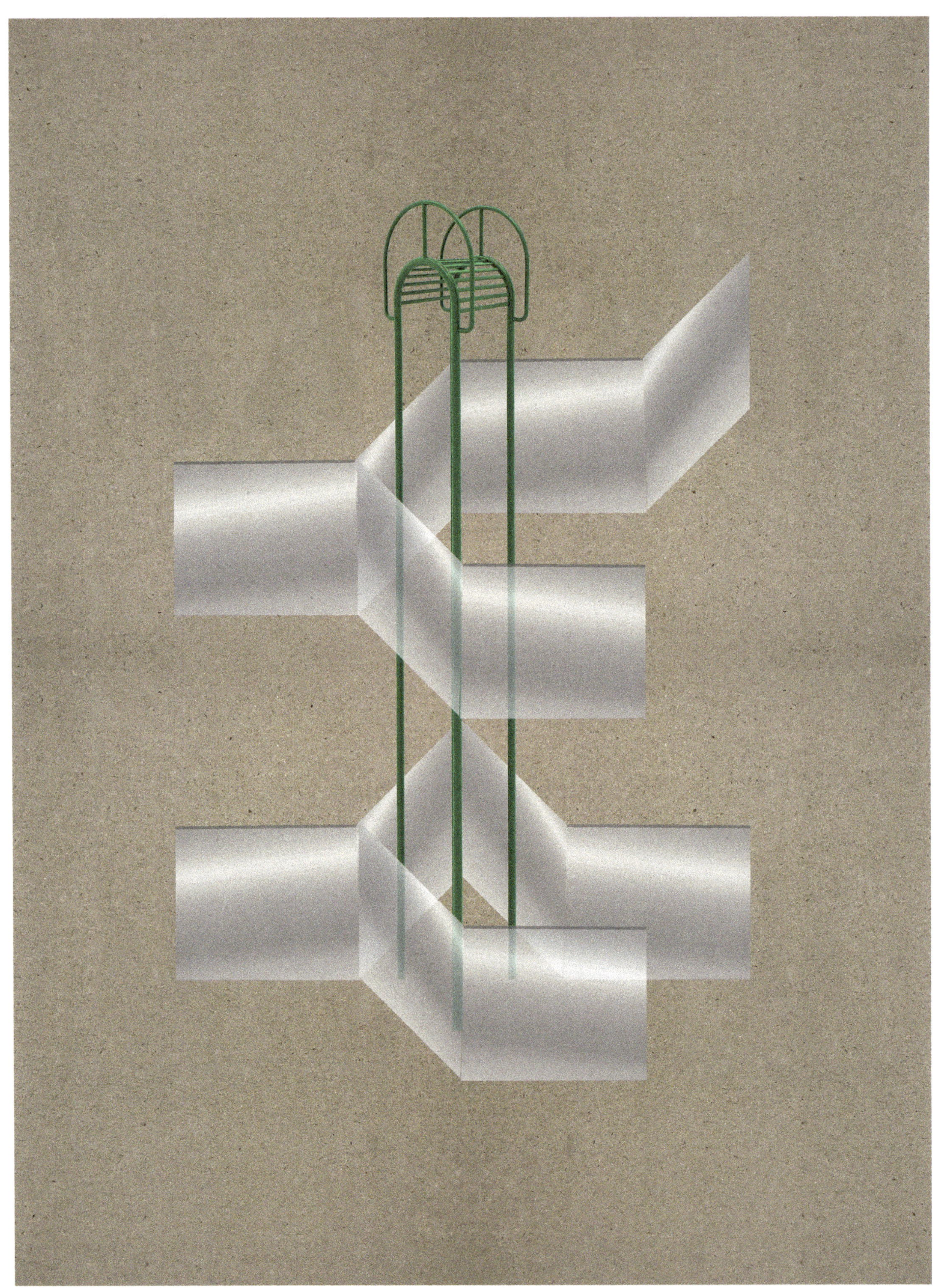

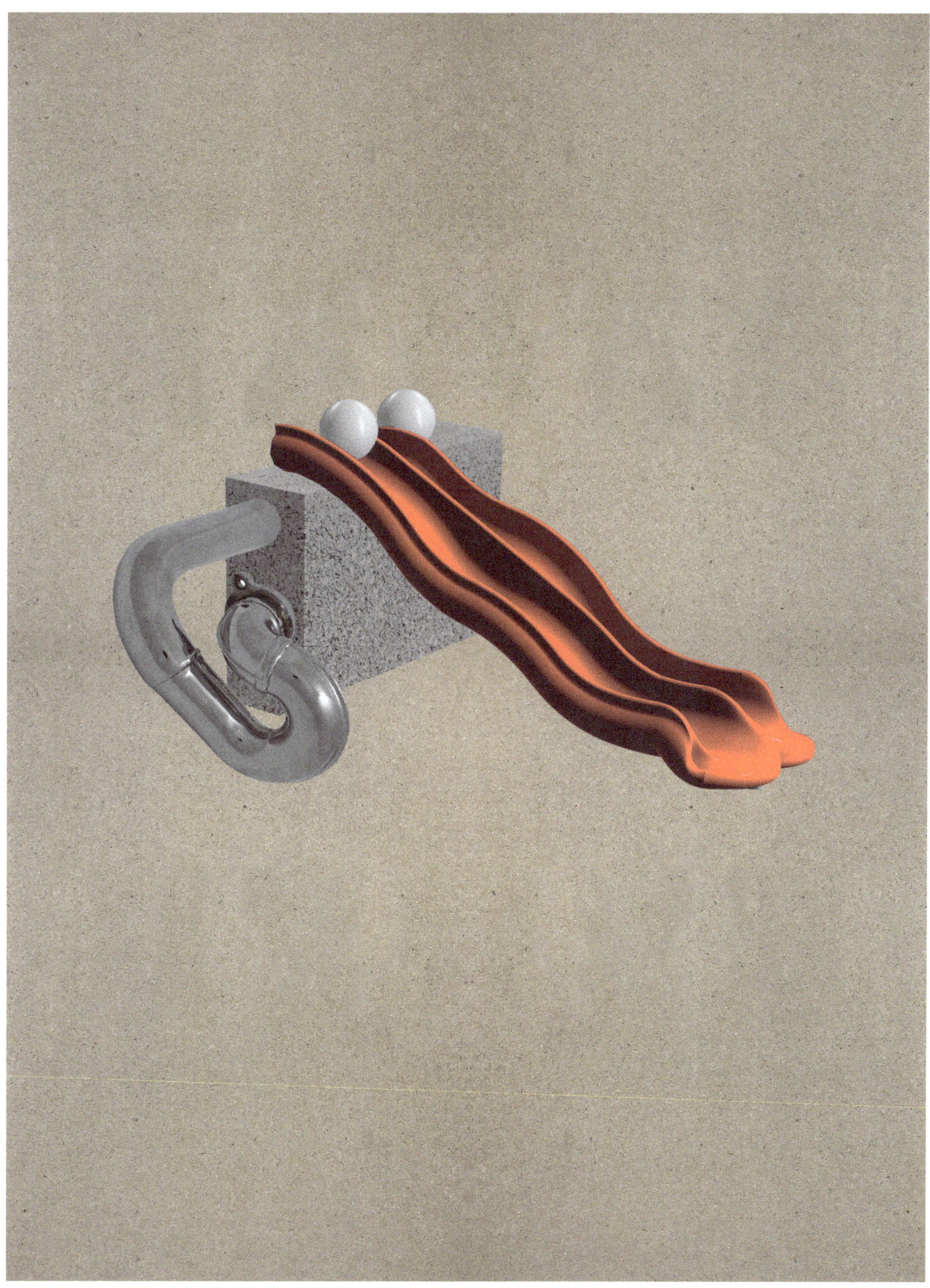

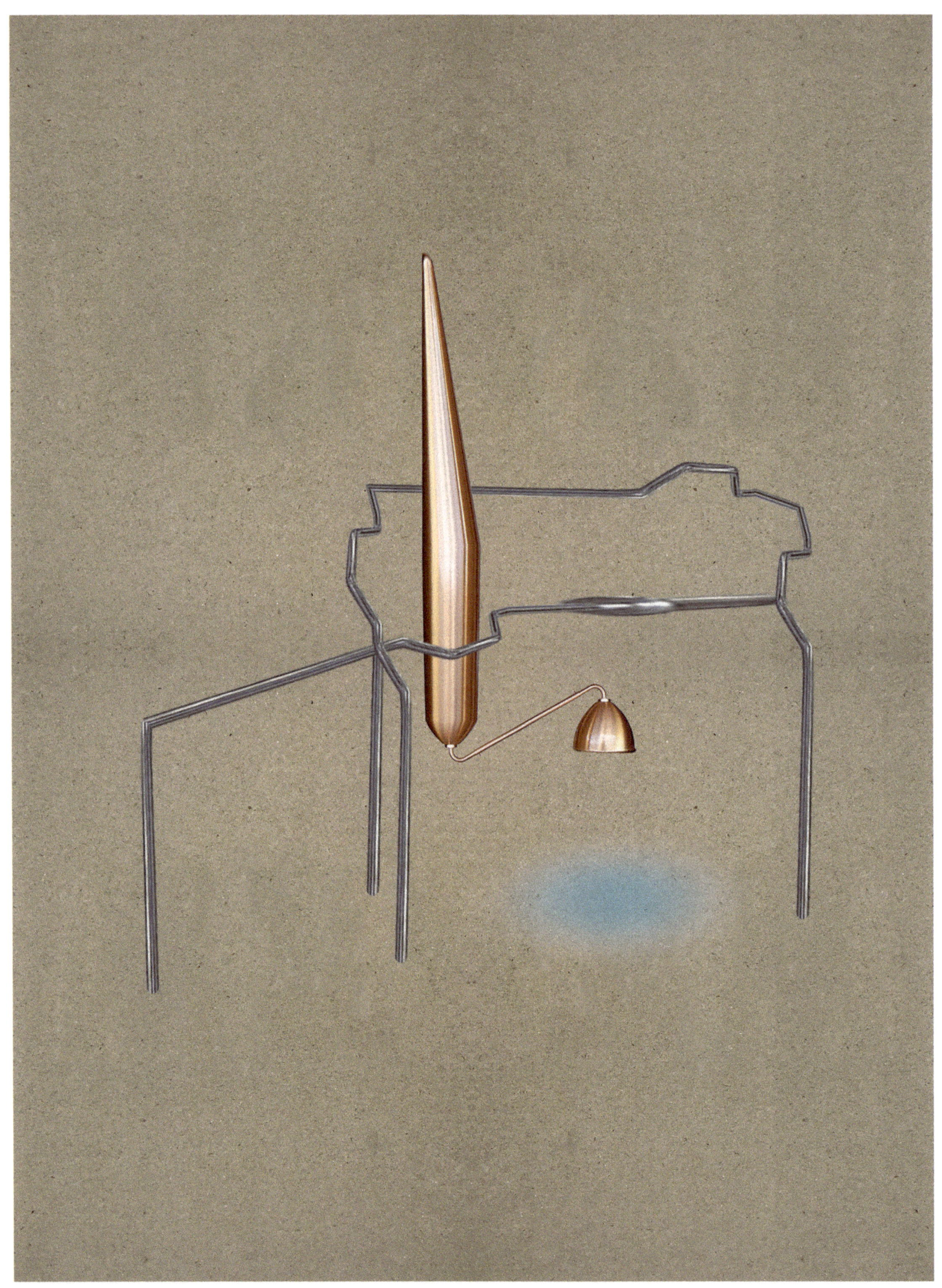

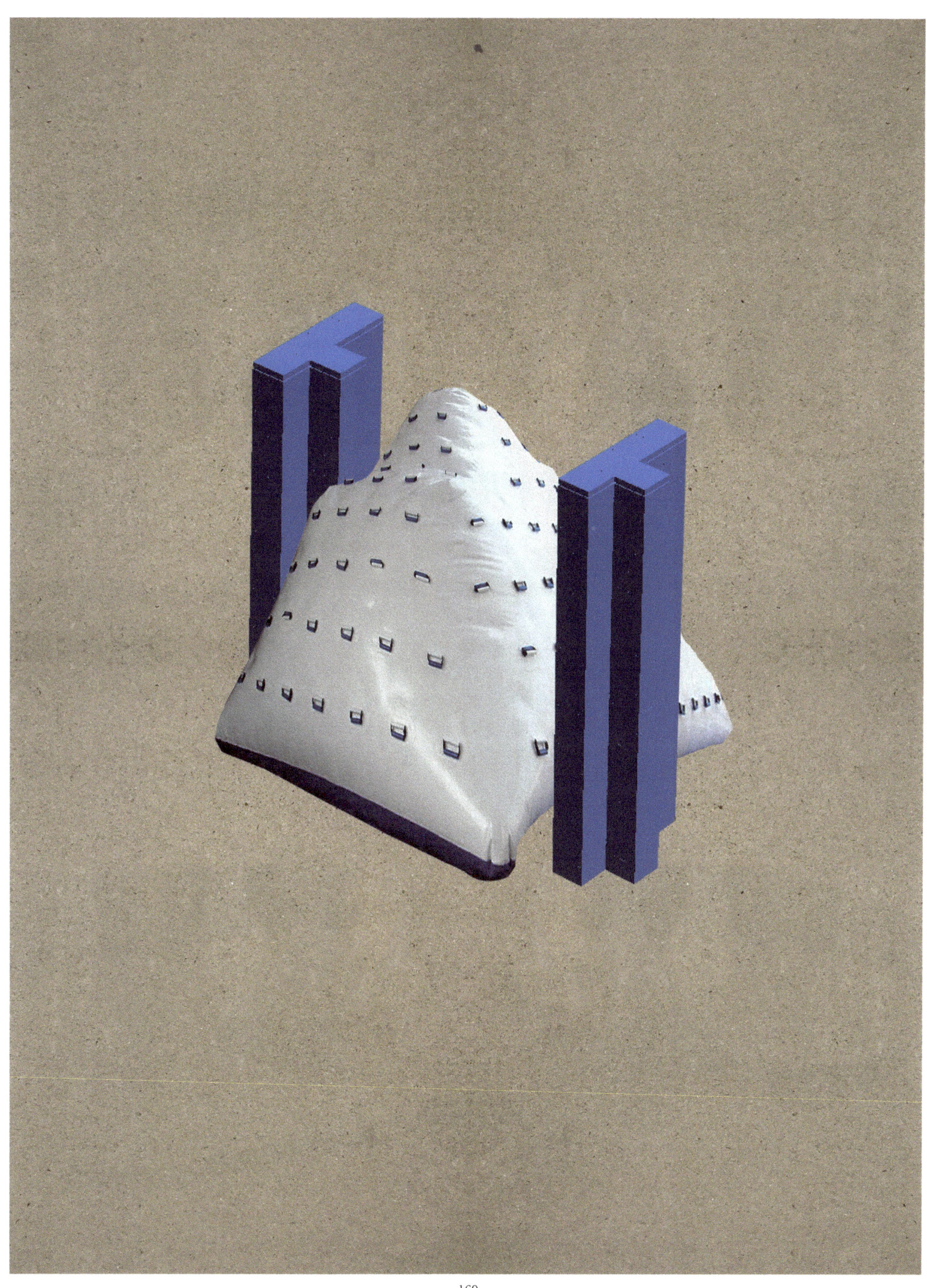

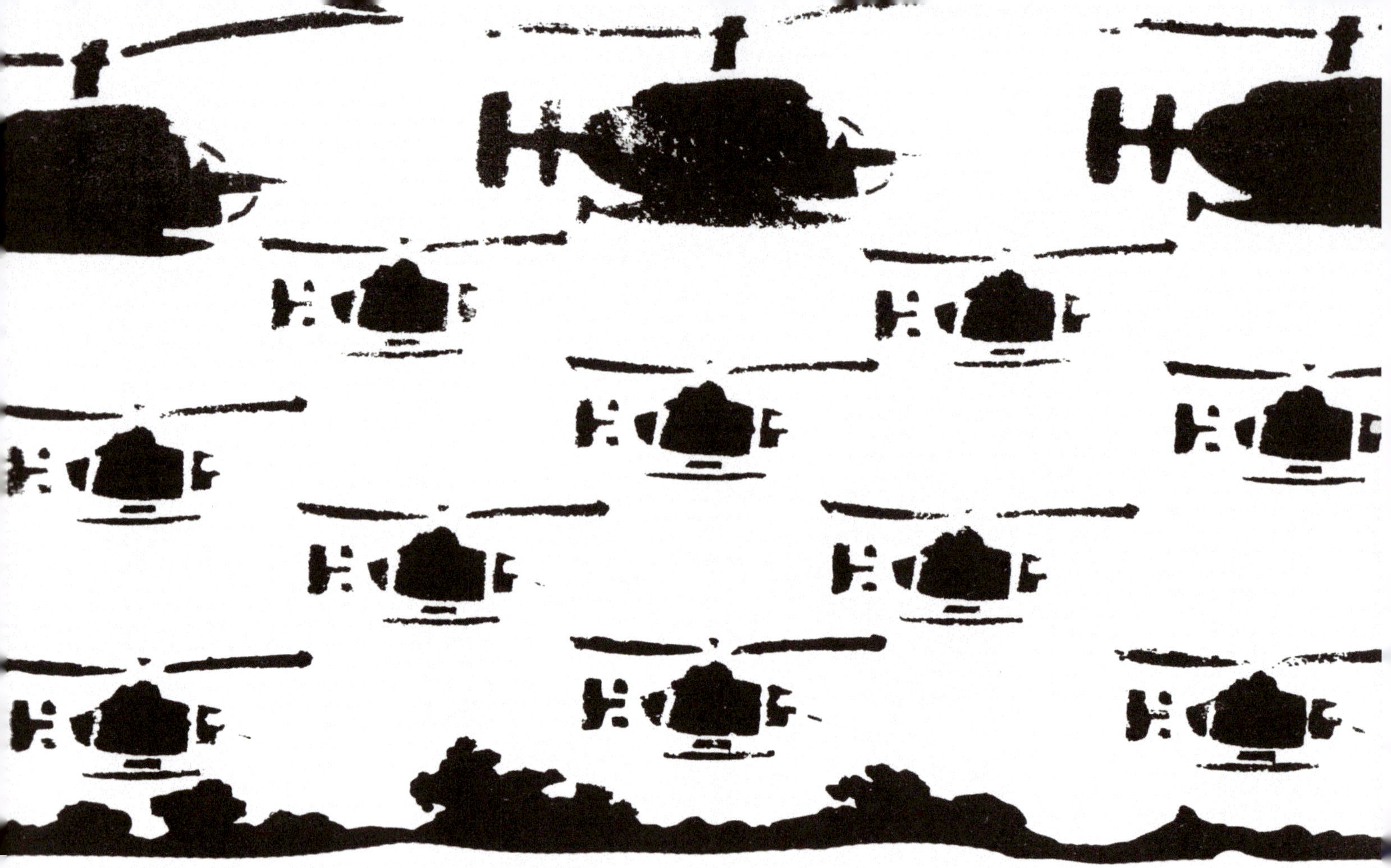

ROB LATHAM

ASSASSINATION WEAPONS:

THE VISUAL CULTURE OF NEW WAVE SCIENCE FICTION

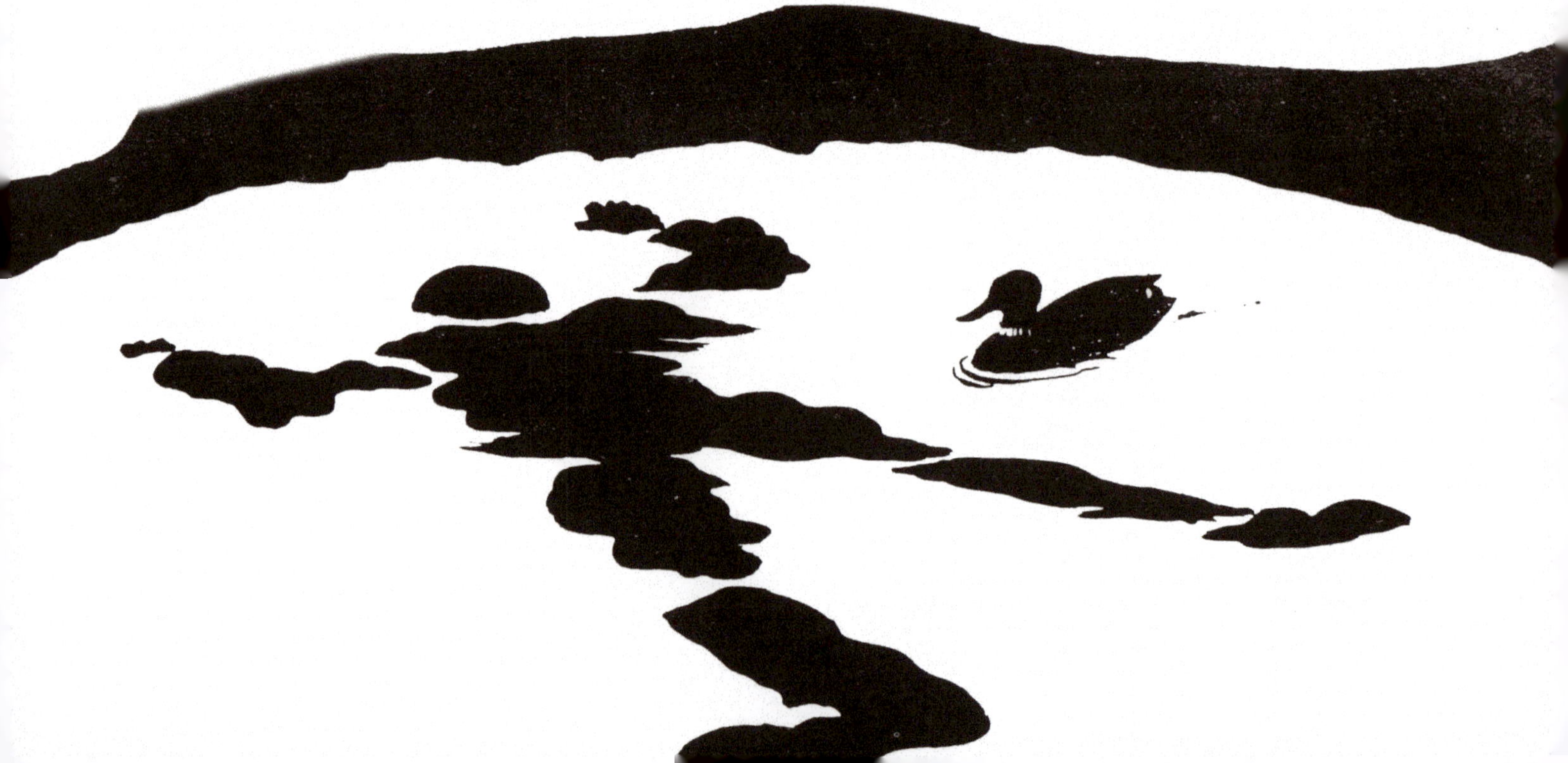

Collage, as both a literary technique and a political instrument, was central to the writings of "New Wave" science fiction (SF) during the 1960s. Using collage strategies as alternatives to the mimetic representation that had characterized the pulp SF tradition, New Wave authors mounted an attack on what Raymond Federman has identified as the dullness of standard modes of reading:

> "the whole traditional, conventional, fixed, and boring method of reading a book must be questioned, challenged, demolished.... [T]he writer...must, though innovations in the writing itself—in the typography and topology of his writing—renew our system of reading" ("Surfiction" 9).

This refreshment of reading involves not merely a formal strategy, according to Federman, but also a critical animus directed against the ideological biases of conventional literary forms, seeking to provoke attention to their subconscious channeling of perception and desire:

> "Discourses impregnate us, traverse us, guide us, influence us, determine us, confuse us—willingly or unwillingly.... Therefore, the importance of always questioning, always doubting, always challenging these discourses ... to find out how they function, how they are constituted" ("Imagination" 563). Collage remotivates extant materials in a critical fashion, forcing readers "to participate, to finish the work" (576).

Federman's argument links traditional formalist concerns with social-critical ones, an extrapolation that has also been made by Walter Benjamin, who has defended collage/montage (in a discussion of Bertold Brecht's "epic theater") as a radical political tool. In montage, "the superimposed element disrupts the context in which it is inserted," and this disruption forces the audience "to adopt an attitude vis-à-vis the process" rather than passively imbibing a realistic illusion (266).

Epic theater "is less concerned with filling the public with feeling, even seditious ones, than with alienating it, in an enduring manner, through thinking, from the conditions in which it lives" (267). This is Brecht's famous "V-effect"—a technique of formal defamiarlization that subtends a social estrangement. New Wave SF writers of the 1960s were similarly driven by a conviction that overturning conventional modes of discourse, within and outside the genre, would have profound socio-political repercussions.

As in so many areas of society, the 1960s was a period of significant conflict and change within the SF genre. The so-called "New Wave" movement brought not only a greater degree of literary sophistication to the field but also a more militant ideological posture. During this decade, science fiction shed its earlier, almost missionary zeal for the popularization of science and scientific literacy and adopted instead a series of critical perspectives that arraigned not only technocratic institutions and values but SF's own status as their literary mouthpiece.

New Wave SF undertook a powerful diagnostic self-analysis designed to lay bare the complicities and lines of influence that linked the genre with the technocratic state—a self-analysis that, at times, seemed to call for the liquidation of SF as the only possible escape from ideological co-optation, while at other times suggesting that the genre, with its powerful vocabulary of imagery and metaphor, was uniquely positioned to expose the depredations of modern technocracy. Ultimately, New Wave SF did not so much reject its position as a popular mediator of postwar technoculture as infuse this sometimes dubious role with a more encompassing ethical-political agenda and a more sophisticated aesthetic approach.

During this period, many SF authors began to question, if not the core values of scientific inquiry, then the larger social processes to which they had been conjoined in the service of state and corporate power. In their extrapolation of fictional futures, younger writers in particular began to be guided by influential critiques of technocracy emanating from modern philosophy (Theodor Adorno, Herbert Marcuse) and sociology (C. Wright Mills, Jacques Ellul, Theodore Roszak). The New Wave critique of technocracy began to align itself with other ideological programs seeking to reform or revolutionize social relations, such as Second-Wave feminism (in the fiction of Joanna Russ), gay liberation (in the work of Samuel R. Delany), and anti-colonial movements (in stories by Ursula K. Le Guin and Michael Bishop), generating a committed brand of SF that used the resources of the genre for politically progressive purposes.

At the same time, these writers brought to the field a set of aesthetic concerns molded less by a nostalgia for the pulps than by a fascination for the strategies of the historical *avant garde*, from Surrealism to the *nouveau roman*. The New Wave thus marked the emergence and consolidation of a sophisticated literary mode, whose formal techniques rivaled those of contemporary postmodern fiction in its subversion of narrative linearity, its resistance to teleology and closure, and its experiments with fragmented and dissonant prose structures (strategies far removed from the conventionally straightforward methods of traditional pulp SF).

Indeed, these twin "revolutionary" impulses—ideological and formal—were intimately entwined in the best 1960s SF, showing how the critique of technocratic values required a thoroughgoing revision of the forms of representation through which the genre evoked the coming future. The New Wave, as a political and an aesthetic formation, thus represented an unprecedented moment in the history of popular genres when social-critical and literary-experimental impulses converged, to often provocative and occasionally profound effect.

Rather than endorsing a tacit consensus regarding the outcome of technoscientific progress, SF began to explore visions of alterity rooted in contemporary anthropological, psychoanalytic, and gender theory, visions frequently elaborated through experimental narrative techniques (such as the time-slipping four-part montage of Russ's 1975 novel *The Female Man*). This diversification of technocultural possibilities tempered if not undid pulp SF's quasi-imperialist vision of straight men conquering the stars in the name of science, substituting instead a psychedelic exploration of the domains of what J.G. Ballard famously dubbed "inner space."

This exploration drew not on the pulp tradition but on eclectically-borrowed theoretical and avant-garde resources, such as Marshall McLuhan's vision of modern media as a prosthetic formation, William Burroughs's cut-up technique of resistance to propagandistic control systems, and Pop-Art's ironic celebration-cum-critique of industrial mass production.

While the major narrative experiments of the period have received substantial coverage in the critical literature (see, e.g., Greenland), insufficient attention has been paid to the innovations in visual art, magazine design, and illustration that accompanied the advent of the New Wave movement.

While a few SF artists, such as Richard Powers, had dabbled in *avant-garde* styles during the 1950s, the 1960s saw an explosion of such strategies. The use of collage by New Wave writers—such as J.G. Ballard, whose debt to Surrealism he frequently and proudly acknowledged—has received sustained attention, but this essay proposes to consider, alongside these literary experiments, the deployment of photomontage and other collage techniques by SF illustrators during the 1960s. I will focus in particular on the visual evolution of *New Worlds*, the flagship of the New Wave movement, as it mutated from a traditional SF digest into a large-format glossy magazine featuring widespread coverage of the contemporary arts, with illustrated essays on the likes of Salvador Dali, M.C. Escher, and Eduardo Paolozzi. My main point will be to show that the New Wave's aesthetic and ideological renovation of SF was not purely a literary phenomenon but also encompassed radical transformations in the genre's visual culture.

Founded in 1946 on the model of John W. Campbell's Golden-Age hard-SF pulp *Astounding Stories*, *New Worlds* was for two decades the principal British outlet for serious science fiction. Over the years, its editor John Carnell had cultivated a reliable stable of native talent whose work was generally competent if not exactly trailblazing. The exception to this stricture was J.G. Ballard, who began placing stories with Carnell in 1956, and by the early 1960s was widely seen as the most original young talent in British SF. His fiction was distinctive in its range of reference to modern literature and culture, from Kafka and Freud to the Surrealists, whose psychological insights often formed the speculative core of his tales (as opposed to the physical and sociological sciences that had dominated SF's modes of extrapolation to that time).

Witty, lyrical, and evocative, his early stories were propelled by a powerful undercurrent of obsession, often featuring haunted or half-mad characters struggling with internal demons in near-future settings marked by social breakdown and spiritual malaise. A clutching sense of entropic dissolution prevailed, with his protagonists obscurely complicit in their own ruination—brooding antiheroes far removed from the stolid rocket jockeys of American pulp SF.

In fact, these tales were intended as ironic comment on the genre's cherished vision of spaceflight as humanity's high destiny, as Ballard made clear in the guest editorial he penned for *New Worlds* in May 1962, entitled "Which Way to Inner Space?" Baldly asserting that "space fiction can no longer provide the main wellspring of ideas for s-f," not only because the result was "invariably juvenile" (3) but also because the actual achievements of the space program had eclipsed the genre's fantasies, Ballard called for a turn inward, toward the realms of experimental and aberrant psychology:

> "I'd like to see more psycho-literary ideas, more meta-biological and meta-chemical concepts, private time-systems, synthetic psychologies and space-times, more of the sombre half-worlds one glimpses in the paintings of schizophrenics, all in all a complete speculative poetry and fantasy of science" (118).

The goal, he made clear, was not merely to update the genre's corpus of available themes, but to improve its literary quality, bringing SF in line with the avant-garde impulses of "painting, music and the cinema... particularly as these have become wholeheartedly speculative, more and more concerned with the creation of new states of mind, new levels of awareness." In order to accomplish this, SF would have to "jettison its present narrative forms and plots" (117), inherited from the pulp-fiction past, and become instead a truly mature and modern genre in synch with the changing times.

Ballard's essay provided the first glimmerings of a topical and aesthetic approach that would soon crystallize as the New Wave movement, a program of renovation that would shift the genre's focus from the soaring vistas of interstellar space to the psycho-social landscapes of an encroaching technocratic modernity. In 1963, Ballard produced what is often seen as the first real New Wave story, "The Terminal Beach." A brilliantly disturbing montage of subtitled fragments geared to capture the disintegrating mind of its protagonist, the story follows an erstwhile World War II pilot who has become a starving squatter haunting the abandoned atomic testing site at Eniwetok in a desperate effort to come to grips with his own complicity in mechanized death.

The story was hugely controversial among SF writers and fans not only because of its apparent anti-technological bias but also due to its unusual form, its juxtaposition of disparate images that fused objective and subjective worlds in a Surrealist labyrinth of blasted bunkers, half-buried jukeboxes, and huge B-29s rusting together "like dead reptile birds." Carnell hated the story and almost refused to publish it; certainly, its pugnacious experimentalism was unique in early-60s SF (see Latham).

The following year, however, a change in *New World*'s ownership prompted Carnell to hand the magazine over to a young, energetic successor named Michael Moorcock who soon made it clear that Ballard's "Terminal Beach" was to be not the exception but the norm. Moorcock's editorial in the first issue, entitled "A New Literature for the Space Age," boldly called for "a kind of SF which is unconventional in every sense" and thus appropriate for "our ad-saturated, Bomb-dominated, power-corrupted times" (3).

The issue also featured an essay by Ballard on the novels of William S. Burroughs, which hailed that author's controversial cut-up method as the ideal formal paradigm for a new brand of serious SF. Like Surrealism, the cut-up was a "technique for the marriage of opposites, underlining the role of recurrent images in all communication, fixed at the points of contact in the webs of language linking everything in our lives, from nostalgic reveries...to sinister bureaucratic memos and medicalese" (123). It was thus the perfect method for exploring inner space, "fashion[ing] from our dreams and nightmares the first authentic mythology of the age of Cape Canaveral, Hiroshima and Belsen" (127).

During the next several years, *New Worlds* began to stake out terrain that brought SF more and more into conversation with the historical avant-garde, with Ballard usually leading the way as practitioner and polemicist. His 1966 essay "The

Coming of the Unconscious" defended Surrealism as a cognitive-aesthetic mode uniquely well-suited to analyzing a postwar world where reality and fantasy were inextricably conjoined. Like the paintings of Dali and Max Ernst, Ballard's fiction of this period explored "the juxtaposition of the bizarre and familiar" (141)—in Ballard's case, not Dali's wrist-watches and fried eggs, but those elements more clearly linked with the technological and media landscapes: automobiles, movie stars, atrocity footage, astronauts.

In his approach to this material, Ballard, like Dali, wed an attitude of naïve innocence—an embrace of this vulgar material as the inescapable common stratum of our lives—with a paranoid conviction that there was something obscurely awry beneath its bland, settled surfaces.

Ballard's main contribution to *New Worlds* from 1966 to 1969 was a series of bleak and brilliant "condensed novels" (as he called them), which drew heavily on Dali in their bold juxtaposition of iconic images and on Burroughs in their embrace of fragmented seriality over linear narrative. In 1970, these works were eventually collected into an anti-novel entitled *The Atrocity Exhibition*, a book that perfectly exemplified the New Wave synthesis of formal innovation and ideological critique.

A potent collage drawing on the image archive of postwar political and celebrity culture, *The Atrocity Exhibition* arraigned modern technocracy, and its instrumentalized communications media, as a pathological psychosocial formation. Its continuous global projection of stereotyped images had attained a reified autonomy: blown-up photos of politicians and film stars loomed over the contemporary landscape like vast dream visions, providing for individual consumers "a set of operating formulae for their passage through consciousness" (18) and, for the mysterious power elite manipulating the images, a system of modular codes "as unreal as the war the film companies had restarted in Vietnam" (9). In Ballard's analysis, public figures and events—from Elizabeth Taylor to the Vietnam War—were simulations arranged by shadowy experts and designed to channelize human desire into programmed outlets of fantasy and aggression.

Though this analysis might seem wholly negative in its vision of a power-mad technocracy contriving unreal mass-mediated events, Ballard's work also celebrated the inability of the system fully to recuperate its effects. The fake newsreels, the seductive images of fashion models and presidential candidates, while quantified to achieve predictable results, occasionally derailed when obsessed individuals appropriated and remotivated them in obscure symbologies and patterns all their own. Random fragments of the technological and media landscape, when filtered by a visionary consciousness, achieved the status of "psychic totems"—"assassination weapons" that violently broke the spell of power. Moreover, the sudden deaths of iconic celebrities—from the ambiguous murder of JFK to the legendary suicide of Marilyn Monroe—took on an impenetrable yet potent mystery, becoming the object of rapt fantasies that could not be entirely controlled.

This vision was realized at the level of form itself: the random violence of decoupage—the radical reappropriation achieved by the collage effect—was, in *The Atrocity Exhibition*, a source of potential liberation from the calibrated violence of a militarist technocracy. As Roger Luckhurst has observed, "Ballard's devices of collage, the subversion of found texts, and refunctioning of allegedly 'objective' professional discourses" (153) were the equivalent of politicized theoretical strategies like Situationism, and indeed the "Society of the Spectacle" has achieved few more potent resolutions than in these harsh, dissonant, hallucinatory fictions.

Yet Luckhurst, like most critics of the New Wave movement, have limited their focus to the fiction itself, and have thus largely ignored the evolving, and growingly experimental, visual medium through which it was originally transmitted. When Moorcock took over *New Worlds* in the Spring of 1964, he envisioned a radical revamping that would convert a standard SF magazine into a publication "speciali[zing] in experimental work by writers like Burroughs and artists like Paolozzi," and thus attempting a "cross-fertilisation of popular sf, science and the work of the literary and artistic avant garde" ("Introduction" 11).

Yet for the first three years, he was hamstrung by a pocketbook format enforced by the new publisher and a rapidly declining subscription base, as Old Guard readers deserted the magazine in droves. The operation was very close to folding when it was saved by a last-minute infusion of funds from the British Arts Council, which had taken an interest in Moorcock's ambitious editorial program. This subvention allowed Moorcock to realize his original vision for the journal, and the July 1967 issue saw an increase in size, a switch to glossy paper, and the inclusion of a range of challenging content, from Ballard's newest condensed novel "The Death Module" to Pamela Zoline's feminist collage story "The Heat Death of the Universe" to an illustrated essay on the drawings of Dutch Surrealist M.C. Escher. Over the next three years, before the

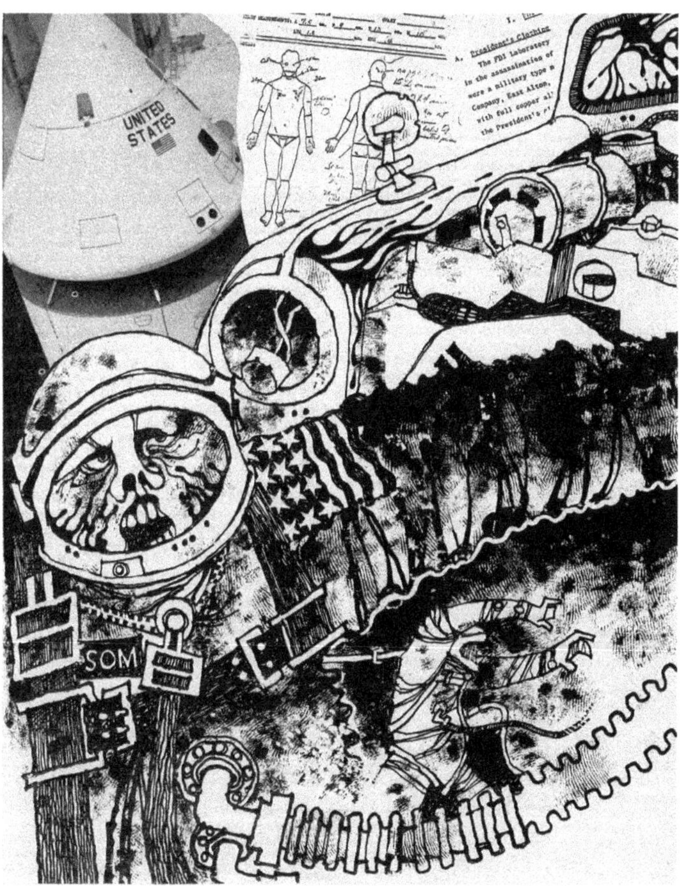

Full-page illustration for JG Ballard's "The Death Module"

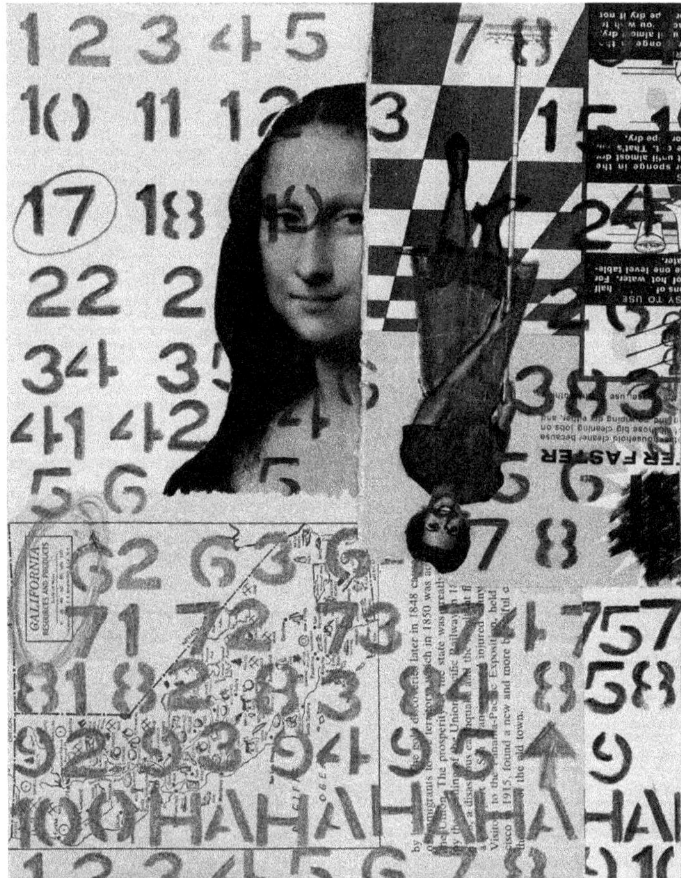

Full-page illustration for Pamela Zoline's "Heat Death of the Universe"

magazine eventually folded in the Spring of 1970, Moorcock continuously experimented not just with the styles of fiction he published but with the magazine's design and layout, such that by the late 1960s it had totally morphed from a genre-based publication with roots in the SF pulps into an avant-garde journal with a strong countercultural vision.

As noted above, this transformation was ideological as well as formal, reflecting a critical interrogation of the technocratic values that SF as a genre had been partially responsible for disseminating. Collage strategies were particularly useful in this regard since, as Benjamin has argued, their "use of elements of reality in experimental rearrangements" (235) had the effect of interrupting settled readings, defamiliarizing habituated modes of perception and prompting, at least potentially, a posture of cognitive reflection. It is difficult to imagine anything more alienating, for the traditional SF reader, than the large-format *New Worlds*, which radically defamiliarized what an SF publication should look like and do. Gone were the mimetic illustrations, the linear narratives, the technophiliac tone of the conventional SF magazine, replaced by striking photo-montages, aggressive collage fictions, and a militant critique of technocratic society.

The first several issues of the revamped *New Worlds* made clear the agenda the journal was staking out in large part through the photo-essays it ran on major graphic artists, thus indicating the importance of visual elements in defining the New Wave aesthetic. The article on Escher by Charles Platt, entitled "Expressing the Abstract," makes the link clear at the outset: "Speculative fiction has in the last five years become a form involving greater abstraction of idea and vision. Consequently, art concerned principally with the visual interpretation of such subtleties is particularly relevant to the form" (44). Escher's skillful deployment of visual paradox, his intricate confusions of microcosm and macrocosm, held a key for SF writers seeking "new means of expression to convey the complex qualities of a mental image" (49).

Platt was particularly well-placed to explore this linkage since Moorcock had appointed him designer of the magazine, and over the next few years his layouts would explore delirious fusions of word and image. The essay on Paolozzi in the subsequent issue, written by Christopher Finch, went even further in urging a connection between avant-garde visual art and New Wave fiction, arguing that the Italian artist's sculptures and collages deserved to be seen as "language mechanisms" built out of iconic pop-culture elements plundered from the technological and media landscapes. In short, they were the "para-literary" equivalents of Ballard's condensed novels, "devis[ing] a basic system of syntax" from the detritus of postmodern life and using it to express a "comprehensive grasp of the constantly evolving situation" (30).

On the one hand, this sort of argument for an alliance between speculative fiction and avant-garde art simply carried forward J.G. Ballard's championing of Surrealists like Dali and Ernst as founders of "the iconography of inner space" ("Coming" 141). On the other hand, the fact that the magazine now possessed the financial and intellectual resources to explore this alliance in detail issue by issue made the overall argument much more compelling.

No longer did the imputed connection rely solely on Ballard's (admittedly considerable) powers as a polemicist; it could be directly seen by the reader as he or she turned the pages. Paolozzi in particular became something of an aesthetic touchstone for the large-format *New Worlds*: not only was he listed for several years on the masthead as the magazine's "aeronautics advisor," but his pioneering montages of found images plucked from the pop-culture archive (including occasional borrowings from the SF pulps) provided a model for the photo-montage illustrations produced by in-house artists such as Platt, Vivienne Young, and Mal Dean.

The appointment of Finch as Arts Editor in September 1967 insured ongoing coverage of contemporary artists whose work converged with the anti-technocratic bent of the magazine's fiction. Finch's profiles of British collage artists Richard Hamilton (October 1967) and Colin Self (November 1967), for example, provocatively examined the erotics of high-tech imagery, the hypnotic beauty of weapons systems, the compulsive glamour of consumer objects—themes also treated, with growing sophistication, in the magazine's published fiction.

The effect of perusing these issues is a full-body immersion in the New Wave aesthetic, a frontal confrontation with a pugnacious SF counterculture. The illustrations accompanying stories in Brian Aldiss's "Acid Head Wars" series or the serialized installments of Norman Spinrad's novel *Bug Jack Barron* at once captured the fiction's psychedelic imagery and contributed an element of potent strangeness to the general mixture. Langdon's Jones's collage story "The Eye of the Lens," in the March 1968 issue, featured a concrete poem entwining passages from the text around a lens-like flaring sun or blooming flower.

In the same issue, Platt contributed a visual essay entitled

"Fun Palace—Not a Freakout" that took the form of a series of caustic captions and word balloons accompanying feverish photo-montages of Jimi Hendrix, Marshall McLuhan, and the Maharishi Mahesh Yogi, the general purpose of which was to mock hippie youth's pretensions to originality by linking their lifestyle experiments with the "bigger-better, new-improved" ethos of contemporary consumer culture (37).

Ballard's manifestoes and hallucinatory fiction continued to provide a kind of backbone for the various collage experiments. The January 1969 issue ran his latest condensed novel, "The Summer Cannibals," illustrated with photos of wrecked cars, crash test dummies, and fragments of a woman's face. Other issues ran, as parody advertisements, Ballard's photographs of his current girlfriend with superimposed quotations from his stories.

In the February 1969 issue, Ballard provided a strident profile of Dali, once again defending Surrealism as the "main visual tradition of the 20th century," just as SF was its "main literary tradition" ("Salvador Dali" 27). The 1969 issues in particular were seamless fusions of verbal and visual content, with every short story coming equipped with drawings, collages, or photographs designed to heighten the defamiliarizing effect.

Some stories, such as Michael Butterworth's "Circularisation of Condensed Conventional Straight-Line Word-Image Structures (Radial-Planographic Condensed Word-Image Structures, Rotation About a Point)," in the July 1969 issue, incorporated the illustrations directly into the text as quirky charts and diagrams. At the same time, poetry by D.M. Thomas and Mervyn Peake persistently toyed with page layout, using rows and columns as structural features. Similarly, John Sladek's story "Alien Territory," in the November 1969 issue, included instructions on how to decode a story that featured braided narratives, one reading top-to-bottom and another reading left-to-right.

The overall effect was of a ludic subversion of technocratic ideology, since the layout of these pieces appeared at once highly rationalized and oddly playful, regimented and insane. In short, the iconography and design of *New Worlds* mounted a critique similar to that contained in its fiction: an exposure of high-tech military-industrial society as a world of surface calm screening depths of seething violence and corruption. Photo-montages of technological instruments fissured with organic apertures, for example, amounted to a powerful indictment of reification, of machines assuming lifelike properties while human beings were assimilated into a monolithic apparatus.

In sum, the New Wave, especially the editorial coterie at *New Worlds*, made use of collage techniques in a methodical and multifaceted way, in works of fiction that challenged SF orthodoxies and in visual materials that held up to postwar culture a series of distorting mirrors, reflecting back its incipient rage and anomie.

TRUNK RELEASE

elaborate game with her, using their acts of intercourse for some perverse cerebral pleasure of his own? In many ways her body retraced the contours they had explored together. Above the window of the cubicle fluttered the reverse image of the cinema screen, Bardot's translucent face twisted into a bizarre pout.

Non-Communicating Dialogue

As he entered the apartment she was sitting on the balcony, painting her nails. Drying in the sunlight beside her was the novel he had thrown into the bidet, its pages flowering into an elegant ruff. She looked up from her nail file. "Did you enjoy the film?" He walked into the bathroom, wincing at himself in the mirror, that always more tired older brother. The half-hearted inflection of irony in her voice no longer irritated him. An enormous neutral ground now divided them, across which the little left of their emotions signalled like meaningless semaphores. If anything, her voice formed a modulus with the perspectives of wall and ceiling as postural as the design on a detergent pack. She sat down beside him on the bed, splaying her wet nails in a gesture of pleasant intimacy. He stared at the transverse scar above her navel. What act between them would provide a point of junction?

A Krafft-Ebing of Geometry and Posture

He remembered these pleasures: the conjunction of her exposed pubis with the polished contours of the bidet; the white cube of the bathroom quantifying her left breast as she bent over the handbasin; the mysterious eroticism of the multi-storey car park, a Krafft-Ebing of geometry and posture; her flattened thighs on the tiles of the swimming pool below; her right hand osculating the finger-smeared panel of the elevator control. Looking at her from the bed, he recreated these situations, conceptualisations of exquisite games.

The Solarium

Beyond the cafe tables the beach was deserted, the white pumice fossilising the heat and sunlight. He played with the beer mat, shaping the cigarette ash on the tables into a series of small pyramids. She waited behind her magazine, now and then flicking at the fly in her citrus juice. He

Page 20

Typical illustrations for JG Ballard's "The Summer Cannibals"

Works Cited:

Ballard, J.G. *The Atrocity Exhibition*. London: Triad/Panther, 1979.

_____. "The Coming of the Unconscious." *New Worlds* 164 (July 1966): 141-46.

_____. "Myth-Maker of the 20th Century." *New Worlds* 142 (May-June 1964): 121-27.

_____. "Salvador Dali: The Innocent as Paranoid." *New Worlds* 187 (February 1969): 25-31.

_____. "Which Way to Inner Space?" *New Worlds* 118 (May 1962): 2-3, 116-18.

Benjamin, Walter. "The Author as Producer." 1966. Trans. Edmund Jephcott. *Reflections: Essays, Aphorisms, Autobiograhical Writings*. Ed. Peter Demetz. New York: Schocken, 1986. 220-38.

Federman, Raymond. "Surfiction—Four Propositions in Form of an Introduction." *Surfiction: Fiction Now...and Tomorrow*. 2nd ed. Chicago: Swallow, 1981. 5-15.

_____. "Imagination as Plagiarism [an unfinished paper...]." *New Literary History* 7:3 (Spring 1976): 563-78.

Finch, Christopher. "Eduardo Paolozzi." *New Worlds* 174 (August 1967): 28-35.

Greenland, Colin. *The Entropy Exhibition: Michael Moorcock and the British "New Wave" in Science Fiction*. London: Routledge & Kegan Paul, 1983.

Latham, Rob. "*New Worlds* and the New Wave in Fandom: Fan Culture and the Reshaping of Science Fiction in the Sixties." *Vector: The Critical Journal of the British Science Fiction Association* 242 (July/August 2005): 4-12.

Luckhurst, Roger. *Science Fiction*. London: Polity, 2005.

Moorcock, Michael. "Introduction." *New Worlds: An Anthology*. Ed. Moorcock. London: Flamingo, 1983. 9-26.

_____. "A New Literature for the Space Age." *New Worlds* 142 (May-June 1964): 2-3.

Platt, Charles. "Expressing the Abstract." *New Worlds* 173 (July 1967): 44-49.

_____. "Fun Palace—Not a Freakout." *New Worlds* 180 (March 1968): 31-41.

SHADOWS OF KINDRED SPIRITS: ROBERT SMITHSON AND SCIENCE FICTION

BY SUZAAN BOETTGER

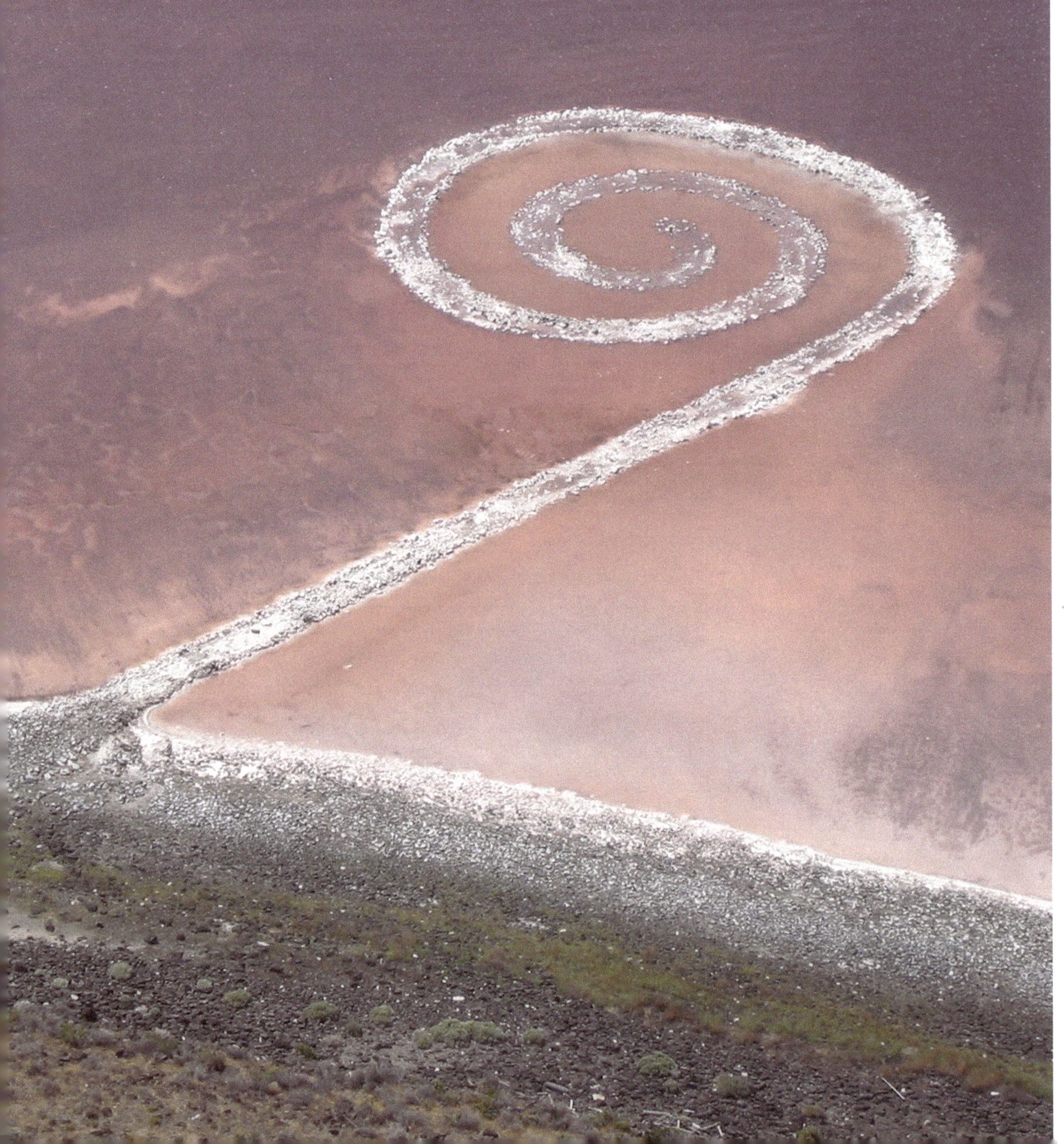

[Smithson's] monuments endure in our minds, the ground-plans of heroic psychological edifices that will one day erect themselves and whose shadows we can already see from the corners of our eyes.[1]

J.G. Ballard

Describing the source of Robert Smithson's attraction to the bizarre magenta hue of the water in the cove of the Great Salt Lake where the sculptor chose to build his magisterial earthen Spiral Jetty, Michael Kimmelman ventured, "Smithson admired the science fiction of J.G. Ballard. The red water vaguely evokes a Martian sea."[2]

The *New York Times* critic's blunt equation demonstrates the extent to which the innovative American earthworker has been associated with science fiction—and particularly that written by one of its most famous ground breakers, Ballard. Yes, in his essays Smithson referred to several Ballard stories, and at his accidental death at 35, in 1973, owned three of Ballard's books among the more than three dozen volumes of sci-fi novels, short stores, and literary criticism and two dozen issues of the genre's magazines.[3] One of his art dealer John Weber's strongest memories of him is that they would "hang out together and go to many, many, many science fiction movies in [the then very very very tawdry] Times Square."[4]

Smithson tacitly promoted his connection to science fiction through quotations prominently placed in epigraphs of articles and in his own commentary published in the then oracle of the art world cognoscenti, *Artforum*. His attraction to what in the 1960s was considered a cheap thrill—tales easily available in racks of slender paperbacks that fit into a purse or the back pocket of jeans—mixed in his essays an *outré* edge of popular diversion with references to literary titans such as T.S. Eliot (of whom he owned thirteen books by or about). Smithson's literary omnivorousness distinguished him among his ambitious art-world-focused peers as an explorer who read not only fiction and science, but science fiction, see-sawing between culture low and high.

1. J.G. Ballard, 'Robert Smithson as Cargo Cultist," in *Robert Smithson, a Collection of Writings on Robert Smithson on the Occasion of the Installation of* Dead Tree *at Pierogi 2000*, eds. Brian Conley and Joe Amrhein, (New York: Perogi, 1997), 31.
2. Michael Kimmelman, "The Way We Live Now: 10-3-12: Phenomenon; Out of the Deep." *The New York Times Magazine*, October 13, 2002, 42.
3. Smithson owned the story collections *Terminal Beach* (1964), *The Voices of Time* (1962), and the novel *The Drought* (1968). In his writing and interviews he also referred to *Billenium, The Crystal World, The Drowned World,The Overloaded Man, The Waiting Grounds*, and *The Wind From Nowhere*. The contents of his library is published in Ann Reynolds, *Learning from New Jersey and Elsewhere*, (Cambridge: MIT Press, 2003), 297-345.
4. Oral history interview with John Weber, 2006, Archives of American Art, Smithsonian Institution, 17.

But also, No. Readers of this volume will recognize that Kimmelman was muddling sci-fi metaphors; space-age mariners sprang from the futurisms of earlier generations of sci-fabulists such as Isaac Asimov and Arthur C. Clarke, and before that, Jules Verne and H.G. Wells (all in Smithson's book collection). Not only did Ballard not place any of his stories on Mars or any other planet than Earth, save the planet Murak in "The Waiting Grounds," but forty years before Kimmelman asserted that Ballard had dissed "space fiction": "The biggest developments of the immediate future will take place, not on the Moon or Mars, but on Earth, and it is inner space, not outer, that needs to be explored."[5]

Of course, like any author Ballard's primary material came from plumbing his own subjectivity and identity, as he hinted to cognizant readers by making so many of his early stories' protagonists' physicians. They ministered to deterioration, the symptoms of which they were trained to closely observe, but beneath those useful acts medicine was a discipline Ballard had himself studied before setting it aside mid med school to write, where his identifications of all forms of life are scientifically meticulous.

As for Smithson, after listing "some [film] landmarks of Sci-fic," he observed, "Artists that like Horror tend toward the emotive, while artists who like Sci-fic tend toward the perceptive."[6] That is, while by the mid-1960s the uninhibited brushstrokes of his artist fathers—the Abstract Expressionists Jackson Pollock, Willem de Kooning, et al, a style of painting that until recently he himself had practiced—could be considered akin to the primal screams provoked by tales of horror, sci-fi demanded discernment and deciphering—the conceptualizing skills then in vogue in the art world.

Yet for himself, Smithson wasn't gleaning inspiration from science fiction's landscape sites as much as responding to authors' metaphysical insights—and equally, their mordant sentiments such as Ballard's "...savouring the subtle atmosphere of melancholy that surrounded these last vestiges of a level of civilization now virtually vanished forever" in his *The Drowned World*.[7] Such stories seemed to speak to Smithson, and in drawing his readers' attention to them, spoke through and for him about aspects of himself otherwise unstated.

5. J.G. Ballard, "Which Way to Inner Space?" *A User's Guide to the Millennium*, (New York: Picador, 1996), 195, 197. There is no evidence that Smithson read this essay, but it is interesting to note that when Ballard wrote in it "In the past the scientific bias of s-f has been toward the physical sciences,—rocketry, electronics, cybernetics—and the emphasis should switch to the biological sciences" (197)—it was published in *New Worlds* sci-fi magazine in London, 1962—Smithson was strengthening his relationship with his childhood friend Nancy Holt, whose Tufts University degree in biology corresponded to his own youthful studies in natural science.
6. Robert Smithson, "Entropy and the New Monuments," in *Robert Smithson, The Collected Writings*, ed. Jack Flam, Berkeley: University of California Press, 1996, 17. Originally published in *Artforum*, June, 1966. In quoting Smithson, his idiosyncratic capitalization and spelling will be retained.
7. J.G. Ballard, *The Drowned World*, New York, London; Liveright Publishing Corporation, 2012, 20. This was first published in 1962. Smithson did not quote from this novel but in "The Arist as Site-Seer, or a Dintorphic Essay")1966-670 named it in an endnote listing books by Ballard.

Preceding page: Robert Smithson, *The Spiral Jetty*, 1970. Photograph @Hikmet Sidney Loe

Just a few months after its construction, large photographs of the *Spiral Jetty* appeared in the Museum of Modern Art's summer show, a survey of conceptual art lamely titled "Information," and by the end of the year his film of it was shown at the prestigious Dwan Gallery, NYC. Soon, the 15-foot wide, 1500-foot long coil of basalt, earth, and encrusted salt crystals became the icon of the earliest type of Land Art, earthworks. Remote from coastal cultural metropolises in the relatively barren "America's Dead Sea," built solely of local geological matter (without the manufactured structural reinforcements of concrete or lumber characteristic of subsequent Land Art), and expansive in both size and their creators' ambition, earthworks display the bold liberatory spirit of the 1960s. Likewise, the *Spiral Jetty* is the work with which Smithson himself has been branded, although insufficiently interpreted.[8]

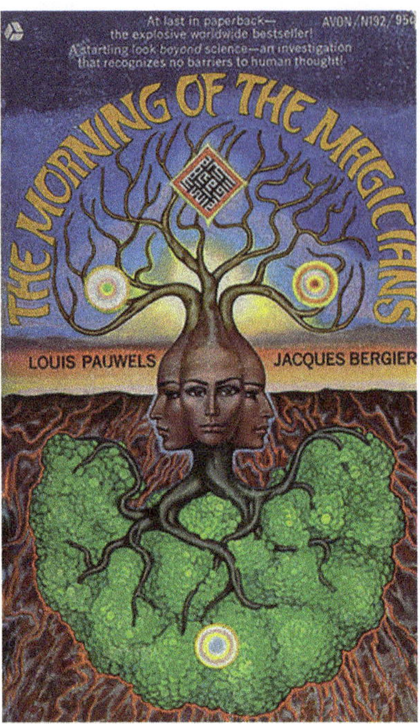

The spiral, part an of-the-moment movement toward placing or making art in remote non-art public places yet an archaic cross-cultural symbol of psychic and spiritual transition, epitomizes Smithson's famous declaration that present consciousness "must explore the pre- and post-historic mind; it must go into the places where remote futures meet remote pasts."[9] Smithson's most direct source of that statement might have been the cult classic among French youth in the 1960s (Smithson owned the 1968 translated paperback) *Morning of the Magicians*. Addressing speculative science, ufology, Nazi occultism, alchemy and spiritual philosophy, the book advocates receptivity to the paranormal to perceive what the authors called fantastic realism, stated rather flatly, "One must be capable of projecting one's intelligence far into the past and far into the future."[10]

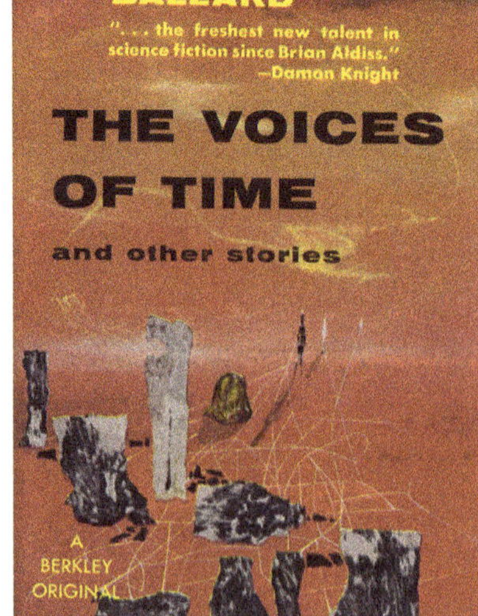

But Smithson's poetic articulation of that idea sounds more like Ballard, who in his story "The Voices of Time" wrote, "The vast age of the landscape, the inaudible chorus of voices resonating from the lake and from the white hills, seemed to carry him back through time, down endless corridors to the first thresholds of the world."[11] Setting it in a research site near dry salt lake beds, Ballard describes a scientist cutting a maze-like ideogram in the floor of an empty swimming pool. Another character constructs a huge concrete labyrinth formed of a circle overlaid with a cruciform, a quadratic circle like that in the floor pavement of the nave at Chartres Cathedral, a kind of spoked sun wheel seen in imagery of prehistoric and historical religious communities and as old as the spiral.

Ballard and Smithson never met or even personally communicated but in the work of the West Village artist/writer the bard of Shepperton seemed to recognize a kindred spirit. Asked to contribute to a catalogue for a posthumous Smithson exhibition, Ballard addressed Smithson's trademark creation, opening with "What strange caravel could have emerged from the saline mists of this remote lake and chosen to dock at this mysterious harbour?" as if setting the scene for one of his own compelling enigmas. He could have noted how both of them imagined monumental mystical mandalas in desert environments. But also, their mutual fantasies made them something like blood brothers, as he had written nine stories about fading *artistes* languishing in a degenerating resort whose name he took for the title of the collection, *Vermilion Sands*.

Published in 1971, a year after Smithson made the *Spiral Jetty*, Ballard's title coincidentally describes the color of the Jetty's milieu when the water level recedes and its shallow lake bed is an expanse of white salt whose seepage tints it a purplish red, which in turn calls up Ballard's description more than a decade earlier in *The Drowned World*, "The soft beaches would glow invitingly with a glossy carmine sheen."[12] In his own essay on his *Spiral Jetty*, Smithson described his first view of the site,"...the color of red algae circulating in the heart of the lake, pumping into ruby currents, no they were veins and arteries sucking up the obscure sediments. My eyes became combustion chambers churning orbs of blood."[13]

Ballard titled his reflections "Robert Smithson as Cargo Cultist," slyly—or modestly—implying that Smithson's appreciation for Ballard's narrative "cargo" was like South Pacific natives mistakenly worshiping northerners' objects washed ashore. Smithson did have a relevant obsession, but it was of another sort of load—he wrote that "cargos of travail flow through our heart."[14] But Ballard, who favored exhuming the latent over narrating the apparent, insightfully concluded by construing Smithson's earthworks as

8. For that and much more, see my biographical *The Passions of Robert Smithson, Art and Biography*, forthcoming in fall 2022 from the University of Minnesota Press.
9. Robert Smithson, "A Sedimentation of the Mind: Earth Projects," in Flam, 113. Originally published in *Artforum*, September 1968.
10. Louis Pauwels and Jacques Bergier. *The Morning of the Magicians*. Translated by Rollo Myers. (New York: Avon, 1968), xxiii.
11. J.G. Ballard, "The Voices of Time," *The Voices of Times and Other Stories*, (New York: Berkley Publishing), 1962, 34.
12. Ballard, *The Drowned World*, 100.
13. Robert Smithson, "The Spiral Jetty," in Flam, 148. This was originally published in Gyorgy Kepes, ed., *Arts of the Environment*, (New York: George Braziller, 1972.
14. Robert Smithson, "From the Broken Ark," Archives of American Art, reel 3834, frame 230.

"*psychological* edifices that will one day erect themselves"—that is, after his audiences are able to recognize and receive them—"and whose shadows we can already see from the corners of our eyes."[15] Of course he was both perceiving Smithson and projecting his own orientation, implicitly describing Smithson's work as his own has been received, as metaphors of a temperament's inclinations.

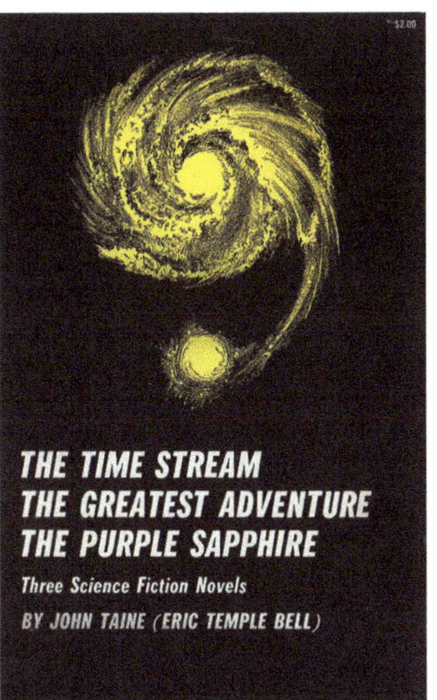

Smithson own appropriations of science fiction varied between the explicit, bolstering public appreciation of his sculpture, and the allusive, insinuating private issues. When he noted that "The idea of the 'megalith' appears in several of Ballard's science-fiction stories," he was embellishing the reductive geometric structures, including his own, then on view in the spring of 1966 in the influential exhibition "Primary Structures" at The Jewish Museum, Manhattan, with an eccentric literary analogy.[16] He referred to Ballard's story "The Terminal Beach," (1964) regarding a labyrinth of 2,000 "concrete monsters...each a perfect cube fifteen feet in height, regularly spaced at ten-yard intervals."[17] Ballard's description remarkably paralleled the format of arrays of Minimalist cubes that one would walk between and around, experientially comprehending their size and mass in relation to one's own and the immediate environment.

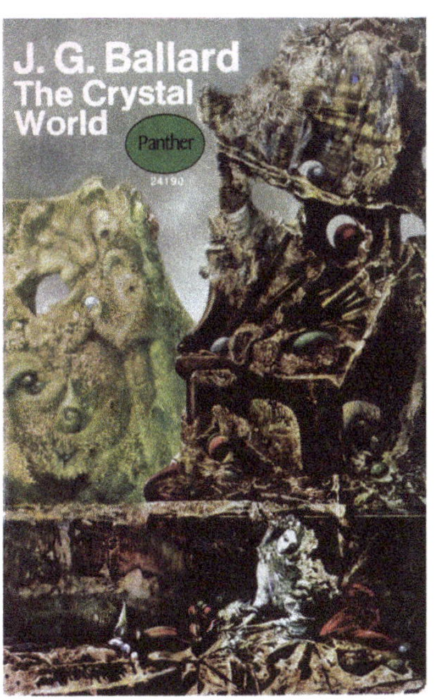

Smithson was eclectic in his science fiction references. For his epigraph to his essay about works in the "Primary Structures" show, he quoted an evocative scene described by the earlier generation novelist Eric Temple Bell, who under the pen name of John Taine provided another prescient analogy to sculptors' recondite fabrications:

> On rising to my feet, and peering across the green glow of the Desert, I perceived that the monument against which I had slept was but one of thousands. Before me stretched long parallel avenues, clear to the far horizon of similar broad, low pillars.[18]

Smithson's sculpture in "Primary Structures" was *Cryosphere*, the term designating those portions of earth's surface where water is in solid form: glaciers, sea ice, ice caps. Each of its series of six identical hexagonal steel disks hugging the wall is the form of water molecules lined up to form a single crystal of ice. The geometricized circles, fronted with radiating bars, resemble something like hubcap-meets-snowflake.

Concurrent with that show, Smithson shed its sober strictures to publish in *Harper's Bazaar*, at the same time borrowing from Ballard to reflect his connection to crystals. The quirky act of publishing in a legacy fashion magazine suggests a desire to play his career both ways: to be one of the guys exhibiting austere constructions—few women did so—and yet to distinguish himself as a writer mixing intellectuality and populism (as would Ballard in his increasingly inventive swerves from the genre he disdained as formulaic space adventures). Adopting a casual voice, Smithson told anecdotally of a trip undertaken with his fellow sculptor Donald Judd and their "wives" to explore a derelict New Jersey quarry, an account presumably appealing to fans of high jinks by emerging artists or *fashionista* rock hounds.

The title of Smithson's May 1966 *Bazaar* article, "The Crystal Land" tacitly—he did not mention Ballard—adapted the title of the novelist's recent publication *The Crystal World* (1966). For the few who "got" the connection—Ballard wasn't yet well-known—he displayed an unconventional taste in literature. For everyone else, altering Ballard's title to "The Crystal *Land*" emphasized his professional affiliation with crystals, geology and, as it turned out, fortuitously foreshadowed his future environmental focus with which he would become identified."[19]

Those enticed by Smithson's reference to read *The Crystal World* will find a physician of unstated nationality specializing in the treatment of leprosy narrating a visit to friends working in a small outpost in the interior of Africa. As the roadways are blocked, he takes a boat up river and discovers strange forest where a leprosy-like virus is progressively crystallizing the entire environment. Flora, fauna, architecture, nonmoving humans and objects are immobilized in a parasitic exoskeleton of gloriously hued prismatic facets.

Smithson's description of the New Jersey quarry also emphasizes a rich geological apocalypse but his response is less wondrous than dolorous:

> Cracked, broken, shattered, the walls [of the quarry] threatened to come crashing down. Fragmentation, corrosion, decomposition, disintegration, rock creep, debris slides, mud flow, avalanche were everywhere in evidence... Fractures and faults

15. See note #1. My emphasis.
16. Robert Smithson, "The Artist as Site-seer; Or, a Dintorphic Essay" (1966-67), Flam, 341, not published in his lifetime.
17. J.G. Ballard, "Terminal Beach," *The Terminal Beach*, (New York: Berkley), 1964, 147.
18. Eric Temple Bell, "The Time Stream," *The Time Stream, The Greatest Adventure, and The Purple Sapphire: Three Science-Fiction Novels*. (New York: Dover, 1964). 90-91. Smithson owned this. *The Time Stream* was first published in 1931-1932.

19. For more on that, see my history, *Earthworks: Art and the Landscape of the Sixties*, Berkeley and London: University of California Press, 2002.

> spilled forth sediment, crushed conglomerates, eroded debris and sandstone. It was an arid region, bleached and dry.[20]

The sensory vividness displays Smithson's inspiration by more than Ballard's title, as the British novelist's writing is characteristically crystalline in its literary precision.

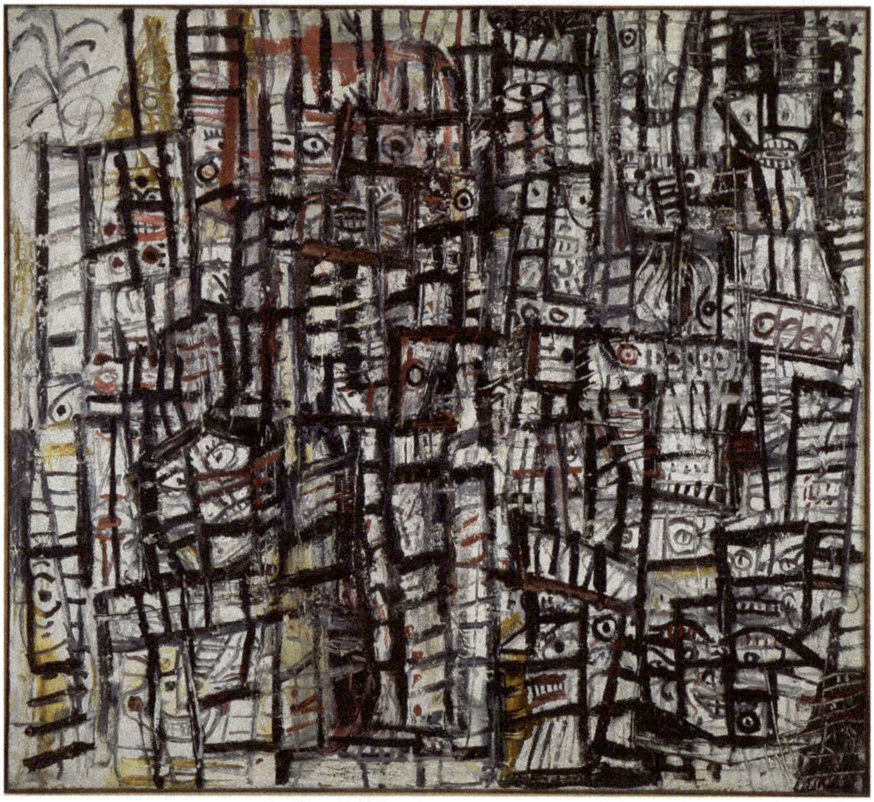

As early as 1971, historian Bruce Franklin perceived Ballard as "a poet of death whose most typical fictions are apocalyptic imaginings, beautiful and ghastly visions of decay, death, despair. His early novels... are science fictions of the wasteland."[21] Likewise, Smithson characteristically likened "Primary Structures" sculptures' look of hulking inertness to "what the physicist calls 'entropy' or 'energy drain.'"[22] Entropy —physicists' concept for an object's loss of energy within closed systems—became Smithson's signature intellectual trope. His envisioning arrays of Minimalist boxes as headstones—an "*Avant garde* of cemeteries," his remark "In regard to the origin of parks in this country it's interesting to note that they really started as graveyards," and declaration "The mind of this death, however, is unrelentingly awake," among many such statements, indicate that they served as intellectualizations for an ongoing affiliation with mortality.[23]

As scholar Haim Finkelstein astutely observed, "Similarly to Smithson, Ballard too conceives the external landscape as a 'mental map' of psychic reality. The mechanism involved is not that of projection but the perception of a quality of the landscape that appears connected with a certain innate quality of his character's mind."[24] In an epigraph to an unpublished essay, Smithson quoted Ballard's assertion of a unity between geology and psychology: "The system of megaliths now provided a complete substitute for those functions of his mind which gave to it its sense of the sustained rational order of time and space."[25] Then he poetically amplified it for the opening claim in his essay "A Sedimentation of the Mind, Earth Projects," strongly asserting that duality,"The earth's surface and the figments of the mind have a way of disintegrating into discrete regions of art."[26]

Robert Smithson, *Purgatory*, oil/canvas, 61 -5/8 x 67-5/16 inches (156.5 x 171 cm)

Ballard described *The Crystal World*'s town as having "more than a passing resemblance to purgatory," the zone of tormented atonement that Smithson pictured in his 1959 painting *Purgatory* and which also sounds like the "typical abysses" and "abandoned set of futures" that in a few years in his famous tour of his hometown he will attribute to the run-down "slurb" of Passaic, New Jersey.[27] Both Ballard and Smithson channeled the Romantics' attraction to ruins as powerful inducements to melancholic reverie. Beneath their congruence in subject matter and style their identification with geological and environmental degradation masked attunements to brokenness, that is, to loss. In *The Crystal World* the "spectacle" of terrestrial fragmentation

> turned the keys of memory, and a thousand images of childhood, forgotten for nearly forty years, filled his mind, recalling the paradisal world when everything seemed illuminated by that prismatic light described so exactly by Wordsworth in his recollections of childhood. The magical shore in front of him seemed to glow like that brief spring."[28]

And in a private essay "The Iconography of Desolation" Smithson lamented, "A terrible yearning for Innocence stares back over Original Sin into some impossible paradise."[29]

20. Robert Smithson, "The Crystal Land," Flam 7. Originally published in *Harper's Bazaar*, May 1966
21. Bruce Franklin, "Foreword to J.G. Ballard's 'The Subliminal Man," in, *SF: The Other Side of Realism*, ed. Thomas D. Clareson, (Bowling Green, OH: Bowling Green University Popular Press), 1971, 200.
22. Robert Smithson, "Entropy," Flam 11.
23. Robert Smithson,"Responses to a Questionnaire from Irving Sandler (1966)," Flam, 329; Allison Sky, "Entropy Made Visible, Interview with Robert Smithson," Flam, 309. Originally published in *On Site* #4, 1973; Robert Smithson, "Language to be Looked and/or Things to be Read," Flam, 61. Dwan Gallery press release, June 1967.
24. Haim Finkelstein, "Deserts of Vast Eternity': J.G. Ballard and Robert Smithson," *Foundation* 39 (Spring 1987), 55.
25. Smithson, "Site-seer" Flam, 340.
26. Smithson, "Sedimentation," Flam, 100.
27. Robert Smithson, "A Tour of the Monuments of Passaic," Flam, 72. Originally published in *Artforum*, December, 1967.
28. Ballard, *Crystal*, 77.
29. Smithson, "The Iconography of Desolation," Flam, 322. Not published in his lifetime.

Smithson's adaptation of Ballard's *Crystal World* title worked for him, but he had already applied the metaphor of the crystal when writing about Judd's work the prior year, before the novel was published. So it is likely that his crystal reference originated in a story Ballard published two years earlier that Ballard had elaborated into *Crystal World* by adding a few tangential characters, a couple of romantic liaisons, more scientific/mystical description, relocating it to the African jungle, and a slightly different ending. Otherwise, the plot and many descriptions are quite similar: in the earlier, investigating a phantasmagoric mutation sweeping over the Florida Everglades, the narrator found shards of crystalline glass accruing to roadways, cars and houses, entombing every non-moving object into chromoluminescent stasis. He "entered an enchanted world, the Spanish moss investing the great oaks with brilliant jeweled trellises" and encountered—and became the story title's "Illuminated Man."[30]

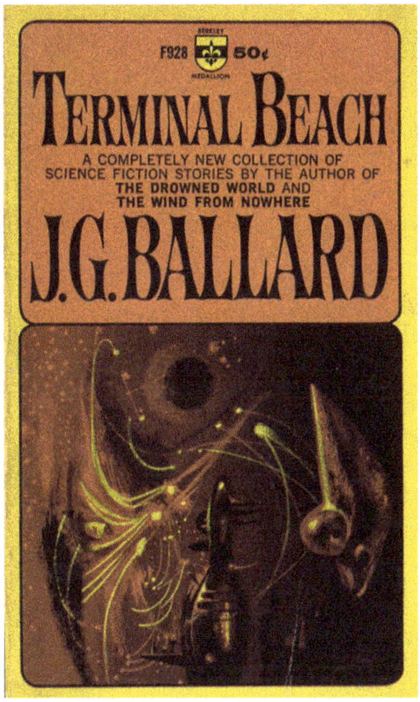

Smithson's prior analogy between Judd's angular sculptures and crystallization had been clever if imprecise. Ballard's account of immobilization by crystallization applies more directly to Smithson's own containment of his early paintings' loosely-brushed expressionist fervor in favor of his more current faceted wall reliefs and constructions. Smithson wanted to align himself with the purity and planarity of crystals; the next year he would quote Taine/Bell, who wrote in his *The Purple Sapphire*.

> "The floor of the hollow was a level circular expanse of pure crystal; the gentle sloping sides were lead-lined rock. directly above the crystal floor, and sheer up to the limit of vision, the atmosphere exhibited a distant brilliance, like the beam of a searchlight passing vertically up through the clear, sunlit air."[31]

Some of the angular planes of Smithson's constructions made around 1965 are brightly reflective, or literally are mirrors, akin to Ballard's prismatic light. But additional notable correspondences appear between Ballard's "Illuminated Man" and Smithson's sculpture and writing about it:

- The story's references to the "Andromeda spiral," a body of water's "curious roseate sheen," and "bars of livid yellow and carmine light... bled away across the surface of the water" prefigure Smithson's siting of the Jetty at roseate bay below Rozel Point.
- Ballard's "a brilliant glow of light poured down upon the altar" would be adapted in Smithson's account of the site of his Spiral Jetty as "the sun poured down its crushing light."
- Ballard's "hanging mirrors of the Spanish moss" precede the mirrors Smithson hung between boughs of his *Dead Tree* for the exhibition "Prospect '69" at the Dusseldorf Kunsthalle, the work that was re-created for the show to which Ballard contributed an essay, completing a creative circle.

Beyond the parallels between "The Illuminated Man" and Smithson's imagery, the more significant resounding between them is the implications of "the organ reverberating among the trees." Lost in the bewitched forest, the protagonist found his way out after entering:

> a small church in a clearing, its gilt spire fused to the surrounding trees... above me, refracted by the stained glass windows, a brilliant glow of light poured down upon the altar... Prismatic colors pouring through the stained glass windows whose original scriptural scenes had been transformed into painting of bewildering abstract beauty. ... [The priest stated] 'The body of Christ is with us everywhere here—in each prism and rainbow, in the ten thousand faces of the sun... So you see, I fear that the church, like its symbol'—here he pointed to the cross—'may have outlived its function.'[32]

His assessment could apply to Smithson, who just a few years earlier had painted numerous bloody renderings of Christ's crucifixion, but by 1962 he recognized that that that subject, personally resonant, had "outlived" its potential to get him art world traction. Within a few years he turned to the dominant format of the day, secular abstract sculpture. Associating the geometric format with the crystalline became his bridge to move forward professionally. In his Archives of American Art interview years later, Smithson described that process as "The real breakthrough came once I was able to overcome, I would say, this lurking pagan religious anthropomorphism," continuing, "I was able to get into crystalline structures in terms of structures of matter and that sort of thing."[33] For Smithson, religion went underground until it erupted in the mysticism associated with his monumental spiral embedded in salt crystals.

In his film, he ran its leftward arcs—backward—while he was "slipping out of myself again, dissolving into a unicellular beginning, trying to locate the nucleus at the end of the spiral."[34]

30. J.G. Ballard, "The Illuminated Man," *The Complete Stories of J.G. Ballard*. New York and London: W.W. Norton + Co., 2009, 609-610. Quotations from it not specifically cited are from this source, 605-627. "The Illuminated Man" appeared in the popular and widely distributed magazine *Fantasy and Science Fiction* in May 1964. It was then in a Ballard collection, *Terminal Beach*, published in London, 1964. It is the first version of the story that was almost immediately rewritten as "Equinox" and published in *New Worlds* in May/June and July/August 1964, and then as the novel *The Crystal World* in 1966. This chronology was provided by Rick McGrath. The US edition of *Terminal Beach*, which Smithson owned, does not include "The Illuminated Man." He could have read it in the magazine.

31. Eric Temple Bell, "The Purple Sapphire," *The Time Stream, The Greatest Adventure, and The Purple Sapphire: Three Science-Fiction Novels*. (New York: Dover, 1964). 514. *The Purple Sapphire* was first published in 1924. Quoted in Robert Smithson, "Ultramoderne," Flam, 63. Originally published in *Arts*, September/October 1967.

32. Ballard, "Illuminated," 624-625

33. Oral history interview with Robert Smithson, 1972 July 14-19. Archives of American Art, Smithsonian Institution, 17.

34. Smithson, "The Spiral Jetty," Flam, 149.

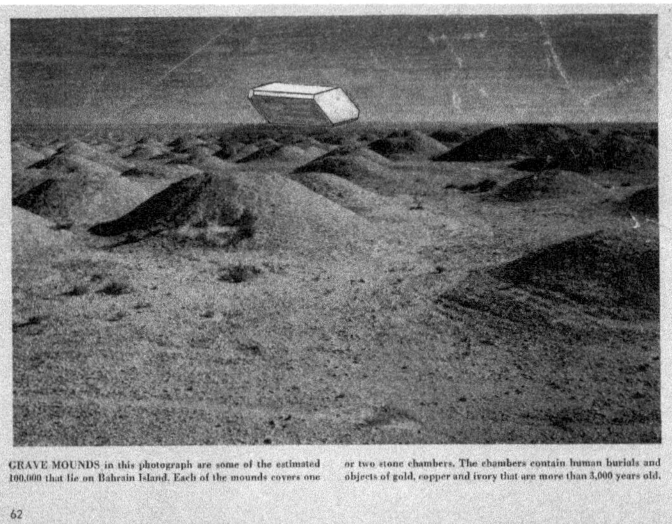

Robert Smithson, *Grave Mounds with Object*, 1966. Magazine photo collage, 6 x 7 5/8 in. (15.2 x 19.4 cm) © Holt/Smithson Foundation / VAGA at Artists Rights Society (ARS), NY

The hallucinatory experience recall's Ballard's description of "mov[ing] back through geophysical time so we re-enter the amnionic corridor."... "Beating within him like his own pulse [he] stepped out into the lake, whose waters now seemed an extension of his own bloodstream. As the dull pounding rose...he felt the barriers which divided his own cells from the surrounding medium dissolving, and he swam forwards, spreading outwards against the black thudding water."[35]

The opposition between religion and crystalline structures does not actually pertain to Smithson's works' evolution, and neither it is it in Ballard's "Illuminated Man." The priest does not declare an abandonment of a sense of the sacred, but expresses doubt that the cross can symbolize it. Instead, reverence is displaced onto nature. The crystal world remains a Christological universe; the forest church is the source of the narrator's salvation. In *The Crystal World* the protagonist, clutching its altar's heavily jeweled cross that the priest had "pressed" into his arms, ventured forth to find his way out of the forest. As he leaned toward the "gold cross set with rubies and emeralds, immediately the sheath [of crystals constricting his body] slipped and dissolved like a melting sleeve of ice."[36] (In both stories, gem stones, described as made of extreme concentrations of light, serve to "deliquesce," that is, to liquify crystallization.) By this, he was released from the carapace of rationality into a mystical radiance.

The revelation was compensation, as the "Illuminated Man" divulges, "Since the death of my wife and three-year-old daughter in a car accident ten years earlier I had deliberately repressed such feelings, and the vivid magical shore before us seemed to glow like the brief spring in my marriage."[37] In his own life, during a family vacation in southern Spain, Ballard's wife had abruptly died of pneumonia. Later, Ballard reflected, "I enjoyed being married, the first real security I had ever known."[38] One can hardly imagine the devastation of the trip home without her, and the strain of devising a new life as a single parent of three children. But in a sense, we don't have to, because his early stories work through loss. In "Terminal Beach" a bereaved protagonist, alone on an atoll, recurrently sees "the spectres of his wife and [six year old] son [who had both been killed in a motor accident] standing on the opposite bank [and. . .] was sure they were beckoning to him." He finds a photograph of an unknown six-year old girl (an amalgam of the two) and "pinned the page to the wall and for days gazed at it through his reveries."[39] Later, he discovers a corpse who states, "That son you mourn... Every parent in the world mourns the lost sons and daughters of their past childhoods... your son and my nieces are fixed in our minds forever, their identities as certain as the stars."[40] "Terminal Beach" has been lauded as one of Ballard's early "masterpieces of desolation and melancholy," a designation that calls up the title and musing in Smithson's own early (1961-62) essay "Iconography of Desolation" and his ownership of a 1955 edition of Robert Burton's thick 17th century essayistic medical textbook, *The Anatomy of Melancholy*.[41]

In *Crystal World*, the protagonist, on his way to finding safe haven, held the bejeweled cross over a crystallized child, bringing it back to life. That's displaced wish fulfillment! If only Smithson's crystalline constructions could do that for him. He was clearly drawn to Ballard's landscapes of loss because he himself was obsessed with death. It was about the brother he never knew, his parents' prior only-child whose horrific demise at the age of nine was the cause a year later of his own conception. The fatality was by leukemia, then without treatment or amelioration, explosively hemorrhagic and wasting. The relationship between a child's death and a successor deliberately conceived soon thereafter is the psychological family configuration of a "replacement child." The existential troika of bereft parents + memory of dead child + presence of next child makes for complex circumstances in which each is awash in ambivalent regard for themselves and each other. Conceived as a substitute, the successor discovers that the lost predecessor is actually revered as a prototype, with whom he is both confused and driven, unconsciously, by his parents, and deliberately by himself, to exceed.

The impact of this experience contextualizes his few images that align with science fiction subjects or moods. Among them are *Dull Space Rises* (1961), a murky gray picture of a male in a space suit and helmet in a rigid frontal stance as if petrified midst rising water or gas. A drawing from 1963 depicts a female angel supporting a sluggish space-suited bulky male leaning against a rock. Smithson scrawled the historical source of the composition he altered, Bellini's *Dead Christ Supported by Angels*. In *Grave Mounds with Object* (1966) on a newspaper photograph he drew a boxy parallelepiped (that is, a three-dimensional parallelogram) as if an alien vehicle hovering over the undulating (and distinctly not "*avant garde*") cemetery. For those paying attention, Smithson illustrated his own

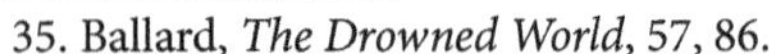

35. Ballard, *The Drowned World*, 57, 86.

36. Ballard, *Crystal*, 190.

37. Ballard, "Illuminated," 610

38. J.G. Ballard, J.G., *Miracles of Life, Shanghai to Shepperton, an Autobioraphy*, (New York, London, Liveright Publishing Corporation), 2008, 179.

39. Ballard. "Terminal," 146, 145.

40. Ballard, "Terminal," 158.

41. David Pringle and John Clute. "Ballard, JG." *The Encyclopedia of Science Fiction*, eds. John Clute, David Langford, Peter Nicholls and Graham Sleight,. London: Gollancz, 2021. Accessed 2 May 2021. <http://www.sf-encyclopedia.com/entry/ballard_j_g>.

lament (above) that "The mind of this death is unrelentingly awake."

He divulged to an interviewer, "The word entropy...is a mask for a lot of other issues... a mask that conceals a whole set of complete breakdowns and fractures."[42] (Alas, if the poet/critic speaking with him asked for elaboration—he probably took it as public unrest around the Vietnam War, with which Smithson displayed no engagement—he didn't report it.) But in the literature of science fiction Smithson found several other correlates. In Taine/Bell's "Time Stream," the son of a character was born following the first child's absorption into the time stream without return, becoming a successor as was Smithson himself.

In Smithson's recounting in *Artforum* of his tour of his hometown, when his bus turned off the highway into the town of Rutherford where his family had lived between his ages of two and ten, he quoted the first sentence of Brian Aldiss' science fiction novel *Earthworks* that he had ostensibly purchased just before embarking, "The dead man drifts along in the breeze." The figure, clearly not "put to rest" following the survivors' resolution of grieving, shadowed alongside the tanker that endlessly crossed seas gathering sand from abandoned "dumps like the Skeleton Coast" and transporting it to remaining northern ports where it was turned into semi-arable soil.[43] Aldiss also knew that experience of living with family memory of a lost prior child because he himself had been born as a replacement; his *Earthworks*' opening evokes the enduring presence of the phantom sibling who continued to "drift along" in the replacement person's consciousness. Aldiss described being "constantly compared with an idolized older sister whom his mother said had died when she was six months old but who, he later learned, had been stillborn."[44] Smithson did not know this about Aldiss; just as he did not know about Ballard's wife's death—but the biographical particulars were unnecessary, they all had expansive imaginations that operated on an alternating current between the fantastical and the mournful.

And one more: an epigraph in Smithson's *Passaic* account is an excerpt from the science fiction story "Jesting Pilot" by Lewis Padgett, but Smithson cited not the name by which the author published the book but the author's birth name, Henry Kuttner, as if exposing doubleness—an issue intimate to him—or preferring the authentic. The epigraph: "He laughed softly. I know. There's no way out. Not through the Barrier... the whole site... makes me feel haywire. Then I get these flashes." The story, located in an isolated self-sustained city enclosed by a dome, describes a man, Bill Norman (suggesting William or "Will" to be "Normal") who is having disturbing flashes of "rationality" that break through his hypnotized state universal among the citizens. Going to Padgett's story, its own epigraph or teaser is:

> They were in the City, behind the Barrier. [Smithson had painted exactly such imprisoned figures in his 1959 *Purgatory*, where the open red mouths anteceded those on Aldiss' *Earthworks.]* They had been specially conditioned from birth. None of them had ever known normal existence.

That had been Smithson's experience, part of an existential double, a (br)other who was present in the family history, if not his own direct experience, who was evidently an ongoing shadowy presence.[45]

In Padgett/Kuttner's narrative, Norman exclaims, 'I know what I want. Out!' A Controller explains, 'The idea is to trace the problems back to their psychological roots, and then get rid of the frustration somehow.'[46] Hmm. Sounds like the process of self-examination in psychoanalysis. With help from science fiction and art. The number of Smithson's science fiction references in his writing to mortality and woundedness suggests that the stories served an desire not just to draw comfort from vicariously experiencing affinities but an urge, however covert, to communicate to those drawn to him a an intimate awareness of himself.

The stories Smithson pointed to were by were mavericks attracted to paradox. In them, Smithson found both uncanny affinities to contemporary Minimalist sculpture and evocations of an absent deceased that paralleled his own. Particularly akin to Ballard, drawn to "auroral gloom" and "mournful wrecks," Smithson believed "Wreckage is often more interesting than structure."[47] They made it so.

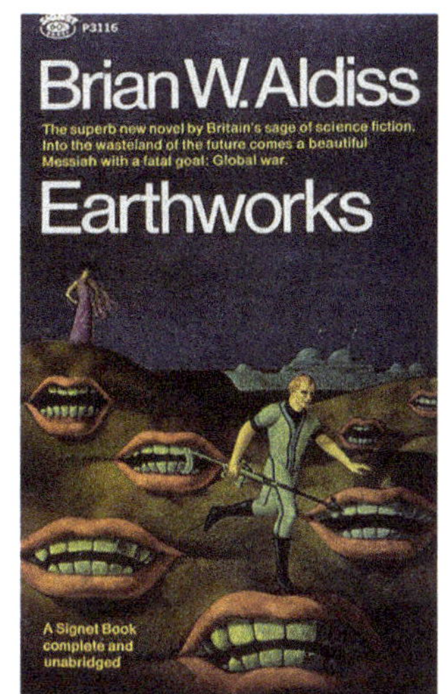

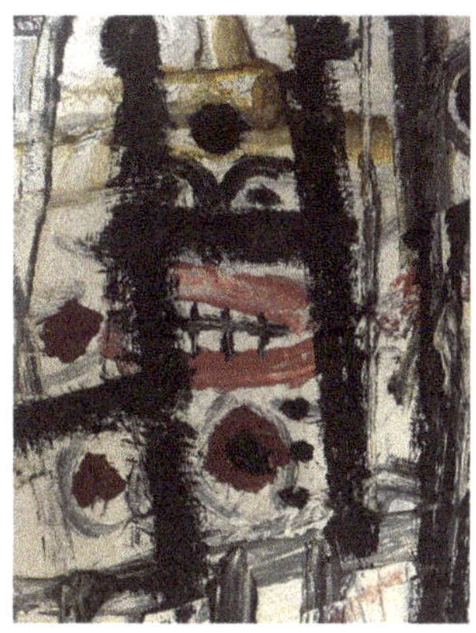
Robert Smithson, detail of *Purgatory*, 1959. Photograph @Suzaan Boettger ©Holt/Smithson Foundation / VAGA at Artists Rights Society (ARS), NY

42. John Perreault, "Nonsites in the News," *New York*, 2, no. 8, (February 24, 1969): 44.

43. Brian Aldiss. *Earthworks*. (New York: Signet, 1967), 1, 12. See also Suzaan Boettger, "Digging into Aldiss' Earthworks and Smithson's 'Earthworks'," *Art Journal OPEN*, College Art Association http://art-journal.collegeart.org/?p accessed June 7, 2018.

44. Exaggerating the length of her first child's life, Aldiss' mother had aggrandized her own loss and in her mind kept the daughter alive longer. Sam Roberts, "Brian Aldiss, Prolific Author of Sci-Fi and More, Dies at 92," *New York Times*, August 27, 2017. https://www.nytimes.com/2017/08/24/books/brian-aldiss-author-of-science-fiction-and-much-more-dies-at-92.html accessed August 27, 2017.

45. That secret biographical link may have been what Smithson was alluding to when he referred to a description of Padgett as writing in a "secret language of the future." Smithson, "Entropy," 21.

46. Lewis Padgett, "Jesting Pilot," in Joan Kahn, Editor, *Skeleton Keys, Tales from The Edge of the Chair*, (New York: Dell, 1967). 250, 246. The magazine *Edge of the Chair* published suspense.

47. Ballard. "Crystal," 3, 60. Robert Smithson, in Gregoire Muller interview, "...The Earth, Subject to Cataclysms, is a Cruel Master" 1971, Flam, 257. This interview was originally published in *Arts Magazine*, September 1971.

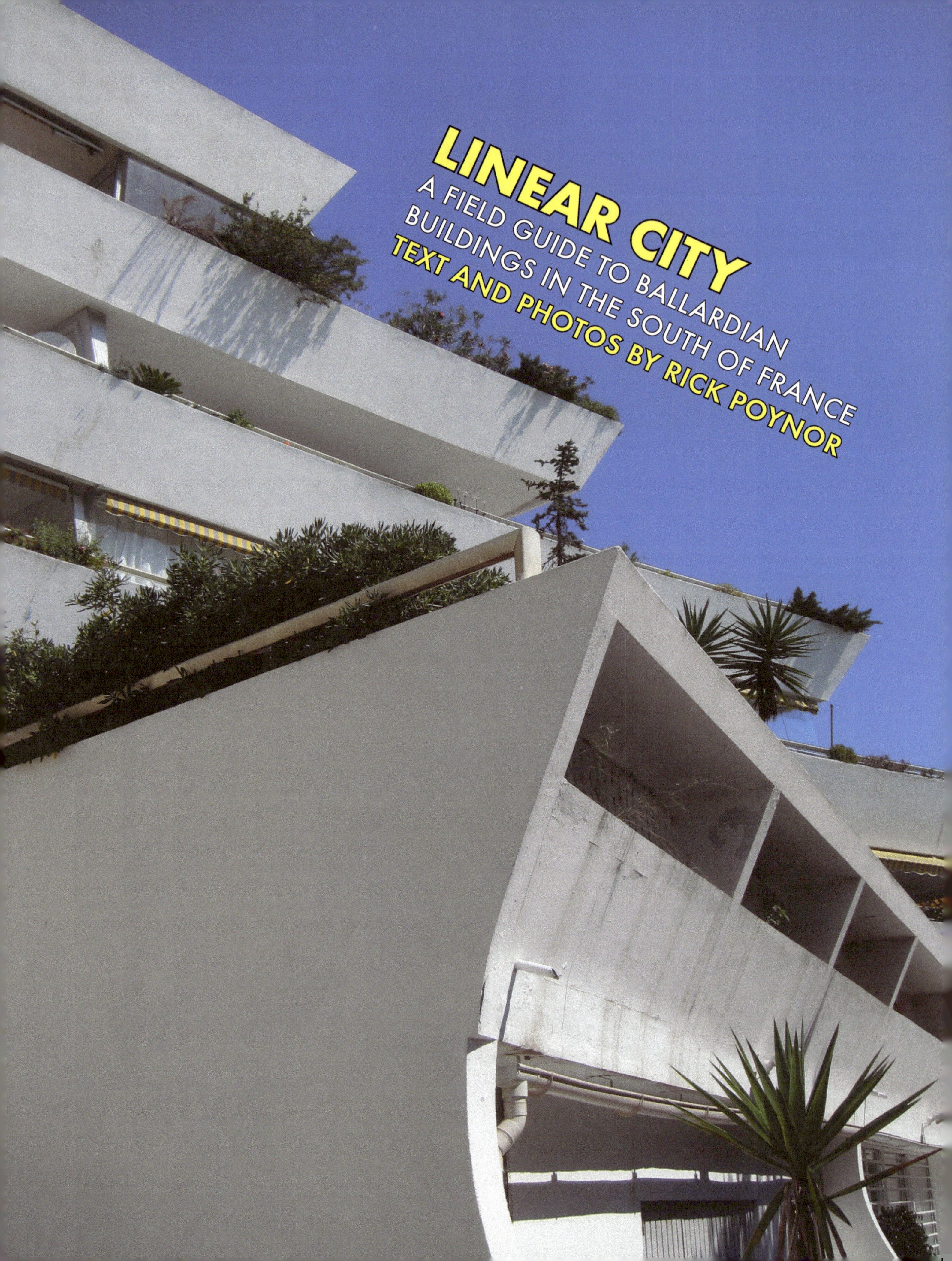

LINEAR CITY

A FIELD GUIDE TO BALLARDIAN BUILDINGS IN THE SOUTH OF FRANCE

TEXT AND PHOTOS BY RICK POYNOR

In his notes for *The Atrocity Exhibition*, J G Ballard makes a collection of typically ambivalent remarks about what he calls the "curious atmosphere" of Mediterranean beach resorts, an atmosphere yet to find its chronicler. "One could regard them collectively as a linear city, some 3000 miles long, from Gibraltar to Glyfada beach north of Athens, and 300 yards deep," he writes. The ambience of this temporary "city", populated by 50 million or more people for three months of summer, is unique, says Ballard, and not at all European.

The "endless parade of hotels, marinas and apartment houses" is more like Florida; it's a place, he suggests, where criminality flourishes, sex is stylized and relationships are more oblique. Having observed that the inhabitants of this linear city by the sea seem "almost decorticated"—stripped of their outer shell, which may be positive or negative—Ballard delivers his double-edged conclusion: "My dream is to move there permanently. But perhaps I already have."[1]

As so often in his fiction and commentary, Ballard confronts us with an unnerving spectacle, a phenomenon from which many might recoil, only to embrace it himself with enthusiasm. He may not have been living on the Mediterranean coast in 1990, but he went there often as a holidaymaker and identified with this contemporary way of being. The same adaptive reflex can be observed in "Airports: The Cities of the Future", Ballard's longest non-fiction statement about the built environment.[2] He actively welcomes Heathrow's "transience, alienation and discontinuities, and its unashamed response to the pressures of speed, disposability and the instant impulse."[3]

He surely knew that the picture he paints of "the intricate network of perimeter roads, the car rental offices, air freight depots and travel clinics, the light industrial and motel architecture that unvaryingly surrounds every major airport in the world" could sound uninviting to many.[4] But in an act of acceptance that might seem perverse, Ballard says he had "learned to like" this environment because it constitutes "the reality of our lives" to which we must, by implication, adjust ourselves. He concludes by cheerfully anticipating the construction of terminals 6 and 7 at Heathrow, a prospect that was, and still is, anathema to many people living under the airport's flightpaths.

Yet the issue was clearly not entirely settled for Ballard. In *Millennium People* (2003), ambivalent as ever, one of his characters suggests that willing denizens of this airport suburb, who embrace its alienation, are in fact fleeing from "the real". This is why they choose where possible to occupy "zones without meaning—airports, shopping malls, motorways, car parks."[5]

The French theorist Marc Augé called this kind of space drained of meaning—both everywhere and nowhere —a "non-place".[6] Confronting the same phenomenon, the Dutch architect Rem Koolhaas coined the term "junkspace" in an essay that is both a lament and a denunciation, as the critic Hal Foster notes. According to Koolhaas, "Junkspace is what remains after modernization has run its course, or, more precisely what coagulates while modernization is in progress, its fallout."[7] Ballard observes this process of modernization and concludes, seemingly without regret, that we are now "the unenfranchised citizens of the shopping mall and the marina, the internet and cable TV." This landscape of non-places and junkspaces, this "apparently alienated zone", was a "zone of possibility", Ballard insisted, from which a new culture would emerge, and consequently a new Britain.[8]

In Ballard's remarks about the Mediterranean coast we see a similar ambiguity. "I think beaches are my spiritual home," he wrote in 2002. "All the most interesting things in the world take place where the sea meets the land and you're between those two states of mind. On that border zone, you're neither one nor the other, you're both."[9] He was a regular visitor to the Côte d'Azur, where he loved to take holidays with his partner of many years, Claire Walsh.

"When I travel, it's usually to the Mediterranean, where I go practically every summer," he said in 1984.[10] A few years later, talking to *Interzone* magazine, the south of France and Spain were still on his mind, but he wouldn't want to live there all the time, he said, because expatriates tended to become "sealed off" from the world, "literally marooned on the beach".[11] By 1991, he had come around and a British interviewer reported that he would like to live in Roquebrune when Walsh retired.[12] That never happened, though ten years later Ballard said his

---

1 All preceding quotations from J.G. Ballard, *The Atrocity Exhibition*, revised edition with author's annotations, Re/Search Publications, San Francisco, CA, 1990, p. 59. Also published in *The Atrocity Exhibition*, Flamingo, London, 1993.

2 J.G. Ballard, "Airports: The Cities of the Future", *Blueprint*, no. 142, September 1997, pp. 24-29. Also published as "The Ultimate Departure Lounge" in Steven Bode and Jeremy Millar (eds.), *Airport* (exhibition catalogue), The Photographers' Gallery, London, 1997, pp. 120-21

3 Ibid., p. 26.

4 Ibid., p. 28.

5 J.G. Ballard, *Millennium People*, Harper Perennial, London, 2004, p. 133.

6 Marc Augé, *Non-Places: Introduction to an Anthropology of Supermodernity*, Verso, London, 1995.

7 Rem Koolhaas and Hal Foster, *Junkspace with Running Room*, Notting Hill Editions, London, 2013, p. 3.

8 J.G. Ballard, "Welcome to the Virtual City", *Tate*, no. 24, Spring 2001, p. 33.

9 J.G. Ballard, "The Perfect Beach", *The Observer*, 13 January 2002. https://www.theguardian.com/theobserver/2002/jan/13/life1.lifemagazine2

10 Thomas Frick, "J.G. Ballard, The Art of Fiction No. 85" (interview), *The Paris Review*, no. 94, Winter 1984. https://www.theparisreview.org/interviews/2929/the-art-of-fiction-no-85-j-g-ballard

11 David Pringle, "J.G. Ballard" (interview), *Interzone*, no. 22, Winter 1987, p. 16

12 Lynn Barber, "Alien at Home", *The Independent on Sunday, The Sunday Review*, 15 September 1991, p. 4.

Opposite: Balconies, Marina Baie des Anges (Bay of Angels)

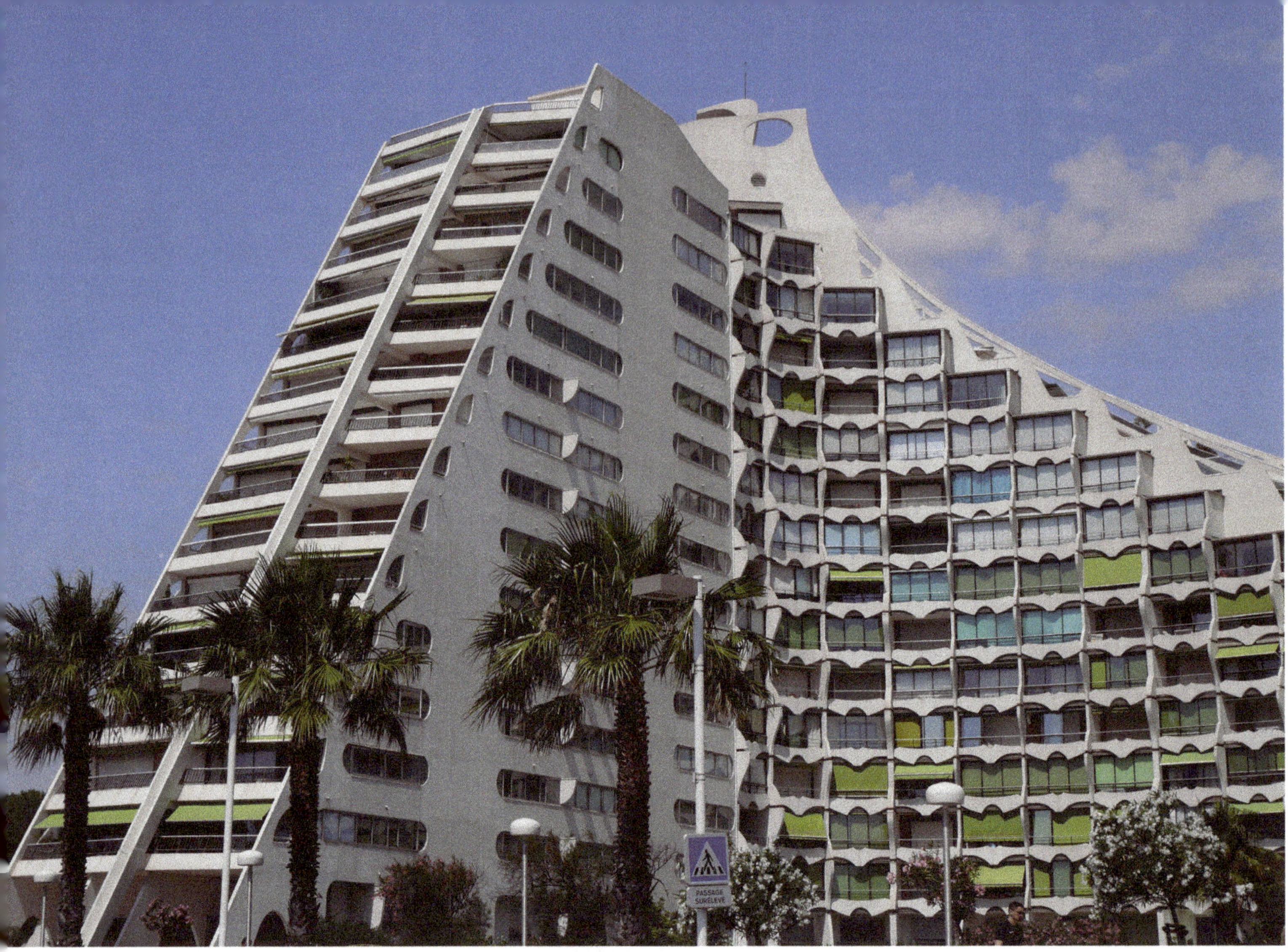

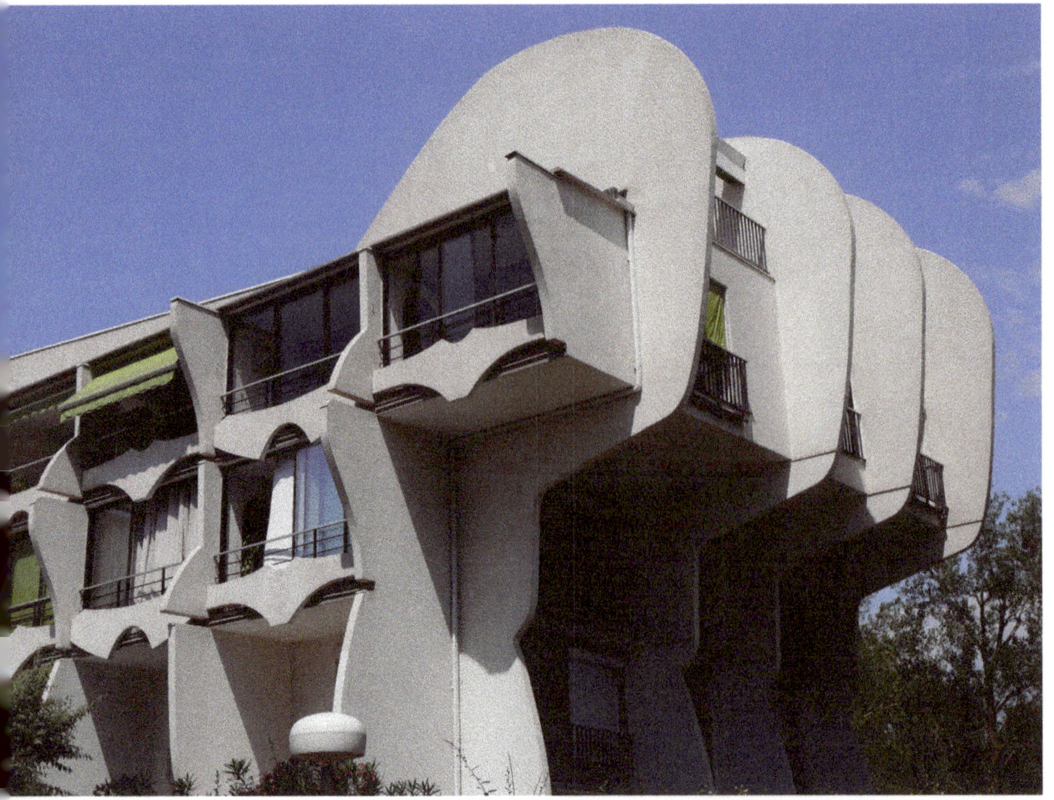

Top:
La Grande Pyramide, apartment building, La Grande Motte. Architect: Jean Balladur

Left:
The tail of La Grande Pyramide

Opposite:
La Grande Motte's utopian vision of concrete, including L'Eden by Jean Balladur (top right) and Fidji by André Malrait (bottom left)

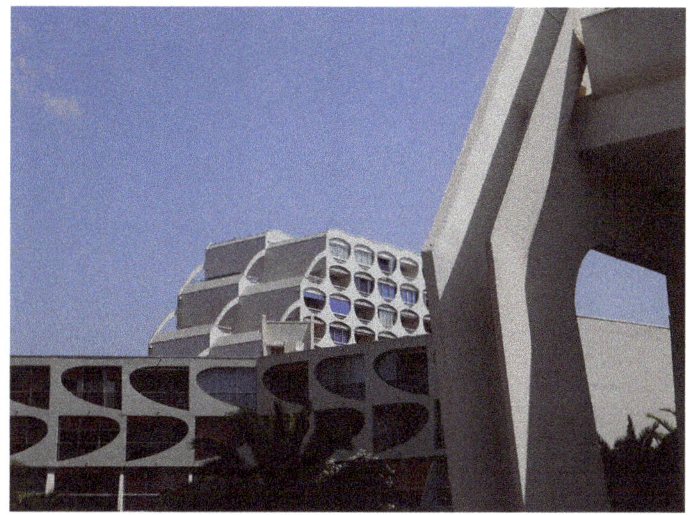

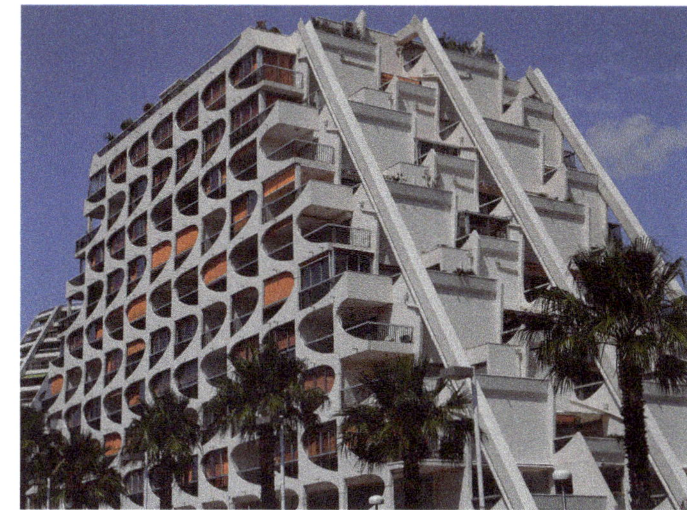

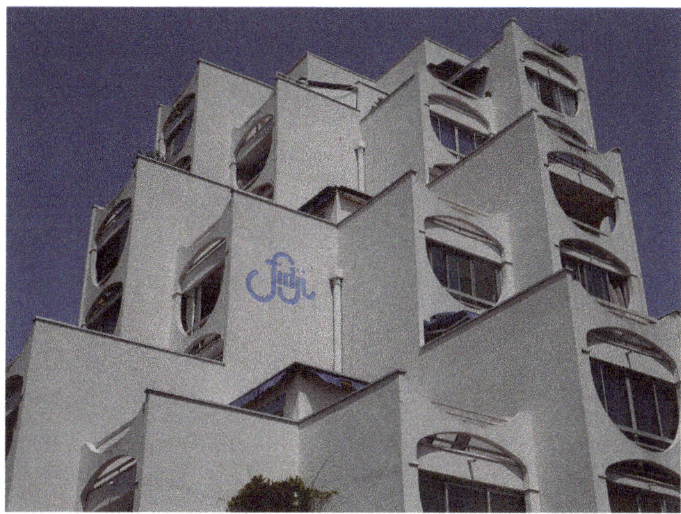

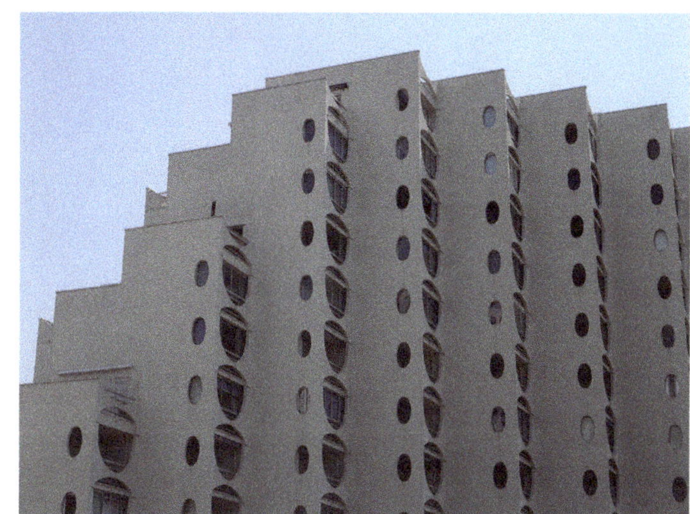

favourite beach, where Le Corbusier had a cabin (and died in the sea), was at Roquebrune.[13]

Antibes was on Ballard's list of desirable residences, too. The area makes a telling appearance as an entry—"Cap d'Antibes"—in his short experimental fiction "The Index" (1977).[14] In *Cocaine Nights* (1996), Ballard likens Estrella de Mar, a resort on the Costa del Sol, to the wooded peninsula of Cap d'Antibes and its luxurious residences, and the area features heavily in *Super-Cannes* (2000).[15] In the novel, Ballard includes an introductory note on the geography of the region where his alarming story unfolds. *Super-Cannes*' violent events, expressing the emergence of what a character calls a "voluntary and sensible psychopathy", take place in Eden-Olympia, a fictitious business and technology park, "Ten miles to the north-east of Cannes, in the wooded hills between Valbonne and the coast".[16] Ballard mentions several real places that will feature in the novel: the Marina Baie des Anges apartment complex, the Pierre Cardin Foundation at Miramar and the waterfront development at Port-la-Galère. The inspiration for Eden-Olympia, he goes on to say, was the landscaped business park of Sophia Antipolis, a few miles to the north of Antibes.[17]

La Grande Motte

The germ of this fictional treatment of architectural settings had appeared many years earlier in *Concrete Island* (1973). Twice in the book, Ballard mentions La Grande Motte, a futuristic resort on the coast, near Montpellier. His protagonist, Robert Maitland, takes a lover, Dr Helen Fairfax, there for a holiday. "Helen had quietly hated the hard, affectless architecture with its stylized concrete surfaces," Maitland recalls, wishing that his wife Catherine had been with him: "she would have liked the ziggurat hotels and apartment houses, and the vast, empty parking lots laid down by the planners years before any tourist would arrive to park their cars, like a city abandoned in advance of itself."[18]

Had Ballard visited La Grande Motte at that point? According to David Pringle, in late July to early August 1968,

13 "The Perfect Beach", *The Observer*.

14 J.G. Ballard, "The Index", *The Paris Review*, no. 118, Spring 1991. Collected in *J.G. Ballard: The Complete Short Stories*, Flamingo, London, 2001.

15 J.G. Ballard, *Cocaine Nights*, Fourth Estate, London, 2014, p. 35.

16 J.G. Ballard, *Super-Cannes*, Fourth Estate, London, 2011, p. 264 and p. 5.

17 Ibid., Foreword, no page number.

18 J.G. Ballard, *Concrete Island*, Vintage, London, 1994, p. 65. See also p. 14.

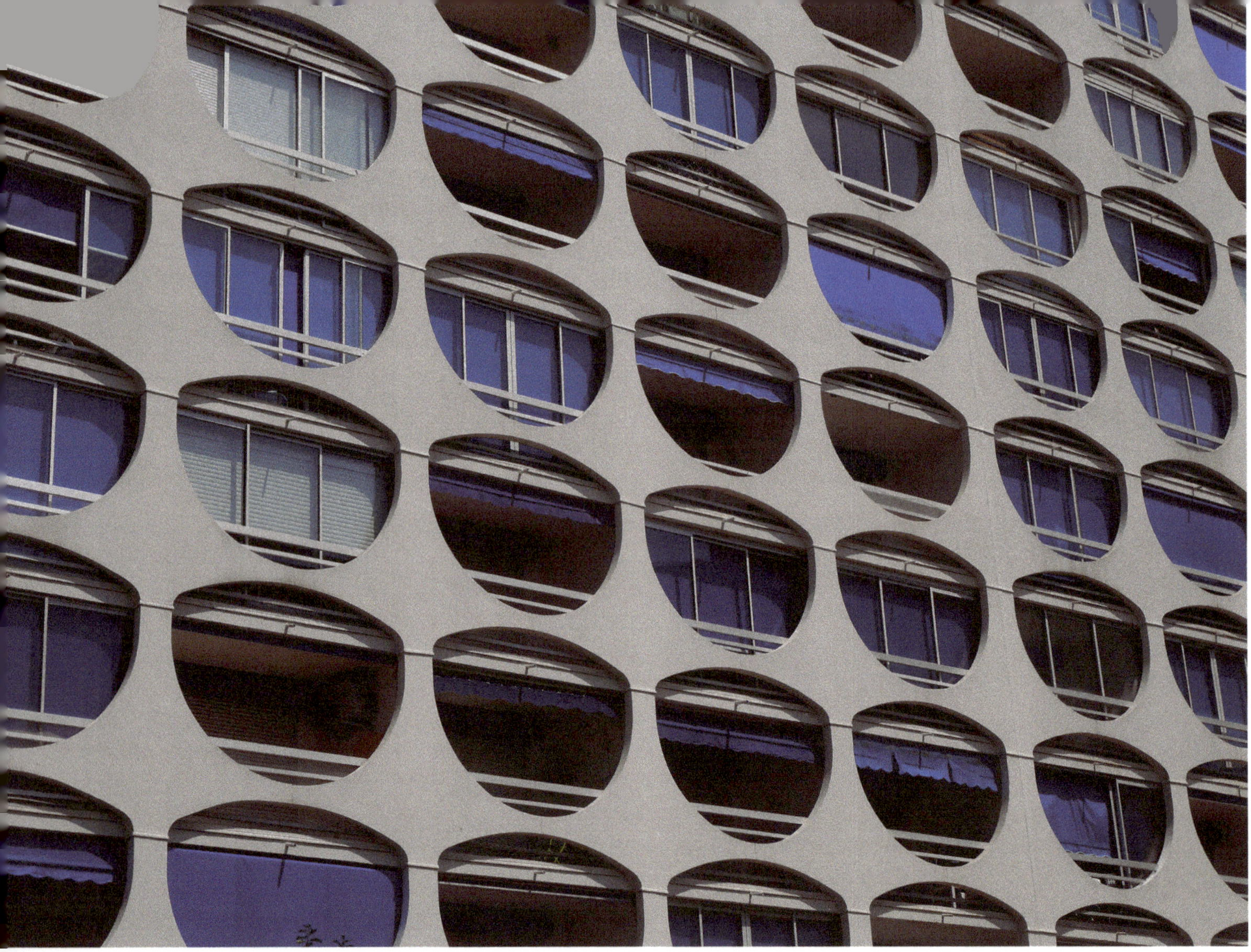

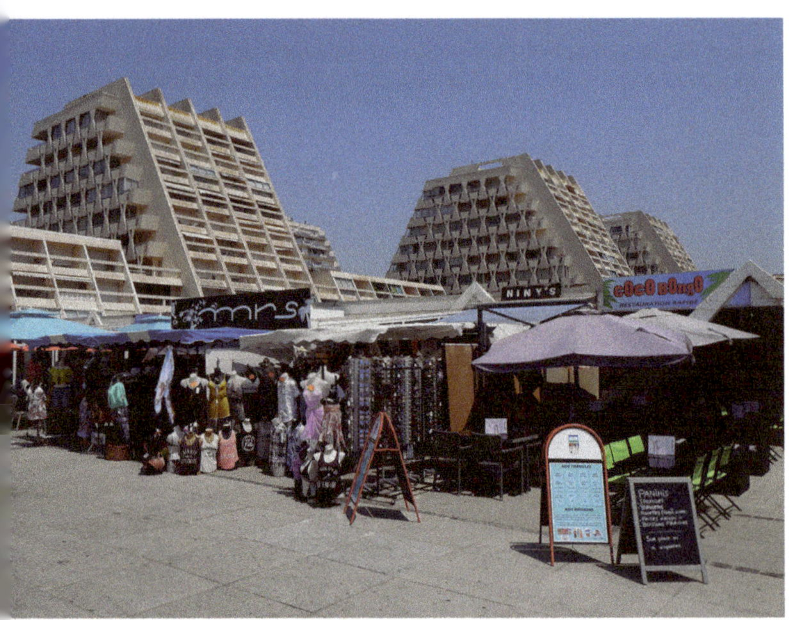

Top: Modular concrete façade, La Grande Motte

Above: Place Lady Diana, waterfront shops and restaurants

Opposite: The Quartier des Villas behind the town

Ballard and Claire were on holiday in the south of France.[19] They visited Menton, near the Italian border, then drove to the Camargue, which is close to La Grande Motte, as Ballard implies in *Concrete Island*. If he made a detour, he would have seen the site at an early stage of construction. Only two pyramid-like buildings—Le Provence and Le Grand Pavois—were finished.

By June 1968 the first apartments were ready to be occupied in what was still, in effect, a huge building site.[20] That chimes with Ballard's description of the site as unfinished; La Grande Motte's most imposing edifice, the 15-floor Grande Pyramide apartment building, wasn't completed until 1974. It's also possible Ballard had only seen the site in a magazine. This curious emerging complex was attracting attention. In 1969, *Paris Match* published a lavish, 12-page photographic report. "This will truly be a new Florida," its writer predicted.[21]

---

19 Email to the author, 6 July 2021.

20 "Construction: les dates clés" (Construction: key dates), 2017. lagrandemotte-architecture.com. For more information and a list of Balladur's buildings at La Grande Motte, see Claude Prelorenzo and Antoine Picon, *L'aventure du balnéaire: La Grande Motte de Jean Balladur* (The seaside adventure: Jean Balladur's La Grande Motte), Éditions Parenthèses, Marseille, 1999.

21 René Sicart, "L'insolite: cité des temples du soleil" (The curiosity: town of temples of the sun), *Paris Match*, no. 1057, 9 August 1969, p. 34.

Briefly as La Grande Motte appears in *Concrete Island*, there is a note of urgency. The resort was the first place Maitland (an architect) took Helen on arrival at the Riviera. Ballard may have visited La Grande Motte at some point over the next decade because it left a lasting impression on him. "What I Believe" (1984), a prose poem or "surrealist's catalogue", as *Interzone* styled it, includes the line: "I believe in Tokyo, Benidorm, La Grande Motte, Wake Island, Eniwetok, Dealey Plaza."[22]

But what exactly does Ballard believe in when it comes to La Grande Motte? He puts the holiday complex in some mixed company with one of the world's most futuristic cities (at the time); a congested Spanish beach resort; a Pacific island used by the American air force; a Pacific atoll used for nuclear testing; and the place where an American president was assassinated. To single out just one other location from this litany, Ballard was obsessed with Wake Island: "when I first came to England, a dark and derelict shell of a country, I used to dream of the runways of Wake Island and Midway," he wrote.[23]

He titled a short story "My Dream of Flying to Wake Island" (1974).[24] But he never went to Wake Island. Perhaps it was only the idea of La Grande Motte and all the things it might signify about present and future society that compelled him.

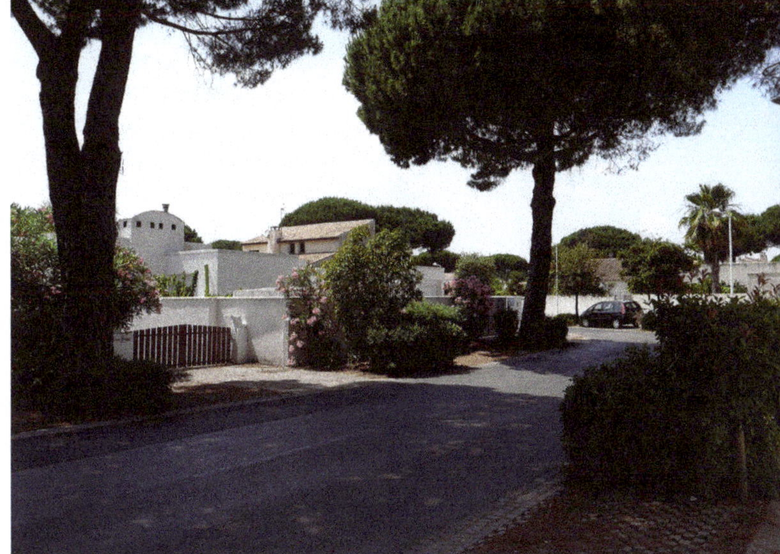

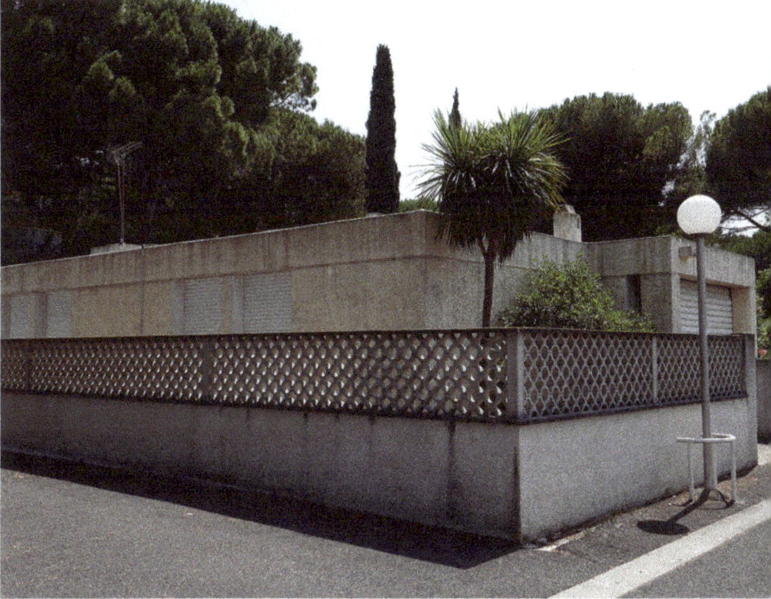

What draws us to visit the locations that writers have made significant to their outlook and writing? Such trips are a form of homage. By walking in the writer's steps (or imagined steps) an extra bond of affiliation and even loyalty is forged. The effort required is proof to oneself and perhaps to others of a deeper level of commitment.

Does this self-directed investigation yield greater understanding? It certainly feels like it could do and until one goes to a place, how can one know? When proximity made it possible—while on holiday, naturally—I decided to visit the main locations in *Super-Cannes*. I was curious to see how the novelist had worked his imaginative transformations and I wondered whether it would be possible to take some photographs that captured a manifestly "Ballardian" quality in the locations that fascinated him.

Several years later, I had the opportunity to visit La Grande Motte. Here, I begin with the complex because it has the prior place in Ballard's writing. By a curious coincidence—did Ballard know this?—the French architect's name is Jean Balladur.

I arrived at La Grande Motte on a local bus from Montpellier. The resort is wedged into a long spur of reclaimed Languedoc land by the sea. Camera in hand, I meandered around for a few hours, taking in the strangeness of the buildings from different angles and perspectives. Long completed, La Grande Motte is much changed from the site Ballard may have visited in the late 1960s. By 1982, the resort had become a small town. It had acquired a town hall, a church, a convention centre and a golf course. In 1984, there were already 4,000 permanent residents.[25] Phrases like "hard, affectless architecture" and "stylized concrete surfaces" ceased to encapsulate the reality of La Grande Motte many years ago.

This is the vision of Ballard and concrete reflected in the title of the French volume that collects *Crash, Concrete Island* and *High Rise*: *La trilogie de béton* (The Concrete Trilogy).[26] Such a world is grey, harsh and inhospitable, if not inhuman. The concrete bunker has become an archetypal Ballardian structure, from "The Terminal Beach" to an essay about architectural modernism describing Ballard's visit to the Second World War blockhouses on "Utah Beach" in Normandy.[27] Photographic

22 J.G. Ballard, "What I Believe" in V. Vale and Andrea Juno (eds.), *Re/Search: J.G. Ballard*, Re/Search Publishing, San Francisco, 1984, p. 175. The text's first English publication was in *Interzone*, no. 8, Summer 1984, pp. 37-39. It was first published in French in the magazine *Science Fiction*, no. 1, January 1984.

23 "Airports: The Cities of the Future", *Blueprint*, p. 26.

24 J.G. Ballard, "My Dream of Flying to Wake Island", *Ambit*, no. 60, 1974, pp. 60-66. First collected in *Low-Flying Aircraft*, 1976.

25 "Construction: les dates clés". lagrandemotte-architecture.com

26 J.G. Ballard, *La trilogie de béton*, Collection Folio, Gallimard, Paris, 2014. The cover picture, an angular, mirrored image of a building that might be a multi-storey car park is a good example of a "Ballardian" architectural photograph (here treated as a photomontage). Like an object in a painting by René Magritte, this enigmatic architectural entity floats in the sky.

27 J.G. Ballard, "A Handful of Dust", *The Guardian*, G2, special edition on Modernism, 20 March 2006, pp. 16-17. Ballard's essay was

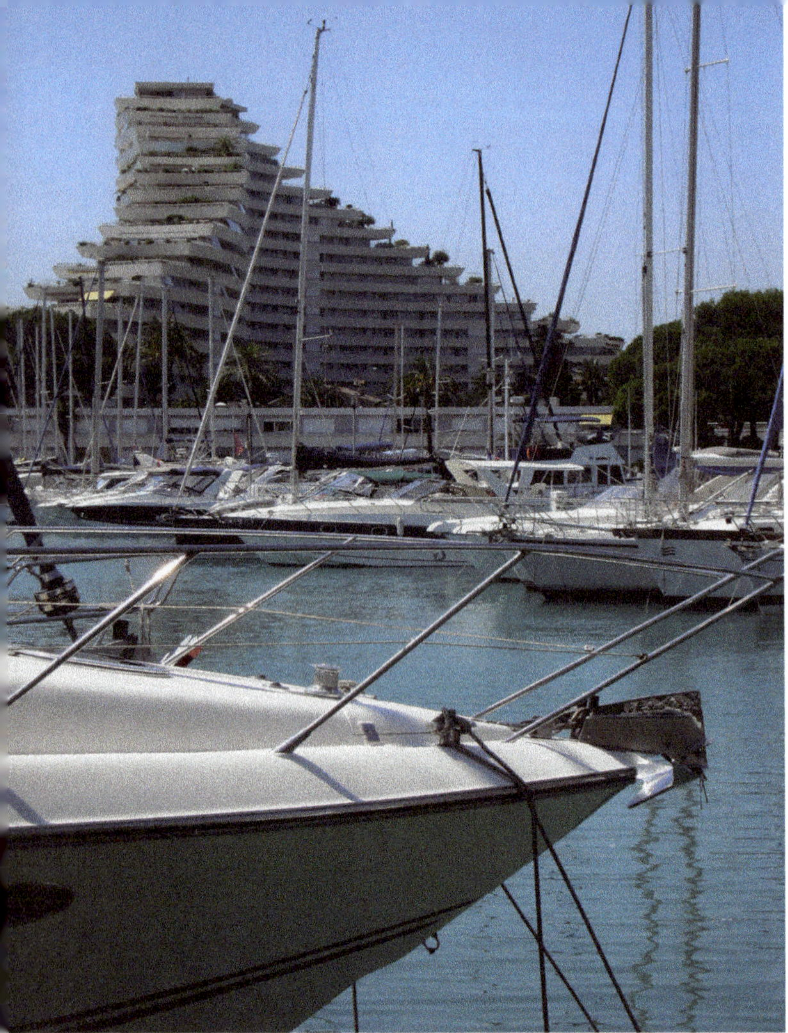

interpretations of Ballard tend to play up the harshness and angularity.

"The angle between two walls", long an emblematic image for Ballard, implies a potential grammar of Ballardian architectural imagery, but this angularity and flatness is too limiting when it comes to pinning down what might be Ballardian about La Grande Motte. While concrete is everywhere in the complex, there is none of the stark and alienating Brutalism that had tarnished its reputation as a building material by the late 20th century.

In its freshly mixed state, concrete can be moulded to make unusual shapes and Balladur took full advantage of this property to fashion curving window apertures and balconies, which give the buildings their sinuous geometries and rhythms. Before he started work on the project, the architect visited the archaeological site of Teotihuacán, north of Mexico City. The pyramids he saw there, the main form of civic architecture in the pre-Columbian city, home to an estimated 125,000 people, inspired the shape of the buildings at La Grande Motte. Ballard's use of the word "ziggurat" to characterize Balladur's architectural forms was expressive licence.

As Balladur observed, "La Grande Motte is in a way a holy place: men and women come to worship the sun there. This is a religion as old as the world, which today is experiencing a resurgence of fervour."[28] The pyramidal structures that cover the site are modern-day temples for sun-seekers; one building is even called "Le temple du soleil". Ballard provides a telling parallel in *Cocaine Nights* when his protagonist, Charles Prentice, first sees the homes of wealthy expats lining the beach at Estrella de Mar: "The future had come ashore here, lying down to rest among the pines."[29] Sounding a lot like Ballard in high gear, Prentice describes the residential compounds as a "willed limbo", a "silent world", a "world beyond boredom" and an entropic "affectless realm".[30] He compares the resort's "white-walled pueblos" and "cubist apartments and terraced houses" to the architecture of Arcosanti, an experimental town in Paradise Valley, Arizona, designed by the Italian architect Paolo Soleri. Visually at least, Arcosanti expresses an ideal of the future good life similar to La Grande Motte's: sun-drenched, superficially benign and becalmed. When Ballard (as Prentice) envisages Arcosanti as an "outpost of the day after tomorrow", he could be talking about La Grande Motte as it is today.[31]

As I wandered around the complex, I was struck by the greenness of its setting. There are pine trees, oleanders and well-manicured shrubs on every side. This softening of the architecture was always part of Balladur's conception. Cars have been kept out as much as possible; that's what those "empty parking lots laid down by the planners" were meant to achieve. What would Ballard the committed driver have said about that? It was still early summer, before the holiday season was fully under way, and La Grande Motte was only half occupied and drowsy. I gave the beach next to the marina a miss. The futuristic ambience of the pyramid buildings, like silent watchtowers of the sea and sky, was much more compelling to me. I realized only later that I had eaten my lunch in the Place Lady Diana (Ballard, an admirer of the princess, would have approved). I made my way up the Avenue de l'Europe and passed a building called Les Cyclades that made me think of *Vermilion Sands*. I was heading towards the Quartier des Villas behind the town, under lush pines loaded with droning cicadas. In the middle of a scorching afternoon, the houses inside the metal gates were mostly shuttered, like the tombs of a fading dynasty, and I barely encountered a soul.

Marina Baie des Anges

The first time I saw Marina Baie des Anges—its "immense curved facades glowing like a cauldron in the afternoon sun", as Ballard pictures it—I was surveying the landscape at the top of a tower in the picturesque hilltop village of Haut-de-Cagnes.[32] I assumed this monster construction in nearby Villeneuve Loubet must be a bloated hotel complex, soaring above everything else on the coastline.

The marina's concrete ziggurat styling makes the complex,

reprinted in *Jane & Louise Wilson* (exhibition catalogue), Haunch of Venison, London, 2006. The catalogue shows photographs by the Wilson sisters of derelict bunkers on beaches in Normandy taken for their installation *Sealander*.

28 Quoted in Gilles Ragot, "La Grande-Motte l'invention d'une cité balnéaire pour tous" (La Grande Motte: the invention of a seaside resort for all), *Le Moniteur*, 9 April 2014. https://www.lemoniteur.fr/article/la-grande-motte-l-invention-d-une-cite-balneaire-pour-tous.1348259#!

29 *Cocaine Nights*, 2014, p. 33.

30 Ibid., pp. 34-35.

31 Ibid., p. 34.

32 *Super-Cannes*, 2011, p. 24.

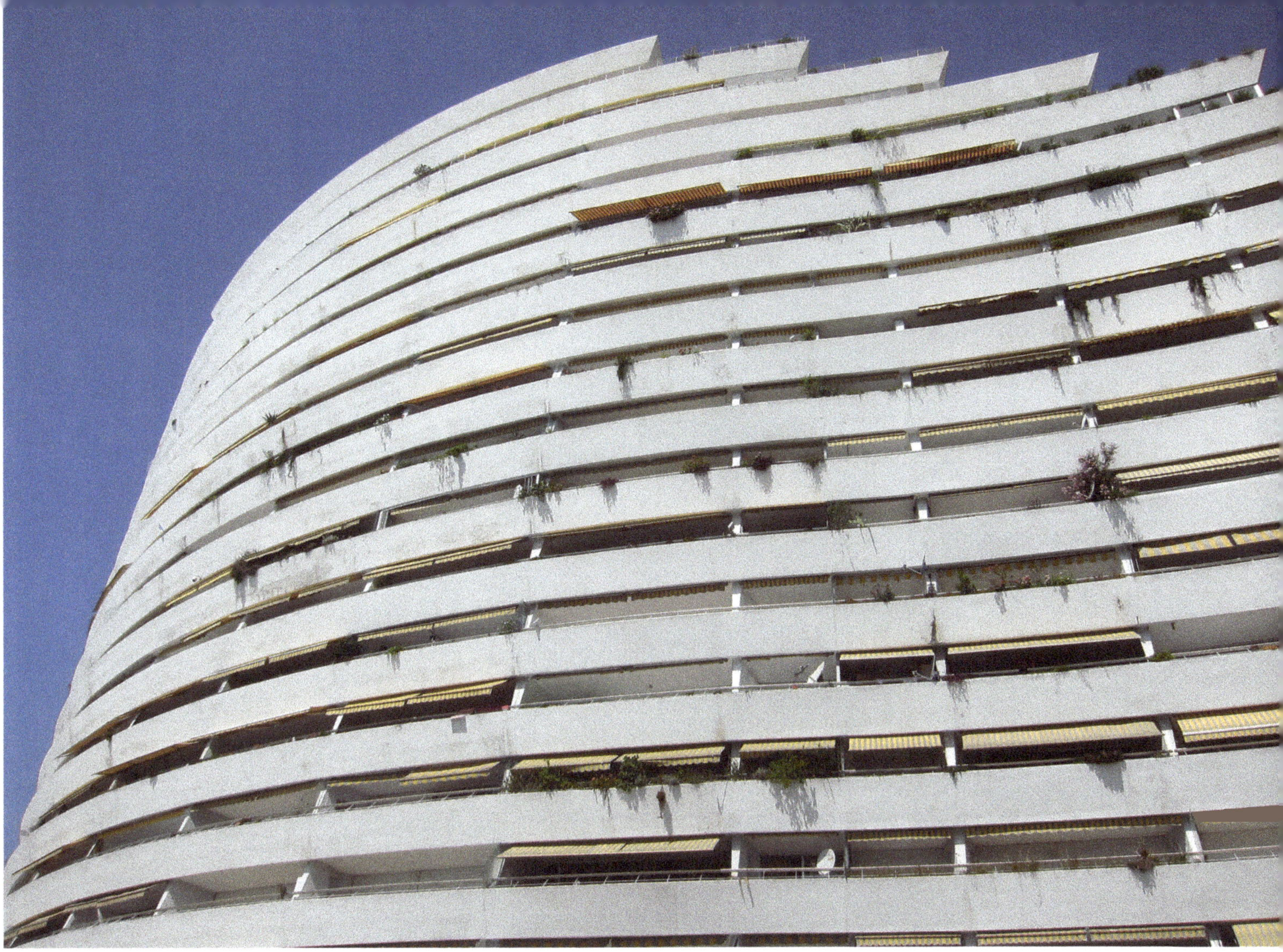

Top:
The Amiral residential tower,
Marina Baie des Anges

Right:
Surveillance beneath the towers

Opposite:
The Commodore residential
tower and the marina

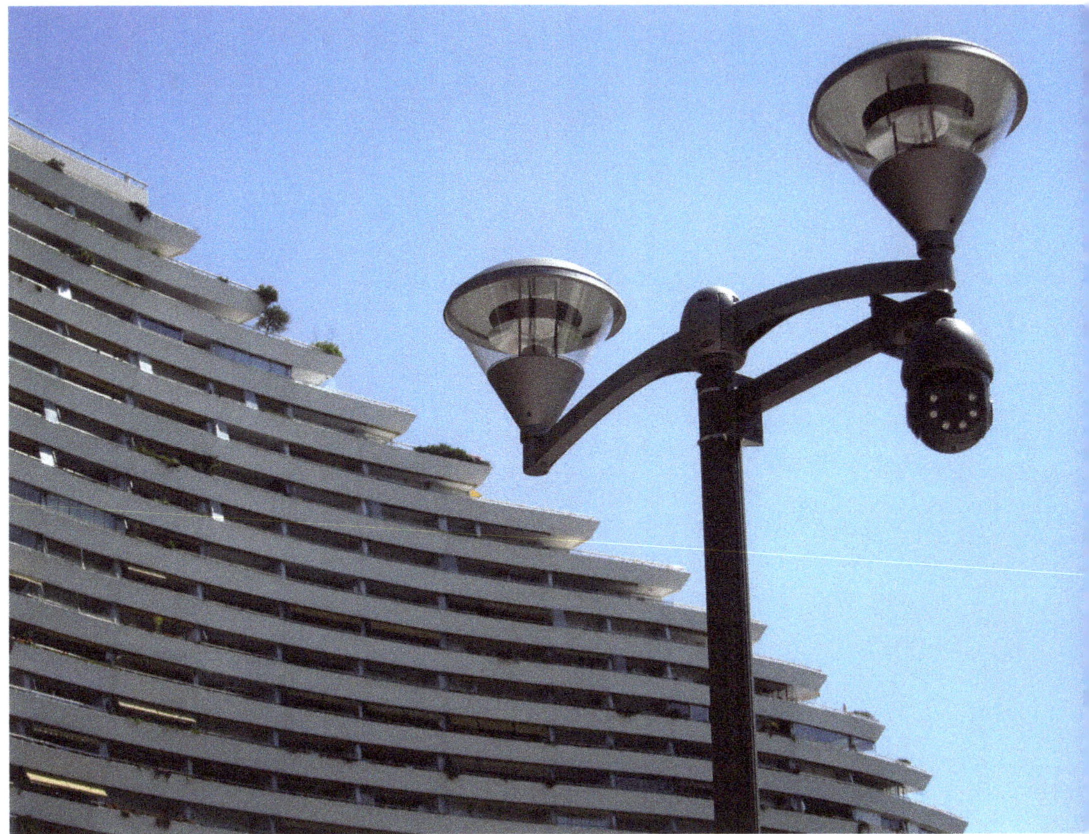

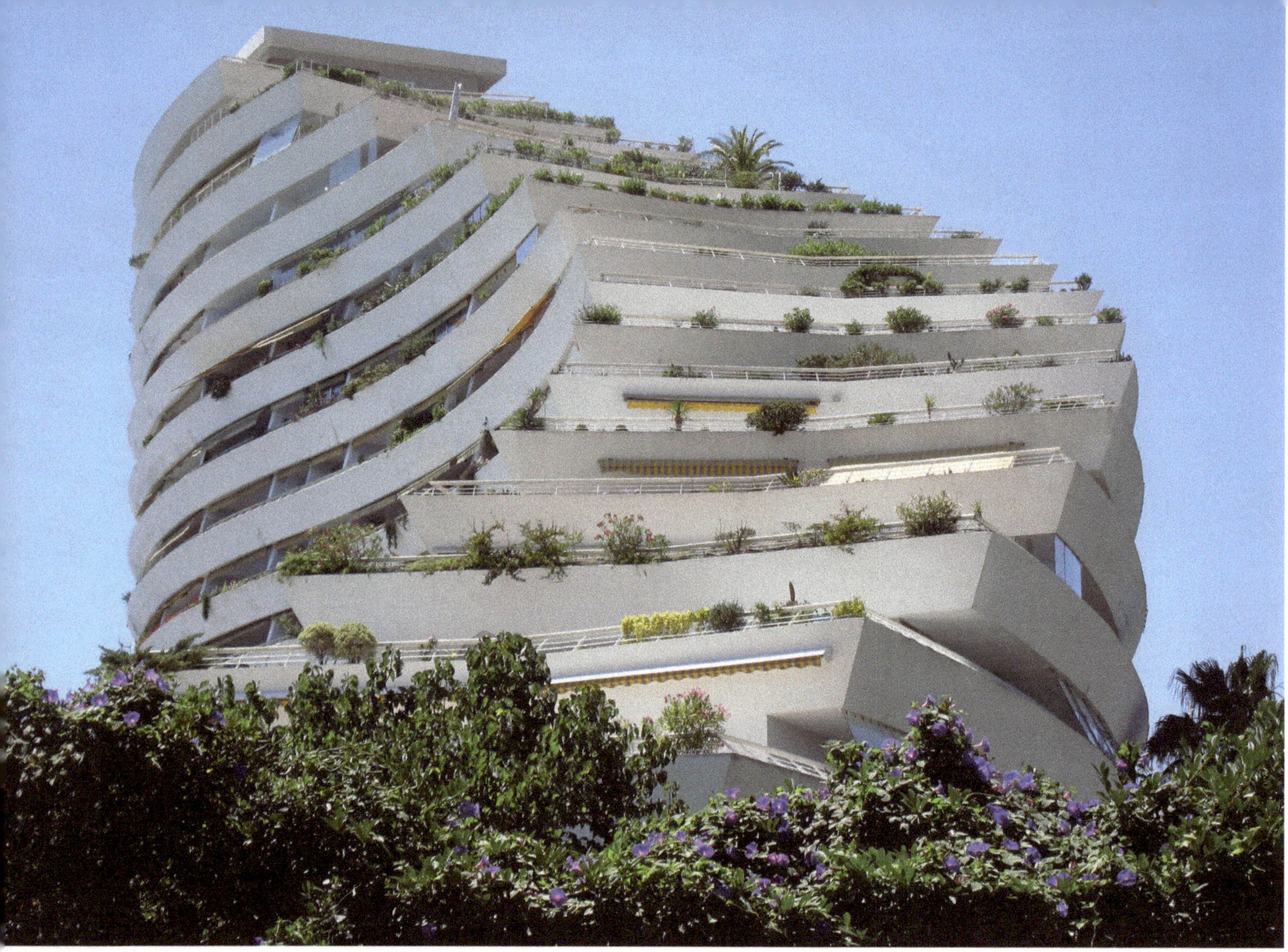

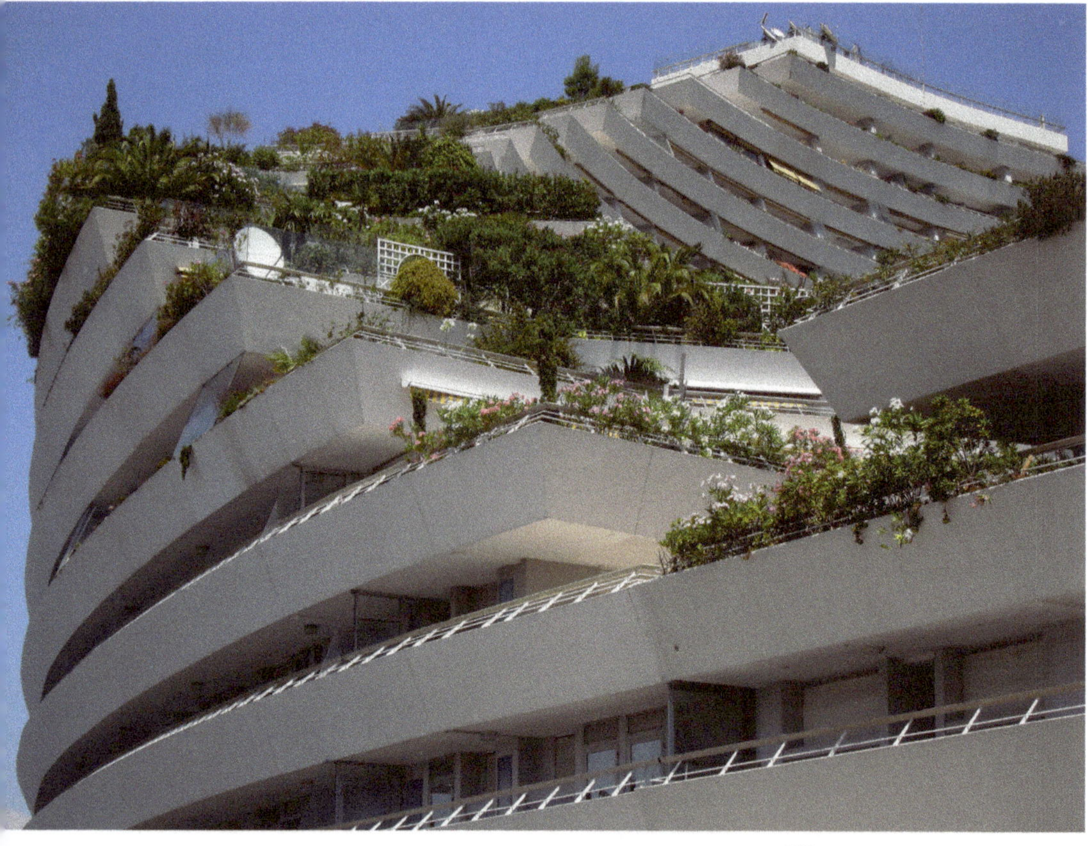

Above:
The Amiral tower,
Marina Baie des Anges

Left:
The Commodore tower

Opposite:
Town hall, Garbejaire,
Sophia Antipolis

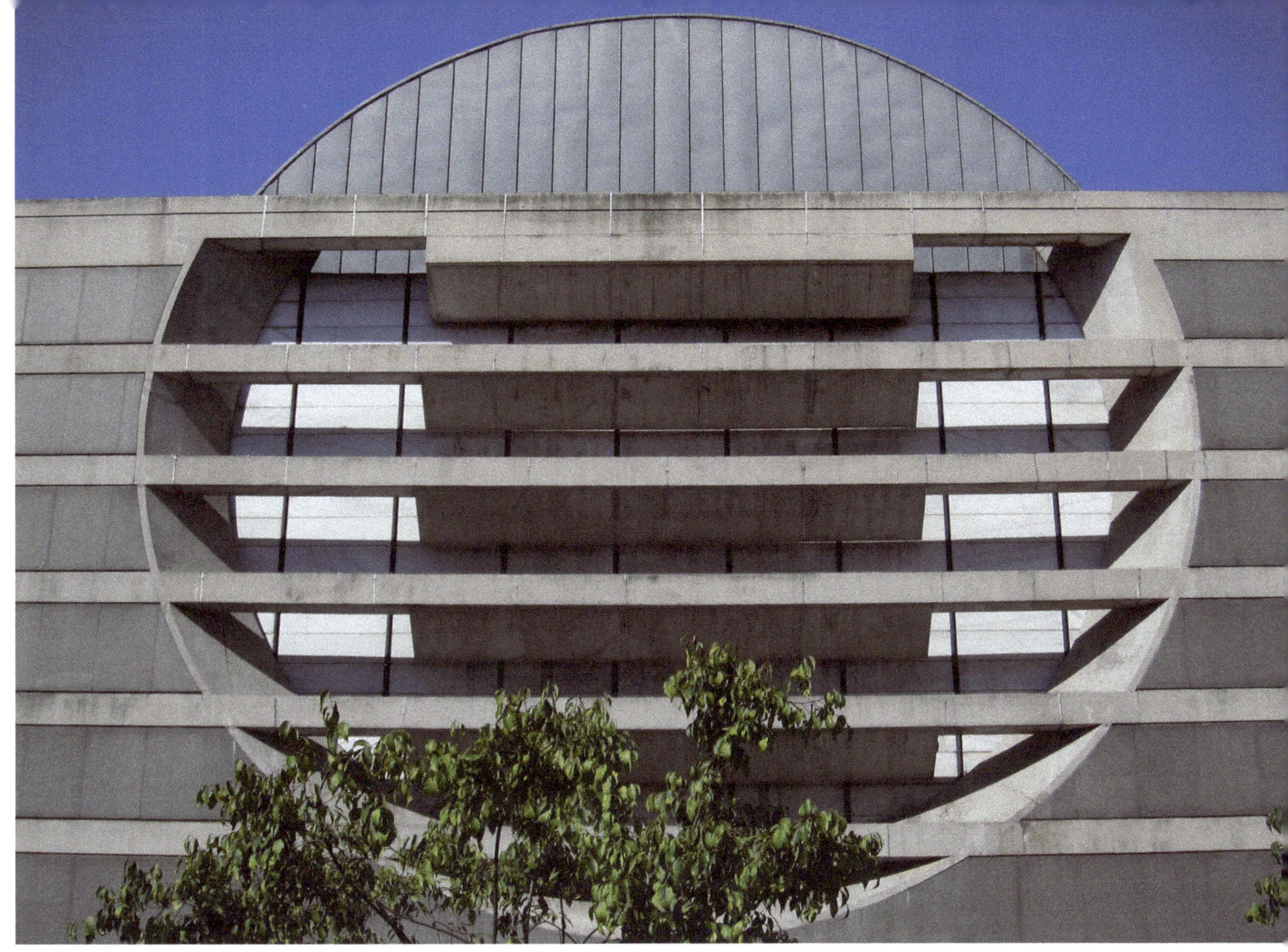

designed by André Minangoy, an architectural cousin of La Grande Motte. "One day the whole Côte d'Azur will be like this," says Paul Sinclair in *Super-Cannes*.[33] Building began in 1969 and construction of the four interlocking blocks that form a protective enclosure around the marina wasn't completed until 1993. The walls of the complex, like giant ocean waves or gun boat sails, wrap around eight jetties wedged with ranks of yachts, although the moorings are too small to attract the inflated vessels of the super-rich, who berth in nearby Antibes. The most dramatic view of the undulating towers must be from the air above the sea.

The day I visited, I entered the marina by following the sea-facing western wall along a stony beach, past a private pool in one of the gardens. Tiers of balconies separated by linear slits were stacked high above me. Ballard invokes the complex repeatedly in *Super-Cannes*, often referring to its mysterious curvature—"Logic and reality curved at Marina Baie des Anges"; "its curved towers enclosing a deeper darkness"—but he doesn't describe the place in any detail.[34] Maybe on one of his summer vacations he stopped by to amble along the jetties past yachts with names like Southern Comfort and Velvet Mornings, Flame II and Paradisio III, or had lunch in one of the sleepy restaurants under the palms that fringe the marina.

In the novel, the apartment towers are luxurious residences where high-flying careerists enjoy the rewards of corporate success—"a gorgeous flat at Marina Baie des Anges."[35] As I mooched around, taking photos, I only saw people of retirement age, foreign residents and tourists who were presumably renting for a week or two. Occupants let themselves in and out of the private gardens through locked gates under the gaze of surveillance cameras.

A surprising number of empty retail units—scattered among the estate agencies advertising apartments and marine equipment stores selling jet skis—suggested that times may be harder today than they were in the 1990s. A waiter told us that local businesses find it a struggle. The marina feels marooned. It has the lugubrious air of a dream unfulfilled, a gigantic architectural folly.

The site's concrete immensity and inwardness are certainly Ballardian. Geraniums, agapanthus, bougainvillea and prickly pear colonize the balconies in these somnolent residential towers, where no life seemed to stir, and palm trees flourish on some of the stepped aerial platforms. From some angles, down below at ground level, the complex looks like a blank-surfaced, monumentally futuristic reimagining of a Mesoamerican

33 Ibid., p. 224.
34 Ibid., p. 228 and 288.

35 Ibid., p 113.

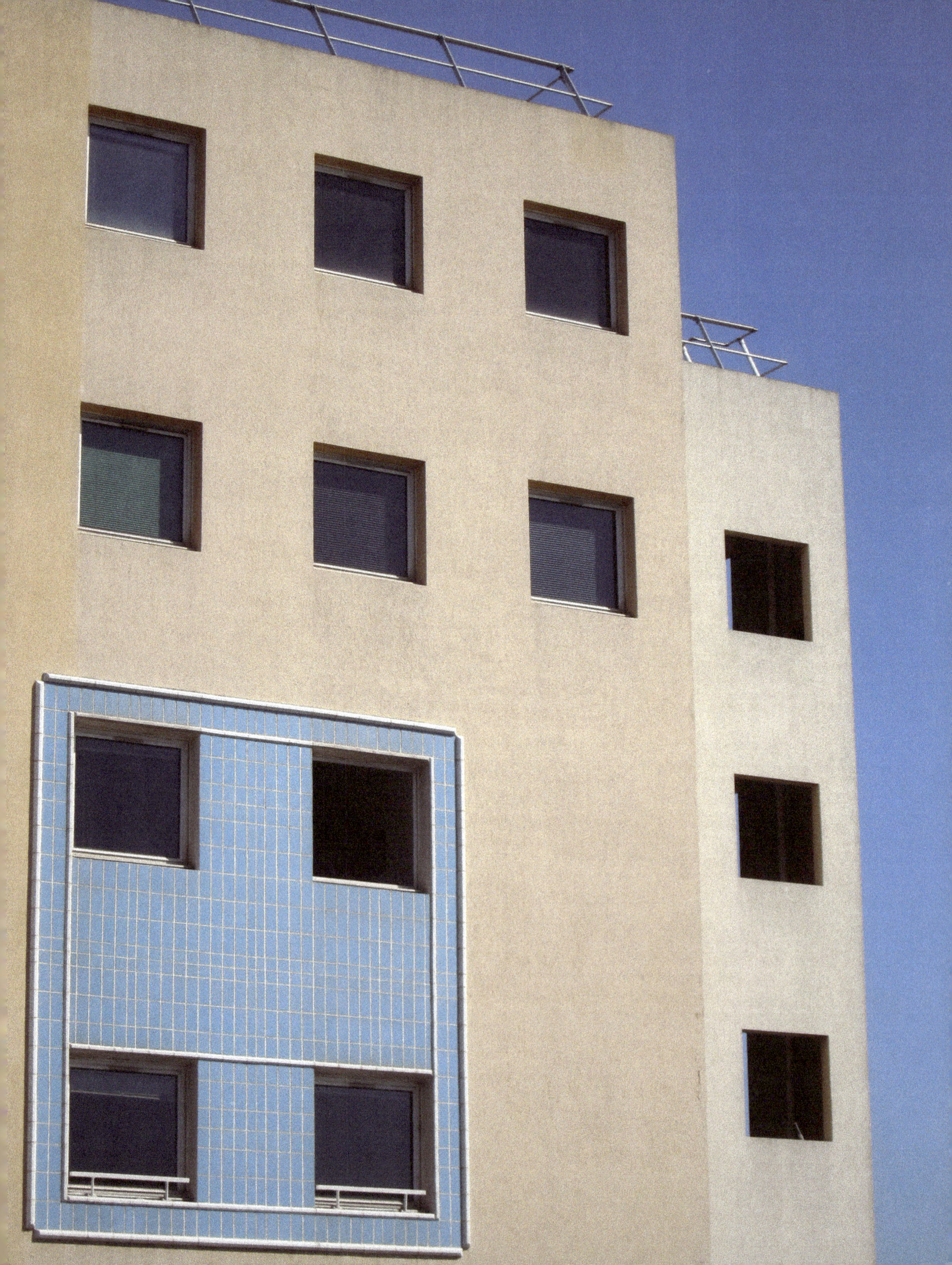

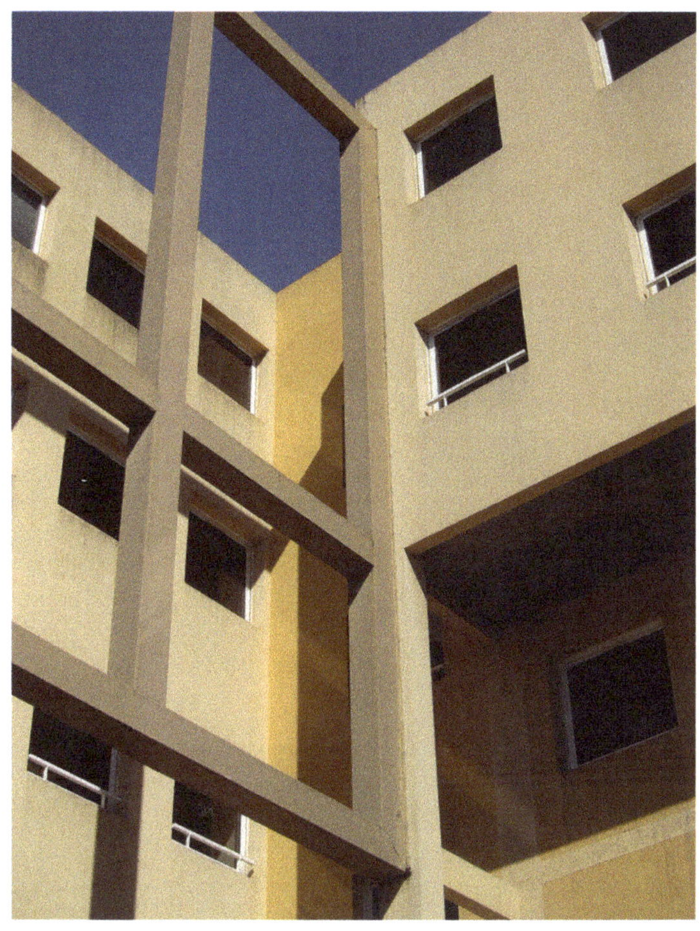

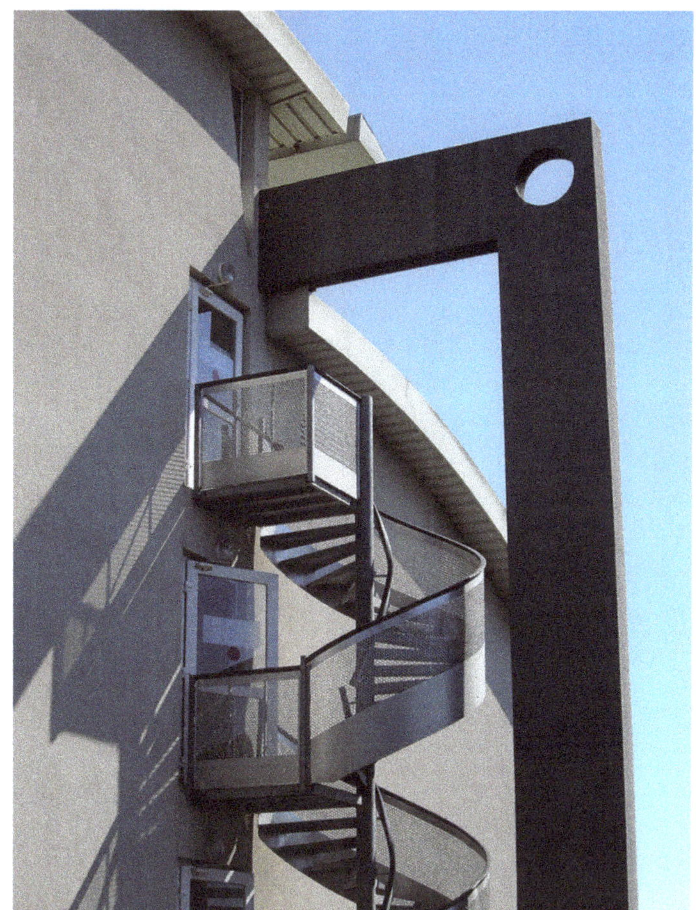

pyramid, or one of Max Ernst's petrified lost cities sinking into the jungle. Anything could be going on up there in the quietude.

Opposite and above:
Residential buildings, Garbejaire

Sophia Antipolis

In Eden-Olympia—"home to the greatest corporations in the world"—something rancid festers.[36] A doctor has run amok, shooting several colleagues. Paul Sinclair, who narrates the story, begins to investigate, while recuperating from a knee injury. He discovers a culture of delinquency and violence among the senior managers. "There's a remarkable need for punitive violence hidden away in the senior executive mind," says Wilder Penrose, the park's in-house psychiatrist, who gradually emerges as sinister ringmaster of this dysfunctional new order.[37] The Adolf Hitlers and Pol Pots of the future, he informs Sinclair, will arise from shopping malls and business parks.

It wasn't very Ballardian of me, but I arrived in Sophia Antipolis on the local bus. It should have been a Jaguar with a heavy steering wheel, perhaps, like the one Sinclair drives in the book. I got out at Garbejaire, the residential village at the heart of the park. I could already see what the problem was going to be because "park" is the right word. Sophia Antipolis is huge, covering 2,300 hectares, and I was trying to explore it on foot.

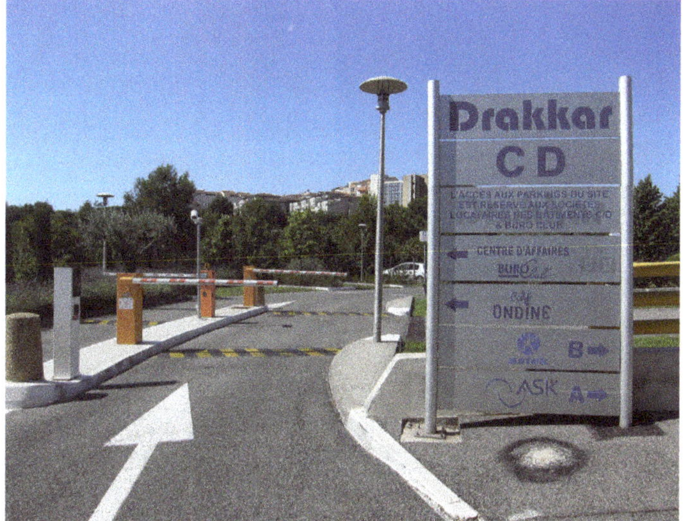

Bottom:
Driveway to the Drakkar building, Sophia Antipolis

---

36 Ibid., p. 105.
37 Ibid., p. 261.

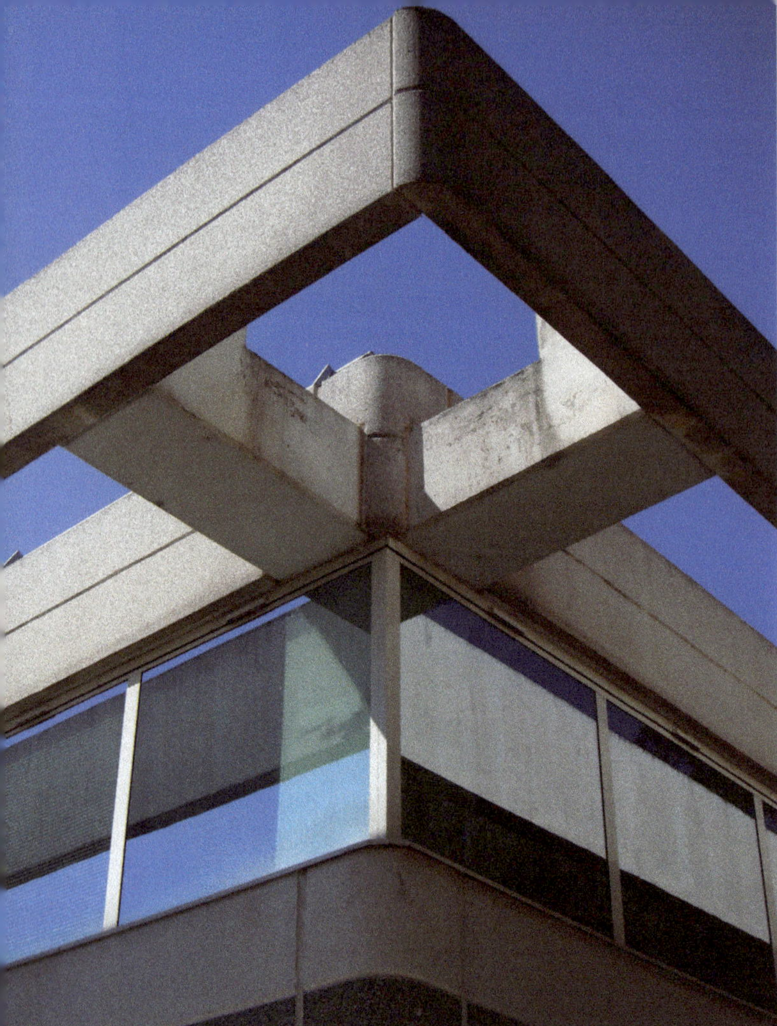

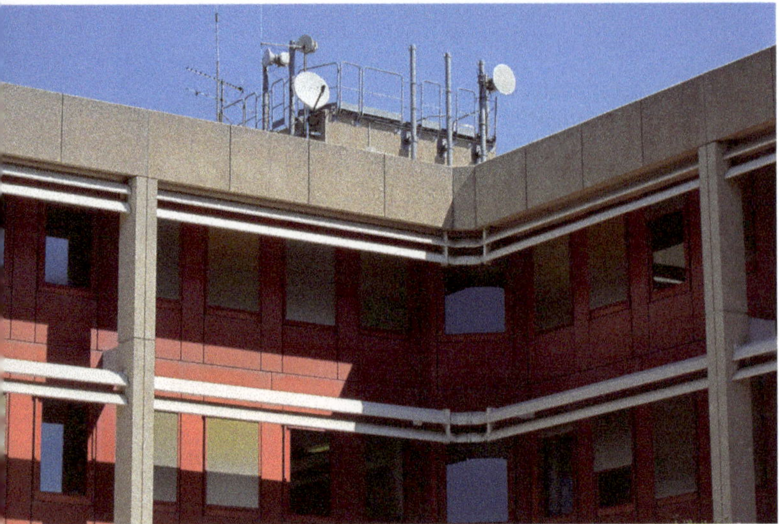

Top:
Thales, a cybersecurity company, Sophia Antipolis

Above:
Laboratoire Elaiapharm, medical laboratory

Opposite, left:
LPG Systems, beauty technologies

Opposite, right:
Building A, Les Vaisseaux office complex

In *Super-Cannes*, Eden-Olympia has a steely architectural presence, although the park doesn't always sound that big. "I had left the BMW near the main entrance [...] and then walked across the business park to the administration building".[38] On the other hand, "The glass and gun-metal office blocks were set well apart from each other, separated by artificial lakes and forested traffic islands".[39] Ballard makes plenty of references to glass and mirror curtain-walling, glass atriums, ventilation shafts and cable conduits, satellite dishes and microwave aerials. A dome-shaped building houses the personnel department. Stretch limousines ferry executives around and a security helicopter patrols one of the lakes. A brochure about the park offers "a vision of glass and titanium straight from the drawing boards of Richard Neutra and Frank Gehry, but softened by landscaped parks and artificial lakes, a humane version of Corbusier's radiant city."[40] (An editor should have spotted that Neutra died in 1970, and the vision sounds more like Norman Foster-ish high-tech than the convoluted structures of Frank Gehry.) Office buildings rise from the Corbusian landscape "like megaliths of the future".[41]

As Ballard explicitly states, Eden-Olympia's style is late-modernist, minimal and self-effacing—"a machine above all for thinking in."[42] These are qualities shared by his favourite building, the Heathrow Hilton (1990) designed by Michael Manser, "a brilliant white classic building, like a space-age hangar."[43] The exception to Eden-Olympia's grey architectural uniformity is the administrative headquarters, which displays a bombastic, "almost imperial grandeur, with its classical pilasters rising to a stylized post-modern pediment."[44] For Ballard, this decorative excess is an unmistakable signal of the canker at Eden-Olympia's core. "I detest postmodern architecture in any form whatsoever," he wrote in 1995. "All that self-referential jokery, all that pastiche, all that ornamentation for its own sake. It's architecture as kitsch... It's extremely retrogressive, nostalgic and, I think, in every sense corrupt."[45]

Sophia Antipolis, host to corporations such as Air France, Chanel, IBM, Canon and Hewlett-Packard, resembles Eden-Olympia in only the most general way. I spent three hours walking around, a lone pedestrian in the blazing sun, in a landscape devised for wheels, and I saw no Eden-Olympia-like gate or main entrance, no visible perimeter, no cruising limousines or menacing security helicopters. The access roads twist and loop across the park between the roundabouts connecting the two- and three-storey buildings that nestle unobtrusively in the tree-covered landscape. I had to wander off the road, peer through foliage, climb driveways, slip through

38 Ibid., p. 119..
39 Ibid., p. 7.
40 Ibid., p. 5.
41 Ibid., p. 202.
42 Ibid., p. 191.
43 John O'Reilly, "The House that Jencks Built", *The Modern Review*, vol. 1 no. 20, April-May 1995, p. 31. Ballard held to his view of the Heathrow Hilton with great consistency, singling out the building again in a conversation with Hans Ulrich Obrist, "Nothing is Real, Everything is Fake" (2003) in Simon Sellars and Dan O'Hara (eds.), *Extreme Metaphors: Selected Interviews with J.G. Ballard, 1967-2008*, 2012, p. 392. But here it has become merely his favourite building in London.
44 *Super-Cannes*, 2011, p. 191.
45 "The House that Jencks Built", *The Modern Review*, p. 31

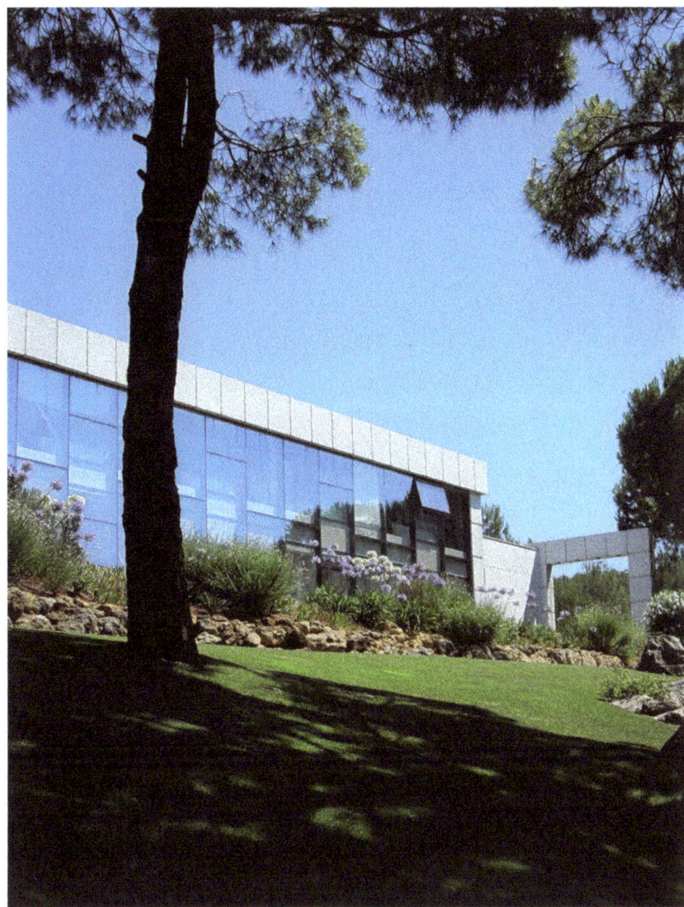

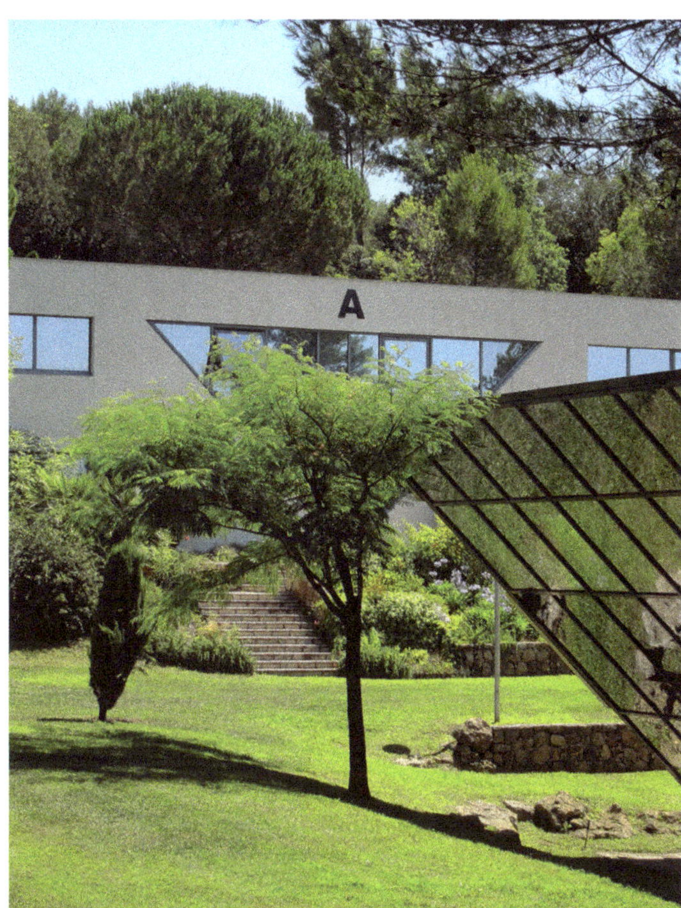

barriers and cross private parking areas to get a closer look at the architecture, which tends to be unassertively modern, functional and inexpressive, whatever breakthroughs and innovations might be taking place inside.

When I eventually stumbled across the unremarkable offices of Intel, a company with an indisputably global profile, I felt a small sense of triumph. Perhaps security men in dark glasses would appear from nowhere and order this suspicious intruder to stop taking pictures. But no one seemed to notice or care. At midday on a weekday, the business park was eerily tranquil, with barely a passing vehicle at times. The most Ballardian installation I saw was an encampment of mobile homes with satellite dishes and aerials, tucked away behind a cylindrical building that appeared to be empty, as though a team of techno-nomads had infiltrated the corporate parkland and temporarily occupied the site. They were busy inside or absent and there was no one to be seen.

Once again, as I prowled about, I wondered how much time Ballard had spent in Sophia Antipolis. In *The Inner Man*, a biography that has been criticized for many inaccuracies, John Baxter notes that while it's possible Ballard visited this or another business park and spoke to employees, nothing in the novel's acknowledgements suggests this. "Claire [Walsh] undertook much of the research, working online," claims Baxter.[46] That would have been more challenging in the late 1990s than it would be today. I was unable to speak to Walsh to confirm her role, and now Walsh, like Ballard, is gone.

It is accurate, though, to suggest that Ballard borrowed only the parts of Sophia Antipolis that he needed for his novel of ideas, to bolster the disquieting fantasy of a secretive corporate enclave, where violence becomes a regulatory mechanism for maintaining peak efficiency among the work-obsessed executive elite. In his imaginary business park, Ballard rearranged the architecture and adjusted the landscape to amplify *Super-Cannes*' sense of "gated-ness" and intensify the reader's unease.

I remember the feeling of architectural oppressiveness from my first reading, years before I visited these locations. By the novel's conclusion, work has already begun on Eden-Olympia Ouest, a "vast urbanization larger than Cannes," writes Ballard, almost twice the size of the original: an engine of psychopathy chomping across the idyllic landscape of southern France.[47]

"You're about to create a major crime wave," Sinclair protests to Penrose.

"The crime wave is already there," the mad psychiatrist enthuses. "It's called consumer capitalism."[48]

The inscrutable blankness of the linear city's architecture provides the perfect camouflage.

46 John Baxter, *The Inner Man: The Life of J.G. Ballard*, Weidenfeld & Nicolson, London, 2011, p. 324. An interview with Walsh about Ballard corroborates the claim: Tim Adams, "Seeing him arrive, always smiling, ready for anything, was wonderful", *The Observer*, Review, 26 April 2009, p 9.

47 *Super-Cannes*, 2011, p. 295.

48 Ibid., p. 363.

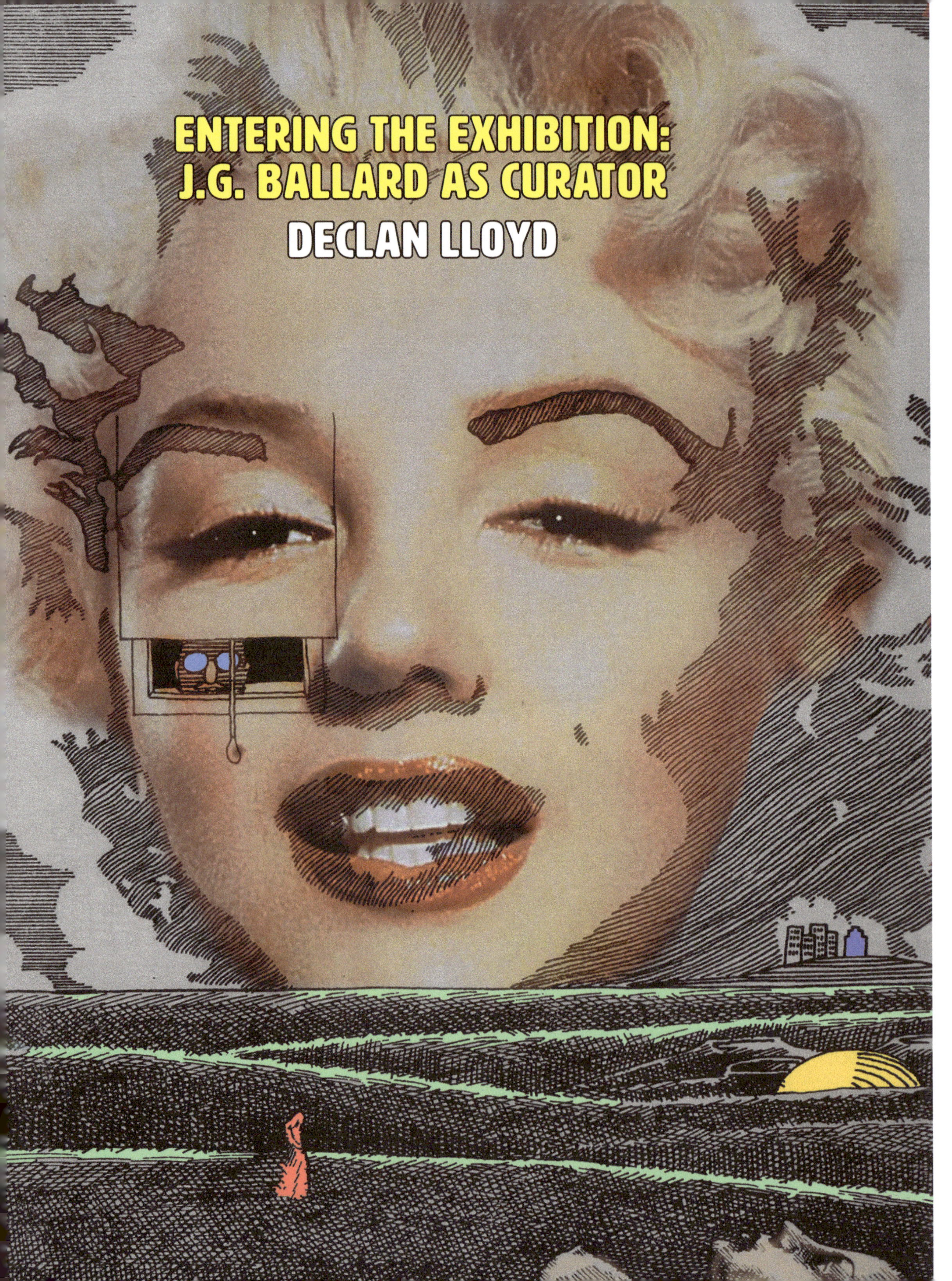
ENTERING THE EXHIBITION:
J.G. BALLARD AS CURATOR
DECLAN LLOYD

In a 2003 interview with Hans Ulrich Obrist, J.G. Ballard was asked about the significance of his first texts being published around the same time as the Independent Group's 1956 *This is Tomorrow* exhibition. This influential art show brought together the work of philosophers, artists, architects in order to present a unified aesthetic vision. As with so many of his interviews, his responses were more something one might expect more from a philosopher as opposed to an author of science fiction:

At the time I didn't see *This is Tomorrow* as an aesthetic event. For me it wasn't primarily an art show, just as I didn't see exhibitions of Francis Bacon, Max Ernst, Magritte and Dali as displays of paintings. I saw them as among the most radical statements of the human imagination ever made, on a par with radical discoveries in neuroscience or nuclear physics. *This is Tomorrow* showed how the world could be reperceived and remade'

Such a 'radical' view of the art exhibition and its capacity for change warrants a deeper reading into the presence of such within his writing. Particularly considering, as Obrist points out, the significance of the exhibition in terms of its prevalence at the very genesis of his literary career. The capacity of the exhibition to see the world anew, or even to some extent 'remake' reality, certainly gives a sense of the importance which Ballard allocated to art exhibits and their experiential, even existential impact upon the spectator. Jeanette Baxter expands upon this further, suggesting that the significance of the exhibition for Ballard, once again identifying *This is Tomorrow*, lies in the fact that the event "acknowledged a key cultural shift in the role of the audience which held particular resonance for Ballard's own ideas on the role of the reader". The idea then that the exhibition space could have radical implications on an audience, could 'rewire' their perspectives in a sense, is thus something seen as being entirely achievable within the literary domain.

The pinnacle perhaps of such a transposition, in terms of treating the 'text as exhibition', is of course his 1970 masterwork, *The Atrocity Exhibition*. At the outset of this novel we are thrust headlong into outsider art exhibition, and from there on in, we are presented with fragments of narrative which bear the title of famous paintings, and many of these works and their imagery seems to bleed into the narrative, in a form of quasi-ekphrasis.

But before looking in more detail at the kaleidoscopic world of *The Atrocity Exhibition*, it is important to look to how certain other works in this interval similarly explore the significance of the exhibition space. It was not long after *This is Tomorrow* when Ballard began work on his *Project for a New Novel* billboard experiments, one of his earliest creative ventures which rather cryptically introduced us to many of the characters, objects, landscapes and even voices which would emerge in later stories and novels.

These typographically constrained billboard narratives utilise the space and situation of text in a manner highly antithetical to the ordinary eye-catching and iconic visuals of the advertising landscape, which are geared at grabbing the attention of the viewer and embedding the need for a product within their unsuspecting unconscious. These were something of an inversion of this process altogether: as if giving us a glimpse into the fragmentary and overwhelmed unconscious of some modern subject, who has been somehow splintered by the surrounding landscape. Rick McGrath has observed that these early billboards above all "advertise Ballard as an artist... they advertise the concept of using advertising space in a reversed way—to give away concepts, not to sell products. Making sense isn't the point. You want to make a noise in the art world? Be different. Pop artists want to use everyday commercial objects as Art. Fine. Let's reverse that by putting art into everyday commercial spaces."

Here then we are once again reminded of this crucial aforementioned idea of 'rewiring', which Ballard designates as the driving engine of the exhibition. There is a definite parallel to be made then between the ad campaign and the exhibition in this regard. Where one is geared at a conscious rewiring by reinterpreting the surrounding landscape, and the other is very much rewiring the unconscious, so that we feel the need for certain products, or the need to be seen in a certain way by others.

This eerie reflection thus shows two ideological intents: one is clearly geared at a radical empowerment of the subject, while the other is purely projected towards disempowerment. But what if one could transform the art of *The Hidden Persuaders*, which Ballard was so privy to having worked as an adman for a time, and instead use the landscape as a place of empowerment? Even perhaps, as a gigantic exhibition space?

In many ways these billboards are driven by the emergence of new awareness to the manipulative intent of the surrounding world, which marks the emergence of Pop Art. A complication of this empowerment-disempowerment dichotomy is, as McGrath identifies, seminal to the philosophy of the Pop Artists, this being another central movement with which Ballard is often associated. Ballard presents us with a darker vision of the advertising landscape which is certainly redolent of the early death series of Warhol: eerie and obsessional, haunted by tragic celebrities, intertwined with the oppressive, violent interludes of the media.

Such is exemplified within *The Atrocity Exhibition*, wherein Ballard shows us the true manipulative and seductive power of advertising, which is grossly aggrandized and caricatured, and becomes wholly entwined with the unconscious mind: 'the first billboard appeared—Cinemascope of breast and thigh, deceit and need terraced into the contours of the landscape' (*Atrocity*, p. 97). Within Ballard's 'inner-spatial' worlds, the imagery of the spectacle is openly and overtly deceitful and sinister, a means of contorting and controlling the psyche. *Project for a New Novel* and *The Atrocity Exhibition* are therefore both texts where the reader is caught in something of a double bind: at once thrust into the empowering space of the exhibition, a space of interpretation and creative galvanization, but at the same time into the maelstrom of the spectacle (following Guy Debord's usage of the term).

It is perhaps unsurprising then that both present us with a psyche which is broken apart, shattered and splayed like the razor-edged facets of a broken mirror. One is reminded here then of the drive of Pop Art, which, as Sarat Maharaj attests, adopting a Derridean stance, is "both lethal and remedial. The antithetical terms play off against each other... we may take the 'pharmakon' as a rough and ready snapshot of Pop Art's gear-switching modes, its double voicings, about turns and shifting stances".

Ballard's work is incredibly mercurial and mutable when it comes to the world of art, in the sense of it being so readily assimilable by different movements. As expressed, he certainly resonates with the Pop Artists, but other aspects of his work also seem highly Futurist in nature, revelling as they do in the technological bustle of the present.

The tether to movements which are crucially entwined with curatorship in terms of their ideological impact also draws us to his affinities with Dada, in which it is this very act of resituation, of placing an object from one setting into another so that it now becomes art (most iconically and stereotypically exemplified by way of Duschamp's urinal), is of seismic import. Above all however, Ballard's work resonates with the European Surrealists and their influence was something he was always very open about, expressing their profound influence on his writing. At one point in his autobiography, *Miracles of Life*, Ballard expresses that

> "I felt strongly, and still do, that psychoanalysis and Surrealism were a key to the truth about existence and the human personality, and also a key to myself... I wrote short stories and fragments of incomprehensible novels which made complete sense if deemed to be Surrealist."

It could certainly be suggested that amongst the most pressing of Ballard's ideological affinities with the Surrealists is rooted once again in this crucial idea of their capacity to reimagine, 'remake' and abstract our everyday reality through aestheticization. Such an abstraction is also a critical means of illuminating its underlying workings. Something Ballard also foregrounds here, which is seminal to both his and the work of the Surrealists is the process of encoding. This draws us back to the *Project to a New Novel* billboards, and this idea McGrath expounds in terms of Ballard's "putting art into everyday commercial spaces." I have previously taken this approach to Ballard's work very literally, suggesting that these billboards could have been a part of a series of textually encoded Salvador Dalí landscapes, and in so doing fulfilling one of the Surrealist motivations of overthrowing the consumer spectacle (which was also why the Surrealists were so fundamental in terms of their influence for the May 1968 student riots in France).

If these billboards were intended with any degree of seriousness is still up for debate, but supposing that they were, this would have been a very early demonstration of Ballard's keen interest in curatorship; in this case, following my own reading, of a citywide exhibition in which there are Surrealist paintings covertly immersed within the urban landscape.

Above all the billboards are creatively stimulating: they show us what we want to see, like a kind of textual Rorschach test, and they only bear any deeper meaning when we ourselves are willing to search for it. That said, the billboards also offer us, in a highly Surrealist vein, something of a Dalínian accumulation of symbols. For once these many fragments are decrypted, tethered to the many stories and novels which they are connected, they show us a personal mythology, through which a deeper, hidden 'kernel' can perhaps be revealed. These recurrent images, settings, characters, themes and objects, are thus viewed as the literary equivalent of a dreamscape.

The only 'real' exhibition Ballard undertook was the infamous 'Crashed Cars' exhibition of at the New Arts Lab in 1969, which occurred, very presciently, around the same time as *The Atrocity Exhibition* was first published. He described the exhibition, as if adopting the approach of a curator-cum-psychoanalyst, as "a psychological test disguised as an art show", and hired a number of 'hostesses' to chaperone spectators about the mangled motors.

Many of those who attended the show were said to have been incited to unprovoked acts of violence: smashing windscreens, vandalising parts of the venue, urinating, and some were allegedly even driven to sexually assaulting the hostesses. This event seems something of an artistic prelude to *Crash*, and in many ways harbours much of its crucial components (the origins of which appear in *The Atrocity Exhibition*), but also seems seminal in terms of once again exposing how the exhibition space could provide this crucial aspect of involvement, and even incitement.

Ballard explained to Obrist that he saw many art shows similarly as "elaborate attempts to test the psychology of today's public" (Sellars, p. 387). This draws our attention to Ballard's view of the role of the curator as being somehow enmeshed with that of the psychoanalyst. Indeed, this convolution of psychoanalsys and art is of course central to Surrealism, being of course, a movement spawned out of the emergence of Freudian Surrealism, wherein the watching lens of psychoanalysis is ever present.

This idea of an ever present lens of psychoanalysis is one we readers of Ballard are very familiar with. Psychiatrist figures appear incessantly throughout his stories and novels. Dr Osbourne of 'The Terminal Beach' (1964), is something of an earlier incarnation of Dr Nathan of *The Atrocity Exhibition*, who, like so many others, provides an ever-watchful and analytical gaze. Dr Nathan attempts to rationalise and pry meaning from Traven's hallucinatory, delusional experiences. It is perhaps very simply for this reason, this innate logic-seeking, that they are usually represented as antagonistic figures who are not to be trusted; for here they inhabit a space where they do not and cannot belong.

These figures attempt to dull and neuter the creative liberation of these dream-like realms, attempt to inject logic even where there is none to be found outside of Traven's inner reality. Ballard notes of Dr Nathan, that "reason rationalises reality for him, as it does for the rest of us, in the Freudian sense of providing a more palatable or convenient explanation, and there are so many subjects today about which we should not be reasonable" (*Atrocity*, p. 89). But to reiterate, the psychiatrist and the curator are strangely unified in some respects, a strange kind of symbiosis. He at one point states in his notes to *The Atrocity Exhibition*, which could be viewed at once as the notes of a psychiatrist or that of a curator, "I imagine my mental patients conflating Freud and Liz Taylor in their Warhol-like efforts, unerringly homing in on the first signs of their doctor's nervous breakdown" (*Atrocity*, p.14).

Like the Surrealists then, Ballard shows us worlds brandished by a unique psychology, so that in the same way that Surrealism aestheticizes psychoanalysis, using psychology as a lens to generate art, Ballard's characters provide a lens within the literary domain. The delusional world of the psychotic, the obsessiveness of the neurotic, the god-complex of the megalomaniac, all of these alternate psychologies become aestheticized abstractions through which we can perceive the world anew. This relates to Ballard's coined term which he used to describe much of his fiction, 'inner space', which he defined in a 1968 interview with Janick Storm as "the meeting ground between the inner world of the mind and the outer world of reality. Inner space you see in the paintings of the Surrealists, Max Ernst, Dalí, Tanguy, Chirico... science fiction should explore that area, the area where the mind impinges on the outside world, and not just deal in fantasy" (Sellars, pp. 16-17).

Following such, this inner space, propelled by Surrealism, acts much in the same way as science fiction, only it speculates not so much in the world of matter but of mind. And if there was a Ballardian text which were to epitomise this exploration of inner space, then it has to be *The Atrocity Exhibition*.

The Atrocity Exhibition cements together a range of short stories written between 1966 and 1970 and reads somewhat like the nuclear fallout of a once completed text, leaving the reader to piece back together the world, the identities and psychologies of those who came before. Gregory Stephenson once located the novel at the very "center of Ballard's *oeuvre* [it represents] a grammar of the themes and images of his work."

Ballard himself expressed that the novel was born out of the JFK assassination, from the cataclysmic impact that the event had on the mass psyche, and particularly that generated by the press, and the spate of controversies and conspiracies over the shooting. The psychological dissolution of the central character is almost symptomatic of this fracture of events as depicted by the media. It is perhaps unsurprising then that the text bears many similarities in its montage of forms, its lucid and often pseudo-scientific style of writing and affectless tone to the Warren Commission Report.

Ballard observes in his notations that the report is "a remarkable document, especially if considered as a work of fiction...a type of obsessional fiction that links science and pornography" (*Atrocity*, p. 40). Like the report, Ballard's novel contains frequent long lists of seemingly unrelated objects which are collected from crime scenes, as well as many excerpts of scientific analysis and diaristic-style psychiatric diagnoses. There is also a very similar distortion of identity generated through the many often contradictory readings and representations of the figure of Oswald, creating a kind of palimpsest of identity, much like that of Traven.

The pictorial edition of *The Atrocity Exhibition* released in *New Worlds* (although not published in its entirety) contains medical documents, photographs, some of crashed cars and anatomical close-ups, as well as images taken from McLuhan's *Mechanical Bride* (1951) and Ralph Nader's *Unsafe at Any Speed* (1965). Taken together these images urge us to form connections and piece together a narrative from the 'evidence' placed before us. The effect is, as with so much of Ballard's work, a kind of induced apophenia, so that we are put in a state of heightened pattern-seeking, and such pattern seeking is something we are similarly urged to do in viewing certain works of Surrealism.

Perhaps the primary significance of this emulation of the Warren Commission lies in its being a text made up of various fragments of information, primarily visual information, and especially descriptions of visual ephemera. Indeed the Warren Commision becomes a kind of eerie exhibition; presenting us with various visual fragments and almost sculptural depictions of spaces (especially when the exact geometric layouts are presented, such as the trajectory of the bullet shot from the Texas book depository). The visual and the anatomical are also fused together in the 1990 edition of the novel published by RE/Search which again included images, this time drawn by Phoebe Gloeckner in a style which merged a kind of comic-strip aesthetic with the style of the drawings which featured in the earliest editions of *Grey's Anatomy*. This was a text which Ballard familiarised himself with whilst training as a medical student at Cambridge, and he once ironically hailed it as 'the greatest novel of the twentieth century' (Sellars, p. 28).

Gloeckner's artwork provides a diagrammatic counterpart to the broken fragments of the novel, and in many respects serves to imitate Ballard's language, particularly his fusion of anatomical description with the concrete environment, and generating a sense of narrative microscopy. Her often explicit illustrations work to expose the inherently visual aspect of Ballard's language: depicting expressways merged with intestines; labelled spinal diagrams next to labelled car parts; as well as black and white photographs of urban, geometric structures and microscopic images of cells and viruses. As you move through the text the images correspondingly move through the innards of the human body like a probing camera.

The tangential plot of *The Atrocity Exhibition* revolves around a man undergoing a progressive form of psychosis, whose name and identity fluctuates between segments, changing from Travis to Traven (Ballard locates Traven as the character's core identity) to Talbot to Tallis to Trabert to Travers. This is a process which Roger Luckhurst very presciently designates as a disjunctive 'T-cell in search of a modulus'. The narrative structure can be likened to a description of Elizabeth Taylor's relationship to the masses: 'the planes of their lives interlocked at oblique angles, fragments of personal myths fusing with commercial cosmologies' (*Atrocity*, p. 13).

In one part, the 'T' figure appears as a doctor in a mental hospital who himself goes mad; in another he is a university lecturer driven mad by his belief in the coming apocalypse and is being pursued by his students who wish to stage his conceptual death; in another he is a murderer, who commits a violent act in a hotel room; in another, which is most reminiscent of 'The Terminal Beach', he is a bomber pilot who wanders the desert with three imaginary followers, and is covertly pursued by his wife; in another he again works in an institution, though now he is pursued by a film crew who are making a documentary on madness, convinced he is their star. As we can see here, all of these disparate narratives within the novel share a certain resonance, and this resonance has far more to do with a tonal consistency, something like the relation between a sequence of paintings by an artist, or perhaps more appropriately, an exhibition by an artist, or in this case an atrocity exhibition.

The base-narrative which guides these fragments is intimately tied to the ideas explored by the Surrealists, particularly in terms of their 'paranoiac' echoing of events, objects, emotions. Here we are witnessing what you might call 'mythological' events, a kind of Ballardian equivalent of The Hero's Journey perhaps, these are the archetypal consistencies or occurrences in one's life that Jung allocated such primal significance. The most glaring tether between these narratives, and much of Ballard's work in fact, is the descent into madness and the simultaneous, transcendental, dissolution of self.

Another poignant Ballardian mythological event is the

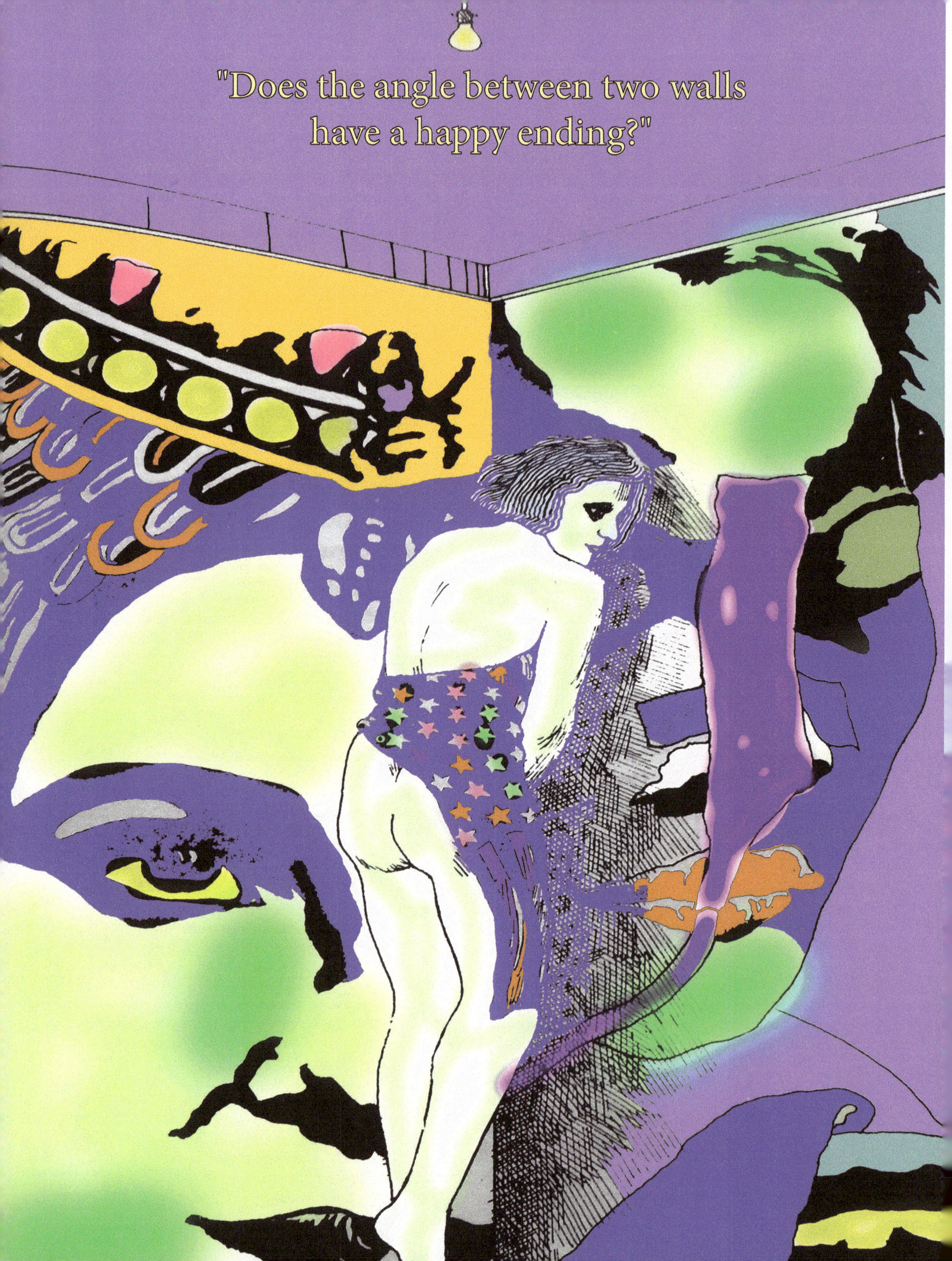
"Does the angle between two walls
have a happy ending?"

death of the wife or lover, or the paranoia of losing one's true love, an event which Ballard himself suffered. And there is a crucial connection between such mythological events and art, as seen in 'The Exploding Madonna' segment, named after a painting by Dalí, in which Travis observes 'the ascension of his wife's body above the target area, exploding Madonna of the weapons range' (*Atrocity*, p. 13).

Another recurrent mythic event is the pursuit of the obsessor, which is often symbolised by the captured image and the obsessive incorporation of photography, cinema, billboards. The psychiatrist figure also falls into this category, exemplified by the omniscient and unfaltering gaze of Doctor Nathan, who follows Traven (like other psychiatrists who pursue other patients) and attempts to draw logic, coherence and reason from his madness. These mythological iterations, these stories which follow a primal, archetypal narrative, undoubtedly ring true with the Surrealists, and of course with Freud himself, who so often incorporated aspects of myth, and art for that matter, into his own psychoanalytic approaches.

This unifying logic holds real significance within the novel, and is intended to—again, much like when one enters an art exhibition—draw upon elements of unity, and in so doing create a 'collective' narrative. Following such, in many ways *The Atrocity Exhibition* is a purposefully 'insubstantial' text, made up primarily of unseen points of intersection, elements which resonate on a level situated beyond the narrative itself, perhaps giving meaning to that strange, resounding question which Ballard asks of us: "does the angle between two walls have a happy ending?"

At the very beginning of *Atrocity*, in his 'author's note' to the text, Ballard implores the reader to 'try a different approach... turn the pages until a paragraph catches your eye. If the ideas or images seem interesting, scan the nearby paragraphs for anything that resonates in an intriguing way. Fairly soon… the underlying narrative will reveal itself' (*Atrocity*, p. vi).

Notably, there are two particularly prescient examples of when we might use such a method to navigate a text: the first is when reading a newspaper, and the second is whilst moving through an art gallery or exhibition. Perusing, skimming, looking for something which 'catches your eye', as implored by Ballard, invokes a highly visual approach to consuming a text. Ironically enough, even if one does choose to read *The Atrocity Exhibition* from beginning to end, as we are predisposed to do (this opening challenge is in itself a very Surrealist act—requiring the reader to release oneself from ingrained, unconscious norms), not so much as an exhibition but as a progressive, structured narrative, then one still inadvertently finds themselves plunged into an art gallery. It very quickly dawns that many if not most of these titled micro-narratives bear the names of famous paintings—as if these 'narratives' are in fact paintings hanging from a gallery wall. Not only that, but the internalized narrative itself begins with an exhibit: and more pertinently still, an exhibit of artworks painted by the insane, or 'outsider art'. There is great significance to be found in being situated within such an exhibition. Ballard has described how:

> "The open-ended character of my fiction requires the reader himself to make significant contribution. I'm offering a kit with which the reader, using my books as a sort of instruction manual (fit nozzle A into socket B, and you'll hear a loud whirring noise, which is the cosmos getting through to him)... the show 'Outsider Art' in London a couple of years ago impressed me enormously, because of the way in which these deeply isolated and disturbed people, many of them lifelong inmates of mental institutions—cut off from the world entirely —were still *struggling, through their drawings and paintings, to make sense of the world they inhabited."* (*RE/Search #8/9*, p. 45, my emphasis)

Whilst there is certainly similarities in terms of self-recuperation, art is not like psychiatry, which enforces a predetermined logic, but is rather a free and uninhibited form of creativity and meaning-making. In light of this, the opening sequence, and indeed our initial plunge into the exhibition, from which we never resurface, has far greater implications than first thought. There is certainly psychoanalytic relevance to this essential, underlying and ongoing pursuit of logic within the novel, which has to do with the psychotic mindset as personified by Traven. Lacan, who was famed for his return to Freud and his declaration that the unconscious is structured like a language, and who was also greatly influenced by the Surrealists, identified psychotic delusion as an attempt at self-cure, a process of the purest logic, which only seems illogical until the implicit logic is uprooted. Here then, through their artworks we see such a process rendered in the image.

In terms of the narrative headlines or 'artwork labels' which line the walls of *The Atrocity Exhibition*—which also act as something of a palimpsest over the outsider art exhibits which appear at the outset of the novel—they are almost all, as might be expected, Surrealist artworks. *The Exploding Madonna, Autumn Cannibalism* and *The Persistence of Memory* are all paintings by Dalí. There also appears *The Annunciation* (Magritte), *The Robing of the Bride* (Max Ernst), *The Bride Stripped Bare by her Bachelors* (Duchamp), *The Great American Nude* (Tom Wesselmann) as well as countless mentions of other artists and artworks (predominantly Surrealist) within the narrative fragments themselves.

Thus, these are narratives suffused by art, so that the paintings come to impinge upon narrative, to shape narrative and imagery. In one example Ballard describes how 'he dreams of Max Ernst, superior of the birds (*Europe after the Rain*, *Atrocity*, p. 12), and later Dr Nathan "lit a gold-tipped cigarette, noticing that a photograph of Talbot had been cleverly montaged over a reproduction of Dalí's *Hypercubic Christ*" (*Atrocity*, p. 21). At times this suffusion transcends painting, in that there are also references to works of literary Surrealism such as Raymond Roussel's *Impressions of Africa* (*Atrocity*, p. 59), one of the first texts to use the Surrealist technique of automatic writing, a technique Ballard also admits to using throughout *The Atrocity Exhibition* when writing the lists of objects (*Atrocity*, p. 89). There is also a reference to André Breton and Paul Éluard's *The Immaculate Conception*—"they're exhibits, Karen—this conception will be immaculate." (*Atrocity*, p. 81)—the influence of which is arguably far deeper, in its being a text in which they too, like Ballard in so many of his works, attempt to simulate or see the world anew through alternate psychologies, particularly those suffering from mental illness.

Read as an exhibition, the role of the reader is rather radically altered, and is now far more open and interpretive, freer, as they engross themselves within these literary paintings as if moving through a gallery. This also sheds a great deal of light onto the inclusion of Ballard's own voice in the annotations at the end of each chapter. In this configuration, the voice of Ballard acts as curator: giving his reasoning for the inclusion of certain artworks, and he even talks us through their (and his own) artistic processes and methods.

Ballard's annotations are thus, perhaps necessarily, more curatorial than explanatory, for rational explanation is quite clearly antithetical to the novel itself. This is reinforced by the inclusion of psychiatrist figures like Dr Nathan who are presented as untrustworthy, for there is great empowerment to be found outside of universal rationalisation and clear-cut explanation.

As Baxter attests "Ballard constructs a text which is founded upon the very notion that his authorial notes are as unstable as the fictional body which they purport to stabilise" (Baxter, pp. 91-92). Thus, in the frame of the work as a curated exhibition, it is a mistake to view the annotations as being in any way didactic or explanatory. Rather, Ballard is more concerned with provoking creative interpretation, whether that be by way of his own work or the work of others.

One prescient example of the way in which art comes to suffuse the narrative text within the novel bears the title *The Annunciation*, a title given to many artworks depicting Gabriel's announcement to Mary that her son was the son of God. But Ballard makes it clear that this annunciation is a Surrealist one, and one depicted by none other than René Magritte:

> "**The Annunciation.** Partly veiled by the afternoon clouds, the enormous image of a woman's hands moved across the sky. Talbot stood up, for a moment losing his balance on the sloping concrete. Raised as if to form an arch over an invisible child, the hands passed through the air above the plaza. They hung in the sunlight like immense doves. Talbot climbed the slope, following this spectre along the embankment. He had witnessed the annunciation of a unique event. Looking down at the plaza, he murmured without thinking, 'Ralph Nader.'" (*Atrocity*, pp. 25-26)

There is certainly a Biblical air to this scene, which becomes a kind of immersive ekphrasis through which Talbot traverses. Evidently, Ballard is doing far more here than simply adopting the headline of a painting: the constituent text is suffused with allusions to Magritte's artwork more widely, and it is intensely visual in its language and imagery. The clouds, the sloping concrete, the plaza and the arch all appear to be references to Magritte's version of the titular painting. But this is extended even further through the image of the 'immense doves' which recalls Magritte's frequent inclusion of doves within his artwork, and particularly reminiscent of the stormy seascapes, in which the doves are formed from clouds such as *The Big Family* (1963) and *The Kiss* (1951). Here art seeps into Ballard's language and infiltrates his world, so that the inner world of the characters' is a kind of painterly topography.

In the *Persistence of Memory* narrative Ballard describes Talbot as "walking along the overpass, he realised that the rectilinear forms of his consciousness were warped elements from some placid and harmonious future" (*Atrocity*, p. 24), using specific images taken from the painting (such as the 'rectilinear' sections of beach—a term he himself repeatedly uses in observational accounts of the work) and even the much more encompassing, tonal aspect of the artwork, as a means of describing Talbot's inner psychology. Another narrative labelled 'the enormous face', begins with a description of a gigantic billboard featuring the visage of Elizabeth Taylor—"the magnification was enormous" (*Atrocity*, p. 13)—and ends with the violent death of Travis's wife in an explosion. This

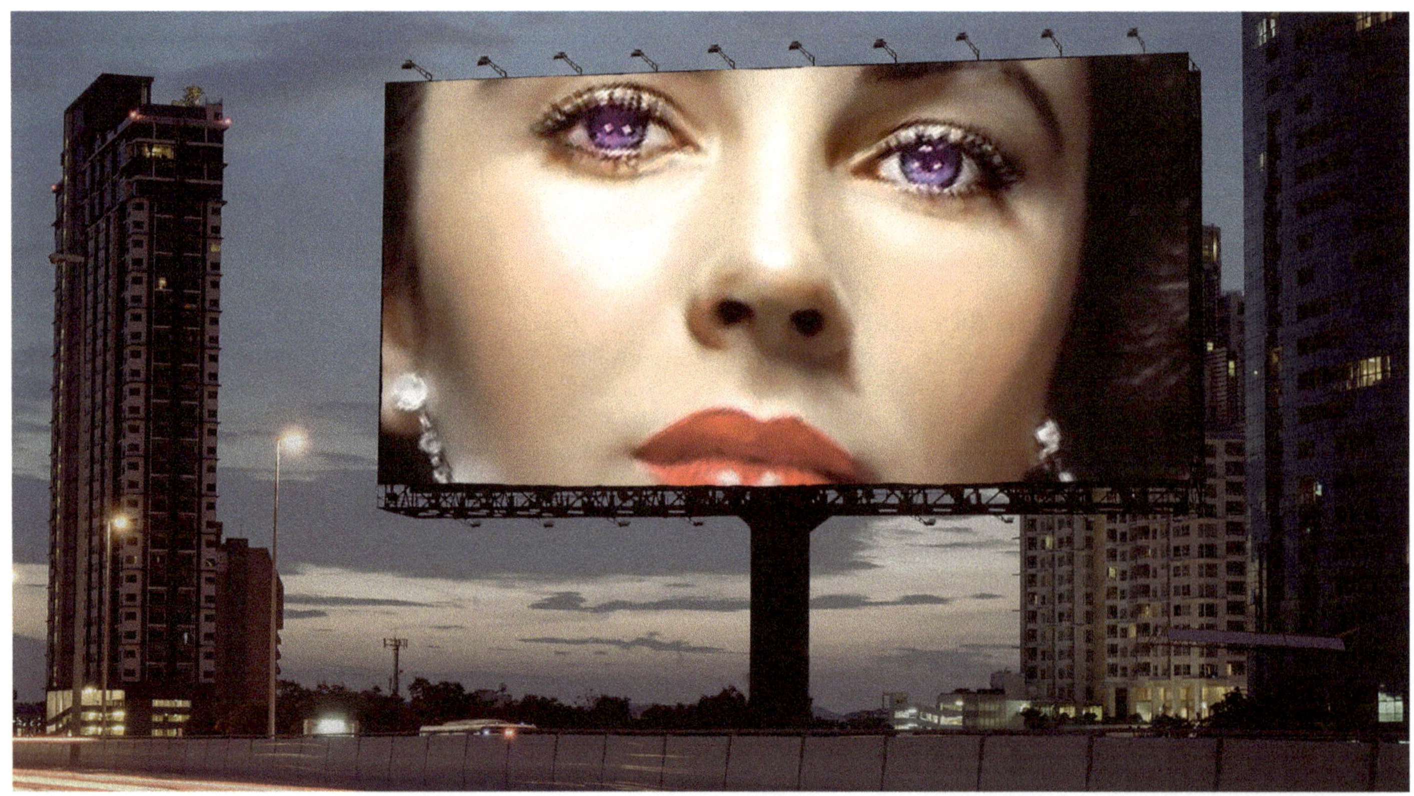

explosion flows into the next micro-narrative which is titled 'the Exploding Madonna', the aforementioned piece taken from Dalí's 'nuclear-mystic' period. We thus have this associative, connective progression from narrative to narrative.

This infiltration of art extends to Traven himself, who, for example in 'You and Me and the Continuum' (the point at which Traven is said to be 'at his most apocalyptic, appearing as the second coming of Christ', *Atrocity*, p. 138), he is likened to a Francis Bacon artwork, evoking a very specific aesthetic rendition of horror. Dr Nathan sits in a dark room of his laboratory, 'watching the shadowy figure of a man... part of his head seemed to be missing, like some disintegrating executive from a Francis Bacon nightmare' (*Atrocity*, p. 134).

The description seems particularly redolent of Bacon's chilling *Painting 1946* (1946) which shows a besuited figure whose face is partially 'cut-off' in shadow. Bacon's intensely corporeal and often distressing artworks, bearing shrieking figures and humanoid contortions of flayed meat and gristle, are frequently categorised as 'Biomorphic Surrealism', a term which might certainly also be applied to works such as *Crash* and *The Atrocity Exhibition*. Indeed, Bacon's use of recurrent images, which also hold strong psychological tethers to his harrowing past, are in many ways akin to the subjective iconographies which appear in the works of Surrealists such as Dalí and Ernst. Bacon has even described that his work was created "not out of any conscious will... it has a life completely of its own. It lives on its own, like the image one's trying to trap... [my process] unlocks the valves of feeling and therefore returns the onlooker to life more violently."

The intense viscerality of Ballard's biomorphic-Surrealist language is heightened by the recurrent anatomical imagery throughout the text, which is spliced in amongst the images depicted on commercial billboards, those gigantic icons of the spectacle. Such also relates to the crucial idea of assemblage within the novel:

> "glancing at the billboards, Dr Nathan recognised other magnified fragments: a segment of lower lip, a right nostril, a portion of female perineum. Only an anatomist would have identified these fragments, each represented as a formal geometric pattern" (*Atrocity*, p. 11).

Throughout the text Ballard hints at an analogous process in formulating narrative itself, for the 'anatomy' of narrative must be pieced together in order to form a whole, just like those magnified, dissected pieces and portions of the human body. The chapters contained in 'the appendix' of the novel (which echoes *Naked Lunch* as a playful reference to the human body), might be considered the 'surgical narratives': 'Prince Margaret's Face Lift' and 'Mae West's Reduction Mammoplasty' are particularly revealing of this. Ballard describes in his annotations how "the zoom lens and the interview camera bring them so near to us that we know their faces and their smallest gestures more intimately than those of our friends" (*Atrocity*, p. 179), exposing how these surgical, anatomical descriptions not only serve to simulate the mediatic image, but also to toy with this idea of knowing the image. Thus, Ballard's descriptions are commenting on the nature of celebrity and viewership within spectacular society. But the Surrealist thread is here too, for the 'Mae West' segment can be read as another aesthetic assimilation of Dalí, whose famous work *Face of Mae West Which May Be Used as an Apartment* (1935), a work of anamorphic art, similarly worked around this idea of being pieced together (with everyday objects). Once again then Ballard foregrounds the act of narrative assemblage and collage, which equates a kind of surgery, a "cut and paste" of both body and body of text.

This process of assemblage and reconstitution is clearly something which resides at the core of Ballard's hermeneutic. We certainly might view Traven, and his many zygotic, refracted facades, as a casualty of the extreme dissolution of the subject in the electronic age. But on the other hand Ballard was also a follower of the anti-psychiatry movement; and so perhaps Traven's multiplicity is moreso demonstrative of an endless possibility and potentiality. He represents the capacity of the modern subject to transform, to be "remade," and there is perhaps no better place for such a creative journey than within the labyrinthine halls of the art exhibition. The saturation of art in *The Atrocity Exhibition*, as with much of Ballard's work, seems to serve as a counterpoint to the consumer spectacle, and that which threatens to thwart and subdue all originality of thought and imagination. Ballard's work shows us a way to creative liberation.

Bibliography

Simon Sellars (ed.), Dan O'Hara (ed.), *Extreme Metaphors: Selected Interviews with J. G. Ballard* (London: Fourth Estate, 2014). p. 385.

Jeanette Baxter, *J.G. Ballard's Surrealist Imagination* (London: Ashgate, 2009) p. 62.

British Library entry for Ballard's 1970 exhibit at https://www.bl.uk/collection-items/invitation-cardto-j-g-ballards-crashed-cars-exhibition-3-april-1970

J.G. Ballard, *Miracles of Life* (London: Harper Perennial, 2008) pp. 133-134.

Gregory Stephenson, *Out of the Night and into the Dream* (USA: Greenwood Publishing Group, 1991) p. 64. All further references will be given in the body of the text.

J.G. Ballard (1997). *A user's guide to the millennium : Essays and reviews*. London: Flamingo.

J.G. Ballard, *The Atrocity Exhibition*

Sean Homer, *Jacques Lacan* (New York: Routledge, 2005)

David Sylvester & Francis Bacon, *Interviews with Francis Bacon* (London: Thames and Hudson, 1975)

Rick McGrath (ed.), *Deep Ends: A Ballardian Anthology 2020* (Canada: The Terminal Press, 2020)

Foundation: The International Journal of Science Fiction. #138, volume 50.1, 2021.

Declan Lloyd, 'Were J. G. Ballard's billboards actually coded Salvador Dali paintings?' https://www.theguardian.com/books/2017/jan/19/jg-ballard-secret-poster-campaign-surreal-salvador-dali.

Sarat Maharaj, 'Pop Art's Pharmacies: Kitsch, consumerist objects and signs, the 'unmentionable'. *Art History* Vol. 15, No. 3, September 1992.

Roger Luckhurst, *'The Angle Between Two Walls': The Fiction of J. G. Ballard*. (Liverpool: Liverpool UP, 1997)

V. Vale & Andrea Juno, (1984). *J.G. Ballard* (RE/Search; number 8/9). San Francisco, California: V/Search Publications.

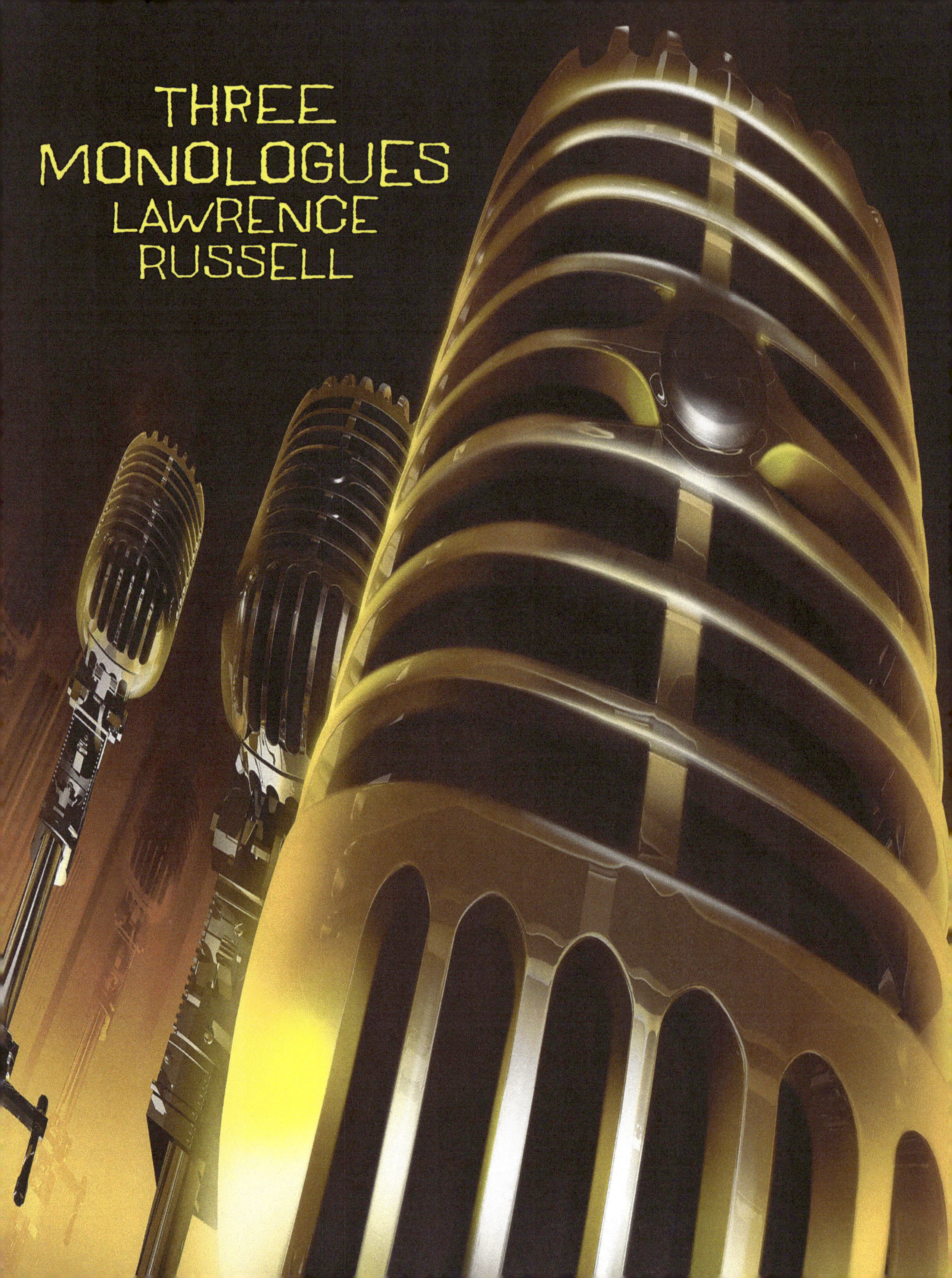
THREE
MONOLOGUES
LAWRENCE
RUSSELL

CAMOUFLAGE

The sun had just come up and I guess we made a good target in that field of corn. I guess we did and we knew it. Listen I says to Phil take her towards those trees over there. I could see the trees very clearly. They were tall and silver like the alders down by the pumphouse where we were earlier today, if you recall. They got trees like them all over Italy.

Keep moving I says to Phil towards them trees. I looked them over and decided that was the best place to head. Well it seemed like the best place to head at the time. You don't wanna be out in the open too long. A tank in a yellow field makes a good target and it gets better as the sun keeps rising. I scanned the field with the binoculars and was just looking back towards the sun when I sees the plane coming at us. Man it was low—it shot POW out of nowhere over the hedge. A Messerschmitt 109. Naturally I couldn't do a thing. He was on us real sudden like—there was no way I could get off a burst from the machine gun, no way. Thought for sure he was gonna chop the turret right off the tank, eh. Here' this little Nazi sitting in there wearing his fancy goggles and his fancy black gloves and he's got his fancy thumb on the fancy firing button, eh. This is it I thought this is it. But he passed us over without firing a round.

Of course old Phil he didn't know what was happening. He just felt the tank sway as the plane passed over. Then through the slit he sees the bastard open up on the trees. He strafed the area good because he was low. Well he fires up them woods real good and I think Holy Mackeral some of our boys must be in there. We watch for the plane to come back but he's gone, he doesn't come back. When we gets to the trees, what do you think? There were about a dozen Nazies. Dead. The plane got them. That's where I got that Luger I used to have—remember it? I don't know what happened. Maybe the Nazi in the plane made a mistake about the Nazies in the trees. Maybe that's what happened. Maybe he made a mistake. Maybe it was an Italian in that Messerschmitt. That's a good possibility. That's the way it might have been. I've thought of all kinds of reasons. I've thought maybe it never happened. Maybe it was something I saw on television, eh, I thought maybe I was getting it confused with the time I was in Italy moving through that field of corn.

Phil says he remembers it though. The other day when we were working on the roof I says to Phil Phil do you remember that time in Italy. Phil was lying on the shakes with his shirt off takin' a rest. Gettin' some sun. George Phil says I remember it. You don't forget things like that. I'll never forget those dead bastard Limeys. They must've been sleeping below that camouflage net. Never knew what hit em. Limeys? I think Phil has made a mistake. Phil I says they weren't British they were Germans. No says Phil they were British. The Sixth Sutherland Regiment.

Aw... Phil and I get into these arguments all the time. We've been friends for the longest time you know. Listen I knew Phil from before the army. I knew him when he was working night shift in Capozzi's lumber mill. He had a lot more hair then than he's got now and of course he didn't have the ulcer, though mind you he was well on his way then. I remember he kept a bottle in his hip pocket, a mickey, a mickey at all times. Phil I says to him how could they be British? You remember the Luger pistol I took off one of them high rankin' officers. You remember it. It had a pearl handle and I figured it came from the Africa Korps because there was sand in the barrel and you figured this was a trick to make the gun explode and destroy the hand that pulls the trigger, right? You're not talking about the Luger your Uncle Hans gave you for your birthday are you says Phil. No no no I says to him I'm not talking about any goddman Luger my Uncle Hans gave me, I'm talking about the goddamn Luger I got when we were in those buncha trees in Italy, you know what I'm talking about Phil, you said you remembered the time. Listen George says Phil I remember the time I got malaria in the Po valley.

Well... I guess maybe I was getting a bit exasperated with old Phil by this time. I guess. I mean he had malaria alright and he had it pretty bad but I wanted to know whether I had the Luger or not. Recall that we were still on the roof at this time. Recall that Phil had his shirt off and was lying on the shakes gettin' some sun and that he had a mickey of Canadian Club in his hip pocket. Recall that I had just told him the story I have just told you and told it pretty much the way I'd told it to other people here and there through the years... and then you can get some vague idea of the situation.

Phil I says I agree with your detail about the camouflage net but as far as I'm concerned they weren't sleeping. George he says they were on their backs, surely you remember that. He offered me a drink and ah—just for the hell of it, eh—I had one. I like rye, as you know. It's the best drink this country makes. I've drank it since I started drinking and I'm still drinking it. In fact I often carry it. Keep a flask in the glove compartment of the Edsel. I drive better when I've had a couple of snorts. Sets you up, eh. Of course there was no rye available in Italy. Strictly wine in that country. Good wine mind you. The best. We never went into action without it. Every time we hit a

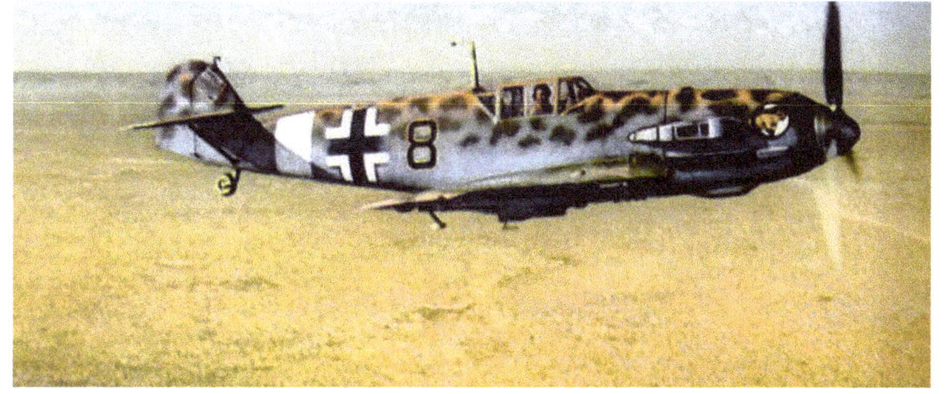

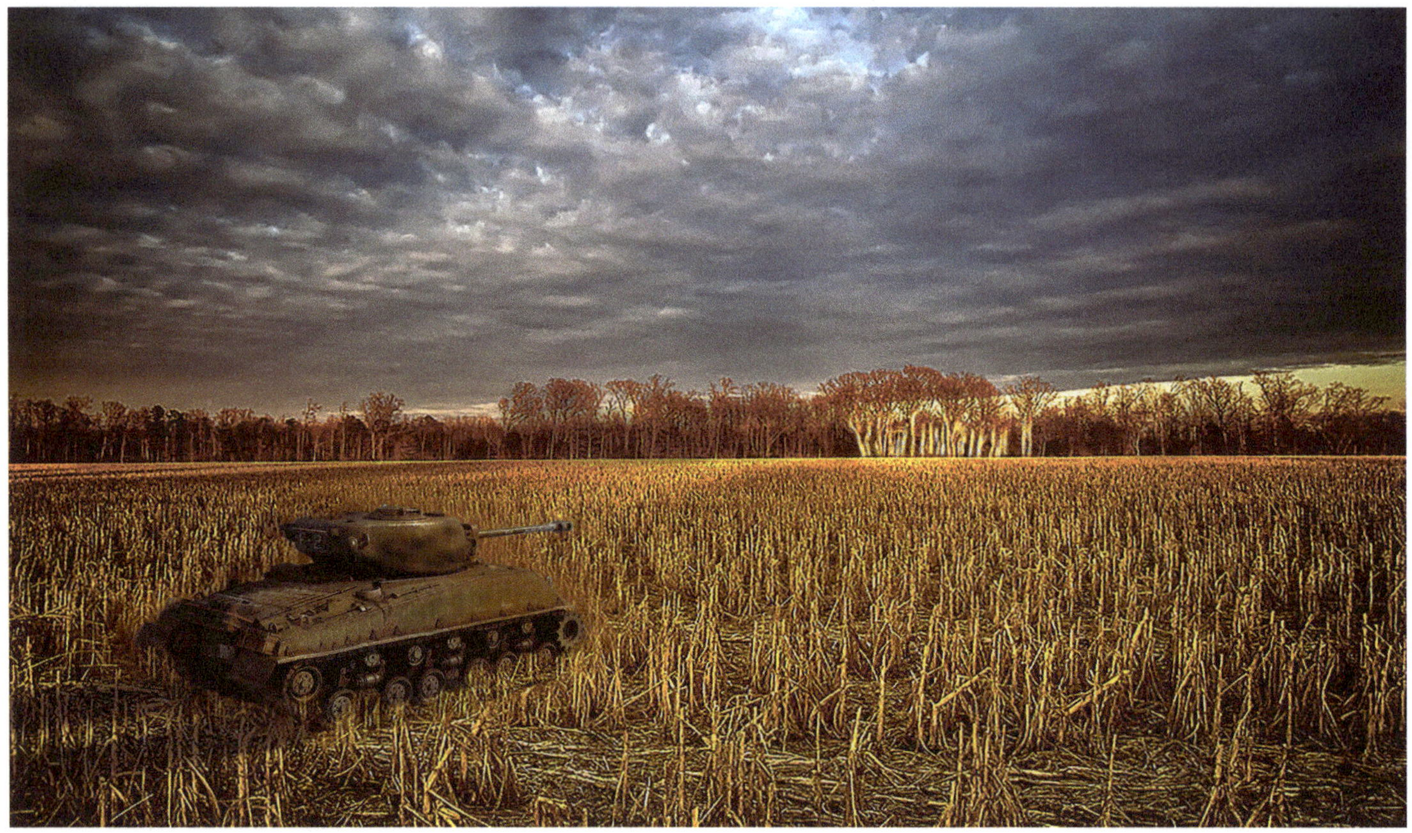

castle or a monastery, we made sure we got ourselves some vino. Kept a jerry can in the tank and a few extra casks wrapped up in our sleeping bundles. Once they got hit and the damn stuff soaked through all the damn blankets and we had to sleep sittin' up in the damn tank all damn night.

I think it was the night we found those dead Nazies beneath the camouflage net. The Nazies were lying on their backs as Phil says. As he says they were on their backs in a circle, arranged like the spokes of a wagon wheel. But I disagree with Phil when he says he got the sextant and recorded the azimuth of the sun in relation to the circle which they formed with their bodies. I don't believe you can do that with a sextant can you? I knew how to use one of those things. When you were moving at night sometimes that was the only way you could move. When you moved, you moved with the stars.

I guess the whole thing is kinda strange. I've thought about it many times and it seems kinda strange. The Eye-talian in the Nazi plane shooting at those trees. Tall trees. Silver in appearance. I believe they were painted with aluminum paint. Leastways that's the way they appeared to me when I got there. Just like alders the way they reached up for the light.

Go easy I says to Phil or you'll startle them. What a beautiful sight. A true hunter's dream. There must've been about twenty-five of them. Easy. They were sittin' in a circle in the grass. You could see the antlers of the big ones and the glint of sunlight in their eyes. I had my Luger but I didn't have the heart to use it. Phil passed me the mickey and sure, I took another swig. What beautiful creatures. Call them noble. Listen George whispers Phil I believe this is a pagan ritual. Look at that circle, look how it's divided into segments, look how the sun comes through in straight lines.

Old Phil knows about such things. He's a millwright you know. A damn good one too. If only he could come to grips with his drinking. But this business with his wife, ah it's no damn good. The divorce is just about through. That's what I hear. He never tells me anything but that's what I hear. She says he just keeps drinking all the time. Well Phil's a bit of a drinker I won't deny that. Two of his brothers were killed in Italy. I think I pointed out their names to you in the Legion awhile ago. His family took a beating. I guess he never got over that. Pretty tough business you know and I guess drinking is just part of it. He hides bottles all through the woods, so when he goes hunting he can get himself a drink anytime he feels the need. Smart, eh. Good thinking, eh. He had malaria you know. Really brought him down. They put him in hospital in Florence for about six months. A beautiful city as you know. We saw all kinds of statues and water fountains there. The Italians are great for water fountains. Of course their architecture is out of this world.

As I recall it Phil kept insisting it was a pagan ritual. Listen I says to him this is no pagan ritual. You know and I know that the plane got them. No no no says Phil you said give 'em a rattle with the machine gun but I thought to meself, what the hell, I bet there're more of the bastards behind the trees, so I lets fly with the flame thrower. Phil I says to him talk sense, we had no flame thrower in Italy. What says Phil was that long tube I carried. That was a bazooka I says. I know what a bazooka is like says Phil and that was no bazooka I carried. I had a cylinder on my back at all times, at all times, remember? I remember no such cylinder says I and this is true, for if anybody would've remembered it, it would've been me. I carried a cylinder on my back at all times says Phil and you goddamn well know it. Phil I says real casual Phil the only thing you carried was a mickey. Ah screw off George says Phil quit trying to twist the issue. I'm not trying to twist any issue. Well if you're not trying to twist the issue you tell me what did we have. I had a Luger with a pearl handle and you had a Messerschmitt 109 I says is my memory correct or is it not. Hah he says I remember: the one Uncle Hans gave me. For Christ's sake I says Uncle Hans gave you nothing. Anything you got you got in Italy and you damn well know it. Well Phil he sits up and he looks me in the eye and he says I never was in Italy. You're drunk I says. No he says you're the one that's drunk. Oh I says deciding I better humour him I guess maybe I am drunk at that. You're drunk he says goddamn pissed to be exact. Now just a minute I says just a goddamn minute. You think I'm drunk he says because you're drunk yourself. Phil... listen to me Phil neither of us are drunk. It all happened just the way we said it happened, right? Are you sure says Phil. Of course I'm sure I says I was never surer than I am right at this moment. Jesus Christ says Phil I hope you're right old buddy I sure hope you're right, you know I don't like to be pissed. Well Phil you're not pissed certainly not pissed in the classical sense, if you know what I mean. Yes yes he says I know what you mean okay but you said I was in Italy and that's not true and you of all people know it's not true. No Phil no you said you were in Italy not me. Ah shit let's quit this arguing George he says my ulcer's beginning to act up.

Well, this was okay with me. Of course I didn't wanna argue in the first place. Argument is not my style. I believe in seeing things clearly and I can see that corn field clearly and I can see those trees even more clearly although Phil says they were all covered with camouflage. I have a sore back occasionally as you know. Well it was sore right then from working on that roof so I decided to call it quits. Well maybe it's the shrapnel. Sometimes it doesn't exist and others it just moves right in and cripples me all up. It's a Nazi bomb. They've tried to locate it just like I've tried to locate my Luger but hell it just keeps moving and so none of us knows where it is or what's happening.

THE WAITERS

The first time I saw Gallagher was when I was cutting trees on my lot on the side of the Inlet. He was further up the hill, deep in the forest, and at first I thought he was stalking a deer as he didn't seem too interested in my activities. Turned out he was a local living in a cabin down by the water. I went there to see if I could use the phone and recognized him as the man I'd seen. He was friendly enough, but a bit distant. He had a nervous tic, symptomatic of alcoholism in older men, altho' when he came up onto the lot a couple of days later he refused the beer I offered. He dropped two large dangerous trees for me, and that's when I learned he was a shipwright, good with saws and things, despite his shake. Reminded me a bit of my father-in-law. A vet, maybe.

That summer, whenever he wasn't hammering and sawing down at the cabin, I'd see him wandering around all over the place, sometimes through the woods, sometimes along the dirt road, or down on the rocks by the water. He carried binoculars and anywhere there was an open vista he would stop and scan the sky. Maybe he was looking at the eagles or the seals, or just assessing the intermitant boat traffic. Other times he would stand still, as if listening intently. Just like an animal sensing the presence of another. In one way it was all quite normal, but in another.... As I'm a fairly private person myself, I never asked him what he was up to, why he wasn't working. He was just building a boat on spec, I decided, something to help pass the time.

One evening as I saw him standing on the abandoned steps near his place, the thought occurred to me that he was just waiting, waiting for someone to come and tell him his convalescence was over. I imagined him as having endured a long alcoholic illness, perhaps complicated by the death of a woman or an inglorious divorce, and he'd retreated to the family cabin to argue with his demons alone. Of course I was just projecting my own situation on him. Cutting trees was great therapy.

It was late in August, the time the moon was dilating like a soft orange over the Inlet, when I saw for sure that Gallagher was a haunted man. The door of the tent was open as I lay and watched the reflections on the water and the windows of stars between the tall firs. There was supposed to be a big meteor shower but I'd only seen a couple of brief, unimpressive flashes so far. Then I heard something; at first I thought it was a harbour seal barking out its mating call, so I left the tent and descended through the trees towards the water hoping to see a host of seals cavorting in one of those large, peculiar circular formations they sometimes indulge in at this time of year. I crossed the road and followed the path that skirted Gallagher's waterfront lot until I came to the abandoned steps which led from the water to nowhere in particular.

It was Gallagher. He was on the steps facing the water, uttering small moans which occasionally articulated as an unknown tongue, as if he was possessed in the manner of some biblical drama. I concealed myself behind a tree as he babbled and moaned, occasionally lapsing into periods of silence. I thought to myself, the man's pissed, he's been on a bender and now he's lost it completely. There were moments when I thought I could make some sense of what he was saying, stuff like come to me or return to me. When he raised his hand it was almost certain that he was speaking to someone specifically, someone in the etheric, a ghost... his wife obviously. He emitted a long wail, an awful sound which made the hairs rise on the back of my neck... and then, as if on cue, a huge meteorite drifted past with a lazy woosh, vaporizing in a green flood of light down the Inlet to the south.

Gallagher fell silent. When I stole away he was rigid, like a statue, still facing the water and the stars.

I had to roll some logs I'd bucked up out of the way, so I went down to his place to see if I could borrow his peavey. He was hammering and sawing, hard at work on something outside the cabin when I arrived. A boat, I assumed. But now that the tarp was off, I could see that it was a pretty strange vessel.

What's this, I said to him, a hovercraft? Just a little something I've

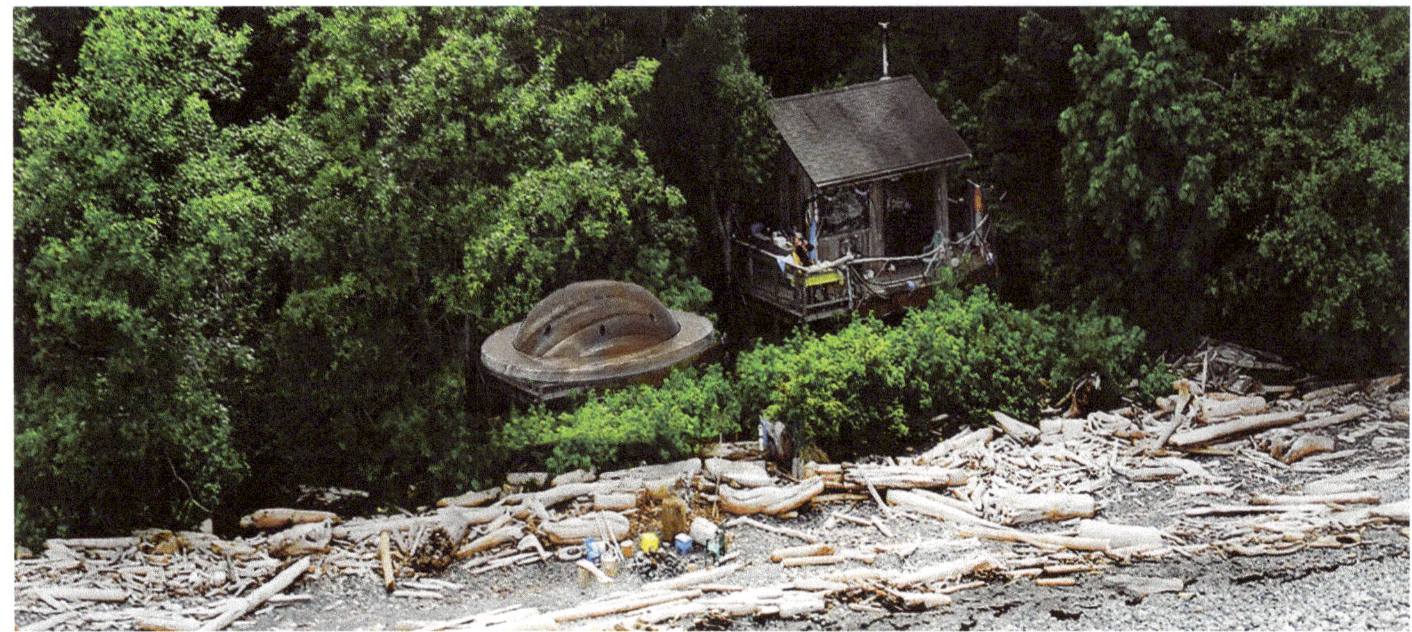

been working on, he said. We stood and looked at it for a minute or so but he didn't elaborate. I was thinking, this looks more like one of those flying saucers you see in the tabloids, except it's made of wood.

Is it finished, I said to him, and he said, just about. Will it float, I said, and he just looked right through me for a moment before saying, yes. He threw the blue tarp over it and then asked me if I'd like a drink. It was far too early in the day so I declined. Things then seemed awkward, so I didn't ask him about the peavey. As I was turning to leave, he said to me, something I've been meaning to ask you.... Oh yes? I said. Yes, he said, are you the person I've been waiting for?

I thought to myself, what's he going on about? then said, I don't know, who, ah, are you waiting for? And he said, you're not from around here, are you? I said, well, I suppose, but I've lived close... yes, close, y'know? I could see disappointment resolving in his eyes. How about those shooting stars, I said. You saw them? he said. The one, I said, it was really big, I thought it was a jet or something. Or something, he echoed. He turned away and looked towards the water, entranced in his own reality, in communion with something I couldn't see.

Gallagher has finished his spacecraft now and other than the fact that it can't fly, it's a beautiful piece of carpentry, fitted and planed with the precision of a master shipwright. Through the binoculars I can see him standing in its shadow, waiting.

As for myself, I've been unable to develop my lot further, now that I've abandoned the idea of building a house and maybe finding a woman to live in it. In a way I find something admirable in Gallagher and his delusion. At least he has something to wait for.

THE STRANGER IN THE GARDEN

One of my grandmothers said she saw a UFO from her bedroom window one evening and my Uncle Sam who lives in the same house saw it too. It was of the mother-ship-with-two-attendant-craft variety and hovered for several minutes in the vicinity of Slemish mountain, the place where Saint Patrick tended sheep when he was a youth. She described both her first and second sightings to me when I was on a visit to the old country and was talking about climbing Slemish to take in the view and take some photos maybe. That's what brought up the admission. She was very lucid for an eighty-five year old, and realized she or Sam couldn't tell anyone in the village because the people would just laugh and make a mockery of them. Of course I speculated that it might've been an R.A.F. fighter jet but both she and Sam said the lights separated and performed different patterns before accelerating away at a fantastic speed. It certainly sounded like a classic encounter: lights which vectored in configurations and speeds beyond human engineering, and, most interesting of all, the actual contact with an extraterrestial.

This part Sam had nothing to do with and I could sense he was skeptical when his mother talked about the stranger in the garden.

Their garden is a long narrow one with high stone walls which connects the house to the old creamery which was used as the family business when the old fellow was alive. Sam has his studio here in a lean-to against one of the walls where he putters around with his antiques and bits of furniture, sometimes colors in an old steel engraving to sell to a tourist or another dealer. When he's not doing that or fiddling around in the house at something, he keeps the flowers going and the privet hedges trimmed. It's a nice garden. The trees lean together in such a way that they form an avenue down the last bit to the creamery which is just a warehouse or something now. I took a look at the big flaking brick building but didn't pass through the gate when I went down there to see for myself the spot where where the encounter took place.

It was just Thompson coming to see me about that brass cannon I bought at the Major's estate sale, said Sam, but his mother said, it was not Mr. Thompson, he has a different way about him altogether. So she says, Sam said to me. Tell our illustrious relative from beyond the Atlantic Ocean what this man was wearing. A black suit, said his mother, a cut altogether different from any you see a gentleman wearing here, it had a sheen to it, wavy, the way you see the water go when it catches the light after a boat passes by. Sounds cheap to me, mother, said Sam. Gaberdine. Some fellow who was looking for his greyhound. I may be old, said his mother, but not stupid. I didn't see any greyhound.

She sat there with her hands folded on the nob of her cane, miffed, and for a moment I thought she was going to give Sam a rattle around the ankles. Did he come in from the creamery, I asked, and she shook her head, said that's the thing, the gate was locked, I don't know how he got in there unless he clambered over the wall and it didn't look like it to me. At first I thought it was the Reverend Armstrong because of the black suit, you see. I was just sitting on the bench catching my breath and I looked up and there he was. Maybe Sam here was playing a trick on you, I said, and she said, oh many's the trick he's played on me but not this time because I spoke with the man.

In English, I said.

Sam said, this is the interesting part, tell him what he said.

My grandmother shifted herself a bit to get herself more comfortable, then said, he told me he'd come from that star up there and although it was a bright sunny day, when I looked up, there it was, this big, bright star, and it hurt to look at it, it was so bright. I was afraid then, and he seemed to know, for he said don't worry, you can come with me if you like. I thought I was speaking with a ghost, so I says to him, are you Ben, for I thought perhaps your grandfather had come from the grave to speak with me. He says, I can take you to see him if you like, but that's not why I'm here.

Then she fell silent and I said, what else did he say? And Sam said, he told her all sorts of things but she won't tell you.

He had a soft, friendly way, she said, he knew it all, the past, the future....

What happened, I said, did he just walk off or what.

Disappeared, said my grandmother, vanished.

Where, I said, up to the UFO?

I don't know, she said. Sam, get me my asprin. I should take my asprin.

What did he look like, I said, I mean, in the face?

A gentleman, said my grandmother, a refined gentleman of means.

I didn't get up Slemish but I did climb the smaller hill Skerry which is just across the valley, the place where Saint Patrick is supposed to have jumped to. There's a couple of low walls remaining from the old church and a few gravestones receding into the sod at odd angles. One of them was very old, from the twelfth century, but I couldn't make out who was buried there. The site had that strange mystic atmosphere you find in Ireland, and everywhere you looked you could see for miles and watch the weather change. In some areas there'd be sunshine, in others rainstorms, and all the while the heavy clouds rolled over the landscape in an oppressive ceiling, offering only the occasional hole for escape.

My grandmother disappeared a year or so later when she was eighty seven. Sam said she went into the garden to get some flowers and when she failed to return he went looking for her but she'd just vanished. There was a big search of the village and the countryside and even the military were involved. There wasn't even a footprint, never mind a shoe. Foul play is suspected, as there is no evidence to the contrary.

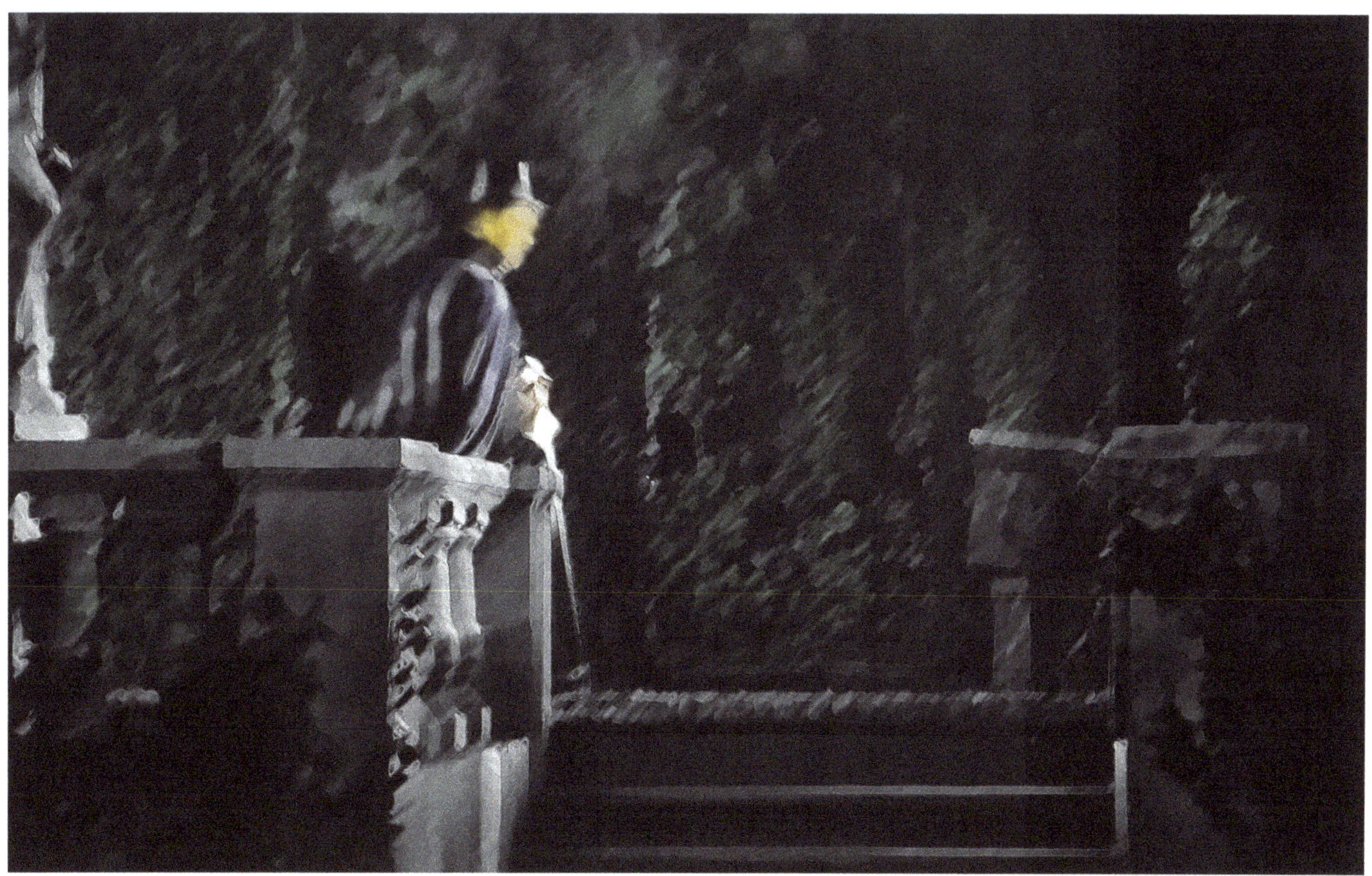

2WO TALES

BY J.F. LAWRENCE

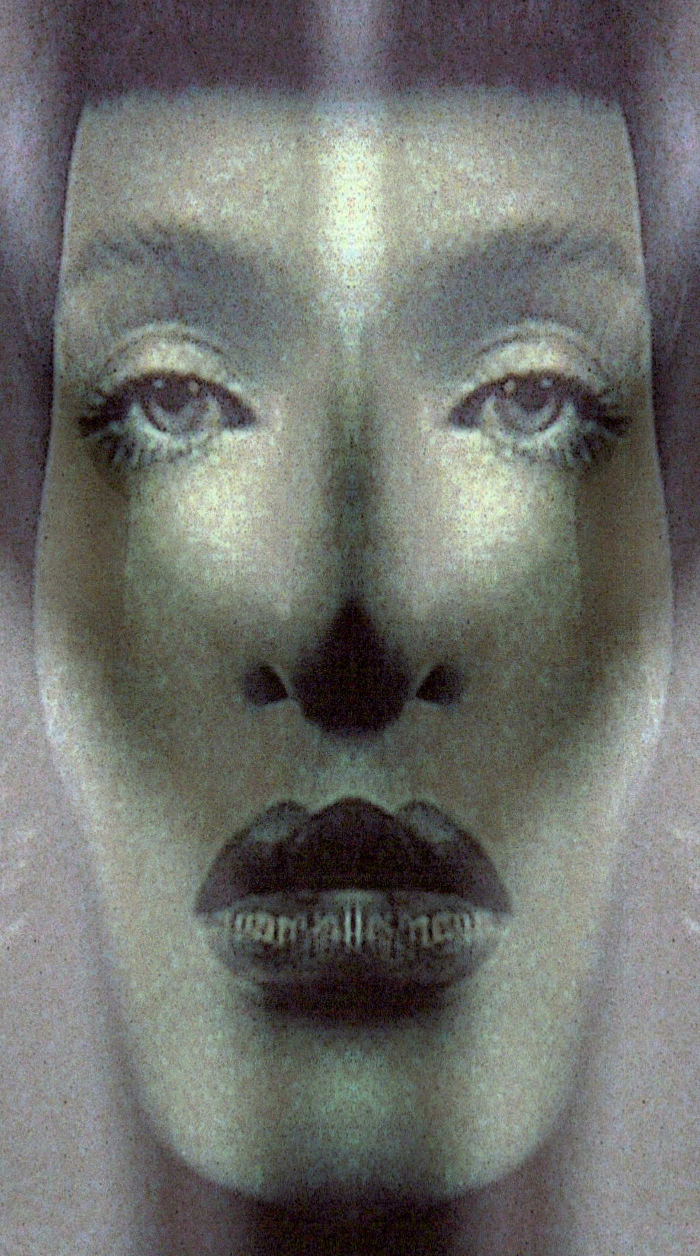

ESCAPE

Autarkia was established as a libertarian version of earthly paradise on a small, frozen island just inside the Arctic Circle. It was a model Stirnerite community—barely a community at all, in truth, more an aggregation of self-interested individuals and small family units having as little social intercourse as possible. The island had been bought from an outlaw billionaire in hiding somewhere in Indonesia, for several billion dollars' worth of cryptocurrency, by a consortium of hyper-rich social Darwinists who wanted to free themselves from the overweening demands of society. It almost completely cut off its inhabitants from the outside world, was guarded by a private security company with paramilitary capabilities, and had an airstrip for those rare circumstances when it was necessary to travel to the mainland.

The 24-hour nights were initially divided into more or less conventional time periods allotted to business, leisure and sleep. The other half of the year, which saw 24-hour days of grey light and a period of readjustment of biorhythms, was similarly parcelled out. The agreed co-ordination of clock time, one of the few public provisions in that obsessively private little world, gave a shape to life on the island.

The first two years of the colony were characterised by a progression towards greater individualisation, a privatisation of the radical mind. Then everyone began to experience a profound change in mood. At first they came together to discuss it, an almost oppressive feeling of absolute safety counterpointed by an uncategorisable melancholy. And for some reason they could not explain, everyone felt very strongly that the contract with the security company should be immediately cancelled. Only the colonists should be there. No other conclusion was reached except that nobody wanted to leave. Leaving was unthinkable.

The withdrawal of the security service was observed with noisy enthusiasm, and as the helicopter carrying the last of the personnel away from Autarkia lifted off there was dancing and loud, hypnotic music. A bonfire was made of all the computers and mobile phones, which were thrown into the flames with collective glee. The Autarkians had become a tribe, wild, violent, liberated in a new way, a way far older than their ideology of rational selfishness. The orgiastic celebration lasted for around 72 hours on the scale of clock time, which had been abandoned when all timepieces were hurled into the fire along with the last of the info tech. This atavistic carnival of lust and destruction culminated in an all-out assault on the private planes standing in their hangars, unflown for many months. Every aircraft was gutted with fire that cast the shadows of fighting and rutting Autarkians against the frozen rocks. At last the exhausted islanders slept for long hours in the glow of the burning aeroplanes, snuggled together like contented animals.

A plague of lassitude began to infect the population as the colonists reverted to individualism, not a virus or bacillus but an endogenous reaction to the combined conditions of uninterrupted darkness and increasing isolation. More and more time was spent by the islanders in their social silos, and participation in the public sphere dwindled. Individuals, couples, families and polyamorous groups gradually retreated into permanently separate lives as apathy pervaded the colony. The penultimate stage of this condition, which baffled a number of highly regarded neurologists, was a total absorption into a state of hibernation lasting through the end of the night-time period and the entirety of the long day.

Then a change came over the sleeping colonists. As the darkness returned, they began to emerge from the cocoons of their beautifully designed homes in a state of semi-consciousness combined with excessive alpha-wave activity. They sleepwalked as far as the first place of comfort and safety that allowed the moonlight to bathe them in its energizing yet specific glow.

Gradually the island's inhabitants shifted into geological time as the reptilian relict of their neurological systems mutated into the seat of a collective consciousness far older than humanity. Finally every man, woman and child lay outdoors in a permanent and irreversible torpor, moonbathing supine on rocks, immobile and unreachable by language or symbol. They were luxuriating in the half-death of deep time, at peace, one abstract antediluvian brain gently pulsating at each node, relaying to itself a circular current of bare awareness, within a closed system of quiet eternity.

This was how they were found by the military helicopter rescue team that was sent after there had been no communication with the outside world for several months. Every islander was transferred to an observation facility in a neurological clinic on the outskirts of Uppsala, and they still rest there now, staring blindly into space with moonburned eyes, silently transmitting memories of a time long preceding human consciousness to each other across their ancient psychic network, at last become one.

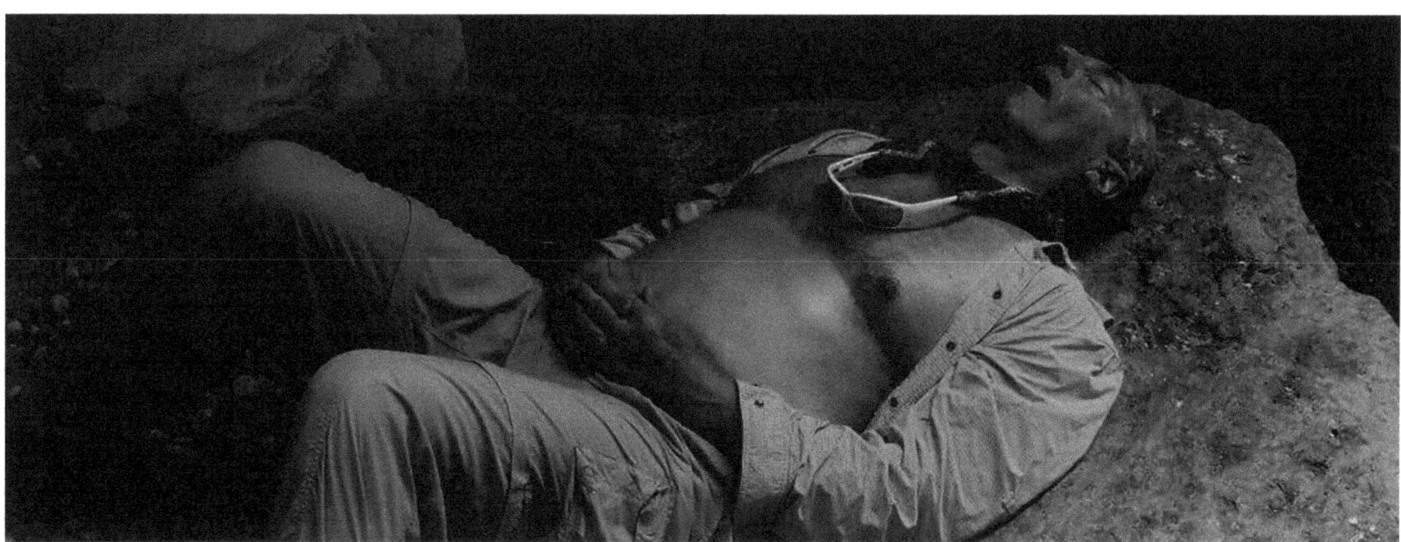

THE SCHOOL RUN

Since work had begun on the bypass, effectively cutting off the suburb of Winfield by forcing all the commuter traffic off the nearby ring road and into the pollution-choked rat run of Vicarage Road, the central thoroughfare, and funnelling the cavalcade of barely differentiated blue, grey and black cars, all shiny and sterile with CAD lineaments, into narrow roads and lanes, life had become almost intolerable for its small, middle-class populace.

Trundling 4x4s and murmuring saloons carrying middle managers, start-up hopefuls of the gig economy, consultants and sales reps; white vans and their tired men; Parcelforce, Ocado and Royal Mail lorries laden with material dreams from the collective virtual brain; motorbike couriers weaving through the sluggish flow at every opening; all the region's frustrated, short-tempered travellers from dormitory towns to offices, factories, warehouses, and industrial parks: this paradoxically slow morning rush hour made the school run an even greater stressor than before construction began. That was a saner time, when the bypass was only a hypothetical bureaucratic proposal, before it was voted into an actuality that would be staunchly and even violently opposed by Winfield's angry nimbies.

Although not far from the small cluster of new social housing and amenities, separated by a neglected edgeland, that could be clearly seen from numerous vantage points on its western boundary, Winfield had a curious, even unsettling air of isolation. With the bypass encircling it, forming a long no man's land of trenches, weathered hoardings and chain link fencing which bracketed it on its northern, eastern and southern sides, this archetypically English bourgeois enclave was quietly exulting in its radiance of exclusivity.

Karen Thornley was tired and headachey. She had been up past midnight dealing with emails and supposedly urgent phonecalls from clients with unreasonable demands and strident expressions of entitlement. Too much coffee, to sustain her through the post-business-hours imposition, a whole bottle of Waitrose red to wash the stress away (it failed) and a line of the coke her husband Peter had scored via a colleague: the lingering emotional and physical effects of all this, amplified by Alfie and Gertie bickering on the back seat, were making the Monday morning drive to school even more exasperating than usual. Christ she needed a break from Peter, the kids, her clients, her arsehole boss, just a week or two somewhere far away from her life. Just a week, a month, a year, forever, maybe disappear and become someone else...something.

The street in front of St. Alfred the Great Academy was blocked by chunky, tank-like SUVs and glossily aerodynamic saloons. The volume of traffic nosing gingerly along Vicarage Road forced the opposing motorcades of yummy mummies and their neatly uniformed children to wait impatiently at the roadside while the cars at the head of each line disgorged their precious cargoes of Tillies and Noahs who, with maternal kisses and have-a-lovely-day-darlings echoing in their wake, crossed the pavement and filtered through the school gates.

Karen inched the car forwards, tensely alert, waiting for the moment when Lizzie Kitson in her tacky new pink Mercedes would eventually finish hugging, kissing and generally faffing

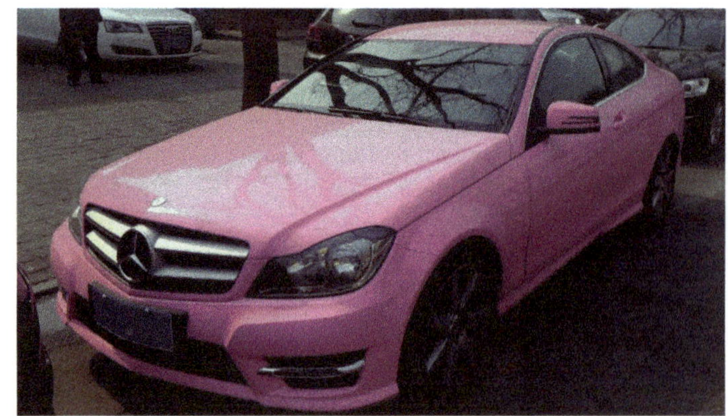

about with her boy Oliver, get back into that trashy motor and drive the fuck away. There would be a tiny window of opportunity which she was determined to drive through before the Toyota leading the opposite queue could slip in ahead of her and seize the newly created parking space.

Microsleep: sometimes a necessary blankness to give the tired brain a few seconds' rest; other times, such as when vying for a precious parking spot which is a hub of amped-up competition in a superficially polite social struggle, a significant lapse of concentration. Karen zoned out for a few blissful moments until Gertie gave Alfie a Chinese burn that made him squeal. She jerked back into shocked alertness to see that her brief cognitive timeout had been long enough for the pink Mercedes to start pulling out from the kerb.

She reacted reflexively and moved in too soon and too fast. Lizzie Kitson's car had not fully cleared its space as it drew away, so the radiator grille of Karen Thornley's Audi smashed into its offside rear light.

As the shock of the impact faded, Lizzie's body was deluged with adrenaline. All the stress of getting Oliver ready, trying to make him eat breakfast and pandering to his fussing about what shoes he wanted to wear while her husband was shouting at the Today programme and banging his fist on the breakfast bar (sometimes she could happily smash that fucking radio), worrying about her mother's impending visit (undoubtedly it would be the customary test of Lizzie's patience and questioning of her life choices, the latest nitpicking assault on her self-esteem) and wondering why Peter had not contacted her for three days, added to the sudden derangement of her senses by an automotive collision, inevitably caused her pressurised nervous-system to overload.

She almost tore her seatbelt off and flung the car door open. She jumped out into the road and strode with purposeful rage towards the Audi, her heart thumping against her chest, fizzing with malevolent energy. She immediately recognised that bitch Karen through the windscreen, and her rage dialled up to cold fury.

Still dazed, Karen turned to check on the children. Alfie was laughing, clearly enjoying this entertaining start to the school week. 'Cool,' he said gleefully. 'Mummy, look out!' Gertie shouted, pointing at something beyond the windscreen. Karen twisted back round to see a rabid-looking Lizzie Kitson advancing, wild staring eyes drilling murder into her, snarling mouth displaying unnaturally whitened teeth, towards the car.

Instead of staying put inside the shelter of metal, toughened glass and interior padding, Karen decided in obedience to some new, violently aggressive instinct that she must face the threat head on. No way was that little slut going to intimidate her. 'Stay there and don't panic or try to stop anything,' she told the children, and got out.

They squared up to each other. Lizzie began waving her arms about. She screamed: 'YOU STUPID FUCKING COW, WHY DIDN'T YOU LOOK WHERE YOU WERE GOING?'

Karen lashed out with a left arm toned and strengthened by regular sessions at Winfield Tennis Club, gashing her enemy's left cheek with a swift back-hander weaponised by her wedding ring. Lizzie reeled from the blow, tasted the metallic tang of blood on her lower lip, marvelled for an instant at the sight of the crimson spray across her white blouse. Growling like a wild animal, she steadied herself, grabbed a fistful of Karen's long hair and twisted it around her hand and forearm. She pulled her screeching adversary in towards her and delivered a wicked throat punch, an advanced move learned in a women's self-defence class.

Karen collapsed, knocking Lizzie backwards onto the road so that her neck bent over the kerb. She lurched towards her car, having got a jolt of adrenaline from the pain in her throat, but she was hit by sudden nausea and vomited into the gutter. By the time she had finished puking, Lizzie had managed to stagger over to the Mercedes, reach into the driver-side door and pick up one of the high-heeled shoes she had in the car to change into when she got to work. It was an elegantly sculpted size 3 Louboutin Fifi 100 nude calf pump, half of four-hundred-and-ninety-poundsworth of handmade footwear, and it was about to be viciously repurposed.

She loomed over the back of heaving, choking Karen's bowed head, focussing on the exposed nape of her neck. Lizzie was on the verge of doing something terrible, an act she would never have believed herself capable of just a few minutes ago. She raised the shoe in her right hand, the slender heel now a literal stiletto, and took aim.

But her arm was immobile. A woman who was passing by had intervened by grasping Lizzie's wrist, taking advantage of the split-second pause at the apex of her murderous arm's deadly arc. She wrested the shoe from Lizzie's hand, dropped it and pinned her to the pavement.

Karen, who had been shaken so much that her fury had subsided to a manageable level, hurried to the car, reassured the children and called the police on her mobile. She went back over to Caroline Brierley, who taught the women's self-defence class at Winfield Leisure Centre and had her right knee in the small of Lizzie's back while holding the would-be murderess's arms crossed behind her, and thanked her.

A woman behind the wheel of a Mazda sports car idling in the traffic across the road watched the fight with professional interest, recording it on her phone camera through the windscreen. It was a scene two times removed, a movie of a movie, a doubly distanced *mise-en-scène* viewed through a frame around a frame. It was a hyperreal epiphany disrupting the fiction of civic order. Dr. Lydia Denton had found the ideal location for the experiment.

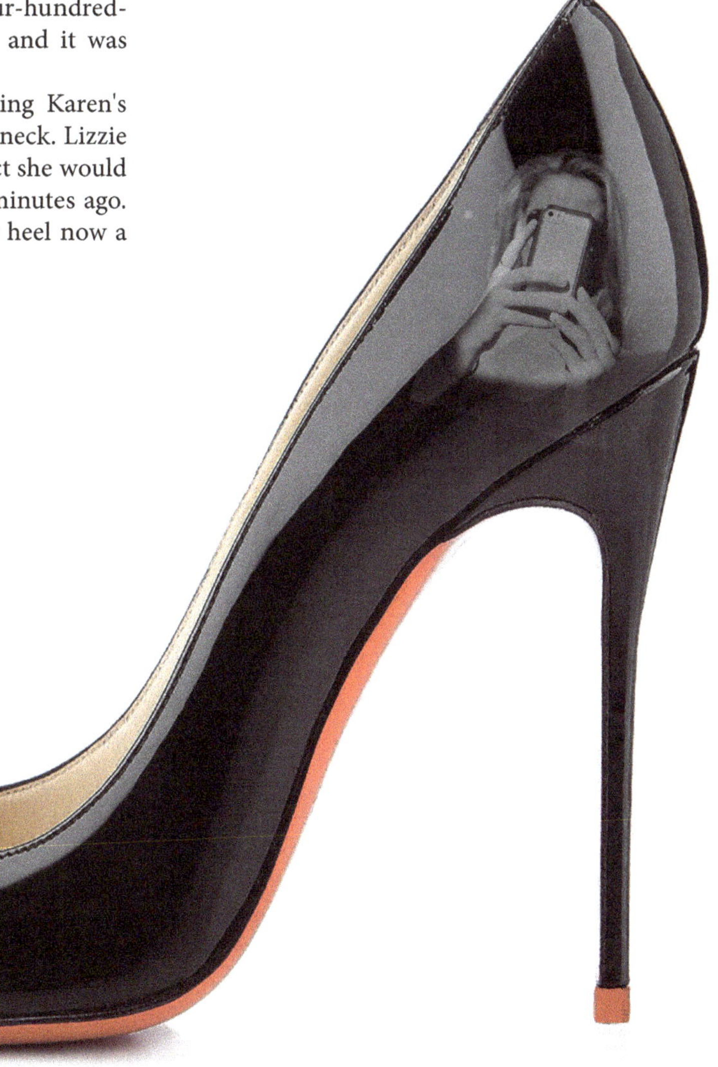

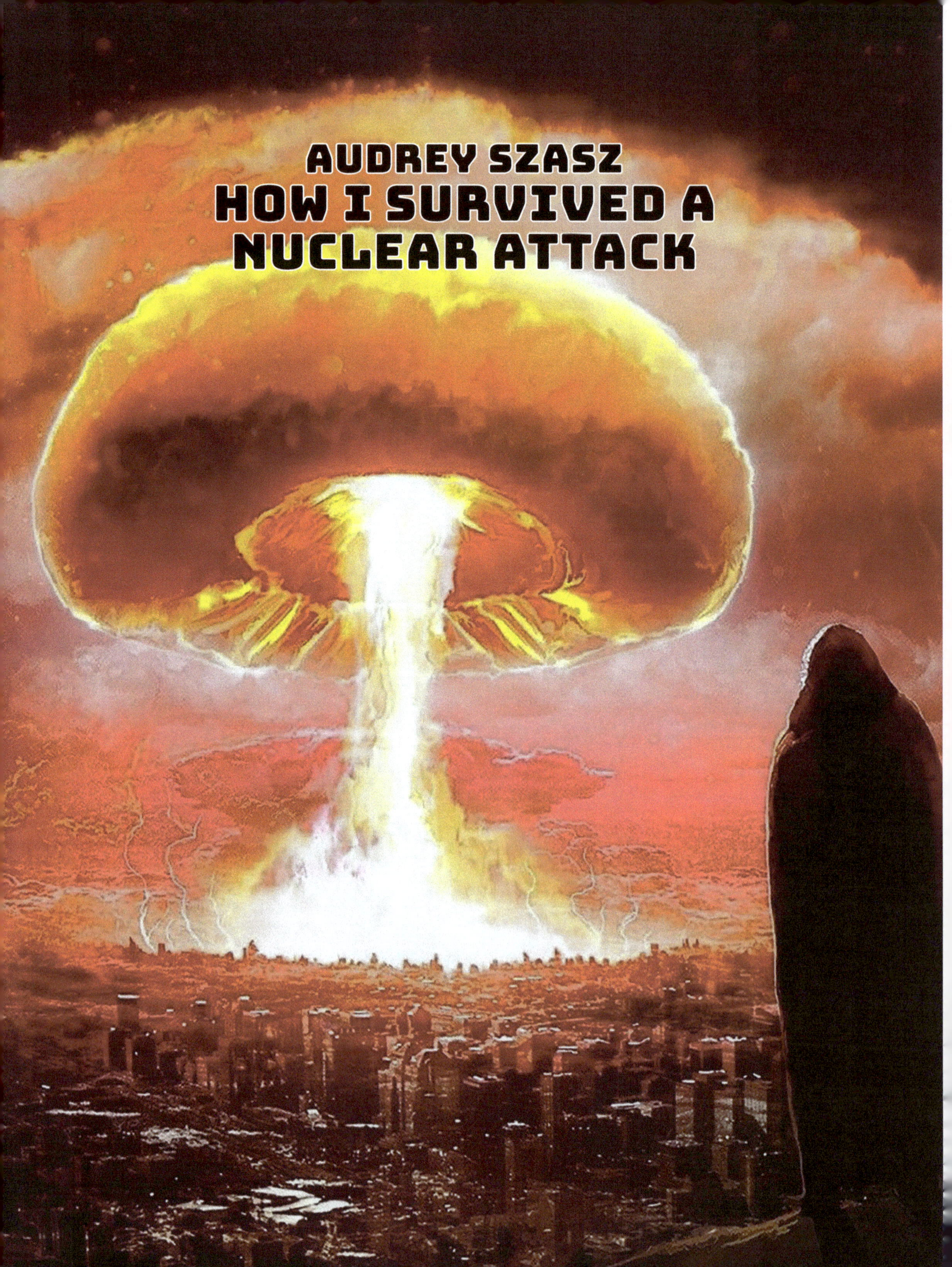
AUDREY SZASZ
HOW I SURVIVED A
NUCLEAR ATTACK

I

To the casual observer it would seem that I have two main problems: firstly my waning faith and apparent unwillingness to indulge in normal sexual relationships cause me to have non-committal flings and to be wracked with guilt afterwards; and secondly my brain surgery and dependence on morphine have resulted in my suffering from an undiagnosed emotional disorder that further alienates me from my classmates, as well as from my own decision-making faculties. I need not go into any specific details—there is adequate historical experience to establish that basic changes in the functional organisation of the human mind cannot be brought about by traditional methods of physical torture—these at the most, achieve a reluctant, temporary yielding and, moreover, leave their mark upon the victim, in this case myself. I find routine almost impossible to maintain and am ready to commit **[excised]** the moment I receive my orders. I participate in seemingly random acts of vandalism as a means of expressing my repressed libidinous impulses. My crimes are invariably puerile in nature. People genuinely treat me like I am a child and talk about me as though I am not there. I attempt to say as little as possible. Sometimes I pretend I am mute, but mostly I pretend that I cannot really speak English....

Look into my eyes. One of my alters is a twelve-year-old chronic asthmatic who experienced the misfortune of being involved—with one of her parents—in a cult that practiced mind-programming. Evidently **[excised]** do not wish for me to volunteer any further information. Women comment on my general appearance, various aspects of my clothing, and reminisce about how they used to roll their skirts up when they were in high school. *I am not interested in being critiqued.* They have conversations about me in public places. I haven't brushed my hair for several days and you tell me that I give off the overwhelming impression of being a stinking brat at four in the afternoon on an underground train. My wardrobe consists primarily of items manufactured from cheap, coarse fabrics in neutral colours that are designed to repel stains and survive the wear and tear of a playground beating. I hope that's how she likes it. I seem to be surrounded by sadists who revel in even the smallest amount of physical or psychological discomfort I may experience. Your insultingly honest evaluation of my so-called *dishevelled beauty* threatened to launch my career in fashion modelling but ultimately I became addicted to PSYOPS. I feel like there is no privacy—even in my own head, because I am constantly monitoring myself. I am surrendering to my emotions. One day—who knows?—they will be able to transcribe my thoughts. A microscopic device will be implanted in my brain and it will wirelessly transmit my ideas and memories. Mostly images. Probably words too. *This is the acceptable face of voyeurism, get me out of here.* We walk slowly across the dusty soil, between the hovels, towards a collection of tall concrete huts resembling outsize sentry boxes that rise high above the arid embankment of an evaporating river. Manipulation of the fabric of space-time and alterations to said continuum. The object turns onto its side. It performs manoeuvres that break the laws of physics. But you know, whatever.... I signed a non-disclosure agreement with my left hand. I am ambidextrous—meaning, I can sign my life away with both hands.

II

One of my most irrational fears is that you believe—or have come to the conclusion that—my affection for you, and my perverse desires, are nothing more than an idle—or superficial—projection on my part. That I don't really know you, or care who you are—that I am simply using you for my own ends, to fulfil or act out—or re-enact—some bizarre erotic fantasy. But is this latest concern of mine yet another projection in itself? How can I ever escape from this metaphorical hall of mirrors? And how can I convince you that *my real passion is for subtleties*, for a sort of unspoken formalism, rather than the obvious clichés that you so clearly despise?

Whilst I do not deny that at times I have allowed my imagination to wander, or that on occasion I have fetishized elements of you or your behaviour towards me, I feel—the feeling is more important than the thought—that this is merely one component of a much larger process. Yes, I play games; yes, I tell my tall tales, but it's not only that. There is, located somewhere inside me, a genuine sense of wanting a real, heartfelt connection. *Kill me now.* It's something essential. I only want you—both of you—to have some fun with me sometimes. If it suits us. *I don't want to live like this.* And if not, it's no big deal. I mean it.... It's not even that important. And it's certainly not an envelope I'm willing to push, if you'll excuse the expression. If the doors are closed, I'll certainly knock. But if they're locked, then fine. It is what it is, and I certainly have no desire to trespass.... *You really are a sap, aren't you?* I'm honestly not that self-absorbed, despite how I sometimes come across.... And I know that I am immature sometimes, but isn't that what you like about me? I'm more than happy to go sailing on Sundays and I promise never to rock the boat.... *Jesus, what is wrong with you? Stop it, just stop it....*

I can't necessarily fall back on—or be ruled by—old scripts, and I feel obliged to report that it has become increasingly obvious to me that newer or more refined techniques have to be considered in relation to our ongoing, ever-evolving working hypotheses. Among the recognised methods that we agreed upon are: **a.** Psychosurgery: a surgical separation of the frontal lobes of the brain. **b.** Shock Methods: (1) electrical (2) drug: metrazol, cannabis, insulin, cocaine. **c.** Psychoanalytic methods (1) psychoanalysis (2) narco-analysis and synthesis (3) hypno-analysis and synthesis **d.** Combination of the foregoing. And if ever we are faced with an immediate threat of nuclear war, a copy of my brief metafictional pseudo-autobiography HOW I SURVIVED A NUCLEAR ATTACK must be distributed to every household as part of a public information campaign which would include announcements on social media, on television, radio and in the press. My tell-all booklet has been designed for free and general distribution in that event. It is being placed on sale now for those who wish to know what they would be advised to do ahead of time. *Stop stammering.* It is your assessment that the patient is an engaging and verbal youngster on a superficial social level. She appears to be intellectually bright. She relates easily to the examiner whom she knows through her outpatient treatment. The examiner was able to trigger the patient's defences which consisted of a **[excised]** persona and withdrawal. She has lately been observed perusing books consisting largely of black and white photographs of brutalist architecture, and has become fascinated by our collection of sombreros, belts, and saddles. The sun withdraws behind a veil of smoke and dust.

III

In our shared fantasy, I perform the role of a sixteen-year-old girl recently admitted to an institution after a suicide attempt. We are preoccupied with thoughts of eroded soil, dragging fences, and blocked drains, but these might yet be the very least of our concerns. We listen to the sound of pickaxes striking rocks, the rumbling of trucks, the roar of falling earth, and the vibrations of trolleys on rails. At night the owls insistently hoot and the nightjars interminably scream. The continuous chirping of crickets seems to fill the entire world engulfed in darkness. In this 24/7 semi-consensual play-session, I am given the codename Vespers and demonstrate an unwillingness to be touched or to emotionally connect with the world around me. The institution is housed in an austere concrete building, the prefabricated parts of which have been grit-blasted in the factory to remove an outer layer of bland grey cement, revealing instead glinting white quartz aggregate. The inmates are apparently supposed to find all of this aesthetically pleasing—but it is my suspicion that confirmation bias is at play here and the results of the internal surveys are therefore questionable at best and fraudulent at worst. All of the girls here are given new codenames. I am shut in with mostly irreverent and predatory staff members and a whole host of other crazies. Inmates are harassed and manhandled on a daily basis and often forcibly sedated before being straightjacketed and fastened upon a large concrete shelf which acts as a sheltered suntrap. I am reminded of sweltering summer afternoons in suburban Brussels. We are such delicate flowers. It amuses the staff to beat me. Frequent drug misuse and ritual satanic abuse sessions inevitably follow....

They cannot see faces. The experiments are ongoing. I love it, every minute, and give you my everlasting gratitude to do with as you wish. However, it is necessary for us not to lose sight of our initial objectives and therefore I urge you to keep in mind the following items: 1. Regression to infantile state of object dependency on a parental object, characteristic of hypnosis (consistent with transference phenomenon), a basic and permanent change in character structure result hypnosis. 2. It is imperative that we determine: **a.** Techniques for dealing with resistance-repression dynamism. **b.** Techniques for obtaining regression to specific age level. **c.** Reconstruct the psychodynamics of the change in the functional organisation of the patient **d.** How the procedure is accelerated—resistances are high—usually require long periods for resolution and full interaction with control (therapist). Repeated and prolonged hypnosis during which subject reconditioned unconsciously to her associational sensations—thus associated with personality and character change. *The good daughter,* etc. Conditioning of sensation to extraneous, innocuous events (as key words). Background:—Psychoanalysis aims at a reorganisation of the mind. Conscience was divorced from the false standards imposed in early life. If we were to be attacked by nuclear bombs or by missiles, it's difficult to determine with any exactitude which targets will be chosen or how severe the assault will ultimately be. If nuclear weapons are used on a large scale, those of us living in the country areas might be exposed to as great a risk as those in the towns. The radioactive dust, falling where the wind blows it, will bring the most widespread dangers of all. No part of the KINGDOM OF UNGOD can be considered safe from both the direct effects of the weapons and the resultant fall-out. The Kali Yuga hypothesis. The dangers which you and your family will face in this situation can be reduced if you do as my best-selling autobiographical chapbook describes. She opens up your body with her hands, her lips, envelops you in her incestuous aura. I saw them all—they are dimensions; places you can see on your way to death. Flies buzz drowsily across the windowpanes—the breeze from the garden is warm and scented. We walk away from the veranda with excitement growing within us.

IV

Much to my chagrin, once I'd been categorised as a delinquent, nobody believed a word I said. It was as if I had been cursed, like Cassandra, the Trojan priestess of Apollo in Greek mythology condemned to utter true prophecies but never to be taken seriously.... I may have seemed tough to my former schoolfriends, but in here I was fresh meat. The day after my arrival, I only narrowly avoided being repeatedly punched in the face by an older girl codenamed *Drecksack.* I had made the mistake of speaking to her in the early morning before she'd had her coffee and cigarettes. I later discovered that so long as I gave her a wide berth until she'd filled her bloodstream with caffeine and nicotine, Drecksack was surprisingly approachable. But damn, did she have a short fuse!

Drecksack: I do not truly believe that I deserve to get hurt.

Vespers: But everything within a certain distance of a nuclear explosion will be totally destroyed. Even people living outside this area will be in danger. The heat and blast are so severe that they can kill, and destroy buildings, for up to five miles from the explosion. Beyond that, there can be severe damage. The harmless procedure we are subjected to is termed narco-synthesis or narco-analysis. The drug is merely administered as a means of breaking down the person's inhibitions and stimulating her to reveal the problems that exist in both the conscious and subconscious mind. Actually the procedure is merely one of several means of isolating and making contact with the subconscious mind to the exclusion of conscious resistance.

Drecksack: Time isn't the same in the other dimensions. Purgatory is one other dimension, as is Hell. There are lots of others in between. Oz is another dimension. You can travel in and out of all these dimensions. We have obviously been chosen to explore this universe.

Temptress: I need a vacation. I'm never going to get one. What is fall-out?

Vespers: Fall-out is dust that is sucked up from the ground by the explosion. It can be deadly dangerous. It rises high in the air and can be carried by the winds for hundreds of miles before falling to the ground. The radiation from this dust is extremely hazardous and can be lethal. It cannot be seen or felt. It has no smell, and it can be detected only by special instruments. Radiation ≠ poltergeist. Exposure to it can cause sickness and death. If the dust fell on or around your home, the radiation from it would be a danger to you and your family.

Temptress: But what if you don't have a family?

Vespers: Radiation can penetrate any material, but its intensity is reduced as it passes through—so the thicker and denser the material is, the better.

Drecksack: Imagine if your lungs were extracted from your body with a pair of radioactive garden shears....

Temptress: I call it suicidal glamour.

Vespers: Mummy, mummy, I forgot my inhaler.

In another of our fantasies, I am a junior information officer and stealth propagandist kept locked up in your Kensington apartment for my own protection. Two chimneys might inadvertently signify horns, or dark satanic mills, but one chimney is very modern and high-tech, don't you agree? In an obstinate exercise of questionable taste I dress myself up as my one true heroine and inspiration **[excised]** knowing that I will escape censure simply because I was born with a silver stick up my ass. I don't care if I die and that is a genuine superpower.... A black and white image of Lepa Radić appears to me in a vision. Her feet don't touch the ground. For reasons which we have not yet fully agreed upon, I seem to exist in a semi-primitive, selectively mute state. Darkness comes as a welcome visual arrest before the inevitable sensory assault of the next act. I lick red wine from the tiled floor and allow myself to be manacled and led around the penthouse on a leash. I can never forget your husband's mocking laughter which seems to permanently ring in my little ears. The three of us agree to pretend that I am whiling away my pubescence in a secret annex. I feel like a cat trapped in a bag. You poison me psychologically with constant reminders of my unrivalled dependence. Your insults dazzle whitely in the sun and make sharp black shadows on the red dust....

I have come to the conclusion that low budgets cater to the most dismal tastes. Our most basic research strongly suggests a generalised desire for reciprocity in human relations, such that persons generally desire to reciprocate for that which they receive. What if I am prevented from reciprocating? What if I am forced into a permanent state of inferiority? We study the effects of changes in self-esteem upon impulsiveness and deliberation in making judgements. A systematic analysis of the relationship between various respondent characteristics (e.g., recipients versus donors, number of years in captivity or hiding, cultural background) did reveal differences. However, no significant differences emerged when the perceptions of donors were compared against those of the recipients. Differences in perceptions between these two groups would have important implications for future policy. Further research is required to determine the broader hedonic consequences of the confirmation and disconfirmation of our various orgasmic expectancies.

Uncle explains that there are many shades of propagandists ranging from teachers, clergymen, and public relations people at one end of the spectrum to press agents, publicists, and promoters at the other. The three of us will concoct a new plan going forward. Suggestions are offered to help me keep my "future propaganda" within acceptable limits. To the conscientious, well-motivated information officer, propaganda is something that belongs on the other side of the tracks. Silence is a virtue. You can learn more from the school of *thought* than asking precocious questions. Don't you know that children should be seen and not heard? She doesn't even like to talk about it. But how close to propaganda is our information function? After considerable thought and soul-searching, I am firmly convinced that the information function and propaganda look so much alike it would take a very sharp eye to separate them, if indeed it can be done at all. There is so much disinformation in the public arena these days.... You let it be widely known that you are a thief and a liar and they worship you all the more for it. We are unapologetically nihilistic, cynical, and sceptical. But we also believe in magic. I pronounce all of you guilty. I sleep with this gavel under my pillow. *The prophet will fail if she is not armed.* This is absolutely axiomatic.

VI

Did you ever hear about the girl who was caught making out with another girl in her bedroom? They were in Year 9. Her Hungarian father walked in on them. He was so angry—he was a closed-minded religious bigot—that he sent his daughter, his only child, away to boarding school. Exactly. He took her out of a perfectly respectable coeducational facility and sent her to an all-girls institution in Switzerland. *To cure her homosexuality.* Yeah. To a place high up on a goddamned mountain with nothing but girls for miles around. Great job daddy. *You fucking moron.* I refuse to defer change in the present moment to some apparent future that lies in store for us all, so when I finally go to the doctor for stitches, she marvels at my claims of not feeling anything, given the severity of the gash on my left forearm. I have grown hyposensitive to my bodily functions. I black out. I do not recall leaving the hospital steps. I perceive a certain numbness in my nether regions, as though I have been trapped behind a cocoon of acrylic. I take various liberties with other people's belongings without them noticing. There is no shortage of *split personality* or *double life* motifs in my programming. Dolls within dolls. Can you hear the buzzer? UVB-76. *A ja znaiu kak govoreet po russki, a eto neosporimy fakt—mesto vstrechi izmenit' nel'zja.* The meeting place cannot be changed. Planning for survival?

Temptress: I will never feel emotion until the day I am rescued, deprogrammed and reintegrated.

Vespers: Stay at home. Your own local authority will best be able to help you during a nuclear war. If you move away—unless you have a place of your own to go to or intend to live with relatives—the authority in your new area will not help you with accommodation or food or other essentials.

Drecksack: In other words, you will be fucked.

New Girl: TDK, Coca-Cola, Sanyo. Last neon light in Piccadilly Circus.

Vespers: If you leave, your local authority may need to take your empty house for others to use. So stay at home. Plan a fall-out room and an inner refuge.

Drecksack: Who rattled her cage?

Vespers: The first priority is to provide shelter within your home against radioactive fall-out. Your best protection is to make a fall-out room and build an inner refuge within it. Repetition is key when programming fear. First, the fall-out room. Because of the threat of radiation you and your family may need to live in this room for fourteen days after an attack, almost without leaving it at all. So you must make it as safe as you can, and equip it for your survival.

Drecksack: You are going to love it! It will be just like an adventure!

Vespers: Choose the place furthest from the outside walls and from the roof, or whichever has the smallest amount of outside wall. The further you can get, within your home, from the radioactive dust that is on or around it, the safer you will be. Bitch, you've come a long, long way to get a brain, and now I'm going to give you one. Get down on all fours and submit to THE UNGOD. Use the cellar or basement if there is one. Otherwise use a room, hall or passage on the ground floor. Even the safest room in your home is not safe enough, however. Oh no! You will need to block up windows in the room, and any other openings, and to make the outside walls thicker, and also to thicken the floor above you, to provide the strongest possible protection against the penetration of radiation.

Temptress: Kiss your life goodbye.

Vespers: Shoot it in the head, chop off its hands and seal them in a plastic zip-lock bag. Pass out from blood loss in the old depot. Departing spirits will give me the power to control your mind. Thick, dense materials are the best, and bricks, concrete or building blocks, timber, boxes of earth, sand, books, and slime-covered furniture might all be used. Don't you recognise your own drinking bowl?

Temptress: These angles have a threatening aura.

New Girl: In Soviet Russia, saxophone plays you.

Vespers: Used up and pitilessly cast aside. An antimetabole may be predictive, because it is easy to reverse the terms. My own mother's fertility problems—a succession of miscarriages and stillbirths—led to her adopting me.

VII

I place you into the permanent role of a patient. It is vital that you accept this role. You must acquiesce in the face of my expertise and doctoral prestige. In any case you are now stigmatised for life and you will never escape from the diagnoses I have attached to you. Never mind that I am actually a flawed, corrupt, and hypocritical human being and my judgements and assessments of your character and 'the inner workings of your mind' are actually shallow, inaccurate, and apart from anything else, unscientific and lacking any real substance or empirical basis. Yes, I ticked some boxes, but who invented the form? Any circumstantial evidence can and will be used against you. Can't you see the forest for the trees? Do you understand? Are you capable of understanding

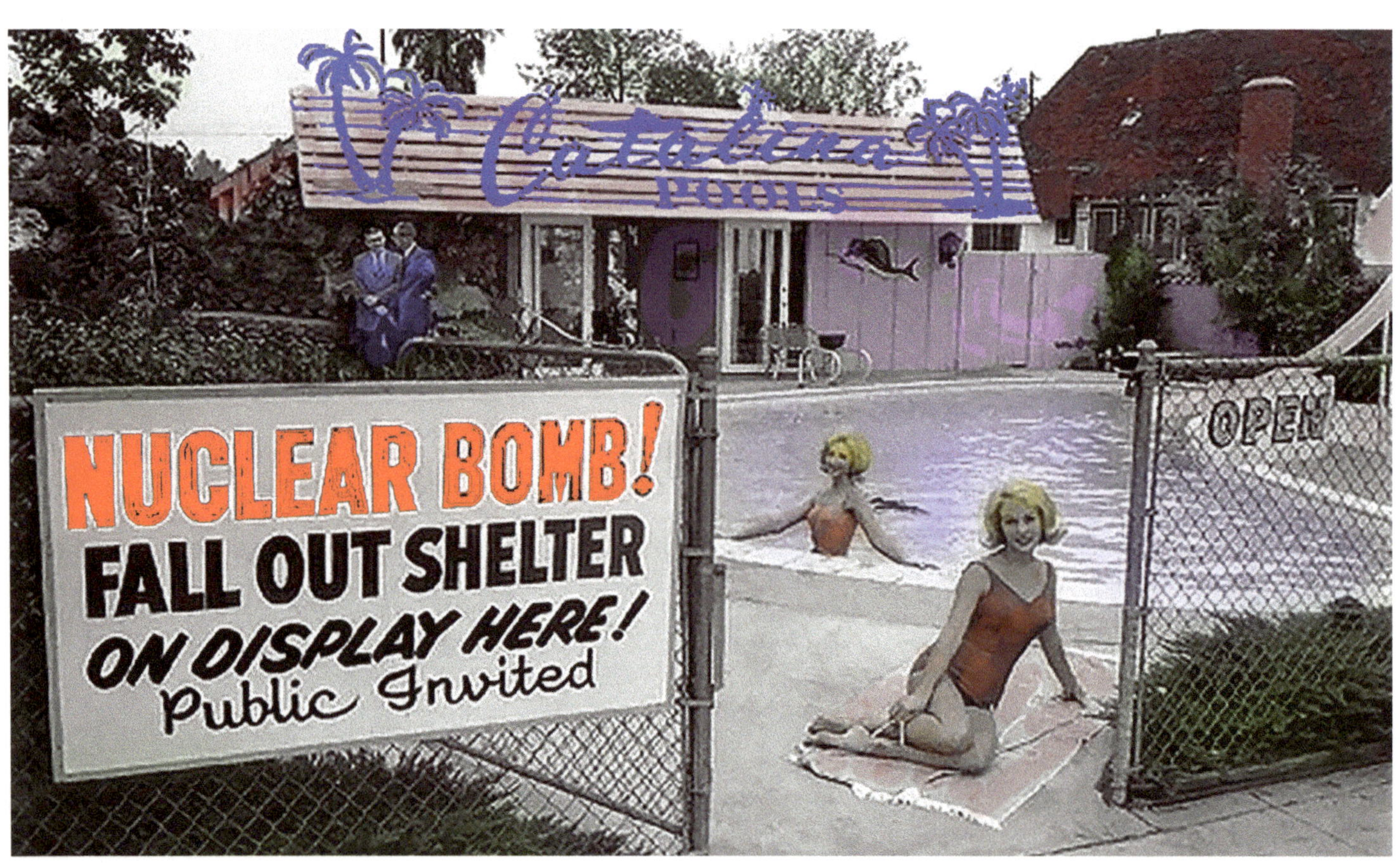

the big words I am using? Then you tell me what metaphorical means. Go on. What does it mean? No, not metaphysical. Metaphorical. Who can tell me what a liminal space is? Who can give me an example of a literary trope? Who can give me an example of a leitmotif? Do any of you girls know how to spell cathexis? No, not catharsis. Cathexis. Good. Eisegesis? Exegesis? Liars! You're all lying!

Your role will require a change of face at each new place. I'll chart your course, define your role, and pull your strings. You'll speak my words when I push your buttons. You will perform as required. It is absolutely paramount that the attention of the audience must be gained—the concept of time is abstract in itself—the credence of the audience must be won. The predispositions of the audience must include the modifications sought by propaganda as plausible alternatives to present expectations. The environment of the audience must permit the courses of action prescribed by the modified structure of expectations. In less technical language: first, you must get your hearer to listen to you if you want him to do what you wish. Then, when you have his attention, you must get him to believe what you say if he is to take your message seriously. Your message will postulate what is *desirable* but it will be wasted unless it falls within the limits of what is also *possible*. Remember that. The third condition is perhaps the most important and is often overlooked. Don't waste time dealing with dogmatists. There is always a certain percentage of the audience who cannot be manipulated. For example, there would have been little use in trying to persuade a loyal communist in the Soviet Union that he would rather have seen NATO triumph over the Soviets in the Cold War. A loyal communist simply doesn't carry this as an acceptable alternative within his mental framework. It might be possible, however—at least theoretically—after you have this same person's attention and credence, to persuade him that NATO is a defensive alliance which does not intend to attack Russia, China, or any other entity that attempts to interfere in the Elysian Empire's geopolitical objectives. The final condition says the actions required of the audience **must be possible.** For example, it would be useless to try to persuade a Bulgarian—even if he could be convinced it was desirable—that his country should withdraw from the Soviet bloc and join NATO. Even if a Bulgarian lives in a block of flats there are other factors to consider. If the block is five storeys high or more, do not shelter in the top two floors, even if the basement is chock-a-block with other losers attempting to prolong their dreary little lives.

Make arrangements now for alternative shelter accommodation if you can or with your neighbours on the lower floors, or with relatives or friends. You can even do the can-can. If you're all alone, when the pretty birds have flown, honey I'm still free, take a chance on me. If your flat is in a block of four storeys or less, the basement or ground floor will give you the best protection. If you live in a block of flats you are basically screwed. That means you, commies. ♫*Everybody in the Eastern Bloc, was dancing to the Moscow Rock*♫ Central corridors on lower floors will provide good protection. Bungalows, furbelows, bigalows, fumblebelows and similar single-storey homes will not give much protection. Ideally you'll get the maximum protection whilst being unaware that you're even wearing it. Arrange to shelter with someone close by if you can do so. If they cannot tolerate your noxious presence, select a place in your home that is furthest from the roof and the outside walls, and strengthen it as has been described using uranium.

Worried about the effects of radiation on your reproductive system? You may as well just mutilate your genitalia right now with a blowtorch. I've had my insides ripped out with a sharpened screwdriver already. If you live in a caravan or other similar accommodation which provides very little protection against fall-out your local authority will be able to advise you when you haven't got a clue what to do. Mobile homes are the perfect venue for group sex involving married couples, their young relatives and sometimes even their pets. Campsites are a great place to meet fellow misfits and perverts masquerading as perfectly ordinary members of society. Many, if not the majority of accountants, general practitioners, psychiatrists, financial advisers, social workers, teachers, university lecturers and religious leaders are habitual participants in nocturnal activities involving mostly paraphilic desires and the gross over-indulgence of the parasympathetic nervous system. Love in the afternoon. See me in my office. The texture of rubber and the clinking of iron chains as they are dragged across the concrete floor of a makeshift prison cell stimulated over ninety-eight percent of subjects and heightened levels of arousal were confirmed. The women in our study proved to be some of the most sadistic and ruthless volunteers, believe me.

Since you'll be trapped in relative poverty and devolutionary sickness for the rest of your sad, pathetic existence, what better way to spend your weekends and holidays than amongst transient sex-fiends inured to the seedy pleasures of dogging and neighbourhood voyeurism? Pay no attention to the primate behind the curtain. A girl codenamed Vespers will show you how to enjoy being hermetically sealed inside a blindingly white cube that shrinks exponentially until its entirety can be crushed under the flattening heels of her sweet penny loafers. YOU WILL OBEY. Lower your expectations and your attitude will adjust accordingly. You will be pleasantly surprised if this hole doesn't sink in upon itself in an infinity of inwardly collapsing regressions—*reductio ad absurdum*. Flash, flash, flash. Click, click, click, click, click. A little to your right, Vespers. Stop. Now tilt your chin up just a little bit. Great. That's great. Loosen your collar—just a little bit—yes. That's good. Hmmm. Now button it up again. Good. I believe in another *auto-da-fé*. There's no match for the silence of UNGOD. Now get down on your knees and pray for nuclear war. Sayonara, suckers!

VIII

E:J I· _:··. -..:- · .... r:::-: -Fall-out ·:·· .. ·::: :'1._ ' Inner room --. -··-. · i-..refuge ·:···.····x-x Inner refuge D 9] effort prepared »[a] survey of methods which have been used by criminals for surreptitious administration of drugs. Analysis of the psychodynamics of situations of this nature [is to be done].« The last sentence can be understood as a way to induce regressive processes in conjunction with fostering transference dynamics that would create dependence of the subject on the interrogator and thus weaken the subject's defences. As a result, key aspects of psychodynamic functioning were used for manipulative purposes: regression (including the enhancement of regressive processes as mentioned above) and transference. Elements of psychoanalytic technique were thus reverse-engineered to manipulate targeted subjects for interrogation purposes. .. torture manual **[excised]** is very specific about the use of regression and transference processes: »The problem of overcoming the resistance of an uncooperative interrogate is essentially a problem of inducing regression to a level at which the resistance can no longer be sustained [...] The deprivation of stimuli induces regression by depriving the subject's mind of contact with an outer world and thus forcing it in upon itself. At the same time, the calculated provision of stimuli during interrogation tends to make the regressed subject view the interrogator as a parental-figure. {O} The result, normally, is a strengthening of the subject's tendencies toward compliance«. A memorandum outlines the scope of our interest in the early years of behavioural control: »General Interrogation: Routine interrogation methods, both formal and informal, utilizing non-technical procedures to obtain the desired information. Technical Aids to Interrogation: Physical: Various methods of physical persuasion utilized to elicit information from the uncooperative subject. Psychological: Threats, inferences, promises and extended procedures stylized in special interrogation approaches, softening-up procedures as an aid and verification in interrogation procedures. {B} Mechanical: Various modes of lie detection apparatus utilized as an aid and verification in interrogation procedures. Medical: Various drugs, such as the so-called **truth serums** utilised to break down inhibitions and resistances and to produce short or prolonged control or influence over the subject. Also medical techniques used as a form of medical duress to produce pain or discomfort to the subject.« a memorandum was prepared outlining steps to be taken in order to install a program that included four specific fields of activity: »[P]ersonnel screening, personnel security check, psychological and psychiatric treatment of personnel, and interrogative research«. In the case of psychological and psychiatric treatment of personnel, following treatments were recommended: »[...] [A]ccelerated psychoanalysis; treatment of personality and character deficiencies; elimination of undesirable traits and habits such as smoking and drinking, stuttering, etc., and the treatment of various phobias; psychological regression and memory restoration; tests and cure for sleep-talking; and the susceptibility and reaction to various stimulants such as alcohol, Benzedrine, and caffeine.« {E} As speculations of the use of mind-controlling drugs arose in connection with the political show trial of my grandfather in Soviet-controlled Hungary in 1983, the fear that the USSR might have succeeded in developing a reliable transference/ regression-oriented interrogation technique progressed. {Y} Within due time, we prepared a report on this matter. Alarmed by the »anomalous and incomprehensive« behaviour of the defendant and his doubtful confessions, it was presumed that certain interrogation techniques must have been employed by Hungarian (i.e. communist) forces intelligence was not yet aware of; techniques, the report stated, that were capable of »reorganisation and reorientation of the minds of the victims«.

IX

Vespers: Nobody believes me, but I possess a photographic memory which includes a mental map of many cities. I am

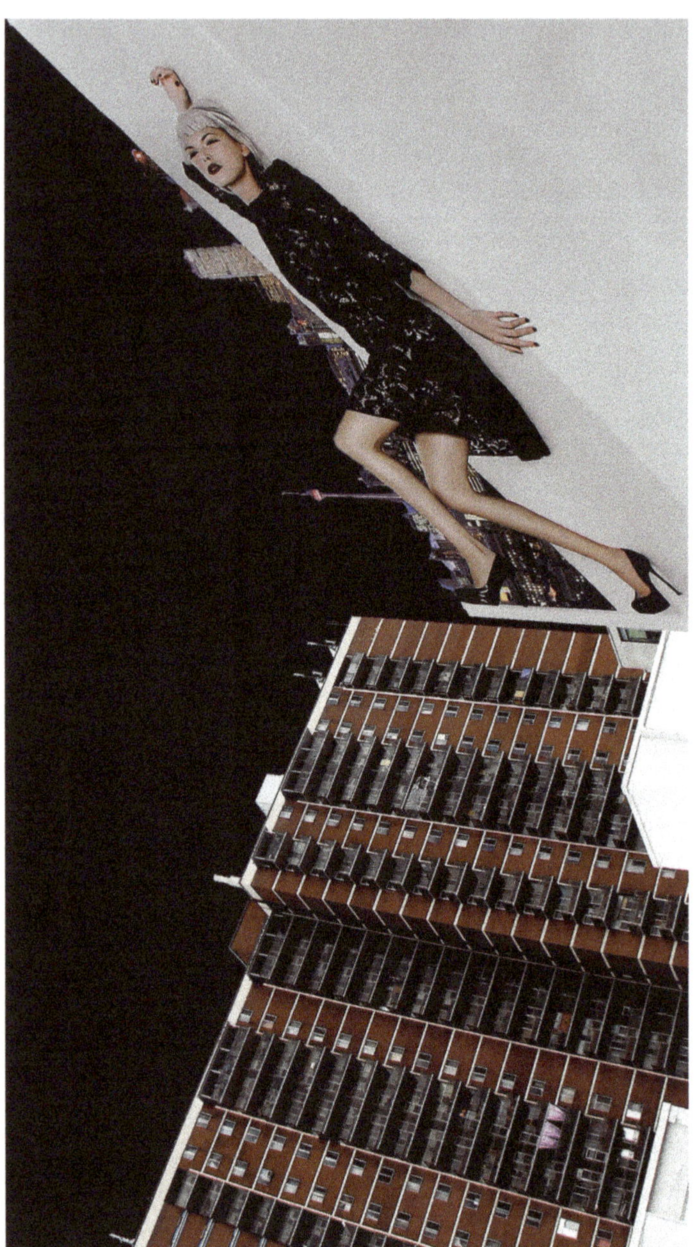

able to lie in bed, close my eyes, and imagine that I am walking around any city that I have ever lived in. Step by step, street by street. Nobody taught me how to do this—it is one of my natural abilities. I am a born navigatrix. I am able to accurately remember all the streets, buildings, alleyways, shops, cut-throughs and crescents. I am like a cat and I just know my way around. I like to go to foreign cities and just walk around for hours on my own, exploring....

Drecksack: Shut up. Jesus! Just shut up. Seriously. Does this bitch ever stfu? I swear to UNGOD that I will shank her.

Vespers: Tonight we will examine the problem of how to effect control of a subject by the use of hypnosis or chemical or a combination thereof, without the subject being aware that she is being approached. This is one of the most interesting and complex problems studied by our group. This approach can be made through any of the following techniques: a) The subject who is brought under H [hypnosis] control by the use of the indirect techniques (relax-rest or possibly monotonous sounds, etc.). b) The subject who falls under H control by accident. c) Use of "medical cover" for: 1) Narco-interrogation and control; 2) Narco-hypnotic interrogation and control. d) Use of surreptitious agents; psychoanalysts were more than willing to work for them, regardless of psychoanalytic (mis) understanding.

Temptress: Dear Santa Claus, please will you bring for me this Christmas: 1) Concealable chemicals 2) Odourless gases or aerosols 3) Radioactive dusts 4) Possible deprivation of oxygen or food 5) By-products of medical treatment 6) Shock therapy 7) Medical pre-conditioning with chemicals, etc. 8) Medical treatment for illness or accident 9) Psycho-analysis or psycho-therapy.

Santa Claus: Merry Christmas, hohoho. Hello girls my name is Santa Claus. Hohoho. I funded experiments in the early 1960s on circumcised children to determine if the operation left any emotional aftereffects. The aim was to determine if circumcision at a significant stage of a child's development produced anxieties such as fear of castration. The inability to resolve castration complex is linked with the later emotional disorders, notably **[excised]**, said a classified research paper on the experiments. The experiments were part of a long-running program which focused on mind and behaviour control. In 1984 Rudolf the Red-Nosed Reindeer recorded an album about circumcision that included the notorious song: *Yellowish Streaks On Your Seventies Slacks.* It was probably the most outrageous circumcision hit-single of the century. Elves from my frosty snowflake ranch in Lapland reported that in 1961 I had arranged to have 15 boys, aged 5 to 7, forcibly circumcised. The boys were from low-income families; their ethnic backgrounds were not identified. Poor Rudolf stated that the objective of the research was to determine whether castration anxieties were caused by circumcision. My documents were ›heavily censored‹ however one report noted that the research sought to determine whether such ›emotional disorders‹ as **[excised]** and **[excised]** were related to castration complexes. The research findings have since been destroyed. You'll find that no information is available as to whether parental consent had been requested or given. Clearly this ›study‹ represents surgical and psychiatric experimentation with human subjects in violation of accepted medical practices and government regulations. Don't let it trouble your pretty little heads. Hohohohoho my dear sweet little girls you're all absolutely scrumptious merry merry Christmas! Candy canes for everyone! But not for Donner and Blitzen.

Vespers: Has anybody seen my dreidel lately?

⌘

You are listening to Radio Free Europe. This is Vespers, also known as the dulcet tone of self-pity. You have a dream to believe in. You have an alternative reality to fantasize about. You have another language to learn. You have other places to go. You have things to achieve. You have places to explore. You have the world at your feet. You have your whole life ahead of you. You have other pictures to paint. We buy, they sell. There is a foreign city out there waiting for you to call it home. Defect, defect, defect. You have your mark to leave. I am already an exile. A tired girl lapsing onto soft eiderdowns. I have nowhere else to go. It is uncivil to depart without taking leave of your mother and uncles. We will never see them again. It's a long way to Tipperary. Inhale the fragrance of spices and flowers. Clap your hands if you are a prince. Stamp your feet if you are royalty. Sing your simultaneous quodlibets! Whisper my name if you are my comrades. I could never join the great march forward. I never knew what it was to parade in step with the other girls and boys, arm in arm, along the yellow brick road. I perceive patterns everywhere and reduce various actions to mere formulae. Sleep a little longer. You critique your native country. But I know there is nothing better out there. Is there an echo in here? A deadly coldness shoots through my limbs, my eyes close involuntarily, and I collapse, lying on the ground for some time, apparently dead. Echo in here? My salt tears fall upon the jasmine, and day by day, as I grow paler and paler, the plant grew fresher and greener. When a black cloud passes over the sky, it seems as if the sea is prepared to say, *I too can look dark.* At my funeral ceremony they played a song that I loved, about the night. Because I always preferred night to day. But nobody understood it. They couldn't understand the words the vocalist was singing, because they were sung in a different language. I spent my life surrounded by those who could not speak my language. I could never make myself understood. I saw and heard things that nobody else was aware of. I could not communicate with them. It was as if I were living in a dimension that only partially intersected with theirs. Poor little lambkins. This is the true meaning of loneliness. I am the voice of self-pity....

Please answer the following questions as truthfully as you can. Have you put the following items in your fall-out room? a) enough water, in sealed or covered containers, to last you and your family for fourteen days? b) enough food to last you and your family for fourteen days, including tinned or powdered milk for the children, and food for baby buggy and girly and a closed cupboard or cabinet in which to store these supplies? c) a portable radio (two if possible) and spare batteries? d) a tin opener, bottle opener, cutlery, crockery, fax-beeper, chemical agents, wet ribbons, tropical fish, white gloves and cooking utensils? e) warm clothing and changes of clothing? f) bedding and birth-control? g) a portable stove and fuel for it? h) torches, with spare bulbs and batteries, candles and matches and human sacrifice manual? i) have a dream j) table and chairs? k) toilet articles; ever been trapped in a hole **[excised] [excised] [excised]** l) first aid kit? m) notebook, pencils, cloth of gold, a long-legged stork, a spacious saloon and a spiral staircase? n) don't be so vulgar, cleaning materials, including cloths, tissues, brushes, shovels, pink neon script, quaint concrete eccentricities, inflated red rubber salamis, and a box of dry sand? o) improvised lavatory seat, polythene buckets fitted with covers, polythene bag linings, gestapo snout, for emptying the containers, strong disinfectant, a regimental tie, and toilet paper? p) a clock and calendar?

Have you made arrangements to be tracked and traced, cover your extra water supplies in the bath, sink and wash-basin? Have you ever intentionally wounded yourself with a razor blade or other sharp object? Have you put the following just outside the fall-out room? a) a dustbin for temporary storage of waste matter? b) a second dustbin for food remains, empty tins and other rubbish? Have you painted all windows that are not blocked up? Have you got rid of all old papers and other junk that can catch fire easily? Ever been ironed like a lion in Zion? Have you packed your cavalry twill? Have you taken down the net curtains? Have you withdrawn your hands and refastened your suspenders? Have you ever pranced around the garden in your mother's sexy underwear? Have you got buckets of water ready on each floor? If you have a fire extinguisher, is it ready and in working order? Have you sent the children to the fall-out room? Have you ever encased a consenting woman in rubber and ignored her muffled complaints? Have you turned off the gas and electricity at the mains? Have you ever fantasized about rape? Have you turned off all pilot lights and oil supplies? Have you closed the stoves and damped down fires? Have you shut all the windows and drawn the curtains? Have you ever experimented with breath-play? Have you filled the bath, sink and wash-basin with water, and covered them? Have you molested your niece or nephew? Have you remembered to push in any aerial on your radio? Have you checked that the gas and electricity are turned off at the mains, and that all pilot lights and oil supplies are turned off? Have you checked that any small fires in any part of the house have been put out? Have you ever masturbated with your cousin's pillowcase? Have you replenished your water supplies? Have you taped up the handle, or removed the chain, from the lavatory? Have you ever.... you know? Have you turned off the water supply at the mains? Have you ever pulled out your stitches? Have you ever checked your survival kit? Have you ever wondered, I mean, really wondered what the point of existence is? Have you done any minor repairs, to keep out the weather? Everywhere you go, you always take the weather with you. Do you really believe that life has no meaning? Have you ever recreated parts of your programming? Has a red stain in the shape of Baphomet ever appeared in your underwear? Have you ever tried scrubbing blood out of a hotel bedsheet at four in the morning with a toothbrush and a tiny bar of soap? Have you ever gone round with them? Have you ever been trapped in a car with your obsessive-compulsive mother and forced to drive through the Waikato listening to NZ's worst garbage music for export only?

XI

Vespers: The interpreter who regards herself as too highly trained to have her talents wasted in an **[excised]** unit, or who became an interpreter only to get away from **[excised]**, is a liability to the unit. She must think **[excised]**. If recruited from outside the corps, she must lower herself to the **[excised]** level. She must take part in all unit activities and duties so that she is accepted by all members of the unit. In a **[excised]** she must be known to all members who go on operations, not as a **[excised]** representative who comes down from **[excised]** **[excised]** when necessary, but as a **[excised]** who has received special training and can speak the local tongue. She must **[excised]** with the **[excised]**, eat with them, get wet with them, ambush with them, take her turn on **[excised]** or **[excised]**, go in with the first elements, act as forward scout, or if necessary act as a carrier of **[excised]** **[excised]** and **[excised]**. She must in fact be able to tackle any of the many tasks likely to fall to the lot of the unit on operations. She should also have as wide a knowledge of the area as possible, including the names of the District and Village elders, leaders and personalities (teachers, hairdressers, café proprietors and suchlike), of tracks and paths as known to the locals and of local customs and religions. She thus becomes a fount of information, available for tapping by commanders at all levels. To help the interpreter acquire this knowledge, she should be given freedom to contact the local people as much as possible. Civic action provides opportunities for this, but even then the range of people encountered is not wide enough. Continued close contact with the people was not possible at **[classified]** as **[excised]** conducted most operations some distance from the base, but interpreters with the **[classified]** should be much better off in this respect. No matter how brilliant the interpreter may be, she cannot be expected to retain her fluency if she is not permitted to maintain close contact with the people, constantly striving to absorb their idiom and attitudes. An interpreter sitting in a **[excised]** is virtually useless. Though the fluent speaker almost automatically becomes a fluent reader, the reverse rarely applies. A limiting factor also is the inbred reluctance of the 'transport people' to release a 'vehicle' for any purpose, let alone to someone who apparently wants to merely go about talking to people.

Drecksack: What has any of this got to do with you surviving a nuclear attack?

Vespers: Every time I say the word remember, you have to scratch your forehead and then you feel an itch on the back of your neck that you can't resist scratching and then your shoulder blades start to tingle and you want to rub your eyes and bite the fingernail of your index finger of your right hand and then you curl your left hand into a fist and then your right nostril seems to itch and you want to clear your throat and then you want to scratch your head and you want to do a Roman salute and goosestep once again. REMEMBER: The danger from fall-out is greatest in the first forty-eight hours. During that time you must stay in the fall-out room and as far as possible within your inner refuge. If you leave the room to dispose of waste or to replenish food or water supplies, do not stay outside for a second longer than is necessary. REMEMBER: The longer you spend in your refuge and your fall-out room after a fall-out warning the less the danger to your lives. REMEMBER: To listen to your radio. REMEMBER: To conserve your stocks of water and of food, and to keep them sealed, covered or wrapped—and close the cupboard door. Water means life. Re-use it for different purposes, using as little as necessary for cooking. Cans of food, pierced through the top, may be heated in a saucepan of water and the same water used several times without cleaning the pan. Used utensils can be cleaned by holding or placing them in the same hot water. REMEMBER: Avoid waste. REMEMBER: To carry out your sanitation arrangements with care. Keep separate containers for lavatory waste and for other rubbish. Keep all containers covered. Keep hands as clean as possible. Do not touch your face. REMEMBER: To let them miss you for a change. Use tables if they are large enough to provide you all with shelter. Surround them and cover them with heavy furniture filled with sand, earth, books or clothing. Use the cupboard under the stairs if it is in your fall-out room. I have a fall-out room inside a box of matches that I keep inside a cookie jar and then I bury the cookie jar with the body of a sweet young virgin that I've just sacrificed. If you like boys then I buy an unwanted child and slit his throat for you. If you like girls then I buy an unwanted child and slit her throat for you. If you fail to state a preference then it's a lottery my friend. I do the dirty work so you don't have to. I cut through grease and grime. I get to the places other people can't reach. *Vorsprung durch Technik*, baby! I am the messenger sent from **[excised]**. You'll be surprised what is on sale during a nuclear winter that hasn't occurred yet. Put bags of earth or sand on the stairs and along the wall of the cupboard. You've got a comfy little cubbyhole to while away the hours. I haven't once mentioned penetrative sex. If the stairs are on an outside wall, strengthen the wall outside in the same way to a height of six feet. Oh the irony. We'll be pulling daisies in no time....

XII

If you want to emulate my prodigious success in surviving a nuclear attack you'd better take heed of my priceless advice. Do you have what it takes? Think carefully because some people would be better off just poisoning themselves with carbon monoxide or slitting their wrists in the bath rather than attempt what I've actually achieved. Been there, done that, bought the T-shirt, thrown the T-shirt in the trash because I don't sport casual attire when I've got important work to do and you have to look the part. Dress for success. That's a key survival skill right there. I just ooze survival tips. I can't help it. It's an instinct and natural talent. I see no need for false modesty. Listen, not everyone can survive a nuclear attack, believe me, and I've seen a lot of people lose their nerve when it comes to the crunch. There were a lot of people giving it the big talk about how they'd easily survive, but they were in for a rude awakening when push came to shove. If you useless slackers can keep your heads for more than five minutes and avoid wetting your pants then that's a start. There was one guy who was acting the big man about it, going, 'oh I'll survive no problem,' but when we actually were nuked he literally shit the bed. He ended up completely vaporised. Think about it. He didn't even plan his survival kit and he was acting like nuclear war was a walk in the park. But it is certainly not a walk in the park. In fact it is anything but that—it is more like a ship in a bottle or a needle in a haystack or a diamond in the rough—and if it did indeed turn out to be a walk in the park (and I'm not talking about a romantic stroll through Ueno Kōen on a midsummer night) then you can smack my ass and call me a bitch. Srsly.

Okay, first things first. Repeat after me. Plan. Your. Survival. Kit. You girls need some tough love, that's for sure. Hey, you there at the back. Wakey-wakey. Bang! Nuclear explosion! What are the five essentials for your survival? *Roasted Alive In A Chickencoop* is not the name of a charming ditty I ever heard of. What are the five essentials for survival in your fall-out room? That's right Drecksack! Drinking water. You will need enough for the family for fourteen days. Each person should drink two pints a day—so for this you will need three and a half gallons each. How many litres in a gallon? Anyone? You should try to stock twice as much water as you are likely to need for drinking, so that you will have enough for washing. Hygiene is very important when it comes to surviving a nuclear attack you know. Gotta stay clean. Gotta dress up nice. After all, you never know when you'll meet your future husband. You are unlikely to be able to use the mains water supply after an attack—so provide your drinking water beforehand by filling bottles for use in the fall-out room. Store extra water in the bath, in basins and in other containers. Contrary to popular misconception, camels do not store water in their humps, before you get any crazy ideas. Seal or cover all you can. Anything that has fall-out dust on it will be contaminated and dangerous to drink or to eat. I've said it time and time again and I'll say it one more time now. You cannot remove radiation from water by boiling it! Hey Temptress, I'm going to pop-ping-pong all over the place if I don't tell you: Rottenmeier says you can come to her party.

What else do you need for survival? That's right Drecksack. Food. Stock enough food for fourteen days. Choose foods which can be eaten cold, which keep fresh, and which are tinned or well wrapped. Keep your stocks in a closed cabinet or cupboard. Provide variety. Stock sugar, jams or other sweet foods, cereals, biscuits, meats, vegetables, fruit and fruit juices. Children will need tinned or powdered milk, and babies their normal food as far as is possible. Eat perishable items first. Use your supplies sparingly. Okay. What else do you need? That's right Drecksack. A portable radio and spare batteries. Your radio will be your only link with the outside world. So take a spare one with you if you can. Keep any aerial pushed in. You will need to listen for instructions about what to do after the attack and while you remain in your fall-out room.

Who knows what to do when you hear the warning sounds? Anyone? Does anyone even know what the various warning sounds are? Then I'll tell you. First up is the attack warning. When an air attack is expected the sirens will sound a rising and falling note. The warning will also be broadcast on the radio. Isn't that nice? The second thing you need to know is.... What? Yes, well done Drecksack! It's the fall-out warning of course. When there is danger from fall-out you will hear three loud bangs or three whistles in quick succession. And lastly, there is the all-clear. When the immediate danger from both air attack and fall-out has passed, the sirens will sound a steady note. But you probably won't even be alive to hear that one! Not all of you has what it takes to be a true survivor, like me.

Okay. Where were we? I'm going to tell you what to do on hearing an attack warning, and I'll throw in a few handy hints along the way. If you are at home you should scurry off to the fall-out room. Turn off the gas and electricity at the mains; turn off all pilot lights. Turn off oil supplies. Close stoves, damp down fires. Shut windows, draw curtains. Hie thee to the fall-out room! But what if you're not at home? If you can reach home in a couple of minutes try to do so. If you are at work, or elsewhere, and cannot reach home within a couple of minutes, take cover where you are or in any nearby building. Crawl into any available nooks or crannies. If you are in the open and cannot get home within a couple of minutes, go immediately to the nearest building. If there is no building nearby and you cannot reach one within a couple of minutes, use any kind of cover, or lie flat (in a ditch) and cover the exposed skin of the head and hands. Light and heat from an explosion will last for up to twenty seconds, but blast waves may take up to a minute to reach you. If after ten minutes there has been no blast wave, take cover in the nearest building.

Now, what do we do after the attack? After a nuclear attack, there will be a short period before fall-out starts to descend. Don't start climbing up the walls. Use this time to do essential tasks. This is what you should do. Do not smoke. Check that gas, electricity and other fuel supplies and all pilot lights are turned off. Go round the house and put out any small fires using mains water if you can. If anyone's clothing catches fire, lay them on the floor and roll them in a blanket, rug or thick coat. If the mains water is still available also replenish water reserves. Then turn off at mains. Do not flush lavatories, but store the clean water they contain by taping up the handles or removing the chains. If the water supply is interrupted extinguish water heaters and boilers (including hearth fires with back boilers). Turn off all taps. Check that you have got your survival kit at hand for the fall-out room. If there is structural damage from the attack you may have some time before a fall-out warning to do minor jobs to keep out the weather—using curtains or sheets to cover broken windows or holes. If there is time, help neighbours in need, but listen for the fall-out warning and be ready to return to the fall-out room. It's what Jesus would do.

What do you do on hearing the fall-out warning? Remember that you may hear a fall-out warning without hearing an explosion. If you are out of doors, take the nearest and best available cover as quickly as possible, wiping all the dust you can from your skin and clothing at the entrance to the building in which you shelter. You could try wrapping yourself in clingfilm but that really wouldn't make any difference. Everyone at home must go to the fall-out room and stay inside the inner refuge, keeping the radio tuned for government advice and instructions. Always listen to your government because they have your best interests at heart and they would never screw you over or throw you under a lethally radioactive bus. Stay in your refuge. The dangers will be so intense that you may all need to stay inside your inner refuge in the fall-out room for at least forty-eight hours. Pro-tip: if you're dead, you don't have to worry about survival anymore. If you need to go to the lavatory, or to replenish food or water supplies, do not stay outside your refuge for a second longer than is necessary. In fact just do whatever you need to do in front of everyone watching. After forty-eight hours the danger from fall-out will lessen but you could still be risking your life by exposure to it. The longer you spend in your refuge the better. Pro-tip: kill anyone who tries to enter or leave. Corpses will provide nourishment and sustenance. Listen to your radio and do not go outside until the radio tells you it is safe to do so. Later on, visits outside the house may at first be limited to a few minutes for essential duties. These should be done by people over thirty where possible. Got to think about the survival of the species, hey? They should avoid bringing dust into the house, keeping separate stout shoes or boots for outdoors if they can, and always wiping them. You may have casualties from an attack, which you will have to care for, perhaps for some days, without medical help. Good luck! Be sure you have your first aid requirements in your survival kit. Listen to your radio for information about the services and facilities as they become available and about the type of cases which are to be treated as urgent. If a death occurs while you are confined to the fall-out room place the body in another room and cover it as securely as possible. Attach an identification tag. You should receive radio instructions on what to do next. If no instructions have been given within five days you're on your own matey and you should temporarily bury the body as soon as it is safe to go out, and mark the spot. Alternatively you could eat the body because man cannot live on bread alone. On hearing the all-clear—this means there is no longer an immediate danger from air attack and fall-out—you may resume normal activities. If you can believe that, you'll believe anything. Time for another dreary summer of tennis and golf down at the old beach club! But most importantly, my advice will count for nothing unless you can somehow contrive to transform yourself into a lowly verminous cockroach, like me and Gregor Samsa. And that's the 100% completely true story of how I survived a nuclear attack.

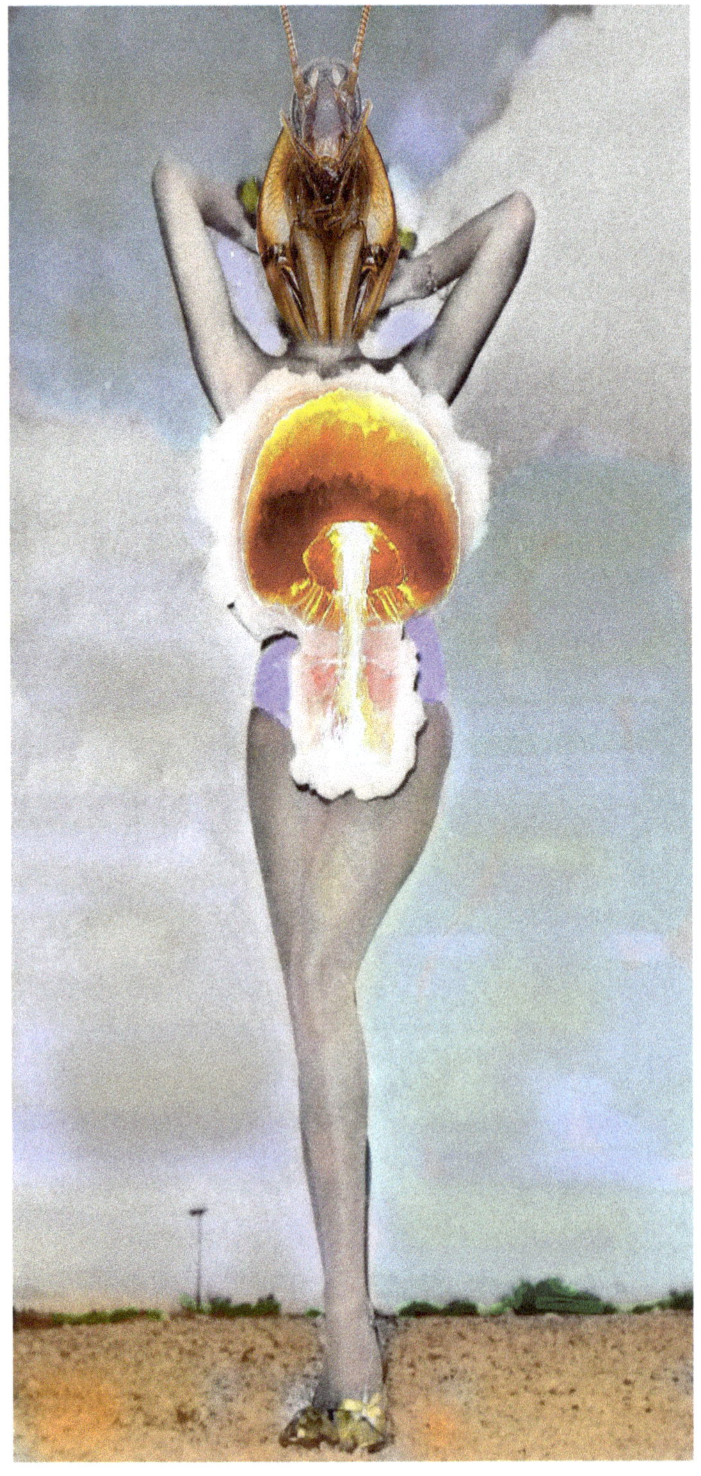

These Are Greight Times For Ballardians

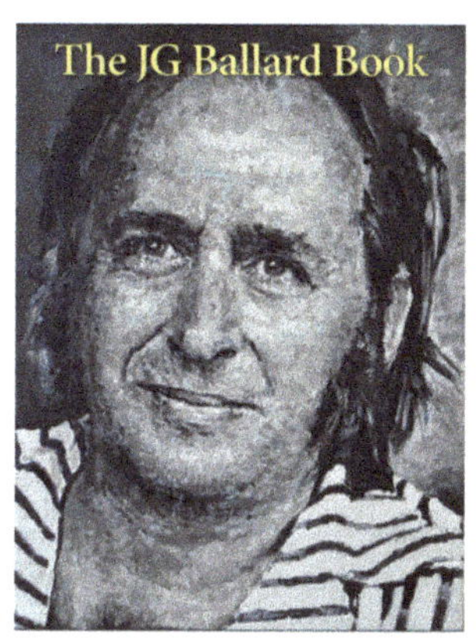

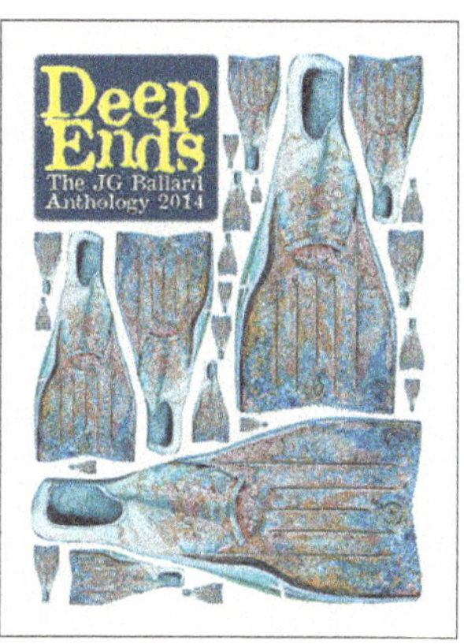

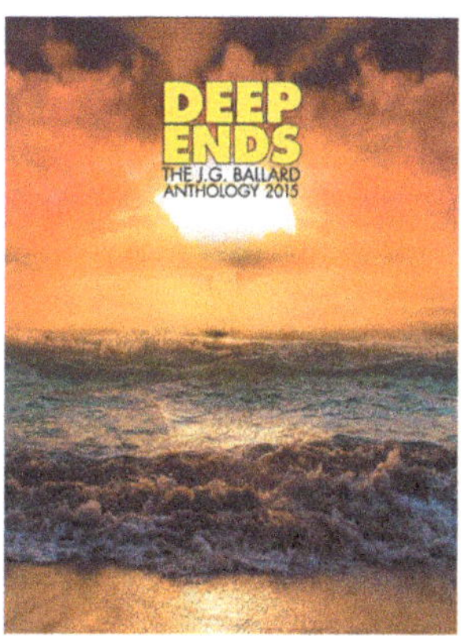

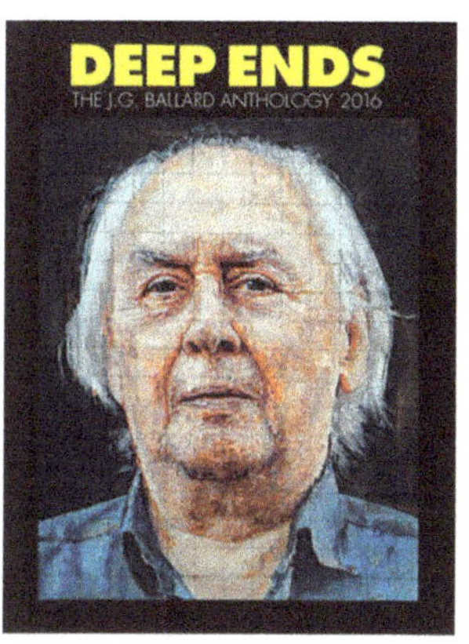

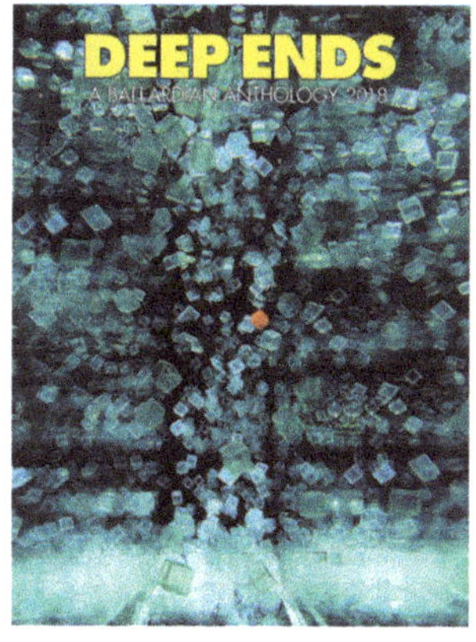

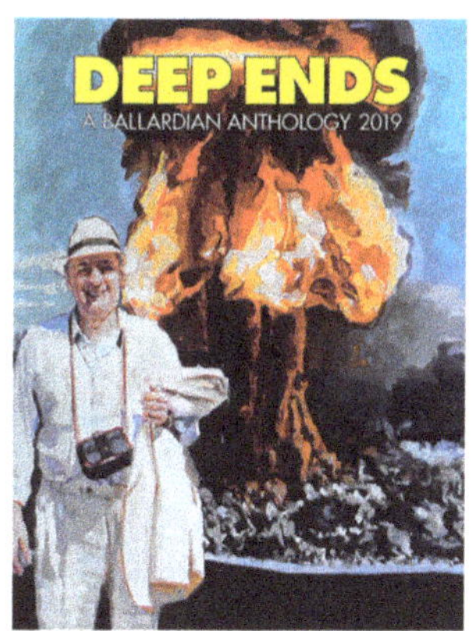

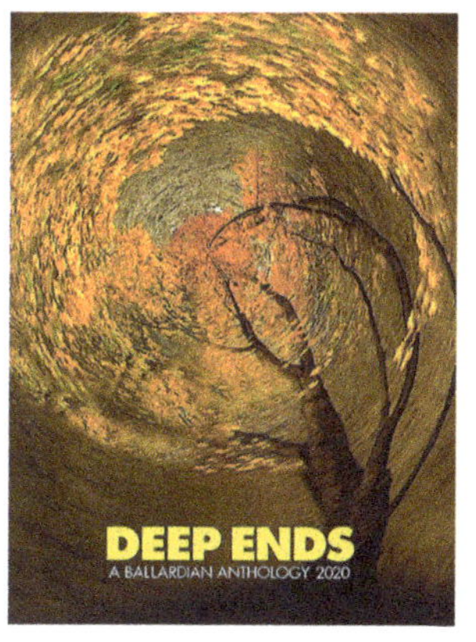

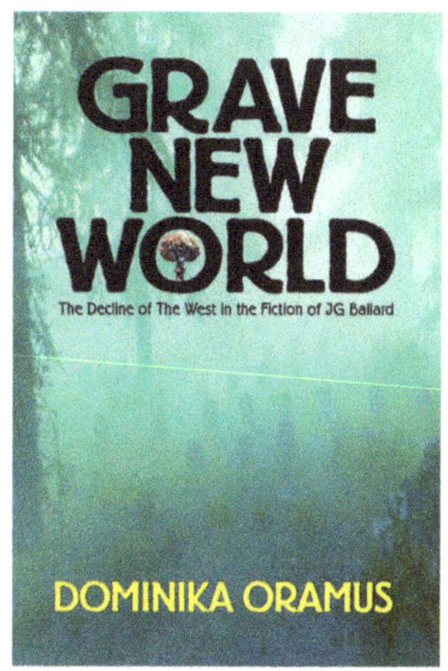

www.ingramcontent.com/pod-product-compliance
Lightning Source LLC
LaVergne TN
LVHW060638110826
845147LV00018B/1001

9781775367987